ACCOUNTING THEORY

A Conceptual and
Institutional Approach

ACCOUNTING THEORY
A Conceptual and Institutional Approach
Third Edition

Harry I. Wolk
Drake University

Jere R. Francis
University of Iowa

Michael G. Tearney
University of Kentucky

COLLEGE DIVISION South-Western Publishing Co.

Cincinnati Ohio

AT 6 OCA

This text was originally developed and produced by PWS-KENT Publishing Company. South-Western will market and sell this and future editions.

Sponsoring Editor: Mark Hubble
Production Editor: Pamela Rockwell
Cover and Interior Design: Pamela Rockwell
Manufacturing Coordinator: Lisa Flanagan

ISBN: 0-538-82158-2

International Student Edition ISBN: 0-534-98637-4

1 2 3 4 5 6 7 8 9 MV 9 8 7 6 5 4 3 2

Printed in the United States of America

FASB Statements copyright by Financial Accounting Standards Board, 401 Merritt 7, P.O. Box 5116, Norwalk, Connecticut, 06856-5116, U.S.A. Reprinted with permission. Copies of the complete documents are available from the FASB.

LIBRARY OF CONGRESS CATALOGING-IN-PUBLICATION DATA

Wolk, Harry I.
   Accounting theory : a conceptual and institutional approach /
Harry I. Wolk, Jere R. Francis, Michael G. Tearney. -- 3rd ed.
   p.   cm.
   Includes bibliographical references and indexes.
   ISBN 0-538-82158-2
   1. Accounting.   I. Francis, Jere R.   II. Tearney, Michael G.
III. Title.
HF5625.W64   1991
657--dc20   91-37701
                                                         CIP

To Our Families

Barbara, Joel, and Josh
Candis, Nathan, and Adam
Barbara, Bryce, and Flint

CONTENTS

Preface   *xv*

Part One
THEORETICAL AND INSTITUTIONAL BACKGROUND   **1**

CHAPTER 1
An Introduction to Accounting Theory   **5**

Accounting Theory and Policy Making   7
The Role of Measurement in Accounting   8
Summary   13
Appendix 1-A: Valuation Systems   14
Questions   *24*
Cases and Problems   *25*
Bibliography of Referenced Works   *26*
Additional Readings   *26*

CHAPTER 2
Accounting Theory and Accounting Research   **28**

Accounting Research and Scientific Method   28
Is Accounting an Art or a Science?   36
Ethics and the Professional Realm in Accounting   38
Directions in Accounting Research   39
Summary   43
Questions   *44*
Cases and Problems   *45*
Bibliography of Referenced Works   *46*
Additional Readings   *47*

CHAPTER 3
Development of the Institutional Structure of Financial Accounting   **49**

The Formative Years, 1930–46   50
The Postwar Period, 1946–59   53
The Modern Period, 1959 to the Present   56

Summary   70
Questions   71
Cases and Problems   72
Bibliography of Referenced Works   74
Additional Readings   75

CHAPTER 4
The Economics of Financial Reporting Regulation   77

Unregulated Markets for Accounting Information   78
Regulated Markets   81
The Paradox of Regulation   87
The Regulatory Process   89
Toward a Political Economy of Accounting   93
Summary   95
Questions   96
Cases and Problems   97
Bibliography of Referenced Works   107
Additional Readings   109

CHAPTER 5
Postulates, Principles, and Concepts   112

Postulates and Principles   113
Basic Concepts Underlying Historical Costing   118
Equity Theories   130
Summary   133
Appendix 5-A: The Basic Postulates of Accounting (ARS 1)   134
Appendix 5-B: A Tentative Set of Broad Accounting Principles
    for Business Enterprises (ARS 3)   135
Questions   139
Cases and Problems   140
Bibliography of Referenced Works   141
Additional Readings   143

CHAPTER 6
Objectives and Standards   145

ASOBAT   147
APB Statement 4   153
The Trueblood Report   155
SATTA   161
The Conceptual Framework Project   166
Concluding Remarks on the Conceptual Framework   183
Summary   183
Appendix 6-A: User Objectives   185
Appendix 6-B: User Diversity   187

Questions   *189*
Cases and Problems   *190*
Bibliography of Referenced Works   *190*
Additional Readings   *193*

CHAPTER 7
Usefulness of Accounting Information to Investors and Creditors   **195**

Accounting Data and Models of Firm Valuation   196
The Information Content of Accounting Numbers   197
The Usefulness of Accounting Allocations   210
Summary   211
Appendix 7-A: Information Economics   212
Questions   *217*
Cases and Problems   *218*
Bibliography of Referenced Works   *220*
Additional Readings   *223*

CHAPTER 8
Uniformity and Disclosure: Some Policy-Making Directions   **225**

Uniformity   226
Disclosure   240
Directions in the Standard-Setting Process   246
Summary   248
Questions   *249*
Cases and Problems   *251*
Bibliography of Referenced Works   *253*
Additional Readings   *255*

Part Two
CONTEMPORARY ISSUES AND ACCOUNTING THEORY   **257**

CHAPTER 9
The Income Statement   **261**

The Relationship Between the Balance Sheet and Income Statement   262
Income Definitions   266
Revenues and Gains   267
Expenses and Losses   270
Current Operating Versus All-Inclusive Income   273
Operating Section Format   275
Nonoperating Sections   276
Earnings Per Share   282
Specialized Subjects Concerning Income Measurement   283
Earnings Management   285

Summary   289
Questions   *289*
Cases and Problems   *290*
Bibliography of Referenced Works   *294*
Additional Readings   *296*

CHAPTER 10
The Balance Sheet   298

Assets   298
Liabilities   309
Owners' Equity   315
Financial Instruments and Off-Balance-Sheet Transactions   318
Classification in the Balance Sheet   321
Summary   322
Questions   *323*
Cases and Problems   *324*
Bibliography of Referenced Works   *327*
Additional Readings   *329*

CHAPTER 11
Statement of Cash Flows   331

Logic Underlying the Statement of Changes in Financial Position   331
The Move to a Cash Flow Statement   335
Requirements of the Cash Flow Statement   338
Cash and Funds Flow Research   340
Summary   342
Questions   *342*
Cases and Problems   *343*
Bibliography of Referenced Works   *345*
Additional Readings   *346*

CHAPTER 12
Conceptual Issues in Accounting for Inflation and Changing Prices   348

Constructing Price Indexes   349
An Overview of Inflation Accounting   351
Income Measurement Systems   358
Special Problems in Measurement and Valuation   370
Summary   376
Appendix 12-A: Current Value Depreciation   377
Questions   *380*
Cases and Problems   *381*
Bibliography of Referenced Works   *382*
Additional Readings   *383*

CHAPTER 13
Problems of Implementing Accounting for Changing Prices and Inflation   385

History of Accounting for the Effects of Changing Prices in the
   United States Prior to SFAS 33   386
Provisions of SFAS 33 and Rejection in SFAS 82 and 89   389
The Failure of SFAS 33   395
Accounting for Changing Prices in Other Countries   399
Summary   402
Appendix 13-A: The Double Counting Effect with Current Costs   403
Questions   *405*
Cases and Problems   *406*
Bibliography of Referenced Works   *409*
Additional Readings   *411*

CHAPTER 14
Income Taxes and Financial Accounting   412

Income Tax Allocation   412
Accelerated Cost Recovery System   425
The Asset-Liability Orientation of SFAS 96   426
Summary   435
Appendix 14-A: Investment Tax Credit   436
Questions   *440*
Cases and Problems   *441*
Bibliography of Referenced Works   *445*
Additional Readings   *447*

CHAPTER 15
Oil and Gas Accounting   448

Conceptual Differences Between FC and SE   450
Standard Setting for Oil and Gas Accounting   452
Reserve Recognition Accounting (RRA)   462
Current Status of Accounting in the Oil and Gas Industry   465
Summary   467
Questions   *467*
Cases and Problems   *468*
Bibliography of Referenced Works   *472*
Additional Readings   *474*

CHAPTER 16
Pensions and Other Postretirement Benefits   476

Overview of Pension Plans   477
Development of Pension Accounting Standards   485
Assessing SFAS 87   491

Economic Consequences   493
Postretirement Benefits Other Than Pensions   495
Summary   499
Appendix 16-A: Mathematical Definitions and Illustrations of
    Actuarial Funding Methods   500
Questions   503
Cases and Problems   505
Bibliography of Referenced Works   507
Additional Readings   509

CHAPTER 17
Leases   510

The Lease Contract   511
Lease Capitalization   514
The Evolution of Lease Accounting Standards   518
Assessing SFAS 13   531
Economic Consequences of Lease Capitalization   532
Summary   535
Questions   535
Cases and Problems   536
Bibliography of Referenced Works   542
Additional Readings   543

CHAPTER 18
Intercorporate Equity Investments   545

Relevant Circumstances   545
Consolidation   547
The Equity Method   556
The Cost Method   557
Defining the Reporting Entity   558
Summary   561
Questions   561
Cases and Problems   562
Bibliography of Referenced Works   565
Additional Readings   567

CHAPTER 19
Issues in International Accounting   568

Translation of Foreign Operations   569
The International Scene   575
International Harmonization of Accounting Standards   577
Summary   585
Questions   586

Cases and Problems 586
Bibliography of Referenced Works 587
Additional Readings 588

Author Index **591**

Subject Index **601**

PREFACE

DURING THE LAST THREE DECADES, standard setting in accounting has become more extensive and more complex. Paralleling this regulatory development, accounting research has grown in importance and sophistication. Also during this period, accounting and other business disciplines have enjoyed increased respectability as academic subjects.

As a result of these developments, courses in accounting theory have arisen in order to synthesize approaches to financial accounting. In this book we provide an overview of accounting theory and policy to sharpen the understanding and analytical abilities of accounting students.

This book is intended for one-semester accounting theory courses at either the senior or graduate levels. It assumes that students are thoroughly grounded in intermediate accounting as well as (for Chapter 18) intercorporate equity investments. At the graduate level, the book is appropriate for courses in MBA programs with accounting concentrations and for MS programs in accounting.

We presume that all instructors will assign the first eight chapters, which are concerned with the elements of accounting theory as well as material on the structure and development of accounting policy formulating agencies. Beyond this point, chapters can be taught in any order although Chapters 12 and 13 (accounting for inflation and changing prices) are linked.

OBJECTIVES OF THE TEXT

Our basic objective is to clearly identify the elements of accounting theory in the first part of this text and then relate them to significant problem areas in accounting in the second part. Both parts bring in extensive coverage of the accounting literature. As the title indicates, we have attempted to integrate the theoretical and institutional aspects of accounting theory. The reader should thus acquire an increased depth of understanding of the major problem areas of accounting and the related standards going well beyond a mere technical grasp of debits and credits.

FEATURES OF THE NEW EDITION

All chapters of the book have been updated where either new standards have been promulgated or new theoretical findings or insights have appeared. Chapter 3 discusses the power struggle in which the FASB is engaged. Chapter 6 presents the view of the conceptual framework as a codificational document. Summary annual reports are discussed in Chapter 8. A major new standard on postretirement benefits (SFAS 106) is discussed in Chapter 16. Coverage of international accounting (Chapter 19) has been greatly expanded. We have also tightened the linkages between the first part of the text on the theoretical and institutional background and the second part of the book on contemporary issues.

The third edition, like its predecessor contains many cases based on corporate annual reports and sources such as the *Wall Street Journal* and *Business Week*. More than a half dozen new cases have been added from these sources and also from existing accounting standards. These cases enable students to relate accounting theory to the real world of business, a task that is essential to their professional growth and development.

Each chapter contains a fairly lengthy group of questions along with several cases or problems that reinforce the textual material or expand upon it. Additional teaching materials are contained in the Instructor's Manual. There is a very extensive list of referenced works and additional readings at the end of each chapter.

ACKNOWLEDGEMENTS

We have accumulated many debts arising from this project. The reviewers of the current and past editions provided valuable reviews, comments, and critiques:

R. Glen Berryman
University of Minnesota

Linda Bowen
University of North Carolina

John Corless
Sacramento State University

Thomas Hogan
University of Lowell

Garry Marchant
University of Texas, Austin

Sharon McKinnon
Northeastern University

Ralph Peck
Utah State University

G. Edward Philips
University of New Mexico

Gary Porter
Loyola University (Chicago)

Frank Rayburn
University of Alabama

Anne Rich
Quinnipiac College

Frederick Richardson
Virginia Polytechnic Institute

H. Lee Schlorff
Bentley College

W. Robert Smith
Georgia State University

Weldon Walker   Jerry Williams
Hardin-Simmons University   Delta State University

Robert Yahr
Marquette University

We would also like to thank Al Bruckner and Kelle Karshick from the editorial staff and Pam Rockwell and Tina Samaha from the production staff of PWS-KENT Publishing Company for their unflagging efforts to make this an outstanding revision. Ginger Wheeler, our typist, did her usual excellent job of turning our drafts into finished manuscript form. We also received many useful criticisms from previous users and other interested parties. We greatly appreciate all of their efforts.

ABBREVIATIONS USED IN THIS TEXT

AAA	American Accounting Association
AcSEC	Accounting Standards Executive Committee
AICPA	American Institute of Certified Public Accountants
APB	Accounting Principles Board (When used with a number it refers to an Accounting Principles Board Opinion)
ARB	Accounting Research Bulletin issued by the Committee on Accounting Procedure
ARS	Accounting Research Study issued by the Accounting Principles Board
ASR	Accounting Series Release issued by the Securities and Exchange Commission
CAP	Committee on Accounting Procedure
EITF	Emerging Issues Task Force
EPS	Earnings Per Share
FAF	Financial Accounting Foundation
FASAC	Financial Accounting Standards Advisory Council
FASB	Financial Accounting Standards Board
FC	Full Costing
FEI	Financial Executives Institute
GAAP	Generally Accepted Accounting Principles
GASB	Government Accounting Standards Board
IASC	International Accounting Standards Committee
IFAC	International Federation of Accountants
NYSE	New York Stock Exchange
OPEB	Postretirement Benefits Other than Pensions
RRA	Reserve Recognition Accounting
SCFP	Statement of Changes in Financial Position
SE	Successful Efforts
SEC	Securities and Exchange Commission
SFAC	Statement of Financial Accounting Concepts issued by the Financial Accounting Standards Board
SFAS	Statement of Financial Accounting Standards issued by the Financial Standards Board
SOP	Statement of Position

Part One

THEORETICAL AND INSTITUTIONAL BACKGROUND

T HE FIRST PART OF THIS TEXT is concerned with what accounting theory is and identifying important current issues pertaining to it. Developments in accounting theory play an important part in the formulation of accounting standards (rules) and their basic underlying concepts. These theoretical issues are linked to institutional developments in financial accounting. The first eight chapters establish a useful framework for analyzing and assessing the important accounting issues examined in the second part of the text.

Theory helps to explain and predict phenomena in a given field; accounting is no exception. The phrase *accounting theory* is commonly used in financial accounting, but it has no standard definition. Therefore, this text takes a broad approach to the interpretation of accounting theory. Chapter 1 discusses the various definitions of accounting theory and its role in the standard-setting process. Accounting theory includes a sizable array of concepts, models, hypotheses, and theories (in the narrow sense) of financial accounting. Many of these concepts have developed in response to needs arising from practice. The rules for recognizing revenues, valuation models, such as current valuation, and general price-level adjustment approaches are examples of need-driven concepts. Because of the insights accounting theory provides into identifying issues and solving problems, it makes an important contribution to the standard-setting process, the second major concern of Chapter 1. The chapter also points out that political factors and economic conditions are two other important influences upon the standard-setting process.

The process of measurement is clearly an activity in which accountants are engaged. Measurement, the process of assigning numbers to the attributes or characteristics of the elements being measured, is closely related to accounting theory and to the formulation of rules by standard-setting agencies. The relationship of measurement to accounting theory is considered not only in Chapter 1 but throughout the book.

Chapter 2 discusses both the deductive and inductive approaches to accounting research. During the last twenty-five years empirical (inductive) research in accounting has become extremely important; hence, the chapter discusses the problem of maintaining researcher neutrality, a very important issue. Agency theory is also introduced in the chapter. These topics lead to the broad question of whether accounting is an art or a science and an examination of the main research directions occurring in accounting.

Chapter 3 describes institutional aspects of accounting. The Securities and Exchange Commission, created in 1934, is empowered to make the accounting rules for enterprises whose securities are publicly traded. As a result of the fact that accounting rules were therefore to be made in the public sector, the Committee on Accounting Procedure of the American Institute of Certified Public Accountants began to take a much more active role in the setting of accounting standards. A good working relationship was established between this private-sector group and the public agency that had the power to make accounting rules. Despite occasional clashes, a close connection has been maintained to this day. The Committee on Accounting Procedure has since been succeeded by two other private-sector rule-making agencies: the Accounting Principles Board and the Financial Accounting Standards Board. How these three groups have operated and developed, their similarities and differences, and relations with the Securities and Exchange Commission and other external groups is the main subject matter of Chapter 3.

Accounting information is a commodity produced by the enterprise and, in the case of publicly traded firms, consumed by a wide variety of outside users. Chapter 4 presents the economic analysis of accounting information, a relatively new outlook. Accounting information is prepared by a monopoly supplier, the firm itself, for consumers — financial analysts — who do not pay for the commodity. Thus the nature of this market raises certain important issues. One important question concerns whether the cost of the regulatory agencies exceeds the benefits. Another important related issue is the economic consequences of accounting standards: the impact that accounting standards have upon the behavior of those who are affected by financial reporting.

Chapters 5 and 6 analyze extensively important documents and committee reports published by the American Accounting Association, the American Institute of Certified Public Accountants, and the Financial Accounting Standards Board. These publications highlight developments in standard setting and summaries of research issues during the last thirty years and reflect the attempt to establish a system of postulates and principles for the Accounting Principles Board and the Conceptual Framework Project of the Financial Accounting Standards Board. Between the time these two bodies were established to formulate a guiding theoretical structure, emphasis shifted to the importance of users of financial statements and their perceived information needs. Two committee reports of the American Accounting Association included in our survey provide an excellent summary of the state of accounting theory at the time. Chapter 5 also includes a brief analysis within a historical cost context of the concepts that have been used, albeit in an informal and unorganized fashion, as a guide for financial accounting rule making. In addition, Chapter 6 examines the conceptual framework developed by the Financial Accounting Standards Board.

Chapter 7 covers important new theoretical work centered largely on the usefulness of accounting information. Much of this work originated in fields outside of accounting but has important implications for the standard-setting process. The chapter's discussion of information economics provides a broad framework for understanding the value of information where uncertainty exists. Appendix 7-A presents the topic in the context of measuring the probabilities and values of the payoffs stemming from the choices facing the decision maker.

As Chapter 7 explains, capital market research is concerned with the response of security prices to accounting information. Of particular importance within capital market research are studies that have attempted to determine whether securities markets are "efficient." While the issue is by no means settled, these studies have generally shown that new information is reflected rapidly and without bias in security prices. Furthermore, the market does not appear to be fooled by changes in accounting methods that have a merely cosmetic effect upon reported income. However, changes in accounting policy that do have either direct or indirect effect upon enterprise cash flows do influence security prices. Studies have also shown that accounting information is useful for assessing risk: the degree of expected variability of accounting earnings. Chapter 7 also examines the role of risk in the determination of security prices — portfolio theory — and the allocation problem in accounting. Allocations are the methods used by accountants to divide costs or revenues among different affected periods. A strict interpretation maintains that there is no way to logically justify one allocation method over another. Nevertheless, income numbers containing allocations still influence security prices and are useful to investors.

The theory section of the text concludes in Chapter 8 with an extensive look at two concepts: uniformity and disclosure. One of the objectives of the Financial Accounting Standards Board, particularly in light of its Conceptual Framework Project, is to bring about greater uniformity in financial accounting. However, uniformity is a concept that has not been definitively established despite extensive discussion in accounting literature. There appear to be two conceptions of uniformity. One ignores the presence of different economic circumstances in broadly similar transaction situations. The other attempts to take into account these differences in underlying circumstances. The chapter analyzes the two conceptions of uniformity in broad cost-benefit terms as well as their application by standard-setting agencies to some situations. The examination of the concept of disclosure reveals that recent developments in capital markets research, the increasing complexity of transactions, and an inability to resolve theoretical issues indicate that disclosure is becoming more important as a means of communicating financial and economic information.

AN INTRODUCTION TO ACCOUNTING THEORY

THE FORM in which accounting information is recorded has been used for hundreds, if not thousands, of years. Luca Pacioli, a fifteenth-century Italian monk and mathematician, first described the double-entry framework, though its origins can be traced back another 300 years. Hence, the formal structure for processing business transactions is at least 700 years old. It should be no surprise that financial and economic information has always been important to owners and managers of enterprises. What is surprising, however, is the durability of the double-entry approach during a period of history in which technology and social institutions — including business itself — have become increasingly complex.

The complex changes directly affecting business include

1. The growth of absentee ownership and increasing importance of stock exchanges, where securities of firms can be bought and sold.
2. The increase in the power of national governments, including the right to tax, to regulate, and (in socialist countries) to own and operate business enterprises.
3. Catastrophic financial upheavals, the greatest of which was the depression of the 1930s, which have undermined the confidence of the public in financial reporting.
4. Prolonged inflationary periods, in which the utility of traditional historical cost-based accounting has come under sharp attack.
5. The growth and development of the multinational corporation.

The fact that these conditions have been particularly prevalent during the last sixty years not surprisingly gave rise to a demand for some amount of uniformity in recording business transactions and presenting financial statements of publicly owned companies. In the United States this demand led to the Securities Act of 1933 and the Securities and Exchange Act of 1934. The latter law created the Securities and Exchange Commission (SEC) and empowered it to prescribe accounting principles for firms whose securities are registered for trading on national and regional stock exchanges. However, since the creation of the SEC, three groups in the private sector have been entrusted with the task of developing and implementing accounting principles for publicly traded corporations: the Committee on Accounting Procedure (CAP, 1936–59), the Accounting Principles Board (APB, 1959–73), and the Financial Accounting Standards Board (FASB, 1973 to the present). The development and accomplishments of these private-sector groups will be discussed in Chapter 3.

We would all undoubtedly agree that because these groups and the SEC have been engaged in formulating financial accounting policy, they must somehow be concerned with something that is identifiable as accounting theory. Although we would be correct, a theory ideally *precedes* the work of rule-making bodies. The subject of accounting theory involves the whole complex of concepts, models, hypotheses, and theories that underlie and influence the work of the rule-making groups.

But even though the phrase *accounting theory* has been used for many years, it has no standard definition.[1] The term is used in this text in a very broad sense. It includes concepts, such as realization and objectivity, that have evolved in response to practical needs; models for valuation methods and other types of accounting alternatives, such as purchase and pooling; and hypotheses and theories based on a more formalized method of investigation and analysis of subject matter used in other academic disciplines such as philosophy, mathematics, and statistics. These newer and more formal approaches to the development of accounting theory are a relatively recent innovation in our field and permeate much of the accounting research going on today. The results of the research process are published in books and academic and professional journals devoted to advancing knowledge of financial accounting as well as of other branches of accounting, such as cost and management accounting, auditing, taxes, and systems. Various facets of accounting theory are discussed throughout this book. This chapter, as its title indicates, provides an introduction to accounting theory.

We begin by briefly examining the relationship between accounting theory and the institutional structure of accounting. One of the objectives of this book is to assess the influence of accounting theory upon the rule-making process. Hence, the approach adopted here is concerned with the linkages (and often the lack thereof) between accounting theory and the institutions charged with developing the rules that are intended to improve accounting practice. Closely related to accounting theory but somewhat separate from it is the process of measurement. **Measurement** is the assignment of numbers to properties or characteristics of objects. Measurement and how it applies to accounting are introduced in this chapter and appear throughout the text. The appendix to

---

[1] For example, the title of a famous work originally published in 1922 was *Accounting Theory*. See Paton (1922).

the chapter briefly illustrates the principal valuation approaches to accounting. These valuation methods are concerned with the measurement of economic phenomena. They are discussed in more depth in Chapter 12, but they are also referred to in the intervening chapters on accounting theory.

ACCOUNTING THEORY AND POLICY MAKING

The relationship between accounting theory and the standard-setting process must be understood within its wider context, as shown in Exhibit 1–1. We caution that Exhibit 1–1 is extremely simplistic. In reality, numerous feedback relationships exist — for example, among the components of the accounting policy environment — also, economic conditions have an extremely heavy influence upon political factors and accounting theory. Economic conditions thus have an important indirect as well as direct effect upon accounting policy making. Nevertheless, Exhibit 1–1 is a good starting point for bringing out how ideas and conditions eventually coalesce into policy-making decisions that shape financial reporting.

Bodies such as the FASB and the SEC, which have been charged with making financial accounting rules, perform a policy function. This policy function is also called *standard setting* or *rule making* and specifically refers to the process of arriving at the pronouncements issued by the FASB or SEC. The inputs to the policy-making function come from three main (though not nec-

EXHIBIT 1–1
The Financial Accounting Environment

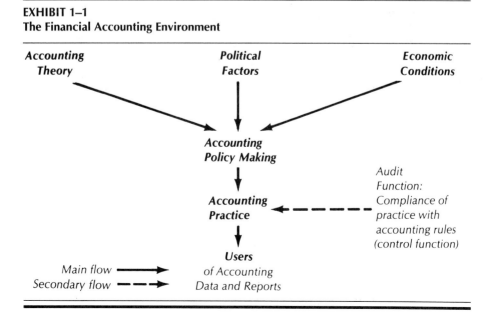

essarily equal) sources. The steep inflation of the 1970s, which was undoubtedly the catalyst that led the FASB to force the disclosure of information concerning price changes, is a classic example of an *economic condition* that impinged on policy making.

Political factors refers to the effect upon policy making of those who are subject to it. Included in this category would be auditors, who are responsible for assessing whether the rules have been followed; preparers of financial statements, represented by organizations such as the Financial Executives Institute; investors, represented by organizations such as the Chartered Financial Analysts; and the public itself, who might be represented by governmental groups such as Congress or by departments or agencies of the executive branch of government. In addition, the management of major firms and industry trade associations are important political components of the policy-making process.

Accounting theory is developed and refined by the process of accounting research. Research is carried out mainly by accounting professors, but many individuals from policy-making organizations, public accounting firms, and private industry also play an important part in the research process.

Standards and other pronouncements of policy-making organizations are interpreted and put into practice at the firm level. Hence, the output of the policy level is implemented at the accounting practice level.

Users may be any of many groups and include both actual and potential shareholders and creditors as well as the public at large. It is important to remember that users not only employ financial statements and reporting in making decisions but are also affected by the policy-making function and its implementation at the accounting practice level.

All facets of the accounting policy environment are important and are considered in this book, but we focus primarily on that part of the track running between accounting theory and the accounting policy function.

THE ROLE OF MEASUREMENT IN ACCOUNTING

Although the main topic of this book is accounting theory, measurement also receives close scrutiny. There is a link between theory formulation and measurement, but they are separate problems. Larson has stated this relationship well:

> First, there is a conceptual category of problems involving the isolation and precise definition of the properties that will be measured. Second, there is a separate category of methodological problems involving the determination of appropriate measurement procedures to be employed in assigning numbers to represent those properties.
>
> Evaluating the explanatory significance of the numbers which ensue from any measurement process depends on having resolved the problems of both categories . . . if the two types of problems are confused with each other and

treated as being essentially one, it is likely that one or the other of the problem areas will go generally unresolved.[2]

Measurement is defined as the assignment of numbers to the attributes or properties of objects being measured, which is exactly what accountants do. Objects themselves have numerous attributes or properties. For example, assume a manufacturing firm owns a lathe. The lathe has properties such as length, width, height, and weight. If we eliminate purely physical attributes (because accounting measures are made in dollars), there are still several others to which values could be assigned. These would include historical cost, replacement cost of the lathe in its present condition, selling price of the lathe in its present condition, and present value of the future cash flows that the lathe will help to generate. Attributes or properties are particular characteristics of objects. It should be clear that we do not measure objects themselves but rather something that might be termed the dollar "numerosity" or "how-muchness" that relates to a particular attribute of the object.

DIRECT AND INDIRECT MEASUREMENTS

If the number assigned to an object is an actual measurement of the desired property, it would be called a *direct measurement*. This does not necessarily mean that it is accurate, though. An *indirect measurement* of a desired attribute is one that must be made by roundabout means. For example, assume that we want to measure the replacement cost of ending inventory for a retail concern. If the inventory is commonly traded, we could determine the replacement cost of the inventory by multiplying the current wholesale price per unit for each inventory type by the quantity held and adding these amounts for all inventory types. This would be a direct measurement. Assume that our retail establishment has a silver fox coat in its inventory, a type of coat no longer commonly traded because of societal changes (animal rights activism, for example). Assume the coat originally cost the firm $1,000 when acquired; we estimate that it could be sold now for only $600. If the normal markup for fur coats were 20 percent on cost, we would estimate the replacement cost to be $500 ($600 ÷ 1.2 = $500). This would be an indirect measurement. Direct measures are usually preferable to indirect ones.

ASSESSMENT AND PREDICTION MEASURES

Another way of categorizing measurements is to classify them as assessment or prediction measurements. *Assessment measures* are concerned with particular attributes of objects. They can be either direct or indirect. *Prediction measures*, on the other hand, are concerned with factors that may be indicative of conditions

---

[2] Larson (1969, p. 44).

in the future.[3] Hence, there is a functional relationship between the predictor (prediction measure) and the future condition. For example, income of a present period might be used as a predictor of dividends for the following period. The market value of marketable securities would be an example of an assessment measure.

THE MEASUREMENT PROCESS

Several elements are brought together in the measurement process. Even when a direct assessment measure is used, that does not mean that there is only one absolutely correct measure. A simple measure of this type, such as a count of cash, depends on several factors:

1. The object itself.
2. The attribute being measured.
3. The measurer.
4. Counting or enumerating operations.
5. Instruments available for the measuring task.
6. Constraints affecting the measurer.

Objects themselves and their attributes differ vastly in type and complexity. How much cash does a small retail firm have? What is the size of the grape harvest in the Napa Valley during the current year? How many inches of topsoil did Iowa lose in 1990? The measurers themselves might have different qualifications. An ambitious junior accountant and a clerk who is somewhat shaky in arithmetic and not overly concerned about the job could bring markedly different talents to a measuring task. Counting and enumerating operations vary from simple arithmetic in a cash count to statistical sampling in inventory valuation. Instruments used by the measurer could include everything from a large computer to a hand calculator to pencil and paper, and the most obvious constraint would be time. Clearly, even a direct assessment measure is not as simple a matter as might first be thought.

TYPES OF MEASUREMENTS

The relationship between the measuring system itself and the attributes of the objects being measured determines the type of measurement.[4] The simplest type of measuring system is the nominal scale. A **nominal scale** is nothing more than a simple classification system, a system of names. Assume that all the students at a university come from Massachusetts, Connecticut, or Rhode Island. If we wish to classify students by state, a 1 might be assigned to Massachusetts students, a 2 to those from Connecticut, and a 3 to Rhode Islanders. In this

---

[3] Chambers does not believe that prediction measures should fall within the scope of measurement theory [Chambers (1968, p. 246)].
[4] Excellent coverage of this topic is given by Mattessich (1964, pp. 57–74).

example, the numbering system serves no other purpose than to classify by state. The same purpose could be achieved by the assignment of a different number for the state of origination — as long as the assignment of numbers to students is done consistently in accordance with the new nominal scale. A chart of accounts provides a good example of nominal classification in accounting.

Next in the order of measurement rigor is the ordinal scale. Numerals assigned in **ordinal** rankings indicate an order of preference. However, the degree of preference among ranks is not necessarily the same. Assume that three candidates are running for office. A voter's ranking might be Abel first, Baker second, and Charles third. However, the voter may see a virtual toss-up between Abel and Baker, either of whom is vastly preferable to Charles. In accounting, ordinal measurement is used to determine liquidity in the balance sheet.

In **interval** scales, unlike ordinal rankings, the change in the attribute measured among assigned numbers must be equal. The Fahrenheit temperature scale is an example. The increase in warmth from 9° to 10° is the same as that from 19° to 20° or any other increase in temperature of 1°.

The ratio scale like the interval scale assigns equal value to the intervals between assigned numbers, but it also has an additional feature. In the **ratio scale,** the zero point must have a unique quality. It does *not*, for example, in the Fahrenheit scale. The zero point on a Fahrenheit thermometer does not imply absence of temperature. Therefore, we cannot say that 8° is twice as warm as 4°; furthermore, 8° divided by 4° is not "equal" to 16° divided by 8°. Using a ratio scale type of measurement in accounting is at least possible because the zero point implies nothingness in terms of dollar amounts. Thus, in accounting, both $100,000 of current assets divided by $50,000 of current liabilities and $200,000 of current assets divided by $100,000 of current liabilities indicate the property of $2 of current assets for each $1 of current liabilities. This is possible only because of the uniqueness of the zero point in accounting.

QUALITY OF MEASUREMENTS

In attempting to analyze the worth of a measure, several qualities might be considered. Since measurers and their skills, tools, and measuring techniques are so important, we might consider agreement among measurers, in the statistical sense, as one criterion. Ijiri and Jaedicke view **objectivity** as the degree of consensus among measurers in situations where a given group of measurers having similar instruments and constraints measure the same attribute of a given object.[5] Objectivity is then defined as

$$V = \frac{1}{n} \sum_{i=1}^{n} (x_i - \bar{x})^2 \qquad (1.1)$$

---

[5] Ijiri and Jaedicke (1966). *Objectivity*, prior to the Ijiri and Jaedicke paper, referred to the quality of evidence underlying a measurement. In the statistical sense developed by Ijiri and Jaedicke, the word *verifiability* has tended to supplant *objectivity*.

where

n = the number of measurers in the group
x_i = measurement of the ith measurer
$\bar{x}$ = mean of all x_i for all measurers involved

In Equation (1.1), Ijiri and Jaedicke have used the statistical measure of variance as a means of quantifying the degree of agreement among measurers. The closer each x_i is to $\bar{x}$, the more objective is the measure and the smaller V will be. A comparison among competing measures in terms of objectivity could thus be made by comparing the Vs in controlled experiments.[6]

In the case of prediction measures, an obvious criterion is how well the task of prediction is accomplished. Assume that users of accounting data for a particular firm presume that dividends are equal to 50 percent of the income of the preceding period. This can be stated as

$$D_{j2} = f(.50I_{j1}) \tag{1.2}$$

where

D_{j2} = dividends of firm j for period 2
I_{j1} = income of firm j for period 1

Very often the predictor — the right-hand term in Equation (1.2) — cannot be known because users are diverse and make predictions in vastly different ways. In these cases, how well prediction is accomplished cannot be quantified. Where it can be, a measure of predictive ability — called *bias* by Ijiri and Jaedicke — can be determined by the following equation:

$$B = (\bar{x} - x^*)^2 \tag{1.3}$$

where

x^* = the value the predictor should have been, given the actual value of what was predicted and the predictive model — such as (1.2) — of users

While (1.3) is a less operational measure than (1.1), it is, nevertheless, an interesting conception for both theory formulation and policy-making purposes.[7]

Two other qualities that are pertinent to both assessment and prediction measures are timeliness and the cost constraint.[8] In terms of financial accounting, timeliness means that financial statement data — which are aggregations of many measurements — should be up to date and ready for quarterly announce-

---

[6] Objectivity tests have been applied by McDonald (1968) and Sterling and Radosevich (1969). Both studies used standard deviation of alternative measurements rather than the variance of Equation (1.1).
[7] Ijiri and Jaedicke (1966, p. 481) combine the objectivity and bias measures into one formula. Objectivity and bias together add up to the relevance of the measure ($R = V + B$).
[8] McDonald (1967, pp. 676–677).

ments of earnings as well as for annual published financial statement purposes (the 10-K and 10-Q requirements of the SEC). Oftentimes, the need for information on a timely basis may conflict with the cost constraint problem.

It is easy to lose sight of the fact that data are costly to produce. Many costs, computer information systems and accounting staffs, are fixed. More precise or accurate measurements, as well as more timely measures, involve expending additional resources. Timeliness and costliness must be borne in mind in the policy-setting process if not in theory formulation.

We will be referring again to problems of measurement throughout this text; however, we must make one observation immediately. Many of the measurements in traditional financial accounting are of neither the assessment nor the prediction variety. Historical cost depreciation and LIFO inventory valuations are numbers that admittedly do not represent any real attributes. Whether these are really measurements is not the primary issue. The important question is whether measurements made by totally arbitrary methods have utility for users.

Sterling refers to methods such as LIFO and FIFO as *calculations* rather than measurements if they do not correspond — that is, attempt to simulate or come as close as possible — to the measurement of real phenomena or attributes.[9] For example, LIFO and FIFO measures of cost of goods sold and inventories are simply cost flow calculations, which are concerned with dividing or allocating historical costs between asset and expense categories. They are not concerned with the measurement of such *real economic phenomena* as the replacement cost of the ending inventory and the inventory that has been sold. The distinction between measurements and calculations is important and should be kept in mind throughout this book.

SUMMARY

Accounting theory, introduced and broadly defined at the outset of the chapter, has no standard definition. We have adopted a very broad definition for the purposes of this text so that we could address many significant issues.

The relationship between accounting theory and policy making (the establishment of rules and standards) shows accounting theory to be one of the three major inputs into the standard-setting process, the others being political factors and economic conditions. There are numerous and complex interrelationships among these three inputs, but Exhibit 1–1 provides a useful basic understanding of the process.

Accounting theory and measurement are closely linked. Accounting theory is ultimately concerned with what information is needed by users; whereas measurement is involved with what is being measured and how it is

---

[9] Sterling (1989, p. 85).

being measured. As a result, there are often trade-offs between objectivity and the usefulness of the numbers being generated by the measurement process. The costliness and timeliness of the information are other important considerations underlying the measurement process.

There are four types of measurements: nominal, ordinal, interval, and ratio scale. Accounting has the potential to be in the ratio scale category. Meaningful comparisons may thus be made among similar accounting measurements for different firms. However, many so-called measurements in accounting are simply calculations in which no meaningful attempt is made to make them correspond to real economic phenomena.

Appendix 1-A briefly illustrates and discusses the principal valuation approaches to accounting. These include historical costs, general price level, exit- and entry-value models of current value accounting, and discounted cash flows.

APPENDIX 1-A: VALUATION SYSTEMS

In recent years much debate in accounting has centered upon the issue of valuation of accounts appearing in the balance sheet and income statement. We believe that many other theoretical issues should precede any attempt to come to grips with the valuation question. However, a basic familiarity with valuation systems enriches the theoretical discussion in this chapter. Consequently, an extremely simple example will be used to illustrate five valuation systems that have been extensively discussed in the literature. Using a simple example is a way to make clear the assumptions and workings of the valuation methods while holding aside, for the moment, many difficult problems that will surface later. The main aspects of each system will be discussed and critiqued here.

THE SIMPLE COMPANY

1. Simple Company was formed on December 30, 1984, by stockholders who invested a total of $90,000 in cash.
2. The owners operate the company and receive no salary for their services.
3. On December 31, 1984, the owners acquired for $90,000 cash a machine that provides a service that customers pay for in cash.
4. The machine has a life of three years with no salvage value.
5. All services provided by this machine occur on the last day of the year.
6. No other assets are needed to run the business nor are there any other expenses aside from depreciation.
7. Dividends declared equal income for the year.
8. The remaining cash is kept in a checking account that does not earn interest.
9. The general price index stands at 100 on December 31, 1984. It goes up to 105 on January 1, 1986, and 110 on January 1, 1987.
10. Budgeted revenues and actual revenues are the same. They are $33,000 for 1985; $36,302 for 1986; and $39,931 for 1987.

11. Replacement cost for a new asset of the same type increases to $96,000 on January 1, 1986; and $105,000 on January 1, 1987.
12. Net realizable value of the asset is $58,000 on December 31, 1985; and $31,000 on December 31, 1986. It has no value on December 31, 1987.
13. Simple Company is dissolved on December 31, 1987. All cash is distributed among the owners.
14. There are no income taxes.

The balance sheet for Simple Company after acquiring its fixed asset is shown in Exhibit 1–2.

VALUATION APPROACHES TO ACCOUNTING FOR THE SIMPLE COMPANY

Historical Cost

Throughout the financial history of the United States, historical costing has been the accepted orthodoxy in published financial statements. But severe inflationary periods in this country as well as in many other nations of the industrial and third worlds has led to an extensive search for a viable alternative to either replace historical costing or serve as a supplement to it. In a period of rising prices, attributes measured by historical costing methods generally have limited relevance to economic reality. The major exception to this is accounts that are either receivable or payable in cash during the short run, such as accounts receivable and payable, as well as cash itself.

The presumed saving graces of historical costing are that its valuation systems are both more objectively determinable and better understood than are competing valuation systems. However, the objectivity issue is by no means to be taken for granted. Even in our simple example, sum-of-the-years'-digits or fixed-percentage-of-declining-balance depreciation (among other methods) might have been selected to create a different balance sheet. And factoring in estimated depreciable life and salvage could produce different results. The understandability of historical costing is largely a function of familiarity. The introduction of new valuation methods obviously requires familiarizing users with their underlying assumptions and limitations.

Historical costing has also been defended as more suitable as a means for distributing income among capital providers, officers and employees, and taxation agencies because it is not based on hypothetical opportunity cost figures.

EXHIBIT 1–2

SIMPLE COMPANY
Balance Sheet
December 31, 1984

Fixed Assets	$90,000	Capital Stock	$90,000

Hence, the presumption is that there would be less conflict among competing groups over the distribution of income. However, this argument is by no means conclusive. As with depreciation, methods selected for income measurement can be easily disputed. Furthermore, opportunity cost valuations may be hypothetical in one sense, but they are surely far more indicative of economic valuation than are historical costs.

Income statements and balance sheets under historical costing are summarized in Exhibit 1–3. Balance sheets on December 31, 1987, in Exhibits 1–3 through 1–7 are prior to final dissolution.

General Price-Level Adjustment

Financial statements based on historical costing combine dollars that were expended or received at different dates. For example, a balance sheet on December 31, 1984, would add together cash that is on hand at that date with the unamortized cost of a building that was acquired in, say, 1960. It is, of course, very well known that a 1960 dollar had considerably greater purchasing power

EXHIBIT 1–3

SIMPLE COMPANY
Income Statements
Historical Costs

	1985	1986	1987	Total
Revenues	$33,000	$36,302	$39,931	$109,233
Depreciation	30,000	30,000	30,000	90,000
Net Income	$ 3,000	$ 6,302	$ 9,931	$ 19,233

Balance Sheet
December 31, 1985

Cash	$30,000		
Fixed Asset (net)	60,000	Capital Stock	$90,000
Total Assets	$90,000	Total Equities	$90,000

Balance Sheet
December 31, 1986

Cash	$60,000		
Fixed Asset (net)	30,000	Capital Stock	$90,000
Total Assets	$90,000	Total Equities	$90,000

Balance Sheet
December 31, 1987

Cash	$90,000		Capital Stock	$90,000

than a 1984 dollar. Consequently, there is a very serious additivity problem under historical costing because dollars of different purchasing power are added to or subtracted from each other. The additivity issue is an aspect of measurement theory.

One possible response to this problem is general price-level adjustment. This refers to the purchasing power of the monetary unit relative to all goods and services in the economy. Obviously, the measurement of this phenomenon is a considerable task. Adjustment is accomplished by converting historical cost dollars by an index such as the Consumer Price Index compiled by the Department of Labor. This index is not really broad enough, as its name implies, to be a true general price index, but it has been advocated as a meaningful substitute.

Except for monetary assets and liabilities — all items receivable or payable in a specific and unalterable number of dollars as well as cash itself — all amounts in financial statements adjusted for price levels would be restated in terms of the general purchasing power of the dollar at a given date, either as of the financial statement date itself or the average purchasing power of the dollar during the current year. Assume, for example, that land was purchased on January 1, 1970, for $50,000 when the general price index stood at 120. On December 31, 1984 — the balance sheet date — the general price index stands at 240. The transformation to bring forward the historical cost is accomplished in the following manner:

$$\$50,000 \times \frac{240}{120} = \$100,000 \tag{1.4}$$

Since it takes twice as many dollars to buy the same general group of goods and services in 1984 as in 1970, the general price-level adjusted cost of the land is, likewise, twice the historical cost.

Adjustments of this type restore the additivity of the dollar amounts on the 1984 statements. However, we must stress one very important point: in no way should the $100,000 figure be construed as the value of the land on December 31, 1984. The historical cost of the land has been merely brought forward or adjusted so that it is expressed in terms that are consistent with the purchasing power of 1984 dollars. Consequently, some individuals see price-level adjustment as a natural extension of the historical cost approach rather than as a separate valuation system.

Exhibit 1–4 shows income statements and balance sheets using general price-level adjustments. Footnotes to the income statements show the calculations for general price-level adjusted depreciation. Purchasing power loss on monetary items is an element that arises during inflation where holdings of monetary assets exceed monetary liabilities. Calculating the purchasing power loss is very similar to the adjustment for depreciation. In the Simple Company case, the cash holding prior to the price-level change is multiplied by a fraction consisting of the general price-level index *after* change in the numerator divided by the general price-level index *before* change in the denominator.

Although a purchasing power loss is certainly real, it is totally different from other losses and expenses, which represent actual diminutions in the firm's

EXHIBIT 1–4

SIMPLE COMPANY
Income Statements
General Price-Level Adjustment

	1985	1986	1987	Total
Revenues	$33,000	$36,302	$39,931	$109,233
Depreciation	30,000	31,500[a]	33,000[b]	94,500
Operating Income	3,000	4,802	6,931	14,733
Purchasing Power Loss	—	1,500[c]	3,000[d]	4,500
Net Income	$ 3,000	$ 3,302	$ 3,931	$ 10,233

Balance Sheet
December 31, 1985

Cash	$30,000		
Fixed Asset (net)	60,000	Capital Stock	$90,000
Total Assets	$90,000	Total Equities	$90,000

Balance Sheet
December 31, 1986

Cash	$63,000		
Fixed Asset (net)	31,500	Capital Stock	$94,500[e]
Total Assets	$94,500	Total Equities	$94,500

Balance Sheet
December 31, 1987

Cash	$99,000	Capital Stock	$99,000[f]

[a] $30,000 \times \dfrac{105}{100} = \$31,500$

[b] $30,000 \times \dfrac{110}{100} = \$33,000$

[c] $(\$30,000 \times \dfrac{105}{100}) - \$30,000 = \$1,500$

[d] $(\$63,000 \times \dfrac{110}{105}) - \$63,000 = \$3,000$

[e] $(\$90,000 \times \dfrac{105}{100}) = \$94,500$

[f] $(\$90,000 \times \dfrac{110}{100}) = \$99,000$

assets of either an unproductive or productive nature. Purchasing power losses do not result in a decrease in monetary assets themselves but rather in a decline in their purchasing power when the general price-level index increases. Consistent with the will-o-the-wisp nature of the loss, if an entry were booked it would take the following form:

Purchasing Power Loss   XXX
   Retained Earnings   XXX

The direct effect in the accounts is thus nil even though a very real type of loss has occurred. Calculations for purchasing power losses on monetary assets are shown below the income statements in Exhibit 1–4.

Current Value Systems

Current value, as the term implies, refers to attempts to assign to financial statement components numbers that correspond to some existing attribute of the elements being measured. There are two valuation systems that fall into the current value category: exit value (very similar to *net realizable value*) and replacement cost (also called *entry value*). As we shall see, entirely different purposes and philosophies underlie each system.

Exit Valuation   This approach is primarily oriented toward the balance sheet. Assets are valued at the net realizable amounts that the enterprise would expect to obtain for them if they were disposed of in the normal course of operations rather than in a bona fide liquidation. Hence, the method is frequently referred to as a process of *orderly liquidation*. Liabilities would be similarly valued at the amounts it would take to pay them off as of the statement date. The income statement for the period would be equal to the change in the net realizable value of the firm's net assets occurring during the period, excluding the effect of capital transactions. Expenses for such elements as depreciation represent the decline in net realizable value of fixed assets during the period.

     The benefit of this system, as proponents of exit-value accounting see it, is the relevance of the information it provides. With this approach the balance sheet becomes a huge statement of the net liquidity available to the enterprise in the ordinary course of operations. It thus portrays the firm's adaptability, or ability to shift its presently existing resources into new opportunities. A point in the system's favor is that all of the measurements are additive because valuations are at the same time point for the balance sheet (and for the same period of time on the income statement) and measure the same attribute. But the principal criticism of exit valuation also involves the same question of relevance: how useful are net realizable value measurements for fixed assets if the firm intends to keep and utilize the great bulk of them for revenue production purposes in the foreseeable future?

     Exhibit 1–5 shows exit-value income statements and balance sheets. As noted above, depreciation amounts represent the decline in net realizable value of the fixed asset occurring during each period.

Replacement Cost or Entry Value   As the name implies, this system uses current replacement cost valuations in financial statements. Both replacement cost and exit values are current market values. Replacement cost will usually be higher for two reasons. First, selling an asset that a firm does not ordinarily market usually results in a lower price than a regular dealer would be able to obtain. A good example is provided by the automobile market. If a person buys

EXHIBIT 1–5

SIMPLE COMPANY
Income Statements
Exit Valuation

	1985	1986	1987	Total
Revenues	$33,000	$36,302	$39,931	$109,233
Depreciation	32,000	27,000	31,000	90,000
Net Income	$ 1,000	$ 9,302	$ 8,931	$ 19,233

Balance Sheet
December 31, 1985

Cash	$32,000		
Fixed Asset (net)	58,000	Capital Stock	$90,000
Total Assets	$90,000		$90,000

Balance Sheet
December 31, 1986

Cash	$59,000		
Fixed Asset (net)	31,000	Capital Stock	$90,000
Total Assets	$90,000		$90,000

Balance Sheet
December 31, 1987

Cash	$90,000	Capital Stock	$90,000

a new car and immediately decides to sell it, he or she usually cannot recover full cost because of limited access to the buying side of the market. Second, "tearing out" and other disposal costs are deducted from selling price in determining net realizable values. Hence, the two different markets can result in significantly different current values.

Replacement cost is ideally measured where market values are available for similar assets. This is often the case for acquired merchandise inventories and stocks of raw materials that will be used in the production process. However, market values are often unavailable for such unique fixed assets as land, buildings, and heavy equipment specially designed for a particular firm. The same is true even for used fixed assets that are not unique, although second-hand markets often exist for these assets. These same considerations of measurement difficulty, however, also apply to the exit valuation system.

In the absence of firm market prices, replacement cost can be estimated by either appraisal or specific index adjustment. Cost constraints may inhibit the use of appraisals, but there are specific indexes applicable to particular segments of the economy — for example, machinery and equipment used in the steel industry. Indexes are essentially averages and if calculated for too wide a segment of the economy, they may not be good representations of replacement cost.

Replacement cost income statements and balance sheets appear in Exhibit 1–6. When replacement costs changed, depreciation was calculated by taking one-third of the new cost. Current value depreciation is a much more complex phenomenon to measure in practice. The holding gain adjustment on the balance sheet offsets the excess depreciation above historical cost.

The principal argument used to justify the replacement cost system over exit values is that if the great majority of the firm's assets were not already owned, it would be economically justifiable to acquire them. On the other hand, fixed assets are sold mainly when they become obsolete or their output is no

---

EXHIBIT 1–6

SIMPLE COMPANY
Income Statements
Replacement Cost

	1985	1986	1987	Total
Revenues	$33,000	$36,302	$39,931	$109,233
Depreciation	30,000	32,000	35,000	97,000
Net Income	$ 3,000	$ 4,302	$ 4,931	$ 12,233

Balance Sheet
December 31, 1985

Cash	$30,000		
Fixed Asset (net)	60,000	Capital Stock	$90,000
	$90,000		$90,000

Balance Sheet
December 31, 1986

		Capital Stock	$90,000
Cash	$62,000	Holding Gain	
Fixed Asset (net)	32,000	Adjustment	4,000
Total Assets	$94,000	Total Equities	$94,000

Balance Sheet
December 31, 1987

		Capital Stock	$90,000
		Holding Gain	
Cash	$97,000	Adjustment	7,000
Total Assets	$97,000	Total Equities	$97,000

longer needed. But advocates of the replacement cost school of thought disagree on some important points. The main one concerns interpretation of holding gains and losses, the differences between replacement cost of assets and their historical costs. The point at issue is whether these gains and losses should be run through income or closed directly to capital. This problem will be discussed in Chapter 12. We should also note that replacement cost can be combined with general price-level adjustment to provide a more complete analysis of inflationary effects upon the firm. This issue will likewise be covered in Chapter 12.

Discounted Cash Flows

Of the systems discussed, only the discounted cash flow approach is a purely theoretical method with virtually no operable practicability on a statement-wide basis. In this system, valuation of assets is a function of discounted cash flows and income is measured by the change in the present value of cash flows arising from operations during the period. Thus, both asset valuation and income measurement are anchored to future expectations.

In Exhibit 1–7 the internal rate of return of the asset is found by discounting the future cash flows at that rate that will make them just equal the cost of the asset (10 percent in this case). Thereafter, income is equal to 10 percent of the beginning-of-period asset valuation and depreciation is "plugged" to bring about this result. Income is also equal to the change in the present value of the cash flows measured at the beginning and end of the period.

In a real situation, the method would be virtually impossible to apply because many assets contribute jointly to the production of cash flows, so individual asset valuation could not be determined. Also, the future orientation of asset valuation and income determination leads to very formidable estimation problems, which would undoubtedly reduce objectivity in terms of the degree of consensus among measurers.

Because of the insuperable measurement problems, the discounted cash flow approach can be implemented only for a very restricted group of assets and liabilities: those where interest and principal payments are directly stipulated or can be imputed. An alternative approach for other assets, whereby assets of the firm would be valued in terms of those attributes assumed to approximate most closely their discounted cash flow in terms of their expected usage, has been advocated.[10] A mixed bag of discounted cash flows, net realizable values, and replacement costs would result.

---

[10] For more detail, see Staubus (1967).

EXHIBIT 1–7

SIMPLE COMPANY
Income Statements
Discounted Cash Flows

	1985	1986	1987	Total
Revenues	$33,000	$36,302	$39,931	$109,233
Depreciation	24,000	29,702	36,298	90,000
Net Income (10% of Beginning-of-period Asset Value)	9,000	6,600	3,633	19,233
Beginning-of-period Asset Value	$90,000	$66,000	$36,298	

Present Value of Cash Flows
December 31, 1984

$39,931 × .7513	$30,000
36,302 × .8264	30,000
33,000 × .9091	30,000 $90,000

December 31, 1985

$39,931 × .8264	$32,999	
36,302 × .9091	33,002	$ 9,000
33,000 × 1	33,000 $99,000[a]	

December 31, 1986

$39,931 × .9091	$36,301	
36,302 × 1	36,302	$ 6,600[b]
33,000 × 1	33,000 $105,603	

December 31, 1987

$39,931 × 1	$39,931	
36,302 × 1	36,302	$ 3,633[b]
33,000 × 1	33,000 $109,233	

Balance Sheet
December 31, 1985

Cash	$24,000		
Fixed Asset (net)	66,000	Capital Stock	$90,000
Total Assets	$90,000	Total Equities	$90,000

(*continued*)

EXHIBIT 1–7   (*continued*)

Balance Sheet
December 31, 1986

Cash	$53,700		
Fixed Asset (net)	36,300	Capital Stock	$90,000
Total Assets	$90,000	Total Equities	$90,000

December 31, 1987

Cash	$90,000	Capital Stock	$90,000

---

[a]$1 rounding error
[b]$3 rounding error

QUESTIONS

1. Why do you think the phrase *accounting theory* has no standard definition but, instead, several possible definitions?
2. Of the three inputs to the accounting policy-making function, which do you think is the most important?
3. How can political factors be an input into accounting policy making if the latter is concerned with governing and making the rules for financial accounting?
4. Is accounting theory, as the term is defined in this text, exclusively developed and refined through the research process?
5. What type of measurement is the measurement of objectivity in Equation (1.1): nominal, ordinal, interval, or ratio scale?
6. "The measurement process itself is quite ordinary and routine in virtually all situations." Comment on this quotation.
7. Can assessment measures be used for predictive purposes?
8. Why are theory formulation and measurement in separate domains?
9. A great deal of interest is generated each week during the college football and college basketball seasons by the ratings of the teams by the Associated Press and United Press International. Sports writers or coaches are polled on what they believe are the top twenty-five teams in the country. Weightings are assigned (twenty-five points for each first place vote, twenty-four for each second place vote, . . . one for each twenty-fifth place vote) and the results are tabulated. The results appear as a weekly listing of the top twenty teams in the nation. Do you think that these polls illustrate the process of measurement? Discuss.
10. Accounting practitioners have criticized some proposed accounting standards on the grounds that they would be difficult to implement because of measurement problems. They therefore conclude that the underlying theory is inappropriate. Assuming that the critics are correct about

the implementational difficulties, would you agree with their thinking? Discuss.

11. Some individuals believe that valuation methods proposed by a standard-setting body such as FASB should be based on those measurement procedures having the highest degree of objectivity as defined by Equation (1.1). Thus, some assets might be valued on the basis of replacement cost and others on net realizable value. Do you see any problems with this proposal? Discuss.

12. What type of measurement scale (nominal, ordinal, interval, or ratio) is being used in the following situations?
    Musical scales
    Insurance risk classes for automobile insurance
    Numbering of pages in a book
    A grocery scale
    A grocery scale deliberately set ten pounds too high
    Assignment of students to advisors, based on major

13. If general price-level adjustment is concerned with the change over time of the purchasing power of the monetary unit, why is it not considered to be a current value approach?

14. How do entry- and exit-value approaches differ?

15. Why is discounted cash flow extremely difficult to implement in the accounts?

16. How do measurement and calculation in accounting differ from each other? Give three examples of each.

CASES AND PROBLEMS

1. Assume that three accountants have been selected to measure the income of a firm under two different income measurement systems. The results for the first income system (M_1) were incomes of $3,000, $2,600, and $2,200. Under the second system (M_2), results were $5,000, $4,000, and $3,000. Assume that users of accounting data believe that dividends of a year are equal to 75 percent of income determined by M_1 for the previous year. Users also believe that dividends of a year are equal to 60 percent of income determined by M_2 for the previous year. Actual dividends for the year following the income measurements were $3,000. Determine the objectivity and bias of each of the two measurement systems for the year under consideration. On the basis of your examination, which of the two systems would you prefer?

2. J & J Enterprises is formed on December 31, 1987. At that point it buys one asset costing $2,487. The asset has a three-year life with no salvage value and is expected to generate cash flows of $1,000 on December 31 in the years 1988, 1989, and 1990. Actual results are exactly the same as plan. Depreciation is the firm's only expense. All income is to be distributed as dividends on the three dates mentioned. Other information:

- The price index stands at 100 on December 31, 1987. It goes up to 104 and 108 on January 1, 1989 and 1990.
- Net realizable value of the asset on December 31 in the years 1988, 1989, and 1990 is $1,500, $600, and 0.
- Replacement cost for a new asset of the same type is $2,700, $3,000, and $3,300 on the last day of the year in 1988, 1989, and 1990.

Required: Income statements for the years 1988, 1989, and 1990 under
Historical costing
General price-level adjustment
Exit valuation
Replacement cost
Discounted cash flows

BIBLIOGRAPHY OF REFERENCED WORKS

Chambers, Raymond J. (1968). "Measures and Values: A Reply to Professor Staubus," *The Accounting Review* (April 1968), pp. 239–247.

Ijiri, Yuji, and Robert Jaedicke (1966). "Reliability and Objectivity of Accounting Methods," *The Accounting Review* (July 1966), pp. 474–483.

Larson, Kermit (1969). "Implications of Measurement Theory on Accounting Concept Formulation," *The Accounting Review* (January 1969), pp. 38–47.

Mattessich, Richard (1964). *Accounting and Analytical Methods* (Richard D. Irwin).

McDonald, Daniel (1967). "Feasibility Criteria for Accounting Measures," *The Accounting Review* (October 1967), pp. 662–679.

McDonald, Daniel (1968). "A Test Application of the Feasibility of Market Based Measures in Accounting," *Journal of Accounting Research* (Spring 1969), pp. 38–49.

Paton, William A. (1922; reprinted 1962). *Accounting Theory* (Accounting Studies Press, Ltd.).

Staubus, George (1967). "Current Cash Equivalent for Assets: A Dissent," *The Accounting Review* (October 1967), pp. 650–661.

Sterling, Robert R. (1989). "Teaching the Correspondence Concept," *Issues in Accounting Education* (Spring 1989), pp. 82–93.

Sterling, Robert R., and Raymond Radosevich (1969). "A Valuation Experiment," *Journal of Accounting Research* (Spring 1969), pp. 90–95.

ADDITIONAL READINGS

Measurement in Accounting

American Accounting Association (1971). "Report of the Committee on Foundations of Accounting Measurements," *Accounting Review Supplement*, pp. 1–48.

———— (1975). "Report of the Committee on Accounting Valuation Bases," *Accounting Review Supplement*, pp. 535–573.

Bierman, Harold (1963). "Measurement and Accounting," *The Accounting Review* (July 1963), pp. 501–507.

Chambers, Raymond J. (1960). "Measurement and Misrepresentation," *Management Science* (January 1960), pp. 141–148.

——— (1965). "Measurement in Accounting," *Journal of Accounting Research* (Spring 1965), pp. 32–62.

——— (1971). "Asset Measurement and Valuation," *Cost and Management* (March–April 1971), pp. 30–35.

——— (1971). "Measurement and Valuation, Again," *Cost and Management* (July–August 1971), pp. 12–17.

——— (1972). "Measurement in Current Accounting Practices: A Critique," *The Accounting Review* (July 1972), pp. 488–509.

Devine, Carl T. (1985). "Accounting — A System of Measurement Rules," in *Essays in Accounting Theory*, Vol. I, *Studies in Accounting Research* #22 (American Accounting Association), 115–126.

Ijiri, Yuji (1967). *The Foundations of Accounting Measurement: A Mathematical, Economic, and Behavioral Inquiry* (Prentice-Hall).

——— (1972). "Measurement in Current Accounting Practices: A Reply," *The Accounting Review* (July 1972), pp. 510–526.

——— (1975). "Theory of Accounting Measurement," *Studies in Accounting Research* #10 (American Accounting Association).

Jaedicke, Robert, Yuji Ijiri, and Oswald Nielsen, eds. (1966). *Research in Accounting Measurement* (American Accounting Association).

Mattesich, R. (1970). "On the Perennial Misunderstanding of Asset Measurement by Means of 'Present Values,' " *Cost and Management* (March–April 1970), pp. 29–31.

——— (1971). "On Further Misunderstandings About Asset 'Measurement' and Valuation," *Cost and Management* (March–April 1971), pp. 36–42.

——— (1971). "Asset Measurement and Valuation — A Final Reply to Chambers," *Cost and Management* (July–August 1971), pp. 18–23.

Mock, Theodore (1976). "Measurement and Accounting Information Criteria," *Studies in Accounting Research* #13 (American Accounting Association).

Moonitz, Maurice (1970). "Price-Level Accounting and Scales of Measurement," *The Accounting Review* (July 1970), pp. 465–475.

Vickrey, Don (1970). "Is Accounting a Measurement Discipline?" *The Accounting Review* (October 1970), pp. 731–742.

ACCOUNTING THEORY AND ACCOUNTING RESEARCH

ACCOUNTING HAS BEEN an academic discipline in colleges and universities for over a hundred years. One of the characteristics associated with an academic discipline is the publication of the ideas it generates in magazines (which academics prefer to call *journals*, a particularly appropriate name for the discipline of accounting). The content of journal articles is often referred to as *research*. Although there are numerous viewpoints about the appropriate content of and approach used in carrying out accounting research, what is particularly interesting for our purposes is the increase in the use of the scientific method in the published research on accounting theory.

In this chapter we first examine **scientific method** and how it relates to accounting research. The term refers to the formal procedures used to derive the laws and principles that govern the so-called hard scientific disciplines, such as physics and chemistry. The application of scientific methodology to softer disciplines, such as accounting — which involves the human behavior of rule makers, preparers, and auditors of financial statements, and of the users of accounting information — has become an important topic in recent years. The role and meaning of theory to a given discipline are affected by whether the discipline is a science. Therefore, we need to consider the questions of whether accounting is, or can be, a science and of the relation of art to science. Accounting theory is largely derived from the research process. Therefore, the chapter concludes by examining what appear to be the main directions of current accounting research as well as some other influences affecting accounting research.

ACCOUNTING RESEARCH AND SCIENTIFIC METHOD

Theories can be extremely useful because they attempt to explain relationships or predict phenomena. Although accounting theory embraces a wide range of philosophical viewpoints, we are particularly concerned in this chapter with the formally developed theories that have been derived from the research process.

In terms of scientific method, a theory is, first of all, nothing more than sentences.[1] It must contain a basic set of **premises** (also called *assumptions* or *postulates*). The premises may be self-evident or they may be constructed so that they can be tested by statistical inference, in which case they are usually called *hypotheses*. Some of the terms in premises may be undefined but other terms may need precise definitions. The words *debit* and *credit* are so well understood by accountants that no definition is necessary. However, the word *liabilities* as used in a theory needs to be carefully defined because several different conceptions of it exist. In the narrowest sense, liabilities can be defined strictly legally — amounts presently due other parties for goods, services, or other consideration already received. However, the definition can be extended to include future cash disbursements for estimated income tax liabilities — straight-line depreciation is used for published financial statement purposes, and accelerated depreciation is used for tax purposes (a legal liability does not exist in this situation). Finally, a theory contains a set of conclusions derived from the premises. The conclusions can be determined either by deduction or induction.

DEDUCTIVE AND INDUCTIVE REASONING

To go from premises to conclusions in a deductive system requires logical reasoning. Empirical data are not analyzed in purely deductive systems. A simple example of a deductive system would be

Premise 1: A horse has four legs.

Premise 2: John has two legs.

Conclusion 1: John is not a horse.

In this simple case only one conclusion can be derived from the premises. In a more complex system, more than one conclusion can be derived. However, conclusions must not be in conflict with each other. Notice that no other conclusion relative to John could possibly be reached from the given premises.

Of course, if we were applying this theory to a real being named John, as opposed to analyzing the logic of a set of sentences, we would have to see and, if necessary, examine John to determine his status. At this point we would be in the inductive realm — because we would be judging the theory not simply by its internal logic but rather by observing the evidence itself. For example, John might be a horse that had two legs amputated. Assuming that the reasoning is valid, a deductive theory can be challenged only by questioning premises or conclusions empirically.

Accounting and economic theorists have developed different income models by means of deductive reasoning. The main source of a firm's income is

---

[1] Scientific method cannot be precisely defined and restricted to a given set of rules or procedures. See AAA (1972, pp. 403–406). For more on accounting and scientific method, see Mattessich (1984).

an increase in wealth resulting from operations during the period. Income has often been defined as the maximum amount that can be distributed to owners and still leave the firm as well off at the end of a period as it was at the beginning of the period.[2] Income thus is conditional, in the definitional sense, on maintaining intact the firm's capital at the beginning of the period. This concept is known as *capital maintenance*. Beginning with the basic premise, capital maintenance, there are at least three different ways to approach well-offness in capital maintenance terms. If we assume that the dollar is stable, historical-cost income measurement is appropriate and capital maintenance is ascertained in unadjusted dollars. In a period of inflation, if we desire to take into account the shrinking general purchasing power of the dollar, revenues and expenses can be measured by restating historical cost figures by appropriate general price-level adjustments. Similarly, income measured by calculating expenses in terms of current replacement costs is geared to a physical capacity concept of capital maintenance. Chapter 12 takes a more extensive look at capital maintenance and other goals and premises of various income systems.

Some deductive approaches to accounting theory have used formalized axioms as the premises of a system from which various rules of accounting can be derived. By *formalized axioms* we mean a set of terms rigorously defined according to the rules and terminology of symbolic logic.[3] Formalized deductive approaches (sometimes called *analytical/deductive* methods) have not met with a great deal of success in accounting theory owing to a limited understanding of symbolic techniques as well as a lack of agreement on the fundamental premises of financial accounting. General deductive reasoning, however, remains extremely important in accounting theory and policy making.

Inductive theories attempt to gather data or make observations in support of a premise or hypothesis.[4] If an individual were testing a pair of dice to see whether they were loaded, he or she might throw each die 100 times in order to check that all sides come up approximately one-sixth of the time. In accounting research, data is gathered through many methods and sources, including questionnaires sent to practitioners or other appropriate parties, laboratory experiments involving individuals in simulation exercises, numbers from published financial statements, and prices of publicly traded securities.

In a complex environment like the business world, a good inductive theory must carefully specify the problem that is being examined. The research must be based on a hypothesis that is capable of being tested, select an appropriate sample from the population under investigation, gather and scrutinize the needed data, and employ the requisite tools of statistical inference to test the hypothesis.

---

[2] Hicks (1961, p. 172).

[3] For an incisive review of this literature, see Willett (1987).

[4] Deductive reasoning prevailed over the inductive form from the time of Ancient Greece down through the Middle Ages. One of the individuals most responsible for shifting emphasis to inductive reasoning was the famous Elizabethan statesman and scholar Sir Francis Bacon. See Eiseley (1962).

One of the criticisms of early inductive or empirical research in accounting was that the relationships expressed were mechanistic. For example, empirical tests were made on the relationship between security prices and changes in accounting methods. However, the question of *why* standard setters or financial managers chose particular alternatives largely remained unanswered. Empirical research that attempts to answer the question of why particular standards are selected by policy makers or why management selects the particular accounting alternatives it chooses has been called *positive research.*[5] **Positive research** attempts to explain behavioral relationships in accounting. It attempts to describe "what is" without making any value judgments as to how things should be, though the researcher must make value judgments, as subsequent sections will demonstrate.

Many examples of inductively derived theories are present in the accounting literature. Watts and Zimmerman, for example, explored the question of how corporate management responds to new standards proposed by the FASB (the board invites written responses from interested parties to exposure drafts of proposed new standards).[6] One of their premises was that management acts in its own self-interest; for example, to increase personal compensation if reported net income increases. However, this is not necessarily the case in large firms if they are subject to antitrust action or regulation because of their dominant market position. In these firms, it may be in management's best long-run interests to have standards that result in lower reported net income. As a result, Watts and Zimmerman hypothesized that management has more incentive to favor standards that lower reported net income when the firm is subject to political pressure. They examined responses to the board's exposure draft requiring general price-level adjusted income calculations in corporate annual reports (the exposure draft was eventually withdrawn). Their findings tended to corroborate the hypothesis that the proposal was supported by larger firms that would have lower income as a result of general price-level adjustment. Similarly, those larger firms that would have higher income using general price-level adjustment tended to be against the proposal.

Several other comments are in order relative to Watts and Zimmerman's study. Their premise concerned potential management reactions to accounting rules that could either increase or reduce income, but the exposure draft on general price-level accounting concerned a supplementary measurement of income rather than the primary measurement of income. The exposure draft (which did *not* become a standard) would have required the publication by most firms of general price-level-adjusted income statements in addition to the primary historical cost statements. Their study concerned whether general price-level-adjusted income was higher or lower than historical cost income. Hence, it appears to have been a very reasonable test of the question of how manage-

---

[5] A discussion of positive research in accounting and a critique of previous empirical work appears in Watts and Zimmerman (1986).
[6] Watts and Zimmerman (1978).

ment reacts to standards that are perceived to increase or decrease measurements of the primary reported income number itself.

However, several other aspects of the study do raise important issues. Solomons, for example, has stated that Watts and Zimmerman's evidence is rather flimsy because it involves a relatively small number of firms (52), a single accounting issue, and a single point in time (the year 1973).[7] Solomons has also noted (from an unpublished study by William Lanen and Meir Schneller) that many of the firms that lobbied in favor of general price-level-adjusted income when that technique appeared to give a lower reported income were not availing themselves of existing techniques, such as accelerated depreciation and LIFO, which would have reduced reported income. The possibility of measurement error also exists relative to the situations where general price-level-adjusted income for 1973 would have been lower than reported historical cost income.

Furthermore, of the nine largest firms that would have had lower general price-level-adjusted income relative to reported historical cost income in 1973, two lobbied *against* the proposed standard, which certainly raises questions about the predictive use of the hypothesis.[8] Moreover, three other firms (Union Carbide, Continental Oil, and International Harvester) also lobbied against the proposed standard even though their general price-level-adjusted income was lower than reported historical cost income for 1973. Since these firms ranked between twenty-two and thirty-four in the Fortune 500 for 1973, it appears that the premise — large firms would be in favor of standards that decrease income — would be applicable only to a very small handful of very large firms (although there were anomalies here as noted above). We raise these criticisms of Watts and Zimmerman simply to show that empirical research in an area involving human behavior is subject to many interpretations and must be used in an extremely guarded and careful fashion if inferences relative to the standard-setting process are to be drawn from the research. There are, however, still other problems with the Watts and Zimmerman's research, which will be considered shortly.

NORMATIVE AND DESCRIPTIVE THEORIES

In addition to the deductive or inductive classifications, theories may also be categorized as normative (prescriptive) or descriptive. **Normative theories** employ a value judgment: contained within them is at least one premise saying that this is the way things *should* be. For example, a premise stating that accounting reports should be based on net realizable value measurements of assets would indicate a normative system. By contrast, **descriptive theories** attempt

---

[7] Solomons (1986, pp. 239–241).

[8] McKee, Bell, and Boatsman (1984) found statistical biases in Watts and Zimmerman's analysis that led them to question the explanatory power and predictive ability of the Watts and Zimmerman hypothesis.

to find relationships that actually exist. The Watts and Zimmerman study is an excellent example of a descriptive theory applied to a particular situation.

Although there are exceptions, deductive systems are usually normative, and inductive approaches usually attempt to be descriptive. These characteristics derive from the nature of the deductive and inductive methods. The deductive method is basically a closed, nonempirical system; its conclusions are based strictly on its premises. The inductive approach, because it tries to find and explain real-world relationships, is, conversely, in the descriptive realm by its very nature.

However, there is the question of whether empirical research can, in fact, be value free (neutral) in its findings because implicit value judgments underlie the form and content of the research itself.[9] This point has also been made by Gunnar Myrdal, the famed Swedish economist, who is quoted by Mattessich:

> Questions must be asked before answers can be given. The questions are an expression of our interest in the world, they are at bottom valuations. Valuations are thus necessarily involved already at the stage when we observe facts and carry on theoretical analysis, and not only at the stage when we draw political inferences from facts and valuations.[10]

Watts and Zimmerman do concede that from the perspective of both researcher and user, values do indeed underlie research.[11] Furthermore, Christenson has discussed the fact that positive research is not concerned with accounting issues per se but rather with the behavior of those who prepare and use accounting data — accountants, management, and users. The choice of issues to be addressed certainly involves values as Myrdal has so forcefully stated. Even though positive research is concerned with a different type of issue — behavioral relationships — than conventional accounting research, this does not necessarily mean that it is value free. An example of the difficulty of maintaining a value-free orientation is provided in a list of "positive" questions provided by a positive researcher. One entry on this list is the following:

> Why has the accounting profession been *cursed* with a strong authoritative bias — resulting in the establishment of professional bodies such as the . . . FASB to rule on "generally accepted accounting techniques"? (emphasis added)[12]

This question certainly contains strong biases of its own. A value judgment is obviously involved in even asking whether standard-setting bodies have or have

---

[9] Tinker, Merino, and Neimark (1982); and Christenson (1983).

[10] Mattessich (1978, p. 236).

[11] Watts and Zimmerman (1990, p. 146).

[12] As quoted in Christenson (1983, p. 4). Sterling (1990) is also very forceful about the point that you cannot study a discipline by studying the behavior of those who practice the discipline. Hence, Sterling sees positive research being concerned with the *sociology* of accounting rather than with the mainstream focus on income determination and wealth measurement.

not been successful. While empirical research attempts to be descriptive, it is virtually impossible for investigators to be totally neutral as they attempt to determine "what is."[13] Recognition of this fact by researchers might well improve the nature and findings of "descriptive" theories.[14]

Finally, on the output side, one of the purposes of positive research is to satisfy "information demand" by managers, auditors, users (financial analysts and creditors), and standard setters.[15] These groups look to positive research to maximize their own welfare.[16] The assumption — which is really a tautology — that individuals act in their own best self-interest appears to be the principal underlying postulate of positive accounting research. Hence, individuals have very normative purposes in mind and may well be in conflict both with members of their own group and with other groups.

GLOBAL AND PARTICULARISTIC THEORIES

A more sharply defined difference between deductive and inductive systems is that the former are sometimes *global* (macro) in content, whereas the latter are usually *particularistic* (micro). Where the premises of deductive systems are total or all-encompassing in nature, their conclusions must be sweeping. Within the context of accounting, examples of the global approach are the theories that advocate one type of valuation system for all accounts, as illustrated in Appendix 1-A. Inductive systems, because they are grounded in real-world phenomena, can realistically focus on only a small part of the relevant environment. In other words, inductive research tends to examine rather narrowly defined questions and problems. Again, the Watts and Zimmerman paper provides a representative example of the particularistic scope of inductive theory.

Many individuals (Nelson, for example) see global theories of accounting at an impasse.[17] The *Statement of Accounting Theory and Theory Acceptance* (1977) of the American Accounting Association regarded the conflict among global

---

[13] Schreuder (1984, pp. 216–218) discusses the view of Max Weber, the noted sociologist, that scientific statements are devoid of normative content and therefore cannot be used for justifying policies. This is an ideal position that appears to cut off pure descriptive research from the policy-making domain. It may thus be a mixed blessing that inductive research cannot be hermetically sealed and kept free from contamination by value judgments!

[14] For a brilliant essay on the pervasiveness of values, see Devine (1985). Devine does note that the separation of facts from values should, insofar as possible, be attempted. The question of values engaged Watts and Zimmerman (1979) in another journal article. In this paper they attempted to show that accounting theories provide "excuses" for particular political purposes. Since this outcome buttressed their own claim for providing "value-free" theories, the question arises as to whether they would have wanted to publish any other "finding." Peasnall and Williams (1986), in refuting Watts and Zimmerman, make a reasonably good case that the leading academic journals attempt to publish research that is largely value free (to the extent that this is possible).

[15] Watts and Zimmerman (1986, p. 340).

[16] Ibid., p. 3.

[17] Nelson (1973, p. 16).

accounting theories as unresolvable at that particular time.[18] Caplan saw the future direction of accounting research in inductive theory because it could shed light on particular questions.[19] Nevertheless, there continue to be important advocates of normative approaches.[20] In fact, the distinction between deductive and inductive research is simply not clear-cut.

COMPLEMENTARY NATURE OF DEDUCTIVE AND INDUCTIVE METHODS

The deductive–inductive distinction in research, although a good concept for teaching purposes, often does not apply in practice. Far from being either/or competitive approaches, deduction and induction are complementary in nature and are often used together.[21] Hakansson, for example, suggested that the inductive method can be used to assess the appropriateness of the set of originally selected premises in a primarily deductive system.[22] Obviously, changing the premises can change the logically derived conclusions. The research process itself does not always follow a precise pattern. Researchers often work backwards from the conclusions of other studies by developing new hypotheses that appear to fit the data. They then attempt to test the new hypotheses.

The methods used by the greatest detective in all literature, Sherlock Holmes, renowned for his extraordinary powers of deductive reasoning are an excellent example of the complementary nature of deductive and inductive reasoning. In one of Holmes's cases, Silver Blaze, a famous race horse, mysteriously disappeared when its trainer was murdered. One element of the case was that the watchdog did not bark when the horse disappeared. Dr. Watson, Holmes's somewhat slow-witted sidekick, saw nothing unusual about the dog not barking. Holmes, however, immediately deduced that the horse was taken from the stable by someone from the household rather than by an outsider. Thus, his list of suspects was immediately narrowed. Holmes was also keenly aware of induction: he systematically observed elements that would increase his knowledge and perceptions. Extensive studies of such diverse items as cigar ashes, the influence of various trades upon the form of the hand, and the uses of plaster of Paris for preserving hand and footprints added considerable depth to his deductive abilities.

In a not dissimilar fashion, inductive research in accounting can help to shed light on relationships and phenomena existing in the business environ-

---

[18] AAA (1977).

[19] Caplan (1972, pp. 437–443).

[20] See Hakansson (1969).

[21] See Carnap (1951, pp. 199–202) and Rudner (1966, p. 66). Bell, who is sharply critical of much empirical work, nevertheless sees a complementary relationship between empirical work and normative questions and issues that must ultimately be decided on what can be called a logico-deductive basis (Bell, 1986).

[22] Hakansson (1969, p. 37).

ment. This research, in turn, can be useful in the policy-making process in which deductive reasoning helps to determine rules that are to be prescribed. Hence, it should be clear that inductive and deductive methods can be used together and are not mutually exclusive approaches despite the impossibility of keeping inductive research value free.

IS ACCOUNTING AN ART OR A SCIENCE?

Both the rule-making structure and the practice of accounting occasionally raise the question of whether accounting is an art or a science. At least one author (in the 1940s) perceived it as a science.[23] However, he did not really set up criteria for defining a science, except his own particular prejudices in terms of valuation issues. Slightly later, another author maintained that accounting was very closely related to the liberal arts.[24] Accounting itself was seen as a "practical art." But that author did not present any real criteria for distinguishing between an art and a science. Certainly we can see that discussing accounting in terms of scientific method and the role of measurement theory in accounting potentially places accounting within the scientific domain.

In an important article and a follow-up book, Sterling has attempted to clarify the position of accounting relative to science.[25] He points out that the arts rely heavily on the personal interpretations of practitioners. For example, one painter might represent a model as having three eyes, whereas another painter might use the conventional two eyes — and a green nose — to represent the same subject. In science, however, he argues that there should be a relatively high amount of agreement among practitioners about the phenomena being observed and measured (notice the relationship of Sterling's definition of a science to the concept of measurement).

Sterling believes that accounting, as presently practiced, is far closer to an art than a science — owing to the way accountants define problems. In the case of depreciation, for example, a great deal of latitude is allowed in our measurements (if that is even the appropriate word) in selecting a depreciation method as well as deciding on an estimated number of years of life and a salvage value. The result is a low degree of objectivity, as well as the fact that no real attribute of the asset or the related expense calculation emerges except for the vague concepts *unamortized historical cost* and *depreciation expense*. A scientific approach, on the other hand, would strive to institute rigorous measurement procedures resulting in economically meaningful attributes, such as replacement cost or net realizable value of the asset or other elements being measured. The intention would be to provide information useful for either predictive or assess-

---

[23] Kelley (1948).
[24] Cullather (1959).
[25] Sterling (1975 and 1979).

ment purposes. These objectives are not being well served under our present rules.

Whether rigidly specified measurement procedures can be instituted to bring about a high degree of consensus among measurers in accounting is, of course, an extremely important question. However, scientists do not always come up with uniform measurements or interpretations of what they are measuring. Two examples from other disciplines should help to clarify this point.

One of the principal functions of econometricians (literally, "economic measurers") is predicting gross national product and related variables, such as the percentage of unemployment. There are several large models that have been constructed in an attempt to predict these variables. The models employ hundreds of simultaneous equations that must be solved by computer to generate the predictions. However, considerable disagreement exists among the models, and their predictions are often far from accurate when the actual results are tabulated. A further complicating factor is that the predictions interact with the results because many large corporations, as well as the federal government, use the services of econometric forecasters, which, of course, influences their actions. Nevertheless, the term *economic science* has been used to describe what econometricians do, though some may dispute the characterization.

Going further afield, we take an example from human anthropology, which is concerned with the study of ancient people and their forebears. In the mid-1970s, an almost complete female skeleton was discovered in a remote desert in Ethiopia. The skeleton of this species, named *Australopithecus Afarensis* (the skeleton itself is affectionately and unscientifically known as "Lucy" because its discoverers jubilantly played "Lucy in the Sky with Diamonds" and other Beatles' songs after the discovery was made), has been subjected to many scientific measurements, including carbon dating, which put Lucy's age at approximately 3,500,000 years. In addition, careful scrutiny of the structure of the leg and thigh bones indicated that the creature walked upright like humans rather than with the shambling gait of members of the ape family. Nevertheless, a huge controversy surrounds this species, *Australopithecus Afarensis*. Some anthropologists, particularly its discoverers, maintain that it is a true ancestor of the line that eventually became humankind. Other anthropologists, though, think that the species is not a true progenitor of humans. It should be noted that the arguments surrounding the species' place are largely deductive in nature. Even though the measurement techniques were carefully specified (though often applied in new and ingenious ways), the answer may never be known for certain unless more evidence is forthcoming. However, no one would dispute that human anthropology is a science.

These two examples demonstrate that science is not always exact and scientists do not always agree on the results of their work. Bearing this in mind, we can say, along with Sterling, that accounting has the potential to become more like a science, an outcome that should be pleasing to all involved. However, accounting is largely concerned with the human element, which is less controllable than the physical phenomena measured in the natural sciences. Consequently, we can expect accounting, along with economics and other social sciences to be less precise in its measurements and predictions than the natural sciences.[26]

ETHICS AND THE PROFESSIONAL REALM IN ACCOUNTING

Related to the question of art versus science is the issue of whether accountants practice a profession. Most accountants, we believe, would view themselves as members of a profession, but there has, in fact, been much discussion of the meaning of that term. We will leave it undefined here and instead consider another occupational group that is universally regarded as a profession: medical doctors. A recent book on the medical profession stated the following about doctors:

> Doctors are not scientists, at least not in their medical roles, because, though they certainly draw on science, what they do is neither objective enough nor oriented to the production of new knowledge – nor should it be. And they are certainly not artists, since aesthetic principles and independent creativity have little or no place in practice, despite everything that has been said about the "art" of medicine. But doctors are craftspeople of the highest order. Sometimes, like engineers, they lean very heavily on science. Sometimes, like diamond cutters, they seem to be coasting along on pure skill. And occasionally, like glassblowers or goldsmiths, what they do verges on art.[27]

Although not specifically stated, the concept of profession is certainly implied in this wonderful description of doctors, and it does suggest the following possible typology for medical doctors and accountants:

Scientist	*Professional*
Medical researcher	Medical doctor
Accounting researcher	Accounting practitioner

Like the medical doctor, the accountant can apply the results of research. As noted, however, it does not appear that accounting is quite ready to fit the scientist/professional mold, though the field has the potential to do so.

One possible reason why accounting may not yet be quite ready for the scientist/professional characterization is that accounting research is conducted separately from accounting practice and accounting education.[28] In other words, research is not taught in the classroom and does not have a large impact upon practice. This separation is stronger in accounting than in the professions

---

[26] See Stamp (1981) for an extended discussion of this point.

[27] Konner (1986).

[28] See Sterling (1973) and, in particular, Lee (1989) for an extensive review of the literature involving accounting research, education, and practice.

of medicine and law. A stronger emphasis on research results in the classroom ultimately might well enhance the interface between the professional and the accounting researcher, as well as have a beneficial effect upon accounting standard setters.[29]

The lack of emphasis on inculcating and fostering professional attitudes and outlooks in students is another drawback to the classification of accounting as a profession. Current accounting education is weak in areas such as ethics, beliefs and attitudes, and professional judgment and responsibility especially where technical issues and training are stressed over moral goals.[30] However, ethical and professional responsibilities are about to play a far more important role in accounting education. It is virtually certain that most accounting programs in the United States will shortly begin including case studies that require ethical and professional considerations. Accounting teachers might also encourage a more professional outlook on the part of students if they were to treat them as budding professionals.[31]

DIRECTIONS IN ACCOUNTING RESEARCH

The approaches discussed below represent particular orientations or directions of accounting research. They represent a significant change over the purely normative research of a generation ago.

THE DECISION-MODEL APPROACH

The **decision-model** approach asks what information is needed for making decisions. From this point of view, financial statements based on entry values, exit values, and discounted cash flows qualify as useful possibilities (see Appendix 1-A). This approach does not ask what information users want but rather concentrates on what information is useful for particular decisions. Thus, its orientation is normative and deductive. A premise underlying this research is that decision makers must be taught how to use this information if they are unfamiliar with it. Sterling advocates the exit-value approach for usefulness in decisions because the selling price of assets is relevant to the decision of keeping or disposing.[32] Also, aggregated exit values of all assets provide a measure of the total liquidity available to the firm.

---

[29] Lee maintains that "short-run" research, which is concerned with solving problems, is potentially welcome to accounting practice, but fundamental research (in areas such as valuation systems) threatens to change the status quo and, thus, remains outside of accounting practice and its satellite, accounting education. Lee (1989, pp. 249–251).

[30] Mayer-Sommer and Loeb (1981, pp. 125, 127).

[31] Ibid., p. 132.

[32] See Sterling (1979, p. 89 and pp. 95–124).

CAPITAL MARKET RESEARCH

A significant amount of empirical (inductive) research shows that prices of publicly traded securities react rapidly and in an unbiased manner to new information. Hence, market prices are assumed to reflect fully all publicly available information. This proposition, which stems principally from the discipline of finance, is known as the *efficient-markets hypothesis*. It has some potentially significant implications for accounting. For example, because information is rapidly reflected in security prices, the impetus for increased disclosure with less concern for choice among accounting alternatives has grown stronger.[33] Since the efficient-markets hypothesis states that the return of a security is based on its risk, other research has attempted to assess the relationship between accounting-based measures of risk (financial statement ratios, for example) and market-based risk measures.[34] The effect of accounting policy choices on security prices has also been extensively tested.

BEHAVIORAL RESEARCH

Behavioral research is another important area of investigation. The main concern of **behavioral research** is how users of accounting information make decisions and what information they need. Notice that this approach is descriptive, whereas the decision-model approach is normative. Much of this research uses laboratory subjects in carefully controlled experimental situations. McIntyre, for example, attempted to find out whether replacement cost information is more useful than historical cost information in evaluating actual annual rate of return.[35] Four middle-sized firms in the tire and rubber industry were analyzed over a three-year period. His subjects were graduate and undergraduate students some of whom received replacement cost financial statements, other historical cost statements, and still others both. The subjects were asked to select the firm that would produce the highest actual annual rate of return during the three years. Actual annual rate of return was defined as

$$r = \frac{1}{n}\left(\frac{\Delta M + D}{M}\right) \tag{2.1}$$

where

n = length of the assumed holding period in years;
D = dividends received during the holding period;
M = market value of the stock at the beginning of the holding period;
ΔM = change in the market value of the stock during the holding period.

Although there were considerable qualifications, McIntyre's findings failed to show any advantage to users of replacement-cost financial statements. But the question of how representative McIntyre's student subjects were relative to the

---

[33] See Beaver (1973).
[34] For example, see Beaver, Kettler, and Scholes (1968) and Bildersee (1975).
[35] McIntyre (1973). For an extended critique of McIntyre's research design, see Dyckman (1975).

broad population of real decision makers is a problem that pervades virtually all behavioral research employing student subjects in laboratory experiments.

AGENCY THEORY

Agency theory is now an extremely important type of accounting research. **Agency theory** studies may be deductive or inductive and are a special example of behavioral research, though the roots of agency theory lie in finance and economics rather than in psychology and sociology. The phrase *positive account-ing research*, coined by Watts and Zimmerman, is virtually synonymous with *agency theory* research in accounting (agency theory studies are also being done in other business disciplines, such as finance and marketing). Its underlying assumption, as we have discussed, is that individuals act in their own best self-interest. Another important assumption of agency theory is that the enterprise is the locus or intersection point for many contractual-type relationships that exist among management, owners, creditors, and government. As a result, agency theory is concerned with the various costs of monitoring and enforcing relations among these various groups.[36] The audit, for example, can be viewed as an instrument for insuring that the firm's financial statements have been sub-ject to a certain amount of internal scrutiny. In addition, the statements them-selves — presuming an unqualified opinion — are assumed to meet the criterion of being in accordance with generally accepted accounting principles. The au-dit, therefore, attempts to give assurances to outsiders, such as owners and cred-itors, about the governance of the enterprise by management. Many agency relationships between parties are defined or governed by accounting numbers. These include bond covenants, which prescribe the maximum level of ratios such as debt to equity; management compensation contracts where bonuses are based on income; and income taxes. As a result, the choice of accounting meth-ods by firms may be influenced by their effect on agency contracts.

One hypothesis of agency theory is that management attempts to maxi-mize its own welfare by minimizing the various agency costs. Notice that this is not quite the same as saying that management attempts to maximize the value of the firm. As in the Watts and Zimmerman study discussed previously, man-agers would presumably select that accounting alternative that maximizes the measurement of income if its own compensation is tied to reported income, provided it perceives that no adverse political effects, such as antitrust action, would result.

Other assumptions about the nature of the firm compete with the agency theory assumption that the firm is the locus or nexus for many contractual types of relationships. Chambers, for example, has described the firm as ". . . a tem-porary coalition of participants in unstable equilibrium."[37] Chambers' coalition view sees the firm — even though it is an artificial entity — playing a stronger

---

[36] See Watts (1977) for more on agency relationships and the role of audited financial statements in an unregulated economy.
[37] Chambers (1990, p. 16).

role vis-à-vis the various participants than it does under agency theory, where the firm per se has virtually no role. In the coalition view, income as a measurement of the economic performance of the firm and economically viable measures of assets and liabilities are important functions of accounting and should be the primary considerations of standard-setting agencies. No such viewpoint exists in agency theory. The point is not that agency theory is either "right" or "wrong"; theories like agency theory and the coalition view are both partial descriptions of the workings and interrelationships of the firm and its constituent participants. Various competing theories and viewpoints may bring important insights to accountants, auditors, users, and standard-setters. No individual approach should be deemed superior to all others, for important contributions may come from any and all sources.

INFORMATION ECONOMICS

Finally, accountants are becoming increasingly conscious of the cost of producing accounting information. This has led to a relatively new field of inquiry for accounting researchers: **information economics.** Information economics research is usually analytical/deductive in nature. With the exception of cash flow accounting, alternatives to the historical cost accounting model would, prima facie, appear to impose additional information production costs upon firms. Whether the benefits of alternative information sets or larger information sets are worth their costs is an important question. The nature of this problem has been succinctly stated by Beaver and Demski:

> . . . . the crux of the argument on behalf of accrual accounting rests on the premise that (1) reported income under accrual accounting conveys more information than a less ambitious cash flow-oriented accounting system would, (2) accrual accounting is the most efficient way to convey this additional information, and, as a corollary, (3) the "value" of such additional information system exceeds its "cost."[38]

These are some of the main directions of current accounting research. Some may be more promising than others, but we believe that all approaches are capable of contributing to our knowledge and providing important insights to the policy process. Sterling and May and Sundem have also expressed a similar view.[39] Many of these approaches will be discussed throughout the text.

A SCIENTIFIC REVOLUTION IN ACCOUNTING?

As should be obvious from this discussion of the many viewpoints in accounting research, it is a field that is presently in a considerable state of flux. Some have predicted a scientific revolution in accounting because of dissatisfaction with

---

[38] Beaver and Demski (1979, p. 43).
[39] Sterling (1979, p. 53) and May and Sundem (1976).

the existing paradigm.[40] A **paradigm** is a shared problem-solving view among members of a science or discipline. In accounting, the shared paradigm has been historical costing, which is based on the concepts of realization and matching and other important tenets, such as conservatism, going concern, accounting entity, and time period.[41] The inability of historical costing to cope with the problems of financial reporting during the 1970s in the wake of severe inflation caused a great deal of dissatisfaction. The effects of inflation at that time combined with the concurrent development of empirical research in accounting as well as other research perspectives led some to see the development of a new paradigm in accounting as possible.

We would question whether this is really the case. Current valuation adherents disagree with each other. Furthermore, with the lessening of inflation during the 1980s, criticism of historical costing has abated. However, influences leading to the development of new paradigms can be very long run in nature. Suffice it to say that the many new research approaches and outlooks in accounting make this an exciting time to be involved with financial accounting. Only time will tell whether a new valuation model or other type of paradigm will emerge as our new orthodoxy.

SUMMARY

One avenue for the development of accounting theory is through research. In reasoning from premises (assumptions) to conclusions, results can be determined either deductively (logically reasoning from premises to conclusions) or inductively (by gathering data to support or refute the hypothesis). Deductive reasoning is generally normative, and, ideally, inductive reasoning is purely descriptive but findings derived from it cannot be totally value free or neutral. Deductive and inductive reasoning are, however, complementary. Clearly, accounting policy making is normative since it is concerned with prescribing choices among accounting methods and requiring particular disclosures.

Whether accounting is an art or a science is a recurring question. In the realm of art, practitioners rather freely use individual interpretations when plying their craft. Science is more rigorous; practitioners should have a relatively high amount of consensus when measuring the same phenomena. There can, however, be strong disagreements in science. Accounting appears to be closer to an art than a science today because there is much free choice in selecting accounting methods and rigorous measurement of phenomena by accountants is presently not a part of our discipline. Ideally, accounting researchers should be scientists in the same way medical scientists are, and accounting prac-

---

[40] The nature of scientific revolutions and dissatisfaction with existing paradigms is described in the very influential work of Thomas S. Kuhn.

[41] Wells has been a strong proponent of the Kuhnian view applied to accounting (Wells, 1976).

titioners should be professionals who utilize the results of the research process as medical doctors do.

Accounting research has taken many directions, including the decision-model approach, capital market research, behavioral research, agency theory, and information economics. Our viewpoint is that all these approaches are potentially valuable in terms of adding to our knowledge about accounting and its environment. However, it does not appear that a scientific revolution has occurred in accounting because historical cost is still the dominant paradigm.

QUESTIONS

1. Do you think that the work of a policy-making organization such as the FASB or the SEC is normative (value-judgment oriented) or positive (oriented toward value-free rules)? Discuss.

2. An individual who was appraising accounting education had the following premises (assumptions):

   (a) Accounting professors used to do more consulting with accounting practitioners than they do today.

   (b) Accounting professors have become more interested in research that is abstract and not practical than used to be the case.

   He therefore concluded that accounting students are not as well prepared to enter the accounting profession as they used to be. What kind of reasoning was the individual using? What is your assessment of his conclusion? Discuss in depth.

3. In 1936 the country was still suffering from the Great Depression. During the presidential election campaign, an extensive survey of voter attitudes was undertaken to find out whether the public preferred the incumbent, Franklin Delano Roosevelt, or the challenger, Alf Landon. The sample was gathered randomly from telephone book listings throughout the country. A preference was found for Alf Landon; however, Roosevelt won re-election by a huge landslide. What type of research was being conducted? Why do you think it failed to make an accurate prediction?

4. Do you think that deductive reasoning, in general, is normative in nature? In accounting, deductive approaches are generally normative. Why do you think this is the case?

5. A frequent argument is that inductive reasoning is value free because it simply investigates empirical evidence. Yet some charge that it is not value free. What do you think is the basis for this charge?

6. Several years ago an author stated that corporate income could be scientifically ascertained, but any type of adjustment for inflation would be pure folly because measurements would tend to become very subjective. Do you agree with the author's appraisal? Comment in detail.

7. Of the four disciplines in the following list, which do you think qualify as sciences and which do not? State your reasons very carefully.

Law
Medicine
Cosmetology
Accountancy
8. Several occupations *within* two of the above-named disciplines are listed below. Which do you think come closest to being scientific and which do not?
Accounting researcher
Chief accountant for an industrial firm
Medical researcher
Doctor (general practitioner)
9. Descriptive research, ideally speaking, should be value free. Do you agree? Why is this ideal unattainable in the actual conducting of research?
10. Why might the managers of very large firms be against accounting standards that would increase their reported income and be in favor of those that would lower their reported income?
11. If Watts and Zimmerman were correct in terms of managers of very large firms being against accounting standards that would raise their income and in favor of those that would lower it, what policy implications would this have for a standard-setting organization such as the FASB?
12. What is the major difference in orientation between positive accounting theory and more overtly normative theories, such as the valuation approaches discussed in Chapter 1?
13. "For a discipline to become a science, the results of experiments and research must be exact." Do you agree with this statement? Discuss.
14. Why, in practical terms, is it impossible to separate deductive and inductive approaches to theoretical reasoning?
15. What particular problems do you see facing disciplines in the areas of business administration and economics, such as accounting and marketing, in moving closer to the scientific realm?
16. What is the relationship among scientific method, accounting research, and accounting policy making?
17. What are the two principal underlying assumptions of agency theory (positive accounting research)? Criticize their role in constructing a theory of accounting.

CASES AND PROBLEMS

1. Agency theory takes the view that the corporation is the locus or nexus of many competing and conflicting interests. List as many of these conflicting groups as you can and discuss in detail the nature of their conflicts with other groups.
2. The concept of profession was discussed in the chapter as a subissue to the art versus science distinction. List and discuss as many traits of a profession as you can.

BIBLIOGRAPHY OF REFERENCED WORKS

American Accounting Association (1972). "Report of the Committee on Research Methodology in Accounting," *Accounting Review Supplement*, pp. 399–520.

—— (1977). *Statement on Accounting Theory and Theory Acceptance* (American Accounting Association).

Beaver, William (1973). "What Should Be the FASB's Objectives?" *Journal of Accountancy* (August 1973), pp. 49–56.

Beaver, William, and Joel Demski (1979). "The Nature of Income Measurement," *The Accounting Review* (January 1979), pp. 38–46.

Beaver, William, Paul Kettler, and Myron Scholes (1970). The Association Between Market Determined and Accounting Determined Risk Measures," *The Accounting Review* (October 1970), pp. 654–682.

Bell, Philip W. (1987). "Accounting as a Discipline for Study and Practice: 1986," *Contemporary Accounting Research* (Spring 1987), pp. 338–367.

Bildersee, John (1975). "The Association Between a Market-Determined Measure of Risk and Alternative Measures of Risk," *The Accounting Review* (January 1975), pp. 81–98.

Caplan, Edward (1972). "Accounting Research as an Information Source for Theory Construction," *Accounting Review Supplement*, pp. 437–444.

Carnap, Rudolf (1951). *The Nature and Application of Inductive Logic* (University of Chicago Press).

Chambers, R. J. (1990). "Positive Accounting Theory and the PA Cult" (unpublished manuscript).

Christenson, Charles (1983). "The Methodology of Positive Accounting," *The Accounting Review* (January 1983), pp. 1–22.

Cullather, James (1959). "Accounting: Kin to the Humanities," *The Accounting Review* (October 1959), pp. 525–527.

Devine, Carl T. (1985). "Description, Phenomenology, and Value-Free Science," in *Essays in Accounting Theory*, Vol. V, *Studies in Accounting Research #22* (American Accounting Association), pp. 1–16.

Dyckman, Thomas R. (1975). "The Effects of Restating Price-Level Changes: A Comment," *The Accounting Review* (October 1975), pp. 796–808.

Eiseley, Loren (1962). *Francis Bacon and the Modern Dilemma* (University of Nebraska Press).

Hakansson, Nils (1969). "Normative Accounting Theory and the Theory of Decision," *International Journal of Accounting* (Spring 1969), pp. 33–48.

Hicks, John R. (1961). *Value and Capital*, 2nd ed. (Oxford University Press).

Kelley, Arthur (1948). "Definitive Income Determinations: The Measurement of Corporate Income on an Objective Scientific Basis," *The Accounting Review* (April 1948), pp. 148–153.

Konner, Melvin (1987). *Becoming a Doctor* (Elizabeth Sifton/Viking).

Kuhn, Thomas S. (1970). *The Structure of Scientific Revolutions* (University of Chicago Press).

Lee, Tom (1989). "Education, Practice and Research in Accounting: Gaps, Closed Loops, Bridges and Magic Accounting," *Accounting and Business Research* (Summer 1989), pp. 237–253.

Mattessich, Richard (1978). *Instrumental Reasoning and Systems Methodology* (D. Reidel Publishing Company).

—— (1984). "The Scientific Approach to Accounting," in *Modern Accounting Research: History, Survey, and Guide* (The Canadian Certified General Accountants' Research Foundation), pp. 1–19.

May, Robert, and Gary Sundem (1976). "Research for Accounting Policy: An Overview," *The Accounting Review* (October 1976), pp. 747–763.

Mayer-Sommer, Alan P., and Stephen E. Loeb (1981). "Fostering More Successful Professional Socialization Among Accounting Students," *The Accounting Review* (January 1981), pp. 125–136.

McIntyre, Edward (1973). "Current-Cost Financial Statements and Common-Stock Investment Decisions," *The Accounting Review* (July 1973), pp. 575–585.

McKee, A. James, Jr., Timothy B. Bell, and James R. Boatsman (1984). "Management Preferences Over Accounting Standards: A Replication and Additional Tests," *The Accounting Review* (October 1984), pp. 647–659.

Nelson, Carl (1973). "A Priori Research in Accounting," in *Accounting Research 1960–1970: A Critical Evaluation*, ed. N. Dopuch and L. Revsine (University of Illinois), pp. 3–19.

Peasnall, K. V., and D. J. Williams (1986). "Ersatz Academics and Scholar-Saints: The Supply of Financial Accounting Research," *Abacus* (September 1986), pp. 121–135.

Rudner, Richard (1966). *Philosophy of Social Science* (Prentice-Hall).

Schreuder, Hein (1984). "Positively Normative (Accounting) Theories," in *European Contributions to Accounting Research*, ed. A. G. Hopwood and H. Schreuder (VU Uitgeverij/Free University Press), pp. 213–231.

Solomons, David (1986). *Making Accounting Policy* (Oxford University Press).

Stamp, Edward (1981). "Why Can Accounting Not Become a Science Like Physics?" *Abacus* (Spring 1981), pp. 13–27.

Sterling, Robert R. (1973). "Accounting Research, Education, and Practice," *Journal of Accountancy* (September 1973), pp. 44–52.

——— (1975). "Toward a Science of Accounting," *Financial Analysts Journal* (September–October 1975), pp. 28–36.

——— (1979). *Toward a Science of Accounting* (Scholars Book Co.).

——— (1990). "Positive Accounting: An Assessment, *Abacus* (September 1990), pp. 97–135.

Tinker, Anthony, Barbara Merino, and Marilyn Neimark (1982). "The Normative Origins of Positive Theories: Ideology and Accounting Thought," *Accounting, Organizations and Society* 7(no. 2): 167–200.

Watts, Ross L. (1977). "Corporate Financial Statements, a Product of the Market and Political Processes," *Australian Journal of Management* (April 1977), pp. 33–75.

Watts, Ross L., and Jerold L. Zimmerman (1978). "Toward a Positive Theory of the Determination of Accounting Standards," *The Accounting Review* (January 1978), pp. 112–134.

——— (1979). "The Demand for and Supply of Accounting Theories: The Market for Excuses," *The Accounting Review* (April 1979), pp. 273–305.

——— (1986). *Positive Accounting Theory* (Prentice-Hall, Inc.).

——— (1990). "Positive Accounting Theory: A Ten Year Perspective," *The Accounting Review* (January 1990), pp. 131–156.

Wells, M. C. (1976). "A Revolution in Accounting Thought?" *The Accounting Review* (July 1976), pp. 471–482.

Willett, R. J. (1987). "An Axiomatic Theory of Accounting Measurement," *Accounting and Business Research* (Spring 1987), pp. 155–171.

ADDITIONAL READINGS

Theoretical Approaches and Problems

Abdel-khalik, A. Rashad, and Bipin Ajinkya (1979). *Empirical Research in Accounting: A Methodological Viewpoint* (American Accounting Association).

American Accounting Association (1971). "Report of the Committee on Accounting Theory Construction and Verification," *Accounting Review Supplement*, pp. 31–80.

Buckley, John, Paul Kircher, and Russell Mathews (1968). "Methodology in Accounting Theory," *The Accounting Review* (April 1968), pp. 274–286.

Carlson, Marvin L., and James W. Lamb (1981). "Constructing a Theory of Accounting — An Axiomatic Approach," *The Accounting Review* (July 1981), pp. 554–573.

Devine, Carl (1960). "Research Methodology and Accounting Theory Formation," *The Accounting Review* (July 1960), pp. 387–399.

Gordon, Myron (1960). "Scope and Method of Theory and Research in the Measurement of Income and Wealth." *The Accounting Review* (October 1960), pp. 603–618.

Ijiri, Yuji (1971). "Logic and Sanctions in Accounting," in *Accounting in Perspective: Contributions to Accounting Thought by Other Disciplines*, ed. R. Sterling and W. Bentz (Southwestern Publishing Co.), pp. 3–28.

Mattessich, Richard (1972). "Methodological Preconditions and Problems of a General Theory of Accounting," *The Accounting Review* (July 1972), pp. 469–487.

Salvary, Stanley C. W. (1989). *An Analytical Framework for Accounting Theory*, McQueen Accounting Monograph Series, Vol. 5 (University of Arkansas, Fayetteville).

Sterling, Robert R. (1970). "On Theory Construction and Verification," *The Accounting Review* (July 1970), pp. 444–457.

Williams, Thomas, and Charles Griffin (1969). "On the Nature of Empirical Verification in Accounting," *Abacus* (December 1969), pp. 143–178.

Theory, Practice, and Research in Accounting

Abdel-khalik, A. Rashad (1983). "Accounting Research and Practice: Incompatible Twins?" *CA Magazine* (March 1983), pp. 28–34.

Mautz, Robert K., and Jack Gray (1970). "Some Thoughts on Research Needs in Accounting," *Journal of Accountancy* (September 1970), pp. 54–62.

Wolk, Harry I., and Roger Briggs (1975). "Accounting Research, Professors, and Practitioners: A Perspective," *International Journal of Accounting* (Spring 1975), pp. 47–56.

Agency Theory

Mills, Patti (1990). "Agency, Auditing and the Unregulated Environment: Some Further Historical Evidence," *Accounting, Auditing & Accountability Journal* 3 (no. 1): 54–66.

Walker, Martin (1989). "Agency Theory: A Falsificationist Perspective," *Accounting Organizations and Society* 14 (no. 5/6): 433–453.

Williams, Paul F. (1989). "The Logic of Positive Accounting Research," *Accounting Organizations and Society* 14 (no. 5/6): 455–468.

Zimmerman, Jerold L. (1980). "Positive Research in Accounting," in *Perspectives on Research*, ed. R. Nair and T. Williams (University of Wisconsin), pp. 107–128.

Information Theory

Feltham, Gerald A. (1972). "Information Evaluation," *Studies in Accounting Research* #5 (American Accounting Association).

Lev, Baruch (1969). "Accounting & Information Theory," *Studies in Accounting Research* #2 (American Accounting Association).

DEVELOPMENT OF THE INSTITUTIONAL STRUCTURE OF FINANCIAL ACCOUNTING

I N CHAPTER 1, we described the role of accounting theory in the standard-setting process. In this chapter we focus on major events that have led to the present institutional arrangements for the development of accounting standards in the United States. In Chapter 19 we briefly examine the standard-setting process in other English-speaking countries as well as attempts to establish uniform accounting standards on an international basis.

In the United States prior to 1930 accounting was largely unregulated. The accounting practices and procedures used by a firm were generally considered confidential. Thus, one firm had little knowledge about the procedures followed by other companies. Obviously, the result was a considerable lack of uniformity in accounting practices among companies, both from year to year and even within the same industry. Bankers and other creditors, who were the primary users of financial reports, provided the only real direction in accounting practices. Bank and creditor pressure was aimed primarily at the disclosure of cash and near-cash resources that could be used for repayment of debt.

The emphasis on debt-paying ability can be traced back to the social and economic conditions in the United States prior to the end of World War I. The American public typically did not invest large sums in private corporations until the 1920s. When the federal government made lump-sum payments for the retirement of Liberty Bonds, the public suddenly had large amounts of available cash. Private corporations were expanding, and both they and government leaders encouraged the public to invest in American business. A "people's capitalism" concept took hold and the number of individual shareholder investors grew tremendously. Unfortunately, financial reporting lagged behind investor needs, so reports continued to be prepared primarily for the needs of creditors.[1]

Not until the stock market crash of 1929 did shareholder investors begin to question whether accounting and reporting practices were adequate to assess investments. The realization that financial reports were based on widely diversified accounting practices and were frequently misleading to current and prospective investors led to the first of three distinct periods in the development of accounting standards.[2] The three periods will be examined carefully in this chapter:

The formative years, 1930–46.

The postwar period, 1946–59.

The modern period, 1959–present.

THE FORMATIVE YEARS, 1930–46

As a result of the stock market crash, the period from 1930 to 1946 influenced accounting practices in the United States more than any other comparable period in our history. The first attempt to develop accounting standards was an agreement between the American Institute of Certified Public Accountants (AICPA) and the New York Stock Exchange (NYSE).

NYSE/AICPA AGREEMENT

In 1930, the AICPA began a cooperative effort with the NYSE that eventually led to the preparation of one of the most important documents in the development of accounting rule making.[3] The AICPA's Special Committee on Cooperation with the Stock Exchange worked closely with the NYSE's Committee on Stock List to develop accounting principles to be followed by all companies listed on the exchange. The NYSE was concerned about the fact that listed companies were using a large variety of undisclosed accounting practices. Initially, the AICPA thought that the best solution was a dual approach: (1) education of the users of accounting reports regarding the reports' limitations and (2) improvement of reports to make them more informative to users. Ultimately, the AICPA's committee suggested the following general solution to the NYSE committee:

> The more practical alternative would be to leave every corporation free to choose its own methods of accounting within . . . very broad limits . . . , but

---

[1] Bedford (1970, pp. 69–70).
[2] Storey (1964, pp. 3–8).
[3] Zeff (1972, p. 119).

require disclosure of the methods employed and consistency in their application from year to year. . . .

Within quite wide limits, it is relatively unimportant to the investor which precise rules or conventions are adopted by a corporation in reporting its earnings if he knows what method is being followed and is assured that it is followed consistently from year to year. . . . [4]

A formal draft of "five broad accounting principles" was prepared by the AICPA's committee and approved by the NYSE's committee on September 22, 1932. This document represented the first formal attempt to develop "generally accepted accounting principles." In fact, the AICPA's committee coined the phrase "accepted principles of accounting." The first five principles were later incorporated as Chapter 1 of Accounting Research Bulletin (ARB) 43.

The joint effort of the NYSE and AICPA had a profound influence upon accounting policy making in the United States during the next fifty years. Reed K. Storey described it this way:

. . . The recommendations [all aspects of the original NYSE/AICPA document] were not fully implemented, but the basic concept which permitted each corporation to choose those methods and procedures which were most appropriate for its own financial statements within the basic framework of "accepted accounting principles" became the focal point of the development of principles in the United States. [5]

FORMATION OF THE SECURITIES AND EXCHANGE COMMISSION (SEC)

The SEC was created by Congress in 1934. Its defined purpose was (and is) to administer the Securities Act of 1933 and the Securities and Exchange Act of 1934. The two acts were the first national securities legislation in the United States. The 1933 act regulates the issuance of securities in interstate markets; the 1934 act is primarily concerned with the trading of securities. The 1933 and 1934 acts conferred on the SEC both broad and specific authority to prescribe the form and content of financial information filed with the SEC.

The SEC initially allowed the accounting profession to set accounting principles without interference. However, statements made by the SEC in 1937 and 1938 indicated that it was growing impatient with the profession. In December, 1937, SEC Commissioner Robert Healy addressed the American Accounting Association (AAA):

It seems to me, that one great difficulty has been that there has been no body which had the authority to fix and maintain standards [of accounting]. I believe that such a body now exists in the Securities and Exchange Commission. [6]

---

[4] American Institute of Accountants (1934, p. 9).

[5] Storey (1964, p. 12).

[6] Healy (1938, p. 5).

Finally, on April 25, 1938, the message the SEC was sending the profession became quite clear. They issued Accounting Series Release (ASR) No. 4, which said,

> In cases where financial statements filed with the Commission . . . are prepared in accordance with accounting principles for which there is no substantial authoritative support, such financial statements will be presumed to be misleading or inaccurate despite disclosures contained in the certificate of the accountant or in footnotes to the statements provided the matters are material. In cases where there is a difference of opinion between the Commission and the registrant as to the proper principles of accounting to be followed, disclosure will be accepted in lieu of correction of the financial statements themselves only if the points involved are such that there is substantial authoritative support for the practices followed by the registrant and the position of the Commission has not previously been expressed in rules, regulations, or other official releases of the Commission, including the published opinions of its chief accountant.[7]

The implicit message was that unless the profession established an authoritative body for the development of accounting standards, the SEC would determine acceptable accounting practices and mandate methods to be employed in reports filed with it.

COMMITTEE ON ACCOUNTING PROCEDURE, 1936–46

In 1933, the AICPA formed the Special Committee on Development of Accounting Principles, but this committee did very little and was replaced by the Committee on Accounting Procedures (CAP) in 1936, which also was relatively inactive until 1938. However, in 1938, prompted primarily by the SEC's new policy embodied in ASR 4, the CAP was expanded from seven to twenty-one members and became much more active.

The CAP originally wanted to develop a comprehensive statement of accounting principles that would serve as a general guide to the solution of specific practical problems. However, most felt it would take at least five years to develop such a statement and by that time the SEC undoubtedly would have lost its patience. Thus, the CAP decided to adopt a policy of attacking specific problems and recommending whenever possible preferred methods of accounting.[8]

The CAP, acting in response to ASR 4, began in 1939 to issue statements on accounting principles that, prima facie, had "substantial authoritative support." During the two-year period of 1938–39, it issued twelve Accounting Research Bulletins (ARBs). The CAP was cognizant of the SEC looking over its shoulder and frequently consulted with the SEC to determine whether proposed ARBs would be acceptable to the commission.[9]

The SEC was initially satisfied with the accounting profession's efforts to

---

[7] SEC (1938, p. 5).
[8] Zeff (1972, pp. 135–137).
[9] Ibid., p. 139.

establish accounting principles. However, it had always let it be known that it was prepared to take over the rule-making process if the profession lagged. The following quotation from the commission's 1939 report to Congress indicates its position clearly:

> One of the most important functions of the Commission is to maintain and improve the standards of accounting practices. . . . the independence of the public accountant must be preserved and strengthened and standards of thoroughness and accuracy protected. I [Chairman Jerome N. Frank] understand that certain groups in the profession [CAP] are moving ahead in good stride. They will get all the help we can give them so long as they conscientiously attempt that task. That's definite. But if we find that they are unwilling or unable . . . to do the job thoroughly, we won't hesitate to step in to the full extent of our statutory powers.[10]

Not all accounting constituents were happy with the way accounting rules were being developed during this period. Members of the AAA favored a deductive approach to the formulation of accounting rules — as opposed to the predominantly informal inductive approach employed by the CAP. Regarding the first four ARBs, the editor of *The Accounting Review* wrote:

> It is unfortunate that the four pamphlets thus far published give no evidence of extensive research nor of well-reasoned conclusions. They reflect, on the other hand, a hasty marshaling of facts and opinions, and the derivation of temporizing rules to which it is doubtless hoped that a professional majority will subscribe. As models of approach in a field already heavily burdened with expedients and dogmatism, they leave much to be desired.[11]

This formative era did not produce a comprehensive set of accounting principles. However, it did make two very important contributions. First, accounting practices, especially in terms of uniformity, improved significantly. Second, the private sector was firmly established as the source for accounting policy making in the United States.[12] When World War II began, the development of accounting rules slowed down significantly. During the war years, the CAP dealt almost exclusively with accounting problems involving war transactions. Of the thirteen ARBs issued between January, 1942, and September, 1946, seven dealt with war-related problems and three with terminology.

THE POSTWAR PERIOD, 1946–59

An even greater economic boom occurred in the postwar period than in the 1920s. Industry required massive amounts of capital in order to expand. The expansion, in turn, created more jobs and more money in the economy. At the

---

[10] SEC (1939, p. 121).
[11] Kohler (1939, p. 319).
[12] Storey (1964, p. 5).

encouragement of stock exchanges, industry began to actively tap money available from the public. In 1940 there were an estimated four million stockholders in the United States. By 1952 the number had grown to seven million and in 1962 it reached seventeen million. Thus, a large portion of the American public had a direct financial interest in corporations.

Corporate financial reports were an important source of information for financial decisions. Thus, financial reports and the accounting rules used to prepare them received wide attention. For the first time, accounting policy making became an important topic in the financial press. The primary problem was one of uniformity or comparability of reported earnings among different companies. The financial press and the SEC brought increasingly heavy pressure to bear on the accounting profession to eliminate different methods of accounting for similar transactions that significantly affected reported net income.

ARB 32 AND THE SEC

The CAP was busy during the postwar period. In total, eighteen ARBs were issued from 1946 to 1953. Although the committee had been quite successful in eliminating many questionable accounting practices of the 1930s, the strategy created a new set of problems during the late 1940s and early 1950s. While eliminating suspect accounting practices, the CAP failed to make positive recommendations for general accounting principles. As a result, there was an oversupply of "good" accounting principles. Many alternative practices continued to flourish because there was no underlying accounting theory. This situation led to conflicts between the CAP and the SEC.

The most publicized conflict dealt with the all-inclusive income statement versus current operating performance. The CAP felt that utilizing current operating performance would enhance comparability of earnings reports among companies and among years for the same company. Any extraordinary gains and losses, it pointed out, are excluded from net income under the current operating performance concept. Consequently, it issued ARB 32 recommending that concept. Upon issuance of ARB 32, the SEC chief accountant wrote:

> [The] Commission has authorized the staff to take exception to financial statements which appear to be misleading, even though they reflect the application of ARB 32.[13]

In 1950, the SEC proposed in an amendment to Regulation S-X the use of the all-inclusive concept. This proposal was in direct conflict with ARB 32. Subsequently, the CAP and the SEC reached a compromise agreement regarding the authority of ARB 32. Thus, the CAP maintained its prominent role in policy making. However, it was very definitely subject to the oversight of the SEC.

---

[13] King (1947, p. 25).

THE PRICE-LEVEL PROBLEM

By the end of 1953, the accounting profession became increasingly concerned with accounting under conditions of changing price levels. The profession turned its attention almost entirely to this problem. As a result, for approximately three years little if any progress was made regarding the development of accounting principles. The main thrust of the price-level debate dealt with depreciation charges. Depreciation charges based on historical costs did not accurately measure the attrition of fixed-asset values in terms of current purchasing power. The result was an overstatement of reported net income. In general, the profession finally decided that to reflect changes in purchasing power would confuse users of financial statements. As a result, it shelved the price-level debate for many years and directed its attention again to the development of standards of financial accounting.

THE CLOSING YEARS OF THE CAP

The years from 1957 to 1959 represented a period of transition in the development of accounting standards in the United States. Criticism of the CAP increased and even pillars of the accounting establishment were critical of its operations. Finally, a president of the AICPA, Alvin R. Jennings, called for a new approach to the development of accounting principles.

Increasing Criticism

During the middle and late 1950s, interest in the development of accounting principles was growing both within and outside the profession. Unfortunately, much of this interest took the form of negative criticism directed toward the CAP. Financial executives and accounting practitioners in the smaller firms complained that they were not given an adequate hearing to express their opinions on proposed ARBs. Many felt that the CAP worked too slowly on pressing issues and refused to take unpopular positions on controversial topics.

Leonard Spacek, the managing partner of Arthur Andersen & Co., shocked the accounting profession with these remarks:

> The partners of our firm believe that the public accounting profession is not in important respects carrying its public responsibility in the certification of financial statements at the present time. We believe that the profession's existence is in peril. Until the profession establishes within its framework (a) the premise of an accepted accounting principle, (b) the principles of accounting that meet those premises, and (c) a public forum through which such principles of accounting may be determined, our firm is dedicated to airing in public the major shortcomings of the profession.[14]

Spacek seemed to be calling for the profession to prepare a comprehensive statement of basic accounting principles. In this he was not alone. In 1957 the

---

[14]Spacek (1969, p. 21).

AAA had published a statement of underlying concepts and definitions in which it at least attempted a deductive approach.[15] From its very inception, the CAP had discarded a formalized deductive approach because it was too time consuming. In fact, the committee had devoted its time to solving specific problems by prescribing rules on a piecemeal basis — without developing fundamental principles of financial accounting, much less a comprehensive theory.

A NEW APPROACH

Alvin R. Jennings delivered a historic speech in 1957 at the AICPA's annual meeting. He suggested a reorganization of the AICPA to expedite development of accounting principles. Jennings emphasized the need for research as part of this process. In other words, he called for a conceptual approach to replace the piecemeal method that had been followed for twenty years by the CAP. The accounting profession was ready to consider Jenning's new approach. The AICPA set up a Special Committee on Research Program, which finished its report in less than a year. This report became the "articles of incorporation" for the Accounting Principles Board (APB) and the Accounting Research Division. The report emphasized the importance of research in establishing financial accounting standards:

> Adequate accounting research is necessary in all of the foregoing [establishing standards]. Pronouncements on accounting matters should be based on thorough-going independent study of the matters in question, during which consideration is given to all points of view. For this an adequate staff is necessary. . . . Research reports or studies should be carefully reasoned and fully documented. They should have wide exposure to both the profession and the public.[16]

The CAP was heavily criticized, perhaps deservedly so, but it represented the profession's first sustained attempt to develop workable financial accounting rules. It issued a total of fifty-one ARBs during its existence. One of these, No. 43, represented a restatement and revision of the first 42 bulletins. Large parts of ARB 43 remain in force to this day. Throughout the CAP's life, ARBs were increasingly recognized as authoritative and had a pronounced effect on accounting practice.

THE MODERN PERIOD, 1959 TO THE PRESENT

The "charter" that created the APB and the Accounting Research Division called for a two-pronged approach to the development of accounting principles. The research division was to be semiautonomous. It had its own director, who had authority to publish the findings of the research staff, and was to be exclu-

---

[15] AAA (1957, pp. 1–12).
[16] AICPA (1958, pp. 62–63).

sively devoted to the development of accounting principles with no responsibilities to the technical committees of the AICPA. In establishing what research projects to undertake, the director of research had to confer with the chairman of the APB. If the two disagreed, the APB as a whole determined what projects the research division would undertake. Results of the projects of the research division would be published in the form of Accounting Research Studies (ARSs). These studies would present detailed documentation, all aspects of particular problems, and recommendations or conclusions. At the outset, two projects were called for in the special committee's report: (1) the "basic postulates of accounting" and (2) a "fairly broad set of coordinated accounting principles" based on the postulates.

In form, the APB was very similar to the CAP. It had from eighteen to twenty-one members, all of whom were members of the AICPA. They represented large and small CPA firms, academia, and private industry. The hope was that the APB's Opinions would be based on the studies of the research division. A two-thirds majority was required for the issuance of an opinion and disclaimers of dissenting members were to be published.

EARLY YEARS OF THE APB

The early years of the APB were characterized by failure and doubt. Research studies called for in the original charter were not accepted by the profession, and the investment credit controversy resulted in a serious challenge to the board's authority by large CPA firms.

ARSs 1 and 3

ARS 1, *The Basic Postulates of Accounting* by Maurice Moonitz published in 1961, did not initially generate much reaction, favorable or unfavorable, from either the APB or the profession generally. Apparently, everyone was awaiting the publication of the companion study on principles before passing judgment. ARS 3, *A Tentative Set of Broad Accounting Principles for Business Enterprises* by Robert Sprouse and Moonitz, appeared in April, 1962. To say the least, this study provoked criticism from all areas. In fact, following the publishing of the text of the study, nine of the twelve members of the project advisory committees on the postulates and principles studies issued personal comments. Only one of the comments was positive. APB Statement 1 expressed the APB's views of the study. The statement said, in part,

> The Board believes, however, that while these studies [1 and 3] are a valuable contribution to accounting thinking, they are too radically different from present generally accepted accounting principles for acceptance at this time.[17]

By issuing that statement, the APB seriously weakened the dual approach to the development of accounting standards.

---

[17] APB (1962).

Investment Credit

In November of 1962 the issuance of APB 2, which dealt with the investment tax credit, caused another problem. The profession as a whole was divided on how to account for the investment credit. Two alternatives existed: (1) recognizing the tax benefit in the year received, designated the *flow-through method*, and (2) recognizing the tax benefit over the life of the related asset, called the *deferral method*. The board chose not to commission a research study on the subject and issued APB 2, which opted for the deferral method. Almost immediately, three large CPA firms made it known that they would not require their clients to follow the opinion. Furthermore, in January, 1963, the SEC issued ASR 96 which allowed registrants to employ either the flow-through or deferral methods. Obviously, these large CPA firms and the SEC had challenged the APB's authority. As a result, APB 4 was issued, which permitted the use of either method.

This successful challenge caused the binding authority of APB opinions to be questioned in the press for several years. Finally, in late 1964 the AICPA's council (the organization's governing body) declared the authority of APB opinions in an Appendix to APB 6. It unanimously agreed that departures from APB opinions must be disclosed in financial statements audited by a member of the AICPA. If the independent accountant concluded that a method being employed had substantial authoritative support, even though it was not contained in a specific accounting principle, this support must be disclosed in footnotes or the auditor's report. Furthermore, the auditor must, if possible, disclose the effect of the departure. If the principle employed did not have substantial authoritative support, the auditor must qualify the opinion, give an adverse opinion, or disclaim the opinion.[18] Thus, as 1964 drew to a close the authoritative nature of APB opinions had been established. However, the two-pronged approach to the development of accounting principles had yet to be implemented.

THE EMBATTLED APB

In the years from 1965 to 1967 further criticisms of the board appeared in the press. The "high-profile" period for the accounting profession had arrived. The diversity of accounting practices was discussed in *Barron's*, *Business Week*, *Dun's Review*, *Forbes*, *Fortune*, the *New York Times*, and the *Wall Street Journal*. Despite the public controversy, the APB compiled an impressive list of accomplishments.

During this period, the APB issued seven opinions, including at least three that were noteworthy. Accounting for the employer's cost of pension plans successfully utilized the desired approach embodied in the charter. ARS 8, *Accounting for the Cost of Pension Plans* by Ernest L. Hicks, reviewed the arguments for

---

[18] Although the term is not defined in APB 6, it has developed a meaning over the years that encompasses—in addition to pronouncements of rule-making bodies and the SEC—opinions of regulatory commissions, provided they do not conflict with statements from other souces, recognized textbooks, leading CPAs, and practices that are commonly followed by business. See Grady (1965, p. 16).

and against various accounting alternatives and the practical problems of each. APB 8 used this research study as a source document. Not only did APB 8 represent the first real application of the two-pronged approach but it also received unanimous approval from the board.

Also adopted unanimously by the board was APB 9, which dealt with the areas of extraordinary items and earnings per share. This opinion eliminated the wide diversity in existing practices for handling extraordinary items. Also, it approved the all-inclusive concept of the income statement.

In another controversial area, income tax allocation, the dual approach was again employed. ARS 9, *Interperiod Allocation of Corporate Income Taxes* by Homer Black, was used as a source of information in the deliberations of the board. Although controversial, APB 11, which required comprehensive income tax allocation, did significantly curtail alternative procedures in practice. Thus, by the close of 1967, the board had finally demonstrated it could function in a meaningful manner.

ARS 7 and APB Statement 4

When the accounting profession failed to accept ARS 1 and ARS 3, another research study was commissioned. Its objectives were to discuss the basic concepts of accounting principles and summarize existing acceptable principles and practices. For this purpose, ARS 7, *Inventory of Generally Accepted Accounting Principles for Business Enterprises* by Paul Grady, was successful. Although the study was well received by the profession, it fell short of the original task assigned to the board in 1958 by the Special Committee on Research Program. Grady codified existing pronouncements (over 50 percent of the study was reproductions of pronouncements) and then tried to derive the profession's existing structure of principles. The study blended inductive and deductive approaches because it took the existing pronouncements and then attempted to deduce accounting principles from the body of accepted pronouncements.

Possibly because of the failure of the APB to accomplish its original task on accounting principles, the Special Committee of the Accounting Principles Board recommended that "at the earliest possible time" the board should set forth the purposes and limitations of financial statements, determine acceptable accounting principles, and define "generally accepted accounting principles."[19]

To accomplish that task, a committee worked for five years to produce Statement 4, *Basic Concepts and Accounting Principles Underlying Financial Statements of Business Enterprises*, which was approved by the APB in 1970. The statement had two purposes:

(1) to provide a foundation for evaluating present accounting practices, for assisting in solving accounting problems, and for guiding the future development of financial accounting; and, (2) to enhance understanding of the purposes of financial accounting, the nature of the process and the forces which shape it,

---

[19] The CPA Letter (1965, p. 3).

and the potential and limitations of financial statements in providing needed information.[20]

APB Statement 4 covered many of the same topics included in ARS 7, but it went beyond that study (as Chapter 6 will show). The statement had no authoritative standing, however. Being an APB *statement*, as opposed to an *opinion*, "it is binding on no one for any purpose whatsoever."[21] Thus, the APB failed in its original charge to set forth the basic postulates and broad principles of accounting, at least in any binding and coherent manner.

Continuing Criticism

Criticism of the standard-setting process continued and was two-pronged: (1) exposure for tentative APB opinions was too limited and occurred too late in the process and (2) the problems with business combinations showed the standard-setting process was too long and subject to too many outside pressures that were not appropriately channeled into the formulation process.

In response to considerable criticism of the exposure process, the APB initiated several important changes that have been carried forward to the Financial Accounting Standards Board (FASB). It introduced public hearings in 1971 and circulated discussion memorandums to interested parties several months prior to the drafting of proposed opinions. These memorandums discussed all aspects of the particular accounting problem and invited interested parties to send written comments as well as to voice their views at the public hearing. After the public hearing, outlines of the proposed opinion were distributed to interested parties for "mini-exposure" in order to determine initial reaction to the proposed opinion. Following that stage, an official exposure draft of the proposed opinion was widely distributed throughout the profession and comments were requested. Ultimately, the opinion required at least a two-thirds favorable vote of the board to be issued. The broadened exposure process prior to issuance of an accounting standard allowed interested parties to be involved in the standard-setting process and tended to alleviate criticism, other than that of timeliness, of the APB.

The controversy over business combinations and goodwill was the most time-consuming and extensively discussed problem the APB faced. In 1963 it published ARS 5, *A Critical Study of Accounting for Business Combinations* by Arthur Wyatt; ARS 10, *Accounting for Goodwill* by George Catlett and Norman Olson, appeared in the latter part of 1968. Both of these studies reached conclusions that were at variance with existing accounting principles. ARS 5 concluded that pooling-of-interests accounting should be discontinued and that goodwill may have two components — one with limited life requiring periodic amortization, the other with unlimited life to be carried forward indefinitely to future periods. ARS 10 concluded that goodwill does not qualify as an asset and

---

[20] The CPA Letter (1970, p. 1).
[21] Moonitz (1974, p. 22).

should be immediately subtracted from stockholders' equity upon completion of the combination.

Business combinations and goodwill received more publicity and discussion than any other subject taken up by the APB. News publications such as *Time* and *Newsweek* had several articles on the subject. Three Congressional committees and the Federal Trade Commission, as well as the SEC, concerned themselves with the merger accounting problem.[22]

A brief review of the various drafts of the proposed opinion on business combinations and goodwill indicates the difficulty in establishing accounting principles on this subject. The initial draft opinion, in July, 1969, proposed that pooling of interests be eliminated and goodwill be amortized over a period no longer than forty years. In February, 1970, another draft opinion allowed pooling of interests when a 3-to-1 size test was met and also required amortization of goodwill over a maximum of forty years. The APB was unable to obtain a two-thirds majority on the draft. Finally, in June, 1970, a two-thirds majority agreed to allowing pooling of interests with a 9-to-1 size test and goodwill amortization restricted to the forty-year maximum. But when the APB met again in July, one member changed his vote. Thus the board was again at an impasse. Finally, the business combination and goodwill subjects were split into two opinions: APB 16 on business combinations, eliminating the size test for a pooling of interests, passed 12 to 6; APB 17 on goodwill, requiring amortization over a maximum of forty years, passed 13 to 5.

The extreme difficulty of arriving at definitive standards of accounting for business combinations and goodwill was certainly in part responsible for the decision to begin a comprehensive review of the procedures for establishing accounting principles. In April, 1971, the AICPA formed two special study groups. One group, "The Study Group on Establishment of Accounting Principles," was chaired by Francis M. Wheat, a former SEC commissioner and a long-time critic of the accounting profession. The other group, "The Study Group on the Objectives of Financial Statements," was chaired by Robert M. Trueblood, a prominent CPA and managing partner of Touche Ross & Co.

The Wheat and Trueblood Committee Reports
The Wheat Committee completed its report in March, 1972. It called for significant changes in the establishment of financial accounting standards. The report made the following recommendations:

1. The establishment of a Financial Accounting Foundation. This foundation would have nine trustees whose principal duties would be to appoint members of the FASB and raise funds for its operation.
2. The establishment of the FASB. The Board would have seven full-time members and would establish standards of financial reporting.

---

[22] Zeff (1972, p. 213).

3. The establishment of the Financial Accounting Standards Advisory Council. This Council, with twenty members, would consult with the FASB for establishing priorities and task forces as well as reacting to proposed standards.[23]

The recommendations were accepted by the AICPA's council in June, 1972; the FASB became a reality on July 1, 1973.

The Trueblood Study Group did not complete its report until October, 1973, after the formation of the FASB. The report identified several objectives of financial statements but did not make any suggestions regarding implementation. It concluded with the following statement:

> The Study Group concludes that the objectives developed in this report can be looked upon as attainable in stages within a reasonable time. Selecting the appropriate course of action for gaining acceptance of these objectives is not within the purview of the Study Group. However, the Study Group urges that its conclusions be considered as an initial step in developing objectives important for the ongoing refinement and improvement of accounting standards and practices.[24]

The FASB has considered the Trueblood Study Group Report in its Conceptual Framework Project. Progress on this project will be reviewed in the next section.

THE CONTEMPORARY PERIOD

The charge to the newly formed FASB was different in one important respect from that given to the APB in 1959. Whereas the APB was to work toward standard setting with a two-pronged approach, the new FASB, although it had a research division, was to establish standards of financial accounting and reporting in the most efficient and complete manner possible. Thus, the FASB was not required to stipulate the postulates and principles of accounting as an underlying framework. Perhaps a tradeoff between "efficiency" and "completeness" was intended. Ironically, FASB statements are more thoroughly researched than prior standards of either the CAP or the APB. The FASB also launched the Conceptual Framework Project, a major attempt to provide a "constitution" for the standard-setting function.

FASB Mechanics of Operations

The structure for establishing financial accounting standards has been modified somewhat since the FASB's founding in 1973. The modifications were the result of recommendations made by the Structure Committee of the Financial Accounting Foundation (FAF) in 1977. Exhibit 3–1 diagrams the organizational structure and its relationship to its constituency.

---

[23] AICPA (1972, pp. 69–82).
[24] AICPA (1973, p. 66).

EXHIBIT 3–1
The Structure of the Board's Constituency Relationships

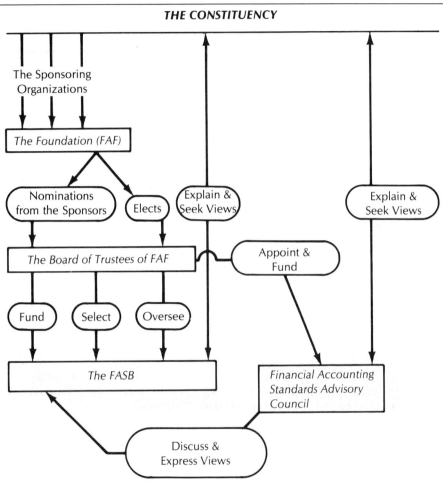

THE CONSTITUENCY

The FAF includes members of the six sponsoring organizations: the AAA, AICPA, Financial Analysts Federation, Financial Executives Institute (FEI), National Association of Accountants (NAA), and Securities Industry Association. The responsibility of the FAF is to elect the board of trustees. The board of trustees has been expanded to accommodate up to two additional members at large from organizations not included in the six sponsoring organizations. To date, one such member has been elected, representing the banking industry. The board of trustees selects FASB members, funds the board's activities, and performs the oversight role.

The FASB includes seven members, each serving a term of five years. Any individual member can serve a maximum of two terms. During their terms of office, the members of the board must maintain complete independence. This not only applies to other employment arrangements (past, present, or future) but also to investments. "There must be no conflict, real or apparent, between the members' private interest and the public interest."[25] The background requirement for board members is simply a knowledge of accounting, finance, and business, and a concern for the public interest. In March, 1979, for the first time the board had a majority of members with backgrounds primarily in areas other than public accounting.

The Financial Accounting Standards Advisory Council (FASAC) is instrumental in the establishment of financial accounting standards. It is also appointed by the board of trustees. The FASAC advises the FASB on its operating and project plans, agenda and priorities, and appointment of task forces, as well as on all major technical issues.

The standard-setting procedure starts with the identification of a problem. A task force is then formed to explore all aspects of the problem. It produces a discussion memorandum that identifies all issues and possible solutions, which is widely circulated to interested parties. The FASB then convenes a public hearing where interested parties may make their views known to the board. Subsequently, an exposure draft of the final standard is issued and written comments are requested. After consideration of written comments either another exposure draft is issued (if significant changes are deemed necessary) or a final vote is taken by the board. Five votes are needed for the issuance of a final standard.

Assessment of the FASB
The FASB experiment in standard setting is perhaps the last opportunity to have the private sector establish financial accounting standards. Even though the SEC has allowed the accounting profession to set standards, the fact remains that the SEC has the legal authority to establish standards whenever it chooses. Both the CAP and the APB made important progress in eliminating poor accounting practices and in standardizing existing practices, but they were not successful in developing a theoretical basis for standard setting. In the early years of the FASB's existence, it too was criticized. Some said it issued too many pronouncements, while others complained that not enough had been issued. Some critics said the board was too conceptual in its approach, but others said it had ignored research and accounting theory. Furthermore, some felt the FASB did not have a significant effect on financial reporting, although others maintained that changes had been too radical.

With all this in mind, a comprehensive review of the board was undertaken by the Structure Committee of the Board of Trustees of the FAF in late 1976. The basic charge of the committee was to "make recommendations to the Board of Trustees regarding any changes in the basic structure of the FASB

---

[25] AICPA (1972, p. 72).

and the FASAC."[26] The committee's report included seventeen major findings. It found overwhelming support for maintaining the standard-setting process in the private sector and for the FASB as the right body to discharge that responsibility. Regarding the standard-setting process, the committee found that

1. the process of establishing a new accounting standard requires careful consideration of the views of all elements of the constituency,
2. the process requires research to assess the possible effects of a proposed standard,
3. a successful standard cannot be imposed by the standard setter, it must be assimilated by the constituency,
4. the assimilation process may require an educational effort to demonstrate the overall value of the proposed new standard.[27]

Since 1977, as a result of the various findings of the Structure Committee, significant changes have occurred. Basically, these changes have increased the involvement of the constituency. Meetings of the FASB, FASAC, the Foundation, task forces, and the Screening Committee on Emerging Problems are now open to the public. Additionally, the board has begun publication of a weekly news bulletin called *Action Alert.* Furthermore, the board has made greater use of available resources outside the FASB staff as well as of task forces. As a result, the board has become sensitive to the potential economic consequences of proposed standards prior to issuance.

The FASB has been quite productive when compared with its predecessors. It has issued over 100 Statements of Financial Accounting Standards as well as numerous interpretations and technical bulletins. If a philosophical trend can be inferred from these standards, it would be that there is a move to "clean up the balance sheet." This has resulted in a more conservative balance sheet with immediate, as opposed to delayed, recognition of events on the income statement. In addition, between 1978 and 1985 the FASB issued six Statements of Financial Accounting Concepts. These statements constitute the conceptual framework, a document which is intended to provide a theoretical underpinning for the assessment of accounting standards and practices. (Chapter 6 takes a critical look at the conceptual framework.) But despite its accomplishments, during the last decade the FASB has once again come under severe attack.

Attempts to Erode the FASB's Power   Several organizations have attempted to restrict or constrict the FASB's legislative powers. When responsibility for standard setting was transferred from the AICPA to the FASB, the AICPA set up the Accounting Standards Executive Committee (AcSEC) in 1972 to perform a liaison function between the AICPA and the FASB. This committee responds to discussion memorandums, invitations to comment, and exposure drafts as

---

[26] FAF (1977, p. 55).
[27] Ibid., p. 18.

well as prepares issue papers for the FASB that can add a subject to the board's agenda.

AcSEC issues two types of pronouncements: (1) Statements of Position (SOP) and (2) Industry Accounting Guides (Guides). Generally, SOPs and Guides deal with narrower, more specialized subjects than FASB Statements. Unlike FASB Statements, neither the SOPs nor the Guides are considered mandatory accounting standards under the AICPA's Rule 203 of the Rules of Conduct, but the FASB has embarked on a program (see Statement of Financial Accounting Standards [SFAS] No. 32) to incorporate the majority of the SOPs and Guides in FASB statements. In addition to its pronouncements, AcSEC periodically prepares Issue Papers covering various accounting practice problems that frequently cause a subject to be added to FASB's agenda. Among the standards that have come up through the AcSEC route are SFAS No. 61, *Accounting for Title Plant*; SFAS No. 63, *Financial Reporting by Broadcasters*; and SFAS No. 65, *Accounting for Certain Mortgage Banking Activities*. AcSEC work that has not yet become embodied in FASB standards is designated "preferable accounting principles" in SFASs 32 and 83, which justify accounting changes in accordance with APB 20.

If fairly narrow industry-type standards have become the province of AcSEC, another group – the Emerging Issues Task Force (EITF) – created in 1984 has concerned itself with highly technical issues, such as financial instruments, which may affect firms in virtually any industry. EITF has also been concerned with specialized problems of financial institutions. Members of this group consist of senior technical partners of the major firms and the chief accountant of the SEC. The Emerging Issues Task Force does not have any formal authority, but its consensus views may well be de facto generally accepted accounting principles (GAAP).[28] One fear is that the EITF may establish excessively complicated and complex standards like those of the Internal Revenue Code, which might result in rule-dominated practice that could erode professionalism.[29]

A further challenge to the FASB's standard-setting powers has come from the Government Accounting Standards Board (GASB) created by the FAF in 1984 to deal with municipal accounting. Unfortunately, its responsibilities overlap with those of the FASB, resulting in an old-fashioned turf battle. Separately issued general-purpose financial statements of such entities as hospitals, colleges and universities, and pension plans are supposed to utilize FASB standards except where the GASB has issued a particular standard covering a specific type of entity or a precise economic practice or activity. As a result of this overlap, GASB standards tend to "muscle out" particular FASB standards for governmental entities. The situation became intolerable for both private and public industries that had previously used FASB standards and preferred to continue to do so. However, some public-sector organizations wanted the dispute settled

---

[28] Wishon (1986, p. 96).
[29] Dyckman (1989, pp. 26–27).

on the basis of public versus private ownership and threatened to withdraw support of FAF if it was not.[30] A tentative compromise has largely agreed to this system. In addition, separately issued general-purpose financial statements of colleges and universities, healthcare organizations, and gas and electric utilities are to be subject to FASB standards unless governing boards of public-sector organizations in these categories decide to be governed by GASB standards.[31]

The AcSEC and EITF were established to solve the problems of particular industries as well as narrow technical issues, and the GASB establishes a different jurisdiction. Two prominent business organizations aimed a much more direct blow at the essence of the way the FASB operates. The FASB, as a separate organization with its own staff and board members, could be neutral in a way that its predecessors could not be. But in July, 1985, the Financial Executives Institute (FEI) and the Accounting Principles Task Force of the Business Roundtable (an organization comprised of the chief executive officers of the most major American corporations) urged a stronger business representation on the FASB itself and among the trustees of the FAF. The major complaints seemed to be the cost of preparing standards (SFAS 96) and the difficulty of understanding them (SFASs 33 and 96). Additional FASB members (one to two members) now come from business under the board's present composition, although the business "takeover" attempt appears to have been effectively parried. Nevertheless, the concerns of business may not have fallen on deaf ears. Indeed, in 1990 the FAF changed the vote required to pass a standard from 4–3 back to the original 5–2. This may be a sign of improvement in FASB operations. If a standard can pass by only a 4–3 margin (as has frequently been the case), it may well indicate that part or all of the standard should be carefully reconsidered.[32]

However, make no mistake about it: the FASB is under strong attack and may not survive. What may ultimately save it is that the only alternative to keeping the primary standard-setting function in the private sector appears to be public-sector takeover by the SEC or a body designated by and subservient to the SEC. Most of those involved would probably agree that this alternative is not a solution.

Congressional Investigations

Although we can make a good case that the standard-setting process is operating better than in the past, this is not a universally held view. We have described challenges to the FASB's legislative authority that have arisen from dissatisfaction. Another source of pressure has been Congressional investigation of the auditing profession and the standard-setting apparatus. Two Congressional

---

[30] Kirk (1989, p. 108).

[31] Ibid.

[32] Dopuch and Sunder (1980, p. 19) were unhappy with the change to the 4–3 vote. Sunder (1989) sees the problem as bureaucratic pressure on the FASB to produce standards because of the relatively large size of its staff and the scope of its operations, as well as the fact that a sizable portion of its revenues stems from the sale of standards, interpretations, and other official documents.

subcommittee reports circulated in late 1976 and early 1977 were highly critical. Congressman John E. Moss was chairman of a subcommittee whose report was particularly critical of the diversity of existing generally accepted accounting principles. The report of the Senate subcommittee, chaired by Senator Lee Metcalf, was directed toward the institutional structure of financial accounting. The report was critical of the concentration of power by the FASB, SEC, AICPA, and the "Big Eight" CPA firms. In essence, the report called for government regulation of the entire profession. Following public hearings, the report was modified significantly to allow standard setting to remain in the private sector.

Many organizational changes have occurred because of these Congressional investigations. The principal purpose of these changes has been to

1. strengthen the auditing process and the independence of auditors,
2. assure compliance with high standards of performance not only of individual CPAs but of CPA firms under an effective self-regulatory system,
3. assure greater participation by public representatives in the affairs of the profession,
4. establish distinctions between public and smaller nonpublic companies for purposes of applying technical standards,
5. enhance the overall effectiveness of the profession in serving public needs.[33]

Furthermore, the SEC must now include a specific section on the accounting profession in its annual report to Congress. In general, since the time of the Congressional investigation these reports have been complimentary to the profession in terms of standard setting and self-governance. The allegation of undue influence over the FASB by the Big Eight public accounting firms has yet to be substantiated by concrete evidence.[34] Brown's research did, however, show a similarity of responses by seven of the Big Eight firms to twelve discussion memorandums of the FASB appearing between October, 1974, and December, 1977.[35] Such similarity assuredly shows a general agreement on issues but absolutely nothing more in terms of the possibility of collusion. It is interesting to note that the resulting FASB statements appeared to be evenly split in terms of "closeness" between the attestors (Big Eight firms) and the preparers of financial statements (as evidenced by corporate respondents and interest groups).[36]

Finally, Congress has continued to scrutinize the public accounting profession. A subcommittee of the House of Representatives, chaired by Congressman John D. Dingell, has been concerned with the laxity of auditors in detecting and disclosing fraud. Because of this concern, the National Commission on Fraudulent Financial Reporting (Treadway Commission) was formed in 1985. Its recommendations are intended to increase the auditor's responsibility for detecting fraudulent financial reporting.

---

[33] AICPA (1978, p. 15).
[34] See Meyer (1974), Rockness and Nikolai (1977), McEnroe and Nikolai (1983), and Moody and Flesher (1986).
[35] Brown (1981, pp. 240–241).
[36] Ibid., p. 243. Brown noted (p. 241) that the FASB's position appeared to be closest to the Financial Analysts' Federation, a group representing user interests.

Current Role of the AICPA

The AICPA has exclusive authority in the private sector for promulgating auditing rules. The committee responsible for this task is the Auditing Standards Board. This board issues Statements on Auditing Standards. Rule 202 of the Rules of Conduct requires AICPA members to adhere to all applicable Statements on Auditing Standards in conducting audits. As a result of the latest Congressional investigation, mentioned above, ten new audit standards were issued in 1988.

Another important role of the AICPA is to curb what has been called "shopping for accounting principles," which involves increasing competition among auditing firms to land clients. As the phrase implies, greater numbers of clients have tried to find an auditor who will either "lowball" its bid to secure a client or will go along with a questionable accounting method that the client desires to employ.[37] In light of these problems, the AICPA has been attempting to strengthen professional standards of conduct and rules of performance and behavior.[38] Finally, the role of AcSEC in the area of standard setting has been previously discussed.

Current Role of the SEC

As mentioned earlier, the SEC is legally empowered to regulate accounting practices. It has, as a matter of policy, been supportive of private-sector standard setting in general and the FASB in particular.[39] In ASR 150, the SEC stated that financial statements based on accounting practices for which there is no substantial authoritative support will be presumed to be misleading. For the first time, accounting standards set in the private sector were formally recognized as having substantial authoritative support. Prior to ASR 150, this support was informal.

The SEC and FASB have had differences of opinion — as in the case of oil and gas accounting, which is examined in Chapter 15. In general, though, their relationship has been cordial and mutually beneficial. The primary differences in accounting standards promulgated by the two groups have been in the area of disclosures. The annual report filed with the SEC, form 10-K, as well as the 8-Q quarterly report require significantly more disclosure of nonfinancial statement information than does the typical annual report to stockholders.

Other Groups

At least three professional associations other than the AICPA have an interest in the standard-setting process in the United States today: the AAA, the FEI, and the IMA (Institute of Management Accounting, formerly the National Association of Accountants).

The AAA has been concerned with accounting standards for many years. From 1936 to 1957 it sponsored several statements on accounting principles. In 1966, a committee appointed two years earlier to develop an integrated state-

---

[37] Sack (1985).
[38] See Anderson and Ellyson (1986), and Connor (1986).
[39] For more on the relationship between the SEC and the FASB, see Sprouse (1987).

ment on basic accounting theory published *A Statement of Basic Accounting Theory*. Parts of this statement subsequently appeared in APB Statement 4, which has become significant in the development of the FASB's Conceptual Framework Project. An AAA Committee issued a report calling for a special commission to study the organizational structure for establishing accounting standards at about the same time the Wheat Committee was being formed. Owing to the formation of the Wheat Committee, the AAA never formed its commission, but the initial committee report reflects the AAA's obvious interest in the development of accounting standards. Zeff has observed that the AAA has played a more important role than is generally acknowledged at crucial turning points in the standard-setting process.[40] Today, the AAA sponsors various research studies on accounting problems. These studies, of which there have been thirty to date, represent a significant contribution to the development of accounting theory. AAA subcommittees also respond to FASB exposure drafts.

The FEI formed a subsidiary, the Financial Executives Research Foundation, specifically to fund various research projects in accounting and related areas. Numerous projects have been published to date. Furthermore, FEI's technical committee on corporate reporting reviews all FASB discussion memorandums and exposure drafts and develops the official FEI position, which is communicated to the FASB. They also frequently participate in FASB public hearings.

Since its formation in 1919 the IMA has conducted research and published reports in the cost and managerial accounting areas. Recently, it has become more interested in external financial reporting and, as a consequence, formed a Committee on Accounting and Reporting Concepts. This committee responds to various FASB projects.

SUMMARY

We have recounted a brief history of the three financial accounting policy-making bodies that have existed in the United States since 1930. Prior to that year, published accounting information was largely unregulated in this country.

As a result of cooperation between the AICPA and NYSE, work on drafting accounting principles was begun. A major impetus was, of course, the creation of the SEC because this body was given the power by Congress to prescribe accounting principles. As a result, the CAP was formed and most of the responsibility for the policy-making function has remained in the private sector. In its life the CAP issued a total of fifty-one ARBs, the most famous being ARB 43. Toward the close of its existence, the CAP was increasingly criticized because it attempted to solve problems on a piecemeal basis without a coherent, underlying theory.

---

[40] Zeff (1984).

The APB was conceived with high optimism. Opinions were to be based upon in-depth research studies, which, in turn, were to be grounded in a set of underlying postulates and principles: in other words, the deductive approach was to come into flower. Unfortunately, the rejection of ARS 3, the broad principles study, virtually put an end to the formalized deductive approach — despite the publication of the conservative ARS 7, which attempted to extract principles from existing rules. Despite considerable progress on many fronts, the very shaky start of the APB combined with its own institutional weaknesses and the fumbling of the business combination issue led to the demise of the APB.

The work of two important committees, one concerned with the organization of a new body and the other with the objectives of financial accounting, preceded the formation of the FASB. Board members were granted much greater independence, and the organization itself was separate from the AICPA. The FASB appears to have weathered a great deal of criticism leveled at it in its early years, but many uncertainties still remain in terms of protecting its legislative jurisdiction and independence, not to mention its very existence.

QUESTIONS

1. How did the APB pave the way for the FASB?
2. In what ways does the FASB differ most markedly from its two predecessors?
3. What is the weakness of Grady's approach in arriving at principles in ARS 7?
4. Do you think that the nonbinding status of the FASB's statements of financial accounting concepts (like that of APB Statement 4) is a good idea or not?
5. Discuss the significance of the SEC's ARS 150.
6. What has been the SEC's role in the evolution of the rule-making process? Why do you think it has generally kept a low profile?
7. What were the politics that led to the demise of both the CAP and the APB?
8. Do you think the Conceptual Framework Project is important to the long-run success of the FASB?
9. Should constituents have input into the FASB decisions, or should the FASB neutrally and independently set standards?
10. Explain how the role and form of research used by the APB and FASB differ.
11. What is the importance of the FAF and FASAC to the success of the FASB?
12. The three attempts at standard setting in the private sector (CAP, APB, and FASB) have all dealt with the need for a theoretical foundation. Why were the CAP and the APB not successful at this endeavor?
13. Can any overall trend be detected in FASB pronouncements? Explain and cite examples to substantiate your opinion.
14. In terms of financial reporting in the future, do you expect greater refine-

ment of measurements appearing in the body of the financial statements or increasing disclosure with less effort directed toward refinement of measurements?

15. What challenges have there been to the FASB's jurisdiction and independence?

16. In late 1990 the "Wyden Amendment" was stricken from the Crime Bill passed by Congress. The amendment would have required reporting by auditors on internal controls. Letters sent by FEI members opposing the amendment were instrumental in its defeat. The AICPA supported the amendment. From an agency theory perspective, why do you think that the AICPA supported the amendment and the FEI was against it? Explain.

CASES AND PROBLEMS

1. During its long tenure, the Committee on Accounting Procedure produced a total of fifty-one ARBs. While the CAP was in existence, another committee, the Committee on Terminology of the American Institute of Accountants (the previous name of the AICPA), prepared certain definitions. Assess their definitions of assets and liabilities (see Chapter 10 for the definitions). Do you see any problems with one committee preparing rules and another making definitions?

   Read Chapter 15 of ARB 43 on unamortized discount, issue cost, and redemption premium on bonds refunded. Why do you think these issues concerned the committee? What were the two acceptable alternatives for dealing with the costs of any issue? Why would the definition of assets be helpful in analyzing a situation of this type? Are there any other situations that might be somewhat analogous to the bond redemption situation?

2. Five so-called broad principles of accounting were prepared by the AICPA's Special Committee on Co-operation with the Stock Exchange and approved by the NYSE's Committee on Stock List in 1932. They were to be followed by all firms listed on the exchange.

   Subsequently, these principles (along with a sixth item) were codified as Chapter 1 of ARB 43 and are printed below.

   (a) Unrealized profit should not be credited to income account of the corporation either directly or indirectly, through the medium of charging against such unrealized profits amounts which would ordinarily fall to be charged against income account. Profit is deemed to be realized when a sale in the ordinary course of business is effected, unless the circumstances are such that the collection of the sale price is not reasonably assured. An exception to the general rule may be made in respect of inventories in industries (such as the packing-house industry) in which owing to the impossibility of determining costs it is a trade custom to take inventories at net selling prices, which may exceed cost.

   (b) Capital surplus, however created, should not be used to relieve the income account of the current or future years of charges which would otherwise fall to be made thereagainst. This rule might be subject to the exception that where, upon reorganization, a reorganized company would be relieved of charges which would require to be made against income if the existing corporation were continued, it might be regarded as permissible to accomplish the same result without reorganization provided the facts were as fully revealed to and the action as formally approved by the shareholders as in reorganization.

(c) Earned surplus of a subsidiary company created prior to acquisition does not form a part of the consolidated earned surplus of the parent company and subsidiaries; nor can any dividend declared out of such surplus properly be credited to the income account of the parent company.

(d) While it is perhaps in some circumstances permissible to show stock of a corporation held in its own treasury as an asset, if adequately disclosed, the dividends on stock so held should not be treated as a credit to the income account of the company.

(e) Notes or accounts receivable due from officers, employees, or affiliated companies must be shown separately and not included under a general heading such as notes receivable or accounts receivable.

(f) If capital stock is issued nominally for the acquisition of property and it appears that at about the same time, and pursuant to a previous agreement or understanding, some portion of the stock so issued is donated to the corporation, it is not permissible to treat the par value of the stock nominally issued for the property as the cost of that property. If stock so donated is subsequently sold, it is not permissible to treat the proceeds as a credit to surplus of the corporation.

Listed below are two principles from ARS 7 as well as some additional comments. This study was done under the auspices of the ARB and was published in 1965.

Principle B-1

In case there are two or more classes of stock, account for the equity capital invested for each and disclose the rights and preferences to dividends and to principal in liquidation.

Principle B-4

Retained earnings should represent the cumulative balance of periodic earnings less dividend distributions in cash, property or stock, plus or minus gains and losses of such magnitude as not to be properly included in periodic earnings. The entire amount may be presumed to be unrestricted as to dividend distributions unless restrictions are indicated in the financial statements.

This principle is closely parallel to the definition of earned surplus in *Accounting Terminology Bulletin No. 1*, paragraph 34, which follows:

The balance of net profits, income, gains and losses of a corporation from the date of incorporation (or from the latest date when a deficit was eliminated in a quasi-reorganization) after deducting distributions therefrom to shareholders and transfers therefrom to capital stock or capital surplus accounts.

Terms such as *principles of accounting* have been used frequently since 1932. Describe what you think the principles might be. Do any of the principles coming from ARB 43, Chapter 1, or ARS 7 qualify as principles as you have construed them? How similar are these two partial groups of principles?

BIBLIOGRAPHY OF REFERENCED WORKS

Accounting Principles Board (1962). "Statement by the Accounting Principles Board," *Statement No. 1* (Accounting Principles Board).

American Accounting Association (1957). *Accounting and Reporting Standards for Corporate Financial Statements and Preceding Statements and Supplements* (American Accounting Association).

American Institute of Accountants (1934). *Audits of Corporate Accounts* (American Institute of Accountants).

American Institute of Certified Public Accountants (1958). "Report of Council of the Special Committee on Research Programs," *Journal of Accountancy* (December 1958), pp. 62–68.

——— (1972). *Establishing Financial Accountants Standards: Report of the Study on Establishment of Accounting Principles* (American Institute of Certified Public Accountants).

——— (1973). *Objectives of Financial Statements: Report of the Study Group on the Objectives of Financial Statements* (American Institute of Certified Public Accountants).

——— (1978). *Report of Progress: The Institute Acts on Recommendations for Improvements in the Profession* (American Institute of Certified Public Accountants).

Anderson, George D., and R. C. Ellyson (1986). "Restructuring Professional Standards: The Anderson Report," *Journal of Accountancy* (September 1986), pp. 92–104.

Bedford, Norton (1970). *The Future of Accounting in a Changing Society* (Stipes Publishing Co.).

Brown, Paul R. (1981). "A Descriptive Analysis of Select Input Bases of the Financial Accounting Standards Board," *Journal of Accounting Research* (Spring 1981), pp. 232–246.

Connor, Joseph E. (1986). "Enhancing Public Confidence in the Accounting Profession," *Journal of Accountancy* (July 1986), pp. 76–83.

The CPA Letter (1965). "Accounting Principles: Committee Identifies the Major Professional Considerations," *The CPA Letter* (June 1965), pp. 3–4.

——— (1970). "APB Approves Fundamental Statements," *The CPA Letter* (November 1970), p. 1.

Dopuch, Nicholas, and Shyam Sunder (1980). "FASB's Statements on Objectives and Elements of Financial Accounting: A Review," *The Accounting Review* (January 1980), pp. 1–21.

Dyckman, Thomas R. (1988). "Credibility and the Formulation of Accounting Standards Under the Financial Accounting Standards Board," *Journal of Accounting Literature,* pp. 1–30.

Financial Accounting Foundation (1977). *The Structure of Establishing Financial Accounting Standards: Report of the Structure Committee, the Financial Accounting Foundation* (Financial Accounting Foundation).

Grady, Paul (1965). "Inventory of Generally Accepted Accounting Principles for Business Enterprises," *Accounting Research Study No. 7* (American Institute of Certified Public Accountants).

Healy, Robert E. (1938). "The Next Step in Accounting," *The Accounting Review* (March 1938), pp. 1–9.

King, Earle C. (1947). "SEC May Take Exception to Financial Statements Reflecting Application of Bulletin No. 32," letter to Carmen G. Glough dated December 11, 1947, *The Journal of Accountancy* (January 1948), p. 25.

Kirk, Donald J. (1989). "Jurisdictional Conflicts and Conceptual Differences," *Accounting Horizons* (December 1989), pp. 107–113.

Kohler, Eric L. (1939). "Theories and Practice," *The Accounting Review* (September 1939), pp. 316–321.

McEnroe, John E., and Loren A. Nikolai (1983). "Voting Patterns of Big Eight Representatives in Setting Accounting and Auditing Standards," *Journal of Business Research* (March 1983), pp. 77–89.

Meyer, Philip E. (1974). "The APB's Independence and Its Implications for the FASB," *Journal of Accounting Research* (Spring 1974), pp. 188–196.

Moody, Sharon M., and Dale L. Flesher (1986). "Analysis of FASB Voting Patterns: Statements Nos. 1–86," *Journal of Accounting, Auditing & Finance* (Fall 1986), pp. 319–330.

Moonitz, Maurice (1974). "Obtaining Agreement on Standards in the Accounting Profession," *Studies in Accounting Research No. 8* (American Accounting Association).

Rockness, Howard O., and Loren A. Nikolai (1977). "An Assessment of APB Voting Patterns," *Journal of Accounting Research* (Spring 1977), pp. 154–167.

Sack, Robert J. (1985). "Commercialism in the Profession: A Threat to Be Managed," *Journal of Accountancy* (October 1985), pp. 125–134.

Securities and Exchange Commission (1938). "Administrative Policy on Financial Statements," *Accounting Series Release No. 4* (Securities and Exchange Commission).

——— (1939). *Fifth Annual Report Fiscal Year Ended June 30, 1939* (Government Printing Office).

Spacek, Leonard (1957). "Professional Accountants and Their Public Responsibility," in *A Search for Fairness in Financial Reporting to the Public* (Arthur Anderson & Co., 1969), pp. 17–26.

Sprouse, Robert T. (1987). "The SEC-FASB Partnership," *Accounting Horizons* (December 1987), pp. 92–95.

Storey, Reed K. (1964). *The Search for Accounting Principles — Today's Problems in Perspective* (American Institute of Certified Public Accountants).

Sunder, Shyam (1988). "Political Economy of Accounting Standards," *Journal of Accounting Literature*, pp. 31–41.

Wishon, Keith (1986). "Plugging the Gaps in GAAP: The FASB's Emerging Issues Task Force," *Journal of Accountancy* (June 1986), pp. 96–105.

Zeff, Stephen A. (1972). *Forging Accounting Principles in Five Countries* (Stipes Publishing Co.).

——— (1984). "Some Junctures in the Evolution of the Process of Establishing Accounting Principles in the U.S.A.: 1917–1972," *The Accounting Review* (July 1984), pp. 447–468.

ADDITIONAL READINGS

History and Development of Regulation in the Private Sector

Burton, John C. (1973). "Some General and Specific Thoughts on the Accounting Environment," *Journal of Accountancy* (October 1973), pp. 40–46.

Carey, John L. (1969 and 1970). *The Rise of the Accounting Profession*, Vols. 1 and 2 (American Institute of Certified Public Accountants).

"History of the Accounting Procedure Committee — from the Final Report," *Journal of Accountancy* (November 1959), pp. 70–71.

Schuetze, Walter P. (1979). "The Early Days of the FASB," *World* (Peat, Marwick & Mitchell, Summer 1979), pp. 34–39.

Spacek, Leonard (1959). *Business Success Requires an Understanding of Unsolved Problems of Accounting and Financial Reporting* (Arthur Andersen & Co.).

Sprouse, Robert T., and Detlev F. Vagts (1965). "The Accounting Principles Board and Differences and Inconsistencies in Accounting Practice: An Interim Appraisal," *Law and Contemporary Problems* (Autumn 1965), pp. 706–726.

Trueblood, Robert M. (1969). "Ten Years of the APB: One Practitioner's Appraisal," *Tempo* (Touche Ross, September 1969), pp. 4–8.

The Securities and Exchange Commission

Blough, Carmen (1967). "Development of Accounting Principles in the United States," *Berkeley Symposium on the Foundations of Financial Accounting* (University of California), pp. 1–14.

Chatov, Robert (1975). *Corporate Financial Reporting* (The Free Press).

Pines, J. Arnold (1965). "The Securities and Exchange Commission and Accounting Principles," *Law and Contemporary Problems* (Autumn 1965), pp. 727–751.

Previts, Gary John (1978). "The SEC and Its Chief Accountants: Historical Impressions," *Journal of Accountancy* (August 1978), pp. 83–91.

Skousen, K. Fred (1987). *An Introduction to the SEC*, 4th ed. (South-Western Publishing Co.).

Voting Patterns and Power in Regulatory Organizations

Haring, J. R., Jr. (1979). "Accounting Rules and the 'Accounting Establishment,'" *Journal of Business* (October 1979), pp. 507–519.

Newman, D. Paul (1981). "Coalition Formation in the APB and the FASB: Some Evidence on the Size Principle," *The Accounting Review* (October 1981), pp. 897–909.

——— (1981). "An Investigation of the Distribution of Power in the APB and FASB," *Journal of Accounting Research* (Spring 1981), pp. 247–262.

THE ECONOMICS OF
FINANCIAL REPORTING
REGULATION

F INANCIAL REPORTING HAS BEEN REGULATED in the United States since the 1930s when Congress empowered the Securities and Exchange Commission (SEC) to regulate financial reporting. However, as noted in Chapter 3, the SEC has allowed accounting policy-making power to remain in the private sector; first with the American Institute of Certified Public Accountants (AICPA), which operated the Committee on Accounting Procedure and the Accounting Principles Board, and then with the Financial Accounting Standards Board (FASB). Oversight is maintained by the SEC, and the authority of the private sector to set accounting policy is derived from the SEC mandate.

Even though financial reporting is a regulated activity and is likely to continue as such, it is useful to evaluate the arguments both for and against formal regulation. Such an evaluation helps us understand the nature of accounting regulation and some of the consequences that flow from it. Arguments for unregulated markets are presented first, followed by arguments for regulated markets. At the conclusion of the first two sections, we assess the merits of the two arguments. Because regulation does exist and is likely to continue, we examine next the nature of regulatory decision making and its influence on parties affected by regulation. This examination aids in understanding how the regulatory process works. Finally, we introduce the notion of a political economy of accounting, which includes the FASB's concern for the economic consequences of accounting regulation.

UNREGULATED MARKETS FOR ACCOUNTING INFORMATION

A recent body of literature has considered the possibility that financial reporting need not be regulated. Several different arguments support the case for unregulated markets. The arguments all relate to the incentives for a firm to report information about itself to owners and to the capital market in general. Agency theory is employed to explain why incentives exist for reliable and voluntary reporting to owners. Wider voluntary reporting to the capital market is attributed to competitiveness in the capital markets. Finally, it is argued that any information not reported voluntarily could be obtained through private contracting.

AGENCY THEORY

The economic theory of agency predicts and explains the behavior of parties involved with the firm. In law, an agent is a person employed to represent another person's interests. The economic theory of agency builds on the legal concept of agency. Agency theory conceives of the firm itself as a nexus (intersection) of agency relationships and seeks to understand organizational behavior by examining how parties to agency relationships within the firm maximize their own utility.

One of the major agency relationships is between the management group and the owners of the firm. Managers are hired by the owners of a firm to administer the firm's activities, thus establishing an agency relationship. Goals of managers and owners may not be in perfect agreement. It is easy to see how the utility-maximizing behavior of managers could be in conflict with ownership interests. Owners are interested in maximizing return on investment, while managers have a wider range of economic and psychological needs, which are satisfied by the employment contract. Because of this potential conflict, owners are motivated to contract with managers in such a way as to minimize conflict between the goals of the two groups. Costs are incurred in monitoring agency contracts with management; and these costs, the argument goes, reduce managers' compensation. Therefore, managers have an incentive to keep the costs low by not being in conflict with owners.

Agency theory posits a conflict between owners and managers that is mitigated to some extent by financial reporting. Routine financial reporting is one means by which owners can monitor employment contracts with their managers. Accountants refer to this traditional type of reporting as *stewardship*, or accountability to the owners of the firm. Agency theory has also been used to explain the demand for audits. The auditor functions as an independent verifier of financial reports submitted by managers to owners.[1] The historical develop-

---

[1] See Ng (1978) and Wallace (1980) for extensions of agency theory to auditing.

ment of both financial reporting and auditing supports the agency theory argument.[2]

Minimizing agency monitoring costs is an economic incentive for managers to report accounting results reliably to the ownership.[3] The incentive comes from the fact that managers are judged and rewarded, at least in part, by how well they report. The reputation of a manager will be enhanced by good reporting; and a good reputation should result in higher compensation because agency monitoring costs are minimized if owners perceive the accounting reports as reliable.

COMPETITIVE CAPITAL MARKETS

Agency theory provides a framework for analyzing financial reporting incentives between managers and owners also suggests why firms would have an incentive to report voluntarily to the capital market even if there were no mandatory reporting requirements: firms compete with one another for scarce risk capital, and voluntary disclosure is necessary in order to compete successfully in the market for risk capital.[4] The ability of the firm to raise capital will be improved if the firm has a good reputation for financial reporting. In addition, good reporting would also lower a firm's cost of capital because there is less uncertainty about firms that report more extensively and reliably; therefore, there is less investment risk and a lower required rate of return.

Incentives would exist to prepare a prospectus voluntarily when raising capital to report regularly in order to maintain continued investor interest in the firm. Companies that perform well have a strong incentive to report their operating results. Competitive pressures would also force other companies to report even if they did not have good results. Silence (a failure to report) would be interpreted as bad news. Companies with neutral news would be motivated to report their results in order to avoid being suspected of having poor results. This would leave only firms with bad news that would not report. Such a situation would also force "bad news" firms to disclose results in order to maintain credibility in the capital market.[5]

Some empirical evidence exists that SEC reporting requirements are not a significant improvement over the voluntary reporting existing prior to the 1933 and 1934 acts. One study concluded that the SEC's prospectus requirements have not significantly affected the quality of securities offered for public subscription. A relatively recent SEC commissioner acknowledged that this conclusion was difficult to refute.[6] A study has also been made of voluntary

---

[2] Watts and Zimmerman (1983).

[3] Holthausen and Leftwich (1983).

[4] The owners of the firm include both debt holders and stockholders under agency theory (Jensen and Meckling, 1976).

[5] See Ross (1979) for a summary of this argument.

[6] Stigler (1975, pp. 78–100). The comments of SEC Commissioner Roderick Hills were quoted in an article which appeared in the *Wall Street Journal*, January 8, 1976, p. 5.

annual reporting prior to the Securities Exchange Act of 1934, which required the 10-K annual report.[7] The basic conclusion in the study was that the reporting requirements mandated by the SEC were already being fulfilled on a voluntary basis. This finding says nothing about the quality or usefulness of the disclosures, but it supports the argument that voluntary disclosure would occur in a competitive capital market.

PRIVATE CONTRACTING OPPORTUNITIES

Another argument in favor of unregulated markets is the presumption that anyone who genuinely desired information about a firm would be able to obtain it, even in the event unregulated markets resulted in less free public disclosure. Any party could privately contract for information with the firm itself, with the firm's owners, or indirectly with information intermediaries, such as stock analysts. If information is truly desired beyond that which is publicly available and free of charge, private individuals would be able to buy the desired information. In this way market forces should result in the optimal allocation of resources to the production of information.

An examination of the stock market reveals that people are willing to contract privately for information. The securities market is as much a market for information as it is a market for securities. Investor newsletters available only by subscription are a good example of paying for private information. A somewhat less formal purchase of information is the use of brokerage firms for investment advice. The cost of investment advice is hidden in commission rates, but it is still a real cost.

Because of private opportunities for contracting additional information, the argument is that market intervention in the form of mandatory disclosure rules is both unnecessary and undesirable. In this view, the demand for information is optimally met when market forces determine the production (supply) and disclosure of accounting information. Some evidence exists of a philosophical shift in this direction by the SEC. An SEC commissioner was quoted as saying the mandatory disclosure system may not be an effective route for transmission of information to the capital markets — and that it serves no purpose to force-feed the investment community with information it does not want.[8] It remains, however, for the SEC to implement a major program for the deregulation of disclosure.[9]

---

[7] Benston (1973).

[8] SEC Commissioner Stephen Friedman, as quoted in *Executive Newsletter* (Peat, Marwick, Mitchell & Co., June 3, 1981), p. 3.

[9] A step toward deregulation is shelf-registration (SEC rule 415). This rule permits the speedier sales of routine offerings of debt and equity securities by large companies. It is not necessary to file a specific prospectus with the SEC for each individual offering of securities. One prospectus can be used for multiple issues within the time period covered by the shelf-registration.

REGULATED MARKETS

Market regulation can be justified on the grounds that it is in the public interest. In this context, two reasons are normally used to defend regulation. One reason is the possibility of a failure in the free market system, referred to as *market failure*, which indicates a suboptimal allocation of resources. Natural monopolies, such as occur in the utilities industry, are an example of market failures requiring regulatory intervention to prevent monopoly pricing. The second reason is the possibility that free markets are contrary to social goals. For example, social welfare programs create income redistributions that modify market-based income distributions. These programs are undertaken to meet social goals of minimum family income and to provide social safety nets for those individuals who are less well off in our society. A philosophical justification of the standard-setting process — called *codification* — is based on these reasons for the regulation of financial reporting.

MARKET FAILURES

There are several arguments favoring regulation because of market failures. The arguments concern the firm as a monopoly supplier of information, the failure of financial reporting to prevent frauds and bankruptcies, and the public-good nature of accounting information and financial reporting.

The Firm as a Monopoly Supplier of Information

One argument is that market failure occurs because the firm is a monopoly supplier of information about itself. This situation creates the opportunity for restricted production of information and its monopolistic pricing if the market is unregulated. Mandatory disclosure would result in more information and a lower cost to society than would be achieved in an unregulated market. Since the firm is a monopoly, it enjoys economies of scale in the production of firm-specific information. However, being a monopoly producer, the firm can underproduce (underreport) information and charge monopolistic prices. The potential for this situation exists in the utilities industry. The regulatory solution in the utilities industry is to permit monopolistic production, but to regulate prices.

With accounting regulation, the argument is that it is better to force mandatory reporting rather than to have individuals competing to buy information privately and at monopolistic prices. In other words, mandatory public disclosure is a cost-effective method of getting firm-specific information to those demanding it. It is a waste of social resources for everyone to be buying the same private information about firms.

The production costs of mandatory reporting requirements may be quite small since most of the basic information is produced as a by-product of internal accounting systems.[10] If marginal information production costs are low, then the social costs associated with mandatory financial reporting requirements may be small. And, as previously noted, mandatory public disclosures could save investors a great deal of money if the alternative is private contracting. The argument is very appealing, though lacking in empirical verification. If the production costs are not low, however, then who bears the cost of producing free public disclosure? Companies will either absorb or pass on regulation costs to consumers; therefore, the owners of the company or the firm's consumers will be subsidizing the information costs. This raises the issue of who bears the costs of financial reporting regulation.

Failures of Financial Reporting and Auditing

The criticisms of accounting practice and the standard-setting process, reviewed in Chapter 3, generally have focused on the alleged low quality of financial reporting, even under regulation. The reasons cited for this are poor accounting and auditing standards, too much management flexibility in the choice of accounting policies, and occasional laxity by auditors.[11] Corporate frauds undetected by auditors and corporate failures not signaled in advance by either financial statements or audit reports are cited as evidence that the financial reporting system is failing to protect the public interest.[12] The argument is that more and better regulation is necessary to raise the quality of financial reporting in order to protect the public from frauds and failures.

A capitalist economy relies on a competitive private-sector capital market. Information is an important part of the capital market infrastructure. Good financial reporting is essential to create investor confidence in the fairness of the capital market so that savings will be channeled into investments. In addition, good information leads to better investment decisions and capital allocation, both of which are socially beneficial. The corollary is that bad financial reporting has the opposite effect. Advocates of regulation doubt if companies can really be trusted to report fully and accurately. In fact, the competitive nature of the capital market could even induce misleading reporting, at least by some companies during the short term. Therefore, regulation of accounting is both necessary and in the public interest to prevent some companies from bad or misleading reporting. This is a counterargument to the notion that a competitive capital market produces good voluntary reporting.

This type of criticism raises useful questions about the value of accounting information and can serve as an impetus for reviewing accounting and auditing standards. It can also be a catalyst for discussing the quantity and quality of mandatory accounting and auditing that would be in the public interest, as well as the amount of regulation needed to achieve these goals. However, corporate

---

[10] Hakansson (1977).
[11] For example, see Briloff (1972) and (1976).
[12] One of the most publicized frauds was Equity Funding. See Seidler, Andrews, and Epstein (1977).

frauds and failures by themselves do not necessarily mean a failure exists in the financial reporting system. Accounting regulation is not going to prevent frauds and failures; risk in investments cannot be eliminated no matter how much accounting and auditing is required, for risk is something that inherently exists in investments. Increased regulation of financial reporting may reduce the likelihood of undetected frauds and failures, but it can never eliminate them. Finally, any argument favoring expanded regulation must also consider the costs of regulation. In all control or regulatory systems, there exists a point where the marginal benefits from more control are less than the marginal costs. It is by no means clear if benefits exceed costs under existing requirements, let alone under potentially expanded regulation.

Accounting as a Public Good

Market failures can also occur with what are called *public goods*. Public goods are commodities that, once produced, can be consumed without reducing the opportunity for consumption by others.[13] This condition exists because of the soft property rights associated with such goods. Examples of pure public goods are radio signals and highways. By contrast, private goods possess hard property rights so that nonpurchasers are, by definition, excluded from consuming the good.

Public goods are underproduced in a free market — owing to what are called *externalities*. An **externality** exists if a producer is unable to internalize (or impose) production costs on all users of the good. In slightly less technical language, the effect of an externality is that the producer of a public good has a limited incentive to produce it because all consumers cannot be charged for the good. The people who consume public goods without paying for them are called *free riders*. True market demand for public goods is not revealed in the market place because free riders are able to use the goods at no cost. The result is that production is less than true market demand. Underproduction of public goods is regarded as a market failure because producers are not motivated to meet the real demand for public goods. The only way in which production can be increased is through regulatory intervention. Inevitably, the cost of free riders must be borne by society as a whole if production is subsidized to meet true demand for public goods.

It appears that accounting information is a public good.[14] It can be freely passed from person to person; each person can consume the content of the information. Because of this characteristic, accounting information has the qualities of a public good. There are two aspects of regulated financial reporting (audited financial statements) that may give rise to social value (externalities) not privately captured. The first is increased comparability of accounting numbers across firms; the second is an increase in confidence in the securities mar-

---

[13] See Bowers (1974) for a good review of the public-good problem.
[14] Gonedes and Dopuch (1974) and May and Sundem (1976).

ket. Both operate to reduce information risk in the capital market and should, as a result, benefit society through a lower required return on risky investments.

But if accounting information is a public good, companies would not have a strong incentive to produce and sell accounting information about themselves in a free market, the opportunities to contract privately for firm-specific information would be restricted, and thus the heart of one argument supporting unregulated markets is seriously challenged. The outcome would be an underproduction of accounting information in an unregulated market. Intervention in the form of mandatory reporting requirements is considered necessary to insure that the real demand for accounting information is met.

SOCIAL GOALS

The other reason for imposing regulation is in order to achieve social goals that are not met by a free market even if there is no market failure. This approach is also justified by a public-interest argument and inevitably involves a normative judgment about how society ought to allocate its resources.

The SEC has always been concerned with what might be termed *fair reporting* and the protection of investors. Fairness of the capital market is a public-interest type of argument. It assumes that the stock market will be fair only if all potential investors have equal access to the same information. This situation is referred to as *information symmetry* and is a laudable goal because the more widely information is distributed, the more competitive the capital market will be. After all, perfect and costless information is an assumption of the economic model of perfect competition. Regulation of insider trading is an application of the information symmetry philosophy. Such regulation attempts to prevent those with unfair access to private information from taking advantage of it. This behavior, it is argued, undermines investor confidence in the fairness of the capital market.

Merino and Niemark are critical of the regulatory focus on information symmetry.[15] In their analysis, they argue persuasively that the rise of corporate economic concentration starting in the late 1800s was at odds with American ideals of pluralism and capitalism. They suggest that the corporate community accepted disclosure and accounting regulation because the alternative was more direct regulation and control. Politicians also accepted disclosure and accounting reforms because they offered the hope of a solution (a belief that increased competition would result from better financial reporting and that this would lessen economic concentration) without making major changes in the structure of the economy. Finally, Merino and Niemark might agree with those who argue that the securities acts "didn't do anything." But this doesn't demonstrate that the unregulated market was therefore all right; instead, they argue that the real underlying need for corporate regulation was (and still is) unmet by the largely cosmetic changes brought about by the securities acts.

---

[15] Merino and Neimark (1982).

THE CODIFICATIONAL JUSTIFICATION OF STANDARD SETTING

In an important monograph published by the AAA, Gaa has provided a meaningful justification of the *standard-setting process* per se.[16] He sees the task of a standard-setting body as providing the "best" standards from the societal point of view.[17] This function occurs in an environment permeated by such problems as managers having interests that do not totally coincide with those of shareholders (the agency theory problem), underproduction of accounting information because it is a public good, and the lack of information symmetry. Gaa's concern is not with the output of the FASB in the form of standards, concepts, interpretations, and the like, but rather with the underlying rationality of the standard-setting process itself.

The *codificational* viewpoint (the term used in the philosophical literature) is not only rational but also evolutionary in the sense that the system is expected to evolve and improve. It thus works best in a relatively open and democratic society rather than in authoritarian societies. Given that financial accounting can be improved by regulation that binds all of the players (publicly owned and traded enterprises), one can generally expect a rational — but not perfect — response from regulating bodies such as the CAP, APB, and FASB. When viewed from the codificational standpoint, members of an organization such as the FASB are expected to have ". . . the ability, the opportunity, and the desire to make a correct decision (or at least, not the desire not to)."[18]

The outputs of a codificational system like accounting standards would not necessarily be correct in terms of deductive logic. Instead, the attitude would be more open-minded: the standards would be evaluated on the basis of whether they work correctly — for example, whether they provide information to users at a reasonable cost. If the standards didn't work, they should be or at least could be amended. The codificational approach is thus pragmatic, evolutionary, and satisficing because maximizing the standards is for all intents and purposes impossible.

Evaluation of the Codificational Approach

Codification works best in an open and democratic society, and given that environment, we can expect problems to be addressed in a rational and appropriate fashion. Codification provides a good idea of what can be expected when democratic societies attempt to resolve difficult distributional problems (how benefits are distributed among competing groups). On the other hand, codification can be viewed as a banal rationalization of the status quo even though, by definition, it assumes that there will be institutional improvements over time in dealing with problems. Chapter 6 has more to say on the codificational viewpoint in relation to the Conceptual Framework Project of the FASB.

---

[16] Gaa (1988).
[17] Ibid., p. 31.
[18] Ibid., p. 123.

ASSESSMENT OF THE REGULATION ARGUMENTS

Since we live in a regulated environment, empirical tests of the free market position are rather difficult. This is why the arguments for an unregulated market are largely deductive. And in spite of the fact that accounting is regulated, precious little is really known about the costs and benefits of regulation. What this means is that the proregulation arguments are also largely deductively reasoned rather than empirically researched. In short, it is impossible to accept either argument as correct. What follows is an attempt to assess the merits of the two arguments and to compare them on points where they address the same issues.

One of the arguments for regulation is that firms are monopoly suppliers of information about themselves. Prima facie, this could be viewed as a market failure. Since the firm is a monopoly supplier of information about itself, it may be cheaper to society to require mandatory free disclosure rather than to have all investors privately contracting for the same information and paying monopolistic prices. The free market counterargument to this is that, owing to competitive pressure for capital, firms have an incentive to report information voluntarily about themselves. Because individuals have alternative investment opportunities, companies are not really able to impose monopolistic prices. They have incentives to report freely in order to attract capital and to lower their cost of capital by being perceived as a good reporting firm. The argument is that where there is perceived information risk due to poor quality reporting, investors penalize such companies by requiring a higher rate of return (to compensate for the extra risk they think they are taking). Proregulators counter that the competitive nature of the capital market provides an incentive for misleading reporting, at least in the short term. The implication is that managers of companies may not pay the penalty for poor or misleading reporting and for this reason may be tempted to manipulate reporting in the short term. If this is true, it would also indicate that owners have not developed good mechanisms for monitoring agency contracts with managers.

Another argument against regulation is that information not voluntarily disclosed by the firm could be obtained through private contracting. However, the viability of private contracting opportunities is questionable because of the public-good nature of accounting information and the free-rider problem.

Finally, it can be argued that mandatory reporting is desirable on social grounds because it creates fairness in the capital market. The less private information there is (and the more that's public), the less wealth transfers between those who have information and those who do not. It is this same principle that is behind insider trading regulations.

The arguments for and against regulation represent deliberate extremes. In reality, voluntary disclosure would probably be substantial for the reasons already cited. Yet there is merit in mandating accounting policies. For example, standardization of accounting policies may lead more quickly to uniformity between companies than would occur in an unregulated market. This may improve the quality of financial reporting and reduce criticisms of it. Mandatory public reporting also enhances the perceived fairness of the capital market and may reduce the total cost to society of acquiring the information. And since most regulated information is produced as a by-product of the firm's accounting system, regulatory costs to the firm appear to be low while benefits to society could be substantial. If, then, regulation is necessary, the codification philosophy justifies the *process* of standard setting, though it does not guarantee that the output of the process is — or even could be — optimal.

Much of the economic argument against regulation maintains that there are incentives for voluntary reporting. However, the focus of accounting regulation is not on mandatory reporting per se; it is on improving the quality of reported information. Accounting regulation is mainly concerned with refining and unifying the rules of recognition and measurement used in the preparation of financial statements. An important implication is that accounting regulation requires a theoretical foundation — given that it is mainly the quality of information that is being regulated. As was evident in Chapter 3, the lack of a theoretical foundation was directly responsible for the collapse of both the Committee on Accounting Procedure (CAP) and the Accounting Principles Board (APB) as standard-setting bodies. By contrast, the FASB has developed a conceptual framework as the basis for standard setting.

THE PARADOX OF REGULATION

If free market pricing does not work because of market failures or is deliberately abandoned for social reasons, it is impossible to know if resources are used to maximize the social welfare, or even to achieve optimality in the more restrictive sense of Pareto-optimality.[19] Market regulation can be justified if there is a market failure (as in the case of public goods) or if the free market produces a result incompatible with social goals. Ironically, though, regulated production and pricing decisions cannot provide an optimal answer to the problem left unsolved by the free market pricing system. This is the paradox of regulation.

Economists have concluded that it is impossible to derive regulatory policies that will knowingly maximize the social welfare. This somewhat gloomy conclusion is the subject of Arrow's well-known *Impossibility Theorem*.[20] Once the free market pricing system is abandoned, there is no way of determining aggregate social preferences. If the pricing system is working, aggregate social preferences are revealed indirectly through supply–demand equilibria, and resources are allocated according to market prices. There is no comparable rule in a regulated market, and for this reason it is difficult to evaluate the benefits of market regulation. Because of this paradox, it is also impossible to know if

---

[19] Pareto-optimality occurs when it is not possible to make anyone better off without making someone else worse off. A Pareto-optimal economy is considered to be efficient. If it is possible to make someone better off at no cost, then the existing allocation of resources is inefficient and involves a waste of resources due to suboptimality.

[20] Arrow (1963).

accounting regulation is producing the optimal quantity and quality of financial reporting.[21]

Economists also argue that public goods supplied in regulated markets tend to be overproduced. This contrasts with underproduction in unregulated markets and gives rise to a second paradox of regulation. The reason for overproduction is that demand is overstated because public goods supplied under regulation are normally subsidized (or even costless) goods. Users overstate their real demand or preference because the good is costless to them. Since accounting information has public-good characteristics, there is a very real danger that overproduction of accounting information occurs in a regulated market. Users of accounting information, such as financial analysts, probably have an insatiable demand for free information about firms.

In determining accounting policy, the FASB could easily be deceived about the level of real demand for new or alternative accounting policies since users do not pay directly for it. The FASB may also be cognizant of the overproduction problem. In recent years, it has paid increasing attention to what is called *standards overload*, particularly as it affects smaller, nonpublicly traded companies. To date, the only relief has been the exemption of some closely held firms from supplemental disclosures. However, the problem of standards overload is still under consideration by the FASB.

The tendency for overproduction in regulated markets can be avoided only if a pricing system can be imposed on public goods, creating nonpurchasers who are effectively excluded from consuming the good.[22] Cable television is an example of how this imposition can be accomplished with television signals. The key is to strengthen property rights over the good so that nonpurchasers are excluded from freely consuming the good. One means of doing this in accounting might be to file company reports with the SEC and charge users for copies of the information. If accounting information were purchased in this manner, there would be incentives for users *not* to pass on the information to free riders. In this way real economic demand for the information could be determined, and production costs could be recovered from the real users of accounting information. The present disclosure system imposes costs on companies rather than on users. Assuming that firms recover the costs indirectly through product pricing, the users of accounting information are being subsidized by the users of the firms' products. This consequence of regulation can be criticized on the grounds of fairness.

In summary, the consequences of regulating accounting, given its public-good nature, are (1) a potential overallocation of social resources to the production of free publicly available accounting information, and (2) a wealth transfer from nonusers to users of accounting information. A wealth transfer occurs because users receive the benefits of free accounting information while non-

---

[21] Gonedes (1972) argued that it was possible to determine optimal accounting regulation. Later thinking, however, has reversed that conclusion. See Demski (1973) and Gonedes and Dopuch (1974).
[22] Demsetz (1970).

users implicitly incur the production costs. But there would also be social costs for *not* regulating financial reporting if there are market failures, or if other socially desirable goals are unmet by free markets.

THE REGULATORY PROCESS

In regulated markets, economic resource allocation is partially determined by the political process. Regulation is essentially a political activity. This is not intended as a criticism, nor is it surprising since regulation is undertaken in the public interest. Ironically, it is unclear exactly what is meant by public interest. Since social welfare cannot be measured (the Impossibility Theorem), there is no criterion for determining what policy will maximize the public interest. Consequently, the notion of public interest is best understood in a political context and with reference to the particular redistribution of income and wealth being advocated. What this means is that there is no way of determining optimal accounting regulation and that regulation will be the outcome of a political as much as an economic process.

Not surprisingly, self-interest models have been used for analyzing regulatory behavior. In a regulated market, individuals or groups who have any stake in the market will be motivated to lobby for their vested interests, to form coalitions with other parties to further strengthen their influence, and generally to try to influence the political system to their advantage.

THE POLITICAL NATURE OF REGULATION

The democratic tradition in the United States means that due process is an important ingredient in the regulatory process. In setting policy, **due process** means that a regulatory agency seeks to involve all affected parties in the deliberations; this is important in maintaining the legitimacy of the regulatory process. In other words, people affected by regulation have an opportunity to have input into the regulatory decision-making process. The due-process tradition goes back to one of the first federal agencies, the Interstate Commerce Commission.[23] It has even been suggested that a regulatory body's method of operation (which includes the principle of due process) is more important to its own political survival than the actual decisions it makes.

Some members of the accounting profession believe that accounting policy setting should be neutral and apolitical.[24] The more widely held view, however, is that accounting policy is inevitably political because of its regulatory nature.[25] In reflecting back on Chapter 3, it is easy to see why both the CAP

---

[23] Krislov and Musolf (1964, p. 185).

[24] For examples of this position, see Armstrong (1977) and Kirk (1978).

[25] Horngren (1973) and Solomons (1978).

and the APB failed as regulatory bodies. These two AICPA committees were regulatory bodies but they lacked the necessary structure to insure their survival. For one thing, they had only a weak mandate to regulate financial reporting. Until the issue of Accounting Series Release (ASR) 150 in 1973, the SEC did not officially endorse private-sector standard setting.[26] What existed was an informal alliance in which the SEC tacitly accepted accounting standards as acceptable for SEC filings. Occasionally, though, the SEC would challenge a specific standard. The investment tax credit produced such a situation. Because of this arrangement, the AICPA's authority to regulate was very weak.

From the SEC's perspective, the arrangement prior to ASR 150 provided security and flexibility. By permitting self-regulation in the private sector, the SEC was shielded from the politics of actually setting accounting policy except when it was expedient to do so. In a sense, the SEC was in a position to use the private sector as a scapegoat if Congress were to challenge the work of the SEC.[27]

The other fatal characteristic of the AICPA committees was the closed-door nature of policy setting. There appeared to be no due process in the determination of accounting and disclosure rules. Although some informal fact gathering and solicitation of the views of interested parties undoubtedly occurred, it was not until late in the life of the APB that formal due-process procedures were implemented. The lack of due process, or at least the apparent lack of due process, sometimes led to a low level of acceptance by affected parties. Ironically, the accounting profession thought a closed-door approach was good because it insulated policy making from outside influence. It believed at the time that accounting policy was primarily a process of identifying the true and correct normative accounting methods. In hindsight, this seems naive, but accounting researchers and policy makers clung strongly to this conviction through the 1960s.

From a regulatory viewpoint at least, the FASB is functioning much more successfully than did earlier regulatory bodies. Its standards were endorsed by the SEC in ASR 150. Due process has been adopted as standard procedure in debating and evaluating accounting policy. As with the legal system, decision making under due process is extremely slow, but this is the nature of democratic politics. Arrow refers to this tendency as *democratic paralysis*.[28] Regulation under a system of due process *is* slow, but the achieving of consensus is what gives legitimacy to the regulation. The problems of the FASB alluded to in Chapter 3 stem from the costliness of implementing standards and, in some cases, their lack of understandability. The mechanism for due process, however, is firmly established in the organizational structure of the FASB.

---

[26] SEC (1973). Accounting standards of the FASB were officially sanctioned as the basis for statutory reports filed with the SEC.

[27] Watts and Zimmerman (1978).

[28] Arrow (1963).

REGULATORY BEHAVIOR

Capture theory and the **life-cycle theory** of regulation both argue that the group being regulated eventually comes to use the regulatory process to promote its own self-interest.[29] When this occurs, the regulatory process is considered captured. The life-cycle theory of regulation argues that a regulatory agency goes through several distinct phases. Although it starts out in the public interest, regulation later becomes an instrument for protecting the regulated group. The regulated parties and the regulatory agency come to see that their interests converge. It becomes very difficult for a regulator to remain truly independent because survival of the regulatory agency itself may depend on how well the policies are accepted by the group being regulated. What often happens is that the regulatory body protects the regulated group from competition. This behavior has been observed in older regulatory agencies — such as the Interstate Commerce Commission, which regulates land transportation; the Federal Aviation Agency, which regulates air transportation; and the Federal Communications Commission, which regulates radio and television licenses. This behavior, by both the regulator and the regulated parties, is explained by the self-interest theory of political behavior.

Capture theory and the life-cycle theory have been applied to the regulation of accounting. From 1976 to 1978, the United States Congress investigated the allegation that accounting regulation had been captured by the Big Eight group of accounting firms.[30] As the predominant auditors of publicly listed corporations, this group has a large stake in the regulation game. In addition, prior to the FASB, accounting regulation was done primarily by AICPA subcommittees, which were undoubtedly heavily influenced by the Big Eight accounting firms. With the implementation of the independent FASB, however, the capture theory argument lost much of its validity. At the time of the Congressional hearings, the FASB had been in operation for several years.

Some changes were made in response to the Congressional hearings, however — for example, restructuring of the AICPA to lessen Big Eight dominance and to increase self-regulation by the AICPA.[31] But the status quo in accounting regulation survived the scrutiny of Congress because capture theory

---

[29] Stigler (1971) and Bernstein (1955).

[30] The Congressional hearings conducted by Senator Lee Metcalf in 1977 and Congressman John E. Moss in 1978 were discussed in Chapter 3. The staff reports prepared for both hearings were highly critical of financial reporting and accounting regulation. After the hearings, the status quo of accounting regulation was maintained, although the SEC, FASB, and AICPA all responded positively to some of the criticisms made during the hearings.

[31] Some of the fallout from the Watergate Congressional investigations was the discovery of corporate slush funds used to make political contributions. Direct corporate political contributions are of course illegal. It was also discovered that some of these funds were used for bribes in foreign countries. Auditors were held publicly accountable for failing to detect these slush funds in their audits. There were also several well-publicized corporate failures in the 1970s in which the auditors' performance was seriously questioned. To some degree, then, the Congressional investigations of the accounting profession reflected a genuine public-interest concern, but they were also part of post-Watergate politics.

and the life-cycle theory are not applicable to financial reporting. The number of parties directly affected by accounting regulation is much larger and more diverse than in older regulated industries. Recent studies of submissions to the FASB found that even the Big Eight group of accounting firms does not have a unified viewpoint, and the group does not dominate policy at the FASB.[32] These studies concluded that decision making at the FASB is pluralistic. Auditors and the other parties affected by accounting regulation, companies that must comply with regulations, and free riders who use the costless information for investment analyses have a divergence of interests, which places the accounting regulator in a more naturally neutral posture than is possible in other regulated industries.

Let's examine the three groups affected by accounting regulation – companies, auditors, and free riders – in greater detail. Management of companies can be expected to respond to regulatory proposals that will affect either the companies or itself personally. All accounting regulation imposes some amount of production cost on firms. One could argue, a priori, that there would be a natural tendency for management to oppose new disclosures or rules that will impose a cost on the firm. On the other hand, some rules may cause specific firms to increase reported net income. Management could have an incentive to support those new proposals that would positively affect reported income and that might increase its own compensation (especially where employment contracts use accounting numbers for bonuses). However, one study found the opposite result. Large regulated companies supported proposed accounting rules that would lower reported net income.[33] The suggested reason was that the self-interest of this type of company was to minimize political costs, such as the possibility of future regulatory intervention, and that lower book profits were consistent with this goal. So, even within the management group there is likely to be a range of reactions to accounting policy proposals.

Auditors are concerned with the auditing implications of financial reporting rules. It would be naive to think the opinion of large accounting firms is not seriously considered in accounting policy deliberations. Many accounting firms maintain regular liaison with FASB personnel and routinely attend policy hearings at the FASB. Auditors could be expected to support regulation that reduces the riskiness of audits – for example, rules that clarify or standardize financial reporting. Auditors have tended to oppose proposed policies that would expand the audit function into subjective areas, such as supplemental disclosures of inflation accounting data and profit forecasts.[34] The reason for this opposition is fairly obvious. If more subjective information is required, the auditor will incur

---

[32] Hussein and Ketz (1980) and Brown (1981).

[33] Watts and Zimmerman (1978). This study was extensively criticized in Chapter 2.

[34] Two areas where the AICPA membership balked were the proposals by the SEC for mandatory financial forecasts (proposed rule No. 33–581 issued in 1975), and ASR 177, also issued in 1975, which required auditors to comment on the preferability of a reported change in accounting policy. Because of the resistance by accounting firms to these two proposed requirements, they were subsequently dropped by the SEC. Auditors would have been placed in the position of attesting to information that was, in the

a greater risk in auditing the information, which would increase the possibility of litigation. Assuming that auditors are risk averse, they would prefer to avoid such risky ventures, if possible.

Finally, free riders may also try to influence the outcome of accounting policy deliberations. As sellers of investment advice, analysts have a strong motivation to demand new accounting information, which they can incorporate into investment counseling and newsletters. As information intermediaries, they can make money simply by summarizing public information for investors who do not have time to sift through it themselves. The lobbying behavior of free riders needs to be watched closely by the FASB because free riders do not have the direct economic interests in information production that management and auditors have. Because they do not, responding to their pressure could easily result in an overproduction situation. It is politically difficult to deal with free riders because they can claim to be acting in the public interest by making the capital market fairer and more competitive through free public reporting. Although this argument is true, it ignores the question of information production costs and who pays for accounting regulation.

The danger of bowing to pressures from special-interest groups has been noted.[35] Accounting policy making should not serve special-interest groups to the detriment of society as a whole, although no real evidence exists that regulation does produce a net social benefit. When regulation is dominated by special interests, its mandate no longer exists because the regulation process has been captured by a vested-interest group. Accounting regulation is likely to continue, and so it is important to understand the nature of regulatory processes. The majority of accounting regulations deal with financial statement refinement and standardization of practices rather than with expanded disclosure. This may mean that the overproduction problem is exaggerated by the critics of regulation. However, as noted before, there is a paucity of hard evidence to support arguments either for or against accounting regulation, so the belief that accounting regulation produces a net social benefit is also offered more hopefully than conclusively.

TOWARD A POLITICAL ECONOMY OF ACCOUNTING

The discussion in this chapter should have made clear by now that financial reporting regulation (or nonregulation) is a social choice that affects different parties in different ways and that there is no "correct" attitude toward it. This has led Cooper and Sherer to argue for the recognition of an explicit *political economy of accounting:*

---

case of forecasts, very subjective, and to comment on the preferability of accounting standards when there were no official guidelines for making such a determination (for example, FIFO versus LIFO inventory methods).

[35] Solomons (1978).

> Our position, that the objectives of and for accounting are fundamentally contested, arises out of the recognition that any accounting contains a representation of a specific social and political context. Not only is accounting policy essentially political in that it derives from the political struggle in society as a whole but also the outcomes of accounting policy are essentially political in that they operate for the benefit of some groups in society and to the detriment of others. . . . Social welfare is likely to be improved if accounting practices are recognised as being consistently partial; that the strategic outcomes of accounting practices consistently (if not invariably) favour specific interests in society and disadvantage others.[36]

That is, accounting policy is not simply a matter of economic efficiency or optimality. It also affects income and wealth distribution (who gets what), and this is necessarily a social and political issue that transcends accounting.

The FASB does, in a limited way, recognize the political economy of accounting. It considers the **economic consequences** of proposed accounting policies, which have been defined as "[T]he impact of accounting reports on . . . business, government, unions, investors, and creditors."[37] The FASB is very sensitive to producer costs and whether or not there are sufficient benefits (to external users) to warrant the imposition of new, costly accounting standards. Indeed, in the late 1970s the FASB began commissioning economic consequences studies to aid in assessing the effects of proposed standards on firms.[38] Unfortunately, these studies have focused primarily on firms, their stockholders, and financial analysts. Other parties, such as creditors, consumers, employees, and even governments, have not been factored into the cost-benefit calculus of financial reporting regulation. Consequently, it is not surprising that such broader questions as the desirability of corporate social responsibility accounting have not been seriously considered.[39] Corporate responsibility reporting is advocated by those who believe that society as a whole has a legitimate (though necessarily pluralistic) interest in corporate behavior, and that the corporation should be made accountable for its behavior over a wide range of activities, including employee and community relations, pollution controls, and compliance with federal laws like the Occupational Health and Safety Act and the Environmental Protection Act.

The FASB only considers costs in the narrowest of senses, producer costs, and benefits are thought of primarily in terms of the information needs of the stock market. An example of this orientation to economic consequences can be seen in the so-called standards overload issue discussed earlier in the chapter.[40] Smaller, nonpublicly listed firms (and their auditors) argue that accounting standards are formulated mainly for larger, publicly traded firms who can afford the costs of accounting regulation and for the benefit of financial analysts who

---

[36] Cooper and Sherer (1984, p. 208). See also Tinker (1980, 1984).
[37] Zeff (1978, p. 56).
[38] For example, FASB (1978), Abdel-khalik (1981), and Griffin and Castanias (1987).
[39] Schreuder and Ramanathan (1984).
[40] For example, AICPA (1983) and FASB (1983).

trade in these firms. For smaller, nonpublic firms, the compliance costs are disproportionately higher and the benefits smaller since the firms' securities are not traded. The FASB is sensitive to the issue and has suspended two disclosure-oriented standards, SFASs 14 and 69, for smaller, nonpublic firms. But the FASB has consistently rejected the argument for differential recognition, measurement, and disclosure rules and has reaffirmed the need for one basic set of accounting standards for all firms.[41]

Research into economic consequences, other than the FASB's, has also focused narrowly on stockholders and managers of firms. One extensive body of research (reviewed in Chapter 7) examined the effects of accounting policies and changes in policies on stock prices. Another extensive body of research has investigated whether the choice of accounting methods or management's preference for certain accounting methods is related to accounting-based contracts; in particular, restrictive covenants in debt agreements that require the maintenance of certain levels of working capital, leverage, or interest-coverage ratios. Another accounting-based contract relates to manager compensation, and here it has been hypothesized that managers choose accounting methods that maximize their compensation under these contracts. The suggestion is that these two contract-based incentives create a preference for income-increasing accounting methods.[42] This line of research has been useful in drawing attention to the literal ways in which accounting data can be used. However, its focus nevertheless is on a very limited aspect of the total social costs and benefits of financial reporting and the regulation of financial reporting. In conclusion, a true political economy of accounting has yet to emerge in either the research literature or in the FASB's policy making.

SUMMARY

The arguments for and against financial reporting regulation force us to consider why we regulate, who benefits, and who pays the costs. These are good questions to pose of any regulatory process. Since regulation is a matter of public interest, the benefits of regulation should clearly be in the public interest and should exceed costs. However, certain individuals benefit directly, while others incur the cost. An analysis of the economic consequences of regulation helps to evaluate these benefits and costs and their fairness.

Regulation is a political process and self-interest may motivate individuals and groups to participate in it. This places the regulator in the role of weighing sometimes conflicting positions and trying to determine what is in the best interests of society as a whole. Due process and neutrality are critical to regulatory success if the regulation is to retain the support of both the regulated parties and society generally. All these objectives are difficult for a regulatory

---

[41] FASB (1986).
[42] Watts and Zimmerman (1978).

agency to accomplish, and there is always the danger that vested-interest groups may capture the regulatory process and divert it to private ends.

The rationale or justification for regulation rests on the public-interest argument. However, a paradox exists. There is no way of determining optimal regulatory policies that maximize the social welfare or the public interest. The best that regulators can do is to try to determine that a net benefit exists – that is, an excess of benefits over costs. Benefits are difficult to identify and measure, although there is evidence that accounting information is useful to investors. (This research is examined in Chapter 7.) Costs are somewhat easier to quantify. There is some reason to believe regulation costs are low because most of the information contained in financial reports is produced as a by-product of firms' accounting systems. Overall, then, there is reason to believe that accounting regulation produces a net benefit to society. However, as was argued in the chapter, there is no way to determine if *either* regulated or unregulated financial reporting results in a socially optimal allocation of resources to the production of accounting information. This indeterminancy, by itself, favors *neither* regulated nor unregulated financial reporting.

QUESTIONS

1. What are the arguments favoring regulation of financial reporting?
2. What are the arguments against regulation of financial reporting?
3. Why is it difficult to evaluate the regulation question?
4. Why does accounting information have the qualities of a public good? What are the implications for information production in both unregulated and regulated markets?
5. Why can't optimal regulation be determined? If optimal accounting regulation cannot be determined, how can a regulatory body such as the SEC or FASB make good decisions?
6. A distinction was made in the chapter between two types of regulation: (a) the refinement and standardization of financial statements, and (b) expanded disclosure. Why is the distinction important in evaluating the regulation question?
7. Who pays for accounting regulation and who benefits?
8. Can accounting standards and policy making be neutral? In what sense is neutrality really important?
9. Arrow (1963) warns that public participation and a consensual approach to social issues can lead to democratic paralysis; that is, to a failure to act due to an inability to agree on goals or objectives. How did such a situation lead to the demise of the APB (review Chapter 3)? Why is the FASB faring somewhat better?
10. Horngren (1973) argues that accounting policies are a social decision and a matter of public interest. Evaluate this statement.
11. Horngren (1973) also believes that accounting standards must be marketed by regulatory bodies. By this he means that affected parties need to be sold

on the benefits of standards. How is this concept consistent with the nature of regulation?

12. It was suggested many years ago that a court should be created to resolve disputes in accounting. In what ways does the FASB function as an accounting court? In what ways is it different?

13. What benefit is the Conceptual Framework Project to the FASB if (a) there is no way of determining optimal accounting regulation and (b) regulatory decision making is a political process?

14. What is meant by a political economy of accounting, and why is it important in evaluating financial reporting in both a regulated *and* unregulated setting?

15. Is corporate social accounting and reporting a legitimate area for the FASB to pursue? Why or why not?

16. How do agency theory and the codificational viewpoint differ in assumptions about the behavior of individuals?

17. Why would codification not be a viable philosophy in authoritarian and totalitarian political regimes?

CASES AND PROBLEMS

1. The table presented by Hussein and Ketz (1980, p. 365) summarizes written responses of Big Eight accounting firms to proposals in exposure drafts, proposals that were eventually adopted in SFASs (see page 98). An *A* indicates agreement, *D* indicates disagreement, and *N* indicates no opinion.

   Required:
   (a) Why might different positions be taken by accounting firms?
   (b) Is there any evidence from this table that policy making has been captured by the Big Eight? Support your answer with an analysis of the responses in the table.
   (c) Does the FASB appear to be responsive to the Big Eight? Should it be?
   (d) What are the limitations of the evidence from this analysis?

2. Benston (1982, p. 102), in an analysis of corporate social accounting and reporting (CSAR), says: "The social responsibility of accountants can be expressed by their forebearing from social responsibility accounting." However, in a critique of Benston's analysis, Schreuder and Ramanathan (1984, p. 414) state:

   > The comments . . . do not purport to convey the message that there is no value
   > at all in analyzing the potential of CSAR from a shareholder perspective and proceed-
   > ing from the (implicit) assumption of perfect and complete markets. We do, however,
   > wish to point out that this may not be the most appropriate perspective as (1) CSAR
   > is addressed toward a more inclusive group of stakeholders and (2) one of its main
   > objectives is to include in the accounting system those aspects of corporate behavior
   > that are decidedly not handled well by the market. Therefore, the perspective implied
   > in Benston's analysis is of very limited value at best.

| | | | | | | Big Eight | | | |
		AA	AY	CL	DHS	EW	PMM	PW	TR

Big Eight Responses to FASB Statements

Issue	Proposal	AA	AY	CL	DHS	EW	PMM	PW	TR
1	FASB No. 2: R&D Costs Expenses	A	N	N	D	D	A	A	A
2	FASB No. 2: R&D Under Contract	N	N	N	A	A	A	A	A
3	FASB No. 5: Overall Reaction	A	D	D	N	A	D	D	A
4	FASB No. 5: Self-Insured Risks	A	A	N	N	N	A	D	A
5	FASB No. 5: Catastrophe Losses of Casualty Insurers	N	A	D	D	N	A	D	A
6	FASB No. 5: Expropriations of Foreign Assets	A	N	N	A	N	A	N	A
7	FASB No. 7: Overall Reaction	N	N	N	D	D	N	D	N
8	FASB No. 7: Same Standards	A	A	A	D	D	A	D	N
9	FASB No. 7: Certain Industries Exempt	A	N	D	N	N	N	N	N
10	FASB No. 7: Start-Up and Similar Costs First	D	D	D	D	D	D	N	D
11	FASB No. 8: Modified Temporal Method	A	D	D	D	N	A	D	D
12	FASB No. 8: Exchange Adjustment to Income	A	D	D	N	N	A	N	N
13	FASB No. 8: Forward Exchange Contract	D	A	A	N	N	N	A	A
14	FASB No. 9: Tax Allocation	A	A	A	A	A	A	A	A
15	FASB No. 9: Transition Method	D	D	A	D	D	D	D	D
16	FASB No. 12: Overall Reaction	A	N	D	D	D	A	A	A
17	FASB No. 12: Lower of Cost or Market	A	A	D	D	D	A	A	A
18	FASB No. 12: All Declines in Income	D	A	A	A	A	D	D	D
19	FASB No. 13: Overall Reaction	D	D	A	A	A	D	N	N
20	FASB No. 13: Lease Classification Criteria	D	D	D	D	D	D	D	A
21	FASB No. 13: Operating Leases on Face of B/S	A	A	N	A	A	A	N	N
22	FASB No. 13: Implementation	A	A	N	N	N	N	N	N
23	FASB No. 14: Overall Reaction	A	A	N	A	D	A	N	N
24	FASB No. 14: Annual Statements	N	N	D	N	N	N	N	D
25	FASB No. 14: Interim Statements	N	N	N	N	N	N	N	D
26	FASB No. 14: Exemption for Small Co.	N	D	D	N	D	D	N	A
27	FASB No. 14: Assets	A	N	N	N	D	D	N	N
28	FASB No. 14: Major Customers	A	N	N	A	A	N	N	N

Reprinted by permission.

Required:
CSAR assumes there is a legitimate interest or "stake" in the corporation beyond the stockholders' interests, and that these other stakeholders' interests are not well served by traditional financial statements. Therefore, it follows that within a broad political economy of accounting, CSAR is an important policy-making issue. Critically evaluate this proposition and indicate your agreement or disagreement and the underlying reasons for your position.

3. Presented on the following pages are extracts from the 1931 annual report of General Electric Company, which at that time was considered to be at the forefront of progressive voluntary reporting.

Compare the report to a contemporary annual report with respect to (1) form, (2) content, (3) explanations of accounting policies, and (4) supplemental disclosures. What effects have fifty years of accounting regulations had on financial reporting? Why is this comparison inadequate in assessing the impact of regulation (that is, the costs and benefits) as well as the question of optimality?

Schenectady, N.Y., March 26, 1932.

To the Stockholders of the
General Electric Company:

Orders received during the year 1931 were $252,021,496, compared with $341,820,312 in the year 1930, a decrease of 26 per cent.

Unfilled orders at the end of the year were $49,308,000, compared with $56,062,000 at the end of 1930, a decrease of 12 per cent.

Committees of the Board of Directors reviewed the valuation of manufacturing plants, investments in associated companies and miscellaneous securities, inventories, and notes and accounts receivable, and the figures used in this report are the result of such reviews.

Associated Companies and Miscellaneous Securities

Investments in associated companies and miscellaneous securities were increased during 1931 by $17,782,549.22, and amounted to $222,592,877.35 before revaluation on December 31, 1931. This amount has been reduced by reappraisal, according to methods stated below, to $179,308,010.36. These investments include advances to associated companies as well as securities, inasmuch as most of the advances are required permanently in the business. The decrease resulting from revaluation was charged in part to the General reserve (page 12) and to other reserves set aside from earnings of previous years.

The larger investments during the year were in Electrical Securities Corporation, United Electric Securities Company, and International General Electric Company, Inc.

Interest and dividends received from associated companies in the United States, and from Canadian General Electric Company, Ltd., and International General Electric Company, Inc., are included in the "Statement of income and expenses" as part of "Income from associated companies and miscellaneous securities." Total income from associated companies and miscellaneous

Comparative Statement of Income and Expenses

	1931	1930
Net sales billed	$263,275,255.37	$376,167,428.42
Less: Costs, expenses, and all charges except interest	234,884,372.57	335,717,167.11
Net income from sales	$ 28,390,882.80	$ 40,450,261.31
Income from other sources: Associated companies and miscellaneous securities	$ 8,657,110.67	$ 13,453,654.25
Interest and discount	3,819,280.21	3,258,498.99
U.S. Government and other marketable securities	21,533.46	1,757,715.15
Royalties and sundry revenue	501,422.20	1,605,334.28
	$ 12,999,346.54	$ 20,075,202.67
Total income	$ 41,390,229.34	$ 60,525,463.98
Less: Interest payments	$ 433,233.73	$ 313,078.69
Addition to general reserve		2,721,470.03
	$ 433,233.73	$ 3,034,548.72
Profit available for dividends	$ 40,956,995.61	$ 57,490,915.26
Less: 6% cash dividends on special stock	2,575,005.15	2,574,952.95
Profit available for dividends on common stock	$ 38,381,990.46	$ 54,915,962.31
Less: Cash dividends on common stock	46,150,256.80	46,150,203.60
Deficit (1931) and surplus (1930) for the year	$ 7,768,266.34	$ 8,765,758.71

securities amounted to $8,657,110.67, which is 4.5 per cent of the average net value of these investments at the beginning and end of the year. This compares with 6.9 per cent returned in 1930.

Your Company's share of income earned by associated companies during 1931 (disregarding revaluations of their securities) exceeded your Company's share of the dividends distributed by approximately $5,000,000, which is equivalent to 17 cents per share of the common stock of your Company outstanding on December 31, 1931.

Condensed Balance Sheet
December 31, 1931 and 1930

Assets

	1931	*1930*
Fixed investments:		
Manufacturing plants at cost, including land, buildings, and machinery	$199,129,732.92	$198,303,962.66
Less: General plant reserve and depreciation	153,068,713.66	152,436,033.08
	$ 46,061,019.26	$ 45,867,929.58
Other property	228,445.67	252,609.47
Furniture and appliances (other than in factories)	1.00	1.00
Patents	1.00	1.00
Total fixed investments	**$ 46,289,466.93**	**$ 46,120,541.05**
Associated companies and miscellaneous securities	**179,308,010.36**	**204,810,328.13**
Current assets:		
Inventories	57,335,498.53	60,063,418.56
Installation work in progress	10,063,820.42	16,229,589.20
Notes and accounts receivable	39,192,433.60	41,676,727,47
Marketable securities (at the lower of par or market) $7,122,820.00		
Cash .. 115,056,113.22	122,178,933.22	141,717,851.25
	$228,770,685.77	$259,687,586.48
Less: Advance payments on contracts	9,684,175.13	17,123,037.38
Total current assets:	**$219,086,510.64**	**$242,564,549.10**
Deferred charges	**241,948.86**	**476,403.83**
	$444,925,936.79	**$493,971,822.11**

Condensed Balance Sheet
December 31, 1931 and 1930

Liabilities and Capital

	1931	1930
3½% Debenture bonds due 1942	$ 2,047,000.00	$ 2,047,000.00
Current liabilities:		
Accounts payable and accrued liabilities	16,301,469.11	28,422,154.65
Dividends payable	12,181,318.95	12,181,296.35
Total current liabilities	$ 28,482,788.06	$ 40,603,451.00
Reserves for self-insurance, workmen's compensation, etc.	4,063,496.81	7,974,385.38
Charles A. Coffin Foundation	400,000.00	400,000.00
General reserve	14,517,597.21*	39,763,664.68
Special stock: Authorized 5,500,000 shares, par value $10; issued 4,292,963½ shares	42,929,635.00	42,929,635.00
Common stock and earned surplus:		
Common stock (authorized 29,600,000 shares no par value; issued 28,845,927 36/100 shares)	180,287,046.00	180,287,046.00
Earned surplus on January 1st	179,966,640.05	171,200,881.34
Deficit (1931) and surplus (1930) for the year (page 5)	7,768,266.34	8,765,758.71
Total common stock and earned surplus	$352,485,419.71	$360,253,686.05
	$444,925,936.79	$493,971,822.11

*After applying $25,246,067.47 in reduction of book value of "Associated companies and miscellaneous securities."

Manufacturing Plants

From the formation of the General Electric Company in 1892, there had been expended on manufacturing plants to December 31, 1930		$327,225,297.35
Added during 1931		9,600,173.80
		$336,825,471.15
Dismantled, sold or otherwise disposed of to December 31, 1930	$128,921,334.69	
Dismantled, sold or otherwise disposed of during 1931	8,774,403.54	137,695,738.23
Cost of present plants	....	$199,129,732.92
General plant reserve and depreciation, December 31, 1930	$152,436,033.08	
Added by charges to income during 1931	8,859,062.05	
Proceeds from sale of dismantled equipment, etc., during 1931	548,022.07	
	$161,843,117.20	
Less: Cost of plants dismantled, sold or otherwise disposed of during 1931	8,774,403.54	153,068,713.66
Net book value, December 31, 1931		$ 46,061,019.26

Investments in associated companies are of a more or less permanent character, and may well be considered as investments in plant and working capital of companies closely associated with your Company in the development of its business on a broader base and in a more effective manner than could be done by your Company itself. Accordingly, investments in associated companies in which your Company has a majority interest are appraised on a basis similar to that used in the valuation of your Company's assets. Investments in other companies are appraised after consideration of cost, net worth, return on investment, market price, if any, and foreign exchange, but in no case is an investment or security appraised at a higher valuation than the market price on a recognized exchange on December 31, 1931, with due allowance for foreign exchange rates.

In determining the value of your Company's investment in International General Electric Company, Inc., these same methods of appraisal were applied to securities of foreign companies held by International General Electric Company, Inc. and its subsidiaries.

Foreign Business

Canadian General Electric Company, Ltd. reported net profit for the year 1931 of $2,308,155, compared with $3,765,798 for 1930. Dividends of 7 per cent were paid on $8,557,750 of preference stock, and 8 per cent on $9,442,250 of common stock outstanding.

International General Electric Company, Inc. conducts the export and foreign business of your Company outside of Canada, and, for 1931, reported a profit available for interest on capital advances and dividends of $2,963,222, compared with $3,897,818 for 1930. Interest and dividends paid in 1931 amounted to $2,846,667, compared with $3,878,619 in 1930.

Electrical Securities Corporation

The capital of Electrical Securities Corporation was reduced $18,750,000 in December 1931, by the surrender by your Company of 750,000 of the 1,000,000 shares of common stock without par value outstanding. As your Company owned all of the common shares, the surrender did not affect its equity position. This action was taken as a result of depreciation in the market price of securities owned by Electrical Securities Corporation, and the amount of the capital reduction was set aside as a reserve against losses on securities.

Earnings of Electrical Securities Corporation for 1931 were $2,675,199, compared with $2,399,048 for 1930, and regular dividends were paid out of earnings at the annual rate of 5 per cent on the preferred stock, and 50 cents per share on the common stock during each of the first three quarters and $2 per share (on the reduced number of shares) in the last quarter.

Current Assets

Inventories

Inventories in factories and warehouses and on consignment have been valued, in accordance with the custom of your Company, at the lower of cost or market. After deducting reserves, they were carried at $57,335,498.53, compared with $60,063,418.56 at the end of 1930.

The following table shows the relation of inventories to shipments billed in each of the last twelve years:

Year	Inventories at end of year	Net billing	Percent of inventories to billing
1920	$118,109,173.99	$275,758,487.57	42.8
1921	64,848,188.87	221,007,991.64	29.3
1922	75,334,561.79	200,194,294.09	37.6
1923	83,746,031.05	271,309,695.37	30.9
1924	68,485,161.08	299,251,869.15	22.9

1925	67,798,190.20	290,290,165.97	23.4
1926	65,295,154.88	326,974,103.84	20.0
1927	67,213,705.87	312,603,771.53	21.5
1928	63,776,149.05	337,189,422.43	18.9
1929	80,835,545.38	415,338,094.39	19.5
1930	60,063,418.56	376,167,428.42	16.0
1931	57,335,498.53	263,275,255.37	21.8

Current and Contingent Liabilities

Total current liabilities amounted to $28,482,788.06, compared with $40,603,451.00 at the end of 1930. Your Company had no notes payable or any obligation bearing its endorsement outstanding, and none of the companies in which your Company owns a majority interest had any funded debt or any loans owing to banks or to the public. Your Company's only contingent liability was that of guarantor for $1,846,724 in connection with the employees home ownership plan (reviewed on page 15), which was adequately secured.

Working Capital

Working capital (total current assets less total current liabilities) amounted to $190,603,722.58, compared with $201,961,098.10 at the end of 1930, a decrease of $11,357,375.52.

General Reserve

The general reserve, which amounted to $39,763,664.68 on December 31, 1930, has been drawn upon in 1931 in connection with the revaluation of associated companies and miscellaneous securities, and on December 31, 1931, amounted to $14,517,597.21.

Capital Stock and Dividends

There were no changes during the year in the special or common stock outstanding. Regular dividends of 15 cents per share on the special stock and 40 cents per share on the common stock were paid quarterly.

Stockholders

On December 18, 1931, there were 150,073 holders of common and special stock, half of this number (exclusive of corporations, institutions, etc.) being women. This compares with 116,750 on December 19, 1930, and 60,374 on December 16, 1929, an increase in 1931 over 1929 of 149 per cent.

Organization Changes

Theodore W. Frech, who was given leave of absence on January 1, 1930, resumed his position as Vice President in charge of the Incandescent Lamp Department in April 1931.

Dana R. Bullen, Assistant Vice President, retired on pension July 1, 1931.

Employees and Payrolls

The average number of employees of your Company during 1931, not including those of associated companies, was 65,516, compared with 78,380 during 1930. Total earnings of these employees amounted to $106,656,000 for 1931 and $140,905,000 for 1930. Average annual earnings per employee were

$1628 and $1798 respectively, a decrease of 9.5 per cent. The cost of living, according to the index of the National Industrial Conference Board, decreased 9.9 per cent from 1930.

Compared with the year 1923, average annual earnings of employees for 1931 were 1.2 per cent more and the cost of living was 13.3 per cent less.

The several plans of extra compensation (or profit sharing), referred to in previous reports, yielded $1,940,257 payable to 1,731 employees for 1931, compared with payments of $3,971,153 to 2335 employees for 1930.

Various Employee Plans

Plans dealing with group life and disability insurance, home ownership, savings, pensions, unemployment, and employment guarantee were described at length in the 1930 Annual Report.

Pensions and Retirement Payments

Company pension and retirement payments aggregating $1,517,667 were made during 1931 to 2141 retired employees, the larger share of which was paid by the Pension Trust. On December 31, 1931, there were 1953 on the pension and retirement rolls, whose average age was 68.0 years, average active service to date of retirement 29.6 years, and average annual payment $885. Pension and retirement payments amounting to $5,513,400 have been made since the inauguration of the plans in 1912.

The General Electric Pension Trust on December 31, 1931 held assets of $20,125,255, compared with $16,505,168 on December 31, 1930.

Contributions by employees to the Additional Pension Plan during the three and one-half years since its establishment amounted, with interest, to $4,098,382. This amount is deposited in a trust fund to the credit of 50,037 employees.

The Additional Pension Plan added $43,275 to pensions paid during 1931.

The Trustees of these two Trusts hold title to their respective assets, which are therefore not reflected in your Company's balance sheet.

PEAT, MARWICK, MITCHELL & CO.
Accountants and Auditors

40 EXCHANGE PLACE, NEW YORK, MARCH 4, 1932.

TO THE BOARD OF DIRECTORS OF THE
   GENERAL ELECTRIC COMPANY,
      120 BROADWAY, NEW YORK.

Dear Sirs:

We have examined the accounts of the General Electric Company for the year ended December 31, 1931, and certify that the Condensed statement of income and expenses and Balance sheet appearing on pages 5–7 of this report are in accordance with the books and, in our opinion, set forth the results of the operations of the Company for the year and the condition of its affairs as at December 31, 1931.

We have confirmed the cash and securities by count and inspection or by certificates which we have obtained from the depositories. The valuations at which the investments in Associated companies and miscellaneous securities are carried have been approved by a Committee of the Board of Directors and, in our opinion, are conservative. Our examination has not included the accounts of companies controlled through stock ownership (other than International General Electric Company, Inc. and G. E. Employees Securities Corporation), but financial statements of these Companies have been submitted to us.

We have scrutinized the notes and accounts receivable and are satisfied that full provision has been made for possible losses through bad and doubtful debts.

Certified inventories of merchandise, work in progress, and materials and supplies have been submitted to us and we have satisfied ourselves that these inventories have been taken in a careful manner, that ample allowance has been made for old or inactive stocks, and that they are conservatively stated on the basis of cost or market, whichever is lower. Provision has also been made for possible allowances or additional expenditures on completed contracts.

Expenditures capitalized in the property and plant accounts during the year were properly so chargeable as representing additions or improvements. Adequate provision has been made in the operating accounts for repairs, renewals and depreciation, and for contingencies.

Yours truly,

PEAT, MARWICK, MITCHELL & CO.

BIBLIOGRAPHY OF REFERENCED WORKS

Abdel-khalik, A. Rashad (1981). *The Economic Effects on Lessees of FASB Statement No. 13, Accounting for Leases* (Financial Accounting Standards Board).

AICPA (1983). *Report of the Special Committee on Accounting Standards Overload* (American Institute of Certified Public Accountants).

Armstrong, Marshall S. (1977). "The Politics of Establishing Accounting Standards," *Journal of Accountancy* (February 1977), pp. 76–79.

Arrow, Kenneth (1963). *Social Choice and Individual Values* (John Wiley).

Benston, George J. (1973). "Required Disclosure and the Stock Market: An Evaluation of the Securities Act of 1934," *American Economic Review* (March 1973), pp. 132–155.

——— (1982). "Accounting and Corporate Accountability," *Accounting, Organizations and Society* 7 (no. 2): 87–105.

Bernstein, Marver H. (1955). *Regulating Business by Independent Commission* (Princeton University Press).

Bowers, Patricia F. (1974). *Private Choice and Public Welfare, the Economics of Public Goods* (The Dryden Press).

Briloff, Abraham J. (1972). *Unaccountable Accounting* (Harper & Row).

——— (1976). *More Debits than Credits* (Harper & Row).

Brown, Paul R. (1981). "A Descriptive Analysis of Select Input Bases of the Financial Accounting Standards Board," *Journal of Accounting Research* (Spring 1981), pp. 232–246.

Cooper, David J., and Michael J. Sherer (1984). "The Value of Corporate Accounting Reports: Arguments for a Political Economy of Accounting," *Accounting, Organizations and Society* 9 (no. 3/4): 207–232.

Demsetz, Harold (1970). "The Private Production of Public Goods," *The Journal of Law and Economics* (October 1970), pp. 293–306.

Demski, Joel S. (1973). "The General Impossibility of Normative Accounting Standards," *The Accounting Review* (October 1973), pp. 718–723.

FASB (1978). *Economic Consequences of Financial Accounting Standards* (Financial Accounting Standards Board).

——— (1983). *Financial Reporting by Privately Owned Companies: Summary of Responses to FASB Invitation to Comment* (Financial Accounting Standards Board).

——— (1986). "Status Report No. 181," *Financial Accounting Series*, November 3, 1987 (Financial Accounting Standards Board).

Gaa, James C. (1988). "Methodological Foundations of Standard-setting for Corporate Financial Reporting," *Studies in Accounting Research* #28 (American Accounting Association).

Gonedes, Nicholas J. (1972)."Efficient Capital Markets and External Accounting," *The Accounting Review* (January 1972), pp. 11–21.

Gonedes, Nicholas J., and Nicholas Dopuch (1974). "Capital Market Equilibrium, Information Production, and Selected Accounting Techniques: Theoretical Framework and Review of Empirical Work," *Studies on Financial Accounting Objectives* (Supplement to *Journal of Accounting Research*), pp. 48–129.

Griffin, Paul A., and Richard P. Castanias II (1987). *Accounting for the Translation of Foreign Currencies: The Effects of Statement 52 on Equity Analysts* (Financial Accounting Standards Board).

Hakansson, Nils H. (1977). "Interim Disclosure and Public Forecasts: An Economic Analysis and Framework for Choice," *The Accounting Review* (April 1977), pp. 396–416.

Holthausen, Robert W., and Richard W. Leftwich (1983). "The Economic Consequences of Accounting Choice: Implications of Costly Contracting and Monitoring," *Journal of Accounting and Economics* (August 1983), pp. 77–117.

Horngren, Charles T. (1973). "The Marketing of Accounting Standards," *Journal of Accountancy* (October 1973), pp. 61–66.

Hussein, Mohamed E., and J. Edward Ketz (1980). "Ruling Elites of the FASB: A Study of the Big Eight," *Journal of Accounting, Auditing and Finance* (Summer 1980), pp. 354–367.

Jensen, Michael, and William Meckling (1976). "Theory of the Firm: Managerial Behavior, Agency Costs and Ownership Structure," *Journal of Financial Economics* (October 1976), pp. 305–360.

Kirk, Donald J. (1978). "How to Keep Politics Out of Standard Setting: Making Private Sector Rule-Making Work," *Journal of Accountancy* (September 1978), pp. 92–94.

Krislov, Samuel, and Lloyd D. Musolf (1964). *The Politics of Regulation* (Houghton Mifflin).

May, Robert G., and Gary L. Sundem (1976). "Research for Accounting Policy: An Overview," *The Accounting Review* (October 1976), pp. 747–763.

Merino, Barbara Dubois, and Marilyn Dale Neimark (1982). "Disclosure Regulation and Public Policy: A Sociohistorical Reappraisal," *Journal of Accounting and Public Policy* (Fall 1982), pp. 33–57.

Ng, David S. (1978). "An Information Economics Analysis of Financial Reporting and External Auditing," *The Accounting Review* (October 1978), pp. 910–920.

Ross, Steven A. (1979). "Disclosure Regulation in Financial Markets," in *Issues in Financial Regulation*, ed. F. Edwards (McGraw-Hill), pp. 177–202.

Schreuder, Hein, and Kavasseri V. Ramanathan (1984). "Accounting and Corporate Accountability: An Extended Comment," *Accounting, Organizations and Society* 9 (no. 3/4): 409–415.

Securities and Exchange Commission (1973). "Statement of Accounting Policy on the Establishment and Improvement of Accounting Principles and Standards," *Accounting Series Release No. 150* (Securities and Exchange Commission).

———— (1975). "Notice of Adoption of Amendments to Form 10-Q and Regulation S-X Regarding Interim Reporting," *Accounting Series Release No. 177* (Securities and Exchange Commission).

Seidler, Lee J., Frederick Andrews, and Marc J. Epstein (1977). *The Equity Funding Papers, Anatomy of a Fraud* (John Wiley & Sons).

Solomons, David (1978). "The Politicalization of Accounting," *Journal of Accountancy* (November 1978), pp. 65–72.

Stigler, George J. (1971). "The Theory of Economic Regulation," *Bell Journal of Economics and Management Science* (Fall 1971), pp. 3–21.

———— (1975). *The Citizen and the State: Essays on Regulation* (University of Chicago Press).

Tinker, Anthony (1980). "Towards a Political Economy of Accounting," *Accounting, Organizations and Society* 5 (no. 1): 147–160.

———— (1984). "Theories of the State and State Accounting: Economic Reduction and Political Voluntarism in Accounting Regulation Theory," *Journal of Accounting and Public Policy* (Spring 1984), pp. 55–74.

Wallace, Wanda A. (1980). *The Economic Role of the Audit in Free and Regulated Markets* (University of Rochester).

Watts, Ross L., and Jerold L. Zimmerman (1978). "Toward a Positive Theory of the Determination of Accounting Standards," *The Accounting Review* (January 1978), pp. 112–134.

———— (1983). "Agency Problems, Auditing and the Theory of the Firm: Some Evidence," *Journal of Law and Economics* (October 1983), pp. 613–634.

Zeff, Stephen A. (1978). "The Rise of Economic Consequences," *Journal of Accountancy* (December 1978), pp. 56–63.

ADDITIONAL READINGS

Abdel-khalik, A. Rashad, ed. (1980). *Government Regulation of Accounting, Accounting Series No. 11* (University Presses of Florida).

Advisory Committee on Corporate Disclosure (1977). *Report of the Advisory Committee on Corporate Disclosure to the Securities and Exchange Commission* (U.S. Government Printing Office).

Benston, George J. (1980a). "Disclosure under the Securities Acts and the Proposed Federal Securities Code," *Journal of Accountancy* (October 1980), pp. 34–45.

———— (1980b). "The Establishment and Enforcement of Accounting Standards: Methods, Benefits, and Costs," *Accounting and Business Research* (Winter 1980), pp. 51–60.

———— (1984). "The Costs of Complying with a Government Data Collection Program: The FTC's Line of Business Report," *Journal of Accounting and Public Policy* (Summer 1984), pp. 123–137.

———— (1985). "The Market for Public Accounting Services: Demand, Supply and Regulation," *Journal of Accounting and Public Policy* (Spring 1985), pp. 33–80.

Breyer, Steven G. (1982). *Regulation and Its Reform* (Harvard University Press).

Bromwich, Michael (1985). *The Economics of Accounting Standard Setting* (Prentice-Hall/Institute of Chartered Accountants in England and Wales).

Chatov, Robert (1975). *Corporate Financial Reporting: Public or Private Control* (The Free Press).

Chow, Chee W. (1983). "Empirical Studies of the Effects of Accounting Regulation on Security Prices: Findings, Problems and Prospects," *Journal of Accounting Literature* (Spring 1983), pp. 73–109.

Cushing, Barry E. (1977). "On the Possibility of Optimal Accounting Principles," *The Accounting Review* (April 1977), pp. 308–321.

Demski, Joel S. (1974). "Choice Among Financial Reporting Alternatives," *The Accounting Review* (April 1974), pp. 221–232.

Foster, George (1980a). "Externalities and Financial Reporting," *Journal of Finance* (May 1980), pp. 521–533.

———— (1980b). "Accounting Policy Decisions and Capital Market Research," *Journal of Accounting and Economics* (June 1980), pp. 29–62.

Fromm, Gary, ed. (1981). *Studies in Public Regulation* (The MIT Press).

Horngren, Charles T. (1972). "Accounting Principles: Private or Public Sector?" *The Journal of Accountancy* (May 1972), pp. 37–41.

Ingram, Robert W., and Eugene G. Chewning (1983). "The Effect of Financial Disclosure Regulation on Security Market Behavior," *The Accounting Review* (July 1983), pp. 562–580.

Kelly, Lauren (1983). "Positive Theory Research: A Review," *Journal of Accounting Literature* (Spring 1983), pp. 111–150.

Kelly-Newton, Lauren (1980). *Accounting Policy Formulation, the Role of Management* (Addison-Wesley).

Leftwich, Richard W. (1980). "Market Failure Fallacies and Accounting Information," *Journal of Accounting and Economics* (December 1980), pp. 193–211.

Leone, Robert A. (1986). *Who Profits: Winners, Losers, and Government Regulation* (Basic Books).

Lindahl, Frederick W. (1987). "Accounting Standards and Olson's Theory of Collective Action," *Journal of Accounting and Public Policy* (Spring 1987), pp. 59–72.

Miller, Paul B. W., and Rodney Redding (1988). *The FASB: The People, the Process and the Politics* (Richard D. Irwin).

Moonitz, Maurice (1974). "Obtaining Agreement on Standards in the Accounting Profession," *Studies in Accounting Research No. 8* (American Accounting Association).

O'Leary, Ted (1985). "Observations on Corporate Financial Reporting in the Name of Politics," *Accounting, Organizations and Society* 10 (no. 1): 87–102.

Owen, Bruce M., and Ronald Braeutigam (1978). *The Regulation Game* (Ballinger).

Peltzman, Sam (1976). "Toward a More General Theory of Regulation," *Journal of Law and Economics* (October 1976), pp. 211–240.

Phillips, Susan M., and J. Richard Zecher (1981). *The SEC and the Public Interest* (MIT Press).

Posner, Richard A. (1974). "Theories of Economic Regulation," *Bell Journal of Economics and Management Science* (Autumn 1974), pp. 335–358.

Puro, Marsha (1984). "Audit Firm Lobbying Before the Financial Accounting Standards Board: An Empirical Study," *Journal of Accounting Research* (Autumn 1984), pp. 624–646.

Puxty, A. G., Hugh C. Wilmott, David J. Cooper, and Tony Lowe (1987). "Modes of Regulation in Advanced Capitalism: Locating Accountancy in Four Countries," *Accounting, Organizations and Society* 12 (no. 3): 273–291.

Solomons, David (1986). *Making Accounting Policy: The Quest for Credibility in Financial Reporting* (Oxford University Press).

Sterling, Robert R., ed. (1974). *Institutional Issues in Public Accounting* (Scholars Book Company).

Watts, Ross L. (1977). "Corporate Financial Statements: Product of the Market and Political Processes," *Australian Journal of Management* (April 1977), pp. 53–75.

———— (1980). "Can Optimal Information Be Determined by Regulation?" in *Regulation and the Accounting Profession*, ed. John W. Buckley and Fred Weston (Lifetime Learning Publication, 1980), pp. 153–162.

White, Lawrence J. (1981). *Reforming Regulation: Processes and Problems* (Prentice-Hall).

Zeff, Stephen A. (1986). "Big Eight Firms and the Accounting Literature: The Falloff in Advocacy Writing," *Journal of Accounting, Auditing and Finance* (Spring 1986), pp. 131–154.

POSTULATES, PRINCIPLES, AND CONCEPTS

THE NEED FOR A THEORETICAL FRAMEWORK in financial accounting has long been felt. The Committee on Accounting Procedure was not concerned with the task of deriving an underlying framework, but both the Accounting Principles Board and the Financial Accounting Standards Board have attempted to develop theoretical foundations as a guide to formulating accounting rules. As briefly mentioned in Chapter 3, the APB attempted to derive a system of postulates and principles but was unsuccessful. The FASB instituted the Conceptual Framework Project, a much longer-term endeavor recently completed, although it could eventually be altered or extended.

Despite the fact that Accounting Research Studies (ARSs) 1 and 3 on postulates and principles were not accepted, these studies represent a milestone in the attempt to provide a unified theoretical underpinning for financial accounting rules by the APB. Consequently, it is important to assess why these studies fell short of the goal of obtaining a framework for opinions. Part of the story has already been told: the project advisors, not to mention the profession at large, felt the principles were too much in conflict with existing notions to serve as a frame of reference for the rules that were sure to follow. A closer look at these early studies will help us understand the FASB's conceptual framework and its prospect for success.

A discussion of postulates and principles would be incomplete without analyzing those concepts that have continued to form an important basis for contemporary historical cost accounting. No matter what form financial statements may take in the future, it is quite likely that many of these ideas will be retained, refined, or modified because they have proved useful in an informal but pragmatic fashion.

Finally, in this chapter we look at another group of concepts that have long played a role in interpreting accounting relationships. These are the so-called equity theories of accounting. They are concerned with the relationship that exists between the firm itself and its ownership interests. Various inferences can be drawn from these relationships, which can have an influence on standard setting.

The two appendices to this chapter are the postulates of ARS 1 and the broad principles of ARS 3. They should be read in conjunction with the discussion of these documents.

POSTULATES AND PRINCIPLES

The facts that the formation of the APB was a watershed in the development of accounting theory and the role of research cannot be overstressed. However, Alvin R. Jennings, in his important speech advocating this new approach to the development of accounting principles, did not propose the formation of a new rule-making body. What he did envision was a new research organization within the American Institute of Certified Public Accountants that would issue statements subject to a two-thirds vote of the Council of the AICPA.[1]

THE SPECIAL COMMITTEE ON RESEARCH PROGRAM

The result of Jennings' ideas was the Special Committee on Research Program, which stressed the need for articulating the basic set of postulates underlying accounting. In turn, the principles were to be logically derived from the postulates. The committee thus advocated a deductive approach. Chapter 2 noted that deductive approaches to theory are basically normative in outlook. The committee gave only bare mention to this fact and its implications in its report:

> The general purpose of the Institute ... should be to advance the written expression of what constitutes generally accepted accounting principles, for the guidance of its members. ... *This means something more than a survey of existing practice.* It means continuing efforts to *determine appropriate practice* and to narrow the areas of difference and inconsistency in practice. ... The Institute *should take definite steps to lead in the thinking on unsettled and controversial issues* (emphasis added).[2]

Although the committee foresaw the need for securing the approval of those who would be subject to the rules of the new APB, it did not anticipate the storm of protest that would erupt in the wake of ARS 3.[3] The committee's conception of postulates and principles was also problematic.

Postulates are generally defined as basic assumptions that cannot be verified. They serve as a basis for inference and a foundation for a theoretical structure that consists of propositions deduced from them.[4] In systems using formal logical techniques, the basic premises are called *axioms* and consist of symbolic notation, and the operations for deducing propositions are mathemat-

---

[1] Jennings (1958, p. 32).
[2] Special Committee on Research Program (1958, pp. 62–63).
[3] See "Comments on 'A Tentative Set of Broad Accounting Principles'" (1963).
[4] Mautz and Sharaf (1961, p. 37).

ically based.[5] The committee's report represented postulates in accounting as few in number and stemming from the economic and political environments as well as from the customs and underlying viewpoints of the business community. The committee thus virtually defined postulates and limited their number for the author of ARS 1. One committee member revealed shortly thereafter that it was not the committee's intention to define postulates.[6]

Broad principles, on the other hand, were not defined by the APB committee, although it did compare them in scope to the definitions and pronouncements that had been issued in four different reports by the American Accounting Association (AAA). These documents and several supplements were published in 1936, 1941, 1948, and 1957. The first two reports contain the word *principles* in their titles but the word was replaced by *standards* in the 1948 and 1957 reports (the 1948 revision also used *concepts* in its title).[7] These reports contain definitions of basic accounting terms, proposed rules for presentation and measurement of accounting data, and concepts to be applied to published financial reports. The material in these reports thus covers a wide variety of topics, only some of which might be considered pertinent to the topic of principles (the basic definitions and concepts, such as disclosure and uniformity).

These reports did not use the definition of principles contained in Accounting Terminology Bulletin No. 1 of the AICPA: "A general law or rule adopted or professed as a guide to action, a settled ground or basis of conduct or practice. . . ."[8] This definition is quite close to the one used in the philosophy of science, a discipline concerned with scientific method. A principle is closely related to a law. Both are considered statements of a true and generalized nature containing referents to the real world as opposed to purely analytic statements whose truth or falsity is self-contained by their internal logic.[9] A law differs from a principle in that the former contains elements observable by empirical techniques, whereas the latter does not. Of course a principle can be empirically tested and, if proven true (or at least not proven false), would become a law. The "truth" of a law or principle does not mean that it is incapable of replacement by newer systems. However, changes — particularly in the case of laws — should be extremely infrequent.

ACCOUNTING RESEARCH STUDY NO. 1

Given his charge by the Special Committee, Moonitz adopted a frame of reference or outlook that was oriented to the problems dealt with by accountants. He rejected a deductive approach rooted in reasoning alone because it was not

---

[5] Morgenstern (1963, pp. 23–24). Some examples of axiomatic deductive systems in accounting include Mattesich (1964, pp. 446–465), Ijiri (1975, pp. 71–84), and Carlson and Lamb (1981).
[6] Mautz (1965).
[7] AAA (1957).
[8] AICPA (1953, pp. 9505–9506).
[9] Caws (1965, p. 85).

broad enough to encompass the experiential and empirical aspects of accounting. Deinzer correctly pointed out, however, that Moonitz did eventually revert to the axiomatic (meaning deductive) method.[10] He did indeed use a deductive type of approach — but without employing symbolic terminology and formal methods — in terms of reasoning to a second level of postulates and some of the principles. However, the postulates themselves are of two decidedly different types. One category (the A and B groups) is made up of general, descriptive postulates that appear to coincide with the committee's charge that postulates should be derived from the economic and political environments and modes of thought and customs from all segments of the community. The second category (the C group) is value judgments. It is this group that may have gone against the committee's charge and definitely labels Moonitz's work as deductive–normative in scope.

The postulates themselves (see Appendix 5-A) are in three groups: the environmental group (A), those stemming from accounting itself (B), and the imperatives (C). Some postulates in the B group appear to stem from the A category, which led to the criticism that no postulates should be reasoned from any others and a similar criticism that postulates were given a rank order. Although these criticisms may have some validity, they could easily be overcome by relabeling. There is no rule that only two levels (postulates and principles) can be used in deductive reasoning. A complex environment, such as that in which accounting operates, can have numerous levels.

A far more telling criticism was that self-evident postulates may not be sufficiently substantive to lead to a unique and meaningful set of accounting principles. This unquestionably appears to be the case with both the A and B groups. If postulates are indeed defined as self-evident generalizations from a particular environment, this raises the question of what their role is in a deductively oriented system where principles form the basis for more specific rules. Of necessity, it appears that postulates must play a more passive role. The principles and rules should not be in conflict with them, but alone they are not sufficiently important to lead to the desired principles and rules.[11] They are thus necessary but not sufficient to lead to a viable outcome.

Hence the key group in Moonitz's set of postulates is the imperatives. These appear to be more like what Mautz has called *concepts* because (1) they are normative in nature and (2) they have developed within the context of accounting practice.[12] The imperatives have the flavor of being objectives that should be strived for, which is also a result of their normative aspect. The key postulate appears to be C-4, stability of the monetary unit. This postulate appears to have two possible outcomes. If purchasing power of the monetary unit is, in fact, not stable, the postulate implies that some form of inflation accounting should be instituted. If, on the other hand, purchasing power of the monetary unit is relatively stable, two further consequences of the postulate arise —

---

[10] Deinzer (1965, p. 111).
[11] Vatter (1963, pp. 185–186).
[12] Mautz (1965, p. 47).

one is that retention of historical cost is justified, owing to stability of the dollar; the other is that a system of current values is still justified, despite general stability of the monetary unit, because demand changes can cause considerable price fluctuation. The dual interpretation of C-4 is a definite weakness of this very important postulate. Perhaps Postulate A-1, usefulness of quantitative data, should lead to current values, but this is certainly not self-evident from the Moonitz postulates. At any rate, the profession was generally silent when the postulates appeared. It was undoubtedly awaiting the appearance of the broad principles study.

ACCOUNTING RESEARCH STUDY NO. 3

There are eight broad principles in ARS 3 (see Appendix 5-B). At least three of them (A, B, and D) deal with the problems of changing prices, which was the point of departure for the profession's rather stinging rejection of the study. It is interesting to note that the summary of the eight principles covers some four and one-half pages, two and one-half of which are devoted to Principle D, the asset valuation principle.

Deinzer very appropriately noted that Principle A — which states that revenue is earned by the entire process of operations of the firm rather than at one point only, usually when sale occurs — was not reasoned from any of the fourteen postulates.[13] It would appear, then, to belong in the B group of postulates. More importantly, Sprouse and Moonitz apparently needed it to pave the way for their value-oriented principles because it underlies the recognition of changes in replacement cost, which leads to holding gains or losses (Principle B-2).

One of the most pointed criticisms of the asset valuation measures prescribed in Principle D was that they are not "additive." That is, although current value dollars are being used, different attributes or characteristics are being measured; hence, they cannot theoretically be combined by addition because Sprouse and Moonitz advocated different current-value characteristics for different asset classes. For example, if inventory can easily be sold at a given market price, net realizable value (selling price less known costs of disposal) should be used (D-2). On the other hand, the value of fixed assets, which are not intended for sale, is rooted in terms of the service they can provide over present and future periods. As a result, Sprouse and Moonitz opted for replacement cost as the appropriate characteristic of measurement for this class of assets (D-3). Obviously, the additivity question, where different attributes are being measured, has strong overtones of measurement theory.

Chambers was the principal critic of the lack of additivity of asset values put forth by the broad principles of ARS 3.[14] Chambers strongly advocated the

---

[13] Deinzer (1965, p. 131).
[14] Chambers (1964, p. 409).

exit-value approach illustrated in Chapter 1 although his position is blurred by his acceptance of replacement cost as a secondary valuation if exit values were unavailable.[15] However, it should be clear that Chambers was attempting to separate conceptual or theoretical issues from measurement problems. Hence, it would almost appear that the additivity issue can be breached only if one's heart is in the right place: the basic theoretical system must be unified in terms of one primary characteristic of assets and liabilities to be measured. Nevertheless, the primacy of conceptual issues over measurement problems cannot be ignored. The answer probably lies in determining which current value elements have most utility for financial statement users, an issue not addressed by Sprouse and Moonitz.

A last criticism to be leveled at ARS 1 and ARS 3 was that a set of postulates should be complete enough to allow no conflicting conclusions to be derived from them. Postulate C-4 says that the monetary unit should be stable. From it, Principle D was derived advocating various current values for different categories of assets. The various choices espoused in Principle D cannot be justified to the exclusion of other possibilities. Hence, the postulate system is not theoretically tight enough to justify it, whether or not one agrees with the resulting principles.

A PERSPECTIVE ON ARS 1 AND ARS 3

ARS 1 and ARS 3 failed for a variety of reasons in addition to the most obvious one – the inability of the profession to abandon historical costs. The postulates and principles themselves had several weaknesses. The postulates were not complete and therefore could not exclude all value systems other than the one prescribed in the principles. Additionally, at least one principle, Principle A, was not derived from any of the postulates. Finally, the question of whether resulting valuations of various assets should be additive (because they advocated different attributes) became an interesting, and probably moot, point.

Even beyond the questions of logic and adequacy of ARS 1 and ARS 3, a number of issues have since made it clear that the Moonitz–Sprouse efforts could not succeed. It appears that Moonitz and Sprouse were commissioned to find those postulates and principles that would lead to "true income"; in other words, to use a single concept of income that would show itself superior to all other challengers. In retrospect, it has become evident that no income measurement can presently be deemed to have such an advantage over competing concepts (see Chapter 6 for further coverage).

Aside from Postulate A-1, which states that "quantitative data are helpful in making rational economic decisions," virtually nothing is said in either study about who are the outside users of accounting data and what their particular

---

[15] For a complete exposition see Chambers (1966). For additional coverage, see Wright (1967) and Chambers (1970).

information needs and abilities might be. It is generally conceded today that users of financial data (with their underlying information needs and abilities to understand and manipulate financial data) cover a broad, heterogeneous spectrum. However, the emphasis on users was not a particularly prominent theoretical accounting issue when ARSs 1 and 3 were published. (User diversity and its implications are discussed later in Chapter 6.) Thus, the postulates and principles approach tended to overlook a theoretical area that has since received a great deal of attention. The rise of the user-needs outlook has produced a new focus on the objectives of published financial statement data. Indeed, as we mentioned, several of the imperative postulates actually began to spill over into the area of financial statement objectives. Formulating the objectives of financial statements and reporting has become an extremely important part of theory formulation; it will be extensively discussed in Chapter 6.

Finally, we note that the commissioning of ARS 1 and ARS 3 occurred at a time when little formal attention was given to what might be called the politics of rule making. By this we mean that under the FASB there is more opportunity to react to potential accounting rules for those who will be subject to them than was the case with the APB.

Some might say that the postulates and principles studies were a dismal failure. As we view events from the perspective of thirty years, we realize that this is not the case. These studies would hold an important place in the history of accounting theory for no other reason than the fact that they were the first attempt in the United States by the practicing arm of the profession to provide a conceptual underpinning for the rule-making function. Furthermore, by examining the difficulties encountered by the APB in drafting a theoretical statement that would meet the approval of those who would be governed by it, the FASB learned valuable lessons for its Conceptual Framework Project.

BASIC CONCEPTS UNDERLYING HISTORICAL COSTING

Many accounting concepts have long influenced accounting rules. These concepts have largely evolved from practical operating necessities, including income tax laws, but have also appeared in several theoretical works written mostly in the formative years (1930–46) of accounting policy-making groups.[16] Perhaps the most outstanding of these was the monograph by Paton and Littleton, *An Introduction to Corporate Accounting Standards*, which approached theory deductively rather than from the point of view of what was being done in practice.[17] This work was not revolutionary, but it did attempt to provide a basic framework that the enterprise could use to assess its accounting practices. The authors hoped that a greater degree of consistency in accounting practice would result from their effort.

---

[16] Chatfield (1974, p. 256).
[17] Paton and Littleton (1940).

Other important works of this period included Canning's attempt to relate asset valuation to future cash flows; separate books by Sweeney and MacNeal that were concerned with accounting for, respectively, the changing value of the monetary unit and the weakness of historical costs; Sanders, Hatfield, and Moore's monograph on deriving the principles of accounting from practice; Gilman's book about refining the concept of income; and Littleton's attempt to derive inductively the accounting principles underlying relevant practice.[18]

The concepts discussed in this chapter have been called *postulates, axioms, assumptions, doctrines, conventions, constraints, principles,* and *standards*. The word *concepts* is probably an accurate overall label for these terms. A **concept** is the result of the process of identifying, classifying, and interpreting various phenomena or precepts.[19] It is thus not part of the formal process of theory formulation but can be used within a theory — as part of the structure of postulates, or in the conclusions deduced from the postulates, or even as the subject of testing in empirical research. Many elements fall into the concept category in accounting, and they are quite rightly considered part of accounting theory. Many have been and will be part of a general theoretical framework for interpreting and presenting financial accounting data as well as individual accounting theories. Indeed, several concepts will be discussed in Chapter 6 in terms of their place in the conceptual framework of the FASB.

Attempts like ARS 1, ARS 3, and those mentioned in Chapter 2 to set up deductive systems of postulates and principles have failed to achieve a high degree of consensus due to lack of rigor in reasoning, overlapping definitions, and different value judgments.[20] Bearing this in mind, we have given the following organization to our discussion of concepts strictly for teaching purposes. The concepts are broken down as follows:

Postulates are basic assumptions concerning the business environment.

Principles are general approaches utilized in the recognition and measurement of accounting events. Principles are, in turn, divided into two main types:

---

[18] Canning (1929); Sweeney (1936); MacNeal (1939); Sanders, Hatfield, and Moore (1938); Gilman (1939); and Littleton (1953).

[19] Caws (1965, pp. 24–29).

[20] For example, Study Group at the University of Illinois (1964). In addition, Anthony has attempted to deductively derive a conceptual framework using premises and concepts: "Premises are *descriptive* statements based on the best available evidence. They are subject to change as new evidence develops. In this framework, concepts are normative statements; they say what financial statement information *should be*. Concepts are deduced from the premises and they must be consistent with the premises and with one another" (emphasis added) [Anthony (1983, p. xi)]. While not labeling his system as postulates and principles per se, Anthony is certainly using a deductive-normative approach in terms of developing underlying rules to guide and support the FASB's ongoing operating standards. Anthony states that his premises are "descriptive statements based on the best available evidence," but many surely contain strong normative overtones. For example, Premise 15 (p. xiii) states that "users are primarily interested in the performance of an entity and secondarily in its status." Premise 15A then states that "between competing accounting practices, the one that provides users with more useful information about performance is preferable to the one that provides more useful information about status" (p. xiii).

Input-oriented principles are broad rules that guide the accounting function. Input-oriented principles can be divided into two general classifications: general underlying rules of operation and constraining principles. As their names imply, the former are general in nature while the latter are geared to certain specific types of situations.

Output-oriented principles involve certain qualities or characteristics that financial statements should possess if the input-oriented principles are appropriately executed.

A schema of these various concepts is shown in Exhibit 5–1.

POSTULATES
Going Concern or Continuity
The going-concern postulate simply states that unless there is evidence to the contrary, it is assumed that the firm will continue indefinitely. As a result, under ordinary circumstances, reporting liquidation values for assets and equities is in violation of the postulate. However, the continuity assumption is simply too broad to lead to any kind of a choice among valuation systems, including historical cost. Fremgen and Sterling have criticized this postulate extensively.[21] Sterling logically demolishes it because the time period of continuity is presumed to be long enough to conclude the firm's present contractual arrangements. However, by the time these affairs are concluded, they will have been replaced by new arrangements. Hence, the implication is one of indefinite life. However, we know that over the long run, many firms do conclude their activities. Therefore, continuity is more in the nature of a prediction than an underlying assumption. Suffice it to say that, aside from ordinarily excluding liquidation values, going concern has little to add to accounting theory.

Time Period
Business, as well as virtually every form of human and animal activity, operates within fairly rigidly specified periods of time. The time period idea is, nevertheless, somewhat artificial because it creates definite segments out of what is a continuing process. For business entities, the time period is the calendar or business year.[22] As a result, of course, financial reports contain statements of financial condition, earnings, and funds flow over a year's time. Since the year is a relatively short time in the life of most enterprises, the time period postulate has led to accrual accounting and to the principles of recognition and matching under historical costing. Furthermore, even though the needs of users have required financial reporting for less than full-year intervals and these interim financial statements have their own problems and sets of rules, APB 28 states in general, however, that accounting methods followed in annual financial state-

---

[21] Fremgen (1968) and Sterling (1968).
[22] For an example holding revenues constant with time as a variable, see Nichols and Grawoig (1968).

EXHIBIT 5–1
Basic Concepts Underlying Historical Costing

POSTULATES	*PRINCIPLES*
Going Concern	*Input-Oriented Principles*
Time Period	
Accounting Entity	• General Underlying Rules of Operation
Monetary Unit	1. Recognition
	2. Matching
	• Constraining Principles
	1. Conservatism
	2. Disclosure
	3. Materiality
	4. Objectivity (also called verifiability)
	Output-Oriented Principles
	• Applicable to Users
	1. Comparability
	• Applicable to Preparers
	1. Consistency
	2. Uniformity

ments must likewise be followed in interim reports. Hence, interim reports must include estimates of annual amounts.

Accounting Entity

When we view the business entity in the context of accounting as well as in its legal form, it is clear that the entity is separate from its owners, but there are two important problems nevertheless.

First is the problem of defining the entity and accounting for the relationship among its parts. Involved here is the question of whether entities should be considered as one unit as a result of one controlling the other(s). In other words, should accounts be combined or should a noncombinative method of showing the relationship be used? If combination is deemed appropriate, the purchase versus pooling question arises: has a new accountability been created and, if so, how? The whole combination issue is made more complex by the presence of foreign operations. Theoretical aspects of these questions are discussed in Chapters 18 and 19.

The second issue related to the question of the accounting entity concerns the relationship between the firm and its owners. While the accounting is separate, the point of interface between the firm and the owners exists in the owners' equity accounts. A number of deductive theories purport to describe this relationship and the role of the owners' equity accounts. These ideas influence our interpretation of what constitutes income, the meaning of equities, and other important issues. The equity theories, as they are called, are discussed later in this chapter.

Monetary Unit

In nonbarter economies money serves as the medium of exchange. As a result, money has also become the principal standard of value and is subject to the measurement process. Thus, financial statements are expressed in terms of the monetary unit of their particular nation. The assumption, for accounting purposes, that the monetary unit is stable became a mainstay of accounting principles and methods. Hence, the historical cost principle became enshrined as a virtually unchallengeable tenet of accounting.

Severe inflation in the United States and other nations of the Western world encouraged a fresh examination of valuation theories and new ways of presenting financial information. However, the subsiding of inflation in the 1980s has restored, for the time being at least, the supremacy of the historical cost principle.

PRINCIPLES

The word *principles* has not been well defined in ARSs of the AICPA. Neither ARS 1 nor ARS 3 precisely defines the word, though the latter contains the phrase *broad accounting principles* in its title. The preface of ARS 7, by Paul Grady, indicated that he regarded accounting principles as synonymous with practices.[23] However, some 400 pages later, Grady identifies principles as postulates derived from "experiences and reason" that have proved useful.[24] Deductively, then, it appears that principles are postulates that have been successful in practice, an interpretation that Grady himself would probably tend to reject.

Perhaps the most useful definition of *principles* in official publications comes from APB Statement 4. **Generally accepted accounting principles,** it says, are rooted in "experience, reason, custom, usage, and . . . practical necessity."[25] Furthermore, they ". . . encompass the conventions, rules, and procedures necessary to define accepted accounting practice at a particular time."[26] This still overlaps with Grady's definition, in which principles are identified with acceptable practice, but it distinguishes principles from postulates even though they stem from practical necessity and related experiences.[27] However, a subset of generally accepted accounting principles, **pervasive principles,** is largely synonymous with the way the term is used in Statement 4:

---

[23] Grady (1965, p. ix).

[24] Ibid., p. 407.

[25] AICPA (1970, p. 9084).

[26] Ibid.

[27] One reason for the overlap is that APB Statement 4 envisions a three-tiered approach to principles. The bottom level, detailed principles, is made up of the actual operating rules themselves, such as the opinions of the APB (AICPA, 1970, p. 9084).

> ... pervasive principles are few in number and fundamental in nature. ... pervasive principles specify the general approach accountants take to recognition and measurement of events that affect the financial position and results of operations of enterprises.[28]

Notice that both definitions of *principles* from APB Statement 4 do not include the idea of permanence that is given to the word in the scientific sense. Pervasive principles in accounting overlap with what we refer to here as *input-oriented principles.*

INPUT-ORIENTED PRINCIPLES

Accounting principles are classified here into two broad types: input-oriented principles and output-oriented principles. The distinctions between these groups are at least somewhat clear. Input-oriented principles are concerned with general approaches or rules for preparing financial statements and their content, including any necessary supplementary disclosures. Output-oriented principles are concerned with the comparability of financial statements of different firms. Although some of these principles apply to preparers of the statements and others to users, there is a close linkage between them.

General Underlying Rules of Operation

Input-oriented principles are further broken down into two classifications: those involved with revenue recognition and with expense recognition. These principles illustrate the primary orientation of historical cost accounting towards income measurement rather than asset and liability valuation.

Recognition　　*Revenue* is defined here as the output of the enterprise in terms of its product(s) or service(s). Notice that this definition says nothing about the receipt or inflow of assets as a result of revenue performance because defining revenue in this way can easily lead to problems in terms of when to recognize revenue as being earned.[29] It is generally conceded that revenues arise in conjunction with all of the operations of a firm.[30] For a manufacturing enterprise, these operations would include acquisition of raw materials, production, sale, collection of cash or other consideration from customers, and after-sale services such as product warranties and guarantees.

Recognition concerns the problem of when to enter revenues and expenses in the accounts. The most prevalent revenue recognition point by far is at the point of sale. Other possibilities may, however, arise; for example, revenue may be recognized in accordance with the firm's "critical event." The critical event, as mentioned above, is that operating function which is the most crucial

---

[28] Ibid.

[29] For further coverage, see Hendriksen (1982, pp. 172–174).

[30] For a classic statement of the idea, see Paton and Littleton (1940, pp. 48–49). Of course, this is also Principle A of ARS 3.

in terms of the earning process.[31] Revenue recognition points are discussed in Chapter 9. Suffice it to say that the revenue recognition principle is the most pervasive in the canon of historical cost accounting.

The Conceptual Framework Project of the FASB states that revenue recognition occurs in accordance with two criteria: (1) the assets to be received from the performance of the revenue function are realized or realizable, and (2) performance of the revenue function is "substantially accomplished."[32] In the latter case revenues are referred to as being *earned*, a commonly used term for revenue performance. This conception of revenue recognition has its roots in that fountainhead of the historical cost approach, the Paton and Littleton monograph mentioned previously.[33] The terms *realized* and *realizable* refer to the conversion or ready convertibility of the enterprise's product or service into cash or claims to cash. **Realized** means that the firm's product or service has been converted to cash or claims to cash, while **realizable** has been defined as the ability to convert assets already received or held into known amounts of cash or claims to cash.[34] *Realization* has often been used as a synonym for *recognition*.[35] The Conceptual Framework Project appears to have been instrumental in having the word *recognition* supplant *realization*.

Matching   *Expenses* are defined as costs that expire as a result of generating revenues. Expenses are thus necessary to the production of revenues. If all expenses could be directly identified with either specific revenues or specific time periods, expense measurement would present few problems. Unfortunately, many important expenses cannot be specifically identified with particular revenues, and they also bring benefit to more than one time period.

The process of recognizing cost expiration (expense incurrence) for categories such as depreciation, cost of goods sold, interest, and deferred charges is called *matching*. Matching implies that expenses are being recognized on a fair and equitable basis relative to the recognition of revenues. Matching is thus the second aspect, after recognition, of the primacy of income measurement over asset and liability valuation in our present system, which is oriented toward historical cost. Matching is currently under extensive attack. First, the historical cost approach often tends to substantially understate expense measurements relative to the value of expired-asset services. Second, the "systematic and rational" methods employed under generally accepted accounting principles tend to be extremely arbitrary: a particular problem can be handled in more than one way. This imprecision is known as the "allocation problem" and is discussed in Chapter 7.

---

[31] Myers (1959).

[32] FASB (1984, p. 28).

[33] Paton and Littleton (1940, p. 49).

[34] FASB (1984, p. 28). Devine contends that the concept of realization ". . . is concerned entirely and exclusively with liquidity." Devine (1985, p. 61).

[35] See AICPA (1970, pp. 9085–9086).

Constraining Principles

The second group of input-oriented principles partially overlaps with the "modifying conventions" mentioned in APB Statement 4. They are described in the following fashion:

> Certain widely adopted conventions modify the application of the pervasive measurement principles. These modifying conventions . . . have evolved to deal with some of the most difficult and controversial problem areas in financial accounting.[36]

The constraining principles either impose limitations upon financial statements, as in the case of conservatism, or provide checks on them, as in the case of materiality and disclosure.

Conservatism Unquestionably, conservatism holds an extremely important place in the ethos of accountants. Indeed, it has even been called the dominant principle of accounting.[37] A classic example of conservatism is the lower-of-cost-or-market valuation for inventories and marketable securities.

Conservatism is defined here as the attempt to select "generally accepted" accounting methods that result in any of the following: (1) slower revenue recognition, (2) faster expense recognition, (3) lower asset valuation, (4) higher liability valuation. However, in some situations some of these criteria can conflict. If so, lower income considerations would take precedence over higher asset valuations in determining whether a method or approach is conservative. For example, in the case of current valuation of assets, one approach — called distributable income — does not include real holding gains in the computation of income. As a result, in an inflationary environment, distributable income often results in higher asset valuations and lower income calculations than would occur under the historical-cost alternative. Therefore, the distributable-income approach to current valuation can be more conservative than historical costing even though, generally speaking, historical cost is assumed to be more conservative.

Several reasons account for the importance of conservatism. As Littleton pointed out, the "lower-of-cost-or-market" notion had the purpose of minimizing inventories for property tax valuation purposes.[38] Then, too, accountants have undoubtedly often had to protect themselves from clients who may have desired to maximize either asset valuation or income measurement to maximize security prices — for example, prior to the stock market crash of 1929. As the conceptual foundations of accounting change in accordance with new theoreti-

---

[36] Ibid., p. 9089.
[37] Sterling (1967). Skinner (1988) found an important example of conservatism. He estimates that at the end of fiscal 1976–77 in the United Kingdom fixed asset lives used for depreciation purposes were equal only to about half of the actual period. He attributes the short write-off periods to conservatism as opposed to factors such as inflation and the equalization of book lives and tax lives.
[38] Littleton (1941).

cal approaches, it is quite likely that conservatism, as a dominating principle, will decline in importance.

Disclosure Moonitz construed disclosure as an imperative postulate (C-5). However, he described it in negative terms: ". . . that which is necessary to make them (accounting reports) not misleading." The fact that it is virtually impossible to quantify the concept of adequate disclosure for users may be the reason for Moonitz's phrasing and for the failure (pointed out by Most) of the Securities and Exchange Commission or AICPA sources to define the concept adequately.[39] Nor has the FASB defined it, though two important SFASs have dealt with it: SFAS 14 on segmental disclosures and SFAS 33 on general price-level and current value data. SFAS 14 requires segmental disclosures by product lines, foreign operations, and major customers where any of these is construed to be a major segment in terms of various quantitative criteria set forth in the statement.

Disclosure refers to relevant financial information both inside and outside the main body of the financial statements themselves, including methods employed in financial statements where more than one choice exists or an unusual or innovative selection of methods.[40] The principal outside categories include

1. Supplementary financial statement schedules, such as those pertaining to SFAS 14 and SFAS 33 (now superseded by SFASs 82 and 89).
2. Disclosure in footnotes of information that cannot be adequately presented in the body of the financial statements themselves.
3. Disclosure of material or major post-statement events in the annual report.
4. Forecasts of operations for the forthcoming year.
5. Management's analysis of operations in the annual report.

There are two important reasons for believing that disclosure will become even more important in the future. First, as the business environment grows more complex, expressing important financial and operating information adequately within the confines of the traditional financial statements becomes more difficult. Second, a considerable body of evidence indicates that capital markets are able to absorb and reflect new information within security prices rapidly. Hence, many who rely on the market-efficiency mechanism consider disclosure per se, as opposed to its particular form, the key factor. The increased dependency on disclosure in the light of market efficiency requires a more extensive examination in Chapter 8.

Materiality Two aspects of materiality in accounting are related but nevertheless distinct. In auditing, materiality refers to the consistency of judgment by auditors given a particular level or standard of materiality accepted in ac-

---

[39] Most (1982, p. 182).
[40] APB 22 (1972).

counting practice. We are concerned here with the latter aspect of materiality, the standard or threshold of materiality that should be employed in accounting practice. *Materiality* refers to the importance of an item (or group of items) to users in terms of its relevance to evaluation or decision making. We can thus view it as the other side of the disclosure coin because what is disclosed should, of course, be material.

The most ambitious attempt to assess quantitative perceptions of materiality was Pattillo's study for the Financial Executives Research Foundation.[41] Pattillo utilized 684 respondents, including preparers of financial statements (financial executives from "Fortune 500" and medium-sized firms), users of accounting information (bankers and financial analysts), auditors, and also academics, to use their own materiality judgments on twenty-eight cases. Pattillo's major findings included:

1. Although many respondents usually use a range of 5 to 10 percent of net income as the boundary of materiality, they did not apply a single absolute dollar or percentage relationship to all situations.
2. Perceptions of materiality differ between groups, with financial executives having the highest percentage threshold of net income and certified public accountants and financial analysts having the lowest overall percentage.
3. Modifying elements, such as the particular characteristics of the firm and the political and economic environment, influence the perception of materiality in particular situations.

Another important empirical study was done by Rose, Beaver, Becker, and Sorter, who attempted to relate materiality to the psychological concept of "sensation," which measures the individual's response to a physical stimulus.[42] Materiality was viewed in this study as the reaction of investor-type individuals to accounting information. The nature of the test was to present simulated financial data for hypothetical firms as of December 31, 1966, and December 31, 1967. The stimulus–response variable was earnings per share. It was always $2.50 for the first year and ranged from $2.00 to $3.00 in the second year at even 10-cent intervals ($2.50 and $2.00, $2.50 and $2.10, etc.). Each of the resulting eleven pairs was presented to 121 MBA students six times in a randomly selected order. Respondents were asked to identify whether earnings per share were "essentially more, essentially the same, or essentially less" in the second year. Upper and lower materiality bounds for essentially more and essentially less were $2.68 and $2.35 as indicated by 50 percent of the responses. The test was repeated for some of the subjects using a $5.00 earnings per share figure in the base year in combination with a $4.00 to $6.00 range in the second year. Materiality responses of essentially more or less were very close in percentage terms to the earlier phase of the study. The authors noted that their subjects responded in a "symmetric, regular and predictable manner" consis-

---

[41] Pattillo (1976).
[42] Rose, Beaver, Becker, and Sorter (1970).

tent with other response patterns to sensory stimuli. Moreover, O'Connor and Collins observed in another study that the nature of the Rose study casts materiality in a predictive context — since information from one period is linked to another period.[43] However, the Rose study is somewhat simplistic because the stimulus is restricted to one variable, perceived changes in earnings per share.[44]

Despite their limitations, these and other empirical studies, using questionnaires and simulated situations, have helped to shed light on the concept of materiality — though it is far from a settled issue.[45] Materiality, along with disclosure, will become an increasingly important issue in the forseeable future. The FASB issued a Discussion Memorandum which outlined many of the factors that influence the judgment of materiality but a standard has never appeared.[46]

Objectivity   In the past objectivity has been interpreted in several different ways, but primarily in terms of the verifiability of evidence underlying transactions that are eventually summarized and organized in the form of financial statements.[47] The concept of quality of evidence was considered apart from those who carry out the measurement function. Now, however, *objectivity* is more commonly thought of in the statistical sense (discussed in Chapter 1) as the degree of consensus among measurers. It is therefore an integral part of the measurement process rather than being either a postulate or principle. APB Statement 4 adopts this outlook although it discusses the concept as a "qualitative objective" of accounting and relabels it *verifiability*.[48] This newer, statistical sense of verifiability also appears in the Statement of Financial Accounting Concepts 2 of the Conceptual Framework Project of the FASB.

OUTPUT-ORIENTED PRINCIPLES

As mentioned earlier, output-oriented principles express qualities that financial statements should possess when viewed from the standpoint of both preparers and users. Of necessity, then, these concepts overlap somewhat as well as com-

---

[43] O'Connor and Collins (1974, p. 174).

[44] Hofstedt and Hughes (1977) used three stimuli variables for assessing materiality. Their study involved a hypothetical situation dealing with the write-down of an investment in an unconsolidated subsidiary. Criteria for materiality concerned the size of the write-down relative to (1) the net income, (2) the balance in the parent's investment-in-subsidiaries account, and (3) the write-down size relative to total book value of the subsidiary involved. In addition, Hofstedt and Hughes used a finer measure for their subjects to indicate perceived materiality than did the Rose group. Hofstedt and Hughes used a scale from 0 to 100 for indicating the need for disclosure, whereas Rose used the cruder response of whether changes in earnings per share were "essentially more . . . the same . . . or less than in the previous year." Unfortunately, the Hofstedt and Hughes study was restricted to only nineteen second-year MBA students.

[45] Pany and Wheeler (1989) applied a number of rule-of-thumb materiality measures to various industries and found sizable differences within and among industries that vary with the particular measure of materiality employed.

[46] FASB (1975).

[47] Paton and Littleton (1940, pp. 18–21).

[48] AICPA (1970, p. 9076). Vatter (1963, p. 190) was an early adherent of the view that objectivity is part of measurement methodology.

plement each other. As viewed here, comparability is a concept that applies to users of financial statements, whereas consistency and uniformity focus on preparers of financial information.

Comparability

Comparability has often been described as accounting for like events in a similar manner, but this definition is too simplistic to be operational.[49] It also applies to those who use financial statements. *Comparability*, viewed here from the user's standpoint, refers to the degree of reliability users should find in financial statements when evaluating financial condition or the results of operations on an interfirm basis or predicting income or cash flows.[50]

Obviously, then, comparability is largely dependent on the amount of uniformity attained in recording transactions and preparing financial statements. Despite the secondary role of comparability relative to uniformity, the cost–benefit relationship between them should be borne in mind: comparability might be improved by more uniformity, but costs may exceed benefits.

Consistency

Consistency refers to a given firm's use of the same accounting methods over consecutive time periods. Consistency is necessary if predictions or evaluations based on a firm's financial statements over more than one time period are to be reliable. Should change occur — because of adoption of a more relevant or objective method — full disclosure must be made to users, and the auditor's opinion must be appropriately qualified.

Consistency is really an aspect of the broader issue of uniformity. Some believe that differing circumstances among firms, particularly when different industries are involved, make it impossible to attain uniformity of accounting techniques on an interfirm basis.[51] Therefore, consistency on an intrafirm basis, with full disclosure when changes occur, would be the most practical goal relative to output-oriented principles.

---

[49] One example is Sprouse (1978, p. 71).

[50] Revsine has conceived a formal model of comparability that is consistent with the output approach advocated here. Revsine's model is based on concepts from the information economics literature. His hypothetical application of the model compares the quality of the information signals received by users in terms of (1) historical cost information systems and (2) current cost (value) information systems. He concludes that historical costing will have a *timing difference* problem; that is, different balance sheet valuations will arise because an older asset will almost never have the same valuation as an exactly similar asset (in terms of type and condition) acquired at the balance sheet date. Hence, historical costing is noncomparable across firms. However, current costing systems have a related problem called the *estimation difference*. It arises because actual current valuations for older assets cannot be directly measured and must therefore be indirectly measured. The difference in valuation between the estimated current valuation and the actual current valuation of exactly similar assets would be the estimation difference. See Revsine (1985).

The timing difference is closely related to representational faithfulness (see Chapter 6), and the estimation difference correlates closely to the principle (concept) of verifiability or objectivity discussed here and in Chapter 1.

[51] For example, see Peloubet (1961, pp. 35–41) and Kemp (1963, pp. 126–132).

Uniformity

Uniformity has been and continues to be an important issue in accounting. But it has several subtle aspects that have not always been fully taken into account. Interpretations of uniformity have included the following:

1. A uniform set of principles for all firms, with interpretation and application left up to the individual entity.
2. Similar accounting treatment required in broadly similar situations, ignoring possibly different circumstances (*rigid uniformity*).
3. Similar accounting treatment that takes into account different economic circumstances (*finite uniformity*).

The second and third definitions differ from the first because they are concerned with the degree of uniformity that enters into interpretation of transactions. The first definition simply prescribes a broad theoretical framework to serve as a basis for interpretation of transactions. The difference between rigid and finite uniformity is best described by illustration. SFAS 2, which requires immediate expensing of research and development costs, is an example of rigid uniformity. Different expectations apply to the broad category of research and development in terms of cash flows that will be received from these costs, but the treatment is uniform even though different patterns of receipt of benefits exist. SFAS 13 is an example of finite uniformity. The statement sets down some rather specific criteria for differentiating between capital and operating leases. Hence, different circumstances are taken into account in distinguishing accounting for the two types of leases (we are not concerned here with the question of agreement in terms of the capitalization criteria themselves). Rigid and finite uniformity are extensively discussed in Chapter 8.

EQUITY THEORIES

The enterprise interfaces with owners in the owners' equity accounts. Several deductive theories have attempted to depict this relationship and are useful in interpreting nonlegal rights and interests in the owners' equity accounts as well as in determining certain components of income. Previously, these normative theories received considerable attention; but today they play a secondary role to newer, empirical research approaches. Nevertheless, they still provide some important insights.

PROPRIETARY THEORY

The *proprietary theory* assumes that the owners and the firm are virtually identical. This theory, which dates back at least as far as the early eighteenth century, is quite descriptive of economies made up largely of the small owner-operated firms that existed prior to the Industrial Revolution.[52]

---

[52] Chatfield (1974, p. 220).

Under proprietary theory, the assets belong to the firm's owners, the liabilities are their obligations, and ownership equities accrue to the owners. The balance sheet equation would be

$$\sum \text{Assets} - \sum \text{Liabilities} = \text{Owners' Equities} \qquad \textbf{(5.1)}$$

Expenses include deductions for labor costs, taxes, and interest but not for preferred and common dividends. In other words, income represents the owners' increase in both net assets (assets minus liabilities) and owners' equities arising from operations during the period. The essentials of the proprietary approach largely coincide with the components of income measurement as it is presently construed in historical cost-based systems, although owners certainly do not exercise the control over owners' equity accounts suggested by proprietary theory. Furthermore, the relationship between the firm and its owners has changed markedly since the advent of the giant corporation in technologically advanced societies.

ENTITY THEORY

Dissatisfaction with the orientation of the proprietary theory led to development of the entity theory. Its chief architect was William A. Paton, long-time professor at the University of Michigan.[53] Under the *entity theory*, the firm and its owners are separate beings. The assets belong to the firm itself; both liability and equity holders are investors in those assets with different rights and claims against them. The balance sheet equation would be

$$\sum \text{Assets} = \sum \text{Equities (including liabilities)} \qquad \textbf{(5.2)}$$

Under orthodox entity theory, there is a dual nature to both the owners' equity accounts and the question of the primary claim to income. Stockholders have rights relative to receiving dividends when declared, voting at the annual corporate meeting, and sharing in net assets after all other claims have been met. Nevertheless, owners' equity accounts do not represent their interest as owners but simply their claims as equity holders. Similarly, net income does not belong to the owners although the amount is credited to the claims of equity holders after all other claims have been satisfied. Income does not belong to capital providers until dividends are declared or interest becomes due. In measuring income, both interest and dividends represent distributions of income to providers of capital. Hence, both are treated the same and *neither* is a deduction from income.

If the entity theory were taken to its logical conclusion, the owners' equity accounts would belong unequivocally to the firm, despite the presence of stockholder claims. Furthermore, income would belong to the firm itself, and, in turn, interest and dividends would both be deductions in calculating it.[54]

Robert N. Anthony has provided an interesting variant on this narrower

---

[53] Paton (1922, pp. 50–84).
[54] Li (1960).

interpretation of the entity theory.[55] The right-hand side of the balance sheet would consist of four main components: liabilities, shareholder equity, equity interest, and entity equity. Shareholder equity would consist of contributed capital, and equity interest would comprise unpaid dividends on both common and preferred stock. Interest cost to the firm would consist of both interest on debt and interest cost on the shareholder equity. Entity equity would be equivalent to retained earnings but would be lower than the latter by the amount of unpaid dividends on both preferred and common stock. The shareholder-equity interest rate suggested by Anthony could either be set equal to the firm's before-tax debt rate or to a specified published rate applicable to all firms set by the United States Treasury Department in accordance with Cost Accounting Standard 414 published by the now defunct Cost Accounting Standards Board.

   Although the entity theory provides a good description of the relationship between the firm and its owners, its duality relative to income and owners' equity in the traditional form has probably been responsible for the fact that its precepts have not taken a strong hold in committee reports and releases of various accounting bodies.[56]

RESIDUAL EQUITY THEORY

The *residual equity theory* is a variant of both proprietary and entity theory. The theory has been developed by George Staubus but its roots also lie in the work of William A. Paton.[57] The residual equity holders are that group of equity claimants whose rights are superseded by all other claimants. This group would be the common stockholders, though its members can change if an event such as a reorganization occurs. Common stockholders are, of course, the ultimate risk takers within an enterprise. Their interest in the firm serves as a buffer or protector for all groups with prior claims on the firm, such as preferred stockholders and bond owners.

   The underlying assumption of the residual equity theory is that information appropriate for decision-making purposes, such as that helpful in predicting cash flows, must be supplied to the residual equity holders. The balance sheet equation under this approach would be

$$\sum \text{Assets} - \sum \text{Specific Equities (including liabilities and preferred stock)}$$
$$= \text{Residual Equity} \qquad \textbf{(5.3)}$$

Although the assets are still owned by the firm, they are held in a trust type of arrangement and management's objective is maximization of the value of the residual equity. Income accrues to the residual equity holders after all other

---

[55] See Anthony (1983, pp. 92–98).

[56] AAA (1957, p. 5) discusses *enterprise net income* in which interest, taxes, and dividends are excluded from the determination of net income; hence, a broad entity theory approach is advocated. Enterprise net income, however, is contrasted with *income to shareholders*, which coincides with proprietary theory.

[57] See Staubus (1961, pp. 17–27) for an overview, and Paton (1922, pp. 84–89).

claims have been met. Interest and preferred dividends (but not common dividends) would be deductions in arriving at income.

The development of the residual equity approach has been relatively recent. It has undoubtedly played a role in the movement toward defining objectives of income measurement with an emphasis on measures that would aid in predicting future cash flows.

FUND THEORY

The *fund theory*, developed by William J. Vatter, backs away from both the entity and proprietary theories because of the inherent weaknesses and inconsistencies of both.[58] A **fund** is simply a group of assets and related obligations devoted to a particular purpose, which may or may not be that of generating income. The balance sheet equation would be

$$\sum \text{Assets} = \sum \text{Restrictions of Assets} \qquad (5.4)$$

The restrictions on the assets arise from both liabilities and invested capital. The invested capital must be maintained intact unless specific authority for partial or total liquidation is given. The restriction on assets also includes the specific purposes for their use mandated by law or contract. Fund theory, therefore, is most applicable to the governmental and not-for-profit areas where endowment funds, encumbrances, and special-asset groups often devoted to specific and separate purposes prevail.

SUMMARY

Despite APB Statement 4's use of the word *principles* to describe several concepts, the postulates–principles approach had, in essence, died out by 1970. Several factors underlie the failure of the postulates–principles approach and the rise of objectives and standards. The failure of ARS 1 and ARS 3 and the difficulty of building on a postulate base have already been discussed. The demise of the APB was certainly one of the reasons for the end of the postulates and principles orientation to standard setting. It is true that by the late 1960s the APB had abandoned this approach despite the publication in 1965 of Grady's ARS 7. Nevertheless, the APB had become identified with postulates and principles, and its decline signaled the obsolescence of this orientation as a theoretical underpinning for the standard-setting process.

Other, more fundamental factors were also at work. New research and committee reports began taking into account such issues as user needs and diversities, which, in turn, led to a focus on the objectives of financial statements, considerations that were barely mentioned in the postulates and principles literature. Indeed, the challenge to income measurement itself posed by the

---

[58] Vatter (1947).

efficient-markets hypothesis and the decline in the search for the one income approach that could be deemed superior to all others — what has sometimes been referred to as *true income* — revealed the need for new outlooks and approaches to income formulation and measurement as well as to the broader topic of financial reporting.

The new outlook began stressing the need for objectives and standards. Several of the concepts that have been loosely labeled as *principles* — disclosure, materiality, and uniformity, for example — will eventually take their place in an objectives-oriented framework. Other concepts, such as going concern, conservatism, and stability of the monetary unit, may diminish in importance.

The emphasis on objectives and standards has also rendered the equity theories of accounting somewhat obsolete. The equity theories are normative–deductive theories based on the relationship between the corporation and its owners. While these theories can provide interesting insights into some problems, their scope is not sufficiently global to permit their extensive use in solving fundamental accounting problems.

Hence, our attention turns next to objectives and standards.[59] Chapter 6 examines important conceptual and institutional pronouncements that occurred after the decline of the postulates and principles approach.

APPENDIX 5-A: THE BASIC POSTULATES OF ACCOUNTING (ARS 1)

Postulates Stemming from the Economic and Political Environment

Postulate A-1. Quantification

Quantitative data are helpful in making rational economic decisions, i.e., in making choices among alternatives so that actions are correctly related to consequences.

Postulate A-2. Exchange

Most of the goods and services that are produced are distributed through exchange, and are not directly consumed by the producers.

Postulate A-3. Entities (including identification of the entity)

Economic activity is carried on through specific units or entities. Any report on the activity must identify clearly the particular unit or entity involved.

Postulate A-4. Time period (including specification of the time period)

Economic activity is carried on during specifiable periods of time. Any report on that activity must identify clearly the period of time involved.

Postulate A-5. Unit of measure (including identification of the monetary unit)

Money is the common denominator in terms of which goods and services,

---

[59] Paton and Littleton noted that the word *standards* has less of a flavor of permanence than does *principles*. Paton and Littleton (1940, p. 4).

Appendices 5-A and 5-B are reprinted by permission of the American Institute of Certified Public Accountants.

including labor, natural resources, and capital are measured. Any report must clearly indicate which money (e.g., dollars, francs, pounds) is being used.

Postulates Stemming from the Field of Accounting Itself

Postulate B-1. Financial statements (Related to A-1)

The results of the accounting process are expressed in a set of fundamentally related financial statements which articulate with each other and rest upon the same underlying data.

Postulate B-2. Market prices (Related to A-2)

Accounting data are based on prices generated by past, present or future exchanges which have actually taken place or are expected to.

Postulate B-3. Entities (Related to A-3)

The results of the accounting process are expressed in terms of specific units or entities.

Postulate B-4. Tentativeness (Related to A-4)

The results of operations for relatively short periods of time are tentative whenever allocations between past, present, and future periods are required.

The Imperatives

Postulate C-1. Continuity (including the correlative concept of limited life)

In the absence of evidence to the contrary, the entity should be viewed as remaining in operation indefinitely. In the presence of evidence that the entity has a limited life, it should not be viewed as remaining in operation indefinitely.

Postulate C-2. Objectivity

Changes in assets and liabilities, and the related effects (if any) on revenues, expenses, retained earnings, and the like, should not be given formal recognition in the accounts earlier than the point of time at which they can be measured in objective terms.

Postulate C-3. Consistency

The procedures used in accounting for a given entity should be appropriate for the measurement of its position and its activities and should be followed consistently from period to period.

Postulate C-4. Stable unit

Accounting reports should be based on a stable measuring unit.

Postulate C-5. Disclosure

Accounting reports should disclose that which is necessary to make them not misleading.

APPENDIX 5-B: A TENTATIVE SET OF BROAD ACCOUNTING PRINCIPLES FOR BUSINESS ENTERPRISES (ARS 3)

The principles summarized below are relevant primarily to formal financial statements made available to third parties as representations by the management of the business enterprise. The "basic postulates of accounting" developed in *Accounting Research Study No. 1* are integral parts of this statement of principles.

Broad principles of accounting should not be formulated mainly for the purpose of validating policies (e.g., financial management, taxation, employee compensation) established in other fields, no matter how sound or desirable those policies may be in and of themselves. Accounting draws its real strength from its neutrality as among the demands of competing special interests. Its proper functions derive from the measurement of the resources of specific entities and of changes in these resources. Its principles should be aimed at the achievement of those functions.

The principles developed in this study are as follows:

A. Profit is attributable to the whole process of business activity. Any rule or procedure, therefore, which assigns profit to a portion of the whole process should be continuously re-examined to determine the extent to which it introduces bias into the reporting of the amount of profit assigned to specific periods of time.

B. Changes in resources should be classified among the amounts attributable to

   1. Changes in the dollar (price-level changes) which lead to restatements of capital but not to revenues or expenses.

   2. Changes in replacement costs (above or below the effect of price-level changes) which lead to elements of gain or of loss.

   3. Sale or other transfer, or recognition of net realizable value, all of which lead to revenue or gain.

   4. Other causes, such as accretion or the discovery of previously unknown natural resources.

C. All assets of the enterprise, whether obtained by investments of owners or of creditors, or by other means, should be recorded in the accounts and reported in the financial statements. The existence of an asset is independent of the means by which it was acquired.

D. The problem of measuring (pricing, valuing) an asset is the problem of measuring the future services, and involves at least three steps:

   a. A determination if future services do in fact exist. For example, a building is capable of providing space for manufacturing activity.

   b. An estimate of the quantity of services. For example, a building is estimated to be usable for twenty more years, or for half of its estimated total life.

   c. The choice of a method or basis or formula for pricing (valuing) the quantity of services arrived at under (b) above. In general, the choice of a pricing basis is made from the following three exchange prices:

      (1) A past exchange price, e.g., acquisition cost or other initial basis. When this basis is used, profit or loss, if any, on the asset being priced will not be recognized until sale or other transfer out of the business entity.

      (2) A current exchange price, e.g., replacement cost. When this basis is used, profit or loss on the asset being priced will be recognized in two stages. The first stage will recognize part of the gain or loss in the period or periods from time of acquisition to time of usage or other disposition; the second stage will recognize the remainder of the gain or loss at the time of the sale or other transfer out of the entity, measured by the difference between sale (transfer) price and replacement cost. This method is still a cost method; an asset priced on this basis is being treated as a cost factor awaiting disposition.

(3) A future exchange price, e.g., anticipated selling price. When this basis is used, profit or loss, if any, has already been recognized in the accounts. Any asset priced on this basis is therefore being treated as though it were a receivable, in that sale or other transfer out of the business (including conversion into cash) will result in no gain or loss, except for any interest (discount) arising from the passage of time.

The proper pricing (valuation) of assets and the allocation of profit to accounting periods are dependent in large part upon estimates of the existence of future benefits, regardless of the bases used to price the assets. The need for estimates is unavoidable and cannot be eliminated by the adoption of any formula as to pricing.

1. All assets in the form of money or claims to money should be shown at their discounted present value or the equivalent. The interest rate to be employed in the discounting process is the market (effective) rate at the date the asset was acquired.

   The discounting process is not necessary in the case of short-term receivables where the force of interest is small. The carrying-value of receivables should be reduced by allowances for uncollectable elements; estimated collection costs should be recorded in the accounts.

   If the claims to money are uncertain as to time or amount of receipt, they should be recorded at their current market value. If the current market value is so uncertain as to be unreliable, these assets should be shown at cost.

2. Inventories which are readily salable at known prices with readily predictable costs of disposal should be recorded at net realizable value, and the related revenue taken up at the same time. Other inventory items should be recorded at their current (replacement) cost, and the related gain or loss separately reported. Accounting for inventories on either basis will result in recording revenues, gains, or losses before they are validated by sale but they are nevertheless components of the net profit (loss) of the period in which they occur.

   Acquisition costs may be used whenever they approximate current (replacement) costs, as would probably be the case when the unit prices of inventory components are reasonably stable and turnover is rapid. In all cases the basis of measurement actually employed should be "subject to verification by another competent investigator."

3. All items of plant and equipment in service, or held in stand-by status, should be recorded at cost of acquisition or construction, with appropriate modification for the effect of the changing dollar either in the primary statements or in supplementary statements. In the external reports, plant and equipment should be restated in terms of current replacement costs whenever some significant event occurs, such as a reorganization of the business entity or its merger with another entity

or when it becomes a subsidiary of a parent company. Even in the absence of a significant event, the accounts could be restated at periodic intervals, perhaps every five years. The development of satisfactory indexes of construction costs and of machinery and equipment prices would assist materially in making the calculation of replacement costs feasible, practical, and objective.

4. The investment (cost or other basis) in plant and equipment should be amortized over the estimated service life. The basis for adopting a particular method of amortization for a given asset should be its ability to produce an allocation reasonably consistent with the anticipated flow of benefits from the asset.

5. All "intangibles" such as patents, copyrights, research and development, and goodwill should be recorded at cost, with appropriate modification for the effect of the changing dollar either in the primary statements or in supplementary statements. Limited term items should be amortized as expenses over their estimated lives. Unlimited term items should continue to be carried as assets, without amortization.

   If the amount of the investment (cost or other basis) in plant and equipment or in the "intangibles" has been increased or decreased as the result of appraisal or the use of index-numbers, depreciation or other amortization should be based on the changed amount.

E. All liabilities of the enterprise should be recorded in the accounts and reported in the financial statements. Those liabilities which call for settlement in cash should be measured by the present (discounted) value of the future payments or the equivalent. The yield (market, effective) rate of interest at date of incurrence of the liability is the pertinent rate to use in the discounting process and in the amortization of "discount" and "premium." "Discount" and "premium" are technical devices for relating the issue price to the principal amount and should therefore be closely associated with principal amount in financial statements.

F. Those liabilities which call for settlement in goods or services (other than cash) should be measured by their agreed selling price. Profit accrues in these cases as the stipulated services are performed or the goods produced or delivered.

G. In a corporation, stockholders' equity should be classified into invested capital and retained earnings (earned surplus). Invested capital should, in turn, be classified according to source, that is, according to the underlying nature of the transactions giving rise to invested capital.

   Retained earnings should include the cumulative amount of net profits and net losses, less dividend declarations, and less amounts transferred to invested capital.

   In an unincorporated business, the same plan may be followed, but the acceptable alternative is more widely followed of reporting the total interest of each owner or group of owners at the balance sheet date.

H. A statement of the results of operations should reveal the components of profit in sufficient detail to permit comparisons and interpretations to be made. To this end, the data should be classified at least into revenues, expenses, gains, and losses.

1. In general, the revenue of an enterprise during an accounting period represents a measurement of the exchange value of the products (goods

and services) of that enterprise during that period. The preceding discussion, under D(2), is also pertinent here.

2. Broadly speaking, expenses measure the costs of the amount of revenue recognized. They may be directly associated with revenue-producing transactions themselves (e.g., so-called "product costs") or with the accounting period in which the revenues appear (e.g., so-called "period costs").

3. Gains include such items as the results of holding inventories through a price rise, the sale of assets (other than stock-in-trade) at more than book value, and the settlement of liabilities at less than book value. Losses include items such as the result of holding inventories through a price decline, the sale of assets (other than stock-in-trade) at less than book value or their retirement, the settlement of liabilities at more than book value, and the imposition of liabilities through a lawsuit.

QUESTIONS

1. Do you think the "broad principles" of ARS 3 are really *principles* as that term is used in science?

2. "Assuming all other things equal, it is possible that the lower-of-cost-or-market method can result in any given year in *higher* income than would be the case under the same inventory costing method *without* the use of lower-of-cost-or-market. If so, then lower-of-cost-or-market cannot be classified as a conservative method." Do you agree with these statements? Discuss.

3. Why is it that postulates stemming from the economic and political climates as well as the customs and viewpoints of the business community would not serve as a good foundation for deducing a set of accounting principles?

4. Why do you think that financial executives appear to have a higher mean for materiality judgments when expressed as a percentage of net income than either certified public accountants or financial analysts?

5. Do you think that the so-called equity theories of accounting are really theories in the scientific sense? If so, how would you classify them?

6. Why do you think the equity theories are less important today than they were, say, thirty years ago?

7. Four postulates (going concern, time period, accounting entity, and monetary unit) were discussed as part of the basic concepts underlying historical costing. Can any of the principles discussed under the same general category be deduced or logically derived from these postulates?

8. How does agency theory (Chapters 2 and 4) differ from the equity theories discussed in this chapter?

9. Does the entity theory or the proprietary theory provide a better description of the relationship existing between the large modern corporation and its owners?

10. Why has the entity theory fragmented into two separate conceptions?

11. Of the nine so-called principles shown in Exhibit 5–1, which do you think are the most important in terms of establishing a historical costing system?
12. How important are the principles in question 11 to establishing a current value accounting system?
13. Postulates are supposed to be tight enough to prevent conflicting conclusions being deduced from them. Is this the case with ARS 1?
14. Is it fair to categorize ARS 1 and ARS 3 as failures?
15. How do the imperative postulates (group C) differ from the other two categories of postulates?
16. Distinguish among the terms *realized, realizable,* and *realization.*
17. How does conventional retained earnings differ from entity equity under the Anthony conception of the entity theory?

CASES AND PROBLEMS

1. Assume the following for the year 1982 for the Staubus company:

Revenues		$1,000,000
Operating Expenses		
Cost of Goods Sold	$400,000	
Depreciation	100,000	
Salaries and Wages	200,000	
Bond interest (8% Debentures sold at maturity value of $1,000,000)		80,000
Dividends declared on 6% Preferred Stock(par value $500,000)		30,000
Dividends declared of $5 per share on Common Stock (20,000 shares outstanding with a par value of $100 per share)		100,000

(a) Determine the income under each of the following equity theories:
   • Proprietary theory
   • Entity theory (orthodox view)
   • Entity theory (unorthodox view)
   • Residual equity
(b) Would any of your answers change if the preferred stock is convertible at any time at the ratio of 2 preferred shares for 1 share of common stock?
2. Critique *A Statement of Basic Accounting Postulates and Principles* by a study group at the University of Illinois (it should be on reserve or otherwise made available to you). Your critique should cover, but not be restricted to, the following points:
   (a) How do the definitions of postulates, concepts, and principles differ?
   (b) Are the examples of postulates, principles, and concepts consistent with their definitions?
   (c) Does this set of postulates, principles, and concepts provide a legislative body with a useful framework for deriving operating rules?

BIBLIOGRAPHY OF REFERENCED WORKS

Accounting Principles Board (1972). Opinion No. 22, *Disclosure of Accounting Policies* (Accounting Principles Board).

American Accounting Association (1957). *Accounting and Reporting Standards for Corporate Financial Statements and Preceding Statements and Supplements* (American Accounting Association).

American Institute of Certified Public Accountants (1953). *Accounting Terminology Bulletin No. 1* (American Institute of Certified Public Accountants), pp. 9503–9517.

——— (1970). "Basic Concepts and Accounting Principles Underlying Financial Statements of Business Enterprises," *APB Statement No. 4* (American Institute of Certified Public Accountants), pp. 9057–9106.

Anthony, Robert N. (1983). *Tell It Like It Was* (Richard D. Irwin, Inc.).

Canning, John B. (1929). *The Economics of Accountancy* (Ronald Press).

Carlson, Marvin L., and James W. Lamb (1981). "Constructing a Theory of Accounting — An Axiomatic Approach," *The Accounting Review* (July 1981), pp. 554–573.

Caws, Peter (1965). *The Philosophy of Science* (D. Van Nostrand Company, Inc.).

Chambers, Raymond J. (1964). "The Moonitz and Sprouse Studies on Postulates and Principles," *Accounting, Finance and Management* (Butterworth), pp. 396–414.

——— (1966). *Accounting, Evaluation and Economic Behavior* (Prentice-Hall).

——— (1970). "Second Thoughts on Continuously Contemporary Accounting," *Abacus* (September 1970), pp. 39–55.

Chatfield, Michael (1974). *A History of Accounting Thought* (The Dryden Press).

"Comments on a Tentative Set of Broad Accounting Principles" (1958). *Journal of Accountancy* (April 1963), pp. 36–48.

Deinzer, Harvey T. (1965). *Development of Accounting Thought* (Holt, Rinehart and Winston).

Devine, Carl T. (1985). "Recognition Requirements — Income Earned and Realized," in *Essays in Accounting Theory*, Vol. II, *Studies in Accounting Research #22* (American Accounting Association), pp. 57–67.

Financial Accounting Standards Board (1975). *An Analysis of Issues Related to Criteria for Determining Materiality* (Financial Accounting Standards Board).

——— (1984). "Recognition and Measurement in Financial Statements of Business Enterprises," *Statement of Financial Accounting Concepts No. 5* (Financial Accounting Standards Board).

Fremgen, James (1968). "The Going Concern Assumption: A Critical Appraisal," *The Accounting Review* (October 1968), pp. 49–56.

Gilman, Stephen (1939). *Accounting Concepts of Profit* (Ronald Press).

Grady, Paul (1965). "Inventory of Generally Accepted Accounting Principles," *Accounting Research Study No. 7* (American Institute of Certified Public Accountants).

Hendriksen, Elden S. (1982). *Accounting Theory*, 4th ed. (Richard D. Irwin).

Hofstedt, Thomas R., and G. David Hughes (1977). "An Experimental Study of the Judgment Element in Disclosure Decisions," *The Accounting Review* (April 1977), pp. 379–395.

Ijiri, Yuji (1975). "Theory of Accounting Measurement," *Studies in Accounting Research #10* (American Accounting Association).

Jennings, Alvin R. (1958). "Present-Day Challenges in Financial Reporting," *Journal of Accountancy* (January 1958), pp. 28–34.

Kemp, Patrick (1963). "Controversies on the Construction of Financial Statements," *The Accounting Review* (January 1963), pp. 126–132.

Li, David H. (1960). "The Nature and Treatment of Dividends Under the Entity Concept," *The Accounting Review* (October 1960), pp. 674–679.

Littleton, A. C. (1941). "A Genealogy for 'Cost or Market,'" *The Accounting Review* (June 1941), pp. 161–167.

———— (1953). *Structure of Accounting Theory* (American Accounting Association).

MacNeal, Kenneth (1939; reissued 1970). *Truth in Accounting* (Scholars Book Co.).

Mattesich, Richard (1964). *Accounting and Analytical Methods* (Richard D. Irwin).

Mautz, Robert K. (1965). "The Place of Postulates in Accounting," *Journal of Accountancy* (January 1965), pp. 46–49.

Mautz, Robert K., and Hussein A. Sharaf (1961). *The Philosophy of Auditing* (American Accounting Association).

Moonitz, Maurice (1961). "The Basic Postulates of Accounting," *Accounting Research Study #1* (American Institute of Certified Public Accountants).

Morgenstern, Oscar (1963). "Limits to the Use of Mathematics in Economics," *Mathematics and the Social Sciences*, ed. J. C. Charlesworth (American Academy of Political and Social Science), pp. 12–39.

Most, Kenneth S. (1982). *Accounting Theory* (Grid Publishing).

Myers, John H. (1959). "The Critical Event and Recognition of Net Profit," *The Accounting Review* (October 1959), pp. 528–532.

Nichols, Arthur C., and Dennis E. Grawoig (1968). "Accounting Reports With Time as a Variable," *The Accounting Review* (October 1968), pp. 631–639.

O'Connor, Melvin, and Daniel W. Collins (1974). "Toward Establishing User-Oriented Materiality Standards," *Journal of Accountancy* (December 1974), pp. 171–179.

Pany, Kurt, and Stephen Wheeler (1989). "Materiality: An Inter-Industry Comparison of the Magnitudes and Stabilities of Various Quantitative Measures," *Accounting Horizons* (December 1989), pp. 71–78.

Paton, William A. (1922; reissued 1962). *Accounting Theory* (Accounting Studies Press, Limited).

Paton, William A., and A. S. Littleton (1940). *An Introduction to Corporate Accounting Standards* (American Accounting Association).

Pattillo, James W. (1976). *The Concept of Materiality in Financial Reporting* (Financial Executives Research Foundation).

Peloubet, Maurice (1961). "Is Further Uniformity Desirable or Possible?" *The Journal of Accountancy* (April 1961), pp. 35–41.

Revsine, Lawrence (1985). "Comparability: An Analytic Examination," *Journal of Accounting and Public Policy* (Spring 1985), pp. 1–12.

Rose, J., William Beaver, Selwyn Becker, and George Sorter (1970). "Toward an Empirical Measure of Materiality," *Empirical Research in Accounting: Selected Studies, 1970* (Supplement to *Journal of Accounting Research*), pp. 138–153.

Sanders, Thomas H., Henry Rand Hatfield, and Underhill Moore (1938). *A Statement of Accounting Principles* (American Accounting Association).

Skinner, R. C. (1988). "The Role of Conservatism in Determining the Accounting Lives of Fixed Assets," *The International Journal of Accounting* (Spring 1988), pp. 1–18.

Special Committee on Research Program (1958). "Report to Council of the Special Committee on Research Program," *Journal of Accountancy* (December 1958), pp. 62–68.

Sprouse, Robert T. (1978). "The Importance of Earnings in the Conceptual Framework," *The Journal of Accountancy* (January 1978), pp. 64–71.

Sprouse, Robert, and Maurice Moonitz (1962). "A Tentative Set of Broad Accounting Principles for Business Enterprises," *Accounting Research Study No. 3* (American Institute of Certified Public Accountants).

Staubus, George (1961). *Accounting to Investors* (University of California Press).

Sterling, Robert R. (1967). "Conservatism: The Fundamental Principle of Valuation in Accounting," *Abacus* (December 1967), pp. 109–132.

———— (1968). "The Going Concern: An Examination," *The Accounting Review* (July 1968), pp. 481–502.

Study Group at the University of Illinois (1964). *A Statement of Basic Postulates and Principles* (Center for International Education and Research in Accounting, University of Illinois).

Sweeney, Henry W. (1936). *Stabilized Accounting* (Holt, Rinehart and Winston).

Vatter, William J. (1947). *The Fund Theory of Accounting and Its Implications for Financial Reports* (University of Chicago Press).

———— (1963). "Postulates and Principles," *Journal of Accounting Research* (Autumn 1963), pp. 179–197.

Wright, F. K. (1967). "Capacity for Adaptation and the Asset Measurement Problem," *Abacus* (August 1967), pp. 74–79.

ADDITIONAL READINGS

Postulates and Principles

Chambers, Raymond J. (1955). "Blueprint for a Theory of Accounting," *Accounting Research* (January 1955), pp. 17–25.

———— (1957). "Detail for a Blueprint," *The Accounting Review* (April 1957), pp. 206–215.

———— (1963). "Why Bother with Postulates?" *Journal of Accounting Research* (Spring 1963), pp. 3–15.

"Comments on the 'Basic Postulates of Accounting.'" (1963). *Journal of Accountancy* (January 1963), pp. 44–55.

Goldberg, Louis (1971). "Varieties of Accounting Theory," *Foundations of Accounting Theory*, ed. W. E. Stone (University of Florida Press), pp. 31–49.

Lambert, S. J. III (1974). "Basic Assumptions in Accounting Theory Construction," *The Journal of Accountancy* (February 1974), pp. 41–48.

Metcalf, Richard (1964). "The Basic Postulates in Perspective," *The Accounting Review* (January 1964), pp. 16–21.

Moonitz, Maurice (1963). "Why Do We Need 'Postulates' and 'Principles,'" *Journal of Accountancy* (December 1963), pp. 42–46.

Popoff, Boris (1972). "Postulates, Principles and Rules," *Accounting and Business Research* (Summer 1972), pp. 182–193.

Tietjen, A. C. (1963). "Accounting Principles, Practices, and Methods," *Journal of Accountancy* (April 1963), pp. 65–68.

Zeff, Stephen A. (1971). "Comments on 'Varieties of Accounting Theory,'" *Foundations of Accounting Theory*, ed. W. E. Stone (University of Florida Press), pp. 50–58.

Basic Concepts

Ashton, Robert H. (1977). "Objectivity of Accounting Measures: A Multirule–Multimeasurer Approach," *The Accounting Review* (July 1977), pp. 567–575.

Barlev, Benzion (1972). "On the Measurement of Materiality," *Accounting and Business Research* (Summer 1972), pp. 194–197.

Bedford, Norton (1973). *Extensions in Accounting Disclosure* (Englewood Cliffs, NJ: Prentice-Hall).

Bedford, Norton, and Toshio Iino (1968). "Consistency Reexamined," *The Accounting Review* (July 1968), pp. 453–458.

Bernstein, Leopold A. (1967). "The Concept of Materiality," *The Accounting Review* (January 1967), pp. 86–95.

Boatsman, James R., and Jack C. Robertson (1974). "Policy-Capturing on Selected Materiality Judgments," *The Accounting Review* (April 1974), pp. 342–352.

Frishkoff, Paul (1970). "An Empirical Investigation of the Concept of Materiality in Accounting," *Empirical Research in Accounting: Selected Studies 1970* (Supplement to *Journal of Accounting Research*), pp. 116–129.

Horngren, Charles T. (1965). "How Should We Interpret the Realization Concept?" *The Accounting Review* (April 1965), pp. 323–333.

Murphy, George (1976). "A Numerical Representation of Some Accounting Conventions," *The Accounting Review* (April 1976), pp. 277–286.

Yu, S. C. (1971). "A Reexamination of the Going Concern Postulate," *International Journal of Accounting, Education and Research* (Spring 1971), pp. 37–58.

Equity Theories

Bird, Francis A., Lewis F. Davidson, and Charles H. Smith (1974). "Perceptions of External Accounting Transfers Under Entity and Proprietary Theory," *The Accounting Review* (April 1974), pp. 233–244.

Goldberg, Louis (1965). *An Inquiry into the Nature of Accounting* (American Accounting Association).

Gynther, Reginald S. (1967). "Accounting Concepts and Behavioral Hypotheses," *The Accounting Review* (April 1967), pp. 274–290.

OBJECTIVES AND STANDARDS

THE POSTULATES AND PRINCIPLES APPROACH largely ignored the question of user objectives, but this issue began to take a more prominent role beginning in the late 1960s in both research and important theoretically oriented monographs and pronouncements sponsored by such organizations as the American Accounting Association (AAA), American Institute of Certified Public Accountants (AICPA), Accounting Principles Board (APB), and the Financial Accounting Standards Board (FASB). In fact, user objectives became an important connecting link among these documents, many of which were attempting to forge a solid theoretical underpinning for financial accounting standards. Therefore, we will examine chronologically (with one exception) the important committee reports and documents that gave rise to objectives and standards in place of the postulates and principles approach.

A good working definition of *standards* was provided by Paton and Littleton:

> Standards should deal ... with fundamental conceptions and general approaches to the presentation of accounting facts. ... Although accounting standards are not in themselves procedures they point toward accounting procedures, that is, toward rules which cover the details of specific situations ... accounting standards should be orderly, systematic, coherent. ... [1]

Standards, as Paton and Littleton also noted, have less of an aura of permanence than is implied by the word *principles*.[2] Our discussion and analysis will include the following works:

---

[1] Paton and Littleton (1940, pp. 5–6).
[2] Ibid., p. 4.

Title	Published By	Year
A STATEMENT OF BASIC ACCOUNTING THEORY (ASOBAT)	AAA	1966
BASIC CONCEPTS AND ACCOUNTING PRINCIPLES UNDERLYING FINANCIAL STATEMENTS OF BUSINESS ENTERPRISES (APB Statement 4)	APB	1970
OBJECTIVES OF FINANCIAL STATEMENTS (Trueblood Committee Report)	AICPA	1973
FASB Discussion Memorandum: An Analysis of Issues Related to CONCEPTUAL FRAMEWORK FOR FINANCIAL ACCOUNTING AND REPORTING: ELEMENTS OF FINANCIAL STATEMENTS AND THEIR MEASUREMENT (Conceptual Framework)	FASB	1976
STATEMENT OF ACCOUNTING THEORY AND THEORY ACCEPTANCE (SATTA)	AAA	1977

Statements of Financial Accounting Concepts:

Title	Published By	Year
No. 1 OBJECTIVES OF FINANCIAL REPORTING BY BUSINESS ENTERPRISES (SFAC 1)	FASB	1978
No. 2 QUALITATIVE CHARACTERISTICS OF ACCOUNTING INFORMATION (SFAC 2)	FASB	1980
No. 3 ELEMENTS OF FINANCIAL STATEMENTS OF BUSINESS ENTERPRISES (SFAC 3)	FASB	1980
No. 4 OBJECTIVES OF FINANCIAL REPORTING BY NONBUSINESS ORGANIZATIONS (SFAC 4)	FASB	1980
No. 5 RECOGNITION AND MEASUREMENT IN FINANCIAL STATEMENTS OF BUSINESS ENTERPRISES (SFAC 5)	FASB	1984
No. 6 ELEMENTS OF FINANCIAL STATEMENTS (a replacement of FASB Concepts Statement No. 3 also incorporating an amendment of FASB Concepts Statement No. 2)	FASB	1985

A general criticism that can be, and has been, leveled at all these works is that they have not broken any new ground. Although largely true, this is not the appropriate issue. New research findings and totally new deductive proposals generally do not come from committee reports and similar documents. Instead, the reports evaluate current positions in either practice or research or a combination of the two. Therefore, the important question is what positions have been adopted or what is the general outlook of the work. From this standpoint, these reports are highly significant. Major financial accounting change is an evolutionary process that will continue to unfold indefinitely. The reports covered here have played and could continue to play an important role in financial accounting research and rule making.

Two short appendices conclude this chapter. One concerns user objectives and the other discusses, by group, who the various users of corporate financial reports are. The appendices relate very closely to the works reviewed and analyzed in the main body of the chapter.

ASOBAT

ASOBAT represented an important change in the work of the AAA. It made a relatively sharp break from the four previous statements and numerous supplements published between 1936 and 1964. The latter were both descriptive and normative in nature, stating general rules or approaches to recording transactions and to presenting financial statements. But the Executive Committee of the AAA in 1964 diverged from the previous approach by giving the committee a charge of developing

> ... an integrated statement of basic accounting theory which will serve as a guide to educators, practitioners, and others interested in accounting. . . . The committee may want to consider . . . the role, nature, and limitations of accounting.[3]

THE DEVELOPMENT OF THE USER APPROACH

The committee's definition of accounting represented a fundamental departure from the past. ASOBAT defined accounting as ". . . the process of identifying, measuring and communicating economic information to *permit informed judgments and decisions by users of the information* (emphasis added)."[4] Perhaps the most widely disseminated previous definition was developed in 1941 and was used in *Accounting Terminology Bulletin No. 1* of 1953, which stated:

> Accounting is the art of recording, classifying, and summarizing in a significant manner and in terms of money, transactions and events which are in part at least of a financial character, and interpreting the results thereof.[5]

The emphasis is on the work and skill of the accountant, with virtually no mention of the user. In further elaborating on the definition and work of the accountant, the *Terminology Bulletin* stated:

> ... it is more important to emphasize the creative skill and ability with which the accountant applies his knowledge to a given problem. . . . The complexities of modern business have brought to management some problems which only accounting can solve, and on which accounting throws necessary and helpful light.[6]

Hence, the accountant is the "grey eminence" who alone is responsible for bringing some semblance of order out of the chaotic affairs of business, and it is up to users to accommodate themselves to this highly skilled practitioner. From the sociological viewpoint, the definition and discussion in the bulletin strongly

---

[3] AAA (1966, p. v).
[4] Ibid., p. 1.
[5] AICPA (1953, para. 9).
[6] Ibid., paras. 11 and 13.

appear to be fortifying the perception of the accountant as a learned professional whose presentation must be accepted by those who do not have his qualifications and credentials.

Emphasis on users and their needs first appears in the literature in the 1950s, an amazingly recent time in light of the long history of accounting.[7]

ORIENTATION TO THEORY

The committee defined theory as ". . . a cohesive set of hypothetical, conceptual and pragmatic principles forming a general frame of reference for a field of study."[8] In applying the definition, it sought to carry out the following tasks:

1. To identify the field of accounting so that useful generalizations about it could be made and a theory developed.
2. To establish standards by which accounting information might be judged.
3. To point out possible improvements in accounting practice.
4. To present a useful framework for accounting researchers seeking to extend the uses of accounting and the scope of accounting subject matter as needs of society expand.[9]

Notice that ASOBAT's definition of theory is a subset of the definition presented in Chapter 1. Our definition is broader because it not only encompasses the ideas expressed above but also applies to valuation systems as well as empirical work in financial accounting.

The ASOBAT definition specifically focused on setting up a framework for evaluating systematic approaches to recording transactions and the presentation of financial statements geared to users. The concern — with the conceptual apparatus for evaluating specific accounting models and rules — is therefore with a **metatheory** of accounting, the topmost part of the theoretical structure for the purposes and goals of accounting information. A metatheory would also be concerned with certain restrictions on published accounting information as well as with delineating criteria or guidelines for selecting among alternatives.

OBJECTIVES OF ACCOUNTING

Since accounting is concerned with user needs, a set of objectives relating to user needs stands at the apex of the metatheory. Below these objectives would be a set of definitions, qualitative characteristics, and supporting guidelines that would facilitate the implementation of the objectives. Despite the importance of objectives, however, ASOBAT covered them rather briefly. Therefore, it appears that ASOBAT assumed that the evaluative framework of standards and guidelines could be largely independent of the objectives themselves.

---

[7] AAA (1977b, p. 10).
[8] AAA (1966, p. 1).
[9] Ibid.

Despite the short shrift given to objectives by ASOBAT, we should discuss them briefly here. The four objectives are these:

1. To make decisions concerning the use of limited resources (including the identification of crucial decision areas) and to determine objectives and goals.
2. To direct and control an organization's human and material resources effectively.
3. To maintain and report on the custodianship of resources.
4. To facilitate social functions and controls.[10]

Making Decisions Concerning Limited Resources

Decision making involves an evaluation of what is expected to happen in the future. These assessments can be done in an informal manner or can involve extremely complex calculations. The discounted cash flow model used in capital budgeting analysis as a means of selecting among competing capital projects is an example of the complex approach. Payback and nondiscounted cash flow methods are simpler — and, presumably, less effective — tools for appraising the likely future. Whether extremely crude or highly complex and refined, the methods used for assessing what will happen in the future are called *decision models*. The capacity to provide information that is useful in the decision-making process pertaining to the future is called *predictive ability*. In the user-oriented approach, the most important objective of accounting is to provide information useful for making decisions.

If all decision makers required the same information, the accounting theory problem would be less difficult. Unfortunately, as ASOBAT recognized, users of accounting reports come from several different groups — creditors, investors, customers and suppliers, governmental agencies, and employees — with widely diverging backgrounds and abilities. Whether user diversity leads to heterogeneous information needs in the different user groups has become absolutely crucial to the future development of accounting (a question that had not fully emerged when ASOBAT was written).

Predictive ability is discussed in ASOBAT in terms of gauging future earnings, financial position, and debt-paying ability. It made an important, though brief, point that accounting reports do not make predictions; rather, users must make predictions, employing inputs from accounting reports as data in their decision models.

Directing and Controlling Resources

This objective is directed toward managerial uses of accounting data. ASOBAT saw managerial needs as different from those of external users but subject to the same four standards of reporting (to be discussed shortly), although the standards themselves may be applied differently. Managerial needs and uses of ac-

---

[10] Ibid., p. 4.

counting data are beyond the scope of this text so we will not be concerned with this objective. However, we should mention that some individuals do not perceive any differences between internal (managerial) and external (financial) uses of accounting data.[11]

Maintaining Custodianship of Resources

The third objective is commonly called *stewardship*. A proper accounting for the use by one party (management) of funds that have been entrusted to it by another party (stockholders) is a relationship extending, in one guise or another, back to the Middle Ages. In modern times, this objective has broadened under conditions of absentee ownership and easy acquisition and disposition of ownership shares through the medium of securities exchanges. The stewardship association has led to the agency theory view of the firm discussed in Chapters 2 and 4.

Facilitating Social Functions and Controls

The last objective appears to be an extension of the stewardship function to society as a whole. Thus accounting is concerned with such areas as taxation, fraud prevention, governmental regulation, and collection of statistics for purposes of measuring economic activity. An issue not addressed by ASOBAT concerns who should bear the costs of producing this additional data.

Though objectives stand at the summit of a metatheory, it is clear that they were not the main concern of ASOBAT. Subsequent reports, however, began to address this topic.

STANDARDS FOR ACCOUNTING INFORMATION

Four standards for evaluating accounting — relevance, verifiability, freedom from bias, and quantifiability — are at the heart of ASOBAT. These standards, the subsequent guidelines for communicating accounting information, and the objectives could be viewed as part of a metatheory of accounting. Like other parts of ASOBAT, the standards appear to be aimed at evaluating published financial statement information. However, they could also be used by a policy-making body to assess proposed rules.

Relevance

Relevance pertains to usefulness in making the decision at hand. It arises directly from the four objectives for various types of information; hence, it is the primary standard. Since there are different user groups with different backgrounds making decisions in different contexts, relevance can be thought of as the major issue of accounting. Further defining relevance, however, was beyond the scope of ASOBAT, save for a few simple and obvious examples.

---

[11] Borst (1981), for example.

Verifiability

Verifiability is synonymous with objectivity as it is defined in Chapter 1. It is thus an aspect of measurement. Chapter 1 stated that it is important to separate theoretical concepts from measurement issues because they involve different domains. The selection of valuation systems in their totality, as well as individual rules for subsets of the systems, should be primarily based on questions of relevance. However, aspects of measurement must also be considered because valuation systems and methods that have a low consensus (in terms of agreement among measurers) might have to be bypassed in favor of approaches that are less desirable from the standpoint of usefulness.

Hence, the selection of methods should not be based on relevance alone without considering verifiability, nor should verifiability take precedence over relevance. Therefore, standards of measurement are a necessary part of the metatheoretical framework. A last point to reiterate here is that *verifiability* appears to have supplanted *objectivity* as the appropriate term for describing the degree of statistical consensus among measurers.

Freedom from Bias

This standard is necessary because of the problem of user heterogeneity as well as the potentially adversarial relationship between management (which, of course, is responsible for statement presentation) and external users. Biases, of course, may be subtle or flagrant and may be extremely difficult to resolve equitably. Suppose, for example, that in the interests of relevance and disclosure, a firm were required to quantify in financial statements or the notes thereto amounts of expected judgments against it in legal cases. An enterprise's own best interests — minimizing legal damages — would conflict with standards of relevance and disclosure because the court's judgment could be influenced by the firm's supposed admission of guilt in financial statements.

Freedom from bias is complementary to the qualitative characteristic of neutrality of SFAC 2, which will be discussed shortly. Neutrality refers to the orientation of standard-setting agencies, whereas freedom from bias is concerned with the preparation of financial statements.

Quantifiability

Quantifiability appears to be very closely related to measurement theory. But while measurement and quantification are both important to the metatheoretical structure, ASOBAT appears, if anything, to have gone too far in emphasizing quantifiability: ". . . it can be said that the primary, if not the total concern of accountants, is with quantification and quantified data."[12] The recent push toward disclosure, emanating largely from the efficient-markets-hypothesis literature, goes beyond mere quantification. One minor problem with a standard that refers largely to the general area of measurement is that since verifiability

---

[12] AAA (1966, p. 12).

is an aspect of measurement theory, verifiability appears to be a subset of quantifiability.

An important point is brought up by ASOBAT in its questioning of why accounting should be restricted to single numbers in financial statements. ASOBAT suggests using ranges and also multiple valuation bases in "side-by-side" columnar arrangements. These possibilities are seen both as responses to the increased data and information needs of users and as possible solutions to the problem posed by heterogeneous user groups. In addition, they might be a means for resolving the overriding problem of choice among accounting methods faced by a rule-making body. Providing more information, known as **data expansion,** could lead, however, to **information overload** on the part of users.[13] Any attempt to circumvent the problem of choice among valuation systems or methods by simply providing more data is subject to the information-processing constraints of users, a point not discussed in ASOBAT.

GUIDELINES FOR COMMUNICATING ACCOUNTING INFORMATION

In addition to the four standards, ASOBAT presents five guidelines for the communication of accounting information:

1. Appropriateness to expected use.
2. Disclosure of significant relationships.
3. Inclusion of environmental information.
4. Uniformity of practice within and among entities.
5. Consistency of practices through time.[14]

The report itself notes that there is overlap between standards and guidelines although it concedes the latter are less fundamental.

Appropriateness to Expected Use
The first guideline basically reiterates the relevance standard although it also mentions timeliness of presentation.

Disclosure of Significant Relationships
Despite its title, this guideline deals with only one aspect of the broad problem of disclosure discussed in Chapter 5. Its concern is with the problem of aggregation of data in which important information may be buried or hidden in the summarizing figures in financial reports. Statement of Financial Accounting

---

[13] Within a given time frame in a "complex environment," such as that provided by financial information, an individual reaches a point where additional information cannot be processed or absorbed. See Revsine (1970b) and Miller (1972). However, disclosure (providing additional information) is seen as important to resolving reporting problems because the market uses a broad informational set. See, for example, AAA (1977a, pp. 20–21). Additional research is needed in terms of both individual abilities to process accounting information and the "black box" effect when going from individuals to the aggregated level of the market.

[14] AAA (1966, p. 7).

Standards (SFAS) 14 on segmental disclosure is one statement that has dealt with this problem.

Inclusion of Environmental Information
As used here, *environmental information* refers to the very broad category of conditions under which data were collected and the preparer's assumptions relative to the uses of the information, particularly if the information is intended for specific rather than general purposes. More detail may well be appropriate where information will be applied to specific uses intended.

Uniformity of Practices Within and Among Entities and Consistency of Practices Through Time
The last two guidelines refer directly to uniformity and consistency as discussed in Chapter 5. ASOBAT desired the type of uniformity that appears to correspond to finite uniformity as that term was previously defined. Finite uniformity cannot be achieved merely by setting it up as a guideline or even a standard. There must be sufficient detail in the theoretical structure, a topic to be further probed in Chapter 8.

CONCLUDING REMARKS ON ASOBAT

ASOBAT can be criticized on numerous grounds. Certainly its guidelines were far too brief to cover the topics adequately. The metatheoretical structure could have been extended and used more appropriate terminology. However, these are carping criticisms. ASOBAT has had an important and beneficial influence on succeeding documents and reports, as will become evident in the remainder of this chapter.

APB STATEMENT 4

APB Statement 4 is a curious document because it was conceived when the rule-making bodies were in transition between theoretical orientations. It appeared when the postulates and principles approach had run its course and objectives and standards were emerging. The statement was published in October, 1970, exactly a half year prior to the formation of the Wheat and Trueblood committees. At that time, the APB was under heavy fire for Opinions 16 and 17 on business combinations and goodwill in addition to broader criticisms, such as inadequacy of research, lack of independence of its members, and lack of sufficient exposure of its work prior to final publication.

The purpose of Statement 4 was to state fundamental concepts of financial reporting to serve as a foundation for the opinions of the APB. This charge from the Special Committee on Opinions of the APB in May, 1965, came at a time when it certainly seemed that the APB would continue indefinitely despite problems that had already begun to surface. Moonitz felt that the report should have been issued as an opinion rather than as a statement — since departures from "generally accepted accounting principles" made in a statement need not be disclosed.[15] Should, however, a theoretical structure — the intended charge to the drafters of the statement — be forced by fiat? Acceptance of a theory cannot be easily mandated, as we will see later in this chapter.

ORIENTATION TO DEFINITIONS

Definition of Accounting

APB Statement 4 started by defining accounting along the newer, user-oriented track that ASOBAT took:

> Accounting is a service activity. Its function is to provide quantitative information, primarily financial in nature, about economic entities that is *intended to be useful in making economic decisions* (emphasis added).[16]

The statement also adopted ASOBAT's very strong emphasis on the diversity of users. Users of financial information are classified into two groups: those with direct interests in the enterprise and those with indirect interests. APB 4 went further than ASOBAT — which had been silent on this issue — by stating that users of financial statements should be knowledgeable and should understand the characteristics and limitations of financial statements. Finally, and in agreement with ASOBAT, it viewed financial statements as being general purpose in nature as opposed to oriented toward a limited group of users.

Other Definitions

Despite its promising start, APB Statement 4 often reverted to useless definitions. It defined assets, liabilities, owners' equity, revenues, and expenses as the "basic elements of financial accounting." All these definitions (save owners' equity, which is a residual) state that they are ". . . recognized and measured in conformity with generally accepted accounting principles."[17] However, the statement is later made that ". . . generally accepted accounting principles incorporate the consensus at a particular time as to which economic resources and obligations should be recorded as assets and liabilities. . . ."[18] Hence, basic accounting terminology was once again defined by whatever was being done in practice. Furthermore, since the document was a statement rather than an opinion and thus carried less enforcement status, the decision not to take a stronger prescriptive position in terms of basic definitions was doubly disappointing.

OTHER ASPECTS OF APB STATEMENT 4

Despite the shortcomings, there are many good aspects of this document, which indicate that its drafters were cognizant of ASOBAT as well as of recent research developments. For example, the fact that accounting is a measurement

---

[15] Moonitz (1971).
[16] APB (1970, para. 9).
[17] Ibid., paras. 132 and 134.
[18] Ibid., para. 137.

discipline is noted in paragraph 67. The section on objectives is obviously heavily grounded in the work of ASOBAT. The standards and guidelines of that report have been combined and largely overlap with the "qualitative objectives" of APB Statement 4. Furthermore, while APB Statement 4 agrees with ASOBAT on the need for finite uniformity, it acknowledges the difficulty of meeting that objective. Finally, APB Statement 4 concurs with ASOBAT on possible conflict among objectives (such as relevance and verifiability) and that the conflict is a very knotty problem which should be resolved in the metatheoretical framework. On the other hand, the statement recognizes the factor of timeliness, which received scant mention in ASOBAT.

Other aspects of APB Statement 4 are less innovative. The "basic features" of financial accounting are largely a rehash of some of the postulates from ARS 1. The pervasive principles and modifying conventions in the section on generally accepted accounting principles consist of those concepts that constitute the heart of the presently ill-defined system of historical costing. The remaining sections of the report, which include statements of the principles of selection and measurement and financial statement presentation, likewise present virtually no theoretical innovation.

CONCLUDING REMARKS ON APB STATEMENT NO. 4

Large parts of APB Statement 4 are restatements of the conventional wisdom of the time, whereas other parts recognize that important evolutionary changes had begun to occur.[19] The conventional wisdom is stated relatively concisely and completely. In fact, the document was often quoted by public accounting firms in papers outlining their positions on various proposals. But the many parts of the document do not tie together as a whole. For example, it is extremely questionable whether the objectives, which largely stem from ASOBAT, can be implemented by means of the various principles derived from the existing body of accounting. This problem is further compounded by the loosely — if not circularly — worded set of definitions. Hence, the document is, to a large extent, justly accused of being all things to all people. Nevertheless, considering its positive aspects as well as the fact that the APB was under heavy fire during the document's drafting, it has served a useful purpose.

THE TRUEBLOOD REPORT

The AICPA formed the Trueblood Committee in April, 1971, at a time when the APB was under heavy criticism but also at a point when some degree of quiet progress was being made in terms of reformulating the structure of accounting theory. The committee was charged with using APB Statement 4 as a

---

[19] Critiques of APB Statement 4 recognized the dual nature of the document. See Ijiri (1971), Schattke (1972), and Staubus (1972).

vehicle for refining the objectives of financial statements as a part of a meta-theoretical structure.

The committee enumerated a total of twelve objectives of financial accounting:

1. The basic objective of financial statements is to provide information useful for making economic decisions.

2. An objective of financial statements is to serve primarily those users who have limited authority, ability, or resources to obtain information and who rely on financial statements as their principal source of information about an enterprise's economic activities.

3. An objective of financial statements is to provide information useful to investors and creditors for predicting, comparing, and evaluating potential cash flows to them in terms of amount, timing, and related uncertainty.

4. An objective of financial statements is to provide users with information for predicting, comparing, and evaluating enterprise earning power.

5. An objective of financial statements is to supply information useful in judging management's ability to utilize enterprise resources effectively in achieving the primary enterprise goal.

6. An objective of financial statements is to provide factual and interpretive information about transactions and other events which is useful for predicting, comparing, and evaluating enterprise earning power. Basic underlying assumptions with respect to matters subject to interpretation, evaluation, prediction, or estimation should be disclosed.

7. An objective is to provide a statement of financial position, useful for predicting, comparing, and evaluating enterprise earning power. This statement should provide information concerning enterprise transactions and other events that are part of incomplete earning cycles. Current values should also be reported when they differ significantly from historical costs. Assets and liabilities should be grouped or segregated by the relative uncertainty of the amount and timing of prospective realization or liquidation.

8. An objective is to provide a statement of periodic earnings useful for predicting, comparing, and evaluating enterprise earning power. The net result of completed earnings cycles and enterprise activities resulting in recognizable progress toward completion of incomplete cycles should be reported. Changes in the values reflected in successive statements of financial position should be reported, but separately, since they differ in terms of their certainty of realization.

9. Another objective is to provide a statement of financial activities useful for predicting, comparing, and evaluating enterprise earning power. This statement should report mainly on factual aspects of enterprise transactions having or expected to have significant cash consequences. This statement should report data that require minimal judgment and interpretation by the preparer.

10. An objective of financial statements is to provide information useful for the predictive process. Financial forecasts should be provided when they will enhance the reliability of users' predictions.

11. An objective of financial statements for governmental and not-for-profit organizations is to provide information useful for evaluating the effectiveness of the management of resources in achieving the organization's goals. Performance measures should be quantified in terms of identified goals.

EXHIBIT 6–1
Hierarchy of Objectives

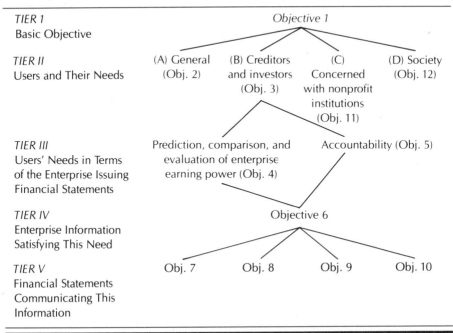

| TIER 1
Basic Objective | *Objective 1* |

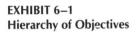

Source: Sorter and Gans (1974), p. 4.

12. An objective of financial statements is to report on those activities of the enterprise that affect society which can be determined and described or measured and which are important to the role of the enterprise in its social environment.[20]

The committee did not indicate a structural order for these objectives, but a study by Anton and another by Sorter and Gans arranged them in a hierarchical framework.[21] Sorter and Gans, it should be noted, were the research director and the administrative director, respectively, of the Staff for the Study Group. Exhibit 6–1 shows the arrangement of Sorter and Gans. The Anton structuring agreed with Sorter and Gans on most major points.

OBJECTIVES OF FINANCIAL STATEMENTS
Objective 1
The topmost objective agrees with the emphasis on the user of both ASOBAT and APB Statement 4. Objective 1 overlaps with the standard of relevance and the guideline of appropriateness to expected use of ASOBAT and the general objectives of APB Statement 4. This objective is not an operational one; rather,

---

[20] AICPA (1973).
[21] Sorter and Gans (1974, p. 4) and Anton (1976, pp. 4 and 5).

it is a very broad statement of a goal or direction for the standard-setting process.

Objective 2

The second objective describes the primary users being served by financial statements. By zeroing in on users with "limited authority, ability, or resources," the Trueblood Committee diverged from its two predecessors. In terms of ability, ASOBAT had nothing to say. To the extent the matter was discussed in APB Statement 4, users were expected to be knowledgeable about financial statements and information. Opting to serve users with limitations may seem an unusual choice in light of the efficient-markets hypothesis — since that body of research states that naive investors are not penalized in an efficient market setting as long as they are properly diversified. However, Sorter and Gans made a curious disclaimer on this point:

> This objective may be the most misunderstood of all objectives. Although it may be interpreted to mean that financial statements should serve those with "limited ability," that was not the study group's intention. . . . Financial statements should not serve special or narrow needs of specific users but rather should serve the general needs of all users. Among the implications of this objective are: 1) that financial statements . . . should provide full disclosure; and 2) that all information should be presented as *simply* as the subject matter allows (emphasis supplied).[22]

"Limited ability," then, may simply be code for full disclosure and broad, general-purpose financial statements. Furthermore, the discussion of the primary user group in the Trueblood Report reveals an extremely important value judgment: while user groups may differ, their economic decisions are essentially similar. This, in turn, leads deductively to the idea that the various user groups have similar information needs and, hence, the justification for general-purpose financial statements with disclosure, as noted in the Sorter and Gans quotation above.

Objective 3

The third objective is on the importance of cash flows. The users mentioned for whom this information is necessary are lenders and investors. Although lenders and investors may well be the most important user groups, it is not totally clear why it was necessary to single them out in light of the committee's value judgment that user decisions and information needs are largely homogeneous. Since the cash flows discussed are future (potential) in nature, they are not susceptible to direct measurement.

Objective 4

Earning power (income), important in its own right, is seen as one of the extremely useful measures for helping to predict, compare, and evaluate cash flow potential. Over the long run, cash flow and earnings have a high correlation.

---

[22] Sorter and Gans (1974, p. 6).

During the short run, earnings may actually be a better predictor of cash-generating potential than cash flows themselves because much of the latter may be either nonoperational or plowed back into the enterprise for the purpose of breeding future cash flows and earnings.

Objective 5

The word *accountability* was used both in the Trueblood Report itself and by Sorter and Gans (Exhibit 6–1) to summarize the fifth objective. It extends beyond the ancient concept of stewardship (which is limited to the functions of safekeeping of assets and insuring that they are used in accordance with investors' purposes).[23] Here, accountability also includes the ideas of effectively and efficiently utilizing assets in order to carry out the enterprise objective of maximizing future cash flows consistent with a given level of risk. As such, accountability and the word *evaluating* used in Objectives 3 and 4 appear to overlap significantly.

Objective 6

The key words in the sixth objective are *factual* and *interpretive*. The difference between these two qualities is connected to the concept of the various enterprise cycles. Cycles can be either broad or narrow. The acquisition, usage, and disposition of a fixed asset would be an example of a broad cycle. The broadest of all cycles would comprise the beginning and end of the enterprise itself. A fairly narrow cycle would be cash to inventory to accounts receivable to cash. From the standpoint of cycles, the broader the cycle is, the more interpretive and the less factual the accounting information is liable to be. For a broad cycle such as acquisition, usage, and disposition of fixed assets, current values of fixed assets may be indicative of progress toward completion of the cycle, although these values may be subject to a great deal of uncertainty.

Generally speaking, the cash flow statement probably provides more factual and less interpretive information than the income statement, which, in turn, has more factual and less interpretive information than the balance sheet. In drawing the distinction between factual and interpretive information, Objective 6 provides the rationale for presenting different types and qualities of information to users.

Objectives 7, 8, and 9

Objectives 7, 8, and 9 call for a balance sheet, an earnings (income) statement, and a funds flow type of statement that will be useful for prediction, comparison, and evaluation of enterprise earning power — without prescribing the format of these statements.

In the statement of financial position (balance sheet), current values are indicative of the present value of future cash flows as determined by the market;

---

[23] *Accountability* is used in a similar manner, extending well beyond the bounds of stewardship, by Ijiri (1975, pp. ix and 10 and 32–35).

hence, these values are useful for predicting, comparing, and evaluating enterprise earning power.[24] Except for cash and, to a slightly lesser extent, accounts and notes receivable, the great majority of assets held represent the results of incomplete cycles. Hence, current valuation, as opposed to historical cost, is a means of presenting interpretive information where incomplete cycles exist. This does not necessarily mean, however, that all historical cost information is factual.

Earnings statements could largely be restricted to a completed earnings cycle basis by eliminating from them expense measurements pertaining to long-lived assets consumed during the period. However, statements of this type would not be as useful as a more complete model in terms of predicting, comparing, and evaluating enterprise earning power. This objective might be further abetted by using current value measurements of expired assets rather than historical cost approaches. The committee itself was divided on the question of whether the earnings figure should include valuation changes relative to unexpired assets. The report appears to call for a multistep income statement where separate amounts are shown for earnings components having different degrees of certainty relative to the factual basis (completion of cycle) of the figures involved.

The statement of financial activities would supplement the other two statements because there would be much less uncertainty about the information presented. The statement could concentrate on highly probable effects on changes in cash (such as revenues and purchases) rather than "narrower" — but even more probable — figures such as cash receipts and cash disbursements. The statement would also show acquisitions and dispositions of fixed assets, changes in long-term debt, and contributions and distributions of capital. In addition, information not shown elsewhere, such as purchase commitments and sales backlog differentials, could also be shown here. All these components would be factual in nature even though some of them (fixed-asset acquisitions, for example) pertain to incomplete cycles.

Objective 10

Financial forecasts are, of course, totally interpretive in nature. As a result, they may be unduly influenced by excessive optimism or pessimism. Furthermore, public accounting firms do not show any great enthusiasm for auditing forecasts. At the present time, the SEC encourages — but by no means requires — firms to make them.[25] Their potential usefulness for predicting, comparing, and evaluating enterprise earning power should be readily apparent.

---

[24] Revsine (1970a) shows that current value income using replacement costs is an indirect measurement of "economic income" (the discounted cash flow approach illustrated in Chapter 1) under conditions of perfect competition. However, replacement cost income is a "mere approximation" of economic income under real-world conditions of imperfect competition. For additional coverage, see Barton (1974).

[25] Rule 175 of the SEC issued in 1979 provides "safe harbors" from liability provisions of the federal securities laws where forecasts are made.

Objectives 11 and 12

Both of these objectives are beyond the general scope of this text so they will not be discussed here. However, accounting for governmental and not-for-profit organizations is an important area — the costs to society that are not borne by business is a fascinating topic. There are many activities carried on by business that are not reported on financial statements.

CONCLUDING REMARKS ON THE TRUEBLOOD COMMITTEE REPORT

The Trueblood Report also contains a short chapter on "qualitative characteristics of reporting" based largely on the standards and guidelines of ASOBAT and the qualitative objectives of APB Statement 4. In addition, there is a brief but useful chapter on the various valuation systems of accounting. The report expresses the belief that different valuation bases are appropriate for different assets and liabilities, a view that ignores the additivity argument.

But it is on its definition of the objectives of financial statements that the report must be evaluated. Critics have pointed out that the objectives are obvious and do not specify operational objectives that could be put into practice.[26] The criticism is true but largely irrelevant. These objectives represented an important step taken toward establishing a meaningful conceptual framework of objectives.

Finally, it is important to reiterate that the Trueblood Report emphasizes the importance of cash flows to users and the relation of earning-power measurements to the generation of future cash flows. The earning-power orientation to income is grounded in the notion that economic income is the change in the present value of future cash flows discounted at an appropriate rate (the discounted cash flow approach was illustrated in Chapter 1).

SATTA

SATTA was commissioned by the Executive Committee of the AAA in 1973. Its overall purpose, similar to that of ASOBAT a decade earlier, was to provide a survey of the current financial accounting literature and a statement of where the profession stood relative to accounting theory. The report accomplished its objectives admirably. However, the results may not be pleasing to accounting theorists and policy makers.

In order to more fully comprehend SATTA, it is necessary to understand its relationship to ASOBAT. Both documents, of course, are products of AAA committees having similarly broad guidelines. ASOBAT attempted to develop metatheoretical guidelines for the evaluation of accounting information and valuation systems. SATTA, on the other hand, took into account the many val-

---

[26]Miller (1974, p. 18).

uation systems of accounting as well as other theoretical considerations and enumerated the reasons why it was impossible to develop criteria that would enable the profession to unequivocally accept a single valuation system for accounting. In effect, then, SATTA is a very cautionary document in terms of the possibility for adopting any one valuation theory.

THEORY APPROACHES IN ACCOUNTING

Classical Approaches

SATTA concisely and efficiently traced and categorized the various valuation systems presented in the literature. Older systems were classified as "classical approaches to theory development."[27] Most of the listings in this group were characterized as primarily normative and deductive and as indifferent to the decision needs of users even though the developers of the models rationalized that their models were superior for user needs to competing alternatives. In some cases, classical writers used what SATTA called an inductive approach, but "inductive" in a rather special sense — a gleaning from the accounting literature itself as well as from observations of practice — instead of the usual sense of a systematic review and analysis of practice.

Decision-Usefulness Approach

Among the contemporary approaches to accounting theory is the large body of research that has concentrated on users of accounting reports, their decisions, information needs, and information-processing abilities. The decision-usefulness approach has been further dichotomized into **decision models** and **decision makers.**

Decision-Model Orientation   The metatheoretical frameworks (or parts thereof) developed in ASOBAT and the Trueblood Report reflect the decision-model orientation. The systems that fall into this category all share the following characteristics: (1) they are normative and deductive since the theoretical system must meet, as closely as possible, criteria of a metatheoretical framework; (2) some form of relevance for particular decisions by a particular user group or groups is stressed; and (3) the relevance criterion is instrumental in measuring the selected attributes of assets, liabilities, and income transactions.

Decision-model approaches often stem from formal investment decision models, such as discounted cash flow.[28] Since decision-model approaches are deemed appropriate for communicating extremely relevant information for de-

---

[27] Older approaches covered the years from 1922 to 1962 — with the single exception of a work by Ijiri in 1975, which was a defense of historical cost accounting based on the importance of accountability. Many of the items listed, however, were current valuation methods.

[28] A good example would be AAA (1969), which used a present value model of gains or losses on long-term debt and equity investments in order to evaluate elements used in financial reports. We should also note that Peasnall has observed that the distinction between the classical and the decision-model approaches is largely artificial because both are normative and deductive. See Peasnall (1978), p. 222.

cision making, a rather unpleasant problem arises if users do not understand or prefer these systems. At least one individual has taken the position that users must be educated to understand the method, an argument consistent with the normative framework of the approach.[29] However, the task of normatively selecting a model and forcing it on users, particularly if they neither prefer nor understand it, is indeed extremely formidable.

Decision-Maker Orientation   The main point about the decision-maker orientation is that it is descriptive rather than normative because it attempts to find out what information is actually used or desired. The assumption is that the information that is desired should be supplied.[30] Hence, in addition to being descriptive, research that falls into the decision-maker category is also inductive (empirical). Much of the behavioral research mentioned in Chapter 2 falls into the decision-maker category.

Although many important "bits" of information have come from the rather extensive research conducted with this approach, no strong position has emerged for particular valuation methods (as will be seen in Chapter 13, current cost disclosures in Statement of Financial Accounting Standards No. 33 were not well understood by users). On the other hand, since the decision-model approach is normative, it has produced advocacy for particular valuation systems.

Information Economics Approach

Information economics as applied to accounting theory does not deal directly with alternative valuation systems. Instead, it is concerned with the issue of costs and benefits arising from information production and usage. Hence, accounting information is viewed as an economic good, an outlook that had not previously been considered in theory formulation. The approach and problems highlighted by information economics are covered in Chapter 7.

DEFICIENCIES OF PRESENT APPROACHES TO THEORY

The overriding message of SATTA relates to why we cannot achieve theory closure — acceptance of a particular valuation system — at this time. Our analysis of this aspect of SATTA will cover the most important issues raised (from the standpoint of accounting theory).

Perhaps the principal problem brought up by SATTA is the diversity of users in terms of their decisions and their possible different information needs. Both ASOBAT and APB Statement 4 recognized the fact that many user groups require information for decision-making purposes. One of ASOBAT's reactions

---

[29] Sterling (1967, p. 106).

[30] Unfortunately, the problem of determining user information preferences appears to be almost totally intractable. Abdel-khalik (1971) developed a stochastic model for measuring preference ordering of users but the model has never been implemented.

to this problem was to call for multiple measures. However, there are perceived limits to the ability of users to absorb and process additional information, so data expansion is not a cure-all.[31] The Trueblood Report, on the other hand, establishes rather early the premise that while there are different user groups, they make similar decisions and have similar information needs. Like ASOBAT, the Trueblood Report is concerned with providing a part of the metatheoretical framework for evaluating theoretical systems and methods from a normative viewpoint. The Trueblood Report is, thus, also closely related to the decision-model school.

SATTA was much more pessimistic than the Trueblood Report about decisions and information preferences both among and within user groups. Venn diagrams illustrate the differences between user homogeneity and user heterogeneity in information needs (see Exhibit 6–2). The circles represent user groups and their information needs. There is a large degree of overlap in the high user homogeneity part of the diagram and much less in the other part.

Heterogeneity of information preferences and needs compounds an already difficult situation. Corporate financial reports and disclosures are a free good. Users do not pay the preparer for the information received, and the information is available to virtually anyone who really desires it. Accounting information is, therefore, a public good rather than a private good. If it were a private good, the information required would be amenable to a market type of solution: it would be determined by supply and demand.

Given user heterogeneity and the public-good character of financial information, the formulation of accounting standards and prescribed methods nec-

EXHIBIT 6–2
Degrees of User Homogeneity of Information Needs

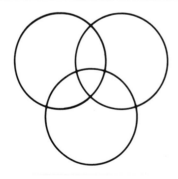

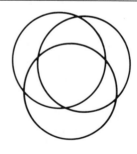

Low User Homogeneity   High User Homogeneity

---

[31] See footnote 13.

essarily reaches an impasse. Providing one set of accounting information rather than another means that one set of users is being favored to the detriment of other user groups. Moreover, different sets of accounting information lead to different security prices, which again means that some individuals are being favored at the expense of others. Furthermore, if a value judgment is adopted which states that a policy-setting organization should not take actions that make one group better off at the expense of another, then accounting policy formulation becomes totally straitjacketed. Hence, SATTA presented a very bleak prospect for theory closure.

SATTA attempted to describe the status of financial accounting theory as of the late 1970s. We do not wish to quarrel with SATTA's conclusion; nevertheless, a few remarks are in order. The assumption that user information needs are heterogeneous is far from proved. The assertions of both homogeneity and heterogeneity proponents are totally a priori in nature.[32] Empirical research is desperately needed to shed some light on this extremely important question. Miller has stated the case very well:

> Certainly I am in favor of on-going research to discover the needs of statement users. But I would not be surprised if users were to indicate that they expect accounting information questions to be resolved by the experts who know something about the merits and helpfulness of accounting measurements. So I believe it is reasonable to expect users to look to the accountant for guidance. This line of reasoning has led me to believe there is a risk that accountants may have been giving too much weight to the lack of (and the desire for) knowledge about users' needs.[33]

Strict adherence to Pareto-optimality is also open to question. In a situation of any social complexity, it will be virtually impossible for any policy-making organization to conform to the very rigid criteria of Pareto-optimality. Pareto himself, a well-known Italian economist, did not see his optimality approach as the sole decision rule.[34] Perhaps what is needed are judiciously applied constraints on policy-setting organizations to control their actions in order to attain the greatest good for the greatest number of individuals. Unquestionably, even this easing of the Paretian reins still leaves organizations such as FASB with a herculean task.

---

[32] Beaver and Demski (1974) lean toward user heterogeneity on an a priori basis. Dopuch and Sunder (1980) see potential heterogeneity among three groups: management, auditors, and users. In turn, the user group is itself heterogeneous. They see the heterogeneity among the three groups at three different levels: desired information in financial statements, desired accounting principles, and desired objectives. As a result they regard attempting to arrive at objectives as a futile exercise, and the FASB's task, therefore, as one of knowing how to mediate among competing interests.

[33] Miller (1974, pp. 19–20).

[34] There are two important points that should be borne in mind relative to Pareto-optimality. First, the status quo should not be treated as a unique Pareto-optimum situation. There are many possible Pareto-optimum situations where change in social rules cannot be made without adversely affecting some parties. Second, Pareto himself did not see his optimality approach as the sole decision rule. Ethics and cost-benefit analysis, for example, could also be used for judging social change. For further coverage see Samuels (1974, pp. 200–206).

CONCLUDING REMARKS ON SATTA

SATTA was a remarkable synthesis of the theoretical financial accounting literature. The jury is still out on the question of heterogeneity of information needs and the application of Pareto-optimality, but it is difficult to argue with SATTA's conclusion. We cannot expect accounting theorists to develop a theoretical framework that will be universally satisfactory. In turn, we can expect the statements and pronouncements of a rule-making group, such as the FASB, which are propounded in an incomplete market setting, to be met with less than full enthusiasm. Hence, a paradoxical situation arose. An important document authored by a distinguished group of academicians took a very pessimistic view of the role and possibilities of accounting theory formulation at exactly the same time that a conceptual framework — a theoretical document — was begun by a rule-making body. We look next at that conceptual framework.

THE CONCEPTUAL FRAMEWORK PROJECT

The Conceptual Framework Project is supposed to embody ". . . a coherent system of interrelated objectives and fundamentals that can lead to consistent standards and that prescribes the nature, function, and limits of financial accounting and financial statements."[35] The Conceptual Framework Project is, then, an attempt to provide a metatheoretical structure for financial accounting. The project, which now appears to be complete, includes six statements of financial accounting concepts (SFACs). It was kicked off by an important discussion memorandum.

DISCUSSION MEMORANDUM

A discussion memorandum is, of course, not the end product of the FASB's deliberations. However, the discussion memorandum for the Conceptual Framework Project was a massive study, perhaps the most extensive ever published by the FASB. In addition, it was widely disseminated and publicized. The discussion memorandum was accompanied by another document pertaining to tentative conclusions of the Trueblood Report on objectives.[36] This latter report accepted the Trueblood Report's user orientation and stress on cash flows but added little more of substance.

The discussion memorandum brought up two new basic issues: (1) three views of financial accounting and financial statements (discussed in Chapter 9) and (2) an outline of the various approaches to capital maintenance. The former might be termed orientations to the financial statements. In both cases, the memorandum attempted to show the various alternatives and possibilities open for adoption, without taking any firm position, in order to elicit responses from

---

[35] FASB (1976b, p. 2).
[36] See FASB (1976a), and FASB (1976c).

the profession. In addition, it presented various definitions for such basic terms as *assets, liabilities, revenues, expenses, gains,* and *losses* — along with a discussion of qualitative characteristics of financial statements (these will be considered in our discussion of SFAC 2).

The most important new issue brought up in the document was capital maintenance. Chapter 2 noted that this concept is concerned with how earnings are measured in terms of maintaining intact the firm's capital (assets minus liabilities) existing at the beginning of the period. This is a problem of overriding importance that should be given a very prominent place in the normative objectives of a metatheoretical structure. It was not considered extensively, if at all, in any of the other documents considered in this chapter. Capital maintenance will be extensively discussed in Chapter 12.

STATEMENTS OF FINANCIAL ACCOUNTING CONCEPTS

The SFACs constitute the finished portion of the Conceptual Framework Project. These statements are analogous to APB Statement 4 in one respect: like that document, these statements do not establish "generally accepted accounting principles" and are not intended to invoke Rule 203 of the Rules of Conduct of the AICPA (which prohibits departures from generally accepted accounting principles). This weakness may be disappointing, but nonetheless provides some important benefits. First of all, the possibility of a crisis arising from a failure to comply with the statements is avoided. Second, the process of arriving at a workable and utilitarian metatheoretical-type structure must be acknowledged as a slow, evolutionary process. Trial and error should certainly be expected, and the tentative nature of the statements may make it easier to change components as the need arises. Unfortunately, the possibility also exists that these statements will have only a purely cosmetic effect.

STATEMENT NO. 1

SFAC 1 is concerned with the objectives of business financial reporting. As such, it is a direct descendant of the Trueblood Report and is generally a boiled-down version of that report, with some necessary value judgments as well as some redundant statements scattered throughout. SFAC 1 continues the user orientation of the other documents reviewed here. Although it acknowledges the heterogeneity of external user groups, it states that a common core characteristic of all outside users is their interest in the prediction of the amounts, timing, and uncertainties of future cash flows. Hence, SFAC 1 maintains that financial statements must be general purpose in nature rather than geared toward specific needs of a particular user group although investors, creditors, and their advisers are singled out among external users.[37] The report also takes the position that users of financial statements must be assumed to be knowledgeable about financial information and reporting, an apparent departure from the

---

[37] FASB (1980, p. 14).

Trueblood Report's statement assuming "limited ability" of users. (We have already noted the potential qualification of the literal meaning of that phrase.)

The statement also notes the importance of stewardship in terms of assessing how well management has discharged its duties and obligations to owners and other interested groups. The notion of stewardship goes beyond the narrow interpretation of proper custodianship of the firm's resources.

Several important value judgments are made throughout the report:

1. Information is not costless to provide, so benefits of usage should exceed costs of production.
2. Accounting reports are by no means the only source of information about enterprises.
3. Accrual accounting is extremely useful in assessing and predicting earning power and cash flows of an enterprise.
4. The information provided should be helpful, but users make their own predictions and assessments.

Finally, the document does not specify what statements should be used, much less their format. Hence, SFAC 1 is an extremely cautious invocation of the Trueblood Committee objectives.

STATEMENT NO. 2

SFAC 2 deals with qualitative characteristics of accounting information. The term *qualitative characteristics* was used in APB Statement 4, but the concepts discussed here proceed directly from ASOBAT. Exhibit 6–3, which comes from SFAC 2, best illustrates the document.

Decision makers stand at the apex of the diagram, a position indicative of the orientation of the financial accounting function to serve the decision needs of users. With regard to users, SFAC 1 previously established that financial statements should be aimed at a common core of similar information needs. Users are also presumed to be knowledgeable about financial statements and information; hence, understandability is recognized in Exhibit 6–3 as a "user-specific quality." However, even if users are assumed to be knowledgeable, information itself can have different degrees of comprehensibility. The quality of understandability is a characteristic influenced by both users and preparers of accounting information. Listed above understandability is the pervasive constraint that benefits of financial information must exceed its costs. The importance of this idea is shown by its place on the diagram. The specific qualitative characteristics of accounting that SFAC 2 has centered on come under the general heading of "decision usefulness," which simply continues the emphasis on decision makers and their needs. The two principal qualities are relevance and reliability.

Relevance

Relevance is a quality carried forward from ASOBAT and is rather awkwardly expressed in SFAC 2 as being "capable of making a difference in a decision by helping users to form predictions about the outcomes of past, present, and fu-

EXHIBIT 6–3
A Hierarchy of Accounting Qualities

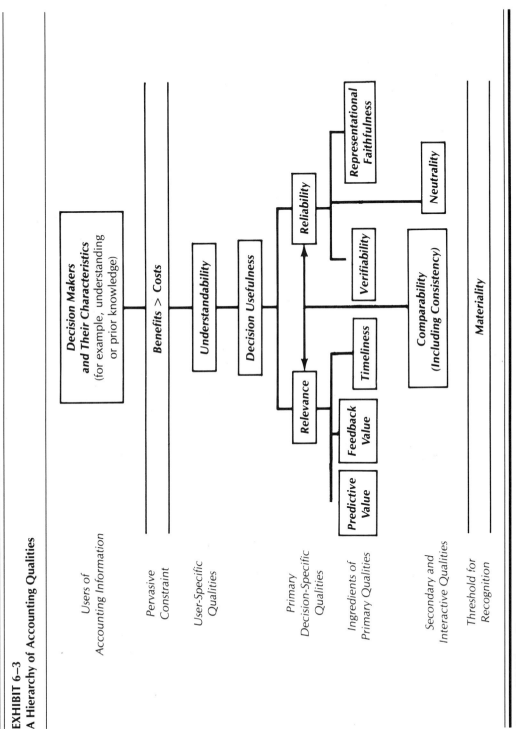

Source: SFAC 2, p. 15.

ture events or to confirm or correct expectations."[38] Relevance has two main aspects — predictive value and feedback value — and one minor one, timeliness.

Predictive Value   Predictive value, as in previous documents, refers to usefulness of inputs for predictions, such as cash flows or earning power, rather than being an actual prediction itself.

Feedback Value   Feedback value concerns "confirming or correcting their (decision makers) earlier expectations."[39] It thus refers to assessing where the firm presently stands and overlaps with how well management has carried out its functions. When viewed broadly, feedback value is closely related to accountability. Information providing this quality must also influence or affect predictive value. Hence, there appears to be a dual meaning to the term *feedback value* that is somewhat confusing. This confusion does not, however, negate the linkage between feedback value and predictive value.

Timeliness   Timeliness is really a constraint on both of the other aspects of relevance. To be relevant, information must be timely, which means that it must be "available to decision makers before it loses its capacity to influence decisions."[40] There is a conflict between timeliness and the other aspects of relevance because information can be more complete and accurate if the time constraint is relaxed. Hence, a trade-off is often present between timeliness and other components of relevance.

Reliability
Reliability is composed of three components: verifiability, representational faithfulness, and neutrality.

Verifiability   Verifiability in SFAC 2 refers, as in previous documents, to the degree of consensus among measurers. It is thus concerned with measurement theory. Unlike aspects of relevance, there is a quantifiable element to verifiability. However, it is unquestionably difficult to measure, so SFAC 2 stops short of specifying how high the degree of verifiability should be.

Representational Faithfulness   Representational faithfulness likewise pertains to measurement theory. It refers to the idea that the measurement itself should correspond with the phenomenon it is attempting to measure. For example, valuation of all fixed assets might be calculated by employing straight-line depreciation for twenty years with no salvage value. There would be an extremely high degree of verifiability but the resulting values would, in most cases, not be representative of the attribute of unamortized cost if this characteristic is supposed to be indicative of the proportion of historical cost that still has economic utility. Individually determined depreciation schedules might represent a better

---

[38] FASB (1980a, p. 21).
[39] Ibid., p. 22.
[40] Ibid., p. 25.

calculation of the attribute of unamortized cost as defined above. Similarly, if replacement cost were selected as the property to be measured, actual market values, if available, would accomplish representational faithfulness, whereas the amount the firm could sell the asset for would not.

It is clear, then, that there can easily be a conflict between verifiability and representational faithfulness, and the need to make a trade-off between these two characteristics of reliability may well arise. Sterling appears to minimize the possibility of a trade-off between representational faithfulness and verifiability. Relevant phenomena pertaining to a decision must be faithfully represented; an unfaithful representation of a relevant characteristic would not be useful for decision-making purposes.[41] Nevertheless, we are still left with the problem of dealing with relevant characteristics (of assets or liabilities) that cannot be easily measured.

Neutrality Neutrality refers to the belief that the policy-setting process should be primarily concerned with relevance and reliability rather than the effect a standard or rule might have on a specific user group or the enterprise itself. In other words, neutrality is concerned with financial statements "telling it like it is" rather than the way a particular interest group, like management or stockholders, might like it to be.

Trade-off Between Relevance and Reliability
It should be clear that trade-off effects are present not only within aspects of relevance and reliability, as previously discussed, but also between relevance and reliability as total concepts. For example, current value figures might be more relevant for predictive purposes than historical costs. However, historical costs might be more verifiable than current value measures. Whether criteria can ever be developed to guide implementation of the many potential trade-offs is a very speculative question.

Conservatism
Conservatism is not shown in Exhibit 6–3 but, curiously enough, it is discussed in SFAC 2, where it is called a *convention*. SFAC 2 is not in favor of deliberate understatements of assets or income or, for that matter, deliberate overstatements. Deliberate understatement conflicts with representational faithfulness, neutrality, and both of the main aspects of relevance. Conservatism is associated with the need for "prudent reporting" by which readers are to be informed where uncertainties and risks lie. Thus, conservatism really appears to pertain to disclosure, an extremely important concept that is not discussed in SFAC 2.

Comparability and Consistency
These qualities are defined essentially the same way that they were defined in Chapter 5. We view these characteristics as being output oriented. Hence, comparability and consistency should be the result of a viable conceptual framework rather than part of the theoretical structure itself.

---

[41] Sterling (1985, pp. 30 and 31), but see p. 29 on the inability to obtain absolute precision.

Materiality

Materiality is also discussed in much the same terms used in Chapter 5. The question that must be raised relative to materiality is whether an item is large enough to influence users' decisions. Materiality is recognized as being a quantitative characteristic, though the profession is not yet ready to implement it in this fashion. Materiality is also a relative concept rather than an absolute one, an aspect that most research in this area has stressed.

STATEMENT NO. 3

SFAC 3 defines ten elements of financial statements. It is obviously a resolution of the definitions presented in the discussion memorandum for the Conceptual Framework Project. Since these definitions were amended in SFAC 6, they will be presented in the discussion of that document.

Several observations are worth making, particularly about what SFAC 3 does *not* include. First of all, it barely mentions the three views of financial accounting in the discussion memorandum. It also does not specify the type of capital maintenance concept to employ. Likewise, it does not address matters of recognition (realization) and measurement as well as "display" in financial statements. Thus, the definitions in the statement seem to be a "first screen" in determining the content of financial statements. It is clear that much work remained to be done in prescribing the properties of these various elements, not to mention their arrangement in financial statements.

SFAC 3 also reveals a reversal of terminology. Throughout the discussion memorandum and SFAC 1, the word *earnings* had supplanted the more commonly used *income*. In SFAC 2 *earnings* had disappeared and *income* was used in paragraphs 90 and 94. Finally, SFAC 3 made the reversal official by designating *income* as the term to indicate the comprehensive or total change in net assets occurring during the period as a result of operations. *Earnings* was reserved as a possible component of income, to be specified at a later date.

STATEMENT NO. 4

SFAC 4 is concerned with objectives of nonbusiness financial reporting. Nonbusiness organizations are characterized by

1. receipts of significant amounts of resources from providers who do not expect to receive either repayment or economic benefits proportionate to resources provided;
2. operating purposes that are primarily other than to provide goods or services at a profit . . . ;
3. absence of defined ownership interests that can be sold, transferred, or redeemed, or that convey entitlement to a share of residual distribution of resources in the event of liquidation of the organization.[42]

---

[42] FASB (1980c, p. x).

SFAC 4 also notes that nonbusiness organizations do not have a single indicator of the entity's performance comparable to income measurement in the profit sector.[43] Since the emphasis in this text is on the profit sector, SFAC 4 is outside the scope of our interest.

STATEMENT NO. 5

The long-awaited SFAC 5 finally appeared in December, 1984, exactly four years after SFAC 4. Since this statement was to deal with the difficult issues of recognition and measurement, it was clear that it would be the linchpin for the success or failure of the entire project. The statement let the cat out of the bag immediately in paragraph 2, which made it quite clear that there would be no extensive attempt to come to grips with the issues of recognition and measurement:

> The recognition criteria and guidance in this Statement are generally consistent with current practice and do not imply radical change. Nor do they foreclose the possibility of future change in practice. The Board intends future change to occur in the gradual, evolutionary way that has characterized past change.[44]

The statement's reliance on the evolutionary process made Solomons angry; he termed it a "cop-out."[45] He was also disappointed with the board's failure to deal with executory contracts in terms of either their possible inclusion within the body of the statement, their disclosure in footnotes, or getting no mention at all.[46]

Scope of the Statement

SFAC 5 makes clear that the concepts discussed apply strictly to financial statements and not other means of disclosure. Indeed, it is almost vehement on the subject:

> ... disclosure by other means is *not* recognition. Disclosure of information about the items in financial statements and their measures that may be provided by notes or parenthetically on the face of financial statements, by supplementary information, or by other means of financial reporting is not a substitute for recognition in financial statements for items that meet recognition criteria (emphasis supplied).[47]

Although it doesn't say so explicitly, SFAC 5 appears to deny one of the main tenets of the efficient-markets hypothesis (Chapter 8), that disclosure outside of the body of the financial statements is as effective as disclosure within the statements themselves.

---

[43] Ibid., p. xi.
[44] FASB (1984, p. 2).
[45] Solomons (1986, p. 122).
[46] Ibid., p. 116.
[47] FASB (1985, pp. 3–4).

EXHIBIT 6–4
Delineation of Formats for Presenting Financial Information

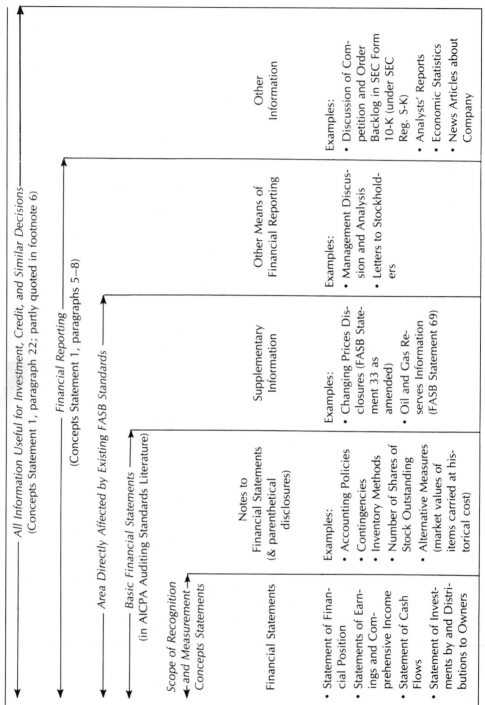

The various formats for presenting financial information are well illustrated in SFAC 5 (Exhibit 6–4).

Earnings and Comprehensive Income

One of the principal concerns of SFAC 5 was the format and presentation of changes in owners' equity that do not arise from transactions with owners. This has been referred to as the matter of "display." **Earnings** would replace net income and would differ from the latter by excluding the cumulative effect on prior years of a change in accounting principle, such as a switch from straight-line depreciation to sum-of-the-years'-digits, for example. Earnings would thus be a better indicator of current operating performance than net income. A hypothetical comparison between the two is shown in Exhibit 6–5.

Accompanying the statement of earnings would be a statement of comprehensive income. The latter is now conceived as a statement that covers all changes in owners' equity during the period except for transactions with owners. The previously mentioned cumulative effect of a change in accounting principle would appear here. Also appearing here would be the income effect of losses or gains (to the extent recognized) of marketable securities that are not classified as current assets as well as foreign currency translation adjustments. Finally, the only two items that are now classified as prior period adjustments

---

EXHIBIT 6–5
Earnings Versus Net Income

	Present Net Income		Earnings	
Revenues		100		100
Expenses		– 80		– 80
Gain from unusual source		3		3
Income from continuing operations		23		23
Loss on discontinued operations	– 10		10	
Income from operating discontinued segment				
Loss on disposal of discontinued segment	12	– 2	– 12	– 2
Income before extraordinary items and effect of a change in accounting principle		21		21
Extraordinary loss	– 6			– 6
Cumulative effect on prior years of a change in accounting principle	– 2	– 8		
Earnings				15
Net Income		13		

Source: SFAC 5, p. 13.

EXHIBIT 6-6
Earnings and Comprehensive Income

+ Revenues	100	+ Earnings	15
− Expenses	80	− Cumulative accounting adjustments	2
+ Gains	3		
− Losses	8	+ Other nonowner changes in equity	1
= Earnings	15	= Comprehensive income	14

Source: SFAC 5, p. 16.

(Chapter 9) would enter into a comprehensive income statement. A quick comparison of earnings and comprehensive income is shown in Exhibit 6-6.

Although the recasting of performance into earnings and comprehensive income may be useful, it is small consolation for not dealing adequately with recognition and measurement criteria.

Recognition Criteria

Recognition criteria refers to when an asset, liability, expense, revenue, gain, or loss should be recorded in the accounts. The fundamental recognition criteria from earlier parts of the conceptual framework are

Definitions. The item meets the definition of an element of financial statements.

Measurability. It has a relevant attribute measurable with sufficient reliability.

Relevance. The information about it is capable of making a difference in user decisions.

Reliability. The information is representationally faithful, verifiable, and neutral.

Although resorting to previous statements logically closed the circle, SFAC 5 needed to do much more work on recognition criteria than its two-page coverage. To take one example, the definitions of elements from SFAC 3 and SFAC 6 are clearly superior to previous definitions. They are necessary in and of themselves, but not sufficient. Solomons notes that the definition of a liability is difficult to apply to pensions:

> Quite apart from the measurement problems resulting from uncertainties, what is an employer's present obligation to the participants in a pension plan? Is it the (discounted) amount of all future payments to all eligible employ-

ees, past and present? Or is it the amount that would be payable if the plan were discontinued at the balance sheet date? Or is it the amount of benefits vested at the balance sheet date? Or is it only the amounts currently due and payable to those who have already retired at the balance sheet date?[48]

Similar examples of the incompleteness of definitions are the liability definition as applied to deferred taxes and the asset definition regarding the level of aggregation (full costing or successful efforts) in accounting for oil and gas exploration costs. Suffice it to say that much greater detail was necessary to successfully implement recognition criteria. Tying recognition criteria to SFACs 2 and 3 barely began the job.

Measurement Attributes

The five measurement attributes that had been extensively discussed in the discussion memorandum of 1976 were dusted off and brought forward in SFAC 5: historical cost, current cost (replacement cost), current market value (exit value), net realizable value (selling cost less any costs to complete or dispose), and present (discounted) value of future cash flows. However, as noted previously, the statement backed away from considering possible criteria for change, which suggests a continued use of present measurement attributes and reliance on an evolutionary approach.

SFAC 5 must be considered a distinct letdown, if not an outright failure. Sterling has made an extremely trenchant point relative to it: by dealing with recognition ahead of measurement, the FASB put the cart before the horse. The issue of when to recognize an element cannot be discussed until we know the measurement characteristics that are to be recognized.[49] This is the shortcoming of SFAC 5. In addition, Miller's analysis of the Conceptual Framework Project and, in particular, SFAC 5 is also of great interest.[50] Miller's views are of particular interest since he was a faculty fellow at the FASB in 1982–83, where he worked on the Conceptual Framework Project. He believes that the first three SFACs would have led to "radical changes" in accounting practice and that therefore SFAC 5 acted as a "counterreformation" to real progress. The linchpin of what Miller calls the "reformation" is the user orientation of SFAC 1 as opposed to the CAP's and APB's emphasis on the needs of auditors. In addition, the move toward the asset-liability viewpoint in the first three documents, as reflected in the definition of assets and liabilities, was a shift toward current valuation and away from matching. The counterreformation, led by the preparer constituency (in particular members of the Financial Executives Institute) and supported by three members of the FASB, appeared when SFAC 5 was being drafted.[51] SFAC 5, particularly paragraph 2's statements to the effect

---

[48] Solomons (1986, p. 121).
[49] Sterling (1985, pp. 43–47).
[50] Miller (1990).
[51] Ibid., p. 28.

that change should occur in a gradual and evolutionary manner, effectively stymied reform, at least for the time being.

SFAC 6

SFAC 6 is a replacement (not a revision) of SFAC 3. Its definitions are virtually identical to those in SFAC 3 except that they are extended to nonbusiness organizations. Likewise, the qualitative characteristics of accounting information of SFAC 2 are extended to nonbusiness organizations. Clearly, then, SFAC 6 added nothing further to the conceptual framework from the perspective of business enterprises.

Perhaps, however, there was a hidden agenda behind the apparent conclusion — at least at this time — of the conceptual framework with a virtual repetition of an earlier segment of the framework. Terminating with SFAC 5 would have meant that the project would end on a low — if not a sour — note. Possibly for this reason the project was concluded by reprising SFAC 3 (with the previously mentioned extensions to nonbusiness organizations).[52] In any event, the definitions of the ten elements of financial statements presented in SFAC 6 (with very slight modification from Chapter 3) are as follows:

1. Assets are probable future economic benefits obtained or controlled by a particular entity as a result of past transactions or events.
2. Liabilities are probable future sacrifices of economic benefits arising from present obligations of a particular entity to transfer assets or provide services to other entities in the future as a result of past transactions or events.
3. Equity or net assets is the residual interest in the assets of an entity that remains after deducting its liabilities. In a business enterprise, the equity is the ownership interest. In a not-for-profit organization, which has no ownership interest in the same sense as a business enterprise, net assets is divided into three classes based on the presence or absence of donor-imposed restrictions — permanently restricted, temporarily restricted, and unrestricted net assets.
4. Investments by owners are increases in equity of a particular business enterprise resulting from transfers to it from other entities of something valuable to obtain or increase ownership interests (or equity) in it. Assets are most commonly received as investments by owners, but that which is received may also include services or satisfaction or conversion of liabilities of the enterprise.
5. Distributions to owners are decreases in equity of a particular business enterprise resulting from transferring assets, rendering services, or incurring liabilities by the enterprise to owners. Distributions to owners decrease ownership interest (or equity) in an enterprise.
6. Comprehensive income is the change in equity of a business enterprise during a period from transactions and other events and circumstances from

---

[52] Miller (1990, p. 29) views SFAC 6 in different terms. He sees it as upholding the progress made in SFACs 1–3 and thus a bulwark against the advocates of the counterreformation represented by SFAC 5.

nonowner sources. It includes all changes in equity during a period except those resulting from investments by owners and distributions to owners.

7. Revenues are inflows or other enhancements of assets of an entity or settlements of its liabilities (or a combination of both) from delivering or producing goods, rendering services, or other activities that constitute the entity's ongoing major or central operations.

8. Expenses are outflows or other using up of assets or incurrences of liabilities (or a combination of both) from delivering or producing goods, rendering services, or carrying out other activities that constitute the entity's ongoing major or central operations.

9. Gains are increases in equity (net assets) from peripheral or incidental transactions of an entity and from all other transactions and other events and circumstances affecting the entity except those that result from revenues or investments by owners.

10. Losses are decreases in equity (net assets) from peripheral or incidental transactions of an entity and from all other transactions and other events and circumstances affecting the entity except those that result from expenses or distributions to owners.[53]

THE CONCEPTUAL FRAMEWORK AS A CODIFICATIONAL DOCUMENT

Now that we have outlined the conceptual framework, it will be instructional to consider what kind of document it is. The postulates and principles approach of ARSs 1 and 3 has been called an example of *foundational standard-setting* because it attempts to provide a logical foundation for deductively deriving "correct," or at least appropriate, accounting standards.[54] On the other hand, the conceptual framework has been likened to a constitution in the sense that alternatives to it could be viewed as either within the law or outside of it.[55] The constitutional approach clearly does not provide as strong a logical structure as does the foundational approach. The conceptual framework, however, is not a legally binding instrument nor does it contain arbitrary elements as a constitution may (such as the number of senators from each state). In Solomons' view, a conceptual framework does not have room for arbitrariness, and so his enthusiasm for the constitutional metaphor diminished.[56]

We have already seen in Chapter 4 that standard setting by an organization such as the FASB has been justified on codificational grounds. *Codification* is a justification of the standard-setting process itself rather than of the individual standards that result from that process. The codificational approach is seen as rational and as one requiring presumably good reasons for the choice of accounting standards, though these are not necessarily the "best" possible standards. Also, it should be understood that codification refers to the process and

---

[53] FASB (1985, pp. ix–x).
[54] Gaa (1988, pp. 103–105).
[55] Solomons (1986, p. 114).
[56] Ibid., p. 115.

not to the individual members (of the FASB) who are responsible for carrying out that process. It should also be remembered that choosing standards by a rational process implies that standards can be changed and improved.

Within the codificational view of standard setting, a conceptual framework makes good sense because it can support and promote the rational nature of that process. Gaa sees the conceptual framework as embodying aspects of both a constitution and a theory.[57] The constitutional view of Gaa differs from Solomons' more legalistic and empowering view. For Gaa, the distributional question concerning who financial information is intended to benefit is involved. As we have seen, SFAC 1 resolved the user-heterogeneity problem through the objective of providing information that is useful to present and potential investors and creditors and other external users who have a reasonable understanding of business and economic activities. The conceptual framework also, in Gaa's view, has theoretical aspects because it does provide criteria for choice when evaluating accounting alternatives. These include factors such as relevance, reliability, and the benefits/costs constraint discussed in SFAC 2, as well as the definitions provided in SFAC 6. These criteria for choice can help or guide the FASB, but they cannot guarantee the best outcome despite the constitutional guideline for information that is useful for actual and prospective investors, creditors, and other outside users.

According to the codificational view, not only can standards be improved upon but the conceptual framework itself is also subject to correction and refinement. This should be kept in mind as we examine some recent critiques of the conceptual framework.

REPRESENTATIONAL FAITHFULNESS VERSUS ECONOMIC CONSEQUENCES

One of the central issues regarding the conceptual framework is whether representational faithfulness or economic consequences should underlie the promulgation of accounting standards. Representational faithfulness is part of the conceptual framework, whereas economic consequences is not. Several recent articles have examined this important issue.

Sole Emphasis Upon Representational Faithfulness

Ruland clearly favors exclusive emphasis on representational faithfulness as an obligation of the FASB in drafting standards.[58] He sees representational faithfulness as sufficient justification for accounting standards. If economic consequences were to be the criterion for standard setting, outcomes of accounting policy making would have to be carefully determined but could by no means be certain.[59]

---

[57] Gaa (1988, pp. 146–161).
[58] Ruland (1984).
[59] Ruland (1989, p. 233).

The Complementary Roles of Representational Faithfulness and Economic Consequences

Ingram and Rayburn have taken a dualistic position relative to the roles of representational faithfulness and economic consequences in the standard-setting process.[60] Unfortunately, difficulties are inherent in achieving representational faithfulness. For example, the definition of assets in SFAC 6 is not complete enough to enable us to determine a unique amount for the unamortized cost of an oil producer's petroleum field holdings. Under the full cost approach, a country or even a continent could be considered a cost center. The components of the definition in SFAC 6 are thus necessary but not sufficient to fully define assets.[61] Even moving to current valuation would not eliminate the problem of levels of aggregation in achieving representational faithfulness (oil well as opposed to an oil field with many wells or even wider aggregational units, such as countries or continents). Hence, in Ingram and Rayburn's view, faithfulness of representation is often a matter of employing measurement rules (or calculation rules as Sterling would have it) rather than "mapping reality"; that is, determining a "true" figure from the representational faithfulness standpoint. Because it cannot employ a relatively easily ascertainable means to objective truth, the standard-setting process necessarily entails a consideration of economic consequences: how users, preparers, and other parties are affected by prospective accounting standards. Ingram and Rayburn conclude that representational faithfulness and economic consequences are not either-or alternatives in the standard-setting process, rather they are complementary to each other.[62]

The Preeminence of the Economic Consequences View

Daley and Tranter's position relative to faithful representations and economic consequences is at the opposite pole from Ruland's.[63] They see economic consequences embodied in the conceptual framework — like the camel gaining access to the tent by slipping its nose under the flap — despite the FASB's attempt to give representational faithfulness primacy in setting accounting standards. The underlying reason for Daley and Tranter's conclusion is that the FASB cannot be neutral in assessing the relevance and reliability of accounting information given the pervasive constraint of the benefits/costs trade-off.

Daley and Tranter view the benefits/costs trade-off as covering a broad gamut of economic consequences issues. For example, they state that

---

[60] Ingram and Rayburn (1989).

[61] For more coverage, see the critique of Dopuch and Sunder (1980, p. 7). The FASB attempted to limit diversity in asset values in SFAS 19, by allowing only successful efforts, but it was forced to suspend SFAS 19 as a result of political pressure. See Chapter 15 for additional information.

[62] While Ingram and Rayburn (1989, p. 65) maintain the balanced view, they state that "good economic consequences . . . are difficult to achieve . . ." while "representational faithfulness . . . is impossible to achieve."

[63] Daley and Tranter (1990).

This process of weighing costs and benefits on differing sectors of our society is not neutral. It cannot be. In the case of marketable equities securities *the decision was clearly that the interests of the insurance industry outweighed the general benefits to financial statement users* of moving to flow-through accounting, even though this method has much support in the conceptual framework. (emphasis added)[64]

However, Ruland interprets the benefits > costs trade-off as a materiality threshold for assessing the usefulness of an accounting standard: benefits to users should be greater than the costs of preparation.[65] Moreover, the discussion of the pervasive constraint of benefits/costs in SFAC 2 focuses mainly upon such issues as the fact that the preparer initially bears the cost of collecting, processing, and disseminating information to users and makes only limited mention of distributional effects on different user groups (for example, the benefit of off-balance-sheet financing for investors as opposed to creditors).[66]

In one sense Daley and Tranter are certainly correct. The benefits/costs trade-off unquestionably involves economic consequences involving the costs of preparing information relative to the benefits to users. Clearly, this aspect of standard setting by its very nature is an inherent part of the process and should thus be viewed as a special type of economic consequence. In other words, standard setters directly affect the cost of information preparation as a result of the standards that they generate. Beyond this point, however, the role neutrality plays is appropriate because it focuses concern upon relevance and reliability (given the benefits > costs constraint) rather than upon other types of economic consequences.

Daley and Tranter do not believe that neutrality can be a component of reliability because the pervasive constraint above reliability (benefits of standards exceeding their cost) of necessity entails economic consequences.[67] We believe that rather than being inconsistent, the problem is one of maintaining a difficult balancing act. The FASB's primary objective is providing useful information for external users subject to the benefits > costs constraint. Information can both be useful for decision making and also involve economic consequences. Neutrality means being concerned primarily with decision usefulness rather than distributive effects.

In reality, the FASB has been concerned with economic consequences beyond the benefits/costs constraint, having commissioned several economic consequences studies. Furthermore, the FASB has not been immune to influence from the political process that results from economic consequences.[68] From a

---

[64] Ibid., p. 19.

[65] Ruland (1989, p. 72).

[66] Paragraph 137 of SFAC 2 mentions factors under the costs of providing information such as loss of competitive advantages and dangers of litigation, which could support the broader Daley and Tranter view of economic consequences, but the main discussion concerns the narrower interpretation of what might be termed the *direct* costs of preparation. See FASB (1980, pp. 54–58).

[67] Daley and Tranter (1990, p. 17).

[68] Ibid., pp. 18–21.

theoretical perspective, taking cognizance of economic consequences by means of research studies should not be objectionable provided it is understood that relevance and reliability are the primary characteristics that standard setters should be concerned with.

CONCLUDING REMARKS ON THE CONCEPTUAL FRAMEWORK

Perhaps the best thing that can be said about the conceptual framework is that the project made it to completion. This does not mean that it cannot be amended and changed in the future, however. The most impressive parts of the project are the qualitative characteristics of SFAC 2 and the definitions of the elements in SFACs 3 and 6, but the failure to come to grips with recognition and measurement criteria in SFAC 5 is very disappointing.[69] Perhaps the project in its present form will be a launching pad for the changes and improvements that are necessary to put financial accounting on a solid theoretical footing.

SUMMARY

The most common thread running through the various documents, reports, and monographs discussed in this chapter is that the field reached the conclusion that financial statements should be relevant to users for decision-making purposes. As a result, the standard-setting bodies turned away from the postulates and principles orientation and toward an objectives and standards orientation.

ASOBAT was the first document based on the new orientation toward user relevance. However, it provided little further detail or explication of user relevance. APB Statement 4 continued the emphasis on user relevance, although it is a curious mixture of the old and new approaches due to the fact that the document appeared at a time of transition. It was clear that the APB would be replaced but the nature of its successor was not apparent.

The first statement to address the issue of user objectives extensively was the Trueblood Report. But although it mentions predictive ability and accountability, the discussion is still not at an operational level. However, a preliminary

---

[69] In an experiment involving twenty-eight former members of the FASB and APB who attempted to use the qualitative characteristics of SFAC 2, only verifiability and costs (as in benefits greater than costs) were found to be operational in terms of having some degree of common meaning to the standard setters. Although these results are not encouraging, the researchers noted that the understanding of the concepts prior to the publication of SFAC 2 could have been considerably lower. In addition, subjects answered questions independently and not in the "give-and-take" atmosphere of the actual standard-setting process. See Joyce, Libby, and Sunder (1982) for further details.

statement of this type can do nothing more than point the way for future efforts.

SATTA was to the 1970s as ASOBAT was to the 1960s. Both are the product of AAA committees that were attempting to summarize the "state of the art" concerning accounting theory. SATTA expressed the opinion that choice among accounting theories (valuation systems) could not be made at that time owing to the diversity of users and their presumably different objectives and information needs.

The FASB's Conceptual Framework Project started up at approximately the same time as the appearance of SATTA. In addition to a discussion memorandum, the project issued six statements of financial accounting concepts. SFAC 1 basically reiterates the objectives put forth in the Trueblood Committee Report. Users are assumed to be knowledgeable about financial statement reporting. The qualitative characteristics of SFAC 2, the most substantive publication to date, center around relevance and reliability. Relevance consists of predictive value and feedback value, both of which are under the constraint of timeliness. Reliability is made up of verifiability and representational faithfulness supported by the neutrality of the underlying standards concerning the desires of vested interests. Many potential conflicts exist among these qualitative characteristics, including the basic conflict between relevance and reliability. SFAC 3 presents basic definitions of accounting terms that serve as a "first screen" for later work in measurement and recognition of these elements on financial statements. SFAC 4 deals with objectives of nonbusiness organizations and is beyond the general scope of this text. SFAC 5 attempts to establish recognition and measurement criteria but largely sidesteps these important issues. The concluding document of the framework, SFAC 6, is a very minor refinement of the definitions of the elements previously done in SFAC 3. It also extends the qualitative characteristics of SFAC 2 to nonbusiness organizations.

The crucial issues discussed in this chapter concern what the objectives of financial statements are, or at least are perceived to be, and what are the information needs of the very heterogeneous users of financial statements. The consensus seems to be that the major objectives are predictive ability and accountability. Accountability is an extension of the traditional stewardship objective to the effective and efficient usage of enterprise resources by management. Minor objectives appear to be capital maintenance measurement and adaptability. Adaptability is best determined by exit valuation of assets, which gives a result that has little if any utility for predictive ability or accountability purposes. Among (and within) all of these objectives, there is some potential conflict. All that can be said about user diversity at this time is that, despite the heterogeneity of groups of users as well as within groups, it has not been proved that the groups have strongly differentiated information needs.

The conceptual framework has been likened to a constitution, but it may be more appropriate to view it from the foundational perspective, which sees standard setting as a logical process even though the standards themselves, both individually and as a group, may be less than optimal. Finally, the hope is that standard setting is primarily guided by representational faithfulness rather than economic consequences. This objective may be extremely difficult to accomplish given a measurement system that is geared to historical costs rather than current values.

APPENDIX 6-A: USER OBJECTIVES

The user objectives stated in such documents as the Trueblood Committee Report and SFAC 1 are quite broad and general. Further specificity may be necessary if policy making is to be appropriately executed. Unfortunately, only a very limited amount of accounting research has focused on this issue. Nevertheless, there appear to be two major areas where broad information is applicable to many user groups. The first of these is referred to as the *predictive ability* objective. The second is an extension of stewardship called *accountability.* Both objectives can be divided into numerous subcategories. Our discussion, however, is restricted to the principal aspects of each objective.

PREDICTIVE ABILITY

Numerous studies have attempted to use accounting data to predict future variables. One group of studies has attempted to predict future income on the basis of present and past income numbers.[70] One of the purposes of these studies was to obtain evidence concerning whether historical cost income, general price-level-adjusted income, or current value income is a better predictor of itself. These studies indicate that historical cost appears to be at least as good a predictor of itself as the other two methods.

However, Revsine has pointed out that income itself is an "artifact." [71] An artifact, in this sense, refers to a number, the determination of which is based on prescribed rules rather than representational faithfulness to the attribute being measured. Furthermore, because there is sufficient latitude in selecting alternative methods (combined with the potential desire of management to smooth income), it is not surprising that historical income appears to be a better predictor of itself than other income measurement methods that intuitively appear to contain numbers more economically relevant. Revsine also suggests that since income is an "artificial construct," its predictive importance lies in the ability to anticipate a real event, such as future cash flows.[72] Finally, since the real event may itself be quite volatile, the predictor should be similarly volatile, whereas the research discussed above was really examining the issue of income smoothing.[73]

Many other studies have focused on the predictive ability of two other sets

---

[70] Simmons and Gray (1969) and Frank (1969).

[71] Revsine (1971, pp. 480–481).

[72] Ibid., p. 487.

[73] Barnea, Ronen, and Sadan (1975) suggest the segregation of recurring income components from the transitory elements in order to facilitate the prediction of cash flows by users. Excluded from recurring income would be extraordinary (nonrecurring and nonoperating) items designated in APB 30, as well as nonrecurring operating factors.

of accounting-generated numbers: quarterly earnings announcements as predictors of annual earnings and financial ratios as predictors of bankruptcy.[74] In both cases, the accounting data — as might be expected — have been highly useful in the predictive process. One cautionary note, however, is that these studies have employed particular models as part of the predictive ability process. Only insofar as users avail themselves of at least roughly similar methods can predictive ability tests be relied upon.[75] The alternative, of course, involves attempting to educate users about what are presumed to be the best predictive models — a task, as noted previously, that could be quite difficult. Another point to keep in mind is that valuation and income methods presumed to be best for one objective, such as predictive ability, may have less utility for other objectives.

ACCOUNTABILITY

We use the word *accountability* to mean a broader concept than the narrower one of stewardship, which is mainly concerned with the safeguarding of assets. This meaning follows Ijiri's usage — the responsibility of management to report on achieving goals for the effective and efficient utilization of enterprise resources.[76] Measurements based on the accountability objective would include earnings per share and return on investment and its components (capital turnover and profit margin). The question of which valuation system provides the best input for these and other accountability-oriented measurements would come under the general scope of recognition and measurement.

   Predictive ability and accountability are separate objectives. One is concerned with data that will be useful in terms of assessing future prospects, whereas the other is concerned with evaluating enterprise performance. Between these two objectives, there is, of course, a linkage of a feed-forward nature. How well a firm is presently doing can certainly be an important input for predictive purposes. Nevertheless, whether the information needed for these objectives differs has never really been determined.[77] Obviously, the problem would be more acute if these objectives had different preferred valuation systems for providing information. Much work of an empirical nature needs to be done to gather evidence to help answer the question.

SECONDARY OBJECTIVES

We see two other possible user objectives for which accounting information can be extremely useful. They are much narrower than the concepts of predictive ability and accountability. One is a measure of **capital maintenance,** which

---

[74] For predictive aspects of quarterly data, see Coates (1972), Brown and Kennelly (1972), and Foster (1977). For financial ratios as predictors, see Beaver (1966) and Elam (1975). For a critical look at the predictive ability objective, see Greenball (1971).

[75] The seminal article on predictive ability and its limitations is Beaver, Kennelly, and Voss (1968).

[76] Ijiri (1975, pp. ix–x).

[77] Devine (1985) sees a rather close link between the predictive and accountability functions and hence identical underlying information needs for both functions. Certainly the case has not been proved that different information is needed for these functions.

gives information about the amount of dividends that can be paid during a period without returning capital to the stockholders. This is covered in detail in Chapter 12. Another possible objective would be that of **adaptability.** This objective is concerned with measuring total liquidity available to the firm. By definition, this is determined by measuring the exit value of the firm's assets minus its liabilities. The exit-value approach is illustrated in Appendix 1-A. An income statement under the exit-value approach measures the change in liquidity occurring during the period as a result of operations.[78] Chambers has been the principal proponent of this system and also of this objective, though Sterling has also advocated it.[79]

A measure of total liquidity available to a firm certainly has some relevance, but we consider adaptability far less important than predictive ability and accountability. Firms that are successful going concerns will probably draw upon only a very small portion of the total available liquidity during relatively short time periods. Adaptability measures would probably be most important to the owners of small, closely held firms and possibly short-term creditors. Consequently, the adaptive approach appears to be more closely linked to the proprietary theory than to the entity theory. Exit-value approaches appear to have limited usefulness for predictive ability and accountability purposes. Indeed, Chambers stoutly denies that accounting figures can have any relevance for predictive purposes.[80]

We have discussed these four objectives in fairly broad terms. More detailed examination of issues, such as attributes to be measured and valuation systems to be employed, should appear in lower levels of the theoretical structure. The topmost level of a metatheoretical framework, which would be concerned with implementing finite uniformity should be a broad statement of objectives. Certainly the development of objectives in SFAC 1 and of qualitative characteristics of financial statements in SFAC 2 indicates a hierarchical ordering in a prescriptive type of metatheoretical framework. Since implementing a set of user objectives implies a fairly large number of information needs on the part of users, user diversity is examined in Appendix 6-B.

APPENDIX 6-B: USER DIVERSITY

Unquestionably, there are a large and diverse number of users of published financial statements.[81] What is not clear, however, is whether their information needs for the various types of objectives discussed in Appendix 6-A can be sat-

---

[78] It is quite unlikely that an exit-value income statement would be particularly useful for either predictive ability or accountability purposes. The sizable declines in exit values for many fixed assets in the early years of usage occur because of market imperfections. These lowered exit values result in excessive depreciation charges, which make the exit-value income statement unrepresentative.

[79] Chambers (1967) and Sterling (1981, p. 119), for example.

[80] Chambers (1968, p. 246).

[81] A good short summary of users and their needs is provided in Stamp (1980, pp. 39–51).

isfied by general-purpose statements prepared under conditions of neutrality. The list of possible user groups is indeed lengthy. It would include

1. shareholders,
2. creditors,
3. financial analysts and advisers,
4. employees,
5. labor unions,
6. customers,
7. suppliers,
8. industry trade associations,
9. governmental agencies,
10. public-interest groups,
11. researchers and standard setters.

Furthermore, even within these groups there is extensive diversity. Shareholders include those whose portfolios are diversified versus those whose aren't, those using professional financial advisers and those who do not, those knowledgeable about financial statements versus those who are uninformed, and actual versus potential owners of securities. Creditors can be segregated into short-term and long-term types. Public-interest groups would include, among others, consumer and environmental groups. Researchers and standard setters include academic accountants, members of the SEC and FASB, and economists. Governmental agencies (such as the Internal Revenue Service, Interstate Commerce Commission, and Federal Trade Commission), unlike the other groups, are often able to acquire by mandate the information that they desire.

Some of the information needs of different user groups may be complementary. For example, short-term creditors may be concerned with liquidity measurements, such as the current or quick ratios, whereas long-term creditors may have greater interest in the composition of capital structures. Serious problems do not appear to exist where there are complementary needs. Perhaps the most serious conflict lies between actual and potential security holders. The former would probably desire information that would maximize security values, whereas the latter would prefer information that would minimize security values (this would change if potential security owners acquire shares). At present it is not clear which types of information are most consistent with the two objectives. Furthermore, these objectives conflict with the neutrality criterion of SFAC 2. Hence, the information that should be supplied to the diverse user groups should still be aimed at the type of objectives stated in Appendix 6-A and SFAC 1.

It may be the case that the diverse user groups have different information needs for their perceived objectives. However, at this time the possibility of diverse user needs is simply an untested proposition. Until the hypothesis becomes validated through empirical testing, the aim of standard-setting organizations should be to produce general-purpose financial statements where rules are determined in a neutral setting with adequate disclosure for knowledgeable users.

Perhaps the most serious problems presented by user diversity involves specialized information needs and the possible distributional effects of different valuation systems. Specialized information needs raise the issue of who should pay for the costs of producing this information. For example, public-interest groups might want information about various types of emitted pollutants (in this particular case, it could be easily argued that the entire society benefits from the publication of pollution information). An example of conflict arising from distributional effects might involve entry-value (replacement costs) versus exit-value information. Since asset values are lower under the latter, security prices may also be lower, which would work to the detriment of existing shareholders relative to other groups. However, an important qualification is that it is simply not clear how the market would adjust in a situation of this magnitude. Under the more conservative exit-value approach, security prices might be largely unaffected. Security returns might simply be higher than what they would have been under the economy-wide use of replacement costs. Consequently, the user heterogeneity problem could be better addressed from the input side by taking user needs into account rather than by examining hypothetical questions involving the distributional effects of various security prices.

QUESTIONS

1. How do objectives differ from postulates?
2. Do you think that the funds flow statement is more "factual" and less "interpretative" than the income statement and balance sheet?
3. Do you think that the standards mentioned in ASOBAT are really standards?
4. Of what importance in a conceptual framework or metatheory are definitions of such basic terms as *assets, liabilities, revenues,* and *expenses?*
5. Are feedback value and predictive value independent of each other or is there some overlap?
6. Why is the problem of heterogeneous users so critical in the development of accounting theory?
7. What is "Pareto optimality" and why is it a very restrictive concept from the standpoint of policy makers?
8. How do the research orientations of accounting in Chapter 2 compare with SATTA's organization of research?
9. What is the relationship between the economic consequences of accounting standards discussed in Chapter 4 and the quality of neutrality presented in SFAC 2?
10. Why must objectives be at the topmost level of a conceptual framework of accounting?
11. What conflicts are present among the four objectives discussed in Appendix 6-A?
12. How does the freedom from bias mentioned in ASOBAT compare to the quality of neutrality mentioned in SFAC 2?

13. The statement of Herbert Miller (footnote 33) is closest to which theoretical approach delineated in SATTA?
14. How has the definition of *accounting* been modified in recent years?
15. What potential conflicts are present in terms of different user needs?
16. Why is putting recognition ahead of the selection of the attribute to be measured analogous to putting "the cart before the horse"?
17. How does earnings as discussed in SFAC 5 differ from net income?
18. What is comprehensive income?
19. Is neutrality inconsistent with the external user primary orientation of SFAC 1 and the pervasive constraint (benefits > costs) of SFAC 2?
20. SFAC 6 is largely a repetition of SFAC 3. Discuss two possible reasons why this repetition occurred.

CASES AND PROBLEMS

1. Discuss as many of the potential trade-offs among the qualities mentioned in SFAC 2 as you can and give either a general or a concrete example of each one.
2. The crucial question brought up in this chapter concerns the issue of whether the admittedly heterogeneous users of financial statements have highly diverse information needs in terms of their underlying objectives. State as carefully as you can (1) why the user groups have largely diverse information needs, and (2) why the user groups may have relatively similar information needs.
3. Analyze three accounting standards promulgated by the FASB and show how economic consequences (rather than representational faithfulness) influenced the shaping of the standard (your professor may suggest particular standards for this case).

BIBLIOGRAPHY OF REFERENCED WORKS

Abdel-khalik, A. Rashad (1971). "User Preference Ordering Value: A Model," *The Accounting Review* (July 1971), pp. 437–471.

American Accounting Association (1966). *A Statement of Basic Accounting Theory* (AAA).

———— (1969). "An Evaluation of External Reporting Practices: A Report of the 1966–68 Committee on External Reporting," *Accounting Review Supplement* (AAA), pp. 79–123.

———— (1977a). *Responses to the Financial Accounting Standards Board's "Tentative Conclusions on Objectives of Financial Statements of Business Enterprises" and "Conceptual Framework for Financial Accounting and Reporting: Elements of Financial Statements and Their Measurement"* (AAA).

———— (1970). "Basic Concepts and Accounting Principles Underlying Financial Statements of Business Enterprises," *APB Statement No. 4* (AICPA), pp. 9057–9106.

—— (1973). *Objectives of Financial Statements* (AICPA).

—— (1977b). *Statement on Accounting Theory and Theory Acceptance* (AAA). American Institute of Certified Public Accountants (1953). *Accounting Terminology Bulletin No. 1* (AICPA, 1973).

Anton, Hector (1976). "Objectives of Financial Accounting: Review and Analysis," *The Journal of Accountancy* (January 1976), pp. 40–51.

Barnea, Amir, Joshua Ronen, and Simcha Sadan (1975). "The Implementation of Accounting Objectives: An Application to Extraordinary Items," *The Accounting Review* (January 1975), pp. 58–68.

Barton, A. D. (1974). "Expectations and Achievements in Income Theory," *The Accounting Review* (October 1974), pp. 664–681.

Beaver, William H. (1966). "Financial Ratios as Predictors of Failure," *Empirical Research in Accounting: Selected Studies 1966* (Supplement to *Journal of Accounting Research*), pp. 71–111.

Beaver, William H., and Joel S. Demski (1974). "The Nature of Financial Accounting Objectives: A Summary and Synthesis," *Studies on Financial Accounting Objectives* (Supplement to *Journal of Accounting Research*), pp. 170–185.

Beaver, William H., John W. Kennelly, and William M. Voss (1968). "Predictive Ability as a Criterion for the Evaluation of Accounting Data," *The Accounting Review* (October 1968), pp. 675–683.

Borst, Duane (1981). "Accounting vs. Reality: How Wide Is the 'GAAP'?" *Financial Executive* (July 1981), pp. 12–15.

Brown, Philip, and John W. Kennelly (1972). "The Information Content of Quarterly Earnings—An Extension and Some Further Evidence," *Journal of Business* (July 1972), pp. 403–415.

Chambers, Raymond J. (1967). "Continuously Contemporary Accounting—Additivity and Action," *The Accounting Review* (October 1967), pp. 751–757.

—— (1968). "Measures and Values: A Reply to Professor Staubus," *The Accounting Review* (April 1968), pp. 239–247.

Coates, Robert (1973). "The Predictive Content of Interim Reports: A Time Series Analysis," *Empirical Research in Accounting: Selected Studies, 1973* (Supplement to *Journal of Accounting Research*), pp. 132–144.

Daley, Lane A., and Terry Tranter (1990). "Limitations on the Value of the Conceptual Framework in Evaluating Extant Accounting Standards," *Accounting Horizons* (March 1990), pp. 15–24.

Devine, Carl T. (1985). "Comments on Prediction, Evaluation and Decision Making," *Essays in Accounting Theory*, Vol. IV, *Studies in Accounting Research* No. 22 (American Accounting Association), pp. 69–81.

Dopuch, Nicholas, and Shyam Sunder (1980). "FASB's Statements on Objectives and Elements of Financial Accounting: A Review," *The Accounting Review* (January 1980), pp. 1–21.

Elam, Rick (1975). "The Effect of Lease Data on the Predictive Ability of Financial Ratios," *The Accounting Review* (January 1975), pp. 25–43.

Financial Accounting Standards Board (1976a). *FASB Discussion Memorandum: Conceptual Framework for Financial Accounting and Reporting: Elements of Financial Statements and Their Measurement* (FASB).

—— (1976b). *Scope and Implications of the Conceptual Framework Project* (FASB).

—— (1976c). *Tentative Conclusions on Objectives of Financial Statements of Business Enterprises* (FASB).

—— (1978). "Objectives of Financial Reporting by Business Enterprises," *Statement of Financial Accounting Concepts No. 1* (FASB).

—— (1980a). "Qualitative Characteristics of Accounting Information," *Statement of Financial Accounting Concepts No. 2* (FASB).

—— (1980b). "Elements of Financial Statements of Business Enterprises," *Statement of Financial Accounting Concepts No. 3* (FASB).

—— (1980c). "Objectives of Financial Reporting by Nonbusiness Organizations," *Statement of Financial Accounting Concepts No. 4* (FASB).

—— (1984). "Recognition and Measurement in Financial Statements of Business Enterprises," *Statement of Financial Accounting Concepts No. 5* (FASB).

—— (1985). "Elements of Financial Statements: A Replacement of FASB Concepts Statement No. 3 (incorporating an amendment of FASB Concepts Statement No. 2)," *Statement of Financial Accounting Concepts No. 6* (FASB).

Foster, George (1977). "Quarterly Accounting Data: Time-Series Properties and Predictive-Ability Results," *The Accounting Review* (January 1977), pp. 1–21.

Frank, Werner (1969). "A Study of the Predictive Significance of Two Income Statements," *Journal of Accounting Research* (Spring 1969), pp. 123–136.

Gaa, James C. (1988). "Methodological Foundations of Standard-setting for Corporate Financial Reporting," *Studies in Accounting Research* No. 28 (American Accounting Association).

Greenball, Melvin N. (1971). "The Predictive-Ability Criterion: Its Relevance in Evaluating Accounting Data," *Abacus* (June 1971), pp. 1–7.

Ijiri, Yuji (1971). "Critique of the APB Fundamentals Statement," *Journal of Accountancy* (November 1971), pp. 43–50.

—— (1975). "Theory of Accounting Measurement," *Studies in Accounting Research* No. 10 (American Accounting Association).

Ingram, Robert W., and Frank P. Rayburn (1989). "Representational Faithfulness and Economic Consequences: Their Roles in Accounting Policy," *Journal of Accounting and Public Policy* (Spring 1989), pp. 57–68.

Joyce, Edward, Robert Libby, and Shyam Sunder (1982). "Using the FASB's Qualitative Characteristics in Accounting Policy Choices," *Journal of Accounting Research* (Autumn 1982, Pt. II), pp. 654–675.

Miller, Henry (1972). "Environmental Complexity and Financial Reports," *The Accounting Review* (January 1972), pp. 31–37.

Miller, Herbert E. (1974). "Discussion of Opportunities and Implications of the Report on Objectives of Financial Statements," *Studies on Financial Accounting Objectives: 1974* (Supplement to *Journal of Accounting Research*), pp. 18–20.

Miller, Paul B. W. (1990). "The Conceptual Framework as Reformation and Counterreformation," *Accounting Horizons* (June 1990), pp. 23–32.

Moonitz, Maurice (1971). "The Accounting Principles Board Revisited," *New York Certified Public Accountant* (May 1971), pp. 341–345.

Paton, William A., and A. C. Littleton (1940). *An Introduction to Corporate Accounting Standards* (American Accounting Association, 1957).

Peasnall, K. V. (1978). "Statement of Accounting Theory and Theory Acceptance: A Review Article," *Accounting and Business Research* (Summer 1978), pp. 217–225.

Revsine, Lawrence (1970a). "On the Correspondence Between Replacement Cost Income and Economic Income," *The Accounting Review* (July 1970), pp. 513–523.

—— (1970b). "Data Expansion and Conceptual Structure," *The Accounting Review* (October 1970), pp. 704–711.

—— (1971). "Predictive Ability, Market Prices, and Operating Flows," *The Accounting Review* (July 1971), pp. 480–489.

Ruland, Robert G. (1984). "Duty, Obligation, and Responsibility in Accounting Policy Making," *Journal of Accounting and Public Policy* (Autumn 1984), pp. 223–237.

———— (1989). "The Pragmatic and Ethical Distinction Between Two Approaches to Accounting Policy Making," *Journal of Accounting and Public Policy* (Spring 1989), pp. 69–80.

Samuels, Warren (1974). *Pareto on Policy* (Elsevier Scientific Publishing Company).

Schattke, R. W. (1972). "An Analysis of APB Statement No. 4," *The Accounting Review* (April 1972), pp. 233–244.

Simmons, John K., and Jack Gray (1969). "An Investigation of the Effect of Differing Accounting Frameworks on the Prediction of Net Income," *The Accounting Review* (October 1969), pp. 757–776.

Solomons, David (1986). "The FASB's Conceptual Framework: An Evaluation," *Journal of Accountancy* (June 1986), pp. 114–124.

Sorter, George H., and Martin S. Gans (1974). "Opportunities and Implications of the Report on the Objectives of Financial Statements," *Studies on Financial Accounting Objectives: 1974* (Supplement to *Journal of Accounting Research*), pp. 1–12.

Stamp, Edward (1980). *Corporate Reporting: Its Future Evolution* (Canadian Institute of Chartered Accountants).

Staubus, George (1972). "An Analysis of APB Statement No. 4," *Journal of Accountancy* (February 1972), pp. 36–43.

Sterling, Robert R. (1967). "A Statement of Basic Accounting Theory: A Review Article," *Journal of Accounting Research* (Spring 1967), pp. 94–112.

———— (1981). "Costs (Historical Versus Current) Versus Exit Values," *Abacus* (December 1981), pp. 93–129.

———— (1985). *An Essay on Recognition* (The University of Sydney, Accounting Research Centre).

ADDITIONAL READINGS

Conceptual Framework

Agrawal, Surendra P. (1987). "On the Conceptual Framework of Accounting," *Journal of Accounting Literature*, Vol. 6, pp. 165–178.

Arthur Young & Company (1977). *Conceptual Framework for Financial Accounting and Reporting* (Arthur Young & Company).

Burton, John C. (1978). "A Symposium on the Conceptual Framework," *Journal of Accountancy* (January 1978), pp. 53–58.

Coe, Teddy L., and George H. Sorter (1978). "The FASB Has Been Using an Implicit Conceptual Framework," *Accounting Journal* (Winter 1977–78), pp. 152–159.

Ernst & Ernst (1977). *Conceptual Framework — Our Analysis and Response* (Ernst & Ernst).

Gerboth, Dale L. (1987). "The Conceptual Framework: Not Definitions, But Professional Values," *Accounting Horizons* (September 1987), pp. 1–8.

Heath, Loyd C. (1988). "The Conceptual Framework as Literature," *Accounting Horizons* (June 1988), pp. 100–104.

Koeppen, David R. (1988). "Using the FASB's Conceptual Framework: Fitting the Pieces Together," *Accounting Horizons* (June 1988), pp. 18–26.

Sprouse, Robert T. (1978). "The Importance of Earnings in the Conceptual Framework," *Journal of Accountancy* (January 1978), pp. 64–71.

Storey, Reed K. (1981). "Conditions Necessary for Developing a Conceptual Framework," *Financial Analysts Journal* (May–June 1981), pp. 51–58.

Objectives of Financial Statements
Bedford, Norton (1974). "Discussion of Opportunities and Implications of the Report on Objectives of Financial Statements," *Studies on Financial Accounting Objectives: 1974* (Supplement to *Journal of Accounting Research*), pp. 13–17.

Cyert, Richard M., and Yuji Ijiri (1974). "Problems of Implementing the Trueblood Objectives Report," *Studies on Financial Accounting Objectives: 1974* (Supplement to *Journal of Accounting Research*), pp. 29–42.

Kripke, Homer (1972). "The Objectives of Financial Accounting Should Be to Provide Information for the Serious Investor," *Corporate Financial Reporting: The Issues, the Objectives and Some New Proposals*, ed. A. Rappaport and L. Revsine (Commerce Clearing House), pp. 94–119.

Most, Kenneth, and A. L. Winters (1976). "Focus on Standard Setting: From Trueblood to the FASB," *Journal of Accountancy* (February 1977), pp. 67–75.

Ronen, Joshua (1974). "A User Oriented Development of Accounting Information Requirements," *Objectives of Financial Statements*, vol. 2, ed. J. J. Cramer, Jr., and G. H. Sorter (American Institute of Certified Public Accountants), pp. 80–103.

Users of Accounting Information
Fraser, I. A. M., and W. Nabes (1985). "The Assumed User in Three Accounting Theories," *Accounting and Business Research* (Spring 1985), pp. 144–147.

——— (1985). "Is Sterling Correctly Valued?" *Accounting and Business Research* (Summer 1985), pp. 246–247.

Gaa, James C. (1986). "User Primacy in Financial Rulemaking: A Social Contract Approach," *The Accounting Review* (July 1986), pp. 435–454.

Sterling, Robert R. (1985). "On Identification of Users and Firms," *Accounting and Business Research* (Summer 1985), pp. 241–245.

7

USEFULNESS OF ACCOUNTING INFORMATION TO INVESTORS AND CREDITORS

I N CHAPTER 4, we suggested that an explicit **political economy of account-ing** recognizes that alternative financial reporting systems (for example, regulated versus unregulated) have both private and social consequences, that in *any* system some people will fare better while others fare worse, and that the choice of system itself is a political as well as an economic act. Consistent with this, the FASB appears to recognize the existence of a diverse and pluralistic user group (see Chapter 6). However, in practice, the FASB has focused on what it calls *primary user groups* (investors and creditors) who are interested in the amounts, timing, and uncertainties of future cash flows.[1] The rationale offered for the investor–creditor focus is that other users either have a commonality of interest with investors and creditors or the means of getting alternative information, such as governments have for taxation purposes and rate-setting bodies for utility pricing. The FASB's cost–benefit calculus is similarly restricted to benefits for investors and creditors, and cost considerations are confined only to producers.

We don't believe that the FASB's focus on producers and the primary user group of investors and creditors fully represents the political economy of accounting. However, the purpose of this chapter is to examine the theoretical and empirical evidence for the usefulness of financial accounting data to the FASB's primary user group, investors and creditors. The chapter concludes with a brief assessment of the usefulness of accounting allocations.

---

[1] Statement of Financial Accounting Concepts (SFAC) 1, paras. 24–30.

ACCOUNTING DATA AND
MODELS OF FIRM VALUATION

Gordon's dividend valuation model is a useful starting point in understanding the potential relationship between accounting data and the value of the firm.[2] This model posits that the value of the firm to stockholders is the present value of future expected dividends to be received by stockholders. Beaver uses the dividend valuation model to formulate the role of accounting earnings in determining firm value.[3] First, present security prices are defined as a function of expected future dividends. Second, future dividends themselves are a function of future earnings. Finally, current accounting income is useful in predicting future earnings; therefore, current income is informative vis-à-vis its predictive ability with respect to future earnings (and ultimately future dividends). So, in this formulation, accounting income has value indirectly through its role in assessing future expected dividends. This, of course, is *predictive* value, which is one of the major arguments for the relevance of accounting information (see the discussion of SFAC 2 in Chapter 6).

More recent work in financial economics regarding the theoretical value of the firm traces back to Miller and Modigliani's seminal work in which they argue that dividend policy is irrelevant to firm valuation.[4] Ignoring the complicating effect of taxes, they show that the value of the firm can be equivalently modeled (independently of dividends) as the present value of future net cash flows, where net cash flows per period are defined as cash flows from operations minus cash investment in assets. This notion of net cash flow is the same used in capital budgeting — present value analysis. Miller and Modigliani's net cash flow model was originally a certainty-equivalent model but has been extended to a more general model in which there is uncertainty as to the future operating cash flows.[5] The attractiveness of the cash flow valuation model for accounting is that it maps directly into the accounting system; that is, cash flows are explicitly measured in accounting systems, whereas dividends are a matter of corporate policy and have nothing to do with accounting systems per se.

Interestingly, the FASB has also adopted (implicitly) the cash flow valuation model. In SFAC 1, the role of financial reporting is characterized as aiding investors, creditors, and others in assessing the amounts, timing, and uncertainty of the enterprise's prospective *net cash flows*. Further, the FASB has asserted that accrual accounting systems, and accrual income numbers in particular, are more useful for this purpose than are simpler cash-based systems:

---

[2] Gordon (1962).
[3] Beaver (1981, Chapter 4).
[4] Miller and Modigliani (1961); see also Fama and Miller (1972).
[5] Miller and Rock (1985) allow only operating cash flows to be uncertain. Francis and Linn (1988a) extend the model to allow *both* operating cash flows and investments to be uncertain.

> ... accrual accounting generally provides a better indication of an enterprise's present and continuing ability to generate favorable cash flows than information limited to the financial effects of cash receipts and payments (SFAC 1, preface).

Beaver agrees with this assertion, arguing that "an accrual can be viewed as a form of forecast about the future. . . ."[6] Francis and Linn, in a further extension of the net cash flow valuation model, use short-term working capital accruals as models for realizable cash flows and argue that yearly cash flows are seriously misstated if the accruals are ignored.[7] There is also empirical evidence that future cash flows are better forecast with accrual data than with cash flow data.[8] And, in stock market studies, security prices do seem to be more highly correlated with accrual income numbers than with either cash or working capital flows.[9]

The implication of this theoretical valuation literature is that accrual accounting systems incorporate the attribute that determines firm valuation — net cash flow data. However, the value to investors of the information in financial reporting does not lie in its role as an historical record; rather, its usefulness lies in its potential for revising investors' assessments of *future* period cash flows. This implies that changes in the firm's economic activity, as represented by accrual income numbers, are expected to continue into the future and for this reason lead to a revision of expected future cash flows.

THE INFORMATION CONTENT OF ACCOUNTING NUMBERS

The usefulness of accounting information to investors has been empirically investigated through the association (or lack thereof) of publicly released accounting data with changes in the firm's security prices. If there is a significant association, then there is evidence that accounting information is useful with respect to firm valuation. These studies also constitute tests of the so-called **efficient-markets hypothesis.**

The efficient-markets hypothesis (EMH) refers to the speed with which securities in the capital market respond to announcements of new information. The classic definition of market efficiency is that (1) the market fully reflects available information, and (2) by implication, market prices react instantaneously to new information.[10] In other words, new information is quickly impounded in the price of the security. If the hypothesis is correct, an item of

---

[6] Beaver (1981, p. 111).
[7] Francis and Linn (1988b).
[8] Bowen, Burgstahler, and Daley (1986) and Greenberg, Johnson, and Ramesh (1986).
[9] Ball and Brown (1968) and Rayburn (1986).
[10] Fama (1970).

information has value to investors only if there is evidence of a price response to the new information. When this occurs, the item of information is said to have **information content.** There are three forms of the efficient-markets hypothesis. The *weak* form says that security prices reflect information contained in the sequence of historical (past) prices; the *semistrong* form says that prices reflect all past and current information that is publicly available; and the *strong* form says that prices reflect all information (both public and private). Most testing has been of the semistrong form, which deals with publicly available information. Much of the information tested has been of an accounting nature — for example, financial statement data and earnings announcements.

The theoretical foundation of capital market or security price research comes from **portfolio theory,** which is a theory of rational investment choice and utility maximization: simply stated, risk can be reduced by holding a portfolio of investments. Risk that can be eliminated in this manner is called ***unsystematic (diversifiable) risk,*** while the remaining portfolio risk is called ***systematic (undiversifiable) risk.*** In portfolio theory, *systematic risk* is defined as the variance of expected investment returns. We conveniently think of expected return as a single number, but in reality it is a probability distribution of possible returns. The larger the variance around the mean of expected returns, the greater the risk associated with the investment. This variance may be quite high in individual stocks, but when evaluated for a portfolio as a whole, it is much lower. The reason for this situation is that variances of individual securities are offset when combined in a portfolio. In this way, it is possible to select a stock portfolio that minimizes risk for a given rate of return. What remains after eliminating all the risk possible is called *nondiversifiable* or *systematic risk* of the portfolio. And that risk which has been eliminated through diversification is called *diversifiable* or *unsystematic risk.* An investor will rationally select a portfolio with a risk-return relation that meets the investor's own utility preferences. The theoretical choice of portfolios is graphically presented in Exhibit 7–1. The capital market line represents alternative portfolios of increasing levels of systematic risk. Since investors are risk averse, the expected portfolio return increases as risk increases. The capital market line is linear only under restrictive conditions, but whether linear or curvilinear, a direct relationship exists between the level of risk and expected returns.

Portfolio theory is the foundation for a related development in finance — the pricing of individual stocks given the concept of diversified portfolios. A model called the ***capital asset pricing model*** has been developed for the theoretical pricing of individual stocks. Its first step is to relate the risk of an individual security relative to the market as a whole. The market is assumed to be a diversified portfolio. A correlation is made between the returns on individual stocks and market returns over a period of time. The correlations are illustrated as a scattergram in Exhibit 7–2. Regression analysis is used to fit a line to the scattergram. The slope of the characteristic line is called ***beta*** and represents a market-based measure of the systematic risk of an individual security relative to the average risk in the market as a whole. If beta equals 1, the returns are perfectly associated and the risks are equal. If beta exceeds 1, the returns on the

EXHIBIT 7–1
Capital Market Line

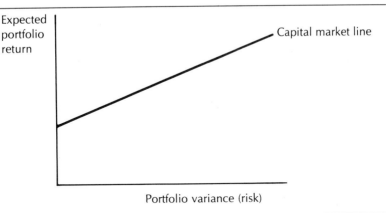

EXHIBIT 7–2
Scattergram of Security Returns Against Market Returns

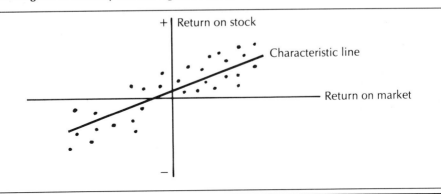

individual stock are greater than the market. In other words, if the rate of return on an individual security is greater than the market average, systematic risk of the security must also be greater because of the direct relationship between risk levels and expected returns. Higher returns must be accompanied by higher risks.

The assumption of the capital asset pricing model is that individual securities are priced solely on systematic risk. Given the assumption of diversified portfolios, it is argued that no one would pay for unsystematic risk. Beta is used to represent systematic risk of individual securities and to predict the risk-based price of securities. A standard two-parameter version of the capital asset pricing model defines the predicted rate of return for an individual security as

$$\bar{R}_j = i + B_j(\bar{R}_m - i) \tag{7.1}$$

where

$\bar{R}_j$ = expected return on security j
i = risk-free rate of return
$\bar{R}_m$ = expected return on the market portfolio
B_j = beta coefficient for security j

The beta term was illustrated in Exhibit 7–2 but it can also be defined statistically as

$$B_j = (Y_{jm}\delta_j\delta_m)/\delta_m^2 \tag{7.2}$$

where

$Y_{jm}\delta_j\delta_m$ = covariance of individual security j and the market-level portfolio m

δ_m^2 = variance on the market-level portfolio returns

Empirical studies in accounting use a simpler approach, called the ***market model,*** in which the risk-free return is dropped and expected returns are defined as

$$\bar{R}_j = \alpha_j + B_j(\bar{R}_m) + e_j \tag{7.3}$$

where

$\bar{R}_j$, $\bar{R}_m$, and B_j are the same as above
α_j = the intercept term illustrated in Exhibit 7–2
e_j = a random error term

Unexpected returns or **abnormal returns** for any time period are captured in the error term e_j in Equation (7.3). A common research approach in accounting studies has been to regress these abnormal returns on accounting variables, such as unexpected reported earnings, for the same time period to determine if there is information content, in which case there would be evidence that firm valuation is correlated with accounting information.

Before reviewing the empirical findings, we should make a few observations regarding the difficulties of doing this type of research.[11] The study of price movements and the pricing mechanism in any market is an imposing task. Determining cause and effect between information and security prices is especially difficult because new information is continuously causing price movements. Since the set of information affecting security prices is large, it is extremely difficult to isolate the effects of one piece of information. This difficulty means that the tests are going to be somewhat crude rather than precise. The research should be examined with this in mind. Failure to find evidence of information content should thus be interpreted cautiously, for the methodology is not always capable of detecting information content. For this reason, the

---

[11] For critiques of the research methodology, see Roll (1977) and Foster (1980).

stronger evidence from efficient-markets research exists where there is information content rather than where there is none.

Another weakness of capital market research is that it is a joint test of both market efficiency *and* information content. The absence of price responses is usually interpreted to mean that the information tested has no information content. This interpretation is correct only if the market is efficient. But what if the market is inefficient? If the market is inefficient, there is no way of determining what the absence of a price response means. This is another reason why the research findings are much stronger when there is evidence of information content.

A final point is that market-based research necessarily considers only the *aggregate* effect of individual investor decision making. That is, the role of accounting information vis-à-vis an individual investor's decision making is implicitly modeled as a black box: an "event," the reporting of accounting information, occurs, and the effect of this event is then inferred from whether or not there was an aggregate (market) reaction. As an alternative, Appendix 7-A presents an investor decision model that explicitly models the role of information in revising expectations about future cash flows at the level of an individual investor.

ACCOUNTING INCOME NUMBERS

The strongest evidence from capital market research concerns the information content of annual accounting earnings numbers. The seminal study, published in 1968, showed that the direction of change in reported accounting earnings (from the prior year) was positively correlated with security price movements.[12] The study also found that the price movements anticipated the earnings results and that there was virtually no abnormal price movement one month after the earnings were announced. This is consistent with the semistrong form of the efficient-markets hypothesis. A later study showed that the *magnitude* as well as *direction* of unexpected earnings are associated with changes in security prices.[13] Quarterly earnings announcements have also shown the same general results.[14]

These results are not surprising. We could expect accounting income to be part of the information used by investors in assessing risk and return. Capital market research has confirmed an almost self-evident proposition. The findings are important, though, in formally linking accounting information with investment decisions and hence with usefulness to investors.

ALTERNATIVE ACCOUNTING POLICIES

A more complex type of securities-price research has examined the effect of alternative accounting policies on security prices. The underlying purpose of these tests is to investigate the so-called naive-investor hypothesis. Research

---

[12] Ball and Brown (1968).
[13] Beaver, Clarke, and Wright (1979).
[14] Brown and Kennelly (1972) and Foster (1977a).

has found that security prices respond to accounting income numbers. Alternative accounting policies — for example, flexibility in the choice of depreciation and inventory methods — can affect reported income numbers. Although these methods affect reported accounting income, there is no apparent impact on company cash flows. These types of accounting alternatives simply represent different patterns of expense recognition or cost allocations.

The question of interest to researchers is whether alternative accounting policies have a systematic effect on security prices. If security prices do respond to income levels that differ solely because of alternative accounting methods, then there is support for the naive-investor hypothesis. On the other hand, if security prices do not respond to such artificial book-income differences, then there is evidence that investors in the market are sophisticated and able to see through such superficial bookkeeping differences. Virtually all the initial research was interpreted as rejecting the naive-investor hypothesis. However, recent research findings have challenged some of the earlier conclusions and reopened what was once considered a closed issue in accounting research.[15]

Alternatives with No Known Cash Flow Consequences

Several studies have compared companies that use different accounting methods. One of the earliest studies compared companies using accelerated and straight-line depreciation methods.[16] The two groups of companies had different accounting income numbers because they used alternative depreciation methods; thus there were differences in income between the two groups of companies due to the use of alternative depreciation accounting methods. There were also differences in price–earnings multiples between the two groups. Companies using accelerated methods had lower earnings but higher price–earnings multiples than companies using straight-line. However, when earnings of companies using accelerated methods were adjusted to a straight-line depreciation basis, the price–earnings multiple between the two groups of companies was not significantly different.

The assessments of the companies in the market did not appear to be affected by arbitrary and alternative accounting income numbers. This finding is often expressed as the market is not "fooled" by arbitrary accounting differences. Other similar research has supported this conclusion. Additional areas tested include purchase versus pooling accounting, expensing versus capitaliz-

---

[15] Hand (1990) believes that some stock prices may occasionally be determined by naive investors who are unduly influenced by bottom-line results. This would be more likely for relatively small firms having a relatively high proportion of stock owned by individual investors. Tinic (1990) urges caution in accepting Hand's results. From the conceptual standpoint, Tinic (1990, p. 785) believes that knowledgeable investors would capitalize on the errors of the naive investors and eventually eliminate the valuation error (belief in the ability of "knowledgeable investors" to spot "mispriced" securities — as opposed to their ability to act on new information — may well require a leap of imagination on the part of EMH enthusiasts). Nevertheless, Tinic does have an open-minded attitude toward evaluating both the EMH and modifications to it such as Hand's viewpoint.

[16] Beaver and Dukes (1973).

ing research and development costs, and recognition versus deferral of unrealized holding gains on marketable securities.[17]

A related area of investigation concerns security-price responses to a reported change in accounting policy by a company. Changes in depreciation policy have been researched, and there is no evidence that the change per se affects security prices.[18] Another area tested has been a change from the deferral to flow-through method of accounting for the investment credit.[19] Again, no price effects were found. Although changes in accounting policies may cause the income number to change (solely because of the policy change), these research studies have not found that security prices respond to the changes. Higher accounting income achieved solely from a change in accounting policy with no apparent real changes in underlying cash flows does not appear to fool the market.

The evidence from the type of research discussed in the preceding paragraphs supports the claim that there is no information content in accounting policy changes, at least where there are no apparent underlying changes in cash flows. This finding has also been interpreted as a rejection of the naive-investor hypothesis. Investors appear to adjust accounting income to compensate for artificial bookkeeping differences with no real substance. That is, investors do not appear to respond mechanistically and naively to changes in reported accounting income numbers.

An Alternative with Cash Flow Consequences:
The LIFO Choice

One type of change in accounting policy that does produce a security-price response is a change from FIFO to LIFO inventory accounting. Changes to LIFO have been associated with a positive security-price movement, even though LIFO lowers accounting income in a period of rising inventory prices.[20] Given the apparent sophistication of investors in other areas of accounting policy differences, what can be the logical explanation for these price responses? The suggested reason for the price response is that LIFO must be adopted for both book and tax purposes. In a period of rising prices, tax expense will be lower for companies that use LIFO, in which case there are real cash flow consequences due to the change in accounting policy. Even though book income is lowered by the use of LIFO, cash flows are higher because the taxable income is lower. Positive security-price responses are therefore consistent with an increase in the value of the firm.

Other studies, however, contradict these findings concerning the effect of the changes.[21] These studies either found no evidence of price response or

---

[17] Hong, Kaplan, and Mandelker (1978), Dukes (1976), and Foster (1977b).
[18] Archibald (1972) and Comiskey (1971).
[19] Cassidy (1976).
[20] Ball (1972), Sunder (1973, 1975), and Biddle and Lindahl (1982).
[21] Abdel-khalik and McKeown (1978), Brown (1980), and Ricks (1982).

found evidence of a negative price response. Either result is contrary to the earlier finding of positive price responses. The recent studies suggest the earlier research may have failed to isolate the real effect of the LIFO change because of a self-selection bias. (This means that companies changing to LIFO had other things occurring simultaneously that confounded the results and may have caused the positive price response.) But if these studies are correct, then there may be some support for the naive-investor hypothesis. There are positive tax benefits associated with the LIFO change that should increase the value of the firm. Yet security-price responses were not positive. Since LIFO will lower accounting book income, a negative price response could be interpreted as a mechanistic response to a lower accounting number, a response made without considering the positive cash flow consequences due to lower taxes.

As discussed at the beginning of this section, security-price research is extremely difficult to conduct and interpret. The LIFO choice issue amply illustrates this point. The early LIFO research rejected the naive-investor hypothesis. Recent research on the LIFO question reopens what was once thought to be a closed issue.

Alternatives with Indirect Cash Consequences

Recent security-price research has been probing a more subtle issue referred to as *indirect consequences*. An **indirect consequence** occurs when an accounting policy change affects the value of the firm through an indirect effect on owners, rather than a direct effect on company cash flows. One such study was motivated by an attempt to explain why securities prices of certain oil and gas companies responded negatively to a mandatory change in accounting policy.[22] The required change from full costing to successful efforts was regarded as simply a change in how exploration costs are allocated to the income statement. Therefore, it was expected that no security-price response would be evident since there was no direct cash flow consequence to the companies.

However, security-price responses were found to exist and since previous research had predominantly rejected the naive-investor hypothesis, a search was made for the existence of some indirect cash flow consequences to explain the price response. The study posited that a change to successful-efforts accounting for oil and gas exploration costs lowered firms' ability to pay dividends in the short term, because of restrictive debt covenants. Therefore, even though the change in accounting policy appeared to affect only book income on the surface, there were indirect cash flow consequences to investors, which might explain the negative price response. This explanation derives from agency theory. When accounting numbers are used to monitor agency contracts, there can be indirect consequences on the firm's owners and creditors from changes in accounting policies. In the case of debt covenants restricting dividend payments, accounting numbers are used to protect the security of bondholders at the expense of stockholders. If an accounting policy change

---

[22] Collins, Rozeff, and Dhaliwal (1981).

lowers accounting income (as could occur in a mandatory change to successful efforts), stockholder returns could be lowered, thus causing a negative price response.

A similar type of study found negative security-price responses for firms using pooling accounting when pooling was restricted by the APB in favor of purchase accounting for combinations.[23] Differences between purchase and pooling accounting appear on the surface to affect only book income with no real cash effects. However, the reduced use of pooling accounting could affect dividend distribution because of debt covenants. Income would normally be lower under purchase accounting than pooling, and the same effect of dividend restrictions as argued in the oil and gas study were also argued in the purchase/pooling study. Another research study along these lines examined the requirement to capitalize leases that had previously been reported as operating leases.[24] There was some evidence of negative price responses for certain companies; this situation could have been due to the existence of debt covenants as well as the adverse effect lease capitalization would have on the firms' future borrowing capacity.

SOME FURTHER QUESTIONS RELATIVE TO MARKET EFFICIENCY

Clearly there is some degree of efficiency present in securities-market transactions. The question is one of how much efficiency exists, which is virtually impossible to answer. However, several recent studies provide evidence that there may be somewhat less than is postulated in the semistrong form of the efficient-markets hypothesis.

Ou and Penman, in a very extensive study, tried to go back to fundamental analysis. **Fundamental analysis** assumes that securities markets are inefficient and that underpriced shares can be found by means of financial statement analysis. This view is directly opposed to the efficient-markets view that prices of securities rapidly reflect all publicly available information (the semistrong form of the hypothesis).

Ou and Penman used traditional accounting measures such as return on total assets, gross margin ratio, and percentage of change in current assets in a multivariate model to predict whether the following year's income would increase or decrease. The time period covered was between 1965 and 1977, the model included almost twenty accounting measures, and approximately 23,000 observations were made.[25] Ou and Penman were able to describe the following year earnings changes correctly almost 80 percent of the time.[26] The key point concerns whether their predictors were capturing information that was not already reflected in security prices but that would be subsequently reflected in security prices and would thus result in abnormal security returns if investment

[23] Leftwich (1981).
[24] Pfeiffer (1980).
[25] Ou and Penman (1989, pp. 303–307).
[26] Ibid., p. 306.

were based on the earnings predictions of their model.[27] Their analysis indicates that this is exactly what would have occurred.[28] They also believed that the excess security returns would not have been attributable to excess risk factors, though they were not entirely sure on this particular point.[29] Ou and Penman's research thus indicates that markets are not as efficient as efficient-markets advocates would like to believe and that fundamental analysis is still important for investment purposes. This study also implies that "better" accounting standards might improve the predictive ability of accounting information, which leads us to Lev's work.

Lev concentrated on an issue that is complementary to the factors in the Ou and Penman study. Specifically, his point is that both over time and within years (cross-sectional studies), the correlation between earnings numbers and stock returns has been exceedingly low.[30] Earnings, in other words, have very little explanatory power (as measured by R^2, the coefficient of correlation) relative to changes in stock prices. Lev believes that one of the principal reasons for this situation lies with the low quality of reported income numbers:

> Research on the quality of earnings shifts the focus to an explicit consideration of accounting issues by calling for a systematic examination of the extent to which the specific principles underlying accounting measurements and valuations, as well as managerial manipulations, detract from the usefulness of earnings and other financial variables. Such research has the potential both to further our understanding of the role of financial information in asset valuation and to contribute meaningfully to accounting policymaking.[31]

Thus the Ou and Penman and Lev papers are complementary because one finds a low explanatory relationship between earnings and stock returns while the other sees a predictive role for accounting data in a market that may be less efficient than presently accepted dogma cares to admit. One article (Lev's) looks directly at the issue of improving accounting measurements while the other may certainly be said to imply this point.[32]

ACCOUNTING INFORMATION AND RISK ASSESSMENT

Capital market research has also investigated the usefulness of accounting numbers for assessing the risk of securities and portfolios. These studies have found high correlations between the variability of accounting earnings and beta, the market-risk measure.[33] The high correlations imply that accounting data may

---

[27] Ibid., pp. 306–309.

[28] Ibid., pp. 309–313.

[29] Ibid., pp. 316–320.

[30] Lev (1980).

[31] Lev (1989, p. 178).

[32] Wyatt (1983) stresses the importance of improving accounting measurements (the quality of earnings issue) given a securities market that is efficient.

[33] Beaver, Kettler, and Scholes (1970), Bildersee (1975), Thompson (1976), Eskew (1979), and Elgers (1980). For a review of the methodological problems in this type of research, see Elgers and Murray (1982).

be useful for assessing risk. Some other research has tried to determine if alternative accounting policies have any effect on risk. The purpose of this type of research is to identify how alternative accounting policies or disclosures may affect the usefulness of accounting numbers for assessing risk. For example, one study tried to determine if unfunded pension benefits (reported in footnotes) affected beta.[34] There was no significant impact. From this evidence, it might be concluded that pension information is not useful for risk assessments. However, other studies found that supplemental segment (line of business) disclosures resulted in a revision of systematic risk, which suggests that such information is useful for risk assessments.[35]

Other studies have tested the association of financial ratios with beta.[36] Some of the ratios and computations tested include dividend payout ratio, leverage, growth rates, asset size, liquidity, and pretax interest coverage, as well as earnings and earnings variability. In general, these tests indicate a strong association between the accounting-based ratios and the market measure of risk, beta.

SUMMARY OF CAPITAL MARKET RESEARCH

Empirical evidence from capital market research is supportive of these statements:

1. Accounting earnings appear to have information content and to affect security prices.
2. Alternative accounting policies with no apparent direct or indirect cash flow consequences to the firm do not seem to affect security prices, though this issue is not entirely settled.
3. Alternative accounting policies that have direct or indirect cash flow consequences to the firm (or its owners) do affect security prices.
4. There are incentives to choose certain accounting policies, where choice exists, owing to indirect cash consequences.
5. Accounting-based risk measures correlate with market risk measures, suggesting that accounting numbers are useful for risk assessment.

In the early 1970s, some argued that capital market research could be used as a basis for (1) choosing the best accounting policies, and (2) evaluating the economic consequences of alternative accounting policies on security prices.[37] Accounting policies that most affected security prices were thought to be most useful. In other words, such policies would have had the most information content. The argument had intuitive appeal, particularly since deductively based

---

[34] Stone (1981).
[35] See Mohr (1983) for a comprehensive review.
[36] For example, Beaver, Kettler, and Scholes (1970), Bildersee (1975), and Thompson (1976).
[37] Gonedes (1972), and Beaver and Dukes (1972).

research had proved unable to resolve the normative accounting theory debate about the most desirable form of accounting. However, the early advocates of security-price research now recognize the limitations of this research for such a use.[38] Reasons for these limitations are the public-good nature of accounting information, the existence of free riders, and the resultant market failure in terms of optimal resource allocation.

In spite of its inability to resolve accounting theory and policy questions, capital market research continues to be useful in empirically evaluating economic consequences of accounting policies vis-à-vis security prices and the usefulness of accounting numbers for risk-and-return assessments. Perhaps more than anything else, though, the impact of capital market research is that it brought a different perspective to accounting theory and policy at a time when the emphasis was primarily on deductively based theory.

SURVEYS OF INVESTORS

Another way of determining the usefulness of accounting information is to ask investors how (if at all) they use annual reports. Surveys of investors have been undertaken in several countries and generally have shown a rather low readership of accounting information.[39] Approximately one-half of the investors surveyed indicated they read financial statements. Institutional investors have shown a much higher level of readership.[40] These surveys, particularly of individual investors, should be interpreted cautiously, however. Individual investors may rely on investment analysts to process accounting information. It would be simplistic to assume accounting information has no usefulness to investors merely because many individual stockholders do not read annual reports in detail.

Another type of survey research has asked investors to weigh the importance of different types of investment information, including accounting information. Several studies of this type have been reported.[41] Accounting information ranks fairly high in importance in these surveys, though not at the top. This status seems to be attributable to the historical nature of accounting information and the reporting-lag effect. More timely accounting information from company press reports, and nonaccounting information such as general economic conditions and company announcements on products and markets, rank ahead of annual reports in perceived importance.

---

[38] Gonedes and Dopuch (1974) argue that the free-rider problem makes it impossible to use capital market research to identify optimal accounting policies. The reason is that production costs cannot be internalized on users because accounting information has characteristics of a public good. See the discussion in Chapter 4. So, even though mandatory information may have information content, there is no way of determining if users would really demand the information in a free market situation.

[39] Epstein (1975) and Lee and Tweedie (1975).

[40] Anderson (1981) and Chang and Most (1977).

[41] See Hines (1982) for a summary of the major investment surveys.

ACCOUNTING DATA AND CREDITORS

Theories underlying the usefulness of firm-specific accounting information to creditors is not as well developed as is the role of accounting numbers vis-à-vis stock prices. It is, however, generally agreed that the price of interest-bearing debt is based on **default risk,** which is defined as the premium in excess of the risk-free interest rate on otherwise identical debt (for example, U.S. Treasury obligations). Thus, firm-specific information, including accounting data, aids creditors in assessing default risk.

Several distinct lines of research have emerged: (1) the usefulness of accounting data in predicting corporate bankruptcy (which encompasses loan default); (2) the association of accounting data with bond ratings wherein such ratings are presumed to proxy for default risk; (3) the association of accounting data with estimates of interest-rate risk premiums on debt; and (4) experimental studies of the role of accounting data in lending decisions. We will present a brief overview of the research findings.

Accounting-based ratios have been very useful in discriminating between firms that subsequently went bankrupt and those that did not.[42] Predictability up to five years prior to bankruptcy has been demonstrated. These findings do not mean that companies with "bad" ratios will necessarily go bankrupt in the future. It simply means that bankrupt companies tend to have financial ratios prior to bankruptcy that differ from nonbankrupt companies. The existence of "bad" ratios does not mean bankruptcy will occur, just that it is more probable. Accounting data has also been associated significantly with both bond ratings and interest-rate risk premiums.[43] Among the important ratios are profitability, earnings variability, and leverage. Research has also been used to evaluate which of alternative sets of accounting data are more highly associated with bankruptcy prediction, bond ratings, and risk premiums. Among the issues examined have been historical cost versus price-level-adjusted income, the effect of lease capitalization versus noncapitalization, and recognition of pension liabilities versus footnote-only disclosure.[44]

Experimental (laboratory) studies have also tested the usefulness of accounting data for creditors. Accounting data in the context of a loan-related decision (for example, loan amount, bankruptcy prediction, and interest rates) are provided to subjects to determine how, if at all, it affects their hypothetical decisions.[45] In these experiments the accounting data are manipulated to see if the judgments are sensitive to whatever manipulations take place; for example, magnitudes of accounting ratios or financial statements prepared under alternative policies (for example, lease capitalization versus noncapitalization). Generally, these studies support the sensitivity of loan-related decision making

---

[42] See Altman (1971), Beaver (1967), and Ohlson (1980).

[43] Cook and Hendershott (1978), Fisher (1959), Horrigan (1966), and Kaplan and Urwitz (1979).

[44] Baran, Lakonishok, and Ofer (1980), Elam (1975), and Reiter (1985).

[45] For example, Libby (1975), Wright (1977), and Wilkins and Zimmer (1983).

to key accounting data and, in this sense, complement the findings based on economic field data.

THE USEFULNESS OF ACCOUNTING ALLOCATIONS

At present, the historical cost accounting model remains the basic framework for financial reporting. Central to this model are revenue recognition rules and the matching of costs to revenues. Many costs are recognized over multiple accounting periods. Some examples include depreciation, organizational start-up costs, goodwill amortization, and bond premium/discount amortization. The recognition of these types of costs over multiple periods is referred to as *accounting allocation.*[46] Allocations have been criticized on the grounds that they are "incorrigible." By this it is meant that there is no obviously correct way to allocate the costs because no single allocation method can be proved superior to another. For example, it cannot be proved that straight-line depreciation is any more appropriate than accelerated depreciation methods.

Another way of describing this dilemma is to say that no allocation is completely defensible against other methods. For this reason, it has been concluded that all accounting allocations are, in the end, arbitrary. Conceptually, this is a very disturbing idea and strikes at the logical core of historical cost accounting. Because of the arbitrariness of accounting allocations, allocation-free financial statements have been advocated as a better way of reporting useful information. Allocation-free accounting can be accomplished by using cash flow statements, exit-price systems (as discussed in Appendix 1-A of Chapter 1), and certain types of replacement cost systems (also discussed in Appendix 1-A of Chapter 1).

However, the fact that accounting allocations are arbitrary does not prove that accounting information is useless. The allocation argument is deductive and examines the logic of historical cost accounting. Usefulness is an empirical question, not a matter of deductive logic. There is no evidence to support the contention that allocation-based financial statements are useless. In fact, there is a great deal of evidence from capital market research that supports the information content of accounting income numbers.

Capital market research in the area of alternative accounting policies does support the arbitrariness of accounting allocations. Alternative policies with no known cash flow consequences have no effect on security prices, which supports the argument that allocations are arbitrary and convey no information to users. However, the research findings also support the fact that investors are not naive and that they are capable of adjusting accounting numbers in order to achieve comparability between companies. In spite of allocations, income numbers are

---

[46]The pioneering allocation research was done by Thomas (1969).

useful and investors appear able to achieve comparability by informally adjusting for the effects of arbitrary allocations.

It must also be remembered that allocations represent only a part of the total accounting information in financial statements. Much accounting information contains no allocations. Even if the allocation criticism is valid, usefulness may still be high. It has also been suggested that the historical cost, allocation-based approach may be the most cost-effective method of reporting financial information about firms.

A policy implication of the allocation research is that the FASB should not try to resolve problems by searching for the best allocation. On the other hand, the FASB should not necessarily avoid allocations. They may be the most cost-effective means of producing financial statements. But the convenience of allocation-type policies should be carefully weighed against allocation-free approaches, which may be less ambiguous and easier to understand. Another implication is that the FASB should reduce flexibility in accounting allocations. Given the evidence from capital market research, there is no compelling reason to permit arbitrary flexibility. Rigid uniformity would be easier to apply and would eliminate some arbitrary differences between companies. It will be recalled that security prices adjust for such arbitrary differences in accounting allocations. In the case of accounting allocations with no real cash flow consequences, a strong argument exists for rigid uniformity.

SUMMARY

This chapter has surveyed the research literature on the usefulness of accounting information to what the FASB calls the *primary* user group of investors and creditors. The picture that emerges is that accounting data are important to investors vis-à-vis security prices and to loan-related decision making by creditors. There should, however, be no illusions about the relative importance of financial reporting for these external users. For example, unexpected accounting earnings explain only a small percentage (around 5 percent) of the firm's revaluation vis-à-vis security prices. Although some of this is due to econometric problems in the research, it is more or less consistent with investor surveys that show accounting information ranking lower in importance than more timely information about the economy, the relevant industry, and the firm itself.

Further, although the evidence supports the usefulness of accounting information to this primary user group, we do not really know just how valuable it is. Thus, we cannot evaluate either the social welfare of the current financial reporting system or the value of hypothetical alternatives, such as current value accounting. The good news for accountants is the systematic evidence that financial reporting is useful. The bad news is that we know very little about how useful it is, and we are unable to infer much about the social benefits of the current investment in accounting information production. Nevertheless, the issue of improving the quality of earnings and other accounting numbers is still alive.

APPENDIX 7-A: INFORMATION ECONOMICS

Information economics is a general framework for determining the value of information to a decision maker. It has been used to study accounting information; the illustrative examples here are based on accounting information.

MODEL FOR INFORMATION EVALUATION

The model for determining the value of information to a risk-neutral decision maker is illustrated with the following example. Assume a decision maker is faced with a choice between two actions (a_j):

a_1 = lend \$1 million to XYZ for one year at 15%.
a_2 = invest \$1 million in government bonds for one year at 12%.

For simplicity, only two alternative future outcomes or scenarios are assumed to be possible. These outcomes are called *states* (s_i):

s_1 = XYZ repays the loan plus interest.
s_2 = XYZ defaults on the loan, and \$200,000 of costs are incurred
      to recover the loan and interest in full.

Based on existing information or knowledge, the subjective probability (ϕ) of each state occurring is considered by the decision maker to be

$$\phi(s_1) = .8$$
$$\phi(s_2) = .2$$

Note that the subjective probability of both states must total 1.0.

The decision problem is summarized by expressing the future value of each action/state combination in a payoff matrix (Exhibit 7–3). Utility is determined by the expected monetary value of each action (a_j) using Bayesian statistics. Letting $E(U|a_j)$ be the utility of each action we have

$$E(U|a_j) = \sum_{i=1}^{s} U(s_i, a_j) \cdot \phi(s_i)$$
$$= U(s_1, a_j) \times \phi(s_1) + U(s_2, a_j) \times \phi(s_2)$$

The expected monetary values of actions a_1 and a_2 are

$$E(U|a_1) = \$(1,150,000 \times .8) + (950,000 \times .2) = \$1,110,000$$
$$E(U|a_2) = \$(1,120,000 \times .8) + (1,120,000 \times .2) = \$1,120,000$$

Given the present information available to the decision maker, action a_2 would be taken since it has a higher utility than action a_1.

EXHIBIT 7–3
Payoff Matrix

s_i / a_j	s_1 XYZ Does Not Default	s_2 XYZ Defaults
a_1 Lend to XYZ	$1,150,000	$ 950,000
a_2 Invest in Government Bonds	$1,120,000	$1,120,000

VALUE OF PERFECT INFORMATION

The next question to consider is the value of what is called *perfect information.* In the preceding example, perfect information means that we would know with certainty which future state, s_1 or s_2, is going to occur. If s_1 occurs (XYZ does not default), the utility maximizing action is a_1, lending $1 million to XYZ. If s_2 occurs (XYZ defaults), utility would be maximized by action a_2, investing in the government bonds. The values of these alternative optimal acts, given the two alternative outcomes, are $1,150,000 (given s_1) and $1,120,000 (given s_2).

The utility of knowing in advance what state is going to occur is defined as

$$E(U|\text{advance state revelation}) = \sum_{i=1}^{s} \{\max_{a \in A} U\,(s_i,a)\} \cdot \phi(s_i)$$
$$= (\$1,150,000 \times .8) + (\$1,120,000 \times .2)$$
$$= \$1,144,000$$

This formula takes the value of the two optimal acts if s_1 and s_2 were to occur and derives the utility of knowing in advance which state occurs. This is done by multiplying these amounts by the subjective probability estimates of s_1 and s_2 based on existing information. The utility of having perfect information is the expected value of the optimal acts, given the original subjective probability of each state occurring. This is computed as $1,144,000. The value of perfect information is the difference between the utility as computed above ($1,144,000) and the utility of $1,120,000 given action a_2 in the original analysis. This amount, $24,000, is the maximum the decision maker would be willing to pay for additional information that reveals the state that will occur.

VALUE OF LESS-THAN-PERFECT INFORMATION

In reality, one could not buy perfect information because future outcomes cannot be known in advance. But new information can cause a revision in the decision maker's subjective probability estimation of each state's occurring. The value of new but less-than-perfect information can also be calculated using Bayesian statistics.

Continuing the previous example, assume a new piece of information can be purchased that is relevant to assessing the probability of default by XYZ. The decision maker believes the predicted ratio of expense to sales for the next year is a good indicator of XYZ's likelihood of defaulting. This predicted information can be extrapolated from historical trends. The new information or signal is designated Y_k, and it comes from an information system called η. For simplicity the new signal (Y_k) can have one of two values:

$$Y_1 = \text{expense to sales ratio} \leq 1$$
$$Y_2 = \text{expense to sales ratio} > 1$$

Given that XYZ does not default, the decision maker believes the probability of receiving signal Y_1 would be .9. This is also defined as $\phi(Y_1|s_1)$, the probability of receiving signal Y_1 given state s_1. The probability of receiving signal Y_2 given state s_1 is, of course, .1 $(1.0 - .9)$.

The decision maker also believes the probability of signal Y_2 given state s_2 to be .7. In other words, the signal Y_2 is *bad news* and would be expected to be associated with default, while signal Y_1 is *good news* and is more likely to be associated with not defaulting. Finally, to complete the analysis, the probability of signal Y_1 given s_2 would be .3 $(1.0 - .7)$. These four probabilities are summarized in Exhibit 7–4.

The probability of actually receiving the signals Y_1 and Y_2 is computed from the formula

$$\phi(Y_k) = \sum_{i=1}^{s} \phi(Y_k|s_i) \cdot \phi(s_i)$$
$$\phi(Y_1) = \phi(Y_1|s_1) \cdot \phi(s_1) + \phi(Y_1|s_2) \cdot \phi(s_2)$$
$$= (.9 \times .8) + (.3 \times .2)$$
$$= .78$$
$$\phi(Y_2) = \phi(Y_2|s_1) \cdot \phi(s_1) + \phi(Y_2|s_2) \cdot \phi(s_2)$$
$$= (.1 \times .8) + (.7 \times .2)$$
$$= .22$$

It is now possible to compute the revised probabilities of each state, given the new signals Y_1 or Y_2. These revisions are based on Bayes Theorem:

$$\phi(s_i|Y_k) = \frac{\phi(Y_k|s_i) \cdot \phi(s_i)}{\phi(Y_k)}$$
$$\phi(s_1|Y_1) = \frac{.9 \times .8}{.78} = .92$$

EXHIBIT 7–4
New Signal Probabilities

S_i \ Y_k	S_1 No Default	S_2 Default
Y_1 Ratio ≤ 1	.9	.3
Y_2 Ratio > 1	.1	.7

$$\phi(s_2|Y_1) = \frac{.3 \times .2}{.78} = .08$$

$$\phi(s_1|Y_2) = \frac{.1 \times .8}{.22} = .36$$

$$\phi(s_2|Y_2) = \frac{.7 \times .2}{.22} = .64$$

These are revised probabilities of states s_1 and s_2, given the receipt of signals Y_1 or Y_2 from information system η.

The final step is to recompute the utility of each action a_1 and a_2, given the revised state probabilities. If signal Y_1 (expenses to sales ratio ≤ 1) is received, the utility of each act is

$$E(U|a_1, Y_1) = (\$1,150,000 \times .92) + (\$950,000 \times .08)$$
$$= \$1,134,000$$
$$E(U|a_2, Y_1) = (\$1,120,000 \times .92) + (\$1,120,000 \times .08)$$
$$= \$1,120,000$$

Action a_1, the loan to XYZ, is the optimal act if signal Y_1 is received.

If signal Y_2 (expense to sales ratio > 1) is received, the utility of each act is

$$E(U|a_1, Y_2) = (\$1,150,000 \times .36) + (\$950,000 \times .64)$$
$$= \$1,022,000$$
$$E(U|a_2, Y_2) = (\$1,120,000 \times .36) + (\$1,120,000) \times .64)$$
$$= \$1,120,000$$

Action a_2, investment in the government bonds, is the optimal act if signal Y_2 is received.

The value of new information from the information system η is derived from the utility of each of the above two optimal acts, given the probabilities of receiving each signal. The formula is

$$E(U|\eta) = \sum_{k=1}^{Y} (U|a_{Y_k}^*,\eta) \cdot \phi(Y_k|\eta)$$
$$= (\$1,134,000 \times .78) + (\$1,120,000 \times .22)$$
$$= \$1,130,920$$

where $a_{Y_k}^*$ is the optimal action given the signal Y_k.

In the original case, given existing knowledge, the expected utility of the decision was \$1,120,000. The expected utility of the decision, given new information Y_k, is \$1,130,920. Therefore, the decision maker would be prepared to spend up to \$1,130,920 minus \$1,120,000, or \$10,920, for the signal Y_k from information system η. This amount would be the point at which the marginal cost of the new information equals the marginal benefit.

Information economics, or decision theory, does not provide answers to normative questions, such as what sets of accounting information are optimal. The analysis can determine only the value of specific information for a narrowly defined decision. Therefore, the question of which are the optimal sets of policies could be analyzed only after calculating the value of each alternative set of policies and then comparing them. This approach would be impossible because there are virtually limitless accounting and disclosure policies that could be prescribed. However, such an approach could be used to assess the net benefits of specific proposals. Another contribution of the information economics model is that it has increased our appreciation of how accounting information is likely to have value in the decision-making process.

A limitation of information economics is that real-world decision makers face more complex decisions (having many more actions and states) than can be illustrated in the model. Human bounds on the ability to process information limit the formal application of decision theory. Thus, real decision-making behavior has been described as "satisficing" rather than as maximizing utility. Another limitation of information economics concerns its generality: unless one assumes that decision makers behave homogeneously, it is impossible to generalize to all decision makers from the analysis of individuals. User diversity is thus a critical issue.

Information has also been deductively analyzed in a multiuser setting.[47] This entails a market-level social welfare analysis of information supply and demand in which accounting information is treated as an economic good. This type of research is very abstract and is based on narrowly defined sets of assumptions concerning economic markets. Information is also treated in a nondescript manner — that is, the analyses are of information markets rather than of specific types of information; for this reason, the conclusions are of a very general nature. These types of deductive analyses try to evaluate market incentives for information production and consumption, as well as the effects on aggregate social welfare or optimality of resource allocation. Some of these

---

[47] See Demski (1973), Gonedes (1980), Hakansson (1977), Ohlson and Buckman (1981), and Verrecchia (1982).

studies also examine the effect of regulation on information markets, but again in a very generalized manner. Because of the abstractness and generality of these analyses, the multiuser setting of information economics has not yielded specific conclusions concerning the value of accounting information. Commenting on this, the *Statement of Accounting Theory and Theory Acceptance* said:

> In summary, the information economics approach offers an explicit individual-demand-based analysis of accounting policy questions. . . . The power of the approach is in isolating general relationships and effects of alternative scenarios. At present, however, the approach is still too general to provide definitive answers. . . .[48]

Perhaps Verrechia best sums it up:

> The relationship between public disclosure and social welfare can be discussed *ad absurdum* by introducing more complicated scenarios. With equal facility and no claim to offer resolution, we can debate the number of angels who can dance on the head of a pin. In the absence of empirical evidence there seems to be no way to determine which set of exogenously specified assumptions is the most reasonable, and even if we could there appears to be no consensus in the literature about what constitutes "social value."[49]

QUESTIONS

1. How is accounting data thought to be useful to investors?
2. How is accounting data thought to be useful to creditors?
3. What is the efficient-markets hypothesis?
4. Why does the concept of market efficiency (with respect to information) have no necessary relation to the quality of accounting information? Why is this distinction important with respect to accounting policy making?
5. What is meant by "information content" and how does capital market research determine the information content of accounting numbers?
6. What are some limitations of capital market research?
7. Describe the general findings from capital market research concerning the information content of accounting numbers and the effects of alternative accounting policies.
8. What is the naive-investor hypothesis; why is it important with respect to financial reporting, and what are the research findings?
9. Why is the choice between the FIFO–LIFO inventory methods an interesting issue in capital market research?
10. Why may accounting policies with no direct cash flow consequences indirectly affect investors or creditors?

[48] American Accounting Association (1977, p. 25).
[49] Verrechia (1982, p. 17).

11. Why is it argued that capital market research cannot determine the optimality of accounting policies even for the limited investor–creditor group?

12. In what ways do you think information useful for investors (in assessing future cash flows) differs from that useful for creditors (in assessing default risk)?

13. How do market-level and individual decision-maker analyses complement one another in studying the usefulness of accounting information to investors and creditors?

14. Recall from Chapter 4 the notion of a political economy of accounting. What other user groups (besides the primary investor–creditor group) could claim to be stakeholders in the firm, and how might their information needs differ from the primary investor–creditor group?

15. Drawing on Appendix 7-A, how does information have "value" in the information economics framework? Compare this to SFAC 2, in which the usefulness of accounting is defined in terms of predictive and feedback value.

16. Do you see any conflict between Lev's paper, which talks about the low correlation between earnings and stock returns, and the Ou and Penman paper, which sees predictive ability in accounting numbers that have not been totally impounded in security prices?

CASES AND PROBLEMS

1. The usefulness of accounting data to investors and creditors for *predictive* purposes is necessarily forward looking. However, under generally accepted accounting principles, financial statements are constructed primarily as an historical record.

   Required:
   (a) What limitation does this impose on the usefulness of financial statements for predictive purposes, and how is this limitation evident from the research reviewed in the chapter?
   (b) Provide examples of important forward-looking events that either are not reported in financial statements or are not reported in a timely manner.
   (c) Why may the feedback value of audited financial statements make them very important to investors and creditors even though predictive value is not necessarily high?

2. Davis, Menon, and Morgan (1982) suggest that four successive metaphors or "images" have shaped our thinking over the past sixty years with respect to financial reporting: accounting as an historical record, accounting as a mirror of economic income, accounting as an information system, and accounting as an economic commodity.

Required:
(a) Who are the users implied by each of the four metaphors?
(b) Which metaphor comes closest to the FASB's view and why?
(c) Which metaphor best characterizes the agency or contracting perspective on the role of accounting data (see Chapter 4)?
(d) Based on the review of financial reporting in Chapter 3 from the early 1900s onward, one can certainly argue that the structure and the substance of accounting is much the same today as it was then. If so, what might this suggest regarding the usefulness of financial reporting, and how is it also consistent with the empirical studies reviewed in the chapter?

3. A retail company begins operations late in 19X0 by purchasing $600,000 of merchandise. There are no sales in 19X0. During 19X1 additional merchandise of $3,000,000 is purchased. Operating expenses (excluding management bonuses) are $400,000, and sales are $6,000,000. The management compensation agreement provides for incentive bonuses totalling 1 percent of after-tax income (before the bonuses). Taxes are 25 percent, and accounting and taxable income will be the same.

   The company is undecided about the selection of the LIFO or FIFO inventory methods. For the year ended 19X1, ending inventory would be $700,000 and $1,000,000, respectively, under LIFO and FIFO.

Required:
(a) How are accounting numbers used to monitor this agency contract between owners and managers?
(b) Evaluate management incentives to choose FIFO.
(c) Evaluate management incentives to choose LIFO.
(d) Assuming an efficient capital market, what effect should the alternative policies have on security prices and shareholder wealth?
(e) Why is the management compensation agreement potentially counterproductive as an agency monitoring mechanism?
(f) Devise an alternative bonus system to avoid the problem in the existing plan.

4. This case draws on the analysis in Appendix 7-A. An investor is considering two $100,000 investments: (1) ABC Company bonds maturing in one year and paying 12 percent interest at maturity, and (2) U.S. Treasury Notes also maturing in one year and paying 7 percent interest at maturity. The investor believes there is a .10 probability that ABC Company will default. If default were to occur, it is estimated that the investor would receive eighty cents on the dollar.

Required:
(a) Determine the expected utility of each investment.
(b) What is the value of perfect information?
(c) Assume the investor can privately contract to obtain ABC Company's profit forecast for the next year. If default were not to occur, there is an

estimated probability of .8 that the profit forecast would be positive, and a .2 probability it would be negative. If default were to occur, the probability of a positive forecast is .4, while the probability is .6 that the profit forecast would be negative. Calculate the utility of each investment based on the new information.

(d) What is the maximum price an investor would be willing to pay for the new information?

(e) Why might this type of private contracting not occur?

(f) Why is this type of analysis difficult to apply to real-world situations for studying economic consequences of alternative accounting policies?

BIBLIOGRAPHY OF REFERENCED WORKS

Abdel-khalik, A. Rashad, and James C. McKeown (1978). "Understanding Accounting Changes in an Efficient Market: Evidence of Differential Reaction," *The Accounting Review* (October 1978), pp. 851–868.

Altman, Edward I. (1971). *Corporate Bankruptcy in America* (Heath).

American Accounting Association (1977). *Statement of Accounting Theory and Theory Acceptance* (AAA).

Anderson, Ray (1981). "The Usefulness of Accounting and Other Information Disclosures in Corporate Annual Reports to Institutional Investors in Australia," *Accounting and Business Research* (Autumn 1981), pp. 259–265.

Archibald, T. Ross (1972). "Stock Market Reaction to Depreciation Switch-Back," *The Accounting Review* (January 1972), pp. 22–30.

Ball, Ray (1972). "Changes in Accounting Techniques and Stock Prices," *Empirical Research in Accounting: Selected Studies, 1972* (Supplement to *Journal of Accounting Research*), pp. 1–38.

Ball, Ray, and Philip Brown (1968). "An Empirical Evaluation of Accounting Income Numbers," *Journal of Accounting Research* (Autumn 1968), pp. 159–177.

Baran, A., J. Lakonishok, and A. Ofer (1980). "The Information Content of Adjusted Accounting Earnings: Some Empirical Evidence," *The Accounting Review* (January 1980), pp. 22–35.

Beaver, William H. (1967). "Financial Ratios as Predictors of Failure," *Empirical Research in Accounting: Selected Studies, 1967* (Supplement to *Journal of Accounting Research*), pp. 71–111.

——— (1981). *Financial Reporting: An Accounting Revolution* (Prentice-Hall).

Beaver, William H., Roger Clarke, and William F. Wright (1979). "The Association Between Unsystematic Security Returns and the Magnitude of Earnings Forecast Errors," *Journal of Accounting Research* (Autumn 1979), pp. 316–340.

Beaver, William H., and Roland E. Dukes (1972). "Interperiod Tax Allocation, Earnings Expectations, and the Behavior of Security Prices," *The Accounting Review* (April 1972), pp. 320–332.

Beaver, William H., Paul Kettler, and Myron Scholes (1970). "The Association Between Market-Determined and Accounting-Determined Risk Measures," *The Accounting Review* (October 1970), pp. 654–682.

Biddle, Gary C., and Frederick W. Lindahl (1982). "Stock Price Reactions to LIFO Adoptions: The Association Between Excess Returns and LIFO Tax Savings," *Journal of Accounting Research* (Autumn, Pt. 2, 1982), pp. 551–588.

Bildersee, John S. (1975). "Market-Determined and Alternative Measures of Risk," *The Accounting Review* (January 1975), pp. 81–98.

Bowen, Robert M., David Burgstahler, and Lane A. Daley (1986). "Evidence on the Relationships Between Various Earnings Measures of Cash Flow," *The Accounting Review* (October 1986), pp. 713–725.

Brown, Philip, and John W. Kennelly (1972). "The Information Content of Quarterly Earnings," *Journal of Business* (July 1972), pp. 403–421.

Brown, Robert Moren (1980). "Short-Range Market Reactions to Changes to LIFO Accounting Using Preliminary Earnings Announcements," *Journal of Accounting Research* (Spring 1980), pp. 38–62.

Cassidy, D. (1976). "Investor Evaluation of Accounting Information: Some Additional Evidence," *Journal of Accounting Research* (Autumn 1976), pp. 212–229.

Chang, Lucia, and Kenneth S. Most (1977). "Investor Uses of Financial Statements: An Empirical Study," *Singapore Accountant* (1977), pp. 83–91.

Collins, Daniel W., Michael S. Rozeff, and Dan S. Dhaliwal (1981). "The Economic Determinants of the Market Reaction to Proposed Mandatory Accounting Changes in the Oil and Gas Industry," *Journal of Accounting and Economics* (March 1981), pp. 37–71.

Comiskey, Eugene (1971). "Market Response to Changes in Depreciation Accounting," *The Accounting Review* (April 1971), pp. 271–285.

Cook, T. Q., and P. H. Hendershott (1978). "The Impact of Taxes, Risk and Relative Security Supplies on Interest Rate Differentials," *The Journal of Finance* (September 1978), pp. 1173–1186.

Davis, Stanley W., Krishnagopal Menon, and Gareth Morgan (1982). "The Images That Have Shaped Accounting Theory," *Accounting, Organizations and Society* 7 (no. 4): 307–318.

Demski, Joel S. (1973). "The General Impossibility of Accounting Standards," *The Accounting Review* (October 1973), pp. 718–723.

Dukes, Roland (1976). "An Empirical Investigation of the Effects of Expensing Research and Development Costs on Security Prices," in *Proceedings on Topical Research in Accounting*, Michael Schiff and George Sorter, eds. (Ross Institute of Accounting Research, New York University).

Elam, Rick (1975). "The Effect of Lease Data on the Predictive Ability of Financial Ratios," *The Accounting Review* (January 1975), pp. 25–43.

Elgers, Pieter T. (1980). "Accounting-Based Risk Measures: A Re-Examination," *The Accounting Review* (July 1980), pp. 389–408.

Elgers, Pieter T., and Dennis Murray (1982). "The Impact of the Choice of Market Index on the Empirical Evaluation of Accounting Risk Measures," *The Accounting Review* (April 1982), pp. 358–375.

Epstein, Mark (1975). *The Usefulness of Annual Reports to Corporate Stockholders* (California State University, Los Angeles, Bureau of Business and Economic Research).

Eskew, Robert K. (1979). "The Forecasting Ability of Accounting Risk Measures: Some Additional Evidence," *The Accounting Review* (January 1979), pp. 107–118.

Fama, Eugene F. (1970). "Efficient Capital Markets: A Review of Theory and Empirical Work," *Journal of Finance* (May 1970), pp. 383–417.

Fama, Eugene F., and Merton H. Miller (1972). *The Theory of Finance* (Dryden Press).

Fisher, L. (1959). "Determinants of Risk Premiums on Corporate Bonds," *The Journal of Political Economy* (June 1959), pp. 217–237.

Foster, George (1977a). "Quarterly Earnings Data: Time Series Properties and Predictive Ability Results," *The Accounting Review* (January 1977), pp. 1–21.

——— (1977b). "Valuation Parameters of Property-Liability Companies," *Journal of Finance* (June 1977), pp. 823–836.

———— (1980). "Accounting Policy Decisions and Capital Market Research," *Journal of Accounting and Economics* (March 1980), pp. 26–62.

Francis, Jere R., and Scott C. Linn (1988a). "An Investigation of Firm Valuation and Its Relation to Operating Cash Flow, Investment and Net Financing" (Unpublished working paper, University of Iowa).

———— (1988b). "Firm Valuation, Cash Flows, and Accrual Accounting: Theoretical and Empirical Analyses" (Unpublished working paper, University of Iowa).

Gonedes, Nicholas J. (1972). "Efficient Capital Markets and External Accounting," *The Accounting Review* (January 1972), pp. 11–21.

———— (1980). "Public Disclosure Rules, Private Information-Production Decisions, and Capital Market Equilibrium," *Journal of Accounting Research* (Autumn 1980), pp. 441–476.

Gonedes, Nicholas J., and Nicholas Dopuch (1974). "Capital Market Equilibrium, Information Production, and Selected Accounting Techniques: Theoretical Framework and Review for Empirical Work," *Journal of Accounting Research* (Supplement, 1974), pp. 48–129.

Gordon, Myron J. (1962). *The Investment, Financing and Valuation of the Corporation* (Richard D. Irwin).

Greenberg, Robert R., Glen L. Johnson, and K. Ramesh (1986). "Earnings Versus Cash Flow as a Predictor of Future Cash Flow Measures," *Journal of Accounting, Auditing, and Finance* (Fall 1986), pp. 266–277.

Hakansson, Nils H. (1977). "Interim Disclosure and Public Forecasts: An Economic Analysis and Framework for Choice," *The Accounting Review* (April 1977), pp. 396–416.

Hand, John R. M. (1990). "A Test of the Extended Functional Fixation Hypothesis," *The Accounting Review* (October 1990), pp. 740–763.

Hines, R. D. (1982). "The Usefulness of Annual Reports: The Anomaly Between the Efficient Markets Hypothesis and Shareholder Surveys," *Accounting and Business Research* (Autumn 1982), pp. 296–309.

Hong, Hai, Robert S. Kaplan, and Gershon Mandelker (1978). "Pooling vs. Purchase: The Effects of Accounting for Mergers on Stock Prices," *The Accounting Review* (January 1978), pp. 31–47.

Horrigan, J. O. (1966). "The Determination of Long-Term Credit Standing with Financial Ratios," *Empirical Research in Accounting: Selected Studies, 1966*, pp. 44–62.

Kaplan, R. S., and G. Urwitz (1979). "Statistical Models of Bond Ratings: A Methodological Inquiry," *Journal of Business* (April 1979), pp. 231–261.

Lee, T. A., and D. P. Tweedie (1975). "Accounting Information: An Investigation of Private Shareholder Usage," *Accounting and Business Research* (Autumn 1975), pp. 280–291.

Leftwich, Richard W. (1981). "Evidence on the Impact of Mandatory Changes in Accounting Principles on Corporate Loan Agreements," *Journal of Accounting and Economics* (March 1981), pp. 3–36.

Lev, Baruch (1989). "On the Usefulness of Earnings and Earnings Research: Lessons and Directions from Two Decades of Empirical Research," *Current Studies on the Information Content of Accounting Earnings (Journal of Accounting Research Supplement, 1989)*, pp. 153–192.

Libby, Robert (1975). "Accounting Ratios and the Prediction of Failure: Some Behavioral Evidence," *Journal of Accounting Research* (Spring 1975), pp. 150–161.

Miller, Merton H., and Franco Modigliani (1961). "Dividend Policy, Growth and the Valuation of Shares," *Journal of Business* (October 1961), pp. 411–433.

Miller, Merton H., and Kevin Rock (1985). "Dividend Policy under Asymmetric Information," *The Journal of Finance* (September 1985), pp. 1031–1051.

Mohr, Rosanne M. (1983). "The Segmental Reporting Issue: A Review of the Empirical Research," *Journal of Accounting Literature* (Spring 1983), pp. 39–71.

Ohlson, James A. (1980). "Financial Ratios and the Probabilistic Prediction of Bankruptcy," *Journal of Accounting Research* (Spring 1980), pp. 109–131.

Ohlson, James A., and A. G. Buckman (1981). "Toward a Theory of Financial Accounting: Welfare and Public Information," *Journal of Accounting Research* (Autumn 1981), pp. 399–433.

Ou, Jane, and Stephen Penman (1989). "Financial Statement Analysis and the Prediction of Stock Returns," *Journal of Accounting and Economics* (Autumn 1989), pp. 295–329.

Pfeiffer, G. (1980). "The Economic Effects of Accounting Policy Regulation: Evidence on the Lease Accounting Issue" (Ph.D. diss., Cornell University).

Rayburn, Judy (1986). "The Association of Operating Cash Flow and Accruals with Security Returns," *Journal of Accounting Research* (Supplement, 1986), pp. 112–133.

Reiter, Sara Ann (1985). "The Effect of Defined Benefit Pension Plan Disclosures on Bond Risk Premiums and Bond Ratings" (Ph.D. diss., University of Missouri).

Ricks, William E. (1982). "The Market's Response to the 1974 LIFO Adoptions," *Journal of Accounting Research* (Autumn 1982), pp. 367–387.

Roll, Richard (1977). "A Critique of the Asset Pricing Theory's Tests: Part 1: On Past and Potential Testability of the Theory," *Journal of Financial Economics* (March 1977), pp. 129–176.

Stone, Mary S. (1981). "An Examination of the Effect of Disclosures Concerning Unfunded Pension Benefits on Market Risk Measures" (Ph.D. diss., University of Illinois).

Sunder, Shyam (1973). "Relationship Between Accounting Changes and Stock Prices: Problems of Measurement and Some Empirical Evidence," *Empirical Research in Accounting: Selected Studies, 1973* (Supplement to *Journal of Accounting Research*), pp. 1–45.

——— (1975). "Stock Price and Risk Related to Accounting Changes in Inventory Valuation," *The Accounting Review* (April 1975), pp. 305–316.

Thomas, Arthur L. (1969). "The Allocation Problem in Financial Accounting Theory," *Studies in Accounting Research #3* (American Accounting Association).

Thompson, Donald J. (1976). "Sources of Systematic Risk in Common Stock," *Journal of Business* (April 1976), pp. 173–188.

Tinic, Seha M. (1990). "A Perspective on the Stock Market's Fixation on Accounting Numbers," *The Accounting Review* (October 1990), pp. 781–796.

Verrechia, Robert E. (1982). "The Use of Mathematical Modelling in Financial Accounting," *Journal of Accounting Research* (Supplement, 1982), pp. 1–42.

Wilkins, Trevor, and Ian Zimmer (1983). "The Effect of Leasing and Different Methods of Accounting for Leases on Credit Evaluations," *The Accounting Review* (October 1983), pp. 749–764.

Wright, William F. (1977). "Financial Information Processing Models: An Empirical Study," *The Accounting Review* (July 1977), pp. 676–689.

Wyatt, Arthur (1983). "Efficient Market Theory: Its Impact on Accounting," *Journal of Accountancy* (February 1983), pp. 56–65.

ADDITIONAL READINGS

Ashton, Robert H. (1982). "Human Information Processing in Accounting," *Studies in Accounting Research #17* (American Accounting Association).

Ball, Ray, and George Foster (1982). "Corporate Financial Reporting: A Methodological Review of Empirical Research," *Journal of Accounting Research* (Supplement, 1982), pp. 161–234.

Demski, Joel S., and Gerald A. Feltham (1976). *Cost Determination: A Conceptual Approach* (Iowa State University Press).

Dyckman, Thomas R., and Dale Morse (1986). *Efficient Capital Markets and Accounting: A Critical Analysis*, 2nd ed. (Prentice-Hall).

Feltham, Gerald A. (1972). "Information Evaluation," *Studies in Accounting Research #4* (AAA).

Griffin, Paul A. (1982). *Usefulness to Investors and Creditors of Information Provided by Financial Reporting: A Review of Empirical Accounting Research* (Financial Accounting Standards Board).

Kaplan, Robert S. (1978). "The Information Content of Financial Accounting Numbers: A Survey of Empirical Evidence," in *Impact of Accounting Research on Practice and Disclosure*, A. Abdel-Khalik and T. Keller, eds. (Duke University Press).

Lev, Baruch, and James A. Ohlson (1982). "Market-Based Empirical Research in Accounting: A Review, Interpretation, and Extension," *Journal of Accounting Research* (Supplement, 1982), pp. 249–322.

Libby, Robert, and B. L. Lewis (1982). "Human Information Processing Research in Accounting: The State of the Art in 1982," *Accounting, Organizations and Society* 7 (no. 3): 231–286.

Ou, Jane, and Stephen Penman (1989). "Accounting Measurement, Price-Earnings Ratio, and the Information Content of Security Prices," *Current Studies on the Information Content of Accounting Earnings (Journal of Accounting Research Supplement*, 1989), pp. 111–144.

Ricks, William E. (1982). "Market Assessment of Alternative Accounting Methods: A Review of the Empirical Evidence," *Journal of Accounting Literature* (Spring 1982), pp. 59–99.

UNIFORMITY AND DISCLOSURE: SOME POLICY-MAKING DIRECTIONS

W<small>E HAVE SEEN</small> in Chapter 6 that the FASB has developed a metatheoretical structure of accounting. Chapter 7 discussed the many new concepts and hypotheses, largely from economics and finance, that may potentially influence a metatheory. Uniformity and disclosure and their potential place in such a structure are the subject of this chapter.

A conceptual framework is a normative structure because both the objectives and standards are the result of choice. If a conceptual framework is in place, it should provide a guide for standard setting. A quasi-deductive relationship thus exists between a metatheoretical structure and rule making. Although theoretical work should obviously be allowed to influence a conceptual framework as it emerges, as well as the rule-making process itself, theory and policy making lie in separate domains. However, Ijiri has pointed out that theory and policy appear to be more intertwined in accounting than in other fields.[1] We have already seen that attempting to combine these functions led the APB to disaster. The FASB has been and will continue to be under pressure from outside bodies and groups over its part in both the conceptual framework and standard-setting activities. Clearly, the issues and concepts that derive from a metatheoretical structure must be as clear and complete as possible in order to minimize discrepancies between the structure and subsequent policy making. In other words, conceptual clarity and completeness are necessary if the resulting standards are to be consistent with the metatheoretical structure.

In this chapter we examine two extremely important conceptual issues

---

[1] Ijiri (1975, pp. 9–11).

that must play an important role in determining the structure and components of a metatheoretical framework: uniformity and disclosure. The FASB's conceptual framework is apparently complete, but it should be remembered that a metatheoretical structure in a discipline such as accounting will always be an evolving instrument, changing in response to new needs and new research findings.[2]

We begin with an analysis of uniformity. It is a topic discussed extensively in the accounting literature and statements and pronouncements of policy-making organizations, but it has not been precisely formulated. The type of uniformity desired should influence the structure of the metatheoretical framework. Information economics (benefits/costs considerations) obviously play a key role in this determination.

An appropriate starting point for understanding uniformity comes, we believe, from an analysis of event types. Events are economic occurrences that require accounting entries. They can be classified as simple or complex. Complex events where "effect of circumstances" exists are broadly similar and might justify different accounting treatments than simple events. Effect of circumstances, or relevant circumstances, are thus economically significant variables that should be identified and categorized.

After defining relevant circumstances, we are in a better position to analyze the uniformity question. In our opinion, there are two concepts of uniformity — finite and rigid uniformity — that have been evolving in the accounting literature. These two approaches to uniformity are discussed in regard to such issues as efficient markets, the allocation problem, and costs and benefits of information.

The uniformity section concludes with an analysis of how certain accounting standards are inconsistent with each other from the standpoint of uniformity. The term *flexibility* is also introduced in this part of the chapter. Finally, we look at the concept of disclosure, focusing on the importance of its potential interaction with the uniformity question. The chapter closes with an assessment of some of the directions the FASB might take relative to the issues discussed in the chapter.

UNIFORMITY

In the accounting literature the concept of uniformity appears to overlap with comparability. For example, Sprouse has stated:

> Finally, because comparing alternative investment and lending opportunities is an essential part of most investor and creditor decisions, the quest for comparability is central. The term comparability is used here to mean accounting for similar transactions similarly and for different circumstances differently. A con-

---

[2] Miller (1985, p. 71), a former faculty fellow at the FASB, takes a similar position.

ceptual framework should foster consistent treatment of like things, provide the means for identifying unlike things, and leave open for judgment the estimates inherent in the accounting process.[3]

Sprouse sees comparability as both a process (accounting for circumstances in accordance with similarities or differences) and an end result of this process (comparing alternatives in order to make a decision). We view **comparability** here only in the latter context, while **uniformity** is seen as the concept that influences comparability. Because comparability is linked to uniformity, the degree of comparability that users can rely on is directly dependent on the level of uniformity present in financial statements.

The relationship between uniformity and comparability espoused here is quite close to the position taken in SFAC 2. Comparability is not an inherent quality of accounting numbers in the sense that relevance and reliability are but instead deals with the relationship between accounting numbers: "The purpose of comparison is to explain similarities and differences."[4] However, SFAC 2 also states, "Comparability should not be confused with identity, and sometimes more can be learned from differences than from similarities if the differences can be explained."[5]

Although uniformity and comparability are usually discussed in terms of the need to account for similar events in a similar manner, no extensive formal attempt has been made to specify the dividing line between similarity and difference. Consequently, a fruitful starting point for examining the uniformity issue is analyzing *events*.

THE NATURE AND COMPLEXITY OF EVENTS

Transactions are economic or financial events that are recorded in the firm's accounts. An **event** has been defined in SFAC 6 as "a happening of consequence to an entity."[6] Transactions occur between entities, between a firm and its employees, and between a firm and investors or lenders. **Transactions** are thus events external to an enterprise. Events that are internal to the firm also require entries in the firm's accounts. Examples would include recognition of depreciation and completion of work-in-process inventories. It is up to the rules of accounting to specify the necessary criteria for event recognition. Rules of recognition are concerned, for example, with the question of when to recognize revenues as being earned.

Another aspect of events that particularly concerns us here is their degree of simplicity or complexity. In a complicated and involved business environment, events are often accompanied by a complex set of restrictions, contingencies, and conditions. For example, in the case of long-term leases, some of the factors would be

---

[3] Sprouse (1978, p. 71).
[4] FASB (1980, p. 45).
[5] Ibid., p. 48.
[6] FASB (1985, p. 46).

1. A clause in the lease providing for cancellation by either party.
2. The proportion of the asset's life the lease period is expected to cover.
3. The possible existence of favorable renewal privileges (either for purchase or rental) at the end of the original lease period.

Some other examples of event complexity would involve situations such as these:

1. Acquisition of common stock for control purposes where the percentage of stock owned may vary.
2. Differing expected usage or benefit patterns of depreciable fixed assets and intangibles.
3. Deferred tax liabilities arising from income tax allocation situations that either grow indefinitely or decrease during the planning horizon.

Before we examine the nature of complex events further, we should mention that there are many events that do not have any significant economic variables that lead to essentially different recording. We denote these as *simple events*. For example, payment for services acquired on account with no discount involved would be a simple event. Some complex events may also be handled with dispatch. Whether the buyer or vendor will pay the freight for acquired inventories is the key issue in recording this event, but under either circumstance it is easily handled. If the buyer pays, the situation comes under the "cost rule," which charges all costs necessary for acquisition and installation to the asset rather than directly to expense. If the seller pays, transportation costs are charged to a freight-out type of account. These situations are similar enough to result in a highly uniform recording of events. Complex events, however, can be considerably more involved than the freight situation and may be much more difficult to resolve. The literature uses the term *effect of circumstances* to describe these situations, but we prefer the less cumbersome *relevant circumstances*.

RELEVANT CIRCUMSTANCES

With regard to the complex events mentioned above, we can say that, while the variables mentioned represent potential economic differences between relatively similar events, there are some subtle differences as well. In the case of leases, all the elements considered would be stipulated in the contract; hence, they would be known at the inception of the lease (except for the expected life of the asset). Similarly, the percentage of common stock owned is a condition that would be known at the time of the transaction. On the other hand, expected usage or benefit patterns of depreciable assets and the question of the drawdown or reversal of deferred tax liabilities pertain to future events.

The Terminology of Relevance

Relevant circumstances are economically significant circumstances that can affect broadly similar events. These economically significant circumstances are general conditions or factors associated with complex events that are expected to influence the incidence or timing of cash flows. As the preceding examples suggest, relevant circumstances are of two general types.[7] Those conditions known at the time of the event will be referred to as *present magnitudes.* Factors that can be known only at a later date shall be called *future contingencies.* Relevant circumstances pertain directly to the event being accounted for and not to the accounting method selected to represent that event. For example, LIFO has different tax implications than FIFO, but its selection would not be the result of a relevant circumstance.

Some considerations concerning future contingencies should be carefully noted. The two cases mentioned above, usage or benefit patterns of fixed assets and the question of reversal of deferred tax liabilities, have some important qualitative differences. In the case of depreciation, we are dealing with an allocation. There are several other relevant circumstances of the future contingency type that are allocations. These include amortization of intangibles, such as goodwill, research and development costs, and depletion of natural resources. One method of avoiding the allocation problem for at least some future contingency problems is by means of current valuations. Hence, depreciation and depletion, at least, could be computed as the difference between market values of their respective assets at the beginning and end of the period. However, in the case of the prospective reversal of deferred tax liabilities arising from an excess of accelerated depreciation for tax purposes over straight-line depreciation for book purposes, the reversal is not an allocation problem but rather a prediction question based on factors such as the pattern of future capital acquisitions and their tax and book depreciation schedules. At present, the prospective reversal of deferred tax credits is a relevant circumstance in the United Kingdom but is not in the United States. The whole tax allocation problem is discussed in depth in Chapter 14.

Future contingencies that are allocations may have limited information content, whereas those that attempt to predict relevant future variables — such as payments of deferred taxes — may have significant information content for users. However, the degree of verifiability of predictive variables that might be selected as factors governing accounting methods becomes important.

A case can certainly be made that one of the principal tasks of a rule-making body should be identifying appropriate relevant circumstances and setting up criteria for how they should govern the recording of events or the format of financial statements. Rule-making bodies have done this in a rather unsystematic fashion in such areas as lease capitalization (SFAS 13); purchase versus pooling (APB Opinion 16); and choice among full consolidation, equity, and cost methods where common stock in another firm is held for control purposes (ARB 51, APB 18, and SFAS 94). Identifying relevant circumstances, not to mention setting criteria to govern choice among accounting methods or for-

---

[7] Sorter and Ingberman have attempted to classify events and establish the cash flow aspect as the key to event recognition. Event recognition centers upon ". . . an actual, required future, or hypothetical cash flow associated with the acquisition and disposition of rights and obligations." Sorter and Ingberman (1987, p. 106).

mat of financial statements, is a formidable task. Whether a conceptual framework can be useful is an important question that will be addressed later in this chapter.

The Role of Management in Relevant Circumstances

Given that relevant circumstances are an extremely important aspect of the uniformity issue, the question arises as to whether management should have the choice of determining them. Weldon Powell, the former managing partner of a Big Eight firm, regarded managerial influence as an important consideration in terms of allowing different methods.[8] For example, if two firms acquired the same type of fixed asset but one intended to use it intensively in the early years whereas the other anticipated relatively even usage throughout its life, then, from Powell's viewpoint, the first firm would be justified in using an accelerated depreciation method and the second could go for straight-line depreciation.

These choices might be valid, but the problem is that selection of accounting methods might be guided by motives different from those dictated by the presumed relevant circumstances. These ulterior motives would include the following:

1. Maximizing short-run reported income if managerial compensation is based on it.
2. Minimizing short-run reported income if there is fear of governmental intervention on antitrust grounds.
3. Smoothing income (minimizing deviations in income from year to year) if it is believed that stockholders perceive the firm has a lower amount of risk than would be the case if greater fluctuations of earnings were present.[9]

Because management is potentially capable of distorting income measurement, Cadenhead favors limiting relevant circumstances to elements beyond managerial control, elements he refers to as *environmental conditions.*[10] Environmental conditions differ between firms and lead to either excessive measurement costs or a low degree of verifiability relative to the preferred accounting method.[11] If environmental conditions possess either of these two qualities, they are designated *circumstantial variables* by Cadenhead. For example, if the valuation of inventories were to be based on the specific identification method, the cost of record keeping would be exorbitant for retail firms having extensive inventories with a low unit value. Also, if the net realizable value of inventories were required, costs of completion and disposal might be extremely difficult to

---

[8] Powell (1965, pp. 680–681).

[9] A very extensive literature in the area of income smoothing or managing income developed during the 1970s. For an excellent summary, see Ronen and Sadan (1981).

[10] See Cadenhead (1970).

[11] The use of LIFO would not be an environmental condition because those electing to use it for tax purposes must use it for financial reporting purposes. Hence, its use for financial reporting purposes is beyond managerial control and is applicable to *all* firms electing it for tax purposes.

estimate in some industries, leading to a low degree of verifiability. Only in cases involving circumstantial variables would Cadenhead allow departure from rigidly prescribed accounting methods.

Despite the importance of relevant circumstances in allowing different accounting treatments in generally similar transactions, little research has been done on the topic. This inattention has led, by default, to two concepts of uniformity that have evolved in both the accounting literature and the standards propounded by rule-making bodies.

FINITE AND RIGID UNIFORMITY

Finite uniformity attempts to equate prescribed accounting methods with the relevant circumstances in generally similar situations. The word *finite* was selected in accordance with the *Random House Dictionary* definition of "having bounds or limits; not too great or too small to be measurable." SFAS 13 on long-term leases provides a good example of finite uniformity. If a lessee has a long-term lease for 75 percent or more of the estimated economic life of an asset, capitalization is required. However, if the lease period is for less than 75 percent of the estimated economic life of the asset, the lease is not capitalized.[12] This lease provision is one of four set down in the standard, any of which is sufficient to require capitalization on the grounds that the lease contract ". . . transfers substantially all of the benefits and risks incident to the ownership of the property . . ." to the lessee, including lower annual rental costs for the property due to the long-term nature of the lease. An obvious difficulty with the 75 percent lease period provision is the fact that it attempts to draw an exact boundary where a continuum exists. Would 70 percent or even 60 percent have been a better break-point between capital and operating leases? The point is very debatable and can never be totally resolved. Furthermore, the door is open to manipulation if management wants noncapitalization. All it has to do is extend, within reasonable bounds, the estimated economic life of the asset or shorten the lease period to just under 75 percent of the estimated economic life.[13]

The Need for an Alternative to Finite Uniformity

Since establishing appropriate criteria for relevant circumstances is difficult and often somewhat arbitrary, an alternative type of uniformity has been implicitly formulated. **Rigid uniformity** means prescribing one method for generally similar transactions even though relevant circumstances may be present. For example, SFAS 2 requires that research and development costs must be expensed even though future benefits may be present. SFAS 96 requires that income tax allocation must be used even if there is no anticipated reversal of deferred tax liabilities during the foreseeable future.

---

[12] Provided none of the other conditions held and there is no bargain lease renewal present. SFAS 13 (1976, para. 7).

[13] For a graphic example, see Wyatt (1983, pp. 58–60).

SFAC 2 appears to accept implicitly the idea of finite uniformity, as the following example reveals:

> For example, to find whether a man is overweight, one compares his weight with that of other men — not women — of the same height. . . . Clearly, valid comparison is possible only if the measurements used — quantities or ratios — reliably represent the characteristic that is the subject of comparison.[14]

But it also implicitly mentions rigid uniformity in the context of improving comparability (by using the same accounting method) in situations where representational faithfulness is not the goal. However, "improving" comparability may, in reality, be counterproductive:

> Improving comparability may destroy or weaken relevance or reliability if, to secure comparability between two measures, one of them has to be obtained by a method yielding less relevant or reliable information. Historically, extreme examples . . . have been provided . . . in which the use of standardized charts of accounts has been made mandatory in the interest of interfirm comparability but at the expense of relevance and often reliability as well. That kind of uniformity may even adversely affect comparability of information if it conceals real differences between enterprises.[15]

An analogy may help to explain the difference between finite and rigid uniformity as well as the greater utility of finite uniformity. Imagine an American diplomat in Europe. In dealing with individuals it is important to know their country of origin but it is not "correct" to ask. Diplomat A can only tell if individuals are European or non-European. Diplomat B is able to tell by the spoken accent whether individuals are (a) Slavic, (b) Scandinavian, or (c) from the rest of Europe. Diplomat C is able to tell by a combination of accent and name the particular country of origin of each individual. The situation faced by Diplomat A is equivalent to rigid uniformity while Diplomat C has achieved finite uniformity; B is in between. The analogies to general event similarity and relevant circumstances are the general European origin and particular country (or region, in the case of B) of birth, respectively. In accounting we presume that if finite uniformity can be attained, it is superior to rigid uniformity from the standpoint of usefulness in decision making or performance evaluation. However, meaningful finite uniformity could be obtained only at a greater cost than rigid uniformity, so the advantage is merely relative and depends on marginal benefits and costs.

Finite and Rigid Uniformity Compared

Finite and rigid uniformity both are based on an underlying rationale. Finite uniformity is based on the belief that accounting methods should attempt to follow economically meaningful circumstances. Consequently, pertinent measures of performance and relevant measures of assets and liabilities should re-

---

[14] FASB (1980a, p. 46).
[15] Ibid., p. 47.

sult. Therefore, the objectives of a conceptual framework, such as prediction of cash flows and evaluation of managerial effectiveness, should be enhanced. In addition, a relatively high degree of comparability between financial statements of different firms should occur.[16] As a result, finite uniformity should help to improve resource allocation because security prices would better reflect the risk-adjusted present value of the firm's cash flows.[17]

Rigid uniformity simply attempts to eliminate alternatives in broadly similar situations. Its immediate link to an objective of accounting would appear to be stewardship, the custodianship of the enterprise's resources and their appropriate usage. Proponents of rigid uniformity might say that the complexity of major business enterprises tends to make comparability of financial statements among firms extremely difficult, if not impossible. Hence the costs of achieving finite uniformity would far exceed its benefits. Rigid uniformity, on the other hand, would not require as extensive a metatheoretical framework and so it could be implemented less expensively.

Both finite and rigid uniformity are oriented toward historical cost accounting. Replacement-cost and exit-value accounting are concerned with deriving specific current values by either direct or indirect methods of measurement. However, both finite and rigid uniformity could be used in conjunction with general price-level adjustment, which is, of course, an extension of historical costing. There are several other areas where finite and rigid uniformity can be further compared and contrasted.

Users of Financial Statements   The focusing of financial accounting theory upon the needs and capabilities of users was extensively discussed in Chapter 6. Finite uniformity relates to this focus from the viewpoint of developing normative models for implementing various objectives of accounting, such as cash flow prediction, and assessing managerial effectiveness in carrying out enterprise goals. Thus, it might be necessary to educate users in their role as decision makers to understand these models. On the other hand, rigid uniformity relates to the perception of users as heterogeneous and of user groups as having different decision needs and capabilities. Decision models cannot be constructed for such users, or the models may be so diverse that they cannot be classified. Given these problems, any attempt to institute finite uniformity would ultimately fail. Therefore, the thrust of a standard-setting body should be to eliminate alternative accounting treatments.

Reliability and Relevance   As defined in SFAC 2 and discussed in Chapter 6, reliability consists of two characteristics: verifiability and representational faithfulness. Verifiability is represented by the degree of statistical consensus reached by accountants in measurements of financial and economic phenomena. Clearly, finite uniformity would be less verifiable than rigid uniformity be-

---

[16] As well as comparability of financial statements over time for the same firm.
[17] For more on the role of security prices relative to resource allocation, see Ronen (1974, pp. 82–86).

cause more judgment would have to be applied to interpret what relevant circumstance is appropriate to a given situation.

Representational faithfulness refers to whether the attribute actually being measured is really what it purports to be. Thus, if the replacement cost of an asset were estimated by a net realizable value measurement, there would be a low degree of representational faithfulness. Since finite and rigid uniformity are approaches to historical costing, neither will be representationally faithful for such assets as inventories and fixed assets. The underlying reason for this is that neither approach measures the real characteristics of assets, such as replacement cost or net realizable value. However, in situations where finite uniformity can be implemented, the results should be more realistic.[18] One such event would be partial income tax allocation in which allocation is used if and only if an actual repayment of tax benefits is forecast. Applications of finite uniformity in areas such as leases may not always be successful. Therefore, in terms of the verifiability issue (which is much more clear-cut than the question of representational faithfulness), rigid uniformity would have a greater degree of reliability than finite uniformity.

In terms of relevance, finite uniformity — since it does attempt to come to grips with different circumstances — should be more relevant than rigid uniformity — with regard to such uses as prediction of cash flows and assessment of managerial effectiveness. Therefore, a trade-off exists: finite uniformity is more relevant but rigid uniformity is more reliable.

Effect on the Audit Function   If finite uniformity were to become a reality, the auditor's role would expand significantly; hence, costs to the firm would increase. The auditor would be concerned not only with the reliability of financial data and its presentation in accordance with a conceptual framework but also with the interpretation of underlying circumstances that gave rise to the data. The auditor must substantiate what circumstances apply to various transactions and whether those circumstances were correctly interpreted by management in terms of the accounting methods selected. Thus, the independent auditor must substantiate monetary amounts and internal controls; but equally important, he or she must audit the circumstances surrounding major transactions.

Relationship to the Efficient-Markets Hypothesis   The principal concern arising from any attempt to institute a system of finite uniformity is the question of costs and benefits. Obviously, costs would be higher with finite, so the question might be whether finite uniformity is needed given that securities markets are presumably efficient. As discussed in Chapter 7, the efficient-markets hypothesis is supported by a considerable body of evidence indicating that all publicly available information is rapidly impounded in market prices of securities.

---

[18] While representational faithfulness is classified under reliability in SFAC 2, it could easily have been put on the relevance side. Sterling (1985, p. 28) is undoubtedly correct when he states that faithful representation of relevant phenomena is the essence of decision usefulness.

Furthermore, many studies have revealed that the market is able to distinguish between real events and accounting changes that are nothing more than allocations devoid of economic content. Therefore, assuming that investors are appropriately diversified, the possibility of their receiving abnormal returns relative to the risk undertaken is relatively small. If so, the principal task of an organization such as the FASB should be in the area of increasing disclosure rather than refining income measurements and assets and liability valuations.[19] Perhaps, then, the presence of efficient securities markets may preclude the development of an extensive finite uniformity system.

The opposing argument is that market efficiency alone does not guarantee optimal resource allocation. To state it in slightly different terms — alternative accounting information (finite versus rigid) can lead to different security prices, which affect important matters such as corporate cost of capital and distribution of wealth among security holders. Finite uniformity should result in security prices that describe a more economically valid relationship between risk and expected return.[20] Thus the quality of information is an important issue. Finite uniformity could increase the quality or fidelity of information provided. Finally, it should be remembered that although there are other means of providing information, the accounting process might well be the most economical means for disseminating this information.[21] The decision, of course, still comes down to the crucial issue of costs versus benefits.

The Role of a Metatheoretical Framework   A metatheoretical framework would play a much more limited role under rigid than finite uniformity. The main functions of a policy-making body under rigid uniformity would be eliminating alternatives for generally similar transaction types and perhaps increasing disclosure. In addition, standards could be promulgated for the presentation of financial statements in terms of how account balances should be listed and grouped.

Under finite uniformity, a metatheoretical structure would have to serve as a guide for developing both standards geared toward common objectives and consistent valuation methods that take into account relevant circumstances. Hence, it would have to provide a framework for an extensive classification system of criteria for the determination of factors affecting the economic substance of transactions.[22] A summary comparison of finite and rigid uniformity is shown in Exhibit 8–1.

---

[19] See Beaver (1973) for additional coverage.

[20] Ronen (1974, pp. 82–86).

[21] Ronen and Sorter (1972, p. 259).

[22] Cyert and Ijiri (1974) provided an interesting approach to a metatheoretical structure. In their system, *constitutional standards* are concerned with determining qualifications or restrictions relative to carrying out the topmost level of the metatheoretical structure, the user objectives. For example, limitations on disclosure requirements would come under this category. Segmental disclosure is illustrative of this problem because although information about product lines and territories is useful to investors, it may also provide information to competitors that could be detrimental to the supplier of the information.

EXHIBIT 8–1
Comparison of Finite and Rigid Uniformity

Type	Possible Objectives	Position Relative to Users	Reliability and Relevance	Audit Function	Efficient-Markets Hypothesis	Metatheoretical Framework
Finite	Prediction of cash flows; assessment of managerial performance	Best normative models should be developed; if necessary, educate users	Lower reliability and higher relevance than rigid	Expanded and more costly	Better quality of information	Extensive
Rigid	Stewardship	Users are heterogeneous in terms of abilities and needs	Higher reliability and lower relevance than finite	Less costly	Goal of FASB should be toward more disclosure	Limited

THE PRESENT STATUS OF UNIFORMITY

Finite and rigid uniformity are, to a certain extent, ideals. At present, a mixed system exists in which some standards attempt to take into account relevant circumstances whereas others are clearly examples of rigid uniformity.[23] A brief survey of extant accounting standards is therefore useful to illustrate the present state of accounting relative to the uniformity question. However, we must make clear several qualifications.

First, the fact that a standard is an example of finite uniformity should not necessarily be construed to mean that the standard cannot be improved or even that the factor selected as the relevant circumstance is appropriate. Second, where rigid uniformity is in effect, the underlying reasons may be attributable to one or more of the following factors: (1) a desire for conservatism, (2) an inability of the standard-setting organization to determine meaningful relevant circumstances, (3) an attempt to increase verifiability of the measurement, (4) recognition of the fact that an allocation is involved, (5) the perception that, given adequate disclosure and an efficient securities market, the costs of implementing relevant circumstances exceed the resulting benefits. Third, another approach to the uniformity problem, usually called *flexibility*, has formed many accounting rules.

Flexibility applies to situations in which there are no discernible relevant circumstances but more than one possible accounting method exists, any of which may be selected at the firm's discretion.[24] The investment tax credit (now defunct) was a good example of flexibility. Holding aside the carryforward problem, which was relatively rare, no relevant circumstance appeared to be present (unless the firm expected to hold the asset for a relatively short period, in which case the government would have recaptured some or all of the investment tax credit benefits). However, APB 4 allowed enterprises to take all benefits immediately in the year of acquisition, or spread them over the useful life of the asset. Either alternative was acceptable.

Another issue that would come under constitutional standards concerns criteria for handling trade-offs among the various elements of relevance and reliability discussed in Chapter 6. These issues have not been addressed in the FASB's conceptual framework. If finite uniformity were being instituted, it might be wise to include a general statement about relevant circumstances and how to implement them, where possible, in the body of the metatheoretical structure.

Below the constitutional standards would be *operating standards* and *prescriptive standards*. The former would be concerned with the form and content of financial statements. The latter would be normative statements leading to the accounting rules themselves. An example of a prescriptive standard would be: ownership interests in other corporations should reflect the degree of control therein. The accounting rules would then attempt to implement the prescriptive standard.

[23] Richardson and Wright have recently suggested an interesting two-tiered approach to uniformity. They are primarily concerned with standards overload and its effect upon smaller firms. "Core" information and standards would be applicable to both large and small firms, thus retaining "uniformity" (p. 51). "Supplemental disclosures would be selectively applied with costs and benefits of information being the crucial issue. How to draw the line between large and small firms is not clear, as Richardson and Wright admit. (Richardson and Wright, 1987.)

[24] Flexibility is sometimes called *diversity*. See Grady (1965, p. 33) for one example.

We will give some examples of each of the three approaches to uniformity. These examples are intended to be illustrative only and do not cover the entire range of policies comprising generally accepted accounting principles. We will highlight relevant circumstances and allowable alternatives; intermediate or advanced accounting texts should be consulted for in-depth discussion of the various methods and other details.

Rigid Uniformity

There are numerous examples of rigid uniformity in official pronouncements of standard-setting bodies. Comprehensive income tax allocation is required by SFAS 96 whether or not deferred tax liabilities are realistically expected to reverse. In the case of research and development costs, despite the presumed presence of future benefits arising from an important proportion of these costs, SFAS 2 requires that they be immediately expensed. SFAS 19 attempted to eliminate "full costing" and allow only "successful efforts" amortization of drilling and exploration costs in the oil and gas industry. (More will be said about oil and gas accounting in Chapter 15.)

Finite Uniformity

Examples of finite uniformity include long-term leases and ownership of common stock of another firm for control purposes. In the former case, any one of four conditions is sufficient to warrant capitalization, whereas the absence of all four results in an operating lease. In the second situation, ownership of various percentage ranges of common stock results in either full consolidation, equity, or cost methods of handling the investment. However, the FASB recognized the fuzziness of stock ownership as a criterion for degree of control when it noted in Interpretation No. 35 that the 20 percent demarcation point between cost and equity methods is to be construed as a guideline rather than an inviolable rule.

These two illustrations of finite uniformity involve situations of present magnitudes. The question of reversal of deferred tax liabilities is a case of finite uniformity where future contingencies are involved. Reversal is seen as a viable circumstance in the United Kingdom, where partial tax allocation must be used, but in the United States it is simply expected to occur though the effective reversal may be in the very distant future. Another case of finite uniformity involving a future contingency involves loss contingencies. SFAS 5 sets up two conditions under which a contingent loss must be charged against income of the current year: (1) the likely occurrence of an adverse future event, such as an expropriation of assets by a foreign government; and (2) the ability to make a reasonable estimate of the amount of the loss. If either or both of these conditions are not met, disclosure of the loss contingency (presumably in the footnotes) should be made if there is at least a "reasonable possibility" of a loss occurring. SFAS 5 can also be interpreted as an example of conservatism because gain contingencies are not mentioned except for the statement that ARB 50 is still in effect relative to them. ARB 50 states that gain contingencies are not reflected in income prior to realization. However, adequate disclosure is to be made, though care must be exercised in order "to avoid misleading implications as to the likelihood of realization."[25]

Flexibility
Flexibility is very prevalent in generally accepted accounting principles. In addition to the investment tax credit, inventory and cost of goods sold accounting is another illustration of flexibility. The actual physical flow of inventory to cost of goods sold does not fall within the definition of relevant circumstances presented here. Nevertheless, firms may choose among FIFO, LIFO, and weighted-average methods as they see fit. If FIFO or weighted average is used, the lower-of-cost-or-market modification is required: lower-of-cost-or-market itself is simply a valuation procedure that has been tacked onto FIFO and weighted-average methods for purposes of conservatism.

Depreciation accounting provides a special example of flexibility. The estimated usage pattern of the asset provides a potential relevant circumstance.[26] However, choice among the many acceptable methods — such as straight-line, accelerated methods, and the annuity method — is again at the user's discretion and need not be related to the estimated pattern of usage.

Another example of flexibility is provided by treasury stock that is acquired for later reissuance. Among the reasons for acquisition are: (1) issuance to employees under stock option plans, (2) acquiring stock of another corporation in a business combination, and (3) temporary investment purposes. The cash flow consequences of these different reasons are simply not clear. It is thus very doubtful that they could be considered as future contingencies. Nevertheless, there are two methods for handling treasury stock acquisitions: the par value and the cost methods. Once again, either method can be used at the firm's option.

Overview of Practice
The present situation in financial accounting can, perhaps, be best understood by means of Exhibit 8–2, which shows a two-by-two matrix with one illustration in each cell. Column I represents situations where relevant circumstances are present. Column II represents situations where relevant circumstances are not present. Row A depicts transactions in which a policy-setting body has treated the situation as if it were finite. Similarly, Row B represents transactions in which a policy-setting body has treated the situation as one of rigid uniformity.

The cells where policy matches the complexity of the situation are IA and IIB. In IA a relevant circumstance is present and the policy-making body has given it recognition. In IIB no relevant circumstance is present and the rule-making organization has attempted to treat the situation with rigid uniformity.

The cells where suboptimization is present are IIA and IB. In IIA no relevant circumstances are present but the policy-setting group has set up criteria

[25] ARB 50 (1958, para. 5).
[26] Powell, (1965, pp. 680–681).

EXHIBIT 8–2
Uniformity and Relevant Circumstances in Practice

Policy Employed	Relevant Circumstances	
	Yes	No
Finite	IA ARB 51, APB 18, and SFAS 94 Ownership of common stock for control purposes	IIA APB 16 Purchase versus pooling
Rigid	IB SFAS 2 Research and development costs	IIB APB 29 Assets acquired by donation

as if relevant circumstances existed. The result is two different methods of treatment that do not appear to have any real basis in fact. In IB relevant circumstances are present but the policy-making group has not been able to implement them, resulting in a situation of rigid uniformity. Situation IIA is more serious than IB. In the former, the standard-setting group has expended resources and taken actions that were not required and indeed led to extremely serious problems in the case of purchase versus pooling. In IB the group restricted alternative treatments because the different circumstances were simply not verifiable.

Finally, we should stress once again that even though cell IA provides a "match" between the standard-setting body's action and the complexity of the situation, it is not necessarily the case that relevant circumstances have been defined and applied optimally; or, even if they have, that the benefits of the standard exceed its costs.

DISCLOSURE

Broadly interpreted, disclosure is concerned with information in both the financial statements and supplementary communications — including footnotes, poststatement events, management's analysis of operations for the forthcoming year, financial and operating forecasts, and additional financial statements covering segmental disclosure and extensions beyond historical costs. *Financial reporting* is often used as an umbrella term to cover both financial statements themselves and the additional types of information mentioned above. For the purposes of our discussion, *disclosure* refers to the whole area of financial reporting and not simply to the financial statements.

THE DISCLOSURE FUNCTION OF THE SEC

It has always been implicitly recognized that disclosure as interpreted by the SEC has two aspects.[27] One of these might be termed *protective disclosure* since the SEC has been concerned with protecting unsophisticated investors from unfair treatment. The other aspect is **informative disclosure,** the full range of information useful for investment analysis purposes. Obviously, there is some degree of overlap between these functions of disclosure.

In its earlier history, the SEC stressed protective rather than informative disclosure. The Securities Act of 1933 required the filing of a registration statement with the SEC prior to the sale of a new issue of securities. Included in the registration statement and the prospectus given to the purchaser is extensive information about the business of the issuer, the securities being sold, and the identity and relevant financial interests of those distributing the securities. In addition, extensive information about the underwriter's compensation and dealings between the corporation and its officers, directors, and principal shareholders must be provided in the registration statement. Much of this information is protective in nature, though there is certainly informative material in the registration statement and the prospectus. The Securities Exchange Act of 1934 extended most of these rules for new issues of securities to sales of existing issues. In effect, then, the intention was to keep the information on the initial registration current.

Several restrictions were put into effect when a firm filed a registration statement: a twenty-day waiting period; delivery of the prospectus to purchasers; and the potential imposition of rather heavy civil liability damages upon the issuer, its officers, directors, and underwriters for filing inadequate or misleading information. It was thought that this package of restrictions would be a strong deterrent against blatant attempts to defraud investors. The SEC also had the authority to invalidate a registration or suspend it if it had already become effective if the information was either incomplete or inaccurate in any material respect.

THE SHIFT TOWARD INFORMATIVE DISCLOSURE

Although the protective and informative aspects of disclosure tended to overlap, the SEC shied away from requiring disclosure of "soft information." However, since approximately the early 1970s, it appears to have shifted its emphasis toward informative disclosure. For example, the commission had always

---

[27] Much of the information on the SEC and the disclosure process was obtained from Anderson (1974).

shunned inflation accounting proposals — despite the presumed importance for informative purposes — very likely on the grounds that the data were not highly verifiable and the average investor would probably not understand the numbers. However, after the FASB exposure draft on general price-level statements came out, the SEC in ASR 190 required for most major firms supplementary disclosures of replacement cost information for depreciation expense, fixed-asset valuation, cost of goods sold, and inventories. It is very likely that the movement toward informative disclosure has occurred as a result of the efficient-markets hypothesis and its conclusion that naive investors are not at a disadvantage in the market as long as they are properly diversified.

The SEC's movement toward informative disclosure was continued by the Advisory Committee on Corporate Disclosure to the SEC. The committee prepared a voluminous report in 1977 summarizing the present state of disclosure and making further recommendations about disclosure. Although stating that the existing disclosure system was adequate and not in need of drastic change, it endorsed the shift away from hard information (as signified by objectively verifiable historical data) toward the soft information embodied in opinions, forecasts, and analyses.

Among the committee's informative-disclosure suggestions were earnings forecasts with a "safe harbors" provision that would protect management from the liability penalties of the federal securities laws, provided projections were reasonable and made in good faith.[28] Other forward-looking informative data recommended by the committee included planned capital expenditures and their financing, management plans and objectives, dividend policies, and policies relative to enterprise capital structure.[29] Other informative disclosures recommended by the committee included standard product-line classifications for segmental reporting, determined on an industry-by-industry basis, and disclosure of social and environmental information if it was expected to affect future financial performance, such as a constant violation of the law.[30]

The SEC acted on the recommendations of the committee by adopting in 1979 Rule 175, which provided safe harbor from the liability provisions of the federal securities laws for projections that are reasonably based and made in good faith.[31]

IMPERFECTIONS OF THE DISCLOSURE PROCESS

The system of disclosure largely in effect today is called *differential disclosure*. The 10-K and 10-Q reports filed annually and quarterly by management with the SEC are basically aimed toward professional financial analysts. They are

---

[28] SEC (1977, pp. 344–365).
[29] Ibid., pp. 365–379. Starting in the late 1970s there has been a growing trend toward inclusion of a voluntary management report in the annual report, focusing on management's assessment of the internal accounting control system. For further details, see Golub (1981).
[30] U.S. Government Printing Office (1977, pp. 380–398).
[31] SEC (1979, p. 19).

more detailed and technical than the annual report going to shareholders. The analysts act as intermediaries by interpreting the SEC filings for the investing public. Beaver believed that the emphasis on more disclosure in the annual report would downgrade the importance of the differential disclosure approach.[32] Differential disclosure should be distinguished from selective disclosure. The latter indicates more information available to some individuals. This constitutes insider information and raises the possibility that those in possession of the insider information may be able to earn an abnormal return.

Although informative disclosure should improve the evaluation of risk and return of enterprises, there are several important qualifications to bear in mind. An important channel of disclosure communication is that between the corporation and financial analysts representing brokerage firms and investment consultants. Several aspects of this arrangement were discussed in Chapter 4. Since financial analysts do not pay for this information, it is likely to be overproduced as compared to the information that would have been available if it were supplied on a market-oriented basis.

However, Brownlee and Young note that timely possession of financial information results in a benefit to the holder (and user) of that information as opposed to later users.[33] Brownlee and Young see financial analysts as aggressive seekers of information that can profitably be sold to consumers (who have an advantage over other consumers who do not have the information on as timely a basis). Thus, they do not see a need for extensive additional disclosures. In effect, through their aggressive information search, security analysts cause the market for financial information to act efficiently in terms of providing adequate and timely information (with those willing to pay for the information better off than those who do not pay, an equitable market-type solution to the problem).[34]

Another argument against regulations that would require the overproduction of disclosure information is the possibility of information overload: the inability of users to process and intelligently utilize all the information provided in financial reports. Still another problem with disclosure, mentioned previously in this chapter, is that of competitive disadvantage. For example, in an area such as segmental disclosure, firms may be somewhat reluctant to reveal information about product lines because they might give vital information to competitors and damage their own favorable market situations. Hence, an inequitable situation may be created, since some individuals will tend to be unfavorably affected, such as present owners of securities of firms whose competitive advantage is revealed. A situation like this would be an economic

---

[32] Beaver (1978, p. 50).

[33] Brownlee and Young (1987, p. 21).

[34] The Brownlee and Young article is the latest in a line of papers that have argued against the need for mandated disclosure by a governmental agency such as the SEC. For example, Benston (1973) argued that the information required by the Securities Acts of 1933 and 1934 could be inferred from other data sources and that voluntary information disclosure plays an important role in information-efficient markets. See Chapter 4.

consequence of an accounting standard. In this particular case, as long as there were no bias relative to firms (in terms of the information being reported), neutrality (SFAC 2) should govern the disclosure: as long as the information required is relevant and reliable, the effect on a particular interest should not be considered.

Lev, however, has made a very strong argument in favor of additional disclosure.[35] Additional disclosure benefits all users. The problem with information asymmetry (which is defended by Brownlee and Young) is that those who do not have information will tend to take defensive measures, such as not dealing in securities where limited information is present, buying diversified portfolios, or even staying out of the market altogether. When this occurs, a "thin" market results and those with additional information do not get the full benefit of their advantage. Hence, on the grounds of equity, Lev would favor additional disclosure (such as management's forecast of earnings), which is beneficial to all parties: those having additional information as well as those not possessing this information.

An additional point that has been mentioned in the disclosure literature is that adequate diversification by the investor may reduce the need for information at the firm-specific level.[36] The investor's concerns, it is argued, are with firm-specific information only insofar as it affects the portfolio. However, separating firm-specific information into categories, that which has no effect on the portfolio and that which is useful in terms of portfolio assessment, appears virtually impossible.

A complementary argument involves the undiversified investor.[37] Because unsystematic risk can be virtually eliminated by proper diversification, the question arises as to responsibilities owed to the undiversified investor in terms of disclosure, since the costs must be borne largely by others (costs passed on to customers of the firm or lower dividends for all stockholders, for example).[38] However, it is difficult to separate information useful specifically for undiversified portfolios and that which is also useful for diversified portfolios — not to mention the difficulty of separating information that is portfolio specific from that which is firm specific. Furthermore, if undiversified investors are also among those possessing less information, a very reasonable hypothesis is that other parties would gain by additional disclosure, the equity argument that all users benefit by additional disclosure, mentioned above. Hence, the cost–benefit argument against additional disclosure to benefit undiversified investors is somewhat mitigated.

Despite the problems of the disclosure process, our value judgment is that, on balance, the operations of securities markets and investors, as a totality,

---

[35] Lev (1988).

[36] Beaver (1978, pp. 46–47).

[37] Ibid., p. 47.

[38] Coffee points out that although finance theory states that rational shareholders will hold diversified portfolios, evidence indicates that significant numbers of investors do not, in fact, possess diversified portfolios. Coffee also points out that it is possible many of these individuals may diversify by owning other risky investments, such as real estate. Coffee (1988, p. 82 and p. 119).

will benefit by expanding the disclosure process. An aspect of the disclosure process that we next examine involves small firms versus larger firms.

Small Firms Versus Larger Firms

A contention is that small firms incur significantly higher costs than large ones in carrying out complex accounting standards or disclosure requirements.[39] Hence, the FASB (and the SEC) has provided some relief to smaller firms.[40] The FASB specifically considers implications of disclosures for smaller firms with the express purpose of requiring disclosures only where they are relevant and cost effective. Furthermore, the FASB established a Small Business Advisory Committee of the Financial Accounting Standards Advisory Council for facilitating communication concerning financial reporting for both small enterprises and small public accounting firms. Nevertheless, balancing costs against benefits in financial reporting for small firms is not an easy task. For example, SFAS 33 on current cost and constant dollar disclosures (essentially similar to general price-level adjustments) was applicable only to firms having either in excess of $125 million of property, plant, and equipment or a billion dollars in total assets; similarly, privately held companies — which are generally smaller than publicly held firms — are exempt from segmental disclosures and earnings per share requirements.

However, recent research suggests that the disclosures of small firms, such as earnings announcements as well as published financial statements, have more information content than the statements for larger firms.[41] The reason for this may be that much less information is publicly available on smaller firms, which makes their published financial statements and related disclosures relatively more important for investors and therefore more comprehensive.[42]

SUMMARY ANNUAL REPORTS

Summary annual reports (SARs) are condensed financial statements that omit or boil down much of the detail contained in the traditional audited financial statements and are a new development in disclosure. Information on property, plant, and equipment as well as expense breakdowns are highly aggregated in SARs and most footnoted information is omitted, though it may appear in the management discussion and analysis. The management discussion and analysis in the SAR, on the other hand, is generally more expansive than the one ap-

---

[39] Atiase, Bamber, and Freeman (1988, p. 18).

[40] Larger firms also receive disclosure benefits. For example, only very large firms can use *shelf registration*, the registration of equity securities for future sale even though the firm has no present intention to issue the securities. See Atiase, Bamber, and Freeman (1988, p. 19).

[41] However, two AICPA committees found that, in addition to it being costly for small enterprises to prepare financial statement information in areas such as tax allocation, leases, and pensions, these enterprises are also providing some information which users either do not need or find confusing. Atiase, Bamber, and Freeman (1988, p. 19).

[42] Ibid., p. 20.

pearing with the traditional audited financial statements in the corporate annual report. The SAR is intended to replace the traditional corporate annual report and to be more understandable.

SARs evolved from a 1983 study sponsored by the Financial Executives Research Foundation (FERF) of the FEI, which was concerned with the readability of corporate annual reports. After some reluctance, in late 1986 the SEC accepted General Motors' proposal to prepare a SAR, but only after General Motors agreed to append the fully audited financial statements including footnotes to the proxy statement mailed to shareholders prior to the annual shareholders' meeting. In addition, shareholders would still be able to acquire upon request copies of the firm's Form 10-K filed annually with the SEC. Approximately forty firms have prepared SARs since 1987 in place of the corporate annual report.

The crucial issue is whether SARs constitute differential disclosure or selective disclosure. As long as Form 10-K is considered publicly available information as well as the fact that audited financial statements are attached in total to the proxy statement, many would undoubtedly see SARs as differential disclosure. Nevertheless, two recent studies do raise significant issues. Nair and Rittenberg question the use of SARs on the basis of the conceptual framework qualitative characteristics of completeness, comparability, and understandability, particularly because of the aggregation procedures that they think do not provide enough detail to elicit a full, meaningful interpretation of enterprise operations.[43] They also observe that while some firms have favorably reacted to SARs, others have expressed considerable skepticism.[44] Lee and Morse did not observe any overt attempts to obscure or mislead users in SARs — as opposed to the full financial statements — but they were concerned with whether SARs can actually provide full disclosure and whether auditors can really comply with GAAP.[45]

We are obviously at a very early stage in the development of SARs. The wide use of SARs would be a revolutionary development in financial reporting.

DIRECTIONS OF THE STANDARD-SETTING PROCESS

Improving the comparability of financial statements by increasing both the degree of uniformity among them and the extent of disclosure raises several issues in terms of possible directions for the accounting profession. Both theoretical and institutional considerations have a bearing on these matters.

Finite and rigid uniformity, as mentioned, are ideals. A standard-setting body would not attempt to impose in one fell swoop either form of system. Such

---

[43] Nair and Rittenberg (1990, pp. 28–31).

[44] Ibid., p. 37.

[45] Lee and Morse (1990, pp. 42–44).

an undertaking would be virtually impossible in a capitalistic and democratic society.

However, given market efficiency, increasing disclosure relative to finite and rigid uniformity should increase the utility of both as well as of any prevailing mixed system (which is by far the most likely possibility). However, we think that increasing the amount of disclosure will tend to give a comparative advantage to rigid uniformity over finite uniformity. To state the case slightly differently, we think that increasing disclosure will lower the benefits/costs differential of finite uniformity compared to the benefits/costs differential of rigid uniformity.

OPTIMAL ACCOUNTING SYSTEMS

Somewhat related to such issues as metatheoretical structures and finite and rigid uniformity are optimal accounting systems or optimal information systems. An **optimal accounting system** is "one for which the expected payoff to a user employing an optimal decision strategy is greater than or equal to the corresponding payoff for any alternative system. . . ."[46] In other words, user utility cannot be improved by alternative financial statement presentations based on any other set of accounting rules. Most, if not all, of the parties engaged in the debate agree that an optimal system is not attainable even if there were no user-heterogeneity problem.[47] The utility of the virtually limitless number of systems of accounting standards would be almost impossible to measure. However, we believe the issue should be addressed somewhat differently. With or without a metatheoretical framework, the development of accounting standards is an evolutionary process. It proceeds on a step-by-step basis. The presence of a conceptual framework or metatheoretical structure is intended to guide the standard-setting process in deriving relevant goals of users consistent with qualitative characteristics and definitions of elements. Therefore, the relevant question is whether a revision of existing standards is better (in terms of whether resulting securities prices better reflect the relationship of risk to return).[48] In other words, accounting information should facilitate the prediction of prospective risk-adjusted cash flows.[49]

The process of setting standards will always be extremely difficult to evaluate. Determining whether securities prices that result after new standards are imposed will better equate risk with return is extremely difficult. Standard setting should also occur within a framework in which benefits exceed costs, an-

---

[46] Marshall (1972, p. 286).

[47] For example, Demski (1973), Cushing (1977), Bromwich (1980), and Benston (1980).

[48] Even a step-by-step basis is fraught with difficulties. The problem lies in the interdependence among standards. As a new — and presumably better — standard is promulgated, it must not decrease the utility of previously enacted standards. See Bromwich (1980) for further analysis. Of course, a conceptual framework should reduce the interdependency problem by making standards consistent in terms of user needs and objectives, but it is no outright guarantee.

[49] See Ronen (1974, pp. 82–86).

other extremely difficult measurement problem. Of course, a program of finite uniformity must have a fairly large degree of homogeneity in information needs of the various user groups, or else failure will surely result. Adding to these difficulties are the workings of the standard-setting group itself. Compromises among board members and political pressures from outside groups are but two of the dangers faced.

MUDDLING THROUGH

All of these difficulties and constraints indicate that a standard-setting body is much more likely to satisfice or just plain muddle through than to attempt to find the presumed holy grail of optimal accounting standards. Even "optimal accounting standards," if such a concept exists other than in the minds of accounting theorists, must be constantly changing as new business conditions and problems emerge. However, muddling through is often the stuff of which good and reasonable progress is made. It is this interaction between the policy-setting process and research (both inductive and deductive) that offers us at least a modest amount of hope that financial reporting will continue to improve.

It is not certain whether there will be an eventual push toward finite or rigid uniformity in conjunction with a meaningful disclosure system. The main consideration here is the question of benefits versus costs. Part of the cost entails extensive research into relevant circumstances in the various valuation areas of accounting. Nevertheless, no matter which way, if either, the profession goes and despite the many qualifications and shortcomings surrounding the development of a conceptual framework, a strong case can be made that the effort is worthwhile. It is possible, of course, that the Conceptual Framework Project is simply a form of window dressing intended to do nothing more than fend off the pressures of critics.[50] The conceptual framework has been strongly criticized, particularly for its avoidance of measurement and recognition criteria, but it still must be viewed as a unique set of documents. It is the first time that a standard-setting body has completed a project of this type. Furthermore, nothing prevents the FASB from amending, extending, or improving the conceptual framework. Despite the well-warranted criticism of the project, optimism is still justified.

SUMMARY

Under finite uniformity, policy-making organizations attempt to take into account relevant circumstances in broadly similar event situations. Policy-making bodies do not attempt to cope with relevant circumstances under rigid unifor-

---

[50]The views of both Peasnell (1982) and Dopuch and Sunder (1980) appear to fall into this category. The latter (p. 17) state that "... a body like the FASB needs a conceptual framework simply to boost its

mity. Their chief concern under rigid uniformity is to limit alternatives, which, in turn, would lead to greater verifiability but less relevance. Relevant circumstances are different economic factors leading to potentially different patterns of cash flows in broadly similar types of event situations.

Although finite uniformity should lead to greater relevance because rule making attempts to take into account appropriate circumstances, it is not at all clear that the resulting additional benefits would exceed the incremental costs of implementation. Certainly a more extensive metatheoretical framework would be needed to delineate the accounting required for relevant circumstances. In addition, extensive empirical research would have to be focused on the search for relevant circumstances.

Finite and rigid uniformity are ideals. It is unlikely that either could ever be totally and consistently applied. At present, examples of both rigid and finite uniformity can be found in various pronouncements of rule-making bodies. One step that might be taken is to eliminate alternatives in event situations where it does not appear that relevant circumstances exist.

The increasing complexity of economic and financial events, along with the rise of the efficient-markets hypothesis, has led to the increasing importance of disclosure in financial reporting. An example would be SFAS 14 on segment reporting. Since approximately 1970, the SEC appears to have changed its primary focus from protective disclosure — which had been its primary emphasis since its inception — to informative disclosure. The increasing emphasis on informative disclosure will probably work to the benefit of rigid uniformity as opposed to finite uniformity — from the benefits/costs standpoint.

SARs, annual reports to stockholders that are greatly condensed in an attempt to make them also more understandable, are an interesting new development. Whether they will really bring about full disclosure is the critical issue that will decide the future of SARs.

An optimal accounting system will never be attained. Although a conceptual or metatheoretical framework can easily be criticized, we believe that efforts to construct them will improve the process of financial reporting.

QUESTIONS

1. Is Cadenhead's conception of circumstantial variables as the only permissible departure from prescribed accounting methods closer to finite or rigid uniformity? Discuss.
2. Do you think management policies should be acceptable as potential relevant circumstances? Discuss.
3. How do present magnitudes differ from future contingencies?
4. Are simple transactions really examples of rigid uniformity? Discuss.

public standing." Much of the Dopuch and Sunder argument against the conceptual framework centers around the presumption of heterogeneous user-information needs in an agency setting.

5. Finite and rigid uniformity would result in different information being received by users of financial statements. What difference would this make in terms of resource allocation when viewed from a macroeconomic standpoint?

6. If the efficient-markets hypothesis is accepted, why does additional disclosure work to the advantage of rigid uniformity rather than finite uniformity?

7. How do protective and informative disclosure differ?

8. Under previous disclosure requirements of the SEC, dividends paid during the past two years to shareholders must be stated in the annual report. This requirement has been broadened: (1) There must be disclosure of any restrictions on the firm's present or future dividend-paying ability. (2) If the firm has not paid dividends in the past despite the availability of cash, and the corporate intention is to continue to forego paying dividends in the foreseeable future, disclosure of this policy is encouraged. (3) If dividends have been paid in the past, the firm is encouraged to disclose whether this condition is expected to continue in the future. Do you think that this broadening of disclosure of dividend policy is primarily protective or informative? Discuss.

9. ASR 242 of the SEC states that relative to payments made to foreign governmental and political officials, ". . . registrants have a continuing obligation to disclose all material information and all information necessary to prevent other disclosures made from being misleading with respect to such transactions." This ASR appeared shortly after the passage of the Foreign Corrupt Practices Act. Do you think this type of disclosure is primarily protective or informative in nature? Discuss.

10. If *uniformity* means eliminating alternative accounting treatments, then surely comparability of financial statements of different enterprises would be improved. Do you agree with this statement? Comment.

11. What are optimal accounting systems and why are they totally unattainable?

12. Do you agree that it is not necessary to provide information for undiversified investors? Discuss.

13. SFAC 6 defines *circumstances* as follows:

> Circumstances are a condition or set of conditions that develop from an event or series of events, which may occur almost imperceptibly and may converge in random or unexpected ways to create situations that might otherwise not have occurred and might not have been anticipated. To see the circumstance may be fairly easy, but to discern specifically when the event or events that caused it occurred may be difficult or impossible. For example, a debtor's going bankrupt or a thief's stealing gasoline may be an event, but a creditor's facing the situation that its debtor is bankrupt or a warehouse's facing the fact that its tank is empty may be a circumstance.

How does this definition of circumstances relate to the definition of relevant circumstances presented in the chapter?

14. SFAS 13 in effect regards a lease period of 75 percent or more as a relevant

circumstance in distinguishing between capital and operating leases. What economic factors (cash flow differentials) lie behind this policy choice?

15. An argument against additional disclosure is that financial analysts aggressively seek this information, which is then sold to their customers, resulting in an adequate market solution to the problem of providing timely and relevant information on securities. Do you agree? Discuss.

16. Why do you think that disclosures of smaller firms appear to have more information content than disclosures for larger firms?

17. What are SARs? Do you believe that they provide selective or differential disclosure?

CASES AND PROBLEMS

1. Refer to either a current intermediate accounting text or a guide to current "generally accepted accounting principles." Give at least one example for each of the four cells of Exhibit 8–2 (your instructor may desire to modify this problem).

2. Using the article by Cyert and Ijiri as background (in *Objectives of Financial Statements*, Vol. 2, AICPA, 1974, pp. 30–35), list as many issues as you can that fall under the categories of (1) constitutional standards and (2) operating standards.

3. Give as many examples as you can of flexibility under current generally accepted accounting principles.

4. Write an essay on trends and developments in the area of disclosure using as background information the following articles cited in the bibliography to this chapter: Beaver (1973), Beaver (1978), Brownlee and Young (1988), Lev (1988). In your discussion, try to answer these points:

   (a) How do Beaver's views on the limitations of disclosure change from the 1973 to the 1978 paper?

   (b) What is the crucial point relative to SEC disclosures that Beaver (1978) makes?

   (c) Why did Beaver not see a "bright future" for differential disclosure? Was he right or wrong?

   (d) How do Lev and Brownlee's and Young's views on disclosure differ?

5. Below are two footnotes from the McKesson Corporation's financial statements, one from the SAR and one from their audited financial statements. Prepare a report indicating where the SAR note lacks completeness compared to the footnote from the audited financial statements (adopted from Nair and Rittenberg, 1990).

Pension Plans (SAR Footnote)*

Substantially all full-time employees of the company not covered by union-sponsored multiemployer plans are covered under company-sponsored defined benefit retirement plans, profit sharing incentive plans and an ESOP. At March

---

*Footnotes reproduced by permission.

31, 1987, the $181 million market value of the assets of the defined benefit plans exceeded the projected benefit obligation for services rendered to date by $9.2 million. A total of 3.7 million McKesson shares, or 8.7% of the shares outstanding, were held for employees in the profit sharing and ESOP trusts at March 31, 1987.

McKesson's GAAP-Basis Pension Footnote

11. Post-Retirement Benefits

Pension Plans

Substantially all full-time employees of the Company are covered under either Company sponsored defined benefit retirement plans or by union sponsored multiemployer plans. The benefits for Company sponsored plans are based primarily on age of employees at date of retirement, years of service and employees' pay during the five years prior to retirement. Pension expense for Company sponsored plans was $0.5 million in fiscal 1987, a negative $1.7 million in fiscal 1986, and $1.7 million in fiscal 1985. In fiscal 1986, the Company adopted Statement of Financial Accounting Standards No. 87, "Employers' Accounting for Pensions" ("SFAS 87") for the Company sponsored defined benefit plans. Pension expense for fiscal 1986 would have been approximately $4.2 million had the Company not adopted SFAS 87. In accordance with SFAS 87, pension expense for years prior to fiscal 1986 has not been restated. Pension expense in fiscal 1985 was reduced by $3.0 million as a result of changed actuarial assumptions for investment return, salary growth and amortization periods.

Net pension expense in fiscal 1987 and 1986 for the Company sponsored defined benefit retirement plan and executive supplemental retirement plan consisted of the following:

	1987	1986
	(in millions)	
Service cost—benefits earned during the year	$ 6.9	$ 3.9
Interest cost on projected benefit obligation	15.1	13.4
Return on assets—actual	(27.7)	(32.2)
—deferred gain	9.2	16.1
Amortization of unrecognized net transition asset	(3.0)	(2.9)
Net pension expense	$ 0.5	$(1.7)

The funded status of Company sponsored defined benefit retirement plans at March 31 was as follows:

	1987	1986	1985
	(in millions)		
Actuarial present value of benefit obligations			
Vested benefits	$138.5	$113.8	$ 84.6
Nonvested benefits	14.3	11.7	8.3
Accumulated benefit obligations	152.8	125.5	92.9
Effect of assumed increase in future compensation levels	19.4	17.8	12.7
Projected benefit obligation for services rendered to date	172.2	143.3	105.6
Assets of plans at fair value	181.4	163.9	141.6
Excess of assets over projected benefit obligation	9.2	20.6	36.0

Unrecognized net loss from experience different from that assumed	27.3	15.6	
Unrecognized net transition asset, recognized over 13 years	(31.6)	(33.9)	(36.8)
Pension asset (liability) recognized on consolidated balance sheet	$ 4.9	$ 2.3	$(0.8)

The projected benefit obligations for Company sponsored plans were determined using a discount rate of 8.5% at March 31, 1987, 9.9% at March 31, 1986 and 12.5% at March 31, 1985, and an assumed increase in future compensation levels at 5% at March 31, 1987 and 6% at both March 31, 1986 and 1985. The expected long-term rate of return on assets used to determine pension expense under SFAS 87 was 11.2% for fiscal 1987 and 11.8% for fiscal 1986. The assets of the plans consist primarily of listed common stocks and bonds.

The projected benefit obligation for the Company's executive supplemental retirement plan is $14.2 million of which $11.5 million is recognized as a liability on the consolidated balance sheet. There is a $2.7 million unrecognized net loss from experience different from that assumed.

The cost of multiemployer retirement plans was $3.0 million in fiscal 1987, $2.8 million in fiscal 1986 and $2.6 million in fiscal 1985.

BIBLIOGRAPHY OF REFERENCED WORKS

American Institute of Certified Public Accountants (1958). "Contingencies," *Accounting Research Bulletin No. 50* (AICPA).

Anderson, Alison Grey (1974). "The Disclosure Process in Federal Securities Regulation: A Brief Review," *The Hastings Law Journal* (January 1974), pp. 311–354.

Atiase, Rowland K., Linda S. Bamber, and Robert N. Freeman (1988). "Accounting Disclosures Based on Company Size: Regulations and Capital Markets Evidence," *Accounting Horizons* (March 1988), pp. 18–26.

Beaver, William (1973). "What Should Be the FASB's Objectives?," *Journal of Accountancy* (August 1973), pp. 49–56.

———— (1978). "Future Disclosure Requirements May Give Greater Recognition to the Professional Community," *Journal of Accountancy* (January 1978), pp. 44–52.

Benston, George J. (1980). "The Establishment and Enforcement of Accounting Standards: Methods, Benefits and Costs," *Accounting and Business Research* (Winter 1980), pp. 51–60.

Bromwich, Michael (1980). "The Possibility of Partial Accounting Standards," *The Accounting Review* (April 1980), pp. 288–300.

Brownlee, E. Richard, and S. David Young (1987). "The SEC and Mandated Disclosure: At the Crossroads," *Accounting Horizons* (September 1987), pp. 17–24.

Cadenhead, Gary (1970). " 'Differences in Circumstances': Fact or Fantasy?" *Abacus* (September 1970), pp. 71–80.

Coffee, John C., Jr. (1988). "Shareholders Versus Managers: The Strain in the Corporate Web," in *Knights, Raiders, and Targets*, John C. Coffee, Jr., Louis Lowenstein, and Susan Rose-Ackerman, eds. (New York: Oxford University Press), pp. 77–134.

Cushing, Barry (1977). "On the Possibility of Optimal Accounting Principles," *The Accounting Review* (April 1977), pp. 308–321.

Cyert, Richard, and Yuji Ijiri (1974). "A Framework for Developing the Objectives of Financial Statements," *Objectives of Financial Statements*, Vol. 2 (American Institute of Certified Public Accountants), pp. 30–35.

Demski, Joel (1973). "The General Impossibility of Normative Accounting Standards," *The Accounting Review* (October 1973), pp. 718–723.

Dopuch, Nicholas, and Shyam Sunder (1980). "FASB's Statements on Objectives and Elements of Financial Accounting: A Review," *The Accounting Review* (January 1980), pp. 1–21.

Financial Accounting Standards Board (1976). "Accounting for Leases," *Statement of Financial Accounting Standards No. 13* (FASB).

—— (1980a). "Qualitative Characteristics of Accounting Information," *Statement of Financial Accounting Concepts No. 2* (FASB).

—— (1980b). "Elements of Financial Statements of Business Enterprises," *Statement of Financial Accounting Concepts No. 3* (FASB).

—— (1985). "Elements of Financial Statements: A Replacement of FASB Concepts Statement No. 3 (incorporating an amendment of FASB Concepts Statement No. 2)," *Statement of Financial Accounting Concepts No. 6* (FASB).

Golub, Steven J. (1981). "Management Reports: Growing Acceptance," *Financial Executive* (December 1981), pp. 26–29.

Grady, Paul (1965). "Inventory of Generally Accepted Accounting Principles for Business Enterprises," *Accounting Research Study No. 7* (American Institute of Certified Public Accountants).

Ijiri, Yuji (1975). "Theory of Accounting Measurement," *Studies in Accounting Research #10* (American Accounting Association).

Lee, Charles, and Dale Morse (1990). "Summary Annual Reports," *Accounting Horizons* (March 1990), pp. 39–50.

Lev, Baruch (1988). "Towards a Theory of Equitable and Efficient Accounting Policy," *The Accounting Review* (January 1988), pp. 1–22.

Marshall, Ronald (1972). "Determining an Optimal Accounting Information System for an Unidentified User," *Journal of Accounting Research* (Autumn 1972), pp. 286–307.

Miller, Paul B. W. (1985). "The Conceptual Framework: Myths and Realities," *Journal of Accountancy* (March 1985), pp. 62–71.

Nair, R. D., and Larry Rittenberg (1990). "Summary Annual Reports: Background and Implications for Financial Reporting and Auditing," *Accounting Horizons* (March 1990), pp. 25–38.

Peasnell, K. V. (1982). "The Function of a Conceptual Framework for Corporate Financial Reporting," *Accounting and Business Research* (Autumn 1982), pp. 243–256.

Powell, Weldon (1965). "Putting Uniformity in Financial Accounting into Perspective," *Law and Contemporary Problems* (Autumn 1965), pp. 674–690.

Richardson, F., and H. Wright (1986). "Standards Overload: A Case for Accountant Judgment," *CPA Journal* (October 1986), pp. 44–52.

Ronen, Joshua (1974). "A User Oriented Development of Accounting Information Requirements," *Objectives of Financial Statements*, Vol. 2 (American Institute of Certified Public Accountants, 1974), pp. 80–104.

Ronen, Joshua, and George Sorter (1972). "Relevant Accounting," *Journal of Business* (April 1972), pp. 252–280.

Securities and Exchange Commission (1979). *Annual Report* (SEC).

Sorter, G., and M. Ingberman (1987). "The Implicit Criteria for the Recognition, Quantification, and Reporting of Accounting Events," *Journal of Accounting, Auditing, and Finance* (Spring 1987), pp. 99–114.

Sprouse, Robert (1978). "The Importance of Earnings in the Conceptual Framework," *Journal of Accountancy* (January 1978), pp. 64–71.

Sterling, Robert R. (1985). *An Essay on Recognition* (The University of Sydney: Accounting Research Centre).

U.S. Government Printing Office (1977). *Report of the Advisory Committee on Corporate Disclosure to the Securities and Exchange Commission (U.S. G.P.O.).*

Wyatt, Arthur R. (1983). "Efficient Market Theory: Its Impact on Accounting," *Journal of Accountancy* (February 1983), pp. 56–65.

ADDITIONAL READINGS

Uniformity and Comparability

Graham, Willard (1965). "Some Observations on the Nature of Income, Generally Accepted Accounting Principles, and Financial Reporting," *Law and Contemporary Problems* (Autumn 1965), pp. 652–673.

Hendriksen, Eldon (1967). "Toward Greater Comparability Through Uniformity of Accounting Principles," *New York Certified Public Accountant* (February 1967), pp. 105–115.

Keller, Thomas (1965). "Uniformity Versus Flexibility: A Review of the Rhetoric," *Law and Contemporary Problems* (Autumn 1965), pp. 637–651.

Langenderfer, Harold (1967). "A Problem of Communication," *Journal of Accountancy* (January 1967), pp. 33–40.

Mautz, R. K. (1972). *Effect of Circumstances on the Application of Accounting Principles* (Financial Executives Research Foundation).

Merino, Barbara, and Teddy Coe (1978). "Uniformity in Accounting: A Historical Perspective," *Journal of Accountancy* (August 1978), pp. 62–69.

Miller, Paul (1978). "A New View of Comparability," *Journal of Accountancy* (August 1978), pp. 70–77.

Olson, Wallace (1977). "Financial Reporting – Fact or Fiction?" *Journal of Accountancy* (July 1977), pp. 68–71.

Revsine, Lawrence (1975). "Toward Greater Comparability in Accounting Reports," *Financial Analysts' Journal* (January–February 1975), pp. 45–51.

Optimal Accounting Systems

Bejan, Mary (1981). "On the Application of Rational Choice Theory to Financial Reporting Controversies: A Comment on Cushing," *The Accounting Review* (July 1981), pp. 704–712.

Chambers, Raymond J. (1976). "The Possibility of a Normative Accounting Standard," *The Accounting Review* (July 1976), pp. 646–652.

Cushing, Barry (1981). "On the Possibility of Optimal Accounting Principles: A Restatement," *The Accounting Review* (July 1981), pp. 713–718.

Demski, Joel (1974). "Choice Among Financial Reporting Alternatives," *The Accounting Review* (April 1974), pp. 221–232.

——— (1976). "An Economic Analysis of the Chambers' Normative Standard," *The Accounting Review* (April 1976), pp. 653–656.

Disclosure

Bedford, Norton (1973). *Extensions in Accounting Disclosure* (Prentice-Hall).

Buzby, Stephen (1974). "Nature of Adequate Disclosure," *Journal of Accountancy* (April 1974), pp. 38–47.

———— (1974). "Selected Items of Information and Their Disclosure in Annual Reports," *The Accounting Review* (July 1974), pp. 423–435.

Chandra, Gyan (1974). "Study of the Consensus on Disclosure Among Public Accountants and Security Analysts," *The Accounting Review* (October 1974), pp. 733–742.

Devine, Carl T. (1985). "Some Problems in Disclosure," in *Essays in Accounting Theory*, Vol. I, *Studies in Accounting Research No. 22* (American Accounting Association), pp. 103–114.

Mautz, Robert, and William May (1978). *Financial Disclosure in a Competitive Economy* (Financial Executives Research Foundation).

Singhvi, Surendra (1972). "Corporate Management's Inclination to Disclose Financial Information," *Financial Analysts Journal* (July–August 1972), pp. 66–73.

Singhvi, Surendra, and Harsha Desai (1971). "Empirical Analysis of the Quality of Corporate Financial Disclosure," *The Accounting Review* (January 1971), pp. 129–138.

Part Two

CONTEMPORARY ISSUES AND ACCOUNTING THEORY

I N THE SECOND PART OF THIS TEXT we attempt to assess important contemporary accounting problems. We review institutional developments, including the evolution of standards, and — wherever possible — the relationship among theoretical concepts, definitions, and issues pertaining to these problems.

The first three chapters are the most general in nature because they are concerned with the present state of the three principal financial statements. Chapter 9 examines the development of definitions of the principal income statement categories: revenues and gains, and expenses and losses. We also examine the income statement within the framework of the current-operating approach versus the all-inclusive approach. The shift toward the all-inclusive approach has guided the evolution of such categories as extraordinary items, prior period adjustments, discontinued operations, and accounting changes. We also discuss briefly other income statement topics, such as earnings per share and income smoothing, and several specialized income statement problems. Chapter 10 reviews the statement of financial position. The main concern is with the development of working definitions of the three main balance sheet elements: assets, liabilities, and owners' equity. We use the three orientations to the relationship between the balance sheet and income statement discussed in the Conceptual Framework Discussion Memorandum (asset–liability, revenue–expense, and nonarticulated) as reference points for the development of the three definitions. The subject matter of Chapter 11 is the statement of cash flows required by SFAS 95. The chapter highlights the move from a funds flow to a cash flow orientation.

One of the principal theoretical problems that has faced policy-making agencies concerns financial reporting in light of inflation and changing prices; the basic models were presented in Appendix 1-A. Chapter 12 provides an extensive theoretical overview of the main issues, including choices between entry and exit values, and computation of purchasing power gains and losses and holding gains and losses. The chapter examines and evaluates various income measurement systems, including general price-level adjustment. One of the key issues concerning current value (cost) systems is the disposition of real holding gains and losses, how that affects the measurement of capital maintenance, and how capital maintenance pertains to general price-level adjustment. We discuss two specialized problems of current valuation systems: measuring current value depreciation when newer technology comes on the market, and whether purchasing power gains on long-term debt during inflation are illusory. Chapter 13 provides an in-depth examination of the failure of the experiment of accounting for changing prices. We cover some questionable choices in the Statement of Financial Accounting Standards (SFAS) 33, measurement problems relative to indexes, and a lack of understanding by users. We end the chapter with a discussion of inflation accounting standards in selected English-speaking countries.

Chapter 14 highlights problems arising in accounting as a result of income taxes, principally income tax allocation. The discussion examines the underlying reasons that led to income tax allocation and analyzes the various positions on the question. The latter are developed within the context of the most important application of income tax allocation: accelerated depreciation for tax purposes and straight-line for financial reporting. We also scrutinize the shift to a modified liability (asset–liability) approach in SFAS 96 and the conceptual inconsistencies of this document. Appendix 14-A discusses the investment tax credit.

Although the subject matter of Chapter 15, oil and gas accounting, pertains to a specialized — though highly important — industry, virtually all facets of accounting theory have some bearing on this unique problem. These include economic consequences, the allocation problem, present valuation and verifiability, uniformity and relevant circumstances, and the politics of standard setting.

Chapter 16, on pensions, emphasizes the recognition of expenses and liabilities for the sponsoring firm and carefully analyzes the move to SFAS 87. The chapter also discusses the economic consequences of pensions. Other postretirement benefits, the subject matter of SFAS 106, is also covered here.

Lease accounting is the subject of Chapter 17. Leases are a good example of an economic condition that influenced standard setting. After World War II, leasing became a popular means of financing the use, if not the acquisition, of fixed assets. One advantage of leasing was "off-the-balance-sheet-financing." The major part of the chapter is concerned with the evolution of lease capitalization methods, beginning with ARB 38, as standard-setting agencies attempted to make purchase and lease accounting more comparable. More types of leases have become subject to capitalization, although the present rules are perhaps not as comprehensive as they might be. The chapter covers the lessee and the lessor, sale and leaseback, and the leveraged lease and concludes with a discussion of the economic consequences of lease capitalization.

Chapter 18 presents a detailed theoretical analysis of intercorporate equity investments. Among the consolidation issues examined is the question of valuation of the assets and liabilities in the combined entity. Purchase, pooling of interests, and the new entity method come under the scope of valuation in a consolidated enterprise. Equity and cost methods are also examined if consolidation is not appropriate.

Chapter 19 examines some international accounting issues. Beginning with foreign currency translation for multinational firms, the chapter continues the consolidation examination from Chapter 18. We survey standard setting in selected English-speaking nations briefly and close with a look at the attempt to harmonize accounting standards throughout the world.

THE INCOME STATEMENT

THE NEXT THREE CHAPTERS examine the income statement, balance sheet, and cash flow statements, respectively, in order to review the conceptual foundation of current financial reporting practices. We emphasize the definitions of accounting elements and the rules of recognition and measurement applicable to each financial statement. It is not our intent to cover all extant accounting standards: such an approach is taken in intermediate accounting textbooks. Rather, we wish to encourage an appreciation of the principles of accounting measurement or calculation embodied in the three basic financial statements.

The first section of the chapter reviews the two basic types of relationship between the balance sheet and income statement: **articulated,** which means the two are mathematically linked; and **nonarticulated,** which means the two statements are independently defined. The basic accounting elements — assets, liabilities, owners' equity, revenues, gains, expenses and losses — are also introduced in the first section.

The chapter then reviews revenue and expense recognition standards. Next, we turn to the controversy over current operating versus all-inclusive income, which has led to the present extended format of the income statement, and discuss the classifications comprising the extended format of the income statement — extraordinary items, accounting changes, discontinued operations, and prior period adjustments (for completeness). Earnings per share is an important "summary indicator" of enterprise performance, and so we touch on its development and future briefly. We also examine several specialized subjects involving income measurement and close with a review of earnings-management research.

THE RELATIONSHIP BETWEEN THE BALANCE SHEET AND INCOME STATEMENT

Two approaches, the articulated and the nonarticulated, have been advocated for defining accounting elements and the relationship between the balance sheet and income statement.[1] Articulation means that the two statements are mathematically defined in such a way that net income is equal to the change in owners' equity for a period, assuming no capital transactions or prior period adjustments. The nonarticulated approach severs the mathematical relationship between the balance sheet and income statement: each statement is defined and measured independently of the other.

ARTICULATION

The accounting elements identified in SFAC 6 are assets, liabilities, owners' equity, revenues, gains, expenses, and losses.[2] Income is calculated from revenues, gains, expenses, and losses. Under articulation, income is a subclassification of owners' equity. Exhibit 9–1 illustrates the articulated accounting model and classification system. For ease of presentation, we take a proprietary approach, in which the net assets are equal to owners' equity.

Under the articulated concept, all accounting transactions can be classified by the model in Exhibit 9–1. There are three subclassifications of owners' equity: contributed capital, retained earnings, and unrealized capital adjustments. Contributed capital is subclassified into legal capital (par value) and other sources of contributed capital (for example, premiums and donated assets). Retained earnings has three subclassifications: income statement accounts, prior period adjustments, and dividends. Because income is a subclassification of retained earnings, the income statement and balance sheet articulate. There are further subclassifications within the income statement itself: the distinctions between revenues and gains, and expenses and losses, and the classification of gains and losses as ordinary or extraordinary. Some accounting transactions bypass the income statement altogether because they are considered to be adjustments of previous years' income. These adjustments are made directly to retained earnings. Dividends represent a distribution of income. The third subclassification of owners' equity, unrealized capital adjustments, arises from a few specific accounting rules. It is discussed later in the chapter and can be interpreted as a type of nonarticulation.

The accounting classification system is rather simple, but this simplicity causes some difficulty because complex transactions cannot always be neatly categorized into one of the classifications in Exhibit 9–1. New types of business transactions challenge the limits of the basic accounting model. For example,

---

[1] FASB (1976).
[2] FASB (1985b).

EXHIBIT 9–1
Accounting Classification System

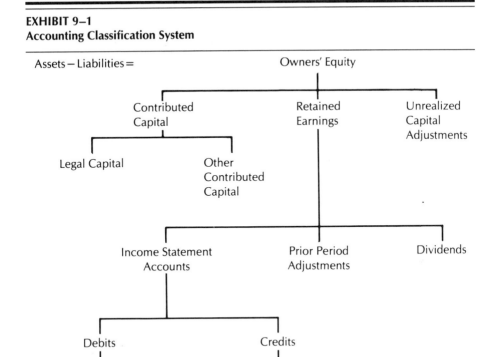

Assets − Liabilities =

Owners' Equity

Contributed Capital

Retained Earnings

Unrealized Capital Adjustments

Legal Capital

Other Contributed Capital

Income Statement Accounts

Prior Period Adjustments

Dividends

Debits

Credits

Expenses

Losses

Revenues

Gains

Ordinary

Extraordinary

Ordinary

Extraordinary

mandatory redeemable preferred stock, because it is stock, has definite owner-ship characteristics; but because it must be redeemed, it also resembles bonds. The SEC prohibits its inclusion in owners' equity. However, a strong case could be made *for* classification as owners' equity. Such complex transactions go be-yond the limits of the accounting classification system. Even so, it is remarkable that the categoric framework used to classify accounting transactions is virtually unchanged since Pacioli's time. It may be that supplemental disclosure is the only way to deal with newer complexities — short of developing an entirely new accounting classification system.

Within the articulated system, there are two alternatives for defining ac-counting elements. One approach, called *revenue–expense*, focuses on defining the income statement elements. It places primacy on the income statement, principles of income recognition, and rules of income measurement. Assets and liabilities are defined, recognized, and measured as a by-product of revenues and expenses. The other approach is called *asset–liability*. It is the antithesis of the revenue–expense approach because it emphasizes the definition, recognition, and measurement of assets and liabilities. Income is defined, recognized, and measured as a by-product of asset and liability measurement.

Revenue–Expense Approach

Since the 1930s, accounting policy has been mainly concerned with the definition, recognition, and measurement of income. Income is derived by matching costs (including arbitrary allocations such as depreciation) to recognized revenues. Both the income statement and balance sheet are primarily governed by accounting rules of revenue recognition and cost matching, and these rules represent a revenue–expense orientation.

One consequence of the revenue–expense approach is to burden the balance sheet with by-products of income measurement rules. As a result, the balance sheet contains not only assets and liabilities (defined in Chapter 10), but ambiguous debits and credits called *deferred charges* and *deferred credits*. These items do not conform to current definitions of assets and liabilities, yet are included in the balance sheet because of deferred recognition in the income statement. An example of a deferred charge is organizational startup costs. These costs are allocated to the income statement over a number of years rather than expensed immediately. Once incurred, organizational costs are a sunk cost and cannot be recovered. Therefore, it is questionable if such costs should be carried forward in the balance sheet. The same is true of some deferred credits. Many of these types of credit balances are not really liabilities; they are simply future income statement credits arising from present transactions that are deferred to future income statements. An example of this type of deferred credit is the investment tax credit accounted for under the deferral method per APB 2. Deferred investment tax credits are not a legal liability; rather, they simply arise from a difference between how the tax credits are treated in the firm's tax return and financial statements.

There are many examples of accounting standards that emphasize the effects of transactions on the income statement somewhat to the exclusion of their impact on the balance sheet. For example, pension accounting under APB 8 was mainly concerned with income statement recognition of pension expenses.[3] Virtually no consideration was given to the question of whether a pension liability exists. The recognition and amortization of intangible assets under APB 17 introduces a dubious debit into the balance sheet (arising from the purchase method of accounting for business combinations) and arbitrarily amortizes it over a maximum of forty years.[4] The question of whether an intangible asset (goodwill) really exists is not addressed.

---

[3] APB (1966a). This has, of course, been superseded by SFAS 87, which does take the balance sheet into consideration.
[4] APB (1970a).

Asset–Liability Approach

The asset–liability approach is directly concerned with measuring and reporting assets and liabilities. In SFAC 6, the FASB defines **comprehensive income** as the change in the firm's net assets (assets minus liabilities) from nonowner sources. The income statement is regarded as simply a way of classifying and reporting on certain changes that have occurred in the firm's net assets. Because assets and liabilities are real, it seems logical that measurement should focus on them. The owners' equity account is merely an invention to make possible the double-entry accounting system. Income and its components (revenues, gains, expenses, and losses) are thus regarded as secondary concepts that are simply a way of reporting on changes in assets and liabilities.

The asset–liability approach focuses on the measurement of net assets. This approach is arguably superior to a revenue–expense approach because, as we have noted, assets and liabilities are real. It is the increase in the value of net assets that gives rise to what we call income, not vice versa. The revenue–expense approach turns things around the other way and implies that changes in net assets are the consequences of "income" measurement. The current value models presented in Appendix 1-A of Chapter 1 are examples of the asset–liability approach.

Although the revenue–expense approach is the basic orientation of current financial reporting practices, some specific accounting standards reflect an asset–liability emphasis. For example, SFAS 2 requires the expensing of research and development costs rather than capitalization because the existence of an intangible asset is considered to be subjective and uncertain.[5] SFAS 7 proscribes loss capitalization for companies that are in the development stage.[6] Previous practice had been to capitalize losses while in the development stage and to write off the losses against future income. The requirement under SFAS 7 keeps a deferred charge out of the balance sheet. Finally, SFAS 87 reoriented sponsor pension accounting toward balance sheet liability recognition rather than the expense-smoothing orientation of previous standards, and SFAS 96 focuses income tax accounting on the recognition of tax "assets" and "liabilities" although conservatism clouds the issue, as will be seen in Chapter 14.[7]

THE NONARTICULATED APPROACH

The possibility for nonarticulated financial statements has not been widely discussed in accounting literature. However, the idea appears to have some merit. There is a great deal of tension between proponents of the traditional revenue–expense approach and the asset–liability approach because revenue–expense proponents are primarily concerned with stabilizing the fluctuating effect of transactions on the income statement and are prepared to introduce deferred charges and deferred credits in order to smooth income measurement. On the other hand, asset–liability advocates are mainly concerned with reporting

---

[5] FASB (1974).
[6] FASB (1975a).
[7] FASB (1985a) and FASB (1987).

changes in the value of net assets, and they are prepared to tolerate a fluctuating income statement that may include unrealized holding gains and losses.

It is evident that the two groups are polarized partly because the balance sheet and income statement are mathematically articulated. Since articulation exists only by custom, the two statements could be severed and both groups might be satisfied with a revenue–expense-based income statement and an asset–liability-based balance sheet. A reconciliation of the two nonarticulated statements could also be included as supplemental disclosure.

Although nonarticulation does not exist, per se, there are some specific accounting standards that create the effect of nonarticulation wherein changes in net asset values are recorded in the balance sheet — but are not recognized in the income statement. SFAS 52 requires the translation of foreign assets and liabilities using end-of-period exchange rates; but gains or losses on the translation arising from exchange-rate changes are not charged to the income statement.[8] Any gains or losses are recorded directly in owners' equity as an unrealized capital adjustment and are recognized in the income statement only if the foreign operations are sold. There is no articulation with the income statement. A similar result occurs when the lower-of-cost-or-market rule is applied to non-current investments under SFAS 12.[9] Temporary losses are not charged to income; they are classified as an unrealized capital adjustment. The losses are recognized in the income statement only if the investments are sold, or if the losses are deemed permanent rather than temporary. In both of these examples, changes have occurred in the measurement of net assets, yet the gains or losses are classified as unrealized and recorded directly in owners' equity.

The treatment of unrealized capital adjustments in SFASs 12 and 52 has been criticized because the income statement is bypassed. Articulation does prevent the bypassing of the income statement in accounting for net assets. An argument favoring articulation is that it maintains the integrity of the income statement by reporting all changes in net assets in the income statement. On the other hand, there is no self-evident reason why net assets need to be measured the same way for both balance sheet and income statement purposes. For example, replacement costs might be most useful for the income statement and exit prices most useful for the balance sheet. Nonarticulation is a concept that deserves more serious consideration than it has received.

INCOME DEFINITIONS

Accounting income has been formally defined in the following ways:

> Income and profit . . . refer to amounts resulting from the deduction from revenues, or from operating revenues, of cost of goods sold, other expenses, and losses. . . .[10]

---

[8] FASB (1982).
[9] FASB (1975b).
[10] Committee on Terminology (1955, para. 8).

> Net income (net loss) — the excess (deficit) of revenue over expenses for an accounting period. . . .[11]
>
> Comprehensive income is the change in equity (net assets) of an entity during a period of transactions and other events and circumstances from nonowner sources.[12]

The first two definitions, from ATB 2 and APB Statement 4, clearly represent the revenue–expense approach. When the primary emphasis is on revenue and expense measurement, it is necessary to have standards that define those elements and specify their recognition and measurement. The third definition, from SFAC 6, represents a clear change in direction to the asset–liability approach. This appears to be the direction that the FASB will take in the future. The impact, if any, on the income statement of the apparent change in direction cannot be foreseen, but it probably will be slight for at least several years because the income statement is largely a legacy of fifty years of accounting standards based on the revenue–expense approach.

REVENUES AND GAINS

Revenues have been defined in the following ways:

> Revenue results from the sale of goods and rendering of services and is measured by the charge made to customers, clients, or tenants for goods and services furnished to them.[13]
>
> Revenue — gross increases in assets and gross decreases in liabilities measured in conformity with generally accepted accounting principles that result from those types of profit-directed activities. . . .[14]
>
> Revenues are the inflows or other enhancements of assets of an entity or settlements of its liabilities (or a combination of both) during a period from delivering or producing goods, rendering services, or other activities that constitute the entity's ongoing major or central operations.[15]

The first definition, from ATB 2, reflects a revenue–expense approach and emphasizes the direct identification of revenue-producing activities. A difference can be detected in the second definition, which is from APB Statement 4. Revenues are defined as an increase in net assets arising from income-producing activities. At first glance, this appears to represent a shift to the asset–liability orientation; however, measurement is said to be based on generally accepted accounting principles, which still implies the revenue–expense orientation. Finally, the third definition, from SFAC 6, does clearly define revenue as an increase in net assets. This represents an asset–liability approach and is consistent with the SFAC 6 definition of comprehensive income.

---

[11] APB (1970b, para. 134).
[12] FASB (1985b, para. 70).
[13] Committee on Terminology (1955, para. 5).
[14] APB (1970b, para. 134).
[15] FASB (1985b, para. 78).

The definition from ATB 2 is similar to the presentation of revenues in Chapter 5, in which revenues were defined as the output of the enterprise in terms of its product or services. However, all three of these definitions, by introducing the issue of how to measure revenues, interject the issue of recognition into the definition. How to measure an element should conceptually be kept separate from the definition since questions of recognition and measurement may well supersede the issue of what is being measured. Recognition is examined in more detail shortly.

Gains and revenues typically have been displayed separately on financial statements. Gains have been defined in the following manner:

> ... revenues ... from other than sales of products, merchandise, or services. ... [16]

> Gains are increases in equity (net assets) from peripheral or incidental transactions ... except those that result from revenues or investments by owners.[17]

The distinction between a revenue and gain once was a subject of considerable controversy. One school of thought believed that only revenues should be reported on income statements. The secondary or peripheral nature of gains means that they did not represent recurring income from the entity's main area of income-producing activities and therefore should be excluded from the income statement. This school of thought has been called the *current operating income concept.* The competing position was called the *all-inclusive income concept.* Its proponents believed that all revenues and gains, regardless of source, should be included in the income statement. There has been an evolution away from the current operating concept to the all-inclusive concept, which is reviewed later in the chapter.

REVENUE RECOGNITION

When is a revenue a revenue? From a theoretical point of view, the answer to this question is clear:

> [Revenues] should be identified with the period during which the major economic activities necessary to the creation and disposition of goods and services has been accomplished.[18]

The practical problem with this definition, however, is the ability to make an objective measurement of the results of those economic activities. Until a verifiable measurement can be made, no revenue can be recognized. Unfortunately, the accomplishment of the "major economic activities necessary to the creation and disposition of goods and services" and the ability to measure those accomplishments objectively frequently occur at different times and in different reporting periods. Finally, as noted in Chapter 6, SFAC 5 is of little help to the

---

[16] APB (1970b, para. 198).
[17] FASB (1985b, para. 82).
[18] Sprouse and Moonitz (1962, p. 177).

general problem of recognition. Although SFAC 5 purports to be the piece of the conceptual framework dealing with recognition, it does little more than reiterate, in an ad hoc manner, concepts from prior SFACs (that is, element definitions, measurability, relevance, and reliability).

Four alternative points in time for recognizing revenue are discussed in the accounting literature and used in accounting practice:

1. During production.
2. At the completion of production.
3. At the time of sale.
4. When cash is collected.

Revenue is recognized during production for certain long-term contracts (see ARB 45 and SOP 81-1); it is recognized at the completion of production for certain agricultural and mining operations (see ARB 43, Chapter 4, paragraphs 15–16); and it is recognized at the time of cash collection when the installment method is used for sales of real estate (see SFAS 66).

Although the topic of revenue recognition has been lively and provocative[19] the fact remains that revenues generally are recognized at the point of sale when legal title is transferred. This norm is clearly expressed in Chapter 1 of ARB 43:

> Profit (revenue) is deemed to be realized when a sale in the ordinary course of a business is effected, unless the circumstances are such that collection of the sales price is not reasonably assumed.[20]

This rule was one of the six originally adopted by the AICPA in 1934 (see discussion in Chapter 3). Exceptions are sanctioned in the accounting rules, as mentioned above, but the general principle is that revenues are recognized at the time of sale.

The vast majority of exceptions to recognizing revenue at the point of sale have evolved because new transactions have emerged that do not fit the mold of traditional transactions. In many instances, but not all, these transactions are peculiar to specific industries. As noted in Chapter 3, the AICPA has been the primary source of the development of accounting standards, particularly revenue recognition standards, as new transactions emerge. Its Accounting Standards Division periodically issues accounting guides (Guides) and used to issue SOPs. These documents, however, are not mandatory and do not have to be followed in practice as do FASB Standards and Interpretations. Perhaps this is why Jaenicke found the accounting practices for revenue recognition that have evolved for these new transactions to be inconsistent in rationale and, often, in outcomes.[21]

In SFAS 32, issued in 1979, the FASB announced that it was embarking on a program of extracting standards from the Guides and SOPs; modifying

---

[19] See complete discussion of revenue recognition concepts in AAA (1965a).
[20] Committee on Accounting Procedure (1953, Chapter 1, para. 1).
[21] Jaenicke (1981, pp. 6–10).

them, if necessary, to be internally consistent with FASB Standards and Concepts; and issuing them as SFASs. To date, thirteen SFASs in this program have been issued: franchise fee revenue (No. 45), revenue recognition when right of return exists (No. 48), product financing arrangements (No. 49), the record and music industry (No. 50), cable television companies (No. 51), motion pictures (No. 53), insurance enterprises (No. 60), title plant (No. 61), broadcasters (No. 63), mortgage banking (No. 65), sales of real estate (No. 66), costs and initial rental operations of real estate projects (No. 67), and an omnibus statement applying to securities dealers, employee benefit plans, and banks (No. 83).

Exceptions to the general rule of recognizing revenue at the point of sale have been sanctioned by the professional literature. Revenue may be recognized during production for long-term construction contracts if reliable estimates of the extent of progress and of the cost to complete can be made and if reasonable assurance of collectibility exists. If immediate marketability at a quoted price exists for a product whose units are interchangeable, revenue may be recognized at the completion of production. Recognizing revenue on a cash basis, either installment or cost recovery, is allowed if no reasonable basis exists for estimating collectibility.

Two additional bases for recognizing revenue have been suggested by many but are not permitted by authoritative literature. Some support recognizing revenue on an accretion basis where product marketability at known prices exists and it is desirable to recognize changes in assets, such as growing timber.[22] Regarding material resources, particularly natural gas and petroleum, many support a view of recognizing revenue on a discovery basis because of the significance of discovery on the earnings process (see discussion in Chapter 15).

Although the norm for revenue recognition is the point of sale, the primary criterion for revenue recognition applied in practice is the completion of the earnings process. In other words, revenue should be recognized when the transaction or event that culminates the earnings process has occurred. Measurement problems must be resolved, however, before revenue is recognized. Attributes that must be measurable are (1) sales price, (2) cash collections, and (3) future costs. If all three can be measured or estimated with reasonable accuracy, then revenue is recognized when the earning process is complete; otherwise, recognition must be delayed until reasonable measurements can be made.

EXPENSES AND LOSSES

Expenses have been defined in the following ways:

> Expense in the broadest sense includes all expired costs which are deductible from revenues. . . . [23]

---

[22] Philips (1963).
[23] Committee on Terminology (1957, para. 3).

> Expenses — gross decreases in assets or gross increases in liabilities recognized and measured in conformity with generally accepted accounting principles that result from those types of profit-directed activities of an enterprise. . . . [24]

> Expenses are outflows or other using up of assets or incurrences of liabilities (or a combination of both) during a period from delivering or producing goods, rendering services, or carrying out other activities that constitute the entity's major or central operations.[25]

The first definition, from ATB 4, represents the traditional revenue–expense orientation. In the second definition, APB Statement 4, a relationship is established between expense and net assets. However, measurement is still based on rules of the revenue–expense orientation. The third definition, SFAC 6, represents a strong asset–liability approach. Again, the FASB may be looking forward in applying this definition. In practice, though, expense recognition continues to be guided by a strong revenue–expense orthodoxy in which expenses are "matched" to recognized revenues.

Losses are defined in APB Statement 4, and in SFAC 6, in a parallel manner to gains. Losses represent a reduction in net assets, but not from expenses or capital transactions. As with gains, the distinction between expenses and losses is not important under the all-inclusive income concept. At one time, however, this was a major issue in accounting.

A good review of the matching-concept literature may be found in a 1964 American Accounting Association committee report.[26] A summary of current expense-recognition rules is found in APB Statement 4. Expenses are classified into three categories:[27]

1. Costs directly associated with the revenue of the period.
2. Costs associated with the period on some basis other than a direct relationship with revenue.
3. Costs that cannot, as a practical matter, be associated with any other period.

A hierarchy exists and the matching concept is based on it. If possible, costs should be matched against the revenues directly produced. If a direct cause-and-effect relationship does not exist, costs should be matched to revenue in a rational and systematic manner. Finally, if there is not even an indirect cause-and-effect relationship, the costs are recognized as period expenses when incurred.

Typically, the third category is the only one that does not give accountants significant recognition problems. Costs incurred in the current period that provide no discernible future benefit as well as costs incurred in past periods that no longer provide discernible future benefits are expensed immediately. The relevant event generally is recognizable: no future benefit. For example, when

---

[24] APB (1970b, para. 134).
[25] FASB (1985b, para. 80).
[26] AAA (1965b).
[27] APB (1970b, para. 155).

a building is destroyed by fire, there is no future benefit; thus, an expense (loss) is recognized immediately.

The first and second categories do provide recognition problems. The first category is basically the application of the matching concept. That is, match costs against revenues that they helped to generate. Some items, such as direct material and labor are relatively clear. Others, however, such as overhead items, require allocation on some basis to the products manufactured. In the absence of a direct means of associating expenses with revenues (cause and effect), costs must be associated with accounting periods on the basis of a "systematic and rational allocation" (category two). The major expense-recognition problem, then, concerns those costs that are clearly not expired in the period incurred but are clearly not associated with the revenues of a particular period.[28]

The standard of expense recognition through allocation does not provide guidance to the events that trigger accounting recognition as does the standard of revenue recognition. Revenue-recognition standards specify not only the amount of revenue to recognize (sales price) but also the period for which the revenue should be recognized (period of sale). Expense-recognition standards aid in determining the amount of expense to be allocated over future years, the cost to be amortized. Those standards, however, prescribe neither how the assets provide their benefit nor when the benefit is provided; thus, they give little practical guidance.[29]

The need for systematic and rational cost allocation over multiple periods cannot be avoided in the existing accounting model. The model based on historical cost, unlike the one based on measuring current value, must allocate the costs incurred. Some examples of these costs include depreciation, organizational startup costs, goodwill amortization, bond premium/discount amortization, and the inventory method (FIFO, LIFO, etc.) used to allocate inventory costs to cost of goods sold. Most accountants share the view that the method of allocation used is nothing more than an arbitrary decision. After extensive study of the subject, Thomas concluded that selection of a particular allocation method over alternative methods is meaningless because the superiority of one allocation method over another can be neither verified nor refuted.[30] This means that there is no obviously correct way to allocate the costs because no single allocation method can be proved superior to another. For example, it cannot be logically demonstrated that straight-line depreciation is any more appropriate than accelerated depreciation methods or that FIFO is more appropriate than LIFO.

Another way of describing this dilemma is to say that no allocation is completely defensible against other methods. For this reason all accounting allocations are, in the end, arbitrary, which is a very disturbing idea that strikes at the

---

[28]Jaenicke (1981, pp. 117–118).
[29]Jaenicke (1981, p. 119).
[30]Thomas (1969) and (1974).

logical core of historical cost accounting. Because of the arbitrariness of accounting allocations, allocation-free financial statements have been advocated as a better way of reporting useful information. Allocation-free accounting can be accomplished by using cash flow statements, exit-price systems, and certain types of replacement-cost systems (discussed in Appendix 1-A of Chapter 1).

Although it is the case that allocations are arbitrary, income statements — which contain allocations — have information content. Capital market research, discussed in Chapter 7, provides strong evidence that this is the case. The usefulness of accounting information is an empirical issue that transcends the deductive logic of the allocation problem.

Nevertheless, the calculation aspect of most expense measurements is one that cannot be easily resolved under historical cost accounting. Perhaps rigid uniformity should be strived for in the absence of meaningful finite uniformity applications. The main point to remember, however, which was discussed in Chapter 7 and noted above, is that accounting income numbers — despite the presence of numerous allocations — has information content for external users.

CURRENT OPERATING VERSUS ALL-INCLUSIVE INCOME

Until 1968, whether certain components of comprehensive income should be displayed in the income statement or the retained earnings statement was a controversial issue, especially with regard to the display of unusual (nonoperating) and infrequently occurring gains and losses. The **current operating** school of thought held that the income statement should contain only normal operating items and that nonoperating items should be reported in the retained earnings statement. The **all-inclusive** school of thought maintained that all components of comprehensive income should be in the income statement and that, as a corollary, the retained earnings statement should reflect only total earnings as reported in the income statement and dividend distributions, in addition to beginning and ending balances.

The current operating advocates contended that the income statement is more useful in assessing management's performance and predicting future years' performance if items extraneous to current management decisions are excluded. They believed that most financial statement users look only to bottom-line net income to assess current performance and to make predictions regarding subsequent years' performance. If material, extraneous, nonoperating, infrequently occurring items are reported in the income statement, financial statement users would be seriously misled and might as a result make incorrect decisions.

Those favoring the all-inclusive concept cited several reasons for their position. First, current operating lends itself to easy manipulation by management because it makes the decision on whether or not an item is extraordinary. Second, financial statement users may be misled because they may not realize substantial gains or losses have been "hidden" in the retained earnings statement. Third, the summation of all income displayed on the income statement for a period of years should reflect the reporting entity's net income for that period. Finally, they pointed out that proper classification within the income statement allows both normal recurring items and unusual, infrequently occurring items to be displayed separately within the same statement.

Historically, the AAA favored the all-inclusive concept. In 1936 the AAA's *A Tentative Statement of Accounting Principles Underlying Corporate Financial Statements* contained the following statement:

> The income statement for any given period should reflect all revenues properly given accounting recognition and all costs written off during the period, regardless of whether or not they are the results of operations in that period. . . . [31]

Conversely, the AICPA consistently favored the current operating concept until APB 9. For example, in ARB 43, the Committee on Accounting Procedure indicated that all extraordinary items should be carried directly to the surplus account.[32] However, in December, 1966, the APB leaned strongly toward the all-inclusive concept in APB 9, which as amended requires that all nonoperating, infrequently occurring items except for prior period adjustments be included in the computation of net income and reported separately on the income statement.[33]

There is empirical research to support the primacy of the current operating income concept. Gonedes, in a capital market study, found that the nonoperating income items had no information content, which suggests that the relevant information for stock valuation is captured by the operating income number.[34] Research on the smoothing of year-to-year income (reviewed later in the chapter) suggests that operating income is better predicted by operating rather than all-inclusive income, which is also supportive of the current operating income concept. However, a later stock market study found that some nonoperating income items were significantly associated with changes in security prices, although the effect was opposite than expected in that nonoperating items representing "bad news" were *positively* associated with stock prices.[35] One interpretation for these results is the so-called big bath theory. The idea here is that when firms come clean with bad news, there is a positive response by the market because the firm has finally recognized in the financial statements that a major problem exists and it is moving to redress the problem. For example, in 1987 Citicorp unexpectedly recognized an enormous $3 billion loss on its for-

---

[31] AAA (1936, section 8).
[32] Committee on Accounting Procedure (1953, Chapter 8, para. 13).
[33] APB (1966b, para. 16).
[34] Gonedes (1978).
[35] Hoskin, Hughes, and Ricks (1986).

eign loans. The day after the announcement, the firm's stock increased in value by about 5 percent (see the *Wall Street Journal*, May 21, 1987, p. 2).

OPERATING SECTION FORMAT

The professional literature has specific guidelines for the format in which non-operating items (extraordinary gains and losses, discontinued operations, and changes in accounting principle) are to be displayed in the income statement. However, specific format guidelines do not exist for the operating section. As a result, at least two formats have evolved and are used in the United States today — single-step and multiple-step.

The single-step income statement focuses on two broad categories, revenues and expenses. All revenues and gains that are not included in one of the nonoperating sections are displayed together and summed for total revenues. This category includes revenues from both primary and secondary operations and gains not meeting the criteria for being extraordinary. Similarly, all costs, expenses, and losses not included in a nonoperating section are displayed together and totaled. Total expenses are subtracted from total revenues to derive net income (loss) before extraordinary items.

The multiple-step statement provides several intermediate steps in arriving at net income before extraordinary items. Net primary revenues are shown first, followed by cost of goods sold, which is subtracted from net revenue to derive gross margin. Operating expenses are then listed and subtracted from gross margin to give income (loss) from primary operations. Other revenues and expenses are then added to or subtracted from income (loss) from primary operations. This classification includes revenues and expenses from secondary sources as well as gains and losses not qualifying as extraordinary. The resulting computation is income (loss) before income tax and nonoperating items. Income taxes on operating income are then deducted to arrive at income (loss) from normal operations.

The single-step format allows more flexibility in reporting than the multiple-step owing to the broader classifications. Many believe, however, the multiple-step is preferable because it provides relevant intermediate subtotals, such as gross margin. The single-step format is common today, but the multiple-step is gaining in popularity.[36] However, it is not at all clear that the multiple-step format discloses anything that is not readily available to financial statements users in the single-step format. Nevertheless, the multiple-step approach may reveal additional information for a class of users who are not adept at making the transformations themselves and who do not rely on financial

---

[36] The frequency of use of the multiple-step format has increased from 38 percent of enterprises in 1978 to 54 percent in 1986. AICPA (1987).

intermediaries. Regardless, it appears the information production costs of the multiple-step approach are extremely small.

NONOPERATING SECTIONS

The nonoperating section of the income statement has expanded since APB 9 and now includes three subdivisions: (1) extraordinary items, (2) accounting principle changes, and (3) discontinued operations. Furthermore, a fourth item, prior period adjustments, is reported in the retained earnings statement. This, of course, represents the continuing dilemma between the current-operating versus all-inclusive concepts.

EXTRAORDINARY ITEMS

How to report extraordinary items has been controversial for many years. The controversy is a good example of the shift away from finite uniformity to rigid uniformity in accounting standards. As we will see, this shift was necessitated because the concept of finite uniformity was thought to be abused in accounting practice; to circumvent that abuse, rigid uniformity became the rule.

The basis of the controversy is the impact that extraordinary items may have on financial statement users' perceptions of the results of operations and projections of future operations for the reporting entity. Evaluating the results of current and past operations and projecting future operations relies heavily on an ability to separate normal, recurring components of comprehensive income from those that are not recurring.

Prior to APB 9, the prevailing standard covering extraordinary items was Chapter 8 of ARB 43, which was a reprint of ARB 32 issued in 1947. The ARBs were vague, as the following quote illustrates:

> [There] should be a general presumption that all items of profit and loss recognized during the period are to be used in determining the figure reported as net income. The only possible exception to this presumption relates to items which in the aggregate are material in relation to the company's net income and are clearly not identifiable with or do not result from the usual or typical business operations of the period.[37]

Needless to say, with no more guidance than the above for the nineteen years prior to APB 9, accounting practice for extraordinary items was not uniform. APB 9 attempted to bring order out of disarray. It required display of all extraordinary items in a specifically designated section of the income statement — as opposed to leaving the decision up to the reporting entity. Also it provided a new definition of "extraordinary items":

---

[37] Committee on Accounting Procedure (1953, Chapter 8, para. 11).

... events and transactions of material effect which would not be expected to recur frequently and which would not be considered as recurring factors in any evaluation of the ordinary operating processes of the business.[38]

Unfortunately, the new definition still proved to be ambiguous. As a result, the APB restudied the problem in 1973 and issued APB 30. This Opinion resorted to rigid uniformity and virtually eliminated the existence of extraordinary items because the definition of and criteria for an extraordinary item were so restrictive. In fact, the APB expressly stated that extraordinary items should occur in only rare situations.[39] For an item to qualify as extraordinary it had to be both unusual in nature *and* infrequent in occurrence. The APB defined these terms as follows:

> *Unusual nature* — The underlying event or transaction should possess a high degree of abnormality and be of a type clearly unrelated to, or only incidentally related to, the ordinary and typical activities of the entity, taking into account the environment in which the entity operates.
>
> *Infrequency of occurrence* — The underlying event or transaction should be of a type that would not reasonably be expected to recur in the foreseeable future, taking into account the environment in which the entity operates.[40]

The environment in which the entity operates is often the controlling factor in applying the two criteria. For example, frost damage to a citrus grower's crop in North or Central Florida would not qualify as extraordinary because frost damage there is normally experienced every three or four years. Conversely, similar damage to a citrus grower's crop in South Florida or Southern California probably would qualify as extraordinary because frost damage there is not experienced on a recurring basis. As a result of APB 30, extraordinary items, other than those specifically allowed (gains and losses from early extinguishment of debt, including gains by debtors from troubled debt restructurings, and tax benefits of loss carryforwards), have practically disappeared from the scene.

The display of an extraordinary item, should one occur, in the income statement is in a specified section entitled "extraordinary items." This section appears just above net income. All items are shown net of tax. Events or transactions that are unusual or infrequent but not both must be displayed with normal recurring revenues, costs, and expenses. If these items are not material in amount, they are not shown separately from other items. If they are material in amount, they are exhibited separately above the caption "income (loss) before extraordinary items." They may not be displayed net of tax. However, normal disclosure practices include a footnote explanation of the item.

---

[38] APB (1966b, para. 21).
[39] APB (1973, para. 23).
[40] Ibid., paras. 19–20.

ACCOUNTING CHANGES

Changes in accounting methods employed by a reporting entity may affect significantly the financial statements of both the current reporting period and any trends reflected in comparative financial statements and historical summaries of the reporting entity. Accounting changes are classified in three broad categories:

1. Change in Accounting Principle — Results from adoption of a generally accepted accounting principle different from a generally accepted accounting principle previously used for reporting purposes. A characteristic of a change in accounting principle is that the change is from one generally accepted that *has been used previously* to another that is *also* generally accepted — for example, changing from straight-line depreciation to an accelerated-depreciation method.
2. Change in Accounting Estimate — Results when a change in a previously estimated item occurs because, through the passage of time, more information for making the estimate is known — for example, the change in estimated life of a depreciable asset where previous depreciation was based on a ten-year life and after five years it is estimated the asset will be used only an additional two years.
3. Change in Reporting Entity — Results when there has been a material change in the reporting entity since the last financial statements were compiled — for example, when the specific group of subsidiaries comprising the reporting entity is significantly different from the specific group reported on the previous reporting period.

Prior to APB 20, there was no comprehensive, consistent standard dealing with accounting changes. That document established standards to be followed for accounting changes.

For all changes in accounting principle, except those specifically excluded by APB 20 and subsequent APB Opinions and FASB Statements, the cumulative effect of changing to a new accounting principle as of the beginning of the period of change is included in comprehensive income on the income statement of the period of change. The amount is displayed in a separate section entitled "accounting changes." This section is below extraordinary items and just above net income. All items are shown net of tax. Prior financial statements are not restated. However, income before extraordinary items and net income computed on a pro forma basis is shown for all periods presented as if the newly adopted principle was applied in those previous years. Furthermore, the effect of adopting the new accounting principle on income before extraordinary items and on net income of the period of change is disclosed in footnotes.[41]

---

[41] APB (1971, paras. 18–22). May and Schneider (1988) report strong evidence indicating that changes in accounting principle occur not for reasons of representational faithfulness but rather to manage earnings. Their evidence suggests that discretionary changes in accounting principle are more likely to be taken if the effect upon earnings is positive rather than negative.

A change in accounting estimate is not reported separately, as is a change in accounting principle. The effects of the change are accounted for in the period of change if that is the only period affected, or in the period of change and future periods if the change affects both on a prospective basis. For example, assume a ten-year life has been used to depreciate an asset, and in the sixth year the life is adjusted to eight years. Depreciation expense for the sixth through eighth years is simply the undepreciated cost at the beginning of the sixth year spread over the remaining three years. In essence, an overstatement of depreciation for the last three years will offset the understatement of the first five years.[42]

For a change in reporting entity, APB 20 requires that financial statements of all prior periods be restated in order to show financial information as if the new reporting entity had existed for all periods. The financial statements of the period of change should describe the nature of and reasons for the change. Furthermore, the effect of the change on income before extraordinary items, net income, and corresponding per share amounts is disclosed for all periods.[43]

Accounting for accounting changes is straightforward; there are clear definitions and reporting requirements. This example of rigid uniformity appears to be working well in accounting practice. The FASB, however, increasingly appears to favor retroactive restatement for accounting principle changes it promulgates in new SFASs. In a majority of its major SFASs, the FASB has either required or encouraged retroactive restatement for a change in accounting principle rather than the method of accounting required by APB 20.

DISCONTINUED OPERATIONS

A special type of nonoperating item requiring specific accounting treatment was recognized by APB 30: discontinued operations. Specifically, the Opinion requires special accounting treatment for gains and losses on the disposal of a segment of a business. The term *segment of a business* refers to a component of an entity whose activities entail a separate major line of business or class of customer. The distinguishing characteristic of a segment of a business is that its activities clearly can be separated physically, operationally, and for financial reporting purposes from the other assets, results of operations, and activities of the reporting entity.[44]

Two dates are of utmost importance in accounting for the disposal of a segment — measurement date and disposal date. The **measurement date** is the date that management commits itself to a formal plan to dispose of the segment.

---

[42] Ibid., paras. 31–32. Nurnberg (1988, p. 18) notes that it is often difficult to determine from annual reports whether the cumulative or prospective basis of correction has been used. His preference for changes in accounting estimates would be to use the retroactive method as long as it appears that benefits exceed costs. [Nurnberg (1988, pp. 21–22).]

[43] Ibid., paras. 34–35.

[44] APB (1973, para. 13).

The plan of disposal includes identification of the segment, method of disposal, expected time required to accomplish disposal, the estimated results of operations of the segment until disposal, and the estimated proceeds to be received on disposal. The **disposal date** is the date of closing the sale of the segment or the date operations cease if disposal is by abandonment.[45]

If a loss is expected on disposal, the estimated loss is recognized in the financial statements of the reporting entity as of the measurement date. On the other hand, if a gain is expected, recognition is deferred until realization, another example of conservatism. The determination of whether a gain or loss is expected is made on the measurement date and includes the following two factors:

1. Net realizable value of the segment after giving effect to any estimated costs directly associated with the disposal.
2. Any estimated income or loss from operations of the segment from measurement date until disposal date.

The two items are combined and if a loss results, it is reported net of tax as a separate component of comprehensive income displayed before extraordinary items on the income statement. In addition to the reported loss, the current year's income statement must display (as a separate component of income before extraordinary items) the results of operations net of tax for the segment being eliminated for the current reporting period prior to the measurement date. Likewise, financial statements of prior years are restated to reflect operations net of tax of the segment being discontinued as a separate component of income before extraordinary items. Errors in estimate of the loss on disposal between the measurement date and disposal date are treated as changes in accounting estimate in the income statement. Additional disclosures in the financial statements for the period that includes the measurement date are the identity of the segment, the expected disposal date, the manner of disposal, a description of the segment's assets and liabilities, and the income or loss for the segment from measurement date to financial statement date. Similar disclosures are required in subsequent financial statements covering the period in which disposal occurs.[46]

Accounting for the disposal of a segment provides some practical problems in identifying whether a particular part of an enterprise qualifies as a segment. These problems, however, are minimal and, in general, rigid uniformity has worked well here. The most serious criticism of accounting for the disposal of a segment involves the complexity of the accounting. Many small enterprises believe that they should be exempt from the requirements of accounting for the

---

[45] Ibid., para. 14.
[46] Ibid., para. 18.

disposal of a segment because of its complexity (as they are exempt from reporting earnings per share and segment reporting).[47]

PRIOR PERIOD ADJUSTMENTS

Accounting for (and the display of) prior period adjustments is quite straightforward. The amount of prior period adjustments is charged or credited to the beginning retained earnings balance. They are exhibited net of tax in the retained earnings statement and are thereby excluded from the determination of net income for the current period.

APB 9 was the first to deal with prior period adjustments and was fairly restrictive. To be classified as a prior period adjustment under APB 9, an event or transaction had to be (a) identified specifically with particular prior periods, not attributable to economic events occurring subsequent to the prior period; (b) primarily determined by persons other than management; and (c) not susceptible to estimation prior to determination.[48] The criteria were thus quite definitive. However, the SEC staff increasingly began to question the application of APB 9. In SEC staff administrative interpretations of APB 9 and later in *Staff Accounting Bulletin No. 8*, it excluded charges or credits resulting from litigation from being treated as prior period adjustments even though this item was illustrated in APB 9 as a specific example of a prior period adjustment. As a result of this and other problems, the FASB reconsidered the concept of prior period adjustments. SFAS 16 is the result of the FASB's reconsideration. It limits prior period adjustments to the following:

1. Correction of an error in the financial statements of a prior period.
2. Adjustments that result from realization of income tax benefits of preacquisition operating loss carryforwards of purchased subsidiaries.[49]

SFAS 16 does not affect the manner of reporting certain accounting changes that are treated, for accounting purposes, like prior period adjustments. This treatment is required for a few specified changes in accounting principle, including changes from LIFO to another inventory method, changes in accounting for long-term construction contracts, and changes to or from the full-cost method used in the oil and gas industry. As mentioned earlier, frequently the FASB requires or permits changes in accounting principle that result from adoption of a new SFAS to be treated like prior period adjustments. Examples of these include SFAS 2, research and development cost; SFAS 4, early extinguishment of debt; SFASs 5 and 11, contingencies; SFAS 7, development stage enterprises; SFAS 12, marketable securities; SFAS 19, oil and gas; SFAS 35, reporting by defined benefit pension plans; SFAS 43, compensated absences; SFAS 45, franchise fee revenue; SFAS 48, revenue recognition when

---

[47] Technical Issues Committee (1982, p. 9).
[48] APB (1966b, para. 23).
[49] FASB (1977b, para. 11).

right of return exists; SFAS 50, records and music; SFAS 52, foreign currency; SFAS 53, motion pictures; SFAS 60, insurance; SFAS 61, title plant; SFAS 63, broadcasters; and SFAS 65, mortgage banking activities.

EARNINGS PER SHARE

The term *summary indicator* was coined by the FASB in its 1979 Discussion Memorandum entitled *Reporting Earnings.*[50] When information is summarized in such a way that a single item can communicate considerable information about an enterprise's performance or financial position, that item is a **summary indicator.** Examples of summary indicators include earnings per share (EPS), return on investment, and the debt-to-equity ratio. The most-used summary indicator to date, and the one that has received the most attention from accounting policy-making bodies, is undoubtedly EPS.

Reporting EPS has been commonplace for many years. However, the decision to report it, the manner in which it was calculated, and where it was reported were entirely at management's discretion prior to APB 9. This Opinion strongly recommended, but did not require, that EPS be calculated and reported in the income statement. It also suggested how hybrid securities, such as convertible debentures, should be handled in the calculation. However, without specific rules, EPS calculations can be manipulated and thus mislead users. Because of the potential for manipulation and the apparent reliance on reported EPS, the APB restudied the subject and, in 1969, issued APB 15.

APB 15, as amended, is a set of rigid rules that accountants must follow to calculate and report EPS. Those rules are designed to result in an EPS number that reflects the underlying economic substance of the capital structure of the reporting enterprise rather than its legal form. Needless to say, the calculations are complex and necessitated the APB's publishing an interpretative booklet of 116 pages. Subsequently, the FASB, in SFAS 21, suspended APB 15 for nonpublic enterprises.

The usefulness of summary indicators in general and EPS specifically (because it is the most published and researched summary indicator) was the subject of an FASB research report entitled *Reporting of Summary Indicators: An Investigation of Research and Practice.*[51] The report found that summary indicators are used to evaluate past performance and predict future performance and financial position. Although EPS remains the most-used single summary indicator, both return on investment and cash flow per share are gaining in popularity. The report concludes that the FASB need not at this time establish additional standards regarding summary indicators, but that it should attempt to educate users away from reliance on a single summary indicator, such as EPS.

---

[50] FASB (1979).
[51] Frishkoff (1981, particularly pp. 17–45).

SPECIALIZED SUBJECTS CONCERNING INCOME MEASUREMENT

Several specialized topics provide important examples of the evolution of and development of a consensus in accounting standards. As will be seen, this evolutionary process frequently takes several years and may have a significant impact on reported earnings. Moreover, these examples will reflect how the lack of a consistent accounting theory framework hinders the establishment of accounting standards.

DEVELOPMENT STAGE ENTERPRISES

A development stage enterprise is any enterprise that "is devoting substantially all of its efforts to establishing a new business" and either has not commenced principal operations or, if principal operations have commenced, has generated no significant revenues as yet.[52] A theoretical question exists as to whether certain costs incurred in the development stage should be expensed or deferred.

There is theoretical justification for deferring costs and operating losses incurred in the development stage because these costs (1) have not generated revenue and (2) provide a future benefit such as the very existence of the enterprise and its ability to operate. Costs incurred in the development stage typically will be in connection with financial planning, exploring for natural resources, developing products and channels of distribution, and establishing sources of supply for raw material. Prior to January 1, 1976, costs of this nature generally were deferred by enterprises in the development stage, while operating enterprises expensed most of these costs. Thus, a dual set of accounting standards existed — one for development stage enterprises and another for operating enterprises — even though there is no relevant circumstance separating the two. SFAS 7 requires that costs of a similar nature be accounted for similarly, regardless of the stage of development of the entity incurring the cost. In other words, the FASB said the nature of the cost, not the nature of the enterprise, determines the appropriate accounting.

Costs incurred by development stage enterprises provide an interesting example of a setting in which multiple accounting theories, although all perhaps equally supportable, can lead to different answers. The FASB certainly made a wise choice in terms of the issue here particularly because it (1) required complete disclosure by the development stage enterprise to avoid misleading financial statement users by heavy initial losses, while at the same time it (2) achieved uniformity on the basis of the nature of the transaction or event that has occurred rather than the nature of the enterprise experiencing the transaction or event. It is interesting to note, however, that this problem is yet another allocation problem. The FASB obviously opted for rigid uniformity in selecting a solution as opposed to finite uniformity, where a relevant circumstance might

---

[52] FASB (1975c, para. 11).

be viewed as the development stage of the enterprise. However, this would be a very broad interpretation of the notion of relevant circumstances.

TROUBLED DEBT RESTRUCTURING

A **troubled debt restructuring** occurs whenever ". . . the creditor for economic or legal reasons related to the debtor's financial difficulties grants a concession to the debtor that it would not otherwise consider."[53] A troubled debt restructuring can have a significant impact on both the creditor's and debtor's income statements. The calculation of the impact (gain or loss) is not obvious, however. It is measured by both the debtor and creditor as the difference between the carrying amount of the obligation immediately prior to restructuring and the *undiscounted* total future cash flows after restructuring. Since APB 21 required discounting, the concept of present value is commonly accepted and used in accounting. However, it does not apply to the restructuring of debt.

If property or an equity interest is exchanged in satisfaction of the debt, the accounting is straightforward. The creditor recognizes a loss for the difference in fair market value of the asset or equity interest received and the carrying amount of the debt. The loss would probably not be extraordinary. The debtor recognizes a gain or loss (not extraordinary) for the difference between fair market value and book value of any property given up. In addition, the debtor recognizes an extraordinary gain equal to the difference in the fair market value of the asset given up and the carrying amount of the debt.

When the terms of the debt are modified, but it continues as an obligation (such as a reduction in interest rate, extension of maturity date, reduction in face amount, or similar modifications), the FASB concluded no transaction or event occurred as long as the total undiscounted future cash flows are equal to or greater than the carrying amount of the obligation. Thus, in this situation no gain or loss is recorded by either party. If total undiscounted future cash flow is less than the carrying amount of the debt, the obligation is reduced to the cash flow amount. The creditor records a loss for the reduction (not extraordinary), while the debtor records an extraordinary gain for the reduction. This again represents an example of rigid uniformity, one that does not appear to be based on any logical economic analysis. Troubled debt restructuring appears to be a triumph of economic consequences over representational faithfulness.

EARLY EXTINGUISHMENT OF DEBT

The early extinguishment of debt provides an interesting example of changing standards and their effect on the income statement. Prior to APB 26, there were three acceptable methods of accounting for the gain or loss on early extinguishment: (1) amortize over the remaining life of the original issue, (2) amortize over the life of a new issue, or (3) recognize currently on the income statement.

---

[53] FASB (1977a, para. 1).

The APB opted for the third alternative and stated that criteria of APB 9 apply in determining whether the gain or loss is extraordinary.

The consensus of the accounting profession was that the gain or loss met the extraordinary classification requirements. Nine months after APB 26, APB 30 was issued. This Opinion altered the criteria for extraordinary status established in APB 9. Under APB 30, the gain or loss from early extinguishment of debt definitely was not considered extraordinary. Thus, in the short period of nine months an item that typically was not given immediate income statement recognition became a mandatory extraordinary item and then a mandatory operating item. The amount involved is frequently very significant in relation to comprehensive income for a given period.

Finally the FASB settled the issue. In SFAS 4, it declared that gains and losses from the early extinguishment of debt, if material, are reported like, and along with, extraordinary items net of the applicable tax effects.[54] The reporting of a gain or loss from early extinguishment of debt provides a good example of where the standard-setting agency gave in to its constituency on a single-line financial statement item but did not change the overall standard (of what qualifies as extraordinary). Obviously, the reason for the concession is the magnitude of the numbers involved.

EARNINGS MANAGEMENT

Earnings management has been defined by Schipper as

> . . . purposeful intervention in the external financial reporting process, with the intent of obtaining some private gain (as opposed to, say, merely facilitating the neutral operation of the process).[55]

Obviously, agency theory studies fall under the category of earnings management since a firm's management may attempt to influence earnings in order to (1) maximize its compensation, (2) avoid the breaching of debt covenants of bond liabilities, which would prevent the payment of dividends, and (3) minimize reported income to lessen the possibility of governmental interference if the enterprise has high political visibility. Other examples of earnings management include attempts to maximize share prices for existing shareholders relative to potential acquiring shareholders where reported income is perceived to be an important determinant of share price, understatement of earnings by management where a leveraged buyout by management is expected to occur, and minimization of earnings by means of higher expense accruals in order to solicit protection from the federal government against foreign competition.[56] If

---

[54] FASB (1975a, para. 8).

[55] Schipper (1989, p. 92).

[56] See Dye (1988) for a two-period analytical model where shareholders selling the firm desire to impress potential acquiring stockholders by means of earnings management. In a leveraged buyout by manage-

these effects are present, the management of earnings constitutes inside information because the market would not be aware of the manipulation. Researchers concede that whether or not earnings has been managed is difficult to detect.[57] One long-discussed example of earnings management is called *income smoothing*, a topic which we examine next.

INCOME SMOOTHING

Given the importance of reported accounting income (see Chapter 7), one hypothesis has been that managers seek to smooth income over time so that a more stable earnings stream with less year-to-year variance would lead to higher firm valuation. In some ways, this argument suggests a naive stock market that cannot unravel accounting data correctly. Ronen and Sadan suggest alternatively that managers smooth income to facilitate better predictions (by outsiders) of future cash flows on which firm value is based.[58]

There are three ways that smoothing can be achieved:

1. The timing of transactions.
2. The choice of allocation methods/procedures.
3. Classificatory smoothing between operating and nonoperating income.

The timing of transactions is a managerial choice rather than an accounting choice, but it is probably the most direct and influential method of manipulating accounting income. Accounting research has focused mainly on the other two approaches. Smoothing can be achieved through the choice of accounting allocation methods, and, prior to APB 30, through the classification of income as operating/nonoperating (it is assumed that the desire is to smooth operating income). After APB 30, little discretion existed in classifying operating and nonoperating income. Several empirical studies have supported the hypothesis that income smoothing is achieved through both accounting-method choice (allocations) and classifications. This latter finding may help to explain why the APB elected to use rigid uniformity in APB 30 concerning nonoperating items rather than the finite uniformity approach used in APB 9.

Although the empirical tests have confirmed income-smoothing behavior, there are several problems with this body of research. First, the underlying theory or motivation for smoothing is not specified clearly enough to make strong predictions as to what smoothed income would look like. Thus, the approach has been to use fairly simple time-series models of income trends over time, but this could mis-specify the smoothed income series and produce mis-

---

ment situation, a conflict of interests on management's part arises. DeAngelo (1986) examined sixty-four management buyout proposals from 1973 to 1982 for firms listed on the New York and American Stock exchanges. She found no evidence of understatement of earnings by means of accrual manipulations. One possible reason why management would choose not to manipulate income is because of the intense scrutiny management is under in these situations and the severe penalties that could result. (DeAngelo, 1986, p. 419.)

[57] See the comments of DeAngelo (1988).

[58] Ronen and Sadan (1981).

leading results. Second, we cannot readily determine what the unsmoothed income series looks like since the firm's entire set of accounting methods, as well as transaction timing, produces the aggregate income results. If we cannot calculate unsmoothed income, it is not easy to determine how, if at all, income has been smoothed. Third, there may be a built-in bias that overstates income smoothing due to inflation. That is, there is likely to be an upward year-to-year drift in the income series due solely to general inflationary effects. So, in light of these possible problems, the evidence in support of widespread income smoothing practices is less convincing than it appears to be at first glance.

Healy takes an alternative approach to studying the income-smoothing issue.[59] First, he argues that smoothing incentives are, in part, related to managerial bonus plans that use accounting income numbers. Healy determined how bonuses are calculated for a sample of firms and then conducted empirical tests to see if accounting decisions are related to this compensation item. Bonuses are usually based on a target income pool with a lower and upper bound, so the incentive is to get income up to the bonus pool (if it is below). But if income is already in the bonus pool, the incentive is to defer income until the next period. In particular, the timing of transactions, especially year-end accruals, can be used to shift income from one year to the next, depending on the status of the bonus pool. Healy's results bear out this type of behavior. Interestingly, there was no indication that changes in accounting procedures were used to manipulate bonus income, although changes in accounting methods did occur when bonus plans were adopted or modified, which suggests that the bonus plan may have been an underlying influence on accounting-method choice, as has been argued in the economic-consequences literature.

More general studies of the time-series properties of accounting income numbers indicate that the series are best described as a random walk with slight upward drift.[60] This means that although there is a slight upward trend from year to year, the best prediction of current-period income is last-period income. These more general time-series studies are not supportive of the smoothing hypothesis. If smoothing were occurring, the trend-line effect should dominate and random-walk prediction models would be inferior to moving-average time-series models in explaining accounting income series.

Debt–Equity Swaps

One situation in which evidence clearly exists that income smoothing has occurred involves debt–equity swaps. The Bankruptcy Tax Act of 1980 provided a tax-free swap of debt for equity applicable to then-solvent firms, a swap that was discontinued by the Deficit Reduction Act of 1984. The swap had to be accomplished through an intermediary, such as an investment banker, acting as a principal — therefore undertaking risk — in the transaction. The bonds, which had a market value significantly less than their book value, were acquired from the bondholders by the investment banker. The bonds were then swapped with

---

[59] Healy (1985).
[60] See Watts and Leftwich (1977) and Albrecht, Lookabill, and McKeown (1977).

EXHIBIT 9–2
Overview of the Debt–Equity Swap

BONDHOLDERS	STOCK MARKET
Sell low-coupon, long-term debt of firm X to investment banker.	Buys newly issued shares made available by the investment banker.

INVESTMENT BANKER

Buys bonds from bondholders and delivers them to firm X in exchange for common stock of the same market value. This stock is then sold, usually via a registered secondary.

FIRM X

Buys back its low-coupon, long-term debt and issues new common stock in return. Transaction generates a one-time reported earnings gain for the swap fiscal quarter.

Source: Hand (1989, p. 590). Reproduced by permission.

the issuing firm for common stock of the same market value as the bonds. The investment banker then sold the shares by means of a registered secondary issue. Details of the debt–equity swap are summarized in Exhibit 9–2.

Under the 1980 tax act, gains on the retirement of the bonds were not taxed, but after July, 1984, the gain constituted either taxable income or reduction of the tax basis of depreciable property or realty which was held as inventory. Hence, the tax could be delayed but not avoided. As a result, there were 291 debt-equity swaps between August, 1981, and July, 1984, but only 2 have occurred since July, 1984.[61] Hand included in his analysis 245 of the 291 swaps occurring during the tax-free swap period. He found strong evidence of the smoothing hypothesis to the extent that the swap gain smoothed unexpected and transitory decreases in year-to-year quarterly earnings per share (four,

---

[61] Hand (1989, p. 591).

eight, and twelve quarters before and after the debt–equity swap occurred).[62] Firms may also have been attempting to avoid onerous sinking fund provisions of their bond indentures, but the evidence was not as clear-cut for this hypothesis. As a result of the swap, firms obviously lowered (improved) their debt-to-equity ratios.

The debt–equity swap was generally a single isolated event rather than a continuing series of events where greater control over income variability might be exerted by management. Nevertheless, Hand's study is one of the most impressive pieces of evidence that we have concerning the presence of the smoothing phenomenon.

SUMMARY

The income statement is based on the historical cost model of revenue recognition and expense matching. That does not mean, however, that it will not change. Some of the changes in the income statement that have occurred in the past fifteen years provide a hint as to what might be expected in the future. It is safe to say, regarding the recognition of revenue, that the FASB is moving toward rigid uniformity. Likewise, in expense recognition, which is largely based on a system of arbitrary allocation, it would not be surprising to see the FASB move toward rigid uniformity.

For the past fifty years, the income statement has been viewed by users of financial statements, as well as by standard setters, as the predominant financial statement. A review of past ARBs and APBs clearly indicates that more time and effort was placed on refining the income statement to the detriment of the balance sheet. Since the inception of the FASB, however, there appears to have been a shift toward "cleaning up" the balance sheet and a movement toward more of an asset–liability approach to the financial statements consistent with the Conceptual Framework Project.

Earnings management has become an important subject for researchers. An important aspect of earnings management is income smoothing by which management attempts to reduce the variance in year-to-year measurements of reported income with the hope of raising security prices. Although some evidence supports the smoothing hypothesis, it is an extremely difficult phenomenon to measure, so we cannot be certain of how widespread the practice is.

QUESTIONS AND EXERCISES

1. What is meant by the *asset–liability* and *revenue–expense* orientations to accounting recognition and measurement?
2. Discuss the advantages and disadvantages of the *nonarticulated* approach.

---

[62] Ibid., pp. 598–602.

Why are SFASs 12 and 52 and prior period adjustments characterized as examples of such an approach?

3. Describe how definitions of income, revenues, and expenses have changed in statements issued by successive standard-setting bodies.

4. In spite of SFAC 6, the revenue-recognition and expense-matching income model more or less underlies accounting practice. Briefly explain how accounting income is calculated and indicate the balance sheet implications.

5. Four points in the revenue cycle, from production through to cash collection, are possible events for revenue recognition. What *relevant circumstances* would justify finite uniformity rather than rigid uniformity for revenue recognition, and which approach is used in practice?

6. What is the *matching concept* and why is there an implied hierarchy for expense recognition?

7. Why is there no matching problem for periodic costs, and what are some examples?

8. What types of costs present matching problems, how are they dealt with, and what are some examples of such costs?

9. Explain why accounting allocations may be considered indefensible and discuss the implications for uniformity and for standard setting by the FASB.

10. In what ways can allocation-free financial statements be prepared? Why may these not necessarily be more *informative*?

11. There has been a trend toward rigid uniformity in the format of the income statement. Explain how and why this has occurred.

12. Why might the distinction between revenues and gains, and between expenses and losses, be important to report yet unimportant as to how they are reported?

13. Describe the incentives that might motivate income smoothing, and the ways that it could be done.

14. Why is income smoothing difficult to research, and what are the research findings to date?

15. Why may interindustry income uniformity be more difficult to achieve than intraindustry uniformity, and what are the implications of this in terms of a conceptual framework project, specific accounting standards, and comparability of accounting income numbers?

16. What is the relationship between earnings management and income smoothing?

17. Is earnings per share an example of finite or rigid uniformity?

CASES AND PROBLEMS

1. Revenue recognition, when the right of return exists, was standardized in 1981 by SFAS 48. Prior to this, SOP 75-1 provided guidance but was not mandatory (which is why the FASB has brought various SOPs into the ac-

counting standards themselves). As a result, three methods were widely used to account for this type of transaction: (1) no sale recognized until the product was unconditionally accepted, (2) a sale recognized along with an allowance for estimated returns, and (3) a sale recognized with no allowance for estimated returns. SFAS 48 mandated revenue recognition for such sales subject to six conditions: (1) the price is substantially fixed or determinable at sale date, (2) the buyer has paid or is obligated to pay the seller, and payment is not contingent on resale of the product, (3) the buyer's obligation would not be changed in the event of theft or physical damage to the product, (4) the buyer acquiring the product for resale has economic substance apart from the seller, (5) the seller has no significant obligations to bring about resale by the buyer, and (6) future returns can be reasonably estimated.

Required:
(a) Discuss the underlying conceptual issues concerning revenue recognition when the right of return exists. Can any (or all) of the pre-SFAS 48 methods be justified?
(b) Indicate the rationale for each of the SFAS 48 tests before a revenue is recognized.
(c) Is SFAS 48 an example of finite uniformity or of circumstantial variables as developed by Cadenhead (see Chapter 8)?

2. Accounting for the transfer of receivables with recourse has been problematic. At issue is whether such a transaction is, in substance, a *sale* in which case a gain/loss would be recognized, or a *financing* transaction, in which case any gain/loss should be amortized over the original life of the receivable. (Note that the receivable could be long term; for example, a sale of an interest-bearing note.) SOP 74-6 concluded that most transfers with recourse are financing transactions based on the argument that a transfer of risk (i.e., no recourse) must exist for a sale to have occurred. In 1983 the FASB reached a different conclusion in SFAS 77. A sale is now recognized if (1) the seller surrenders control of future economic benefits embodied in the receivable and (2) the seller's obligation under the recourse provisions can be reasonably estimated. If these conditions are not met, the proceeds from a transfer are reported on the balance sheet as a liability.

Required:
(a) What is the critical issue in interpreting the nature of this transaction? How does interpretation of the critical issue lead to the two different viewpoints?
(b) Explain why the SOP 74-6 view represents a revenue–expense orientation, while the SFAS 77 represents an asset–liability orientation.

3. Under APB 25, no cost of employee stock options is recognized as long as the exercise price is equal to or greater than the market price on grant date. In 1986, the FASB proposed a major change in accounting for the cost of stock options. The *Wall Street Journal*, February 28, 1986, page 23, reported:

Stock options are probably the most widely used method of long-term compensation, says Charles Peck, a compensation specialist at the Conference Board.

But the Financial Accounting Standards Board may soon change all that. The standard-setting body has "tentatively decided" that companies should estimate some value for most stock option plans and charge that value to the company's earnings statement when the options are issued, says Ken Gerdesmeier, a board project manager. Currently, options are accounted for simply as shares outstanding. . . .

If the proposal passes, estimates Robert S. Kay of Touche Ross Financial Services Center, large companies' earnings could be reduced as much as 5%. Similar consequences at smaller companies would reduce their capacity for growth, says Bruce Overton, president of the American Compensation Association. . . .

The accounting board's proposal should be opened for public comment this spring, and a final decision is slated for early next year. Most observers think that the proposed change will probably be implemented, and that "it will be hard to structure any plans using stock that will escape the dragnet," says Mr. Kay at Touche Ross.

Still, some accountants expect companies to devise ways to keep the popular benefit. "There are many ways to skin a cat," says Mr. Dieter of Arthur Andersen. "Companies will figure out something. The creative juices won't start flowing until (they) know what the regulations are."

Reprinted by permission of The *Wall Street Journal*, © 1986. Dow Jones & Company, Inc. All Rights Reserved Worldwide.

In addition, there are these following observations about stock options and new companies:

New companies have a particular problem of raising capital and attracting talented managers. These managers often receive part of their compensation in the form of stock options. The FASB has proposed that companies granting stock options take an immediate charge against earnings. If this occurs, the National Venture Capital Association estimates that pre-tax earnings of new ventures could be reduced by 20 percent to 40 percent.

This proposed new rule has particularly dangerous implications for start-up companies, which rely heavily on stock options because of limited funds.

Required:
(a) Discuss major conceptual issues concerning expense recognition and valuation of the cost of employee stock options.
(b) What types of negative economic consequences are suggested here and in the discussion of start-up companies, and should these be taken into consideration by the FASB?
(c) What is implied by the comment that "companies will figure out something. The creative juices won't start flowing until (they) know what the regulations are."

4. In 1983, a number of computer software companies reported use of an accounting procedure that was investigated by the SEC. The accounting policy is to capitalize the cost of developing computer software and amortize it over the life of the software (usually three to five years). This procedure is

used by large and small companies, but the impact is more pronounced on smaller, new companies, in which a greater portion of their activity is devoted to software development.

An article in the *Wall Street Journal*, April 8, 1983, page 4, noted:

> ... the procedure has a bigger effect on small companies that specialize in software, such as Comserv. Comserv's president, Richard Daly, said the company's deferred expenses totaled $11.3 million last year with the method. Its net income in the period was $2.5 million, and its assets (including the software costs) $53 million, he said.
>
> The issue, while somewhat arcane to non-accountants, is important to the software industry, which produces computer programs and related equipment. For the past few months, some computer software concerns and their trade group, the Association of Data-Processing Service Organizations, have been negotiating the issue with SEC aides. Mr. Daly of Comserv, defending the practice, said small companies wouldn't be able to invest as much cash in their own growth if they couldn't use the method.
>
> "The costs of developing these (software) products have gone up tremendously" in recent years, Mr. Daly said. His company's products include computerized systems to help manage inventory and ordering at auto and other manufacturing plants. If companies charged the development costs to their income, they would be under greater pressure to keep the costs down so they can show a decent profit, he said.
>
> Reprinted by permission of The *Wall Street Journal*, © 1983. Dow Jones & Company, Inc. All Rights Reserved Worldwide.

The SEC's concern was whether this accounting policy was consistent with SFAS 2 concerning the expensing of research and development costs as incurred. In 1985, SFAS 86 treated software-related research and development costs the same as in SFAS 2.

Required:

(a) Evaluate the software capitalization argument with reference to SFAS 2.

(b) Why is the choice of accounting policies (expensing vs. capitalization) more likely to affect smaller companies?

(c) Comment on the claim that small companies "wouldn't be able to invest as much cash in their own growth if they couldn't use [capitalization]." Is this a real economic consequence?

(d) If you were an FASB member, how would you have voted on this issue?

5. SFAS 15 defines a *troubled debt restructuring* as whenever ". . . the creditor for economic or legal reasons related to the debtor's financial difficulties grants a concession to the debtor that it would not otherwise consider." No gain (to the debtor) or loss (to the creditor) is recognized so long as the total restructured future cash flows from interest and principal payments are equal to or greater than the book value of debt. This accounting standard was issued in the mid-1970s when New York City and other municipalities were defaulting on their bonds and restructuring them. More recently, U.S. banks have been affected by the restructuring of their loans to foreign coun-

tries. In 1987, Citicorp *voluntarily* recognized a large loss on some of its already restructured foreign loans. The *Wall Street Journal*, May 20, 1987, pages 1, 24–25, reported:

> Citicorp chairman John S. Reed threw down the gauntlet yesterday to major bank competitors and big debtor countries alike by adding $3 billion to its foreign and domestic loan reserves. . . .
>
> By sharply increasing the bank's reserves against future loan losses to $5 billion, or 39% of the $12.8 billion in loans to its six biggest Third World borrowers, the action roughly puts the bank in the same position as that achieved in recent years by major lenders in Europe and Japan, which have already increased their reserves. The bigger its reserves, the less vulnerable a bank presumably is to threats by borrowers to default on their loans. Then, such a bank can be more aggressive in negotiating [restructured] repayment schedules with them. . . .
>
> Why did the 48-year-old Mr. Reed take this step now? "The marketplace has been marking down these [bank] stocks to extremely low levels," speculates Mr. Crowley, the Keefe Bruyette analyst. "It doesn't believe banks' earnings and balance sheets. What Mr. Reed is doing is facing up to that."
>
> Reprinted by permission of The *Wall Street Journal*, © 1987. Dow Jones & Company, Inc. All Rights Reserved Worldwide.

Required:

(a) What deficiencies in SFAS 15 contribute to banks' financial credibility problems?

(b) John Maynard Keynes said that if you borrow a little money, the bank owns you, but if you borrow a lot of money, you own the bank. How does this "accounting" move strengthen Citicorp's negotiating position with Third World debtors?

(c) Explain why economic consequences of the accounting for troubled debt restructuring are international in scope and may even tie in explicitly to U.S. government policies toward Third World debtor nations.

BIBLIOGRAPHY OF REFERENCED WORKS

Accounting Principles Board (1966a). "Accounting for the Cost of Pension Plans," *APB Opinion No. 8* (AICPA).

——— (1966b). "Reporting the Results of Operations," *APB Opinion No. 9* (AICPA).

——— (1970a). "Intangible Assets," *APB Opinion No. 17* (AICPA).

——— (1970b). "Basic Concepts and Accounting Principles Underlying Financial Statements of Business Enterprises," *APB Statement No. 4* (AICPA).

——— (1971). "Accounting Changes," *APB Opinion No. 20* (AICPA).

——— (1973). "Reporting the Results of Operations," *APB Opinion No. 30* (AICPA).

Albrecht, W. Steve, Larry L. Lookabill, and James C. McKeown (1977). "The Time-Series Properties of Annual Earnings," *Journal of Accounting Research* (Autumn 1977), pp. 226–244.

American Accounting Association (1936). *A Tentative Statement of Accounting Principles Underlying Corporate Financial Statements* (AAA).

——— (1965a). "The Matching Concept," *The Accounting Review* (April 1965), pp. 368–372.

——— (1965b). "The Realization Concept," *The Accounting Review* (April 1965), pp. 312–322.

American Institute of Certified Public Accountants (1987). *Accounting Trends and Techniques* (AICPA).

Barnea, Amir, Joshua Ronen, and Simcha Sadan (1976). "Classificatory Smoothing of Income with Extraordinary Items," *The Accounting Review* (January 1976), pp. 110–122.

Committee on Accounting Procedure (1953). "Restatement and Revision of Accounting Research Bulletins," *ARB No. 43* (AICPA).

Committee on Terminology (1955). "Proceeds, Revenue, Income, Profit, and Earnings," *Accounting Terminology Bulletin No. 2* (AICPA).

——— (1957). "Cost, Expense and Loss," *Accounting Terminology Bulletin No. 4* (AICPA).

DeAngelo, Linda (1986). "Accounting Numbers as Market Valuation Substitutes: A Study of Management Buyouts of Public Stockholders," *The Accounting Review* (July 1986), pp. 400–420.

——— (1988). "Discussion of Evidence of Earnings Management from the Provision for Bad Debts," *Studies of Management's Ability and Incentives to Affect the Timing and Magnitude of Accounting Accruals* (Supplement to the *Journal of Accounting Research*, 1988), pp. 32–40.

Dye, Ronald A. (1988). "Earnings Management in an Overlapping Generations Model," *Journal of Accounting Research* (Autumn 1988), pp. 195–235.

Financial Accounting Standards Board (1974). "Accounting for Research and Development Costs," *Statement of Financial Accounting Standards No. 2* (FASB).

——— (1975a). "Reporting Gains and Losses from Extinguishment of Debt," *Statement of Financial Accounting Standards No. 4* (FASB).

——— (1975b). "Accounting for Certain Marketable Securities," *Statement of Financial Accounting Standards No. 12* (FASB).

——— (1975c). "Accounting and Reporting by Development Stage Enterprises," *Statement of Financial Accounting Standards No. 7* (FASB).

——— (1976). *FASB Discussion Memorandum: An Analysis of Issues Related to the Conceptual Framework for Financial Reporting: Elements of Financial Statements and Their Measurement* (FASB).

——— (1977a). "Accounting By Debtors and Creditors for Troubled Debt Restructuring," *Statement of Financial Accounting Standards No. 15* (FASB).

——— (1977b). "Prior Period Adjustments," *Statement of Financial Accounting Standards No. 16* (FASB).

——— (1979). *Reporting Earnings* (FASB).

——— (1982). "Foreign Currency Translation," *Statement of Financial Accounting Standards No. 52* (FASB).

——— (1985a). "Employers' Accounting for Pensions," *Statement of Financial Accounting Standards No. 87* (AICPA).

——— (1985b). "Elements of Financial Statements," *Statement of Financial Accounting Concepts No. 6* (FASB).

——— (1987). "Accounting for Income Taxes," *Statement of Financial Accounting Standards No. 96* (FASB).

Frishkoff, Paul (1981). *Reporting of Summary Indicators: An Investigation of Research and Practice* (FASB).

Gonedes, Nicholas J. (1978). "Corporate Signaling, External Accounting, and Capital Market Equilibrium: Evidence on Dividends, Income, and Extraordinary Items," *Journal of Accounting Research* (Spring 1978), pp. 26–79.

Hand, John R. M. (1989). "Did Firms Undertake Debt-Equity Swaps for an Accounting Paper Profit or True Financial Gain?," *The Accounting Review* (October 1989), pp. 587–623.

Healy, Paul M. (1985). "The Effect of Bonus Schemes on Accounting Decisions," *Journal of Accounting and Economics* (1985), pp. 85–107.

Hoskin, Robert E., John S. Hughes, and William E. Ricks (1986). "Evidence on the Incremental Information Content of Additional Firm Disclosures Made Concurrently with Earnings," *Journal of Accounting Research* (Supplement 1986), pp. 1–32.

Jaenicke, Henry R. (1981). *Survey of Present Practices in Recognizing Revenues, Expenses, Gains, and Losses* (FASB).

May, Gordon S., and Douglas Schneider (1988). "Reporting Accounting Changes: Are Stricter Guidelines Needed?," *Accounting Horizons* (September 1988), pp. 68–74.

Nurnberg, Hugo (1988). "Annual and Interim Financial Reporting of Changes in Accounting Estimates," *Accounting Horizons* (September 1988), pp. 15–25.

Philips, G. Edward (1963). "The Accretion Concept of Income," *The Accounting Review* (January 1963), pp. 14–25.

Ronen, Joshua, and Simcha Sadan (1981). *Smoothing Income Numbers: Objectives, Means, and Implications* (Addison-Wesley).

Schipper, Katherine (1989). "Earnings Management," *Accounting Horizons* (December 1989), pp. 91–102.

Sprouse, Robert T., and Maurice Moonitz (1962). "A Tentative Set of Broad Accounting Principles for Business Enterprises," *Accounting Research Study No. 3* (AICPA).

Technical Issues Committee (1982). *Sunset Review of Accounting Principles* (AICPA).

Thomas, Arthur L. (1969). "The Allocation Problem," *Studies in Accounting Research #3* (American Accounting Association).

——— (1974). "The Allocation Problem: Part Two," *Studies in Accounting Research #9* (American Accounting Association).

Watts, Ross L., and Richard W. Leftwich (1977). "The Time Series of Annual Accounting Earnings," *Journal of Accounting Research* (Autumn 1977), pp. 253–271.

ADDITIONAL READINGS

Revenue Recognition

Horngren, Charles T. (1965). "How Should We Interpret the Realization Concept?" *The Accounting Review* (April 1965), pp. 323–333.

Mobley, Sybil C. (1966). "The Concept of Realization: A Useful Device," *The Accounting Review* (April 1966), pp. 292–296.

Myers, John H. (1959). "The Critical Event and Recognition of Net Profit," *The Accounting Review* (October 1959), pp. 528–532.

Storey, Reed K. (1959). "Revenue Realization, Going Concern and Measurement of Income," *The Accounting Review* (April 1959), pp. 232–238.

Thomas, Arthur L. (1966). "Revenue Recognition," *Michigan Business Reports No. 49* (Bureau of Business Research, Graduate School of Business Administration, University of Michigan).

Windal, Floyd (1961). "The Accounting Concept of Realization," *Occasional Paper No. 5* (Bureau of Business and Economic Research, Michigan State University).

Matching

Carroll, Thomas J. (1974). "The Accountants' Extraordinary Dilemma," *World* (Summer 1974), pp. 14–19.

Most, Kenneth S. (1974). "A Proposal for the Abolition of 'Extraordinary Events' and Transactions," *Singapore Accountant* (1974), pp. 23–29.

Snaveley, Howard J., and Allan H. Savage (1970). "Clean Surplus vs. Current Operating Performance — Gaps in APB Opinion No. 9," *New York Certified Public Accountant* (February 1970), pp. 124–129.

Earnings Management

Elliott, John A., and Wayne H. Shaw (1988). "Write-Offs as Accounting Procedures to Manage Perceptions," *Studies on Management's Ability and Incentives to Affect the Timing and Magnitude of Accounting Accruals* (Supplement to the *Journal of Accounting Research*, 1988), pp. 91–119.

Lambert, Richard A. (1984). "Income Smoothing as Rational Equilibrium Behavior," *The Accounting Review* (October 1984), pp. 604–618.

McNichols, Maureen, and G. Peter Wilson (1988). "Evidence of Earnings Management from the Provision for Bad Debts," *Studies on Management's Ability and Incentives to Affect the Timing and Magnitude of Accounting Accruals* (Supplement to the *Journal of Accounting Research*, 1988), pp. 1–31.

Trueman, Brett, and Sheridan Titman (1988). "An Explanation for Accounting Income Smoothing," *Studies on Management's Ability and Incentives to Affect the Timing and Magnitude of Accounting Accruals* (Supplement to the *Journal of Accounting Research*, 1988), pp. 127–139.

THE BALANCE SHEET

THE PREVIOUS CHAPTER presented two approaches to the financial statements: the revenue–expense and asset–liability orientations. The revenue–expense orientation, which emphasizes income recognition and measurement, has dominated financial reporting practices since the 1930s. Through its Conceptual Framework Project, however, the FASB has moved toward an asset–liability viewpoint, in which comprehensive income is passively defined as the consequence of changes in the firm's net assets.

Today's balance sheet is thus a mixture of both orientations. The traditional historical-cost income model determines much of the recognition and measurement in the balance sheet. There are newer areas, however, in which asset–liability valuation is the focus in accounting standards; in these cases the income statement becomes of secondary concern. There are also instances in which the so-called nonarticulated approach is used; that is, changes in assets and liabilities are recognized in the balance sheet but are not recognized in the income statement. Finally, a class of transactions broadly referred to as *financial instruments* are often unrecognized in the balance sheet under current rules. The FASB has, as an interim measure, required expanded disclosure of these so-called off-balance-sheet transactions.

This chapter reviews the three balance sheet elements of assets, liabilities, and owners' equity. Definitions and their evolution are considered first, then principles of recognition, and finally rules of measurement or calculation for specific types of assets, liabilities, and owners' equity. The classification of accounting elements in the balance sheet is considered in the final section of the chapter.

ASSETS

In discussing assets, liabilities, and owners' equity, we present the evolution of definitions first because definitions are necessary for classifying business transactions into the appropriate categories (as illustrated in Exhibit 9–1). The next step is to define the point in time when elements are recognized in the balance sheet. Finally, we review the attributes to be measured for specific types of assets, liabilities, and owners' equity.

DEFINITION OF ASSETS

The definition of **assets** is important because it establishes what types of economic events will appear in the balance sheet. It identifies the elements to be recognized, measured, and reported in the balance sheet. A definition of assets should be solely concerned with the criteria for classifying accounting transactions as assets. As indicated in Chapter 1, the attribute to be measured should be stated independently of the object to be measured. Many definitions of assets can be found in accounting literature. However, the accounting profession in the United States has made only three formal attempts to define assets:

> Something represented by a debit balance that is or would be properly carried forward upon a closing of books of account according to the rules or principles of accounting (provided such debit balance is not in effect a negative balance applicable to a liability), on the basis that it represents either a property right or value acquired, or an expenditure made which has created a property or is properly applicable to the future. Thus, plant, accounts receivable, inventory, and a deferred charge are all assets in balance-sheet classification.[1]

> Economic resources of an enterprise that are recognized and measured in conformity with generally accepted accounting principles. Assets also include certain deferred charges that are not resources but that are recognized and measured in conformity with generally accepted accounting principles.[2]

> Assets are probable future economic benefits obtained or controlled by a particular entity as a result of past transactions or events.[3]

The first definition emphasizes legal property but also includes deferred charges on the basis that they are "properly" included with assets. A distinction is made between assets and deferred charges but both are considered to be assets. The justification is that deferred charges relate to future period income statements. They are included with assets solely because of income statement rules that defer the recognition of these costs as expenses until future periods. This aspect of the definition represents a revenue–expense approach to the financial statements.

The second definition emphasizes that assets are economic resources. These are defined as "the scarce means available . . . for the carrying out of economic activity."[4] Assets are perceived to be more than legal property; anything having future economic value is an asset. For example, a lease agreement

---

[1] Committee on Terminology (1953, para. 26).

[2] APB (1970a, para. 132).

[3] FASB (1985, para. 25).

[4] APB (1970a, para. 57).

that grants the lessee property use rights (though not ownership rights) would satisfy this broader definition. Deferred charges are separately identified in this definition but are still grouped with assets.

The third definition is a further evolution of the concept that assets are economic resources. Key characteristics of an asset are its capacity to provide future economic benefits, control of the asset by the firm, and the occurrence of the transaction giving rise to control and the economic benefits. The capacity to provide economic benefits has also been called *future service potential.* It means that an asset is something that will produce positive net cash flows in the future. These cash flows may occur in one of two ways: in a direct market exchange for another asset, or through conversion in a manufacturing operation to finished goods (which are then exchanged for another asset in a market exchange). SFAC 6 also attempts to reconcile this definition with certain types of deferred charges. Some deferred charges, it argues, do benefit the cash flows of future periods. For example, prepaid costs are deferred charges that will reduce future period outflows of cash. However, other deferred charges, such as organizational startup costs, are sunk costs and do not have any impact on future cash flows.

The "economic resources" approach represents a broader concept of assets than the legal property concept and is consistent with the economic notion that an asset has value because of a future income (cash) stream. The genesis of this broader definition can be found in both economic and accounting literature. It represents an emphasis on control of assets rather than legal ownership. Because the concept of economic resources is broad, it encompasses a wide variation in (1) methods of realizing the future benefits and (2) determining the probability of realizing future benefits. The only subclassification reported within the asset group is the current-noncurrent distinction. This tells very little, though, about how the benefits are to be realized and the probability of realizing the benefits. Classification of assets is discussed further in the final section of the chapter.

The breadth of the economic resources concept has led some accountants to prefer a narrower concept of assets based on the notions of exchangeability and severability.[5] According to this narrower viewpoint, an accounting asset should represent only those economic resources that can be severed from the firm and sold. This narrower asset definition would reduce variation in the reporting of assets in terms of the realization of future benefits — because having value only from productive use would be excluded by this narrower definition. Assets held for use can be argued to have a higher risk of realizing future benefits than assets held directly for sale. It follows that a balance sheet that excludes such assets would have less uncertainty regarding the realization of future benefits.

The severability–exchangeability approach does highlight a weakness in economic value theory. Economic value is often reduced to the one dimension

[5] Chambers (1966) and Arthur Andersen and Co. (1974).

of market exchange prices. An asset may have value in use to its owner but there may not be an external market due to the nature of the asset. For example, the relocation or installation costs of secondhand manufacturing equipment may preclude a market for such goods. But assets held for use still have the potential to generate future cash flows even though they are not directly saleable. The severability–exchangeability approach is very conservative and seems to restrict unnecessarily what is included in the balance sheet as an asset.

Definitions of assets have evolved from a narrow legal orientation to a broader concept of economic resources. As the definition has broadened, the boundary around what is and what is not an asset has become hazy and ambiguous. It might seem that accountants have not been very successful at defining one of the basic accounting elements. However, the legal profession has also had difficulty in defining assets. In law, the following terms have similar but distinctly different meanings: *property, property rights, ownership, title,* and *possession.* There is no clear, unambiguous asset concept in law. A FASB discussion memorandum expressed the opinion that legal definitions and concepts are not helpful in formulating accounting definitions of assets.[6]

EXECUTORY CONTRACTS

A long-standing problem in accounting has been the question of how to account (if at all) for mutually unperformed executory contracts.[7] A mutually unperformed **executory contract** is a contract unperformed by both parties. The traditional accounting view is that no recognition is required in financial statements because a binding exchange has not yet occurred. The contract is prospective. Two examples of such contracts are employment contracts and long-term purchase agreements. In both cases, neither an asset nor a liability is recorded under present practices. However, it can be argued in the case of an employment contract that the employer incurs a liability to pay future wages and receives a benefit in the form of securing future employee services. Similarly, a long-term purchase agreement could be considered a liability for future payments and an asset for future purchases made under the agreement. However, conventional accounting wisdom regards such contracts as too uncertain and contingent for accounting recognition.

There is nothing in the asset definitions presented above that would exclude recognition of executory contracts. The exclusion is by custom and seems to rest on the belief that a binding transaction has not yet occurred. Solomons was not pleased with the FASB's inability to decide whether executory contracts should be booked, merely disclosed in footnotes, or simply omitted from the statements.[8] Indeed, the omission of executory contracts can lead to some rather strange entries when losses arise. For example, when a price decline occurs in the case of purchase commitments, a debit to a loss account is offset by

---

[6] FASB (1976b, para. 122).
[7] Executory contracts were discussed in accounting literature as early as Canning (1929).
[8] Solomons (1986, p. 116).

a credit to a liability account. The credit is certainly unique because no liability exists for the amount of the obligation itself because of its executory nature. However, no other type of account fits the credit, so the liability account is employed in the spirit of its being the least obnoxious type to use.[9] The suggestion to book executory contracts is certainly deserving of attention.

RECOGNITION AND MEASUREMENT OF ASSETS

As noted in Chapters 6 and 9, SFAC 5 is more or less intended to be broad enough to encompass extant accounting practices. It says little that is new with respect to the complex issue of recognition. Thus this chapter, as does Chapter 9, draws on more theoretically grounded work in discussing the recognition of assets and liabilities.

The following "pervasive principle" has been stated about the initial recognition and measurement of both assets and liabilities:

> Assets and liabilities generally are initially recorded on the basis of events in which the enterprise acquires resources from other entities or incurs obligations to other entities. The assets and liabilities are measured by the exchange prices at which the transfers take place.[10]

Hence, assets are initially recognized when the transaction transferring control occurs. At this point in time, a potential exists for future economic benefits. Assets are measured at the market value (exchange price) of the consideration exchanged or sacrificed to acquire the assets and place them in operating condition. This is called *historical acquisition cost*. However, in no case should an asset be recorded in an amount greater than its cash equivalent purchase price. When the consideration is nonmonetary, the market value of the asset received may provide a more reliable basis for measuring acquisition cost. This reflects a primary concern for measurement reliability.

The remainder of this section reviews how specific types of assets are measured in periods subsequent to acquisition. As will be seen, numerous attributes are measured, such as original acquisition cost (historical cost), historical cost less cumulative charges to income (book value), replacement cost, selling prices, net realizable value (selling price less disposal costs), and net realizable value less normal markups. This eclectic approach to accounting measurement violates the additivity principle of measurement theory. The resulting balance sheet may convey relevant information to users, but from the viewpoint of pure measurement theory it can be criticized for a lack of additivity. One often suggested solution to the additivity problem is multicolumn reporting, with each column representing a different attribute of measurement.[11] However, expanded reporting might confuse users because of information overload.

---

[9] The inapplicability of the credit to a liability in the case of purchase commitments as well as examples of how to book this type of executory contract appears in Gujarathi and Biggs (1988). For other arguments in favor of recognizing executory contracts as part of general accounting practice, see Hughes (1978), Ijiri (1975, pp. 129–140), and Ijiri (1980).

[10] APB (1970a, para. 145). See also FASB (1984, para. 67).

[11] American Accounting Association (1966) and Stamp (1980).

Receivables

Receivables are carried at historical cost, adjusted for an estimate of uncollectible amounts. The attribute being measured is an approximation of net realizable value. However, a true measure of net realizable value would be the selling price of receivables through factoring — less any estimated liability for recourse due to nonpayment by the debtors. Since factoring involves present value discounting, the accounting approximation of net realizable value is overstated by the amount of interest implicit in factoring.

Investments Not Subject to Equity Accounting

SFAS 12 requires that marketable equity securities be valued at the lower of historical cost or current market value.[12] Marketable securities are grouped into two portfolios representing current and noncurrent investments. The cost or market rule is applied to each portfolio as a whole. Any write-down to market value is recorded as a charge to income for the current portfolio and is charged to owners' equity as an unrealized capital adjustment for the noncurrent portfolio. This is an example of nonarticulation since an asset change is not recognized as part of earnings. If a write-down is considered permanent, however, the loss is recognized in the income statement even for the noncurrent portfolio. Other investments (besides marketable equity securities) are also accounted for by the lower-of-cost-or-market rule. However, each investment is evaluated on an individual rather than a portfolio basis.

Investment portfolios of financial institutions, such as insurance companies and mutual funds, are subject to specialized industry practices.[13] Generally, current market prices are used to measure the value of securities, and the resulting gains or losses are reported in the income statement.

Investments Subject to Equity Accounting

Equity securities in an amount of 20 percent to 50 percent of the outstanding voting stock are normally accounted for using the equity method under the requirements of APB 18.[14] When equity accounting is used, the investment no longer represents a real attribute of measurement. It is best described as adjusted historical cost, with the adjustment determined by the rules of equity accounting. The investment is increased for the equity share of investee income after eliminating any profit arising from investor–investee transactions and is reduced for amortization of any purchase differential and dividends paid by the investee company.

It can be argued that an investment accounted for by equity accounting may approximate the current selling price of the securities. However, there is no compelling reason to believe this to be true. The attribute being measured is a unique accounting concept. There is no direct measurement of the attribute

---

[12] FASB (1975c).

[13] Industry-specific accounting policies are recommended in industry accounting and audit guides and *Statements of Position* issued by the AICPA. The FASB is in the process of reissuing *Statements of Position* as formal accounting standards.

[14] APB (1971a).

by reference to a market price. The attribute does not exist in the real world; it can be derived only by applying the rules of APB 18. This peculiar effect on the balance sheet represents another example of the revenue–expense approach to accounting policy. The main emphasis of equity accounting is on the income statement, with less concern given to the introduction of a dubious measurement in the balance sheet.

Investments in excess of 50 percent are generally reported through consolidation with the investor's (parent company's) own accounts. This topic is examined further in Chapter 18.

Inventories

Ending inventory is calculated by first determining the quantity on hand, then multiplying this quantity times the unit acquisition cost. An arbitrary choice must be made as to the assumed unit cost, and this depends on the flow assumption selected. Major alternative flow assumptions are FIFO, LIFO, and weighted average. The attribute being calculated is historical cost in all methods. However, the result is arbitrary because unit prices will differ depending on the flow assumption. A FIFO pricing of inventory will price the cost of goods sold assuming the oldest stock is sold first. Ending inventory is priced at the most recent unit cost. The reverse is true with LIFO. Goods are assumed sold from the most recent purchases, leaving ending inventory as the oldest units on hand. It is not necessary that goods actually flow in the manner assumed by the inventory pricing system, and this is why the methods are arbitrary. Hence flexibility is present in inventories and cost-of-goods-sold accounting. The waters of inventory accounting are, of course, muddied by the tax benefits of LIFO and the concomitant requirement that LIFO inventories must be used for financial reporting purposes. Other inventory pricing systems exist in specialized industries; for example, dollar-value LIFO, retail inventory, process costing, and job order costing.

Accounting Research Bulletin (ARB) 43 requires a lower-of-cost-or-market rule to be used in inventory calculation.[15] *Market value* is defined as replacement cost, but a range is established in which replacement cost must fall. The upper limit is net realizable value and the lower limit is net realizable value less a normal markup. The upper and lower limits are used only if replacement cost falls outside the range. These upper and lower limits reduce fluctuations in accounting income between periods when inventory is written down. This policy reflects a concern for the income statement effect of inventory write-downs.

In summary, inventory is carried out at the lower-of-historical-cost-or-market (replacement) cost. However, historical cost is an arbitrary amount owing to the required assumption concerning the flow of goods. If replacement cost is lower than historical cost, the actual calculation may be one of replacement cost, net realizable value, or net realizable value less a normal markup. This variety exists because there are upper and lower limits on the value

---

[15] Committee on Accounting Procedure (1953).

of replacement cost that may be used in applying the lower-of-cost-or-market rule.

Self-Constructed Assets and Manufactured Inventories

The measurement problem with regard to self-constructed assets concerns the identification of the costs incurred to create the asset. The problem of cost identification applies to any type of asset that is self-constructed or manufactured rather than purchased. Two specific problem areas are inventory production and the treatment of interest costs.

A controversy surrounds the calculation of certain costs of manufactured inventory. Two methods are discussed in accounting literature: variable costing and full absorption costing.[16] Only variable production costs are charged to inventory under variable costing. All fixed costs, such as overhead allocations and supervisory salaries, are expensed as period costs. Full absorption costing, on the other hand, attempts to assign all costs, both fixed and variable, to the production of inventory. This approach requires the development of arbitrary overhead rates based on assumed production levels.

ARB 43 requires the use of full absorption costing, arguing that a better estimate of the total production cost is achieved with full absorption costing. From a measurement viewpoint, however, the attribute being calculated under full absorption costing is not clear. Since some fixed costs are incurred over a wide range of production, it is questionable if fixed costs are part of the direct, unavoidable sacrifice required to produce inventory. This accounting debate is not resolved by the definition of assets presented in SFAC 6.

SFAS 34 requires the addition of interest costs on borrowed funds to the acquisition cost of self-constructed assets if the amount is significant.[17] The requirement applies to assets constructed for use or sale but not to routine inventory production. This policy is justified on the grounds that interest on borrowed funds is part of the total sacrifice required to acquire the asset. In addition, SFAS 34 also mentions that the revenues of future periods will be benefited by the costs — such as interest — that are part of the acquisition of a resource.[18] This view is very definitely a matching orientation, which, in turn, gives a revenue–expense orientation to the asset rather than the asset–liability view used in the Conceptual Framework. Similar practices apply to the capitalization of property taxes and insurance costs on land and buildings that are being readied for production. In fairness, however, it should be noted that SFAS 34 preceded by a year SFAC 3, which first defined the elements.

One of the major criticisms of SFAS 34 is that it imputes an interest cost regardless of whether any specific debt has been incurred to finance the asset construction. In such cases, the interest cost is only a *notional charge*, or *opportunity cost*, rather than an actual incurred cost. Moreover, Means and Kazenski show that there are several possibilities for determining the amount of interest

---

[16] See Sorter and Horngren (1962) for a good summary of these issues.
[17] FASB (1979).
[18] Ibid., pp. 2–3.

to be capitalized.[19] The problem does not lie in the flexibility of choice among different methods, however, but rather in establishing verifiability: too many means of calculating a specifically desired amount. Another criticism is that interest is not added to the acquisition cost of other assets. Interest is usually treated as a period expense and is classified as a financing cost. Therefore, SFAS 34 is inconsistent with general accounting policies for interest expense recognition, because it adopts a revenue–expense rather than an asset–liability orientation and does not resolve verifiability problems in the measurement of interest to be capitalized.

Assets Subject to Depreciation or Depletion

The historical acquisition cost of assets that are depreciated or depleted is allocated over estimated useful life. Depreciation allocation is achieved by any of several arbitrary methods: straight-line, sum-of-the-years' digits, declining-balance, and units-of-production. There are no relevant circumstances that dictate any one method in a particular situation. The policy choice is subject only to the constraint of consistency from year to year.

Specialized depreciation systems are used in certain situations. These systems include group and composite depreciation, the replacement and retirement methods, and the inventory-depreciation system. All these systems are simpler to apply than regular methods and are acceptable only on the grounds that the results do not vary materially from conventional depreciation methods.

Costs of natural resources are depleted rather than depreciated. Depletion costs are allocated over useful life in the same manner as depreciable assets. The units-of-production method is used, in which an estimate must be made of the total expected production. Yearly depletion cost is based on the pro rata amount of production. These depletion costs are charged to inventory and become expensed when the inventory is sold. Depletion in the oil and gas industry is discussed in Chapter 15.

The balance sheet carrying value for assets subject to depreciation and depletion is historical cost less cumulative allocations of cost to the income statement. This amount is called *book value* and is the result of cost allocation (see Chapter 9). Book values do not represent real attributes and therefore cannot be directly measured. They can only be calculated by applying the rules specified in the depreciation or depletion method being used. This is another example of a unique accounting attribute and is the result once again of the revenue–expense orientation to the financial statements.

Nonmonetary Exchanges of Similar Assets

APB 29 establishes a unique rule to account for nonmonetary exchanges of similar assets. The rule is contrary to the general principle of using the value of the economic sacrifice to measure the transaction.[20] In a nonmonetary exchange the sacrifice to obtain a new asset consists of a traded-in asset and pos-

---

[19] Means and Kazenski (1988).
[20] APB (1973).

sibly some cash. Under APB 29, the new asset is recorded at the book value of the traded-in asset (rather than market value), plus any additional cash consideration. As with other asset acquisitions, the cash equivalent purchase price sets an upper limit on the recorded value. The rationale for this policy is that an exchange of similar assets represents a continuation of the underlying earning process. It is as though the former asset is embodied in the new asset, thus justifying no recognition of a gain or loss on the disposal of the old asset. Any implied gain or loss is recognized indirectly through subsequent depreciation. This accounting policy is at variance with general accounting practices. One reason for its existence may be that Internal Revenue Service regulations follow a similar (though not identical) procedure.

Intangible Assets

Assets can be classified into tangible and intangible assets. Physical substance is the distinguishing criterion, but it is not a definitive characteristic because some assets (such as accounts receivable, investments, and capitalized lease rights) are legally intangible in nature, yet are not so regarded by accountants. Assets more commonly thought of as intangible are copyrights, patents, and trademarks. Also considered to be intangible assets are purchased franchise rights and purchased goodwill.

All intangible assets are initially recorded at the sacrifice incurred to acquire the assets. Like assets subject to depreciation and depletion, intangible assets are calculated at historical cost less cumulative charges to income. As stated before, book value is a unique accounting attribute of measurement and represents the revenue–expense orientation. APB 17 brought some order to intangibles by requiring straight-line amortization of costs over a period not exceeding forty years.[21] If a shorter period of economic benefit exists, it should be used. Copyrights, patents, and franchise agreements all have finite legal lives that can be used to determine a more specific period of future economic benefit. In these circumstances a specific amortization period that reflects useful economic life can be determined. It can be argued that amortization of intangibles (such as trademarks and purchased goodwill) is not necessary because they have an unlimited life. APB 17 rejected this notion in favor of compulsory amortization. Prior to APB 17, it was common not to amortize goodwill. APB 17 can best be understood as an attempt to bring rigid uniformity to a subjective area of practice, one where flexibility resulted in poor comparability.

Until SFAS 2, research and development costs were capitalized and classified as an intangible asset.[22] The justification was that future benefits existed in the form of probable future patents or products having economic value. However, the uncertainty of realizing these benefits led to the uniform policy in SFAS 2 of expensing all research and development costs as incurred. This is another example of a situation where the concern about measurement reliability led to rigid uniformity. Obviously, some research and development expendi-

---

[21] APB (1970b).
[22] FASB (1974).

tures would satisfy the asset definition in SFAC 6. The FASB's policy in SFAS 2 emphasizes verifiability over representational faithfulness or relevance.

Deferred Charges

There are two distinct types of deferred charges. One type represents prepaid costs, which provide a future benefit in the form of reduced future cash outflows for services — for example, prepaid insurance. Prepayments are normally allocated to the income statement on a straight-line basis over the period of future benefit. The other type of deferred charge represents a cost that is being deferred from expense recognition solely because of income measurement rules. This type includes organizational startup costs and deferred losses on sale–leasebacks (discussed in Chapter 17). Most deferred charges are amortized in the same manner as intangible assets except where specific requirements apply.

SUMMARY OF ASSET MEASUREMENT

This is by no means a comprehensive review of all assets. Some topics were omitted because they are covered in later chapters; for example, deferred tax charges, leased assets, and capitalization of oil and gas exploration costs. Individual assets in the balance sheet may represent one of many attributes, some of which are unique accounting concepts and have no real-world meaning. Book values of depreciable assets and investments accounted for under equity accounting are two examples of unique accounting attributes. Such a situation is uncomfortable, at least in terms of measurement theory. However, as stated at the outset of this section, an eclectic balance sheet may still convey relevant information to users. A summary of asset measurement is presented in Exhibit 10–1.

   Three distinct types of assets appear in balance sheets: those held for sale, those that have economic value through use in production, and deferred charges. The benefits of these assets are derived differently and represent differing degrees of certainty and measurement reliability. Assets held for sale and measured at net realizable value (such as receivables) represent a high degree of certainty as to realization as well as measurement reliability. Assets held for production represent more uncertainty as to the realization of future economic benefits due to the inherent uncertainty of manufacturing. Furthermore, historical cost gives little indication of the productive value of such assets. Finally, certain types of deferred charges do not have any direct effect on future cash flows.

   Because of the wide variation in asset realization and measurement, it is very difficult to interpret assets in the aggregate. In terms of additivity, it is questionable if a balance sheet should really be added. It is added, of course, and used for ratio analysis. However, relevance or usefulness may be impaired because of the additivity problem. This problem is further compounded when data are aggregated across separate legal entities to prepare a consolidated balance sheet. See Chapter 18 for a further discussion of consolidated reporting issues.

EXHIBIT 10–1

Summary of Asset Measurement

Asset	*Attribute(s)*
Receivables	Approximation of net realizable value.
Investments (not subject to APB 18)	Cost, lower-of-cost-or-market, or market, depending on the type of investment and the reporting entity.
Investments (subject to APB 18)	Unique accounting attribute (equity accounting).
Inventories	Cost, replacement cost, net realizable value, or net realizable value less normal markup.
Self-constructed assets	Full-absorption costing for inventory, and capitalization of interest for noninventory assets.
Assets subject to depreciation or depletion	Unique accounting attribute (book value).
Nonmonetary exchanges of similar assets	Book value of old asset plus cash.
Intangible assets	Unique accounting attribute (book value).
Deferred charges	Unique accounting attribute (book value).

LIABILITIES

DEFINITION OF ACCOUNTING LIABILITIES

Definitions of accounting liabilities have evolved over time in a manner similar to that of definitions of assets. The three major statements on liabilities are

> Something represented by a credit balance that is or would be properly carried forward upon a closing of books of account according to the rules or principles of accounting, provided such credit balance is not in effect a negative balance applicable to an asset. Thus the word is used broadly to comprise not only items which constitute liabilities in the popular sense of debts or obligations (including provision for those that are unascertained), but also credit balances to be accounted for which do not involve a debtor and creditor relation. For example, capital stock and related or similar elements of proprietorship are balance sheet liabilities in that they represent balances to be accounted for, though these are not liabilities in the ordinary sense of debts owed to legal creditors.[23]

---

[23] Committee on Terminology (1953, para. 27).

Economic obligations of an enterprise that are recognized and measured in conformity with generally accepted accounting principles. Liabilities also include certain deferred credits that are not obligations but that are recognized and measured in conformity with generally accepted accounting principles.[24]

Liabilities are probable future sacrifices of economic benefits arising from present obligations of a particular entity to transfer assets or provide services to other entities in the future as a result of past transactions or events.[25]

The first definition implies an entity theory view of the firm because no distinction is made between owners' equity and liabilities. The entity theory views the firm as a self-sufficient enterprise separate from its owners, and both liabilities and owners' equity are sources of external capital for which the firm is accountable. The other two liability definitions do not mention owners' equity, which seems to imply a proprietary view of the firm in which owners' equity represents owners' residual interest in the net assets.

The liability portion of the first definition emphasizes legal debts. In the second definition, the liability concept is broadened to mean economic obligations. APB Statement 4 defines *economic obligations* as the responsibility to transfer economic resources or provide services to another entity in the future. This parallels the change in the asset definition. In addition, deferred credits are identified separately but are still considered to be a part of liabilities.

The third and most recent definition continues the emphasis on economic obligations rather than legal debt and drops deferred credits. Deferred charges were similarly dropped from the asset definition. SFAC 6 elaborates on the definition by listing three essential characteristics of an accounting liability:

1. A duty exists.
2. The duty is virtually unavoidable.
3. The event obligating the enterprise has occurred.

Most liabilities are contractual in nature. **Contractual liabilities** result from events in which a liability arises that is either expressly or implicitly contractual in the legal sense of the term. SFAC 6 indicates that a duty can also arise from constructive and equitable obligations as well as legal contracts. A **constructive obligation** is one that is implied rather than expressly written. SFAC 6 specifically mentions the accruals of noncontractual vacation pay and bonuses. An employer duty may exist if such payments have been made in the past even if there is no written agreement to pay them in the future. **Equitable obligations** are an ambiguous, gray area of common law in which a duty is not contractually present but which may nevertheless exist due to ethical principles of fairness (called *equity*). The example given in SFAC 6 concerns the responsibility of a monopoly supplier to deliver goods or services to dependent customers. In spite of their mention in SFAC 6, equitable obligations are not presently recognized in balance sheets.

---

[24] APB (1970a, para. 132).
[25] FASB (1985, para. 35).

Contingent liabilities are a subset of accounting liabilities. SFAS 5 defines these as "an existing situation, or set of circumstances involving uncertainty as to possible gain or loss to an enterprise that will ultimately be resolved when one or more future events will occur or fail to occur." [26] Only losses are recognized, owing to conservatism. A loss contingency (contingent liability) is accrued if (1) it is probable that a liability has occurred, or an asset has been impaired, and (2) it can be reliably measured. Examples of contingent liabilities given in SFAS 5 are product warranties and pending or threatened litigation. The definition of a contingent liability is consistent with the SFAC 6 definition, with the additional proviso concerning feasibility and reliability of measurement.

Finally, there are **deferred credits.** Although not specifically mentioned in the most recent definition, they continue to be part of the liability section in the balance sheet under present practices. There are two different types of deferred credits. One type represents prepaid revenues; for example, magazine or newspaper subscriptions. There is a contractual duty to provide a future good or service, and a liability clearly exists in such a situation. The other type of deferred credit is more ambiguous and arises from income rules that defer income statement recognition of the item. Two examples of this second type of deferred credit are investment tax credits (APB 2) and deferred gains on sale-leaseback transactions (SFAS 13).[27] These types of items impose no obligations on the firm to transfer assets in the future. Rather, they are simply past transactions being deferred from the income statement until future periods.

In summary, accounting liabilities include five distinctly different types: contractual liabilities, constructive obligations, equitable obligations, contingent liabilities, and deferred credits. As with assets, there is considerable variety within the liability group but not to the degree that occurs within assets. This is because most liabilities are contractual in nature. Of the remaining noncontractual liabilities, contingent liabilities are disclosed separately, and deferred credits are identifiable in the balance sheet. As a result, there is a natural subclassification of liabilities that can easily be inferred from the balance sheet. This is not the case with assets.

RECOGNITION AND MEASUREMENT OF LIABILITIES

APB Statement 4 and SFAC 5 indicate that liabilities are measured at amounts established in the transaction, usually amounts to be paid in the future, sometimes discounted.[28] The general principle is that liabilities are measured at the amount established in the exchange. For current liabilities, such as accounts payable, this represents the face value of the obligation to be settled in the future. For noncurrent obligations, the measurement represents a present value calculation based on current interest rates. An example is bonds, which are re-

---

[26] FASB (1975b).
[27] APB (1962) and FASB (1976a).
[28] APB (1970a, para. 181) and FASB (1984, para. 67).

corded at the net proceeds received. The net proceeds represent the stream of interest payments and principal repayment discounted at the current market rate of interest. If the stated interest rate on the bonds is at the current rate, the present value, net proceeds, and face value are all equal at the time of issuance. If the stated interest rate differs from market rates, a premium or discount will occur. The nondiscounting of current liabilities is justified on the grounds of immateriality; that is, the present value is not materially different from the non-discounted future value.

Notes Payable with Below-Market Rates of Interest

Under APB 21 notes payable with below-market interest rates must be discounted.[29] The purpose of the discounting is to adjust the note to an equivalent note having the market rate of interest. The discount is then amortized over the life of the note in order to adjust periodic interest expense to a market rate. By this procedure the real economic value of the transaction is measured at imputed market prices and is consistent with the general principle of discounting noncurrent liabilities at the market rate of interest. An identical procedure is required for notes receivable with below-market interest rates.

Bonds Payable

As noted previously, bonds are initially recorded at the net proceeds of the transaction. The net proceeds are equal to the present value of future interest payments and principal repayment, discounted at the market rate of interest, less any bond issue costs. It is necessary to create a bond premium or discount account if the stated interest rate differs from the market rate. The carrying value of bonds in subsequent balance sheets represents the face value of the bonds plus unamortized premiums or minus unamortized discounts. This is the book value of bonds and is analogous to book value of depreciable assets. Book value of bonds payable is another example of a unique accounting attribute. The book value of bonds must be calculated instead of measured directly. A direct measurement of bonds is not made after they are initially recorded.

Premiums and discounts are amortized to income over the term of the bonds by the effective interest method (APB 21). This has the effect of adjusting interest expense to the market rate that existed at the time of issue. Straight-line amortization is also permitted if the results are not materially different from the effective interest method.

Convertible Bonds

Bonds may have a feature permitting an exchange of bonds for common stock. It is typical for convertible bonds to have a lower coupon interest rate than conventional bonds. The reason for this is that investors are willing to pay a price for the conversion option, and the price is paid in the form of lower inter-

---

[29] APB (1971c).

est rates. For this reason, convertible bonds have elements of both debt and owners' equity. The foregone interest can be thought of as capital donated to the firm in exchange for this privilege.

Two policies have been used to account for convertible bonds. One approach is to treat convertible debt as conventional debt until conversion. This is the method required under APB 14.[30] The other approach is to segregate an amount of the debt as the price paid for the conversion privilege and to add this amount to contributed capital. Interest on the face amount of the debt is imputed, using the market rate for nonconvertible debt that existed at the time of issue. This more complex approach was adopted in APB 10, suspended almost immediately in APB 12, and superseded in APB 14.[31] The reason for suspension was perceived measurement difficulties arising from the potential for subjectivity in choosing the market interest rate. So long as a subjective choice could be made, the results were of questionable reliability. Because of the perceived measurement problems, APB 14 established a simpler method of accounting by treating convertible debt as regular bonds.

Convertible debt highlights the limitations of the accounting classification system (see Exhibit 9–1). The balance sheet is incapable of subtle distinctions, such as those implied by convertible versus conventional bonds. However, APB 15 requires recognition of the conversion feature in earnings per share (EPS) calculations.[32] Bonds meeting the cash yield test are treated as if they are converted for primary EPS calculations, if the effect is dilutive. Bonds not meeting the cash yield test are treated as if they are converted for fully diluted EPS, if the effect is dilutive. The limitations of accounting classification are more easily overcome with EPS rules, however, because EPS is a supplemental disclosure rather than part of the financial statements.

When convertible debt is converted, a gain or loss is not normally recognized. The rationale for not recognizing a gain or loss is that, since the security has both debt and equity characteristics, the conversion represents only a reclassification of the security from debt to equity. This procedure is inconsistent with SFAS 4, which deals with accounting for early retirement of debt.[33] Because convertible debt is initially accounted for as conventional debt, it would be logical to recognize a gain or loss on conversion. Conversion represents the equivalent of early debt retirement. In other words, two separate transactions are implied by APB 14. The first is the recording as conventional debt, then there is the equivalent of early retirement and the issue of common stock in exchange for debt retirement. Since no initial recognition is given to the conversion feature prior to conversion, it is inconsistent to ignore gains and losses on the grounds that the conversion merely represents a reclassification from debt to equity. APB 14 is therefore logically inconsistent.

---

[30] APB (1969a).
[31] APB (1966), APB (1967b), and APB (1969a).
[32] APB (1969b).
[33] FASB (1975a).

Debt with Stock Warrants

APB 14 requires that a value be assigned to detachable stock warrants which may accompany the issue of debt. This policy is inconsistent with the treatment of convertible debt. The reason for the two different policies is that a convertible bond is argued to be either debt or equity at any one time; it cannot be both simultaneously. Detachable warrants, however, permit the holder to own simultaneously both debt and equity (if the warrant is exercised). Therefore, part of the proceeds can be thought of as a direct payment for the right to buy stock. And since a market price is readily determinable for stock warrants, the measurement problem encountered with convertible debt does not occur.

In theory, there is little distinction between convertible debt and debt with detachable stock warrants. In both cases an amount of money is being paid in the transaction for the right to acquire stock. However, the money paid for this privilege is clearly identifiable in the case of detachable warrants traded in the market. It is a more subjective calculation in the case of convertible debt. Hence, considerations of verifiability have led to two different accounting policies for two similar areas of accounting.

SUMMARY OF LIABILITY MEASUREMENT

Like assets, liabilities are recognized when the transaction giving rise to the obligation occurs. There are many different types of accounting liabilities just as there are many different types of assets. Unlike assets, however, the different types of accounting liabilities are more easily recognized in the balance sheet. The different types of accounting liabilities represent differing degrees of obligations to the firm. For example, not all accounting liabilities represent legal debt, so in the case of bankruptcy some accounting liabilities would be ignored. The certainty of differing types of obligations also differs, as well as the reliability of measurement. Legal debt has a high probability of being paid and has a high degree of measurement reliability as well. Certain types of deferred credits, on the other hand, do not represent future cash flows at all. Contingent liabilities often have a lower degree of verifiability than other accounting liabilities. All these characteristics must be considered in evaluating accounting liabilities. As with assets, it is difficult to interpret liabilities in the aggregate because of these differences.

In the case of current liabilities, liabilities are initially measured at face value of the future obligation. There is no present value adjustment. Noncurrent liabilities are initially measured at the present value of future interest and principal repayments. The current market rate of interest is used as the discount rate. This is not a subjective measurement because market values of debt are established in exactly the same manner — the discounting of a stream of payments at the market rate of interest. A premium or discount may exist that is amortized to the income statement over the term of the debt. Book value of debt is used in subsequent balance sheets. This is a unique accounting attribute representing face value of debt adjusted for any unamortized premiums or discounts. Once again, this book value represents the revenue–expense orientation and the historical-cost allocation process (see Chapter 9).

OWNERS' EQUITY

DEFINITION OF OWNERS' EQUITY

Owners' equity is defined as the stockholders' residual interest in the net assets of the firm. This definition represents the proprietary theory according to which stockholders are perceived to be owners of the firm. It will be recalled from the liability definition in ATB No. 1 that no clear distinction was made between liabilities and owners' equity. However, APB Statement 4 and SFAC 6 do make a distinction between the two: APB Statement 4 offers a passive definition of owners' equity as the excess of the firm's assets over its liabilities. The same approach is also taken in SFAC 6. Both definitions imply a proprietary ownership of the firm by the stockholders.

In a sole proprietorship, owners' equity can be represented by a single owner's equity account. The corporate form of ownership gives rise to a legal distinction between contributed capital and earned capital (retained earnings). In the past, in most states dividends could be legally paid only from retained earnings, but the Model Uniform Business Corporation Act, which many states are expected to pass, will allow dividends to be paid out of either contributed capital (including the capital stock account) or retained earnings. Hence, traditional distinctions within owners' equity accounts may become less important than has been the case. We will maintain, however, the usual distinctions even though the owners' equity situation is in flux. So a typical breakdown of total owners' equity will include contributed capital and retained earnings. Contributed capital may be subclassified into legal capital and other capital. Legal capital represents the limited liability of stockholders. If shares are fully paid up, there is no additional stockholder liability. Legal capital is measured at par value, or at the issue price if the stock is no par. Other contributed capital includes stock premiums, donated capital, capital from the reissue of treasury stock, and capital from the issue of stock options and warrants.

A third component of owners' equity (see Exhibit 9–1) represents unrealized gains or losses. As indicated previously, certain changes in net asset values are recognized in the balance sheet; but instead of these amounts being charged to the income statement, they are classified as capital adjustments. The sources of these adjustments are unrealized portfolio losses for noncurrent marketable securities (SFAS 12) and unrealized foreign exchange gains or losses from the translation of foreign net assets into dollars (SFAS 52).

RECOGNITION AND MEASUREMENT OF OWNERS' EQUITY

Owners' equity transactions can be of two types — capital transactions or income-related transactions. *Capital transactions* represent the direct contributions or withdrawals of assets by owners. *Income-related transactions* represent income statement transactions and prior period adjustments that pertain to income of previous periods. This chapter deals only with capital transactions.

Income-related transactions were discussed in Chapter 9. The general principle of measurement for all capital transactions is the same as for assets and liabilities: the market value at the time of the transaction. These values are then carried forward *unchanged* in subsequent balance sheets.

Contributed capital is measured by the value of assets contributed to the firm by stockholders. It is possible to contribute services rather than assets, in which case the value of the services is used to measure contributed capital. If the value of contributed assets or services exceeds the legal capital of issued stock, the excess is recorded as a premium. Other sources of contributed capital include conversions of convertible debt and the issue of detachable stock warrants with debt (discussed earlier in the liability section of the chapter). Two other sources of contributed capital are the reissue of treasury stock and the issue of employee stock options. The measurement of these capital transactions is discussed below.

Retained earnings is equal to the cumulative income or loss of the firm as measured by the rules of income determination, less cash dividends declared. Stock dividends also affect the balance of retained earnings and are discussed in the following section.

Stock Options

Employee stock option plans (ESOPs) are considered a form of deferred compensation to employees if there is a bargain purchase price established in the plan. If a bargain purchase does exist, the accounting recognition and measurement focuses on the value of the bargain purchase option. The value represents additional compensation and a corresponding amount is credited to other contributed capital. Employee services are deemed to be exchanged for the right to buy stock below market price. Measurement at four different points in time has been discussed in the literature. The four dates are the grant date, receipt date by the employee, the first exercisable date, and the actual exercise date. The actual value to the employee is known with certainty only on the exercise date. If measurement occurs any earlier, it must be based on the estimated value of the option to the employee.

APB 25 requires the bargain amount of stock options to be allocated as a periodic expense from the grant date through the period of service required to receive the benefits.[34] The bargain amount is measured by the difference between market price and the stock option exercise price on the measurement date. The measurement date is defined as the point in time when both the number of options and the exercise price are known. Usually the grant date and measurement date are one and the same, in which case the measurement is straightforward. A deferred compensation expense account is debited and contributed capital is credited for the total bargain purchase. The deferred compensation expense is amortized over the number of periods required to exercise the options. The debit is a contra-capital account.

---

[34] APB (1972).

If either the number of shares or exercise price is unknown at grant date, a yearly estimate must be made of both. In such a situation it is also necessary to estimate the market price of the stock at the future measurement date. Having made these necessary estimates, one must make a yearly accrual of the estimated additional compensation expense arising from the options. This results in a debit to expense and a credit to contributed capital, just for an estimate of the current period cost. The entire bargain purchase is not recognized because it is not yet determinable. However, an estimate is made of the bargain purchase and the pro rata effect on yearly compensation expense. At the measurement date (the point when both number of shares and exercise price is known) the actual compensation cost is measured by subtracting the option price from the market price on that date. The actual bargain value of the ESOP at the measurement date, less previous yearly expense recognition based on estimates, is debited to deferred compensation expense and amortized over the remaining service period required to exercise the options. A corresponding amount is credited to contributed capital. This procedure represents a change in accounting estimate and any adjustment is made prospectively as required under APB 20.[35]

Contributed capital is credited for the bargain purchase element in an ESOP. The rationale for this policy is that employee services are being exchanged for the opportunity to buy stock below market price. This amount is considered to be part of the consideration given by these shareholders for the right to buy stock under an ESOP.

In 1986, the FASB announced its intention to review accounting for ESOPs.[36] To date, no formal action has been taken. However, preliminary indications are that a major change will be made. Specifically, an economic value would be assigned to the option when issued (even if not issued at a bargain price), and this amount would be recognized immediately in the income statement as employee compensation expense. The rationale for the change is that compensation is being paid in noncash form, but the transaction is not being recognized in the income statement.

Treasury Stock

U.S. corporations are permitted to trade in their own securities. However, state laws and accounting policies prohibit companies from recognizing income on such transactions. This prohibition is intended to discourage stock price manipulations. Reacquired stock is classified as a contra-account to outstanding stock. The stock is still legally issued but is not considered to be outstanding.

Two methods may be used to account for treasury stock, the cost and par value methods. The methods differ only in terms of the accounts used, but the net effect on owners' equity is the same. This is an example of flexibility since there is unconditional choice in the selection of the accounting policy. However, it makes very little difference since the only effect is on subclassifi-

---

[35] APB (1971b).
[36] See the *Wall Street Journal*, February 28, 1986, page 23.

cations within owners' equity. When treasury stock is reissued, the difference between reissue price and carrying value of the treasury stock is recorded as contributed capital.

Stock Dividends

ARB 43 requires two separate accounting policies for stock dividends, depending on the size of the dividend.[37] Large stock dividends are defined as those over 25 percent and are accounted for by reclassifying retained earnings to contributed capital based on the par value of the stock issued. Small stock dividends are defined as those less than 20 percent. The accounting policy is to reclassify retained earnings to contributed capital on the basis of the market value of the stock and using predividend market prices to value the dividend. A gray area exists from 20 percent to 25 percent in which either method may be used.

Some attempts have been made to use the size of the dividend to define relevant circumstances. However, because total market value of outstanding stock should not change on account of stock dividends, little support can be given to using the predividend market price per share to value the transaction. All that has occurred is an increase in the total number of shares. The market price per share should decline exactly in proportion to the dilutive effect of the new shares. If the price is not diluted, other new information exists that causes investors to revise their assessment of the stock.[38]

Using the par value to measure a stock dividend makes more sense given that the total market value of outstanding stock should be unchanged. It can even be argued that a stock dividend is no different in principle from a stock split in which no change is recorded in owners' equity. This is unacceptable for stock dividends, though, because the dollar amount of legal capital has increased. So, reclassification of retained earnings to contributed capital is necessary because there has been an increase in legally issued capital.

It is difficult to justify finite uniformity that is based on the size of the dividend. This does not appear to be a relevant circumstance justifying two accounting methods. For both large and small dividends, market price per share should fall in accordance with the dilutive effect of the stock dividend. Therefore, use of predividend market prices is a hard policy to defend.

FINANCIAL INSTRUMENTS AND OFF-BALANCE-SHEET TRANSACTIONS

Financial instruments are contracts involving a financial asset of one entity and a financial liability (or equity) of another entity. The FASB defines a financial instrument as cash, evidence of an ownership interest in an entity, or a contract that both

---

[37] Committee on Accounting Procedure (1953).
[38] Capital market research supports the argument there is no theoretical change in the value of the firm due to the dividend per se. See Foster (1986) for a review of this research.

1. Imposes on one entity a contractual obligation (1) to deliver cash or another financial instrument to a second entity or (2) to exchange financial instruments on potentially unfavorable terms with the second entity.
2. Conveys to that second entity a contractual right (1) to receive cash or another financial instrument from the first entity or (2) to exchange other financial instruments on potentially favorable terms with the first entity.[39]

Some financial instruments are quite familiar and their accounting is straightforward: for example, cash held on demand deposit, trade receivables, notes, bonds, and common and preferred stock. Other instruments are highly complex and their use is motivated by management's desire to exploit tax laws, to hedge other assets/liabilities of the entity against market risks (for example, interest rate and foreign exchange hedges), and to achieve off-balance-sheet financing in order to "create" a more favorable-looking balance sheet (also one of the appeals of leasing).

The FASB has issued several pronouncements dealing with specific financial instruments: SFAS 13 addresses the accounting for leveraged leases (discussed in Chapter 17), SFAS 76 deals with in-substance defeasance of debt, SFAS 77 concerns the sale of receivables with recourse, and FASB Technical Bulletin No. 85-2 discusses accounting for collateralized mortgage obligations.[40] There are numerous instruments in existence, however, and new ones are being created all the time.[41] This led the FASB in 1986 to put the general question of off-balance-sheet financing on its agenda, which resulted in SFAS 105.

SFAS 105 deals with disclosure only. The standard requires disclosure of credit risk (the risk that debtors will not meet their obligations), market risk (potential loss arising from fluctuations in market price, which could impair the value of the financial instrument), and cash requirements of financial instruments (data about future contractual cash payments/receipts arising from financial instrument contracts) for off-balance-sheet financial instruments.[42] In addition, information on concentrations of credit risk must be shown for both on- and off-balance-sheet types of credit instruments. *Concentrations* refers to an aggregation of similar financial instruments where similar economic characteristics, similar business or industry, or similar geographic region are present. The FASB did not, however, specify a materiality threshold for determining the various possible concentrations of credit risk.[43]

SFAS 105 is presumably only the first stage in the FASB's examination of off-balance-sheet risks. Other phases of the project will deal with additional risk aspects as well as recognition, measurement, and classification issues regarding

---

[39] FASB (1990, p. 3).
[40] A collateralized mortgage obligation is a debt security that is secured by a "pool" of mortgage loans receivable. Interest and principal payments on the mortgages are then accumulated to pay interest/ principal on the collateralized mortgage obligations.
[41] See Stewart and Neuhausen (1986) for a listing of some of the current financial instruments.
[42] FASB (1990, p. 7).
[43] Ibid., p. 49.

financial instruments.[44] Hence the financial instruments project is indeed ambitious in its projected scope and coverage.

Financial instruments do not readily conform to the transaction classification system depicted in Exhibit 9–1. As a consequence, some of these transactions are not recognized until such time as cash flows or other realization occurs — that is, an accrual basis of accounting is not always used. This is not surprising considering the complex character of many financial instruments. Consider the two instruments described in paragraphs 35 and 36 of SFAS 105 below:

> A more complex example is a forward contract in which the purchasing entity promises to exchange $100,000 cash for a U.S. Treasury note and the selling entity promises to exchange a U.S. Treasury note for $100,000 cash 6 months later. During the six-month period, both the purchaser and the seller have a contractual right and obligation to exchange financial instruments. The market price for that Treasury note might rise above $100,000, which would make the terms favorable to the purchaser and unfavorable to the seller, or fall below $100,000, which would have the opposite effect. Therefore, the purchaser has both a financial asset, similar to a call option held, and a financial liability, similar to a put option written; the seller has a financial asset, similar to a put option held, and a financial liability, similar to a call option written.
>
> An interest rate swap can be viewed as a series of forward contracts to exchange, for example, fixed cash payments for variable cash receipts computed by multiplying a specified floating-rate market index by a notional amount. Those terms are potentially favorable or unfavorable depending on subsequent movements in the index, and an interest rate swap is a financial asset and a financial liability to both parties.

What makes these two securities complex is that they simultaneously contain features of *both* assets and liabilities. In addition, the terms of these instruments are variable (pegged to some market indicator) so that the economic "value" of the asset and/or liability is continuously changing and is only known with certainty when the contract is settled.

In our view, the question of recognition can be dealt with by applying the conventional criteria and carefully delineating the elements comprising the financial instruments. This is exactly what was done with leveraged leases in SFAS 13 when the transaction was separated into its constituent financial assets and/or liabilities for each of the parties to the transaction. But the more ambiguous question is whether measurement is sufficiently objective to recognize the transactions on an accrual basis. If the answer is no, then the FASB's interim step of supplemental disclosure may be the only feasible resolution of the problem.

---

[44] Byington and Munter (1990, p. 42).

CLASSIFICATION IN THE BALANCE SHEET

ARB 43 requires classification of assets and liabilities based on liquidity. Two classifications are used — current and noncurrent. *Current* is defined as the firm's operating cycle or one year, whichever is longer. The operating cycle is the time required to go from materials acquisition to cash collection from revenues. Operating cycles will differ from firm to firm and industry to industry. A liquidity ranking within the current and noncurrent groups is also normally made, though it is not required by any specific accounting standard.

The current–noncurrent approach gives only a crude indication of a firm's liquidity. Current assets cannot be used to assess critical cash flow capacity because the operating cycle may be a year or even longer. In addition, the current asset grouping contains some assets that do not affect current cash flows at all; for example, deferred charges and credits. Other classifications might be better for the assessment of liquidity. For example, a monetary–nonmonetary classification system combined with a current–noncurrent classification would give a better understanding of future cash flows. The problems of liquidity measurement are considered further in Chapter 11 in terms of the cash flow statement.

Another way of subclassifying assets would be according to those held for exchange (sale), those held for use, and those representing deferred charges. This would provide some additional information about how economic benefits will be realized and the uncertainty surrounding realization. As indicated earlier in the chapter, considerable variation exists in the asset group. As a general rule, the realization of future benefits will be more uncertain from production than from exchange. A classification system based on this approach would communicate relevant information about how the benefits will be realized and give some awareness of the relative risks concerning the realization of the benefits. A case could also be made that the most relevant information to report would be net realizable values for assets held for sale and replacement costs for assets held for production (assuming replacement would, in fact, occur).

More detailed reporting could also be made of liabilities. There are five distinctly different types of accounting liabilities: contractual, constructive, equitable, contingent, and deferred charges. Separate classifications by type would assist in evaluating the nature of the different types of obligations. As mentioned earlier in the chapter, it is relatively easy to group liabilities into these classifications. It would also aid the reader of balance sheets to know which liabilities are legally enforceable in the event of bankruptcy and which ones are not. As with assets, liabilities also have differing degrees of certainty concerning realization.

Finally, from a pure measurement viewpoint, classifying assets by the attribute being measured might aid in understanding the eclectic nature of measurement in the balance sheet. Numerous asset attributes are measured and reported in a balance sheet. It is not always clear from reading a balance sheet just how much variation there is in asset measurement. By custom, a balance sheet is added. In terms of measurement theory, the accounting elements in a balance sheet are not additive because of the different attributes being measured. This does not mean that balance sheets or financial ratios lack relevance, but the additivity question does raise an important issue concerning usefulness.

SUMMARY

Definitions of accounting elements determine the types of economic events that are recognized as accounting transactions and how they are classified in the accounting classification system illustrated in Exhibit 9–1. Yet it is apparent that the definitions are of a general nature and that the transactions we recognize in accounting are derived as much from tradition as from the definitions of elements themselves. This may be inevitable. However, the value of good definitions from a policy-making perspective is that they enable policy makers to categorize and understand new types of transactions. Definitions should also aid in identifying those areas of existing practice that are inconsistent. Classification is fundamental in any science to understanding the nature of the discipline. The same is true of accounting classification and the understanding of economic events reported in the financial statements.

Historical cost is widely considered to be the basis of measurement in accounting, but it is very clear that many other types of measurement are embodied in current practices. The many attributes involved in asset measurement were summarized in Exhibit 10–1. Liability measurement is less eclectic than asset measurement, but it too has variation. Face amount of debt is measured for current liabilities, and noncurrent debt is initially measured at discounted present values. Capital transactions in owners' equity basically represent the historical amounts of the transactions. However, as was evident, there are different ways of determining the values of some capital transactions, for example, treasury stock transactions and stock dividends.

This chapter should make it clear that accounting policy and practice are pragmatic. There is no single valuation model on which accounting practice is based. Departures from historical costs are frequent and are made for many reasons. The lower-of-cost-or-market rule represents balance sheet conservatism. Some accounting practices have come about because of verifiability reliability problems — for example, the treatment of convertible debt. Other departures are undertaken because more relevant information may be conveyed by the reporting of current values — for example, the use of current exchange rates to translate foreign operations. As stated throughout this chapter, the balance sheet violates the concept of additivity. However, it must be remembered that accounting policies are the result of a political process and inevitable compromises. Finally, measurement purity per se does not insure that accounting information will be useful or relevant.

QUESTIONS

1. What are the characteristics of assets, liabilities, and owners' equity, and how have they evolved over time?

2. Why is it difficult to define the basic accounting elements?

3. Why are asset and liability definitions important to the theoretical structure of accounting? Why are definitions important to policy-setting bodies?

4. Numerous attributes are measured in the balance sheet. What are the different attributes? Why is this practice criticized?

5. What do aggregated balance sheet totals represent? This data is used for ratio analysis. How useful do you think ratio analysis is?

6. Three approaches have been advocated concerning the definition of accounting elements and the relationship between the balance sheet and income statement. What are the three approaches and how do they differ?

7. What is the meaning of "owners' equity" in the balance sheet? Why are certain unrealized gains or losses included in owners' equity?

8. What are deferred charges and deferred credits, how do they come about, and do they conform to asset and liability definitions?

9. Why have mutually unperformed executory contracts traditionally been excluded from financial statements? Can this practice be justified in terms of asset and liability definitions? How relevant is this approach for professional sports franchises?

10. What is the purpose of balance sheet classification? How useful is the information produced from a classified balance 'sheet? What are some alternative classification systems that could be used?

11. As a potential investor, what do you feel would be the most useful attribute of measurement for each of the following: inventories held for sale, inventories held for production, and long-term debt? Would your answer differ if you were a potential lender? What if you were a manager of a company? What measurement problems are illustrated by this question?

12. Why is it difficult to determine the historical acquisition cost of self-constructed assets? Do definitions of accounting elements and general principles of recognition and measurement resolve the controversy over full absorption costing and variable costing of manufactured inventory?

13. The limitation of the accounting classification system depicted in Exhibit 9–1 was referred to throughout the chapter. What is meant by this? Give some examples. Why is the accounting classification system the foundation of the accounting discipline?

14. Employee stock option plans represent a classic accounting measurement problem involving the trade-off between relevance and reliability. Explain why this is so. Does relevance or reliability seem to dominate in the accounting requirements of APB 25?

15. Based on your reading of this chapter, plus your general knowledge of ac-

counting standards, identify as many examples as you can of measurement flexibility in the statement of financial position.
16. What are credit risk, market risk, and concentrations of credit risk?

CASES AND PROBLEMS

1. Review a recent annual report. Identify all attributes of measurement explicitly identified in the balance sheet and accompanying notes. Notice which items are not specified. Group the accounting elements by attribute. How thorough is the explanation of measurement in the balance sheet? Identify any unusual assets or liabilities. How useful is the current–noncurrent distinction for assessing liquidity? Based on your review, what level of user sophistication do you think is necessary to understand how the balance sheet numbers have been derived? How useful do you think the balance sheet is? What are its limitations and how might it be improved, especially from a communication viewpoint?

2. A paradox exists as to why more firms do not use LIFO in order to get tax savings (LIFO can generally be used for tax purposes only if it is also used for financial reporting). A study by Granof and Short (1984) reported that as few as 5 percent of public companies use LIFO exclusively. They go on to state (p. 324):

> The implication that large numbers of firms, including such giants as IBM and ITT, "voluntarily" pay additional taxes is not intuitively appealing. Such firms have the ability to hire tax specialists as well as academic consultants familiar with research into the efficiency of capital markets. In most cases, it seems more reasonable to assume one or more of the following: (1) certain costs associated with the use of LIFO have not been identified; (2) certain conditions may exist that prevent a company from receiving the benefits normally associated with LIFO; (3) certain benefits are associated with the use of methods other than LIFO which have not been identified in the literature.

An incentive to use FIFO rather than LIFO could be accounting-based management compensation plans. LIFO, of course, lowers reported earnings. Still, it is difficult to believe that managers would allow their companies to pay substantial extra taxes in order to slightly increase their own personal compensation. And since the tax benefits of LIFO are well known, there is nothing to prevent boards of directors from requiring it. Therefore, assume there are good company-related reasons *not* to use LIFO. What might some of these good reasons be? After compiling your list, compare your reasons to the findings of Granof and Short (1984) and Hilke (1986).

3. The FASB's *Status Report No. 177*, July 7, 1986, reported:

> On May 14, 1986, the Board added to its agenda a project on financial instruments and off balance sheet financing.
>
> Board members and staff have been studying issues raised by the Board's

Emerging Issues Task Force (EITF) concerning various kinds of financial instruments and transactions. Issues identified include accounting for repurchase agreements, interest rate and currency swaps, collateralized mortgage obligations, offsetting nonrecourse liabilities against related assets, put and call options, risk participations in bankers' acceptances, unusual preferred stock, and financial guarantees. Many of the instruments and transactions are said by critics to constitute "off balance sheet financing"; others are said to defer losses unjustifiably or recognize gains prematurely. In addition to those kinds of recognition and measurement issues, there has been criticism of the adequacy of disclosure about financial instruments. While many of these matters primarily concern banks, savings and loans, investment banks, and other financial institutions, innovative financial instruments and transactions have given rise to financial reporting issues in all kinds of business enterprises. . . .

The Board decided that the recognition and measurement problems should be approached as several separate, though related, questions, including:

- Whether financial assets should be considered sold if there is recourse or other continuing involvement with them, whether financial liabilities should be considered settled when assets are dedicated to settle them, and other questions of derecognition, nonrecognition, or offsetting of related financial assets and liabilities;
- How to account for financial instruments and transactions that seek to transfer market and credit risks — for example, futures contracts, interest rate swaps, options, and forward commitments, nonrecourse arrangements, and financial guarantees — and for the underlying assets or liabilities to which the risk-transferring items are related, how financial instruments should be measured — for example, at market value, amortized original cost, or the lower of cost or market;
- How issuers should account for securities with both debt and equity characteristics; and
- Whether the creation of separate legal entities or trusts affects the answer (which may not need to be addressed in this project since it is already being addressed in the Board's project on the reporting entity.)[45]

How do these new financial instruments create problems for the accounting classification system shown in Exhibit 9–1? What issues are raised in the FASB's report regarding principles of recognition and measurement?

4. SFAS 76, para. 3, states that a debt is extinguished for financial reporting purposes in any of the three following circumstances:

    a. The debtor pays the creditor and is relieved of all its obligations with respect to the debt. This includes the debtor's reacquisition of its outstanding debt securities in the public securities markets, regardless of whether the securities are cancelled or held as so-called treasury bonds.

    b. The debtor is legally released from being the primary obligor under the debt either judicially or by the creditor and it is probable that the debtor

---

[45] Reprinted by permission.

will not be required to make future payments with respect to that debt under any guarantees.

c. The debtor irrevocably places cash or other assets in a trust to be used solely for satisfying scheduled payments of both interest and principal of a specific obligation and the possibility that the debtor will be required to make future payments with respect to that debt is remote. In this circumstance, debt is extinguished even though the debtor is not legally released from being the primary obligor under the debt obligation.

The third situation (c) is commonly called *in-substance defeasance* because the debt is treated as retired, though legally it has not been discharged. In general, the offsetting of assets and liabilities in this manner is not considered to be an acceptable accounting practice. Critically evaluate whether in-substance defeasance is consistent with the SFAC 6 definition and discussion of liabilities. Is finite uniformity present with regard to (b) and (c) above?

5. Quoted below are excerpts from a *Wall Street Journal* article of September 27, 1990, by Kevin G. Salwyn and Robin Goldwyn Blumenthal entitled "Tackling Accounting, SEC Pushes Changes With Broad Impact," which is concerned with listing financial assets at current value:

> The Securities and Exchange Commission is shaking up the world of accounting. . . .
>
> The overhaul, so far, is a sedate one in a notoriously sedate field. But it could radically change companies' financial reports, and so the way companies are evaluated by investors. Even small variations in accounting can translate into big changes in stock prices, and some of the contemplated rule changes aren't small.
>
> "This isn't evolutionary, it's revolutionary," comments Christopher J. Steffen, chief financial officer at Honeywell Inc.
>
> Right now, the SEC is focusing solely on debt securities and certain types of loans held by banks and other financial institutions. Next to be affected will probably be other companies with significant financial assets. Finally, much of corporate America, ranging from General Motors to a Silicon Valley startup, may feel pressure to revise the way it accounts for assets.
>
> Although no one is suggesting that the SEC will revamp financial statements altogether, it wants to force companies to go a long way toward putting up-to-date values on assets currently on their books at historical cost—the original purchase price. It has launched a campaign in Congress and with the accounting profession to get fast action.
>
> "If accounting standards aren't adequate to give an accurate picture of a firm's condition, they're not doing the job they need to do," says SEC Chairman Richard C. Breeden. . . .
>
> The agency's focus on accounting is another indication of its renewed scrutiny of corporate America, and its shift away from targeting Wall Street stock-trading abuses. The SEC recently adopted rules making it easier for companies to sell debt directly to large institutions and is awaiting congressional approval to toughen enforcement against wrongdoing by corporate officials.
>
> Sweeping changes in corporate accounting won't come easily. Many companies oppose, and are lobbying against, any change that could raise costs, skew numbers or reduce reported profits. Banks especially are leery of any change

that could make their balance sheets look worse. And SEC officials themselves are wary of doing anything that might make U.S. companies less competitive with foreign rivals, or trigger, through accounting advantages, foreign takeovers of U.S. companies. . . .

Under today's standards, financial companies — banks, thrifts and insurance concerns — holding stacks of investment securities can make their own judgments on whether to use historical accounting or current, "market" standards. "Financial-institution balance sheets should have the words 'once upon a time' on top of them," Mr. Breeden says scornfully. "They are a statement of history." Under the SEC plan, recently rejected by an industry accounting panel, only current values of a financial company's securities would be listed on the balance sheet and reflected in quarterly profit-and-loss statements. . . .

But James W. Otto, chief financial officer of Ameritrust Corp., a Cleveland-based banking company, says marking assets to current value "would be a very significant and costly effort that wouldn't be useful. . . . It's an estimation of the liquidation value of a company that is totally irrelevant to a going concern."

Moreover, Mr. Otto adds, "A majority of the assets and liabilities don't have a ready market." Therefore, he argues, "some very subjective assumptions" would be needed to arrive at current values for those assets and liabilities.[46]

In light of the above, answer the following questions:
(a) Why do you think the SEC is focusing on financial assets of banks and other financial institutions first?
(b) Why do you think financial executives (such as Mr. Otto) are strongly opposed to the proposal?
(c) What type of actions would you expect corporate America to take in opposing a ruling of this sort?
(d) A representative of Citicorp (which is against the proposal) made the following comment: "You wouldn't want anything that would cause portfolio managers to make business decisions based on accounting rather than economic impacts." Does this statement make sense? Comment.

BIBLIOGRAPHY OF REFERENCED WORKS

Accounting Principles Board (1962). "Accounting for the Investment Credit," *APB Opinion No. 2* (AICPA).
——— (1966). "Omnibus Opinion — 1966," *APB Opinion No. 10* (AICPA).
——— (1967a). "Accounting for Income Taxes," *APB Opinion No. 11* (AICPA).
——— (1967b). "Omnibus Opinion — 1967," *APB Opinion No. 12* (AICPA).
——— (1969a). "Accounting for Convertible Debt and Debt Issued with Stock Purchase Warrants," *APB Opinion No. 14* (AICPA).
——— (1969b). "Earnings Per Share," *APB Opinion No. 15* (AICPA).
——— (1970a). "Basic Concepts and Accounting Principles Underlying Financial Statements of Business Enterprises," *APB Statement No. 4* (AICPA).

────── (1970b). "Intangible Assets," *APB Opinion No. 17* (AICPA).

────── (1971a). "The Equity Method of Accounting for Investments in Common Stock," *APB Opinion No. 18* (AICPA).

────── (1971b). "Accounting Changes," *APB Opinion No. 20* (AICPA).

────── (1971c). "Interest on Receivables and Payables," *APB Opinion No. 21* (AICPA).

──────(1972). "Accounting for Stock Issued to Employees," *APB Opinion No. 25* (AICPA).

────── (1973). "Accounting for Nonmonetary Transactions," *APB Opinion No. 29* (AICPA).

American Accounting Association (1966). *A Statement of Basic Accounting Theory* (AAA).

Arthur Andersen and Co. (1974). *Accounting Standards for Business Enterprises Throughout the World* (Arthur Andersen and Co.).

Byington, J. Ralph, and Paul Munter (1990). "Disclosures About Financial Instruments," *The CPA Journal* (September 1990), pp. 42–48.

Canning, John B. (1929). *The Economics of Accountancy* (Ronald Press).

Chambers, Raymond J. (1966). *Accounting, Evaluation and Economic Behavior* (Prentice-Hall).

Committee on Accounting Procedure (1953). "Restatement and Revision of Accounting Research Bulletins," *ARB No. 43* (AICPA).

Committee on Terminology (1953). "Review and Resume," *Accounting Terminology Bulletin No. 1* (AICPA).

Financial Accounting Standards Board (1974). "Accounting for Research and Development Costs," *Statement of Financial Accounting Standards No. 2* (FASB).

────── (1975a). "Reporting Gains and Losses from Extinguishment of Debt," *Statement of Financial Accounting Standards No. 4* (FASB).

────── (1975b). "Accounting for Contingencies," *Statement of Financial Accounting Standards No. 5* (FASB).

────── (1975c). "Accounting for Certain Marketable Securities," *Statement of Financial Accounting Standards No. 12* (FASB).

────── (1976a). "Accounting for Leases," *Statement of Financial Accounting Standards No. 13* (FASB).

────── (1976b). *FASB Discussion Memorandum: An Analysis of Issues Related to Conceptual Framework for Financial Reporting: Elements of Financial Statements and Their Measurement* (FASB).

────── (1979). "Capitalization of Interest Cost," *Statement of Financial Accounting Standards No. 34* (FASB).

────── (1982). "Foreign Currency Translation,"*Statement of Financial Accounting Standards No. 52* (FASB).

────── (1984). "Recognition and Measurement in Financial Statements of Business Enterprises," *Statement of Financial Accounting Concepts No. 5* (FASB).

────── (1985). "Elements of Financial Statements," *Statement of Financial Accounting Concepts No. 6* (FASB).

────── (1990). "Disclosure of Information about Financial Instruments with Off-Balance-Sheet Risk and Financial Instruments with Concentrations of Credit Risk," *Statement of Financial Accounting Standards No. 105* (FASB).

Foster, George (1986). *Financial Statement Analysis* (Prentice-Hall).

Granof, Michael H., and Daniel G. Short (1984). "Why Do Companies Reject LIFO?" *Journal of Accounting, Auditing, and Finance* (Summer 1984), pp. 323–333.

Gujarathi, Mahendra R., and Stanley F. Biggs (1988). "Accounting for Purchase Commitments: Some Issues and Recommendations," *Accounting Horizons* (September 1988), pp. 75–82.

Hilke, John C. (1986). "Regulatory Compliance Costs and LIFO: No Wonder Small Companies Haven't Switched," *Journal of Accounting, Auditing, and Finance* (Winter 1986), pp. 17–29.

Hughes, John S. (1978). "Toward a Contract Basis of Valuation in Accounting," *The Accounting Review* (October 1978), pp. 882–894.

Ijiri, Yuji (1975). "Theory of Accounting Measurement," *Studies in Accounting Research # 10* (American Accounting Association).

——— (1980). *Recognition of Contractual Rights and Obligations: An Exploratory Study of Conceptual Issues* (FASB).

Means, Kathryn M., and Paul M. Kazenski (1988). "SFAS 34: A Recipe for Diversity," *Accounting Horizons* (September 1988), pp. 62–67.

Solomons, David (1986). "The FASB's Conceptual Framework: An Evaluation," *Journal of Accountancy* (June 1986), pp. 114–124.

Sorter, George H., and Charles T. Horngren (1962). "Asset Recognition and Economic Attributes — The Relevant Costing Approach," *The Accounting Review* (July 1962), pp. 391–399.

Stamp, Edward (1980). *Corporate Reporting: Its Future Evolution* (Canadian Institute of Chartered Accountants).

Stewart, John E., and Benjamin S. Neuhausen (1986). "Financial Instruments and Transactions: The CPA's Newest Challenge," *Journal of Accountancy* (August 1986), pp. 102–112.

ADDITIONAL READINGS

Measurement of Assets and Liabilities in General

American Accounting Association (1972). "Report of the Committee on Accounting Valuation Bases," *The Accounting Review* (supplement to Volume 47), pp. 535–573.

Henderson, M. Scott (1974). "Nature of Liabilities," *The Australian Accountant* (July 1974), pp. 329–334.

Kulkarni, Deepak (1980). "The Valuation of Liabilities," *Accounting and Business Research* (Summer 1980), pp. 291–297.

Ma, Ronald, and Malcolm C. Miller (1978). "Conceptualizing the Liability," *Accounting and Business Research* (Autumn 1978), pp. 258–265.

Moonitz, Maurice (1960). "The Changing Concept of Liabilities," *Journal of Accountancy* (May 1960), pp. 41–46.

Sprouse, Robert T. (1971). "Balance Sheet — Embodiment of the Most Fundamental Elements of Accounting Theory," in *Foundations of Accounting Theory*, Williard E. Stone, ed. (University of Florida Press), pp. 90–104.

Staubus, George J. (1973). "Measurement of Assets and Liabilities," *Accounting and Business Research* (Autumn 1973), pp. 243–262.

Sterling, Robert R., ed. (1971). *Asset Valuation and Income Determination* (Scholars Book Company).

Walker, Robert G. (1974). "Asset Classification and Asset Valuation," *Accounting and Business Research* (Autumn 1974), pp. 286–296.

Warrell, C. J. (1974). "The Enterprise Value Concept of Asset Valuation," *Accounting and Business Research* (Summer 1974), pp. 220–226.

Measurement of Specific Assets and Liabilities

Anthony, Robert N. (1975). *Accounting for the Cost of Interest* (Lexington Books).

Barden, Horace G. (1973). "The Accounting Basis of Inventories," *Accounting Research Study No. 13* (AICPA).

Beidleman, Carl R. (1973). "Valuation of Used Capital Assets," *Studies in Accounting Research No. 7* (American Accounting Association).

Chasteen, Lanny G. (1973). "Economic Circumstances and Inventory Method Selection," *Abacus* (June 1973), pp. 22–27.

Clancy, Donald K. (1978). "What Is a Convertible Debenture? A Review of the Literature in the U.S.A.," *Abacus* (December 1978), pp. 171–179.

Coughlan, J. D., and W. K. Strand (1969). *Depreciation; Accounting, Taxes and Business Decisions* (Ronald Press).

Gellein, Oscar S., and Maurice S. Newman (1973). "Accounting for Research and Development Expenditures," *Accounting Research Study No. 14* (AICPA).

O'Connor, Melvin C., and James C. Hamre (1972). "Alternative Methods of Accounting for Long-Term Nonsubsidiary Intercorporate Investments in Common Stock," *The Accounting Review* (April 1972), pp. 308–319.

Storey, Reed K., and Maurice Moonitz (1976). "Market Value Methods for Intercorporate Investments in Stock," *Accounting Research Monograph No. 1* (AICPA).

Measurement of Owners' Equity

American Accounting Association (1965). "The Entity Concept – Report of the 1964 Concepts and Standards Research Committee," *The Accounting Review* (April 1965), pp. 358–369.

Boudreaux, Kenneth J., and Stephen A. Zeff (1976). "A Note on the Measure of Compensation Implicit in Employee Stock Options," *Journal of Accounting Research* (Spring 1976), pp. 158–162.

Melcher, Beatrice (1973). "Stockholders' Equity," *Accounting Research Study No. 15* (AICPA).

Scott, Richard A. (1979). "Owners' Equity, the Anachronistic Element," *The Accounting Review* (October 1979), pp. 750–763.

Smith, Ralph E., and Leroy F. Imdieke (1974). "Accounting for Stock Issued to Employees," *Journal of Accountancy* (November 1974), pp. 68–75.

STATEMENT OF CASH FLOWS

$\mathbf{I}$N 1987, the FASB mandated a statement of cash flows.[1] This statement superseded the previously required statement of changes in financial position (SCFP). The SCFP reported on changes in assets, liabilities, and owners' equity account balances. Inclusion of a SCFP in the annual report was recommended by APB Opinion No. 3 in 1963, but it was not required.[2] The SEC made it mandatory for statutory filings beginning in 1971.[3] In response to the SEC action, APB 19 was issued in 1971. It superseded APB 3 and made the statement mandatory for financial reporting.[4]

The transition from a funds flow statement to a cash flow statement reflects the FASB's interest in cash-basis reporting as an important supplement to the accrual-based income statement and balance sheet. In substance, the cash flow statement is the SCFP with *funds* defined as cash. APB 19 allowed flexibility on this point, and most firms elected to define funds as net working capital. Because the cash flow statement is simply a special case of the more general SCFP, the chapter begins with an analysis of the logic underlying the SCFP. The rationale for moving to a cash definition of *funds* is discussed in the next section, and the chapter concludes with a review of related theoretical and empirical research.

LOGIC UNDERLYING THE STATEMENT OF CHANGES IN FINANCIAL POSITION

APB 19 stated that the reporting objectives of the SCFP are to (1) complete the disclosure of changes in financial position, (2) summarize financing and investing activity, and (3) report funds flow from operations. These three items of

---

[1] FASB (1987).
[2] APB (1963).
[3] SEC (1970).
[4] APB (1971).

information cannot be directly obtained from an income statement and comparative balance sheets because of the manner in which data is aggregated in these two financial statements. Therefore, new information is reported in a SCFP even though it summarizes the same transactions reported in an income statement and comparative balance sheets. In other words, the SCFP is a different way of classifying and reporting accounting transactions than occurs in a balance sheet and income statement. However, since it relies on definitions and measurements of accounting elements from the other two financial statements, it may be described as a derivative financial statement.

The underlying logic can be summarized as follows:

$$\text{TRANSACTION CREDITS} = \text{TRANSACTION DEBITS} \quad (11.1)$$

There are two balancing sections in the statement of changes in financial position. These are called *sources of resources* and *uses of resources*, respectively. Sources of resources are defined as transaction credits. Transaction credits arise from increases in liabilities and owners' equity and decreases in assets. Increases in liabilities and owners' equity represent new capital available to the firm from external sources, such as debt and stock issues, and internal sources, such as net income. Proceeds from the disposal of assets (asset decreases) also generate internal sources of resources available to the firm.

Uses of resources are defined as transaction debits. Transaction debits arise from decreases in liabilities and owners' equity and increases in assets. Decreases in liabilities and owners' equity represent a reduction in the firm's

---

EXHIBIT 11–1

Standard Format of the Statement
of Changes in Financial Position

Sources of Resources
(transaction credits)

1. Increases to the "fund balance" accounts.
    a. From net income.
    b. From other sources.
2. Other sources of resources.
3. Decrease, if any, in the fund balance for the period.

Uses of Resources
(transaction debits)

1. Decreases to the "fund balance" accounts.
    a. From net losses.
    b. From other sources.
2. Other uses of resources.
3. Increase, if any, in the fund balance for the period.

---

capital. These types of transactions include debt retirement, capital reductions from many sources including treasury stock purchases, dividend payments, and of course net losses. Asset increases represent new investment, which is also a use of the firm's resources. In all cases, the firm's available resources decrease as a result of debit transactions.

The basic structure outlined in Equation (11.1) forms the logic of the SCFP. However, the SCFP is successor to an earlier financial statement called the *funds flow statement*. In a funds flow statement, certain balance sheet accounts are defined as comprising what is called the *fund balance*. The purpose of the statement was to show how the fund balance accounts increased from income and other sources and decreased from losses and other uses. The funds flow concept represented the liquid, usable, and available resources of the firm. As such, it was an operating statement closer to cash flow accounting than accrual accounting. It was typical for *fund balance* to be defined as working capital accounts.

The funds flow statement affected the structure of the SCFP. In both the sources and uses sections of the SCFP, transactions are subclassified into those affecting the fund balance and those affecting other accounts. The effect of net income on the fund balance is also reported separately. This complex structure of the SCFP is illustrated in Exhibit 11–1. It must be emphasized, though, that the basic logic is still as defined in Equation (11.1). The more complex format in Exhibit 11–1 is only a more detailed way of classifying transaction debits and credits, and it incorporates a funds flow statement within the SCFP.[5]

The evolution from the funds flow statement to the SCFP represents an expansion of reported information. The funds flow statement included only the transactions listed under points 1a and 1b in Exhibit 11–1. Transactions not affecting fund accounts were excluded. The result was a report on the change in fund balance and how this change came about. The emphasis in funds flow reporting focused much more narrowly on liquidity.

By adding the transactions listed under point 2 in Exhibit 11–1, a comprehensive summary is made of all changes in financial position, not just those pertaining to fund balance accounts. This approach is referred to as the *all-inclusive* or *all-resources* SCFP. The types of transactions listed under point 2 pertain to investment and financing activities not affecting fund accounts. Examples include the conversion of convertible debt to common stock, stock issued for nonmonetary assets, dividends paid in property rather than cash, and nonmonetary exchanges of assets. APB 19 opted for the all-inclusive approach rather than the narrower funds flow statement. However, it is apparent that a funds flow statement is still contained within the SCFP.

---

[5] Ketz and Largay (1987) noted difficulties in determining whether an event or transaction fell into the operating, investing, or financing category on the SCFP. Moreover, intrafirm inconsistencies are relative to classification on the income statement and the SCFP. For example, Ketz and Largay (1987, p. 13) note that a $946,000 gain on the sale of marketable securities by Evans & Sutherland in 1985 was included in operating income on the income statement but was deducted from funds provided by working capital on the SCFP.

The preparation of the SCFP requires four distinct steps. The initial step is to define those balance sheet accounts making up the fund balance accounts. APB 19 permitted any one of four definitions: cash, cash plus near cash (short-term marketable securities and other temporary investments), quick assets, and working capital.

The next step is to determine the effect of income statement transactions on the fund balance. Income (or loss) must be carefully analyzed and adjusted for any items not affecting the fund balance. For example, if funds are defined as working capital, all income statement debits and credits that have no corresponding credits and debits to current assets and current liabilities are excluded. Depreciation expense is an example. The credit to accumulated depreciation is to a nonfund account. After adjustments have been made to income, the adjusted number is classified as a source of resources if the amount is a credit balance (adjusted net income) and as a use of resources if the amount is a debit balance (adjusted net loss). This classification corresponds to point 1a in Exhibit 11–1. Major adjustments to income when funds are defined as working capital are shown in Exhibit 11–2.

The third step is to analyze all nonincome statement transactions in nonfund accounts. There are two possible types: transactions involving one fund account and one nonfund account, and transactions involving two nonfund accounts. When a transaction involves a fund and nonfund account, the transaction classification corresponds to point 1b in Exhibit 11–1. If a fund account is debited and a nonfund account is credited, the credit to the nonfund account would be classified as a source of resources because it is a transaction credit. An example would be a debit to cash and a credit to bonds payable for the issue of new debt. If a fund account is credited and a nonfund account is debited, the transaction would be classified as a use of resources because there is a debit to a nonfund account. An example would be a debit to assets and a credit to cash for the purchase of assets. These types of transactions represent investment and financing activity.

Transactions in which both the debit and credit affect nonfund accounts are classified as both sources and uses of resources. The debit represents a use of resources and the credit is classified as a source of resources. An example of this type of transaction is the conversion of convertible debt. The accounting transaction would be recorded as a debit to bonds payable and a credit to contributed capital. The debit is classified as a use of resources and the credit is classified as a source of resources. These types of transactions correspond to point 2 in Exhibit 11–1. They represent investment and financing transactions but differ from the types in point 1b because there is no effect on fund accounts.

Finally, the balancing item in the SCFP is the change in the fund balance itself. The change is classified as a source or use of resources, depending on whether the balance has decreased or increased, respectively. The fund balance represents the equivalent of an asset account, so the change is reported in the same manner as a change in any other asset. A credit (decrease) represents a source of resources, and a debit (increase) represents a use of resources. This item corresponds with point 3 in Exhibit 11–1.

EXHIBIT 11–2
Examples of Nonfund Adjustments to Income When
Funds Are Defined as Working Capital

Elimination of Income Statement Credits

1. All book gains (both ordinary and extraordinary) arising from asset disposals, debt retirement, and debt restructuring.
2. Amortization of premiums on debt.
3. Amortization of discounts on investments.
4. Extraordinary gains arising from a change in accounting principle.
5. Equity accounting investment income in excess of cash dividends.
6. Amortization of deferred investment tax credits.
7. Amortization of deferred gains from sale–leaseback transactions.
8. Tax expense in excess of taxes payable due to deferred taxes.

Elimination of Income Statement Debits

1. All book losses (both ordinary and extraordinary) arising from asset disposals, debt retirement, and debt restructuring.
2. Amortization of discounts on debt.
3. Amortization of premiums on investments.
4. Depreciation, depletion, and leasehold amortization.
5. Amortization of intangible assets and deferred charges.
6. Tax expense reductions relating to reversals of deferred taxes.
7. Extraordinary losses arising from a change in accounting principle.
8. Equity accounting investment losses (less cash dividends).
9. Amortization of deferred losses from sale–leaseback transactions.
10. Compensation expense due to the issue of employee stock options.

All transactions in nonfund accounts are to be included in the statement of changes in financial position. This is true even if the transactions have no direct effect on fund accounts. When funds are defined as working capital, nonfund transactions are restricted to nonmonetary transactions, such as nonmonetary exchanges of assets and the conversion of convertible debt to common stock. Of course, when funds are defined as cash, there are many additional accounting transactions that do not affect cash. Therefore, the narrower the definition of funds, the greater the number of nonfund transactions to be reported separately. This is one reason why a working capital definition of funds minimizes the cost of producing a SCFP.

THE MOVE TO A CASH FLOW STATEMENT

SFAC No. 1 lists three general objectives of financial reporting. The first of these is very broad and simply states: "Financial reporting should provide information that is useful to present and potential investors and creditors and other users in making rational investment, credit, and similar decisions."[6] Two additional objectives can be thought of as specific ways of meeting the first objective. These are (1) reporting information about the firm's net resources and changes in those resources and (2) reporting information useful in assessing future cash flows. These two reporting goals have motivated the FASB's adoption of a cash flow statement. In SFAC 5, the FASB makes the following claims about a statement of cash flow:

> It provides useful information about an entity's activities in generating cash through operations to repay debt, distribute dividends, or reinvest to maintain or expand operating capacity; about its financing activities, both debt and equity; and about its investing or spending of cash. Important uses of information about an entity's current cash receipts and payments include helping to assess factors such as the entity's liquidity, financial flexibility, profitability, and risk (para. 52).

An earlier FASB discussion memorandum suggested that cash flow data are a useful supplemental disclosure because they

1. provide feedback on actual cash flows,
2. help to identify the relationship between accounting income and cash flows,
3. provide information about the quality of income,
4. improve comparability of information in financial reports,
5. aid in assessing flexibility and liquidity, and
6. assist in predicting future cash flows.[7]

In one way or another, all of the points above deal with the limitations of accrual accounting. This is not to say accrual data is uninformative, but, rather, that cash flow data can supplement the income statement and balance sheet.

It is obvious that cash flow is necessary in assessing past cash flows (point 1). It follows that cash flow is also necessary in understanding the actual cash flow being generated from operations (point 2) — that is, the relationship between accounting income and cash flows. The third point also relates to the cash flow component of accounting income. *Quality of income* is a term used by financial analysts to describe this relationship. The higher the correlation between accounting income and cash flows, the better the quality of earnings. The quality-of-earnings concept reflects an awareness that accounting income comprises many noncash accruals and deferrals and that it does not necessarily give a good indication of liquidity.

The fourth point deals with the uniformity problem. Owing to flexibility in the choice of some accounting policies, comparability between companies may not be achieved. As indicated in Chapter 8, many areas of accounting fail to achieve uniformity. Cash flow from operations is a simpler measurement and is subject to fewer arbitrary choices of accounting policy. For this reason, cash flow measurement is more uniform than income measurement and results in a

---

[6] FASB (1978, para. 34).
[7] FASB (1980).

higher level of comparability. Thus, cash flow statements have been advocated as a way of dealing with the arbitrariness of income measurement.[8] There is an appealing simplicity to cash flow when contrasted with the abstractness and complexity of accounting income.

The fifth point concerns the use of cash flow data to assist in assessing a firm's financial flexibility and liquidity. **Flexibility** is the ability of the firm to adapt to new situations and opportunities. **Liquidity** is the capability for quick conversion of assets to cash. Cash being generated internally from operations gives an indication of both liquidity and flexibility. Cash flow represents internal resources available for debt servicing and repayment, new investment, and distributions to stockholders. This was the original reason for requiring a funds flow statement.

Liquidity information is also contained in the balance sheet. As noted in Chapter 10, however, the current–noncurrent classification system is a poor guide to liquidity; this is because some current items are deferred charges or credits that have no impact on future cash flows. Other assets such as inventory may not be readily converted into cash. Within the current group of assets, very few are actually convertible to cash within a short period of time. And since the attribute of measurement reported in the balance sheet is normally something other than net realizable value, it is not possible to determine how much cash will be generated from assets. A balance sheet presents nothing more than a crude ranking of liquidity. As a consequence, the balance sheet in its present form reveals very little about liquidity and flexibility. A cash flow statement, on the other hand, gives insight into the cash-generating potential of operations.

The exit-price accounting system illustrated in Appendix 1-A to Chapter 1 is intended to measure flexibility of the firm in terms of the amount of cash that could be realized from nonforced liquidation of assets.[9] However, even exit-price measurement is only a crude indicator of liquidity and flexibility. Although such a measurement system might provide an estimate of the cash conversion value of a firm's resources, it is the speed of conversion that ultimately determines both liquidity and flexibility. How useful exit-price accounting is for assessing a firm's flexibility is therefore questionable. In addition, a firm is more likely to raise capital incrementally rather than by selling all its assets. In a normal situation, a firm would not sell its productive assets to raise new capital needed for new investment opportunities. A firm is more likely to use either new capital or cash realized from assets being held for sale, such as inventories.

The sixth and final point suggests that cash flow data are useful for predicting future cash flows. It makes sense that past cash flow data would be useful for predicting future cash flows. However, it is unclear if cash flow, funds flow, or accounting income are better predictors of future cash flows. The expanded disclosure philosophy would maintain that all potentially useful information

---

[8] This is due to arbitrary allocations in the determination of accounting income. See Thomas (1969) and the discussion in Chapter 9.

[9] Chambers (1966) used the term *adaptability*, but it means the same thing as *flexibility* in the context being used here.

should be disclosed, holding aside the question of costs. However, in the case of a SCFP, there is only minimal cost in presenting the information since it is nothing more than a different way of summarizing and classifying accounting transactions for the period.

The preceding discussion points to the rediscovery of cash-basis accounting as an important supplement to accrual-based financial statements. It is also necessary to understand why cash flow supplanted the more general concept of funds flow. During the FASB's deliberations that led up to the cash flow statement, a consensus emerged that funds should be defined as cash rather than net working capital mainly because net working capital is a poor measure of liquidity. Three reasons for this are that (1) deferred charges and credits are included in net working capital but have no cash flow consequences, (2) conversion of current assets can take a year or longer if the firm's operating cycle exceeds one year, and (3) items like inventory are carried on a cost basis and thus do not explicitly reveal the cash flow potential of the inventory. In light of these ambiguities, cash flow reporting appeals because of its straightforwardness and literal interpretation — cash is cash is cash (with apologies to Gertrude Stein).

REQUIREMENTS OF THE CASH FLOW STATEMENT

The structure of the cash flow statement subclassifies cash receipts and payments into operating, financing, and investing activities. This contrasts with the sources/uses framework of the SCFP. However, the three-way classification approach more clearly segregates cash flows into functionally meaningful categories of operating flows, net financing flows, and net investment flows. By contrast, the two-way sources/uses framework focuses mechanically on the narrow accounting debit–credit relation illustrated in Exhibit 11–1.

Cash is defined as literal cash on hand or on demand deposit, plus cash equivalents. Cash equivalents are highly liquid investments that are convertible to known amounts of cash and that have short-term maturities (generally, an original maturity of three months or less). Like APB 19, the cash flow statement requires all *noncash* (that is, nonfund) investing and financing transactions to be reported as a supplement to the cash flow statement, either in a schedule or in a narrative format. Again, this approach represents the all-inclusive or all-resources concept of funds flow reporting. It presumably assures that *all* the firm's transaction debits and credits are accounted for and presented in the cash flow statement and illustrates the point made at the outset of the chapter that the SCFP is an alternative schema for classifying and reporting all of the firm's transactions. An example of the suggested format is illustrated in Exhibit 11–3.

On the cash flow statement, cash flows are segregated into those stemming from operating activities, investing activities, and financing activities. Although this organization provides more classificational consistency — which should lead to greater comparability — than the SCFP (see footnote 5), three members of the FASB dissented from the statement because they believed that interest and dividends received arise from investing activities rather than from

---

EXHIBIT 11–3
Illustration of the Cash Flow Statement in Accordance with SFAS 95 (Direct Method)

COMPANY M
CONSOLIDATED STATEMENT OF CASH FLOWS
FOR THE YEAR ENDED DECEMBER 31, 19X1
Increase (Decrease) in Cash and Cash Equivalents

Cash flows from operating activities:		
Cash received from customers	$13,850	
Cash paid to suppliers and employees	(12,000)	
Dividend received from affiliate	20	
Interest received	55	
Interest paid (net of amount capitalized)	(220)	
Income taxes paid	(325)	
Insurance proceeds received	15	
Cash paid to settle lawsuit for patent infringe- ment	(30)	
Net cash provided by operating activities		$1,365
Cash flows from investing activities:		
Proceeds from sale of facility	600	
Payment received on note for sale of plant	150	
Capital expenditures	(1,000)	
Payment for purchase of Company S, net of cash acquired	(925)	
Net cash used in investing activities		(1,175)
Cash flows from financing activities:		
Net borrowings under line-of-credit agreement	300	
Principal payments under capital lease obliga- tion	(125)	
Proceeds from issuance of long-term debt	400	
Proceeds from issuance of common stock	500	
Dividends paid	(200)	
Net cash provided by financing activities		875
Net increase in cash and cash equivalents		1,065
Cash and cash equivalents at beginning of year		600
Cash and cash equivalents at end of year		$1,665

Source: FASB (1987, p. 44).

operating activities, as stated in paragraph 22 of the standard, and that interest paid is an element of financing activities rather than an operating cost, as noted in paragraph 23.[10]

The standard states that operating cash flows may be presented using

---

[10] FASB (1987, p. 10).

either the *direct* or *indirect* methods. The direct method reports literal cash flows related to income statement classifications (revenues, cost of sales, etc.). By contrast, the indirect or reconciliation method starts with accrual income and adjusts it for the noncash items in it. More new information is reported with the direct method, and the FASB appears to favor it. However, in both the exposure draft and the eventual accounting standard, the FASB acknowledged that the direct method may be more costly since not all companies currently organize their accounting records in such a way that produces the necessary data. If the direct method is used, however, a separate schedule shall reconcile net operating cash flow with net income (as illustrated in Exhibit 11–4). In other words, the indirect or reconciliation method must be used either alone or as a supplement to the direct method. Several members of the FASB believe that allowing the use of the indirect method will impede user understanding and will diminish the quality of financial reporting.[11] Exhibit 11–4 also shows the supplemental schedule of noncash investing and financing activities required whether the direct or the indirect method is the primary vehicle for displaying net cash from operating activities.

CASH AND FUNDS FLOW RESEARCH

Two long-standing advocates of cash flow reporting, Lawson and Lee, have argued that cash flow reports are necessary to report on the firm's performance.[12] That is, liquidity (cash flow) is an integral part of the firm's performance. Lee puts it even more strongly: ". . . cash flow and not profit is the end result of entity activity. Profit is an abstraction; cash is a physical resource."[13] Although there is some ambiguity over whether cash flow reports are superior to accrual statements or just an important supplement to them, Lawson and Lee have nevertheless made a strong case. As discussed in Chapter 7, the cash flow valuation model from the financial economics literature presents a similar viewpoint: cash flows of the firm are the ultimate determinant of firm value, not accrual accounting income. But there is also a growing body of capital market research evidence that accounting accruals are informative over and above literal cash flows vis-à-vis the firm's security prices.[14]

One interpretation of this body of research is that *both* cash flows and accruals are more useful together than either one alone; that is, both are useful in evaluating the firm's performance and prospects. From this perspective, then, the cash flow statement is complementary to accrual statements, and *new* information is provided through the decomposition of accrual data in its cash flow and accrual components. Finally, a number of surveys of investors and analysts

---

[11] Ibid., p. 11.
[12] The seminal works are Lawson (1972) and Lee (1971). For later work, see Lawson (1985) and Lee (1985).
[13] Lee (1985, p. 93).
[14] See Chapter 7 for a review of this research.

EXHIBIT 11–4
Indirect or Reconciliation Method of Presenting
Net Cash Flows From Operating Activities

Reconciliation of net income to net cash provided by operating activities:

Net income		$ 760
Adjustments to reconcile net income to net cash provided by operating activities:		
Depreciation and amortization	$ 445	
Provision for losses on accounts receivable	200	
Gain on sale of facility	(80)	
Undistributed earnings of affiliate	(25)	
Payment received on installment note receivable for sale of inventory	100	
Change in assets and liabilities net of effects from purchase of Company S:		
Increase in accounts receivable	(215)	
Decrease in inventory	205	
Increase in prepaid expenses	(25)	
Decrease in accounts payable and accrued expenses	(250)	
Increase in interest and income taxes payable	50	
Increase in deferred taxes	150	
Increase in other liabilities	50	
Total adjustments		605
Net cash provided by operating activities		$1,365

Supplemental schedule of noncash investing and financing activities:

The Company purchased all of the capital stock of Company S for $950. In conjunction with the acquisition, liabilities were assumed as follows:

Fair value of assets acquired	$1,580
Cash paid for the capital stock	(950)
Liabilities assumed	$ 630

A capital lease obligation of $850 was incurred when the Company entered into a lease for new equipment.

Additional common stock was issued upon the conversion of $500 of long-term debt.

Disclosure of accounting policy:

For purposes of the statement of cash flows, the Company considers all highly liquid debt instruments purchased with a maturity of three months or less to be cash equivalents.

Source: FASB (1987, p. 45).

have consistently shown that cash (funds) flow data are used for investment analysis but that conventional profitability based on accrual data dominates over the liquidity focus of cash or funds flow.[15] However, a more recent survey commissioned by the Financial Accounting Foundation found that funds flow data were increasing in importance while accrual data were decreasing in importance.[16] All of this suggests that cash flow plays a secondary but important and perhaps increasing role in assessing overall firm performance and prospects.

SUMMARY

The cash flow statement with funds simply defined to be cash (and near-cash equivalents) is a special case of the more general statement of changes in financial position. It is a derivative statement because it is based on the accounting transactions already summarized in the income statement and balance sheet. However, new information is reported through the decomposition of the data into cash flow and accrual components and through reclassifying of the data into operating flows, net financing flows, and net investment flows. While some classificational problems remain, the change from the SCFP to the cash flow statement should bring about greater consistency among firms as well as providing information that is more useful for predictive purposes and so should enhance comparability.

Research concerning the usefulness to investors of cash and funds flow data is supportive of the contention that they are informative above and beyond accrual data. The opposite also holds true (accruals are informative above and beyond cash flow data), which is generally consistent with the well-known proposition that finer or more detailed sets of information are more informative than coarser ones.[17] These findings are, in a general way, also supportive of the FASB's disclosure-oriented approach to standard setting (see Chapter 8).

QUESTIONS

1. Why is the statement of cash flows a special case of the SCFP?
2. Explain how cash flow data complement the income statement and balance sheet.
3. How does the cash flow statement articulate to the balance sheet and income statement?
4. What is the "quality of earnings" concept, and how does cash flow reporting relate to it?

---

[15] For example, Clarkson (1962), Hawkins and Campbell (1978), Backer and Gosman (1978), and Lee (1983).

[16] Louis Harris and Associates, Inc. (1980), cited in FASB (1980, p. 31).

[17] This is known as the "fineness" theorem. See Mohr (1983) for a discussion in an accounting context.

5. Why is cash flow reporting advocated as an alternative to accounting income by such critics of accounting allocations as Thomas (1969)?

6. What attribute is being measured in the cash flow statement, and how well is representational faithfulness achieved? Compare this to when funds are defined as working capital.

7. Why does the *direct* method of reporting cash flows from operations potentially convey more information than the *indirect* method?

8. Why is there more new information in a SCFP when funds are defined as cash?

9. Why is the three-way classification system in the cash flow statement more informative than the two-way source/use classification?

10. How does the source/use classification reflect the structure of double-entry accounting?

11. Why do you think the FASB moved to a cash basis for the SCFP rather than retain the widely used working capital basis?

12. What is the purpose of reporting noncash items in the cash flow statement?

13. Why is the cash flow statement called a *derivative statement*?

14. The chapter suggests that liquidity and flexibility data do not compose a central feature of accrual accounting. Explain why this is so.

15. What do research findings indicate concerning the relevance of cash and funds flow data?

CASES AND PROBLEMS

1. Presented in the Exhibit for Case 1 (page 344) is a graph of accounting income, cash flows from operations, and working capital flows from operations for W. T. Grant Company, a retailer which filed for bankruptcy in 1976. As late as 1973, the company's stock was selling for twenty times earnings. What does the chart indicate concerning the usefulness of income, cash, and funds flows? What could explain the significant differences between working capital flows and cash flows?

2. This case is adapted from Appendix B of the exposure draft leading up to the FASB's standard on cash flow reporting.[18] Prepare in good form a Statement of Cash Flows. Use the direct format. The following information is about the activities of Company D, a diversified multinational corporation with interests in manufacturing and financial services, for the year ending December 31, 19XX:

   (a) Company D purchased new property, plant, and equipment for $4,000. The company also sold some of its equipment with a book value of $1,900 for $2,500.

   (b) Company D entered into capital lease transactions for the use of new equipment, and the related lease obligation was $750.

---

[3] Adapted with permission of the Financial Accounting Foundation.

EXHIBIT FOR CASE 1

W. T. Grant Company Net Income, Working Capital and Cash Flow From Operations For Fiscal Years Ending January 31, 1966 to 1975.

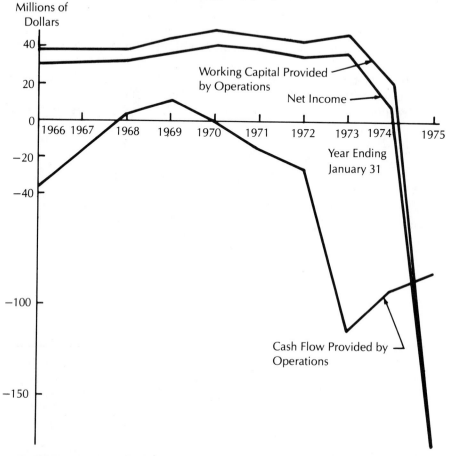

Source: Largay and Stickney (1980).

(c) Company D purchased all the common stock of Company ABC for $900 in cash. Company D thereby acquired Company ABC's working capital other than cash (a net current liability of $100) and its property, plant, and equipment valued at $3,000, while assuming Company ABC's long-term debt of $2,000.

(d) Cash borrowed by Company D for the year consisted of short-term debt of $75 and long-term debt of $1,250.

(e) Company D paid $300 on its short-term debt and $125 on capital lease obligations during the year.

(f) Company D issued $750 in common stock during the year, $250 of which was issued to settle long-term debt and $500 of which was issued for cash.

(g) Company D paid $450 as dividends to its stockholders during the year.

(h) Company D's financial services activities during the year included purchases and sales of investment securities amounting to $4,700 and $5,000, respectively. Lending activities produced new loans of $7,500 and collections of loans of $5,800. Customer deposits in its banking subsidiary increased by $1,100.

(i) Company D's operations for the year resulted in:

Net income	$ 3,000
Depreciation and amortization	1,500
Deferred taxes	150
Changes in operating working capital items other than cash:	
Increase in inventory	4,000
Decrease in accounts receivable	2,000
Increase in accounts payable	1,150
Changes in interest accruals:	
Increase in interest earned but not received	350
Increase in interest accrued but not paid	100
Cash received from customers for sales of goods	10,000
Cash dividends received	700
Cash paid to suppliers, employees	6,000
Cash paid for interest, taxes	1,750

(j) The effect on cash and cash equivalents of changes in the exchange rate for the year was $100.

3. Select a public company that uses the *direct* method of reporting cash flows from operations. Using only the balance sheet and income statement, estimate operating cash flows using the *indirect* method. If you are unable to reconcile the two amounts, why do you think this was the case, and what are the implications for comparability between the two methods?

BIBLIOGRAPHY OF REFERENCED WORKS

Accounting Principles Board (1963). "The Application and Source of Funds," *APB Opinion No. 3* (AICPA).

—— (1971). "Reporting Changes in Financial Position," *APB Opinion No. 19* (AICPA).

Backer, Morton, and Martin L. Gosman (1978). *Financial Reporting and Business Liquidity* (National Association of Accountants).

Chambers, Raymond J. (1966). *Accounting, Evaluation and Economic Behavior* (Prentice-Hall).

Clarkson, Geoffrey P. E. (1962). *Portfolio Selection: A Simulation of Trust Investment* (Prentice-Hall).

Financial Accounting Standards Board (1978). "Objectives of Financial Reporting by Business Enterprises," *Statement of Financial Accounting Concepts No. 1* (FASB).

—— (1980). *FASB Discussion Memorandum: An Analysis of Issues Related to Reporting Funds Flows, Liquidity, and Flexibility* (FASB).

—— (1984). "Recognition and Measurement in Financial Statements of Business Enterprises," *Statement of Financial Accounting Concepts No. 5* (FASB).

—— (1987). "Statement of Cash Flows," *Statement of Financial Accounting Standards No. 95* (FASB).

Hawkins, David F., and Walter J. Campbell (1978). *Equity Valuation: Models, Analysis and Implications* (Financial Executives Research Foundation).

Ketz, J. Edward, and James A. Largay III (1987). "Reporting Income and Cash Flows from Operations," *Accounting Horizons* (June 1987), pp. 9–17.

Largay, James A., and Clyde P. Stickney (1980). "Cash Flows, Ratio Analysis and the W. T. Grant Company Bankruptcy," *Financial Analysis Journal* (July–August 1980), pp. 51–54.

Lawson, G. H. (1971). "Cash-Flow Accounting," *Accountant* (October 1971), pp. 586–589; (November 1971), pp. 620–622.

—— (1985). "The Measurement of Corporate Performance on a Cash Flow Basis: A Reply to Mr. Egginton," *Accounting and Business Research* (Spring 1985), pp. 99–112.

Lee, T. A. (1972). "A Case for Cash Flow Reporting," *Journal of Business Finance* (Summer 1972), pp. 27–36.

—— (1983). "A Note on Users and Uses of Cash Flow Information," *Accounting and Business Research* (Spring 1983), pp. 103–106.

—— (1985). "Cash Flow Accounting, Profit and Performance Measurement: A Response to a Challenge," *Accounting and Business Research* (Spring 1985), pp. 93–97.

Louis Harris and Associates, Inc. (1980). "A Study of the Attitudes Toward and an Assessment of the Financial Accounting Standards Board" (Louis Harris and Associates, Inc.).

Mohr, Rosanne M. (1983). "The Segmental Reporting Issue: A Review of the Empirical Research," *Journal of Accounting Literature* (Spring 1983), pp. 39–71.

Securities and Exchange Commission (1970). "Adoption of Article 11A of Regulation S-X," *Accounting Series Release No. 117* (SEC).

Thomas, Arthur L. (1969). "The Allocation Problem," *Studies in Accounting Research #3* (American Accounting Association).

ADDITIONAL READINGS

Anton, Hector R. (1962). *Accounting for the Flow of Funds* (Houghton Mifflin, 1968).

Drtina, Ralph E., and James A. Largay III (1985). "Pitfalls in Calculating Cash Flow from Operations," *The Accounting Review* (April 1985), pp. 314–326.

Gombola, Michael J., and J. Edward Ketz (1983). "A Note on Cash Flow and Classification of Patterns of Financial Ratios," *The Accounting Review* (January 1983), pp. 105–114.

Gonedes, Nicholas J. (1969). "The Significance of Selected Accounting Procedures: A Statistical Test," *Empirical Research in Accounting: Selected Studies, 1969* (Supplement to *Journal of Accounting Research*), pp. 90–123.

Heath, Loyd C. (1978a). "Financial Reporting and the Evaluation of Solvency," *Accounting Research Monograph No. 3* (AICPA).

—— (1978b). "Let's Scrap the Funds' Statement," *Journal of Accountancy* (October 1978), pp. 94–103.

Huefner, Ronald J., J. Edward Ketz, and James A. Largay III (1989). "Foreign Currency

Translation and the Cash Flow Statement," *Accounting Horizons* (June 1989), pp. 66–75.

Ijiri, Yuji (1978). "Cash-Flow Accounting and Its Structure," *Journal of Accounting, Auditing and Finance* (Summer 1978), pp. 331–348.

Jaedicke, Robert K., and Robert T. Sprouse (1965). *Accounting Flows: Income, Funds and Cash* (Prentice-Hall).

Johnson, Orace (1970). "Towards an 'Events' Theory of Accounting," *The Accounting Review* (October 1970), pp. 641–653.

Kafer, Karl, and V. K. Zimmerman (1967). "Notes on the Evolution of the Source and Application of Funds," *International Journal of Accounting Education and Research* (Spring 1967), pp. 89–121.

Kochanek, Richard F., and Corine T. Norgaard (1988). "Analyzing the Components of Operating Cash Flow: The Charter Company," *Accounting Horizons* (March 1988), pp. 58–66.

Lee, T. A., and A. W. Stark (1987). "Ijiri's Cash Flow Accounting and Capital Budgeting," *Accounting and Business Research* (Spring 1987), pp. 125–131.

Mason, Perry (1961). "Cash Flow Analysis and the Funds Statement," *Accounting Research Study No. 2* (AICPA).

Nurnberg, Hugo (1989). "Depreciation in the Cash Flow Statement of Manufacturing Firms: Amount Incurred or Amount Expensed?" *Accounting Horizons* (March 1989), pp. 95–101.

Rosen, L. S., and Don T. DeCoster. "Funds' Statements: A Historical Perspective," *The Accounting Review* (January 1969), pp. 124–136.

Salamon, Gerald L. (1982). "Cash Recovery Rates and Measures of Firm Profitability," *The Accounting Review* (April 1982), pp. 292–302.

Sorter, George H. (1969). "An 'Events' Approach to Basic Accounting Theory," *The Accounting Review* (January 1969), pp. 12–19.

——— (1982). "The Emphasis on Cash and Its Impact on the Funds Statement — Sense and Nonsense," *Journal of Accounting, Auditing and Finance* (Spring 1982), pp. 188–194.

Thomas, Barbara S. (1983). "Deregulation and Cash Flow Reporting: One Viewpoint," *Financial Executive* (January 1983), pp. 20–24.

Yu, S. C. (1969). "A Flow of Resources Statement for Business Enterprises," *The Accounting Review* (July 1969), pp. 571–582.

CONCEPTUAL ISSUES IN ACCOUNTING FOR INFLATION AND CHANGING PRICES

INFLATION CAN BE DEFINED very simply as the rise in the average price level for all goods and services produced in an economy. We are all, of course, painfully aware of this phenomenon. It has wracked the United States fairly continually since the end of World War II and particularly since 1973 in the wake of the Arab oil boycott. Prices finally began moderating in the early 1980s, although the world events of 1990 could lead to a new inflationary cycle. It is fairly safe to say that inflation has posed the single greatest problem that we face in accounting theory. Finally, it should also be noted that, even in the absence of inflation, individual prices are always changing because of shifts in supply and demand for individual products and services.

Under a historical cost-based system of accounting, inflation leads to two basic problems. First, many of the historical numbers appearing on financial statements are not economically relevant because prices have changed since they were incurred. This is, of course, the problem of representational faithfulness discussed in SFAC 2 as an element of the primary quality of reliability. Second, since the numbers on financial statements represent dollars expended at different points of time and, in turn, embody different amounts of purchasing power, they are simply not additive. Hence, adding cash of $10,000 held on December 31, 1990 with $10,000 representing the cost of land acquired in 1955 (when the price level was significantly lower) is a dubious operation because of the significantly different amount of purchasing power represented by the two numbers.

Because of these two underlying problems, several aspects of the relevance quality are badly impaired under historical costing. It is quite likely that predictive value is diminished as a result of using and combining dollars of different purchasing power. Using financial reporting to determine accountability is similarly restricted owing to the basic shortcomings of historical costing, as is comparability among financial statements of different firms. Perhaps the principal deficiency resulting from the fundamental weaknesses of historical costs lies in the area of capital maintenance. Under historical costing, income is usually overstated relative to amounts that can be distributed to stockholders without reducing the beginning balance of the enterprise's net assets. Thus many "dividends" are really liquidating in nature, rather than derived from earnings (as they appear to be under historical costing).

The purpose of this chapter is to examine some of the principal financial reporting responses to inflation and changing prices. A better appreciation of the complexities of inflation accounting can be gained as a result of seeing how price indexes are devised. Consequently, the chapter begins by using a very simple example to illustrate how price indexes are constructed. An in-depth examination of the various accounting responses to inflation and changing prices comes next. Included in this section is an explanation of basic terms such as *holding gains* and *purchasing power gains*. With the various approaches to inflation in place, the third section presents a related series of simple examples showing the principal theoretical approaches to the problem. Of central importance here will be capital maintenance proofs, which underlie several of the methods. The concluding section of the chapter discusses two particularly difficult problem areas: (1) determining current value depreciation, and (2) purchasing power gains on long-term debt during inflation.

CONSTRUCTING PRICE INDEXES

In order to measure the change in the level of prices occurring during a particular time period, a price index must be constructed. A **price index** is a weighted average of the current prices of goods and services; these averages are related to prices in a base period, and their purpose is to determine how much change has occurred.

Price indexes may be narrowly constructed to determine the changing level of prices in a particular segment of the economy, such as capital equipment used in the steel industry, or broadly constructed for ascertaining the change in prices for all goods and services of an economy. The first type is called a *specific price index* and the second a *general price index*. For both types of indexes, considerable statistical sampling must be done because the number of goods and services involved, as well as the number of transactions occurring, may be very large. Hence, sampling error may easily occur, particularly if the weighting of certain transaction types is not representative of their actual occurrence during the period.

A simple example of price index construction is useful in terms of understanding the accounting process of price translation used in inflation accounting. Assume an economy in which only two goods, X and Y, are produced and consumed. The prices and quantities of X and Y sold during three periods are shown in Exhibit 12–1.

EXHIBIT 12–1

PRICES AND QUANTITIES OF X AND Y
SOLD DURING THREE TIME PERIODS

Time Period	Commodity X		Commodity Y	
	Price	Quantity	Price	Quantity
P_0	2.00	100	1.00	100
P_1	2.20	95	1.05	105
P_2	2.42	90	1.10	115

Our illustration includes two of the widely used types of indexes. The **Laspeyres index** is computed from the following formula:

$$I_n = 100 \cdot \frac{\sum_i P_{ni} \cdot Q_{oi}}{\sum_i P_{oi} \cdot Q_{oi}} \tag{12.1}$$

where

I_n = index number for year n
P_{ni} = price at period n of commodity i
P_{oi} = price at period o (the base period) of commodity i
Q_{oi} = quantity sold in period o of commodity i
$\sum_i$ = sum over all items

Substituting in the formula the transactions for commodities X and Y and using P_o as the base period, the indexes for P_1 and P_2 are

$$P_1 = 100 \cdot \frac{(2.20 \cdot 100) + (1.05 \cdot 100)}{(2.00 \cdot 100) + (1.00 \cdot 100)} = 108.33 \tag{12.1a}$$

$$P_2 = 100 \cdot \frac{(2.42 \cdot 100) + (1.10 \cdot 100)}{(2.00 \cdot 100) + (1.00 \cdot 100)} = 117.33 \tag{12.1b}$$

The index tells us that prices in P_1 are 8.33% higher than in the base year and 17.33% higher in P_2 relative to the base year. In P_2 prices rose 9% relative to P_o (117.33 − 108.33). Prices rose 8.3% in P_2 relative to P_1 [(117.33/108.33) − 1]. The latter calculation, in effect, substitutes P_1 as the base year.

Another frequently used price index is the **Paasche index.** It is computed by means of the following formula:

$$I_n = 100 \cdot \frac{\sum_i P_{ni} \cdot Q_{ni}}{\sum_i P_{oi} \cdot Q_{ni}} \tag{12.2}$$

where

Q_{ni} = quantity sold in period n of commodity i

Again substituting in the formula the transactions from Exhibit 12–1 and using P_o as the base period, the indexes for P_1 and P_2 are

$$P_1 = 100 \cdot \frac{(2.20 \cdot 95) + (1.05 \cdot 105)}{(2.00 \cdot 95) + (1.00 \cdot 105)} = 108.22 \qquad \textbf{(12.2a)}$$

$$P_2 = 100 \cdot \frac{(2.42 \cdot 90) + (1.00 \cdot 115)}{(2.00 \cdot 90) + (1.00 \cdot 115)} = 116.71 \qquad \textbf{(12.2b)}$$

Paasche index calculations state that prices in P_1 are 8.22% higher than in the base year and 16.71% higher in P_2 relative to the base year. Compared to P_1, the price rise in P_2 is 7.84% $[(116.71/108.22) - 1]$. P_1 is used as the base year in the latter calculation.

As this example shows, Laspeyres indexes use base-year quantities only, whereas Paasche indexes employ current-year quantities. Whereas Laspeyres calculations may be somewhat "purer" because they employ base-year quantities throughout, Paasche calculations take into account movement into goods and commodities that have become relatively cheaper, as can be seen even in this very simple illustration. As a result, Paasche indexes may better reflect technological change since lower costs should result from using improved technology. On the other hand, because changes in quantities are largely ignored, Laspeyres indexes are less costly to construct.[1] The Wholesale Price Index (of the Department of Commerce) and the Consumer Price Index (prepared by the Department of Labor) are both Laspeyres-type indexes. SFAS 33 required Laspeyres indexes for general price-level adjustment.

Price index calculations are obviously extremely complex. In addition to the far more important problem of possible sampling error, the fact that several index types exist indicates that a conceptual problem of measurement is also present. Nevertheless, it appears to be far better to attempt to measure the results of inflation, no matter how crudely accomplished, than to ignore the problem.

AN OVERVIEW OF INFLATION ACCOUNTING

In discussing responses to inflation, one distinction must immediately be stressed: that between general purchasing power adjustment and current valuation. The difference in purpose and approach was briefly discussed in Chapter 1. General price-level adjustment is concerned with the change in purchasing power of the monetary unit over time relative to all goods and services produced by the economy. Adjustment is accomplished by taking the historical cost of an item and multiplying it by a fraction consisting of the general price index for the current period in the numerator divided by the general price index existing at the time of acquisition. Hence, if the price of land acquired for

---

[1] For more on these points, see Weil (1976, pp. 101–104).

$10,000 in 1954, when the price index was 80, were being restated into 1989 dollars, when the index was 220, the calculation would be

$$\$10,000 \times \frac{220}{80} = \$27,500$$

The $27,500 does not in any sense, except by pure coincidence, represent the value of the land in 1989.[2] The cost has simply been translated into the number of 1989 dollars having purchasing power equivalent to the number of dollars originally expended in 1954. Of course our examination of price index construction in the previous section shows that this is no easy measurement task.

Current valuation — also called *current cost* — represents an attempt to derive the specific value or worth for a particular point or period in time of assets, liabilities, expenses, and revenues. The two types of current valuation, referred to in Chapter 1, are called *entry* and *exit values*.[3] *Entry value* refers to replacement cost in markets in which the asset, liability, or expense is ordinarily acquired by the enterprise. *Exit valuation* refers to the net realizable value or disposal value of the firm's assets and liabilities in what has been termed a system of "orderly liquidation."[4] Both measures are examples of opportunity costs and both are certainly relevant in some decision situations, such as capital budgeting. The underlying arguments, both pro and con, for these measurements require a closer examination.

ENTRY VALUES

One of the principal arguments of entry-value adherents is that in most cases, value in use to the firm is best represented by replacement cost. In order to understand the meaning of "value in use" for assets, three valuations must be compared: present value of future cash flows attributable to the asset (PV), entry value or replacement cost (EV), and exit or net realizable value (NRV).[5]

---

[2] If the land was restated in 1988 to $26,250 when the index was 210, the $27,500 can also be determined by taking $26,250 × (220/210).

[3] The terms appear to have first been used by Edwards and Bell in their classic work with regard to three different time dimensions: past, current, and future. See Edwards and Bell (1961, pp. 74–80). Today the terms *entry value* and *exit value* used alone are understood as referring to the present time dimension.

[4] Edwards and Bell (1961, p. 76) denote *exit value* as being net of removal costs and transport and installation costs that the seller might have to bear. For major fixed-asset installations, these costs might be considerable. Sterling, in his conception of exit value, attempts to measure the *net* amount of cash that would be received from the immediate sale of an asset (Sterling, personal correspondence). Hence, for a major asset such as a printing press, exit value would be the firm's selling price less any tearing out costs. On the other hand, for an asset such as an oil deposit, exit value would consist of the selling price of the asset *as it is* in the ground. See Sterling (1979, p. 220). Chambers does not even appear to treat the issue in his major work. However, his definition of *current cash equivalent* does not appear to take these reductions into account. See Chambers (1966, pp. 201–202, 208–209, and 218), for example. For exit values to be representationally faithful to the concept of measuring the total funds available to the firm, selling price net of costs of disposition appears to be the most appropriate measure. Of course, these costs would fall heaviest in the first year of an asset's use.

[5] There has been an extensive discussion and analysis of "value in use" and the relation of these concepts in the literature. See, for example, Solomons (1966, pp. 122–125), Bell (1971, pp. 26–31), Parker and

Possible Ordering Combinations

With three value types, six possible ordering combinations can occur:

1. NRV>PV>EV
2. NRV > EV > PV
3. PV > EV > NRV
4. PV > NRV > EV
5. EV > PV > NRV
6. EV > NRV > PV

All three measures would be identical for cash. PV and EV would appear to be virtually identical for accounts and notes receivable net of allowance for doubtful accounts. NRV would be lower, as evidenced by factoring of accounts receivable and discounting of notes receivable. EV is higher than NRV for marketable securities due to the effect of commissions. The crucial assets — because of their materiality — are inventories held for resale, productive fixed assets, and possibly intangibles. Our analysis, therefore, concentrates on inventories and fixed assets.

An asset should be held for use as long as PV > NRV. If, on the other hand, NRV > PV, the asset should be sold. Consequently, in situations 3, 4, and 5 assets will be held for use, whereas in 1, 2, and 6 they should be sold. Situations 3, 4, and 5 would definitely appear to be applicable to the majority of fixed and intangible assets. Assets should continue to be used and replaced as long as situations 3 and 4 prevail because productive usage (represented by PV) predominates. Situation 3, in fact, would be expected to be the single most predominant circumstance for productive fixed assets. Situation 4 would be highly unusual. Since NRV is greater than EV, the asset should be sold as well as used, though primary use would continue to be productive because PV > NRV. In situation 5 the asset should continue to be used productively but should not be replaced.

In cases 3, 4, and 5, PV represents value in use to the firm. However, since PV is based on estimating and discounting future values, it will assuredly be less verifiable than either EV or NRV. Given the choice between EV and NRV as a proxy for PV, it should be borne in mind that the latter will almost always be lower than the former for three reasons: (1) NRV includes the effects of tearing out costs and other disposal-related elements; (2) since the enterprise is only a sporadic seller of productive fixed assets, it may be able to communicate with only a limited number of potential buyers of the asset; (3) since the firm does not ordinarily deal in the productive asset, perceptions of its quality may be more negative than is warranted. The difference between EV and NRV is thus brought about by special considerations that are totally unrelated to productive usage represented by PV. Therefore, EV appears to be a better indicator of

---

Harcourt (1969, pp. 15–20), and Ashton (1987). Even though exit value and net realizable value are often used synonymously, there is a technical difference. Net realizable value is a future cash inflow from selling an asset less present and future cash outflows to complete, dispose, and sell the asset. In some interpretations (inventory valuations, for example), normal profit margin is also deducted. Exit value, on the other hand, is a present price rather than a future price.

economic value than NRV for productive fixed assets and intangibles. For these assets EV would thus appear to have greater utility for purposes such as predictive ability and accountability.

Situations 1, 2, and 6, where resale is appropriate, would be applicable to inventories. Case 6 indicates that the item should be sold but not replaced. NRV represents selling price of inventories less costs of completion and selling. The main difference between NRV and EV is the unrealized income element, even though both are a form of current value. A case might therefore be made for NRV for inventories resulting in multivaluation bases for assets, but this treatment leads to the additivity problem.[6] Consequently, on the basis of analysis of value in use for inventories and fixed assets, if one valuation base is to be selected, an extremely strong case can be made for EV.

Measurement Problems

There are numerous estimation difficulties in determining current entry valuations. Direct measurements are preferable to indirect ones because they are more representationally faithful, more verifiable, and usually less expensive to produce.

Direct measurement for inventories would be accomplished by obtaining the current selling price in the market where goods are normally acquired by the firm — or the current manufacturing cost if the firm usually produces them. There should be no problem for commonly acquired items, but manufactured goods present a more complex situation. Current costs of raw materials, direct labor, and variable overhead are relatively easy to find out. Fixed overhead costs, particularly depreciation, are more difficult. Consequently, indirect measurement of the fixed overhead element of manufactured inventories by means of specific index adjustment may have to be employed.

In the case of fixed assets, direct measurement would be accomplished by finding the selling price in the used-asset market for the same type of asset in the same condition as that being valued. Appropriate secondhand valuation is possible only for a relatively small proportion of fixed assets. The replacement cost of the majority of fixed assets would have to be indirectly measured by means of appropriate specific index adjustment.

EXIT VALUES

The underlying rationale of exit valuation is totally different from that for entry value. Exit-value adherents see the firm in a constant state of flux. Over a long enough period of time, a firm will indeed turn over the majority of its productive assets. Exit-value balance sheets provide a measure of the firm's adaptability: the capacity to switch out of its present asset structure into new opportunities. *Exit valuation* denotes the selling price that can be received from the firm's assets when sold through a process of orderly liquidation, that is, a situation in

---

[6] Indeed, Sprouse and Moonitz (1962, p. 57) opted for net realizable value of inventories in their broad principles study.

which the firm continues operations, as opposed to the larger discounts arising in forced liquidation circumstances.[7]

Under exit valuation, the balance sheet becomes the principal financial statement. The income statement shows the increase in the firm's adaptive ability resulting from operations during the period. However, the income statement under exit valuation is likely to severely limit predictive ability and accountability because of disproportionate declines from purchase price to exit valuation that arise immediately after an asset is acquired, as discussed above. Indeed exit-value partisans deny that accounting numbers can have significance for predictive-ability purposes.[8]

Exit values are a form of opportunity cost. They represent the sacrifice to the enterprise of holding its existing package of assets. Unquestionably, exit values also provide numbers that are additive. On balance, however, despite a small but vocal number of supporters, the preponderance of opinion among both researchers and members of standard-setting bodies is strongly disposed toward replacement costs. The advantage of entry values is comparative, rather than absolute. Both numbers have relevance based on the particular situation. Capital budgeting analyses, for example, require the exit values of currently owned assets that may be disposed of and the entry values of assets that may be acquired. Both measures can be criticized on grounds of what can be termed "inapplicability." What is the significance of replacement cost if the asset is already owned? It is a matter, perhaps, of avoided sacrifice. Similarly, how meaningful is exit valuation if the present intention is to keep the asset? In this case it is a matter of opportunities foregone.

Unquestionably, both measures have relevance. Our value judgment agrees with the majority. Although exit values have importance, the great majority of an enterprise's assets will virtually never be converted into cash during any given short-run period. Furthermore, the weakness of the exit-value-oriented income statement in terms of user objectives other than adaptive ability has already been discussed. Conversely, the value-in-use analysis, particularly as applied to productive fixed assets, is indeed persuasive. Thus, the balance of our current value discussion will concentrate on the entry-value alternative.

PURCHASING POWER GAINS AND LOSSES

Purchasing power gains and losses arise as a result of holding net monetary assets or liabilities during a period when the price level changes. **Monetary**

---

[7] *Orderly liquidation* refers to disposal of assets in the usual course of business operations where the firm is not forced to accept heavily discounted prices. See Chambers (1966, p. 204). Of course, it would be impossible, by definition, to have an orderly liquidation of an enterprise's entire stock of nonmonetary assets.

[8] Sterling (1979, pp. 125–136) contrasts measurements concerned with objective assessments of existing attributes of assets with forecasts of future phenomena, which are subjective and personal in nature. Chambers (1968, pp. 245–246) is far more vehement in his views. He strongly contrasts measurement of existing phenomena and any goal of predictive ability, which he sees as being tied to the process of "valuation."

EXHIBIT 12–2

PURCHASING POWER GAINS AND LOSSES

	State of the Economy	
State of the Enterprise	Inflation	Deflation
Net Monetary Asset Position	Purchasing Power Loss	Purchasing Power Gain
Net Monetary Liability Position	Purchasing Power Gain	Purchasing Power Loss

assets and liabilities include cash itself and other assets and liabilities that are receivable or payable in a fixed number of dollars. These include accounts and notes receivable and payable and also long-term liabilities.[9]

Purchasing power gains and losses arise because monetary items, which are fixed in terms of the number of dollars to be received or paid, gain or lose purchasing power as the price level changes. The potential for gains and losses is summarized in Exhibit 12-2 where "net monetary assets" refers to total monetary assets exceeding monetary liabilities and the converse is true for "net monetary liabilities."

Purchasing power gains and losses are determined by measuring the purchasing power of the monetary items available to a firm and comparing it with the actual amount of the net monetary accounts. A simple example should clarify the method of measurement. Assume a firm's activity in its monetary elements is summarized in the T-account that follows:

Net Monetary Assets

Beginning balance	$10,000		
1st quarter net inflows	8,000	2nd quarter net outflows	$12,000
3rd quarter net inflows	13,000		
4th quarter net inflows	6,000		
	37,000		$12,000
Ending balance	$25,000		

The general price index shows the following for the year:

Beginning index	180
1st quarter	192
2nd quarter	197

---

[9] For an excellent discussion and analysis of the monetary versus nonmonetary distinction, see Heath (1972).

3rd quarter   205

4th quarter   210

   To measure the purchasing power gain or loss for the year stated in terms of the purchasing power of the dollar during the 4th quarter, the beginning balance and the subsequent changes in net monetary items are restated in terms of their purchasing power measured in 4th-quarter terms. This is done by multiplying these elements by a fraction consisting of the 4th-quarter index in the numerator, divided by the index at the time the net change occurred or when the item was on hand (in the case of the beginning balance). This is shown in the following T-account:

Net Monetary Assets (in terms of 4th-quarter purchasing power)

$\$10,000 \times \dfrac{210}{180} = \$11,667$	
$8,000 \times \dfrac{210}{192} = 8,750$	$12,000 \times \dfrac{210}{197}$ $\qquad$ $\$12,792$
$13,000 \times \dfrac{210}{205} = 13,317$	
$6,000 \times \dfrac{210}{210} = \underline{6,000}$	$\underline{}$
$39,734$	$\underline{\$12,792}$
$\underline{\$26,942}$	

   The ending balance in the price-level-adjusted T-account shows the monetary purchasing power available to the firm measured in 4th-quarter dollars. Since this is more than the actual amount of net monetary assets at the end of the year, the firm has lost purchasing power by holding net monetary assets during a period when the value of the dollar was declining.

   All systems of both general purchasing-power-adjusted income and current value income include purchasing power gains and losses as an element of income. The measurement itself, however, may be in either general or specific purchasing power terms.[10] Classification would be as a nonoperating component of income.

HOLDING GAINS AND LOSSES

Just as monetary items are subject to a gain or loss as the price level changes, nonmonetary assets (which we will call *real assets*) are subject to a gain or loss as a result of change in their value. **Holding gains and losses** on real assets can be divided into two parts: (1) monetary holding gains and losses, which arise purely because of the change in the general price level during the period; and (2) real holding gains and losses, which are the difference between general

---

[10]For a discussion of the choice, see Gynther (1966, pp. 155–158).

price-level-adjusted amounts and current values. Monetary holding gains and losses are capital adjustments only; they are not a component of income. The disposition of real holding gains and losses is an important theoretical issue affecting the determination of income; we will examine that issue shortly.

Holding gains and losses can also be classified from the standpoint of being realized or unrealized in the conventional accounting sense.[11] A simple example should clarify these relationships. Assume that a piece of land was acquired for $5,000 on January 2, 1990, when the general price index was 100. One-tenth of the land was sold on December 31, 1990, for $575. The entire parcel of land was valued at $5,750 on December 31, 1990. The total real and monetary holding gains are computed in the following manner:

Current value on December 31, 1990	$5,750
General price-level-adjusted historical cost on Dec. 31, 1990 $\left(\$5,000 \times \dfrac{110}{100}\right)$	5,500
Total real holding gain	$ 250
General price-level-adjusted historical cost on Dec. 31, 1990	$5,500
Historical cost	5,000
Total monetary holding gain	$ 500

The total holding gain comprises the algebraic sum of the real and monetary holding gains or losses. Hence, if all the facts were the same except that the current value of the land was $5,400 on December 31, 1990, there would have been a total real holding loss of $100. Holding gains and losses are realized by the process of selling the asset or, in the case of a depreciable asset, using it up over time.[12] The division of the holding gains in the example is summarized in Exhibit 12–3.

With the concepts of holding gains and purchasing power gains and losses in place, we now take up an examination of income measurement systems that attempt to cope with the inflation problem and their underlying rationales.

INCOME MEASUREMENT SYSTEMS

This section illustrates by means of a relatively simple example both income statements and balance sheets that use different theoretical approaches to the inflation problem. Our principal focus, however, will be on the income statement because it poses many significant theoretical issues. Balance sheets using general price-level adjustment and current valuation for capital maintenance purposes are shown in Exhibits 12–8 and 12–10.

---

[11] A good example is shown by Edwards (1954).
[12] See Edwards and Bell (1961, pp. 112–114) for further details.

EXHIBIT 12–3

ANALYSIS OF HOLDING GAINS

| | Holding Gain Type | | |
State	Real	Monetary	Total
Realized	$ 25	$ 50	$ 75
Unrealized	225	450	675
Total	$250	$500	$750

GENERAL PRICE-LEVEL ADJUSTMENT (GPLA)

The one additional point that should be added to the discussion of GPLA in Chapter 1 concerns the type of capital maintenance it provides. Historical costs measure capital maintenance in terms of unadjusted dollars. GPLA goes one step further; capital maintenance is measured in terms of general price-level-adjusted dollars.[13]

CURRENT VALUE APPROACHES

The three approaches to current value discussed here are oriented to entry-valuation methods. All will show current operating income (revenues minus expenses computed on a replacement cost basis). Therefore, current operating income should have user relevance from the standpoint of accountability and, quite possibly, of predictive ability. The methods differ in terms of disposition of real holding gains and the resulting type of capital maintenance measure.

Distributable Income (DI)

Under DI, real capital gains are considered to be capital adjustments.[14] The resulting capital maintenance is in physical capital terms because income is equal to the excess of revenues over expenses measured in replacement cost terms. The purchasing power gain or loss is computed by using a Paasche type of index to measure the change in the replacement costs of the operating assets used by the enterprise.

---

[13] Hendriksen (1982, pp. 224–225) suggests that price-level adjustment of real accounts can be achieved by use of specific indexes as well as by a general price-level index. He suggests three possible specific indexes: (1) investment goods in general, (2) capital goods generally acquired by the industry of which the enterprise is a member, and (3) goods similar to those that the firm itself has been investing in during past periods. The resulting capital maintenance measures would be entity-theory oriented.

[14] Revsine (1973, pp. 34–35 and 128–129) uses the term *distributable operating flows*, but it is the same as *distributable income* as used here. The same concept has also been called *disposable income* by Zeff (1962, pp. 617–621).

Realized Income (RI)

As the name implies, realized components of real holding gains are routed through income.[15] The resulting capital maintenance measure is generally quite similar to that provided under GPLA even though the statements are totally different in other respects. The reason is that replacement-cost measures of expenses, by definition, exceed historical costs by realized portions of monetary and real holding gains. When realized real holding gains are run through income, the result is generally similar to income determination under GPLA.

Earning Power Income (EPI)

All real holding gains arising during the period, whether or not realized, are components of income under EPI.[16] This method has been advocated on the grounds that real holding gains are an indicator or "signal" to users that real future earnings of the firm in the future are expected to increase.[17] Future income is expected to rise on the presumption that real holding gains indicate an increasing demand for goods and services provided by the particular enterprise. EPI is thus recommended for predictive-ability reasons.

Unfortunately, the rationale underlying EPI has several drawbacks. If productive assets and resources are used by several industries, increasing demand for final product in some industries may drive up the cost of inputs for all firms — including those that experience no such increase in demand for final product. Therefore, the real holding gain may be quite illusory for many firms in terms of signaling future increases in income. Another possibility is that real holding gains may stem from supply-side conditions rather than from demand. A good example is the OPEC cartel's control over petroleum prices, particularly during the 1970s.

Capital maintenance under EPI is geared to treating total real holding gains arising during the period as elements of income (these are also referred to as *realizable real holding gains*).[18]

AN ILLUSTRATION

Assume that W-F-T Company had the historical cost balance sheet on December 31, 1991, shown in Exhibit 12–4. The fixed assets were acquired on January 2, 1990. They are expected to have a seven-year productive life with no salvage value. The merchandise inventory was acquired during 1991. The historical-cost income statement for 1992 is shown in Exhibit 12–5. Revenues resulted from cash sales. No other transactions occurred during 1992 except for those indicated by the income statement.

---

[15] Edwards and Bell (1961, pp. 117–119) use the term *realized profit* similarly to the way *realized income* is used here. It is also similar to *current real income* as used by Bell (1986).

[16] *Earning power income* was used by Zeff (1962, p. 617). It is more descriptive than the term *business profit* used by Edwards and Bell (1961, pp. 119–122).

[17] For an interesting critique, see Revsine (1981a, pp. 347–348).

[18] We are indebted to Philip W. Bell for clarifying the issue of capital maintenance where EPI is used.

EXHIBIT 12–4

W-F-T COMPANY BALANCE SHEET
December 31, 1991

Assets

Cash		$15,000
Merchandise Inventory		15,000
Fixed Assets	$28,000	
Less: Accumulated Depreciation	8,000	20,000
Total Assets		$50,000

Liabilities and Owners' Equities

5% Bonds Payable	$10,000
Capital Stock	20,000
Retained Earnings	20,000
Total Liabilities and Owners' Equities	$50,000

EXHIBIT 12–5

W-F-T COMPANY INCOME STATEMENT
For the Year Ending December 31, 1992

Revenues		$15,000
Operating Expenses		
Cost of Goods Sold	$ 6,000	
Depreciation	4,000	10,000
Operating Income		5,000
Bond Interest Expense		500
Net Income		$ 4,500

For purposes of replacement-cost valuation, the firm is using appropriate specific price indexes for inventories and fixed assets in lieu of direct measurements of replacement cost. One of the hallmarks of current value accounting is that measurements of asset values and expenses are expected to be realistic approximations of the economic values they are intended to portray. In other words, they are expected to have a high degree of representational faithfulness. We assume in this illustration that specific index adjustment of straight-line historical cost depreciation provides a measure of current value depreciation that is representationally faithful. More will be said shortly about measuring current values.

General and specific price indexes are shown in Exhibit 12–6. For simplicity in this example, we assume that prices change once and for all in 1991 and 1992 on January 1.

General Price-Level Adjustment

The GPLA income statement for 1992 and the translations from historical cost to GPLA is shown in Exhibit 12–7. The purchasing power loss is computed by taking the net monetary assets on December 31, 1991, of $5,000 (cash of $15,000 less bonds payable of $10,000) and multiplying it by (110 − 105)/105, which equals $238. The numerator represents the change in general purchasing power in 1992 relative to 1991.

A capital maintenance proof is shown in Exhibit 12–8. Since the beginning and ending balance sheets under historical costing are not expressed in units of the same general purchasing power, a common unit of measurement must be used. Because GPLA income for 1992 was stated in terms of the general purchasing power of the dollar in 1992, the two encompassing balance sheets are likewise stated in the same way. Monetary assets and liabilities in the opening balance sheet must be restated to cost them in units of 1992 purchasing power. No restatement, however, of monetary items in the ending balance sheet is made because they are, by definition, expressed in terms of purchasing power in 1992.

Notice that the difference between opening and closing net assets is equal to income for the year computed under GPLA. Hence, GPLA income is the maximum that can be distributed as dividends and still leave the enterprise as well off (in terms of GPLA-adjusted owners' equities) at the end of the year as it was at the beginning of the year.

GPLA adjustment brings additivity to both the balance sheet and income statement because dollars of the same general purchasing power are used throughout. GPLA adjustment can be construed as adhering to the proprie-

---

EXHIBIT 12–6

GENERAL AND SPECIFIC PRICE INDEXES

Index Type	Year		
	1990	1991	1992
General price index	100	105	110
Specific price index applicable to firm's merchandise inventory	100	110	120
Specific price index applicable to firm's fixed assets	100	102	105

EXHIBIT 12–7

GENERAL PRICE-LEVEL ADJUSTED
INCOME STATEMENT

For the Year Ended December 31, 1992

	Historical Cost	Conversion Factor	GPLA
Revenues	$15,000	—	$15,000
Operating Expenses			
Cost of Goods Sold	6,000	$\dfrac{110}{105}$	6,285
Depreciation	4,000	$\dfrac{110}{100}$	4,400
Total Expenses	10,000		10,685
Operating Income	5,000		4,315
Other Expenses			
Bond Interest	500		500
Purchasing Power Loss on Net Monetary Assets	—		238[a]
Total	—		738
Net Income	$ 4,500		$ 3,577

[a] $\dfrac{110 - 105}{105}$ ($15,000 − $10,000)

EXHIBIT 12–8

CAPITAL MAINTENANCE UNDER GENERAL PRICE-LEVEL ADJUSTMENT

	(1) 12/31/91	(2) Conversion Factor	(3) Restated in 1992 Dollars	(4) 12/31/92	(5) Conversion Factor	(6) Restated in 1992 Dollars	(7) Net Change in 1992 Dollars[a]
Cash	$15,000	110/105	$15,714	$29,500	—	$29,500	$13,786
Merchandise Inventory	15,000	110/105	15,714	9,000	110/105	9,429	(6,285)
Fixed Assets	28,000	110/100	30,800	28,000	110/100	30,800	—
Less: Accumulated Depreciation	(8,000)	110/100	(8,800)	(12,000)	110/100	(13,200)	(4,400)
Total Assets	50,000		53,428	54,500		56,529	3,101
5% Bonds Payable	(10,000)	110/105	(10,476)	(10,000)	—	(10,000)	476
Owners' Equity (Net Assets)	$40,000		$42,952	$44,500		$46,529	$ 3,577

[a] Column 6 minus Column 3

tary-theory approach mentioned in Chapter 5. The reason underlying the proprietary orientation is that general purchasing power would be more representative of the orientation of the owners of the enterprise than would specialized asset indexes.

Distributable Income

DI is a replacement-cost approach that attempts to measure the maximum dividend that can be paid to stockholders without impairing the level of future operations. This is accomplished, as mentioned previously, by deducting from revenues the current value (replacement cost) of expenses incurred during the period. Holding gains must be treated as capital adjustments. Hence, there is no distinction between monetary and real holding gains. The DI statement for 1992 is shown in Exhibit 12–9.

The purchasing power loss on net monetary assets was determined by a Paasche type of specific index geared to the firm's mix of real assets:

$$I_2 - I_1 = \frac{\sum_i (P_{ni} \cdot Q_{ni})}{\sum_i (P_{oi} \cdot Q_{ni})} \frac{\sum_i (P_{(n-1)i} \cdot Q_{ni})}{\sum_i (P_{oi} \cdot Q_{ni})} \qquad (12.3)$$

EXHIBIT 12–9

DISTRIBUTABLE INCOME STATEMENT

For the Year Ended December 31, 1992

	Historical Cost	Specific Index Conversion Factor	Current Value
Revenues	$15,000	—	$15,000
Operating Expenses			
Cost of Goods Sold	6,000	$\frac{120}{110}$	6,545
Depreciation	4,000	$\frac{105}{100}$	4,200
Total Expenses	10,000		10,745
Current Operating Income	5,000		4,255
Other Expenses			
Bond Interest	500		500
Purchasing Power Loss on Net Monetary Assets	—		292
	—		792
Current Net Income (Distributable)	$ 4,500		$ 3,463

where

$I_2 - I_1$ = change in the firm's weighted average of its specific asset holdings from last year to this year

$P_{(n-1)i}$ = price of the ith commodity in the previous year (I_1)

Substituting from our example, we have

$$\frac{\left(\$20,000 \cdot \frac{105}{100}\right) + \left(\$15,000 \cdot \frac{120}{110}\right)}{\$20,000 + \left(\$15,000 \cdot \frac{100}{110}\right)}$$

$$-\frac{\left(\$20,000 \cdot \frac{102}{100}\right) + \left(\$15,000 \cdot \frac{110}{110}\right)}{\$20,000 + \left(\$15,000 \cdot \frac{100}{110}\right)} = 5.84\% \qquad (12.3a)$$

The denominators of the two terms are expressed in base-year prices (1990) for the composition of real assets held at the end of 1991. The two terms in the numerator are stated in 1992 and 1991 prices, respectively. The resulting 5.84% rise in the firm's weighted average of real assets is multiplied by the $5,000 of net monetary assets shown on the December 31, 1991 balance sheet to arrive at the specific purchasing power loss of $292.[19]

A capital maintenance proof in the specific purchasing power of the enterprise is shown in Exhibit 12-10. The beginning and ending balance sheets are shown in terms of 1992 replacement costs. Beginning-of-period monetary items are adjusted by the firm-specific index to make them comparable in specific purchasing power to the ending monetary items. Once again the net asset differential equals income.

The firm-specific measure of capital maintenance shown in Exhibit 12–10 becomes less relevant as the probability increases that the enterprise will invest in assets outside its present industry. DI is a measure oriented toward entity theory because it is geared to the enterprise maintaining its productive capacity (in real terms).

Realized Income

In the last two methods to be illustrated, general price-level adjustment and replacement costs are both employed with holding gains segregated into monetary and real portions. Under RI, the realized portion of real holding gains is added back to income. If a general price-level index is used to determine purchasing power gains or losses on monetary items, the resulting bottom line is quite consistent with GPLA adjustment even though the income statement organization is totally different.

The reason is that the adding back of the realized real holding gain com-

---

[19] For an extensive discussion of specific price index construction, see Tritschler (1969, pp. 99–124).

EXHIBIT 12–10

DISTRIBUTABLE INCOME CAPITAL MAINTENANCE

	(1) 12/31/91	(2) Specific Conversion Factor	(3) Restated in 1992 Dollars	(4) 12/31/92	(5) Specific Conversion Factor	(6) Current Value in 1992 Dollars	(7) Net Specific Change[a]
Cash	$15,000	1.0584	$15,876	$29,500	—	$29,500	$13,624
Merchandise Inventory	15,000	$\frac{120}{110}$	16,364	9,000	$\frac{120}{110}$	9,818	(6,545)
Fixed Assets	28,000	$\frac{105}{100}$	29,400	28,000	$\frac{105}{100}$	29,400	—
Less: Accumulated Depreciation	(8,000)	$\frac{105}{100}$	(8,400)	(12,000)	$\frac{105}{100}$	(12,600)	(4,200)
Total Assets	50,000		53,240	54,500		56,118	2,879
5% Bonds Payable	10,000	1.0584	10,584	10,000	—	10,000	584
Owners' Equity (Net Assets)	$40,000		$42,656	$44,500		$46,118	$ 3,463

[a]Column 6 minus Column 3

ponent of cost of goods sold and depreciation leaves in effect only the GPLA component of these expenses that are beyond historical cost. It should be understood that the change in the general purchasing power of the dollar is reflected in specific price indexes. Therefore, the real holding gain element can be determined by taking the general price-level component out of the specific index. This is done in the footnote of the RI income statement shown in Exhibit 12–11.[20]

Earning Power Income

EPI includes in income all real holding gains arising during the year. The concept does not appear to be strongly rooted in either entity or proprietary theory. It might be loosely related to the residual-equity theory because of the presumed predictive usefulness of the real holding gains arising during the year. (If a capital maintenance proof is desired, beginning-of-period real-asset balances must be adjusted by the general price-level change occurring during the year 1992).[21] If purchasing power gain or loss on monetary items is computed,

[20] The monetary and real holding gains shown in Exhibit 12–11 are based on changes from the preceding year, except for the fixed assets that were purchased during 1990. The real change was related to the 1990 acquisition date for the fixed assets. The realized real holding loss is also equal to the excess of general price-level adjusted depreciation of $4,400 shown in Exhibit 12–7 and current value depreciation of $4,200. No capital maintenance proof is shown because net income is exactly the same as GPLA-adjusted income.

[21] The real holding gain arising during 1992 included in income must be calculated from the preceding year ($ − 371 in footnote b to Exhibit 12–12) rather than from the base year ($ − 400 in Exhibit 12–12).

EXHIBIT 12–11

REALIZED INCOME STATEMENT

For the Year Ended December 31, 1992

	Historical Cost	Conversion Factor	Current Value
Revenues	$15,000	—	$15,000
Operating Expenses			
Cost of Goods Sold	6,000	$\dfrac{120}{110}$	6,545
Depreciation	4,000	$\dfrac{105}{100}$	4,200
Total Expenses	10,000		10,745
Current Operating Income	5,000		4,255
Other Revenues and Expenses			
Bond Interest	500		500
Purchasing Power Loss on Net Monetary Assets	—		238
Realized Real Holding Gains and Losses			
Cost of Goods Sold			(260)[a]
Fixed Assets			200[b]
Total			678
Current Net Income (Realized)	$ 4,500		$ 3,577

[a]Specific index change for 1992 relative to 1991 minus the general index change for 1992 relative to 1991: [(120 − 110)/(110)] − [(110 − 105)/(105)] = 4.33%. The 4.33% is multiplied by the historical cost of goods sold of $6,000 to arrive at $260.
[b]Same procedure for fixed assets as for cost of goods sold: (5/100) − (10/100) = −5%, which is multiplied by depreciation of $4,000 to arrive at −$200. Notice that this is also the difference between current value depreciation of $4,200 and GPLA adjusted depreciation of $4,400.

we lean toward use of the general price-level index in the measurement; but theory is still inconclusive on this question. The EPI statement is shown in Exhibit 12–12.

THE ISSUE OF CAPITAL MAINTENANCE

Referring back to the capital maintenance proofs, GPLA and RI measure financial capital maintenance (in dollars adjusted for the change in general purchasing power), whereas DI provides a measure of physical capital maintenance. The latter is accomplished by not including any real holding gains or losses in income and using an index of price changes applicable to the firm's real assets

EXHIBIT 12–12

EARNING POWER INCOME STATEMENT

For the Year Ended December 31, 1992

	Historical Cost	Conversion Factor	Current Value
Revenues	$15,000	—	$15,000
Operating Expenses			
Cost of Goods Sold	6,000	$\dfrac{120}{110}$	6,545
Depreciation	4,000	$\dfrac{105}{100}$	4,200
Total Expenses	10,000		10,745
Current Operating Income	5,000		4,255
Other Revenues and Expenses			
Bond Interest	500		500
Purchasing Power Loss on Net Monetary Assets	—		238
Real Holding Gains			
Inventories			(649)[a]
Fixed Assets			400[b]
Total			489
Current Net Income (Earning Power)	$ 4,500		$ 3,766

[a] The entire inventory of $15,000 is now multiplied by 4.33% computed in Exhibit 12–11.

[b] Realizable holding gain is determined in three steps:

(1) Compute the holding gain for a two-year-old asset:

Estimated replacement cost of a similar two-year-old asset *after* the price rise ($28,000 × 1.05 × 5/7)	$21,000
Estimated replacement cost of a similar two-year-old asset *before* the price rise ($28,000 × 1.02 × 5/7)	20,400
Total holding gain	$ 600

(2) Break the $600 into its real and monetary components:

Since specific prices have increased by 3% (105 − 102) and general prices have risen by 5% (110 − 105), the real price rise from 1991 to 1992 is −2%.

(3) The holding gains are:

Monetary ($20,000 × .05)	$ 1,000
Real ($20,000 × −.02)	− 400
Total	$ 600

The division of the holding gain shown above determined the specific and general price-level changes relative to the base year 1990. The splits could also have been based on the change in price levels from the previous year, 1991. The computation would have been:

Total holding gain (from the specific index)		Monetary holding gain		=	Specific or real holding gain
$(\dfrac{105 - 102}{102})$ = .0294	−	$(\dfrac{110 - 105}{105})$ = .0476		=	− .0182
$20,400		$20,400			$20,400
× .0294		× .0476			× −.0182
$ 600		$ 971			$ −371

The $20,400 is the estimated replacement cost at the beginning of 1992 *before* the price rise. The presence of two possible methods is yet another example of the allocation problem.

for the calculation of the purchasing power gain or loss on net monetary liabilities or assets. A heated debate has arisen concerning the question of which capital maintenance measurement is more appropriate.[22]

The financial capital maintenance approach is the less controversial of the two types of measurements. This is because the measurement itself is in dollars and the dollars themselves are denominated in terms of general purchasing power. This type of measurement, particularly if the Consumer Price Index is used, would have more applicability for investors (owners) than for the enterprise itself. Consequently, financial capital maintenance has a decided proprietary-theory orientation.

Physical capital maintenance is more ambiguous in its meaning than financial capital maintenance because, while measured in dollars, it purports to be maintaining capital productivity of the enterprise, a measurement which is not easy to translate into dollars. One of the problems surrounding physical capital maintenance is that the firm may go into new endeavors requiring totally different investments in plant and equipment than those currently held (and which were used in the physical capital maintenance measurement).[23] However, as Milburn has noted, if capital maintenance is seen as part of a measure of well-offness pertaining to a past period without regard to what the firm might attempt in the future, the problem can be put into perspective.[24] Physical capital maintenance, because it is concerned with maintaining productive capacity, has an entity-theory orientation. The choice really comes down to proprietary- versus entity-theory orientations. Milburn himself appears to favor financial capital maintenance but purely on definitional grounds: real (and realized) holding gains should be construed as an element of income.[25]

---

[22] See Sterling and Lemke (1982).

[23] Sterling (1982, pp. 18–24).

[24] Milburn (1982, pp. 100–101).

[25] Milburn (1982, p. 102). For a position favoring physical capital maintenance because of the inapplicability of closing any portion of real holding gains to income, see Samuelson (1980). Revsine takes an

SPECIAL PROBLEMS IN MEASUREMENT AND VALUATION

The state of our knowledge and techniques relative to price changes and inflation accounting procedures is still quite primitive. In this section we examine two problems: (1) current valuation of fixed assets that are partially obsolete and (2) inclusion of long-term debt in the measurement of purchasing power gains and losses.

DEPRECIATION AND PARTIAL TECHNOLOGICAL OBSOLESCENCE

Current valuation of fixed assets and depreciation become particularly difficult when technological obsolescence arises. *Technological obsolescence* occurs when new machinery and equipment come on the market that provide productive services similar to those of existing assets at a lower total cost of production. Typically, we would expect discounted cash flow analyses to occur, with some firms opting for the newer technology and other firms maintaining their existing assets. In the latter case, the assets held are partially obsolete.

In terms of depreciation expense, the debate is whether replacement cost depreciation should be measured in terms of the best available technology on the market or the technology that is actually used by the firm.[26] The appearance of new technology on the market generally depresses the price of older machinery and equipment. In fact, in an efficiently operating market where a new asset and an old asset provide similar output services, such as passenger miles for airplanes, the market would depress the cost of old technology so that cost per unit of output for old and new technology — including cost of the asset — would be equal.[27]

A simple example will show how the obsolescence write-down might be determined in the absence of actual market values. Assume that an enterprise owns a cement plant. A technological improvement occurs in which variable costs per unit decrease. The facts of the case are summarized in Exhibit 12–13. Assume that the appropriate cost of capital is 10 percent. For simplicity, we

---

entity-theory approach and also favors physical capital maintenance on the grounds that real holding gains constitute an ambiguous signal for future cash flows because future revenues per unit could either increase, decrease, or remain the same. In other words, the relation between rising current costs per unit and future revenues can be very tenuous. See Revsine (1982, pp. 84–85).

[26] Wright (1965, pp. 167–181) favors basing depreciation on the best available alternative on the grounds that it will "... indicate what the firm can expect to earn in the long run if it continues to follow its present general policies" (p. 175). There is thus an element of predictive ability underlying Wright's reasoning. Wright is critical of Edwards and Bell, who favor computing depreciation related to the actual fixed assets owned. Edwards and Bell (1961, p. 271), however, have a more limited accountability objective with regard to evaluating past business decisions.

[27] See Solomons (1962, pp. 28–42) and Revsine (1979, pp. 306–322) for extensive discussion. Backer (1973, pp. 205–206) and Weil (1976, pp. 89–104) suggest valuation methods grounded on the equalized cost-per-unit-of-output approach.

EXHIBIT 12–13

PARTIAL TECHNOLOGICAL OBSOLESCENCE

	Old Asset	New Asset
Original cost	$1,400,000	$2,000,000
Replacement cost prior to appearance of new technology	$1,050,000	
Estimated total life	10 years	10 years
Present age	5 years	
Annual productivity	200,000 bbl.	200,000 bbl.
Variable cost	$.90 per bbl.	$.50 per bbl.

ignore income taxes and assume that all production occurs at the end of the year.

The first step is to translate into equal annual-cost terms the purchase price of the new technology. This is done by dividing the $2,000,000 cost by the present value of an ordinary ten-year annuity at 10 percent per period. The result is $325,491 ($2,000,000 ÷ 6.14457). Because the firm's present technology is less efficient, we deduct the excess variable costs of production of $.40 per barrel ($.90 − $.50) and multiply by the annual production of 200,000, to yield an amount of $80,000, which is deducted from the $325,491 to arrive at a value equivalent of the old equipment relative to the new. Because there are only five years left in the old machinery, the $245,491 is multiplied by the present value of a five-year annuity at 10 percent (3.79079) to arrive at an estimated replacement cost of $930,605. The obsolescence write-down is thus $119,395 ($1,050,000 − $930,605). Obsolescence write-downs are a type of real holding loss.

The new estimated market value of $930,605 represents, in essence, a break-even value of the old technology of the firm. If the exit value the firm could receive exceeds this figure, the new technology should be acquired because the time-adjusted rate of return determined by capital budgeting calculations would exceed the 10 percent cost of capital. Similarly, if the exit value is less than $930,605, the old technology should be retained because the time-adjusted rate of return would be less than 10 percent.

An obvious question of verifiability must be raised about the determination of the estimated replacement cost and obsolescence write-down. Annual productivity and years of life are predictions. Thus, they may not be highly verifiable. The trade-off between relevance and reliability is obviously a key factor in replacement cost measurements. Furthermore, the method illustrated here can apply only to fixed assets that are homogeneous in terms of the output of their productivity. The determination of current value depreciation in the absence of market value quotations is even more dubious from the standpoint of verifiability. Further discussion of current value depreciation appears in Appendix 12-A of this chapter.

PURCHASING POWER GAINS ON LONG-TERM DEBT

The usual assumption that the firm makes a gain on its long-term debt during inflation because bondholders will be repaid with cheaper dollars has been seriously questioned.[28] Bondholders surely understand that if inflation continues, the repayment of principal to them will have less purchasing power than the dollars originally lent to the enterprise. Consequently, the interest rate is made up of two components: (1) the required return, which consists of the risk-free rate plus a risk premium based on the issuer's credit standing; and (2) an additional element equated to the expected rate of inflation during the period of the debt. As a result, it is posited that there will be a gain only if the actual rate of inflation is greater than the anticipated rate. Conversely, there will be a loss if the actual rate is less than the anticipated rate. The nature of this gain and loss and the implications for capital maintenance measurement require a closer look.[29]

Assume that an enterprise is formed on December 31, 1989. It purchases one asset costing $2,000 with a life of two years and no salvage value. The asset was acquired by issuing $1,000 of common stock and selling one bond, also at $1,000. The bond carries interest of 15 1/2 percent as a result of a 5 percent basic interest rate and an anticipated inflation rate of 10 percent $(1.05 \times 1.10 = 1.15 \frac{1}{2})$. Revenues of $3,000 are earned each year, the only expenses are depreciation and bond interest, and all income is distributed to stockholders as a dividend. For simplicity, income taxes are ignored. Finally, we assume that the actual rate of inflation is 10 percent per year (beginning in early 1990) and that the replacement cost for the fixed asset likewise increases by 10 percent a year. Current value statements for 1990 and 1991 are shown in Exhibit 12–14.

Notice that distributable income has been used without recognizing the purchasing power gain on the bonds. A capital maintenance proof is shown in Exhibit 12–15. In line with the changed conception of purchasing power gains on long-term debt, the beginning balance of bonds payable is *not* restated in end-of-year dollars. A similar capital maintenance proof could likewise be provided for 1991.

That the exclusion of bonded debt from the purchasing power gain is correct rests upon one additional assumption: the $1,100 of cash equal to the depreciation of 1990 is invested in a separate fund, which earns a return equal to the anticipated rate of inflation (10 percent), which is not made available for dividends.[30] As a result, the cash accumulated exactly equals the replacement cost of $2,420 of the fixed asset at the end of 1991 [($1,100 × 1.1) + $1,210 = $2,420]. The purchasing power computation in SFAS 33 required the inclusion of long-term debt. On the basis of this analysis, we would recommend its exclusion in any future inflation accounting standards.

---

[28] See Kaplan (1977, pp. 369–378), Bourn (1976, pp. 167–182), and Revsine (1981b, pp. 20–29).

[29] This illustration was adpated from Revsine (1981b).

[30] This problem is discussed in Vancil and Weil (1976, pp. 38–45) and in Nichols (1982, pp. 68–73).

EXHIBIT 12–14

CURRENT VALUE INCOME STATEMENTS
For the Year Ending December 31, 1990 and 1991

	1990	1991
Revenues	$3,000	$3,000
Expenses		
Depreciation	1,100[a]	1,210[b]
Bond Interest	155	155
Total Expenses	1,255	1,365
Net Income	$1,745	$1,635

[a] Replacement cost of $2,200 ÷ 2 years = $1,100. Replacement cost is $2,000 × 1.1.

[b] Replacement cost of $2,420 ÷ 2 years = $1,210. Replacement cost is $2,200 × 1.1.

EXHIBIT 12–15

CAPITAL MAINTENANCE SCHEDULE

	(1) 12/31/89	(2) Conversion Factor	(3) Restated in 1990 Dollars	(4) 12/31/90	(5) Conversion Factor	(6) Restated in 1990 Dollars	(7) Net Specific Change[b]
Cash	—			$ 2,845[a]	—	$ 2,845	$ 2,845
Fixed Assets	$ 2,000	$\frac{110}{100}$	$ 2,200	2,000	$\frac{110}{100}$	2,200	—
Less: Accumulated Depreciation	—		—	(1,000)	$\frac{110}{100}$	(1,100)	(1,100)
Total Assets	2,000		2,200	3,845		3,945	1,745
15½% Bonds Payable	1,000		1,000	1,000	—	1,000	—
Owners' Equity	$ 1,000		$ 1,200	$ 2,845	—	$ 2,945	$ 1,745

[a] Before payment of dividends

[b] Column 6 minus Column 3

When there is a change in the expected rate of inflation, the market adjusts by raising or lowering the market value of the bonds. From the viewpoint of physical capital maintenance, these gains and losses are irrelevant in terms of their effect on income. This viewpoint is geared to the entity theory. From the viewpoint of financial capital maintenance, redistribution between bondholders and stockholders occurs if the expected rate of inflation is greater than the actual rate. The price of the bonds increases — with a gain to that group and an offsetting loss by stockholders. The converse also applies. Notice that the gain or loss is the change in market value of the bonds rather than a purchasing power gain or loss. The financial capital maintenance approach represents an application of proprietary theory.

A simple example will illustrate these relationships. Assume in the example just used that the actual rate of inflation proves to be 8 percent rather than 10 percent. From the enterprise standpoint, capital maintenance occurs, as long as (1) current value depreciation is used without any recognition of real holding gains (distributable income) and (2) funds equal to the current value depreciation are invested at 8 percent for the purpose of asset replacement. Assuming that the inflation rate goes up 8 percent at the beginning of 1990 and once again at the beginning of 1991, the result would be as shown in the distributable income statements for 1990 and 1991 in Exhibit 12–16. The fact that the actual rate of inflation (8 percent) differs from the expected rate of 10 percent, which is being earned by the bondholders, will have no effect on the capital maintenance proof as long as purchasing power gains or losses on long-term debt are excluded (as above). The cash accumulated from reinvesting the funds gathered from depreciation should equal the replacement cost of $2,332.80 [($1,080 × 1.08) + $1,166.40 = $2,332.80].

However, as mentioned above, bondholders have gained at the expense of stockholders because the expected rate of inflation (10 percent) exceeds the actual rate of inflation (8 percent). The bonds had an interest rate of 15 1/2 percent allowing for a 10 percent inflation rate. Had the actual rate of inflation been anticipated, the bonds would have carried an interest rate of 13.4 percent or [(1.05 × 1.08) − 1]. Assuming that the bonds are two-year bonds with interest payable at year end, the market value of the bonds should rise to $1,034.84, a gain of $34.84 for the bondholder. This is shown in Exhibit 12–17.

The sum of the present values from Exhibit 12–17 is equal to $1,034.84 ($136.68 plus $898.16). In a perfectly operating capital market, this should be the market value of the bonds carrying an anticipated inflation rate of 10 percent with an actual rate of 8 percent. Notice in Exhibit 12–18 that this is exactly what the stockholders lose in excess interest payments to bondholders because

---

EXHIBIT 12–16

CURRENT VALUE INCOME STATEMENTS

	1990	1991
Revenues	$3,000	$3,000
Expenses		
Depreciation	1,080[a]	1,166.40[b]
Bond Interest	155	155
Total Expenses	1,235	1,321.40
Net Income	$1,765	$1,678.60

[a] Replacement cost of $2,160 ($2,000 × 1.08) ÷ 2 years = $1,080.
[b] Replacement cost of $2,332.80 ($2,160 × 1.08) ÷ 2 years = $1,166.40.

EXHIBIT 12–17

PRESENT VALUE OF BONDS WITH EXPECTED RATE OF INFLATION OF 10% AND ACTUAL RATE OF 8%

	Dec. 31, 1990	Dec. 31, 1991	Total Present Value Jan. 1, 1990
Interest	$155	$155	
Principal	—	$1,000	
Total	$155	$1,155	
Discount Factor	× .88183[a]	× .77763[b]	
Present Value on Jan. 1, 1980	$136.68	$898.16	$1,034.84

[a] $\dfrac{1}{1.134} = .88183$

[b] $\dfrac{1}{1.134^2} = .77764$

EXHIBIT 12–18

LOSS TO STOCKHOLDERS BECAUSE ANTICIPATED RATE OF INFLATION IS GREATER THAN THE ACTUAL RATE

	Dec. 31, 1990	Dec. 31, 1991	Total Present Value Jan. 1, 1990
Actual Interest (15½%)	$155	$155	
Interest at the actual rate of inflation (13.4%)[a]	$134	$134	
"Excess" interest paid to bondholders	21	21	
Discount factor at 13.4%	× .88183	× .77763	
Present value of differential interest	$18.52	$16.33	$34.85

[a] $(1.05 \times 1.08) - 1 = 13.4\%$

of the excess of anticipated inflation over actual inflation when discounted at the actual interest rate of 13.4 percent. As mentioned previously, the stockholders loss of $34.85 ($18.52 plus $16.33) should just offset the gain in the market value of bonds. This is merely a redistribution between different capital-providing groups. The corporation itself has not gained or lost in real capital maintenance terms. Hence, the proof reiterates that an entity view should be taken when determining purchasing power gains or losses on monetary items and that bonds payable should be excluded. The inclusion of bonds payable is a proprietary orientation because the gain or loss in purchasing power on the bonds is borne by the shareholders.

In actual practice, however, it would be virtually impossible to distinguish between anticipated and unanticipated rates of inflation. Furthermore, changes in perceived risk relative to the individual firm also bring about changes in the market value of the bonds. Therefore, any attempt to equate price changes in bonds to gains or losses of shareholders would present difficult measurement problems.

However, as a matter of consistency in valuation and presenting additional information to users, long-term debt could be shown at market value where current values are being employed. The difference between current value and unamortized historical cost would appear as an element of owners' equity and would not go through income under an approach that is entity-theory oriented (such as distributable income).

SUMMARY

Coping with inflation and changing prices has presented an extremely serious challenge to accounting theory. The literature has discussed numerous methods of grappling with these problems.

General price-level adjustment is largely an extension of historical costing. Under this method, unamortized costs of nonmonetary assets and liabilities are adjusted for the change in the general level of prices that has arisen since incurrence of these costs. The results in both the balance sheet and income statement would be additive because they are stated in terms of the current general price level. Capital maintenance is likewise measured in terms of the general level of prices. The results, however, should not be confused with current valuation. It is merely a matter of restatement of historical costs in terms of the change in the general level of prices.

Current valuation can be expressed in terms of either entry or exit values. The latter measure appears to be most useful in terms of measuring the ability of the firm to move into new asset holdings because existing assets (and liabilities) are measured in terms of their disposal value. From the standpoint of user-information needs, exit values appear to be relatively limited. Entry values seem to have more utility than their exit-value counterparts.

Under entry-value approaches, the main point of difference concerns disposition of real holding gains. Disposable income recognizes no real holding gains as income. The resulting capital maintenance measure is in physical capital terms, an approach oriented toward entity theory. Realized income, as the name implies, recognizes realized real holding gains as income elements. The results are frequently quite close to general price-level-adjusted measurements of income, but the orientation of the statement is totally different. Earning power income runs all real holding gains through income in the period when they arise. The intention is that users would receive a signal of higher (or lower) future income. Unfortunately, holding gains may result from either supply-side problems, causing price rises above the average, or price rises may be generated by increasing demand for resources in only a limited number of industries.

Two special problems have concerned theorists. One is whether current value depreciation should be equated to presently owned fixed assets or the most efficient technology of the type under consideration. In an efficiently operating used-asset market, the price of older technology would be depressed to the point where operating costs per unit of output of old and new technology would tend to be equated. However, the measurement of holding losses due to partial obsolescence as well as current value depreciation is still very difficult.

The other issue concerns whether purchasing power gains should be picked up on long-term debt during inflationary periods. Holders of long-term debt obviously understand that during inflationary periods they will receive dollars having less purchasing power than those that were lent. Consequently, long-term debt includes an interest element compensating holders for the expected purchasing power decline that they will suffer. As a result, the firm would have a purchasing power gain if the actual rate of inflation exceeds the expected rate. However, the measurement problems are, once again, exceedingly difficult to overcome. A possible substitute might be to show long-term debt at market value rather than unamortized historical cost with the difference being an element of owners' equity.

APPENDIX 12-A: CURRENT VALUE DEPRECIATION

The valuation of fixed assets in the absence of direct market quotations when improved technology comes on the market was discussed in the body of this chapter. Determining current value depreciation is an even stickier problem because depreciation is, of course, an allocation that makes it difficult to justify one measure over another.

EFFICIENT SECONDHAND MARKET VALUATION

One possibility for the valuation of fixed assets would be to equate the total cost of production per unit of output — including interest and depreciation — of old equipment with the best available technology. There would be a tendency toward this condition in an efficient market: all relevant cost and production figures relative to both new and used assets would be available to all participants in the market.

EXHIBIT 12–19

ANNUAL COST OF PRODUCTION OF
BEST-AVAILABLE TECHNOLOGY

Cost of new asset	$2,000,000
Present value of all production costs associated with new asset (200,000 units per year × $.50 × 6.14457)	614,457
Total present value of all costs	2,614,457
Divide by present value of a 10-year annuity at 10%	÷ 6.14457
Total annualized cost	$ 425,491[a]

[a] Annual costs can be determined by taking the annual cost of the asset of $325,491 ($2,000,000 ÷ 6.14457) and adding it to the annual variable costs of $100,000.

Using the information in Exhibit 12–13, the resulting new determination of theoretical replacement cost of the old asset is $930,605. The total annual cost of the new technology is shown in Exhibit 12–19. The present value of all costs is divided by the present value of a ten-year annuity of 10 percent to arrive at the equalized annual total cost of $425,491 including interest.

Exhibit 12–20 now takes the total annual cost of the best technology of $425,491 and applies it to the old asset. The resulting "present value" depreciation is a variant of the present valuation approach discussed in Chapter 1. Interest at 10 percent on the beginning balance of the fixed asset is added to the variable costs and depreciation is "forced" to make the total equal to $425,491. It should come as no surprise that the total accumulated depreciation equals the original simulated market value of $930,605 because this was "equated" with the price of the new technology. The resulting annual carrying values of the fixed asset are likewise simulated market values.

COMPLEXITIES OF PRESENT VALUE DEPRECIATION AS A SURROGATE FOR REPLACEMENT COST DEPRECIATION

Unfortunately, too many drawbacks surround present value depreciation, drastically limiting its potential usefulness. In addition to the troublesome problem of being an allocation, present value depreciation can become exceedingly complex when factors such as uneven annual production, changing production costs as the asset ages, and various tax considerations are contemplated. These complications also lead to the question of the degree of verifiability that would exist — since several estimations must be made about the future in order to measure depreciation of the current period. The same criticism applies, of course, to many present value types of measurements.

Since the measurement is supposed to give an estimation of replacement cost, the question might be raised as to whether the market actually does behave in this manner — as opposed to whether it should behave this way. This question concerns descriptive versus normative behavior. The issue here is basically an

EXHIBIT 12–20

ANNUAL COST OF PRODUCTION OF
PRESENTLY OWNED TECHNOLOGY

Year	1	2	3	4	5
Total costs of best technology (from Exhibit 12–19)	$425,491	$425,491	$425,491	$425,491	$425,491
Variable costs	$180,000	$180,000	$180,000	$180,000	$180,000
Interest at 10% on beginning asset balance	93,061	77,818	61,050	42,606	22,318
Depreciation (by deduction)	152,430	167,673	184,441	202,885	223,173[a]
Total costs of presently owned equipment	$425,491	$425,491	$425,491	$425,491	$425,491
Beginning-of-period asset balance	$930,605	$778,175[b]	$610,502	$426,061	$223,176

[a]$3 rounding error.

[b]($930,605 − $152,430). Succeeding years are calculated the same way.

empirical one and can be answered only by study of the market behavior of fixed asset prices.[31]

Another problem arises in the event of frequent improvements in technology. Recalculations of both obsolescence and present value depreciation must be made — which may be expensive.

There is still another question about the appropriate interest rate to use. The firm's cost of capital was used here, but perhaps the rate of interest used by the market in arriving at asset values is appropriate — because market efficiency has been assumed in these examples.[32]

Finally, all of the aforementioned difficulties logically lead to two other major enigmas. First is the question of users and their objectives: the issues here are whether present value depreciation would have more information content than presumably cruder methods, such as straight-line depreciation of current

---

[31] Beidleman (1973) attempted to use statistical models for determining the elements underlying the valuation of used capital assets.

[32] See Boatsman and Baskin (1981, pp. 38–52) for application of the capital asset pricing model to the valuation of used assets.

values; also, one must ask whether users even understand present value concepts. Second, as a result of these qualifications, the question of benefits versus costs of current value depreciation must be given very careful consideration.

All these issues raise very grave doubts about the utility at this time of present value depreciation as a substitute for direct market measurement of value declines in fixed assets.

QUESTIONS

1. Why do Paasche-type indexes tend to take into account technological changes, whereas Laspeyres indexes do not?
2. Do you believe that exit-value measurements should or should not deduct tearing out and other disposal costs from the selling price of assets?
3. Why are exit values generally considered to be less useful than entry values?
4. Why are the bottom-line income statement results quite similar between GPLA- and RI-type income statements?
5. What is the major purpose of EPI, and why is it likely that the objective will often not be achieved?
6. Why is GPLA oriented to the proprietary theory?
7. Why is DI primarily entity-theory oriented?
8. Why are beginning balance sheets restated in capital maintenance proofs?
9. What type of capital maintenance proof can be applied to EPI measurements?
10. A firm has a net monetary liability balance of $10,000 on January 1, 1992. During the first third of the year, the balance decreased to $7,500. During the second third of the year, the balance increased to $12,500. During the last third of the year, the balance increased to $20,000. The general price index was 100 during the first third of the year, 110 during the second third, and 106 during the last third.

    Required: Compute the purchasing power gain or loss for the year.

11. A plot of land costing $200,000 was acquired on January 1, 1992. The price level was 120 on that date. One-quarter of the land was sold on December 31, 1992, for $60,000 when the general price level was 180.

    Required: Compute the following gains:
    (a) Realized real holding gain.
    (b) Unrealized real holding gain.
    (c) Realized monetary holding gain.
    (d) Unrealized monetary holding gain.

12. What is the argument against including bonds payable as a monetary liability in the purchasing power gain or loss computation?

13. Price-level adjustment may be accomplished by using specific price indexes as well as a general price-level index. One possibility is to use a weighted-average price index for the firm's own mix of assets. What are the dangers here?
14. What is present value depreciation, and why is the prospect of its eventual adoption by a policy-making organization extremely doubtful?
15. Why, in an efficient market, should partially obsolescent technology and new technology providing the same services have equalized total annual costs of production for the same quantity of output?
16. Contrast financial capital maintenance with physical capital maintenance.

CASES AND PROBLEMS

1. Using the balance sheet and income statement shown in Exhibits 12–4 and 12–5, construct the following types of income statements for 1992:
   (a) GPLA
   (b) DI
   (c) RI
   (d) EPI
   Use the following general and specific indexes:

	1990	1991	1992
General price index	100	110	106
Specific price index applicable to the firm's merchandise inventory	100	103	97
Specific price index applicable to the firm's fixed assets	100	115	125

2. Show capital maintenance proofs for GPLA and DI in Problem 1 above.
3. An asset is acquired at a cost of $10,000 with a five-year life and no anticipated salvage value. Straight-line depreciation is considered appropriate. The asset was acquired on January 1, 1990. Price indexes for the five years are

	1990	1991	1992	1993	1994
Fixed asset index	100	95	108	120	125
General price index	100	110	115	112	125

Required:

(a) Compute the current-value depreciation for each year.
(b) What is the realized real holding gain for the years 1991–1994?
(c) What would the holding gain be under EPI for the years 1991–1994?

BIBLIOGRAPHY OF REFERENCED WORKS

Ashton, R. K. (1987). "Value to the Owner: A Review and Critique," *Abacus* (March 1987), pp. 1–9.

Backer, Morton (1973). *Current Value Accounting* (Financial Executives Research Foundation).

Beidleman, Carl (1973). "Valuation of Used Capital Assets," *Studies in Accounting Research* #7 (American Accounting Association).

Bell, Philip (1971). "On Current Replacement Costs and Business Income," in *Asset Valuation*, Robert Sterling, ed. (Scholars Book Co.), pp. 19–32.

——— (1986). *Current Cost/Constant Dollar Accounting and Its Uses in the Managerial Decision-Making Process* (University of Arkansas: McQueen Accounting Monograph Series).

Boatsman, James, and Elba Baskin (1981). "Asset Valuation with Incomplete Markets," *The Accounting Review* (January 1981), pp. 38–53.

Bourn, Michael (1976). "The 'Gain' on Borrowing," *Journal of Business Finance and Accounting* (Spring 1976), pp. 167–182.

Chambers, Raymond J. (1966). *Accounting, Evaluation and Economic Behavior* (Prentice-Hall).

——— (1968). "Measures and Values," *The Accounting Review* (April 1968), pp. 239–247.

Edwards, Edgar (1954). "Depreciation Policy Under Changing Price Levels," *The Accounting Review* (April 1954), pp. 267–280.

Edwards, Edgar, and Philip Bell (1961). *The Theory and Measurement of Business Income* (University of California Press).

Gynther, R. S. (1966). *Accounting for Price-Level Changes: Theory and Procedures* (Pergamon Press).

Heath, Loyd (1972). "Distinguishing Between Monetary and Nonmonetary Assets and Liabilities in General Price-Level Accounting," *The Accounting Review* (July 1972), pp. 458–468.

Hendriksen, Elden (1982). *Accounting Theory*, 4th ed. (Richard D. Irwin).

Kaplan, Robert (1977). "Purchasing Power Gains on Debt: The Effect of Expected and Unexpected Inflation," *The Accounting Review* (April 1977), pp. 369–378.

Milburn, J. Alex (1982). "Discussion," in *Maintenance of Capital: Financial versus Physical*, R. R. Sterling and K. W. Lemke, eds. (Scholars Book Co.), pp. 95–103.

Nichols, Donald (1982). "Operating Income and Distributable Income Under Replacement Cost Accounting: The Long-Life Asset Replacement Problem," *Financial Analysts Journal* (January–February 1982), pp. 68–73.

Parker, R. H., and G. C. Harcourt (1969). "Introduction," in *Readings in the Concept and Measurement of Income*, R. H. Parker and G. C. Harcourt, eds. (Cambridge University Press), pp. 1–30.

Revsine, Lawrence (1973). *Replacement Cost Accounting* (Prentice-Hall).

——— (1979). "Technological Changes and Replacement Costs: A Beginning," *The Accounting Review* (April 1979), pp. 306–322.

——— (1981a). "'The Theory and Measurement of Business Income': A Review Article," *The Accounting Review* (April 1981), pp. 342–354.

——— (1981b). "Inflation Accounting for Debt," *Financial Analysts Journal* (May–June 1981), pp. 20–29.

——— (1982). "Physical Capital Maintenance: An Analysis," in *Maintenance of Capital: Financial Versus Physical*, R. R. Sterling and K. W. Lemke, eds. (Scholars Book Company), pp. 75–94.

Samuelson, Richard A. (1980). "Should Replacement Cost Changes Be Included in Income?" *The Accounting Review* (April 1980), pp. 254–268.

Solomons, David (1966). "The Determination of Asset Values," *Journal of Business* (January 1962), pp. 28–42.

——— (1966). "Economic and Accounting Concepts of Cost and Value," in *Modern Accounting Theory*, Morton Backer, ed. (Prentice-Hall), pp. 117–140.

Sprouse, Robert, and Maurice Moonitz (1962). "A Tentative Set of Broad Accounting Principles for Business Enterprises," *Accounting Research Study No. 3* (AICPA).

Sterling, Robert (1979). *Toward a Science of Accounting* (Scholars Book Co., 1979).

——— (1982). "Limitations of Physical Capital," in *Maintenance of Capital: Financial versus Physical*, R. R. Sterling and K. W. Lemke, eds. (Scholars Book Co.), pp. 3–58.

Sterling, Robert, and Kenneth W. Lemke (1982). *Maintenance of Capital: Financial versus Physical* (Scholars Book Co.).

Tritschler, Charles (1969). "Statistical Criteria for Asset Valuation by Specific Index," *The Accounting Review* (January 1969), pp. 99–124.

Vancil, Richard, and Roman Weil (1976). "Current Replacement Cost Accounting, Depreciable Assets, and Distributable Income," *Financial Analysts Journal* (July–August 1976), pp. 38–45.

Weil, Roman (1976). "Implementation of Replacement Cost Accounting: The Theory and Use of Functional Pricing," in *Replacement Cost Accounting: Readings on Concepts, Uses & Methods*, Richard Vancil and Roman Weil, eds. (Thomas Horton and Daughters), pp. 89–104.

Wright, F. K. (1965). "Depreciation and Obsolescence in Current Value Accounting," *Journal of Accounting Research* (Autumn 1965), pp. 167–181.

Zeff, Stephen (1962). "Replacement Cost: Member of the Family, Welcome Guest, or Intruder?" *The Accounting Review* (October 1962), pp. 611–625.

ADDITIONAL READINGS

Inflation and Changing Prices

Beaver, William (1979). "Accounting for Inflation in an Efficient Market," in *The Impact of Inflation on Accounting: A Global View*, V. K. Zimmerman, ed. (Center for International Education and Research in Accounting, University of Illinois), pp. 21–42.

Bierman, Harold (1981). *Financial Management and Inflation* (Free Press).

Brinkman, Donald (1977). "Replacement Cost/Current Value Accounting," in *Handbook of Modern Accounting*, 2nd ed., S. Davidson and R. Weil, eds. (McGraw-Hill), pp. 46-1 to 46-49.

Bruns, William, Jr., and Richard Vancil (1976). *A Primer on Cost Replacement Accounting* (Thomas Horton and Daughters).

Chambers, Raymond J. (1975). *Accounting for Inflation: Methods and Problems* (Department of Accounting of the University of Sydney).

Largay, James, III, and John Leslie Livingstone (1976). *Accounting for Changing Prices* (Wiley/Hamilton).

Lee, T. A. (1975). *Income and Value Measurement: Theory and Practice* (University Park Press).

Moonitz, Maurice (1974). *Changing Prices and Financial Reporting* (Stipes Publishing Company).

Revsine, Lawrence (1974). "Replacement Cost Accounting: A Theoretical Foundation," in *Objectives of Financial Statement Vol. 2: Selected Papers*, Joe Cramer and George Sorter, eds. (AICPA), pp. 178–198.

Revsine, Lawrence, and Jerry Weygandt (1974). "Accounting for Inflation: The Controversy," *Journal of Accountancy* (October 1974), pp. 72–78.

Sterling, Robert (1975). "Relevant Financial Reporting in an Age of Price Changes," *Journal of Accountancy* (February 1975), pp. 42–51.

Summers, Edward, and James Deskins (1970). "A Classification Schema of Methods for Reporting Effects of Resource Price Changes (with Technical Appendix)," *International Journal of Accounting* (Fall 1970), pp. 101–120.

Vancil, Richard (1976). "Inflation Accounting – The Great Controversy," *Harvard Business Review* (March–April 1976), pp. 58–67.

Zimmerman, V. K., ed. (1979). *The Impact of Inflation on Accounting: A Global View* (Center for International Education and Research in Accounting, University of Illinois).

General Price-Level Adjustment

Davidson, Sidney, Clyde Stickney, and Roman Weil (1976). *Inflation Accounting* (McGraw-Hill).

Holding Gains and Losses

Dickens, Robert, and John O. Blackburn (1964). "Holding Gains on Fixed Assets: An Element of Business Income?," *The Accounting Review* (April 1964), pp. 312–329.

Drake, David F., and Nicholas Dopuch (1965). "On the Case for Dichotomizing Income," *Journal of Accounting Research* (Autumn 1965), pp. 192–205.

Prakash, Prem, and Shyam Sunder (1979). "The Case Against Separation of Current Operating Profit and Holding Gains," *The Accounting Review* (January 1979), pp. 1–22.

Zeff, Stephen A., and W. David Maxwell (1965). "Holding Gains on Fixed Assets – A Demurrer," *The Accounting Review* (January 1965), pp. 65–75.

Purchasing Power Gains and Losses

Bradford, William (1974). "Price-Level Restated Accounting and the Measurement of Inflation Gains and Losses," *The Accounting Review* (April 1974), pp. 296–305.

Gringyer, John (1978). "Holding Gains on Long-Term Liabilities – An Alternative Analysis," *Accounting and Business Research* (Spring 1978), pp. 130–148.

Capital Maintenance

Edwards, Edgar (1961). "Depreciation and the Maintenance of Real Capital," in *Depreciation and Replacement Policy*, J. L. Meij, ed. (North-Holland), pp. 46–136.

Philips, G. Edward (1990). "Inflation Adjustments to Income in Entry and Exit Price Systems," *Abacus* (September 1990), pp. 185–191.

Pratt, Dennis J. (1988). "Capital Maintenance Adjustment Under the Financial (Real) Capital Concept," *Abacus* (September 1988), pp. 170–178.

Revsine, Lawrence (1981). "Let's Stop Eating Our Seed Corn," *Harvard Business Review* (January–February 1981), pp. 128–134.

Current Value Depreciation

Lewis, W. Arthur (1977). "Depreciation and Obsolescence as Factors in Costing," in *Studies in Accounting*, 3rd ed., W. T. Baxter and S. Davidson, eds. (Institute of Chartered Accountants in England and Wales), pp. 210–233.

Lowe, Howard (1963). "The Essentials of a General Theory of Depreciation," *The Accounting Review* (April 1963), pp. 293–301.

Wright, F. K. (1964). "Towards a General Theory of Depreciation," *Journal of Accounting Research* (Spring 1964), pp. 80–90.

PROBLEMS OF IMPLEMENTING ACCOUNTING FOR CHANGING PRICES AND INFLATION

THE FASB FINALLY CAME TO GRIPS with inflation by instituting SFAS 33 in September, 1979. The standard required certain current cost (value) and constant dollar (adjusted historical cost) disclosures to supplement the primary historical-cost-based financial statements. Because of the importance of this departure from historical costs, the standard was issued on a probationary status for a five-year period.

The early 1980s saw an abatement of the very steep rate of inflation that had occurred in the United States since approximately 1973. This single factor was probably more instrumental than any other in leading to the elimination of the constant dollar disclosure (SFAS 82) and making the current cost disclosure voluntary (SFAS 89). However, there were other factors at work that led to the rejection of SFAS 33. Because inflation could easily return, not to mention the fact that huge amounts of assets shown on balance sheets were acquired at prices far below their current costs, it behooves us to carefully examine standards relating to accounting for changing prices both in the United States and other English-speaking nations.

We begin by examining the history of accounting for changing prices in the United States prior to SFAS 33 and then discuss the main elements of SFAS 33, 82, and 89, taking a more careful look at the problems of SFAS 33. These problems include (in addition to the aforementioned slackening of the rate of inflation) measurement errors in current cost indexes used by preparers and questions of relevance and understanding of the SFAS 33 disclosures. The chapter closes with a brief survey of the state of inflation accounting in other English-speaking countries.

HISTORY OF ACCOUNTING FOR
THE EFFECTS OF CHANGING PRICES
IN THE UNITED STATES PRIOR TO SFAS 33

Accountants had been warned about the fallacy of measuring business transactions in terms of historical cost. For decades, economists warned about the problem of assuming that the monetary unit is stable and that the measurement of historical cost income and capital is correct. Even if the general price level remains fairly stable, considerable price movement occurs as a result of changes in supply and demand. Accountants in the United States have realized for over fifty years the potential impact on reported accounting numbers of the effects of changing prices, whether specific or general in nature. In fact, some corporations restated their primary financial statements for the effects of changes in specific prices during the 1920s. In 1932 W. A. Paton perhaps summed up best the unsettled nature of accounting for the effects of changing prices that existed sixty years ago:

> It is evident that this whole problem is an unsettled one, with much to be said on both sides. It is a question to be determined on its own merits with particular reference to the sound needs of business management and not on the basis of tradition. The accountant in general will do well to concentrate his attention on the development of methods of bringing revaluations and their subsequent effects onto the books in a manner which will not impair the integrity of original cost figures, nor lead to misinterpretation of financial reports, rather than take the position that the effects of revaluation are outlawed as far as accounting records are concerned.[1]

Accounting organizations, such as the American Accounting Association and the American Institute of Certified Public Accountants, have discussed accounting for the effects of changing prices in their publications for nearly half a century. Both organizations strongly supported the historical cost model in the mid-thirties. The AAA made this statement: "Accounting is . . . not essentially a process of valuation, but the allocation of historical costs and revenues to the current and succeeding periods."[2] The AICPA adopted the following as one of its first six rules: "Profit is deemed to be realized when a sale in the ordinary course of business is effected, unless the circumstances are such that the collection of the sale price is not reasonably assured."[3]

By the early fifties, however, both organizations began to modify their positions. In 1951 the AAA issued *Supplementary Statement No. 2*, "Price Level Changes and Financial Statements." The statement recommended that financial statements should be stated in units of general purchasing as a supplement

---

[1] Paton (1932, p. 6).

[2] AAA (1936, p. 61).

[3] AICPA (1953, p. 6007). The six rules were adopted by the institute membership in 1934 and reprinted as part of Chapter 1 of *Accounting Research Bulletin (ARB) 43*.

to the primary historical cost statements.[4] In 1952 the AICPA sponsored a study on changing concepts of income. Its report stated:

> Corporations whose ownership is widely distributed should be encouraged to furnish information that will facilitate the determination of income measured in units of approximately equal purchasing power, and to provide such information wherever it is practicable to do so as part of the material upon which the independent accountant expresses his opinion.[5]

The AAA continued to support price-level restated financial statements in their 1957 and 1966 reports. Likewise, the AICPA in *Accounting Research Study No. 6* in 1961 and *Accounting Principles Board Statement No. 3* supported general price-level adjusted statements. Without making any commitments to either general price-level or current value concepts, the Trueblood Committee reaffirmed the need to recognize changing prices in financial statements.[6]

Shortly after its inception, the FASB issued an exposure draft entitled "Financial Reporting in Units of General Purchasing Power." The draft proposed to require the presentation, as supplementary information to the balance sheet and income statement, units of general purchasing power. The FASB deferred action on its exposure draft because the SEC issued ASR 190, which reversed the SEC's long-standing position of forbidding the presentation of information other than historical cost.

ASR 190 required certain registrants (approximately the nation's 1000 largest enterprises) to disclose as supplementary information in their form 10-K

> . . . the estimated current replacement cost of inventories and productive capacity at the end of each fiscal year for which a balance sheet is required and the approximate amount of cost of sales and depreciation based on replacement cost for the two most recent full fiscal years.[7]

The replacement cost disclosures required by ASR 190 differed from the requirements of SFAS 33. In general, the SEC required that replacement-cost information reflect the probable effect of replacement by new, more efficient, productive assets. For example, if replacement of current equipment would probably result in lower labor costs, those anticipated lower labor costs should be reflected in the supplementary disclosures.

At first glance, it seems the need to consider the effects of changing prices in financial reports has followed a rather evolutionary development; actually, the opposite is true. For nearly forty years, the majority of the literature on the subject dealt with the possibility of restating historical cost financial statements for changes in general price levels, not the adoption of a new measurement

---

[4] Committee on Concepts and Standards Underlying Corporate Financial Statements (1951).
[5] Study Group on Business Income (p. 105).
[6] Study Group on the Objectives of Financial Statements (1973, p. 14).
[7] SEC (1976, General Statement).

system. Price-level restated financial statements continue to use historical cost as the measurement system but alter how historical cost is reported — that is, units of constant dollars rather than units of nominal dollars. A current cost approach, however, changes the basic measurement system to one of current values rather than historical costs.

Accountants in general and accounting organizations, such as the AAA, AICPA, and FASB, tended to favor price-level restated historical cost until the SEC's rather dramatic action of issuing ASR 190. Why the accounting profession tended to favor price-level restated historical cost over current cost is purely conjecture, but several possible reasons exist. The methodology of restating historical cost for changes in units of currency is generally easier than measuring current cost. It involves merely obtaining an externally derived index, such as the Consumer Price Index (CPI), and multiplying that index by the historical cost.[8] If agreement can be reached regarding the appropriate index to use, auditing the result is simple and any third-party liability resulting from the audit is minimal.

The SEC's action, however, changed the evolution of accounting for changing prices in the United States. ASR 190 resulted in the FASB immediately reconsidering its position (price-level restatement at that time) and led to the dual approach adopted in SFAS 33. This development (ASR 190) moved the development of accounting for changing prices significantly forward. It was not an evolutionary step but more a reflection of the thinking of the then-chief accountant of the SEC, John C. Burton. Burton's background was academic, and he firmly believed that if any changes in financial reporting were needed because of changing prices, those changes should be made to the measurement system itself in order to permit the system to report more useful information to the users of financial reports. The following quotation best exemplifies Burton's thinking:

> [Inflation] creates greater distortions when the historical monetary unit approach to measurement is used. It is obvious that matching historical monetary costs against current revenues will not give a good approximation of the long-run average net cash inflow at current activity levels under conditions of rapidly changing costs. . . .[9]

This seems to be a strong argument for a measurement system using current economic costs. Under such an approach, expenses would be based on the current cost of replacement of particular assets sold or used. In this way, the matching process would show a long-run average cash flow figure based on current costs at the times transactions occur. Although the ease of application (of general price-level adjustments) cannot be denied, since no new economic measurements must be made, Burton had serious doubts as to whether any significant benefit would be achieved from such a system. Certainly, the impact of Burton's position on accounting for changing prices cannot be overempha-

---

[8] Fabricant made a strong plea for common dollar restatement largely on the grounds of a high degree of verifiability. Fabricant (1978).

[9] Burton (1975, p. 69).

sized. It is quite possible that the FASB would not have considered current cost had Burton not been the SEC's chief accountant.

PROVISIONS OF SFAS 33 AND REJECTION IN SFAS 82 AND 89

In SFAS 33, the FASB decided to keep nominal historical costs as the basis of primary financial statements. SFAS 33 specified that the effects of changing prices should be presented as supplementary information in annual reports. As discussed in Chapter 12, there are several approaches to accounting for the effects of changing prices. The FASB realized that a consensus could not be obtained on which method of accounting should be adopted. The proponents of a constant dollar approach as well as those of a current cost approach both held quite strong views about the usefulness of one to the exclusion of the other. As a result, the FASB concluded that enterprises should report supplementary information under both of these fundamentally different measurement approaches.

Not all enterprises had to comply with SFAS 33; those to which it applied were

> ... public enterprises that prepare their primary financial statements in U.S. dollars and in accordance with U.S. generally accepted accounting principles and that have, at the beginning of the fiscal year for which financial statements are being presented either:
> a. Inventories and property, plant, and equipment [excluding goodwill or other intangible assets] (before deducting accumulated depreciation, depletion, and amortization) amounting in aggregate to more than $125 million; or
> b. Total assets amounting to more than $1 billion (after deducting accumulated depreciation).[10]

SFAS 33 defined a "public enterprise" as one

> ... (a) whose debt or equity securities are traded in a public market on a domestic stock exchange or in the domestic over-the-counter market (including securities quoted only locally or regionally) or (b) that is required to file financial statements with the Securities and Exchange Commission.[11]

Approximately 1200 enterprises were affected directly by SFAS 33. In addition, the FASB encouraged those not affected to experiment with disclosing changing price information.

For constant dollar reporting, the SFAS required disclosure of

> a. Information on income from continuing operations for the current fiscal year on a historical cost/constant dollar basis ...

---

[10] FASB (1979, para. 23).
[11] FASB (1979, para. 22).

    b. The purchasing power gain or loss or net monetary items for the current fiscal year. . . .

The purchasing power gain or loss on net monetary items shall *not* be included in income from continuing operations.[12]

Regarding current cost, the following had to be disclosed:

    a. Information on income from continuing operations for the current fiscal year on a current cost basis . . .

    b. The current cost amounts of inventory and property, plant, and equipment at the end of the current fiscal year . . .

    c. Increases or decreases for the current fiscal year in the current cost amounts of inventory and property, plant, and equipment, net of inflation. . . . [13]

The increases or decreases in current cost amounts were *not* to be included in income from continuing operations, which indicates primarily a distributable-income orientation, though one without purchasing power gains or losses.[14] Constant dollar revenue and expense calculations were computed by the method indicated in Chapter 12. Restatements, however, were in terms of the average price index prevailing during the year rather than the end-of-year index.

CONSTANT DOLLAR DISCLOSURES

SFAS 33 did not require a comprehensive application of constant dollar accounting to each element of income from continuing operations. Instead, the FASB required application to those elements of income from continuing operations most significantly affected by inflation — cost of goods sold and depreciation, depletion, and amortization. Revenues and other expenses were assumed to already reflect average current-year dollars; thus, no restatement was necessary. To simplify the calculations for some enterprises, those that used LIFO inventory procedures in their primary financial statements did not need to restate cost of goods sold, because LIFO should approximate average current-year dollars, assuming no liquidation of prior-years' LIFO layers.

    The purchasing power gain or loss on net monetary items was determined by restating to constant dollars the beginning and ending balances of net monetary items as well as restating transactions in monetary items that occurred during the year. Again, the FASB required restatement by using the average CPI for the current fiscal year rather than the end-of-year CPI. Exhibit 13–1 illustrates a method of calculating the purchasing power gain or loss under the provisions of SFAS 33. The FASB did not specify exactly how the purchasing power gain or loss should be calculated, but Exhibit 13–1 is based on examples provided in Appendix E of SFAS 33. The purchasing power gain or loss was shown separately and was not part of constant dollar income from continuing operations or current cost income from continuing operations.

---

[12] Ibid., para. 29.

[13] Ibid., paras. 29 and 30.

[14] Ibid., para. 30.

EXHIBIT 13–1
Illustration of Calculating Purchasing Power Gain or Loss under SFAS 33

Net Monetary Liability Position:			
January 1			$40,000
December 31			30,000
CPI:			
January 1			250
December 31			270
Average for the Year			260

	Nominal Dollars	Conversion Factor	Constant Dollars
January 1	$40,000	260/250	$41,600
Net Change During Year	(10,000)	*	(10,000)
December 31	30,000	260/270	(28,889)
Gain			$ 2,711

*Assumed to be in average constant dollars.

CURRENT COST DISCLOSURES

The current cost disclosures focused on specific price changes for individual assets rather than price changes caused by general inflation. Current cost measurements typically could be made for assets presently owned and used by the enterprise but not for technologically improved assets that might replace existing assets. In an efficiently operating used-asset market, user costs per unit of output for old and new assets should be reasonably close. As with constant dollar disclosures, SFAS 33 did not require a comprehensive application of current cost to each element of income from continuing operations. Only cost of goods sold and depreciation, depletion, and amortization needed to be restated at current cost. The FASB also allowed considerable flexibility in how an enterprise could determine current cost amounts. It provided examples of the types of information an enterprise may want to use but indicated that "enterprises are expected to select types of information appropriate to their particular circumstances. . . ."[15] Again, as with constant dollar disclosures, an enterprise using LIFO inventory procedures could assume cost of goods sold reported in the primary financial statements represented a good approximation of current cost. Although using the same amounts for constant dollar and current cost may appear inconsistent, the board's reasoning was that both represent the average dollars for the year and that historical cost and current cost are identical at the time of purchase.

The SFAS 33 approach to computing holding gains on fixed assets and inventories is illustrated in Exhibit 13–2 using a specific price index (other methods of measurement will be discussed shortly). The steps to calculate the

---

[15] Ibid., para. 60.

EXHIBIT 13–2
Calculation of Change in Current Cost Amounts Net of Inflation

---

Current Cost Amount			
January 1			$100,000
Current value depreciation for the year			12,000
Acquisitions during the year			15,000
December 31			120,000

	Current Cost	Conversion Factor	Average Dollars
January 1	$100,000	260/250	$104,000
Depreciation	(12,000)		(12,000)
Acquisitions	15,000		15,000
December 31	120,000	260/270	115,556
Net Increase	$ 17,000		$ 8,556
Increase in Current Cost (nominal dollars)			$ 17,000
Increase in Current Cost (constant dollars)			8,556
Inflation Component			$ 8,444

---

increases or decreases for the current fiscal year in the current cost amounts of inventory and property, plant, and equipment, net of inflation, are as follows:

1. Determine the current cost amounts at the beginning and end of the year.
2. Convert those amounts to average dollars for the current year.
3. The change in current cost amounts determined in (1) less the change in current cost average dollar amounts determined in (2) represents the inflation component of the increase in current cost amounts.

Perhaps the major measurement problem involved determining the current cost of enterprise fixed assets. The holding gain shown in Exhibit 13–2 of $8,556 is the real holding gain arising during the current year. If it were combined with adjusted current cost income from continuing operations, the result would be earning power income (excluding purchasing power gains or losses on net monetary items). However, the requirement was that holding gain information was to be shown separately and was not to be reflected in the current cost income from continuing operations number.

SPECIALIZED INDUSTRY PROVISIONS

Pending further study, the FASB exempted certain specialized industries from the current cost provisions of SFAS 33 because of the difficulty in determining current cost amounts and the lack of usefulness of such amounts for those industries. The industries exempted were forest products; mining, and oil and gas producers; and real estate. Subsequently, the FASB issued SFASs 39, 40, and 41 regarding current cost disclosures for these industries. SFAS 39 required the application of SFAS 33 current cost provisions to mining and oil and gas producers. However, SFAS 69 (see Chapter 15 for discussion) reversed SFAS 39's current cost provisions for oil and gas producers. These producers did not need to disclose current costs unless they had significant inventory and property, plant, and equipment apart from oil and gas operations.[16] SFAS 40 continued the exemption provisions of SFAS 33 for the forest products industry. SFAS 41 required real estate enterprises to apply SFAS 33 current cost provisions.

Motion picture producers complained that determining the current cost of completed films in inventory was impossible. After considerable deliberation, the FASB agreed and issued SFAS 46, which exempted motion picture producers from the current cost provisions of SFAS 33. The investment industry also complained to the FASB about the current cost provisions of SFAS 33. Its complaint was that the calculations were confusing and the results misleading. As a result, the FASB issued SFAS 54 exempting investment companies from the current cost provisions of SFAS 33.

OVERVIEW OF SFAS 33

There are several facets of SFAS 33 that are worthy of comment. The overall format adopted in SFAS 33 of disaggregation rather than aggregation of information is significant. It indicates that the board itself had not decided whether real holding gains and losses and purchasing power gains and losses are part of income from continuing operations. Also, it points out the board's confidence in the disclosure mechanism, possibly based on a belief in market efficiency as opposed to a particular aggregation of information. It leaves the problem of aggregating information to the user. For example, realized income may be estimated by taking the difference between the current cost and price-level-adjusted depreciation and cost of goods sold and adding these estimates of realized real holding gains to income from continuing operations.

Although SFAS 33 clearly did represent an experiment, some of the decisions made by the board appear to be suboptimal. The choice of the CPI as a measure of general inflation is not a good decision on theoretical grounds. Its selection implies a strong proprietary-theory orientation. Both APB Statement No. 3 and the 1974 FASB ED recommended use of the gross national product implicit price deflator (GNP deflator), which is an index of changes in prices of all producer and consumer goods and services. Certainly, the GNP deflator would provide a better index of the impact of changing prices on American businesses than the CPI. Both indexes tend to move in the same direction and presumably the FASB chose the CPI because it is calculated and published more frequently than the GNP deflator.

A problem encountered in the real world is the fact that prices change daily throughout the year (in Chapter 12 all price changes for a year were assumed to occur on the first day of the year). The FASB attacked the problem by requiring restatement into average-for-the-year dollars. The benefits of using

---

[16] FASB (1982c).

the average index for the year is that transactions occurring during the year do not have to be restated and an estimation of the index at the end of the year does not have to be made. Hence, using average prices for the year could be less costly and more timely. Of course, if transactions occurring during the year are not representative of average prices for the year, the measurement would not have representational faithfulness. Moreover, it produces results that could be slightly confusing and also probably less useful than end-of-the-year prices. A strong case could still be made for end-of-year prices rather than average prices. SFAS 33 did permit use of year-end prices if comprehensive financial statements were prepared rather than minimal disclosures.

For SFAS 33 purposes, long-term debt was considered a monetary liability in calculating the purchasing power gain or loss. As was pointed out in Chapter 12, the appropriateness of its inclusion is questionable because of the inflation effect built into the determination of interest rates. Moreover, many enterprises are beginning to issue long-term debt with "inflation-proof features." An example is Sunshine Mining's silver-indexed bonds. These bonds provide that the principal repayment is tied to the price of silver. The repayment for each $1000 face-value bond is the greater of $1000 or the current market price of 50 ounces of silver. Bondholders may receive silver in lieu of cash at maturity.[17]

SFAS 82

SFAS 82, issued in late 1984, eliminated the constant dollar income disclosures that had previously been required by SFAS 33. It appears that this information confused users and may have caused "information overload" because of the presence of similar current cost income disclosures. As a result, the board obviously felt that the cost of the constant dollar income disclosures exceeded the benefits of the information.

SFAS 89

The other shoe dropped, so to speak, on the remaining part of SFAS 33 approximately two years after the appearance of SFAS 82. The parts of SFAS 33 that remained in effect — current cost income measurement, purchasing power gain or loss, and holding gain information (as well as the five-year summary of selected financial disclosure) were "encouraged" but not required. Thus, the board beat a hasty retreat from the problem of accounting for changing prices. As a possible sop to those advocating the need for financial reporting to take into account changing prices, the standard, in Appendix A, included a guide for those firms still desiring to present supplementary information showing the effects of changing prices. Little that was new appeared in Appendix A that had not previously appeared in Appendix E of SFAS 33.

The most interesting aspect of SFAS 89 is that it passed only by a four-to-three vote. The comments of the dissenters were extremely enlightening. David Mosso stated his belief that the issue of changing general and specific prices

---

[17] Swieringa (1981, p. 166).

is the most important problem that will be faced by the FASB during this century.[18] He was against the passage of SFAS 33 but was also against making the remaining sections of it voluntary in SFAS 89. Despite SFAS 33's shortcomings, he saw it as a base on which to build in future years. Making it voluntary would essentially destroy this hard-won base. Raymond Lauver agreed with these sentiments.[19] In addition, given the shortcomings of SFAS 33, Lauver felt it quite understandable that SFAS 33 was not being widely used after only five years of dissemination. Robert Swieringa agreed with both Mosso and Lauver and also saw a loss of systems and data continuity: essentially the fixed costs of installing and capturing current cost data.[20] Hence, if inflation returns, systems that were removed would have to be installed once again.

The obvious factor leading to the retreat in accounting for changing prices was the slowing down of the inflation rate. However, other factors also played a role, as we shall see in the next section.

THE FAILURE OF SFAS 33

One extremely important reason for the demise of SFAS 33 has already been mentioned: the dramatic decline in the early 1980s of the rate of inflation. It is important to recognize the other reasons for its lack of success in order to avoid the pitfalls of implementing another standard if inflation returns in the United States and a new standard has to be forged. This critique is broken down into two main sections. The first concerns measurement problems in terms of determining current cost depreciation amounts. The second involves the predictive ability of SFAS 33 disclosures and users' perceptions of the relevance of current cost information. Much of the latter information comes from surveys of various user groups.

MEASUREMENT PROBLEMS IN APPLYING SFAS 33

The current cost of the firm's assets, from which depreciation is calculated, can be determined in numerous ways as noted in paragraphs 58–60 and 179–180 of SFAS 33. Exhibit 13–3 diagrams these methods.

Direct-Estimation Methods

Direct pricing can be accomplished by determining the cost of a new asset similar to that owned by the firm, a used asset of the same age and condition as that owned by the firm, or even a new, technologically improved asset providing the same services.[21] In the last case, an allowance should be made for the technolog-

---

[18] FASB (1986, p. 2).

[19] Ibid., p. 3.

[20] Ibid.

[21] Much of the information on measurement methods comes from Swanson and Shriver (1987) and Shriver (1987).

EXHIBIT 13–3
Estimating Current Costs of Assets

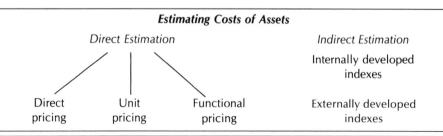

Estimating Costs of Assets

Direct Estimation	*Indirect Estimation*
	Internally developed indexes
Direct pricing Unit pricing Functional pricing	Externally developed indexes

ical improvements of new assets. These prices would be the starting point for determining current cost depreciation. Swanson and Shriver note evidence that obsolescence write-downs for less advanced technology were not frequently made where the prices of technologically improved assets were used as the basis for determining current cost depreciation.[22]

Unit pricing and functional pricing are conceptually quite similar. Unit pricing is used primarily for buildings. Current construction costs per square foot are multiplied by the total square footage to derive total current cost. Functional pricing is applicable to process-oriented plants such as cement plants, chemical plants, and petroleum refineries. Current costs for these types of operations are figured per unit of capacity, such as a ton of cement or a barrel of oil. Current cost of the plant is then determined by taking total capacity times the cost per unit of capacity. Let us next examine the indirect estimation methods to see the full extent of current cost measurement methods.

Indirect Estimation Methods

The current cost of assets using indirect estimation methods is based on the indexing of historical costs. Externally developed indexes were, by far, more frequently used than internally developed indexes — based on estimations and sampling techniques pertaining to the firm's own composition of assets — or any other method for determining current costs. The obvious advantage of this method lies in the minimization of costs. Probably the most frequently used of the specific indexes is the Producers Price Indexes (PPI), a series of fifteen major asset groups that are, in turn, broken down into more than one hundred subgroup indexes.

Swanson and Shriver have raised several issues concerning measurement error due to usage of the PPI.[23] First of all, a firm's mix of machinery and equipment may not be the same as that in the index. That is, the weighting of the machinery and equipment in the index may be significantly different from the enterprise's holdings of machinery and equipment. Thus, price changes in the index may not be representative for the firm. Second, the accuracy of the

---

[22] Swanson and Shriver (1987, p. 72).
[23] Ibid., pp. 73–76.

indexes has been challenged because of their use of outdated pricing data and other pricing errors. Finally, those external indexes that include the effects of technological change and are applied to older assets will overstate the current cost of the nontechnologically improved assets.

This wide variation in ways to estimate current costs of depreciable assets as well as their potential for measurement errors certainly raised questions about the degree of verifiability and representational faithfulness in current cost measurements. Hence, users may have felt, particularly if they were aware of the disparity in current cost estimation, that the numbers did not have a high degree of reliability. Also, the degree of comparability among firms would be relatively low.

A last point is that current cost estimation of fixed assets is necessary to determine current value depreciation. Paragraph 61 of SFAS 33 presumed that depreciation methods, estimations of useful life, and salvage values should be the same for current cost, constant dollar, and historical cost methods. Different methods, however, were allowed if depreciation methods for historical costing were intended to take into account the changing price problem (by shortening the estimated life or using an accelerated method, for example). Since depreciation methods are seldom selected to show the remaining value of the asset, paragraph 61 appears to be self-defeating even if current cost was accurately determined. A better method might have been to determine the change in current cost for the firm's assets at the beginning and end of period (after restating the beginning current cost in end-of-year price-level terms) and adjusting for acquisitions and dispositions.

INUTILITY OF SFAS 33 DISCLOSURES

There are several reasons why SFAS 33 disclosures were perceived as not useful. One reason, already discussed, is the large number of possible measurement methods perhaps coupled with an intuitive feeling that current cost measurements may not be correct. This ties in with the analysis made above of errors in specific index preparation and application as well as the failure of direct pricing measures to account for technological obsolescence in arriving at current cost estimations of depreciable assets (not to mention determining current cost depreciation from current cost of assets). In this section, we briefly review two types of empirical studies: (1) studies that attempt to correlate securities prices or returns with current cost income and historical cost income reporting, and (2) surveys of various user groups to ascertain if current cost disclosures were useful in making decisions.[24]

Correlation and Prediction Studies

In an extensive study involving 731 calendar-year firms reporting SFAS 33 current cost disclosures between the years 1979–81, Beaver and Landsman found that historical cost income correlated more closely with changes in security

---

[24] An excellent analysis of the empirical literature is done by DeBerg and Shriver (1987).

prices than current cost income and several other current cost measures.[25] They advanced several possible reasons for this finding. First, since historical cost earnings are reported quarterly (as well as annually) and current cost disclosures are made on an annual basis only, the information content of current cost disclosures may have already been anticipated in the historical cost disclosure. Therefore, whether quarterly current cost disclosures would provide additional information content is a moot question and one for which the issue of costs versus benefits of information would have to be taken into account very closely. The second reason advocated by Beaver and Landsman concerns the lack of a well-defined theoretical relationship between SFAS 33-type disclosures and security returns. Many theorists, such as Bell, Chambers, and Sterling, have advocated powerful a priori (deductive) reasons for advocating one or another current value (cost) system, but Beaver and Landsman saw the theoretical issue in predictive terms: the ability of current cost income to provide information about variables such as future cash flows that historical cost earnings do not provide. Beaver and Landsman pointed out certain "double counting" aspects to asset values under current costing, which they evidently believed interfered with the predictive ability of current cost income disclosures. This double counting problem is illustrated in Appendix 13-A.

Bublitz, Frecka, and McKeown attempted to replicate and extend the work of Beaver and Landsman.[26] They criticized the Beaver-Landsman study on certain statistical grounds including multicollinearity (intercorrelation among the independent variables), and they extended the study to 1983 and introduced some new variables. Bublitz, Frecka, and McKeown did find better overall predictive power for current cost variables over historical cost numbers.

Several other studies have attempted to assess the predictive power of current cost variables as opposed to historical cost measures.[27] These studies were in general agreement with Beaver and Landsman. Although predictive studies generally have not found current cost disclosures to have the predictive ability of historical cost numbers, it is important to keep several factors in mind: (1) the number of studies is not large relative to the importance of the topic; (2) many of these studies are beset by statistical problems that are not easy to resolve; (3) many theoretical issues about the linkage of current costs to predictive variables have not been well resolved.[28]

---

[25] Beaver and Landsman (1983). Bildersee and Ronen believed that focusing upon the relation between securities price changes and different types of income measures examined the wrong independent variable. They attempted, instead, to use current cost expenses as components of quantity indexes to assess an enterprise's increased productive capacity, which, in turn, would help to assess future cash flows. Despite shortcomings in published current cost data, the current cost information had a slightly stronger correlation with residual security returns than did historical cost variables. See Bildersee and Ronen (1987).

[26] Bublitz, Frecka, and McKeown (1985).

[27] For further detail, see DeBerg and Shriver (1987, pp. 60–64) and Cormier (1989).

[28] Predictive studies involve a very wide range of both dependent and independent variables as well as measurement techniques. They can reveal surprising interrelationships between historical costs and current values. For example, Swanson, Shearon, and Thomas used eight different models for predicting

User Surveys

User surveys have studied how individual users employ current cost data. Numerous studies of individual users of ASR 190 data were done between the years 1978 and 1980; these have been summarized and analyzed by Frishkoff.[29] Roughly 70 percent of the more than forty studies reported on saw little or no usefulness in the ASR 190 disclosures.

The number of studies involving individual users of SFAS 33 data is far smaller at this point. Studies have been made of managers of the 229 largest Fortune 500 firms, auditors whose clients expressed interest in SFAS 33 data, and professional financial analysts. All three groups in general displayed a fairly limited usage or interest. Nevertheless, there were important individual cases of application. General Electric management, for example, has used inflation-adjusted data for several of its divisions, which provided insights into return on investment, product-line profitability, and inventory levels. Although most of the evidence is negative, it must be remembered that such factors as measurement error and lack of familiarity have impeded a wider use and adoption of current cost data.

ACCOUNTING FOR CHANGING PRICES IN OTHER COUNTRIES

The economic phenomenon of inflation has not been limited to the United States. Indeed, the majority of the countries in the world have experienced inflation, many at higher rates and for a longer period of time than the United States.

The International Accounting Standards Committee (IASC) issued International Accounting Standard (IAS) 15, "Information Reflecting the Effects of Changing Prices." The IASC recognized the lack of an international consensus on methods for reflecting the effects of changing prices, but it believed that the situation would be improved if enterprises whose primary financial statements were based on historical cost also provided supplementary information reflecting the effects of price changes (for more on the function of the IASC, see Chapter 19). As a result, the IASC does not recommend one method to the exclusion of others but allows each enterprise to choose how to reflect the effect

---

one-year-ahead forecasts of current cost income. The best predictive model – based on lowest mean absolute error as a percentage of sales – used financial analysts' forecasts of the next year's sales times the estimated current cost profit margin for the forecast year (estimated current cost income of the forecast year divided by forecast sales) plus estimated historical cost income for the forecast year less historical cost income for the current year. It is interesting that the estimated change in historical cost income improved the predictive ability of forecasted current cost income. See Swanson, Shearon, and Thomas (1985).

[29] Frishkoff (1982).

of changing prices. IAS 15 calls for disclosure on either a constant dollar basis or current cost basis. It recommends the following information:

1. The amount of the adjustment to or the adjusted amount of depreciation of property, plant, and equipment.
2. The amount of the adjustment to or the adjusted amount of cost of sales.
3. The adjustments relating to monetary items, the effect of borrowing, or equity interests, purchasing power gain or loss when such adjustments have been taken into account in determining income under the accounting method adopted.
4. The overall effect on results of the adjustments described in (1) and (2) and, where appropriate, (3), as well as any other items reflecting the effects of changing prices that are reported under the accounting method adopted.[30]

IAS 15 came into effect for periods beginning on or after January 1, 1983. Its experimental nature, like that of SFAS 33, can be clearly detected.

Standards on accounting for the effects of changing prices have been implemented in many countries. In this section, we will briefly review some of those requirements for selected English-speaking countries. The countries selected are those countries that have been experiencing inflation at or close to the level experienced in the United States and that have a standard-setting process similar to ours. A common thread can be detected in the standard-setting process regarding changing prices in all countries reviewed: the process is a lengthy one that in most cases, as in the United States, started with constant dollar restatement of historical cost financial statements and concluded with current cost financial statements. It should be noted that, as in the United States, many of these standards have been allowed to lapse.

THE UNITED KINGDOM

The experience of the United Kingdom is similar to that of the United States. In 1973 and 1974, an ED and proposed standard called for constant-dollar-restated historical-cost financial statements. This approach was debated extensively and eventually discarded in favor of a current cost approach. A final standard was issued in March, 1980.

Like the U.S. standard, the U.K. standard did not cover all enterprises but only the largest ones, estimated to be no more than one percent of all enterprises.[31] Unlike the U.S. standard, however, the U.K. standard required a comprehensive current cost income statement and balance sheet in addition to the historical cost financial statements. Either the historical cost or current cost statements could be the primary financial statement with the other as supplementary disclosure.

---

[30] International Accounting Standards Committee (1981, para. 24).
[31] International Accounting and Financial Report (1980, p. 5).

One of the principal differences in the U.K. approach to measuring current cost income is known as the "gearing adjustment."[32] The British model basically takes the distributable income format. The gearing adjustment, which was extremely controversial, recognized that part of the real holding gain was attributable to debt capital. Assume that realized real holding gains on inventories and depreciable assets is £100 and that 30 percent of total long-term capital (debt and equity) is long-term debt. The gearing adjustment would be £30 and would be listed between current cost operating profit and current cost profit before taxes. Notice that the gearing adjustment is based on the idea that the holding gain attributable to debt capital presumably accrues to the benefit of equity capital.[33] It thus appears to be oriented toward proprietary theory.

As inflation fell in the United Kingdom after 1980, many firms stopped publishing current cost financial statements. Therefore, the standard (Statement of Standard Accounting Procedure 16) was withdrawn in 1985. Prospects do not seem particularly strong for its replacement at this time.

CANADA

Canada's experience with inflation is also similar to our own, but constant-dollar-restated historical-cost financial statements were not required. The discussion started in 1974 with a guideline for preparation of constant-dollar-restated historical-cost financial statements. It ended in 1982 with a standard that was a five-year experiment like ours, which likewise did not require comprehensive remeasurement of financial statements but rather selected supplemental disclosures. Only about 300 enterprises were covered by the standard but only about 25 percent published data in line with it. The specific rules required these disclosures:

1. The current cost of goods sold, and depreciation, depletion and amortization, or the current cost adjustments for these items.
2. Income on a current cost basis — income before extraordinary items adjusted for the above charges, with income tax on an historical cost basis.
3. The amount of the changes during the reporting period in the current cost amounts of inventory and property, plant, and equipment.
4. The carrying values of inventory and property, plant, and equipment on a current cost basis at the end of the reporting period.
5. Net assets after these current cost changes attributable to general inflation.
6. The gain or loss in general purchasing power from holding net monetary items.[34]

---

[32] A good explanation of the gearing adjustment appears in Whittington (1983, pp. 168–183).

[33] A spirited and complex debate occurred in the United Kingdom that finally resulted in Statement of Standard Accounting Practice 16 in 1980. The intricacies of the various proposals and positions are covered in Tweedie and Whittington (1984, pp. 81–153).

[34] World Accounting Report (1982, p. 4).

AUSTRALIA

In Australia, constant-dollar-restated historical-cost financial statements were extensively discussed but not put forth as an ED. Rather, drawing from the experience of the United Kingdom, Canada, and the United States, current-cost disclosures were more seriously considered. A provisional standard (similar to an exposure draft) was issued, calling for supplemental disclosure of current cost information. The current cost disclosures are very similar to SFAS 33; however, purchasing power gains and losses are separated into current, which includes normal trading monetary items, and noncurrent, which relates to long-term nonoperating items. This was an attempt to acknowledge that long-term debt is not the same as short-term debt because of expected rates of inflation affecting interest rates on long-term debt (see Chapter 12).

The standard-setting bodies were unable to reach agreement on a final standard, however, and abandoned plans to make current cost disclosures mandatory. A special practice statement was issued to provide guidelines for those who chose to disclose current cost information, but no enterprise was required to disclose anything regarding changing prices.[35]

NEW ZEALAND

The experience in New Zealand has been similar to that of other English-speaking countries. A constant dollar exposure draft in 1974 gained little support. It was followed by a major report in 1976 advocating current costs for depreciation and cost of goods sold. There were two major differences in this report from those of other countries. The purchasing power gain or loss was based on monetary assets only and the gearing adjustment (see the United Kingdom) was based on total holding gains, not just the realized portion.

This report was followed by an exposure draft and an accounting standard. The standard required supplementary current cost information to be published for financial periods beginning on April 1, 1982. The standard was not well received. In fact, it was largely ignored; less than 10 percent of companies listed on the stock exchange published the full data required by the standard.[36]

SUMMARY

SFAS 33 was a probationary standard that required both constant dollar and current-cost-adjusted income from continuing operations to be published as supplemental to the primary historical cost statements. In addition, it required purchasing power gains and losses on monetary items and total holding gains,

---

[35] World Accounting Report (1983, p. 14).
[36] Nobes and Parker (1985, pp. 260–261).

broken into the inflationary component and the real component, to be disclosed separately.

SFAS 82 eliminated the constant dollar disclosures, and SFAS 89 made the current cost disclosures voluntary. The slowing down of the inflation rate was probably the main reason leading to the rejection of accounting for changing prices. In addition, measurement error quite likely hindered usage of current cost disclosures. Measurement error problems included not allowing for technological obsolescence where direct pricing was used as well as problems with externally derived specific indexes. In this latter case, the indexes may not have been accurate due to factors such as using out-of-date prices. In addition, the mix of assets in the specific index may have differed significantly in many cases from firm-specific mixes. The measurement error problems were largely concerned with reliability.

Empirical studies indicated that current cost disclosures did not have as high a correlation with security prices as historical costs. One of the reasons for this may be that the information from current cost disclosures has already been impounded in security prices when the current cost disclosures are released. Surveys of various user groups, such as managers and financial analysts, on the utility of current cost disclosures were likewise discouraging.

The experience of other English-speaking countries largely parallels our own. Constant dollar approaches were generally abandoned in favor of voluntary current cost disclosures, but enthusiasm has not been high.

There are several points that should be kept in mind about the current cost experience. If inflation should return, we will have to cope with the problem of changing prices. And even though inflation has abated, a high proportion of assets are in use that were purchased when lower price levels held sway.

APPENDIX 13-A: THE DOUBLE COUNTING EFFECT WITH CURRENT COSTS

Beaver and Landsman have pointed out in their monograph some theoretical inconsistencies. In this appendix we will use their example to explain their point.

Beaver and Landsman assume perfect and complete markets. There is no opportunity for abnormal returns, and transaction costs are zero. Furthermore, market prices exist for all assets, claims, and services.

NOMINAL AND REAL RATES OF RETURN

Assume that an asset with a one-year life is purchased for $1,000 and it returns a cash flow of $1,100 in a year. The price index is 100 at the beginning of the year and has risen to 106.8 at the end of the year. From this information Beaver and Landsman determine the *nominal* rate of return and *real* rate of return.

The nominal rate of return is the time-adjusted rate of return on the asset ignoring the effect of inflation. The nominal rate of return is 10 percent determined by taking the income of $100 and dividing by the initial investment of $1,000. Similarly, multiplying the $1,100 by .9091 (present value of $1 received in a year discounted at 10%) also gives the $1,000 investment.

The real rate of return eliminates the effect of inflation, which is ignored in nominal rates of return. In eliminating the effect of inflation, we take the investment at the beginning of the year and convert it into end-of-year dollars:

$$\$1,000 \times \frac{106.8}{100} = \$1,068$$

Now take the income, after adjusting for inflation, and divide by the adjusted investment base to derive a real rate of return of 3%:

$$\frac{\$1,100 - \$1,068}{\$1,068} = \frac{\$32}{\$1,068} = 3\%$$

Notice also that $1,100 multiplied by the present value of $1 at 3% (.97087) also equals $1,068, which can be considered as the inflation-adjusted investment.

THE CURRENT VALUE DEPRECIATION PROBLEM

Let us now extend to a two-year time span in order to illustrate the "double counting" problem. An asset with a cost of $1,000 has a two-year life with no salvage value. Expected (and actual) cash flows are $744 at the end of Year 1 and $391 at the end of Year 2. The asset has a nominal rate of return of 10%, which is determined by discounting the cash flows:

$$\$744 \times .9091 = \$676$$
$$\$391 \times .8264 = \underline{\$323}$$
$$\underline{\underline{\$999}}$$

Beaver and Landsman then determine the nominal economic depreciation (the decline in the present value of future cash flows as shown in Chapter 1 in this text). Since the only remaining cash flow, at the end of Year 1, is the $391, which is now only one year away, the present value of the remaining cash flows in $356 ($391 × .9091) and depreciation is $644 for Year 1 ($1,000 − $356) and $356 for Year 2. These depreciation amounts result in a 10% return on investment for each year when the income is divided by the beginning-of-year asset value (with a very slight rounding).

Beaver and Landsman then restate the economic depreciation, this time casting it into real terms. The cash flows are reduced by the constant inflation of 6.8%:

$$\text{Year 1: } \$744 \times \frac{1.00}{1.068} = \$697$$

$$\text{Year 2: } \$391 \times \frac{1.00}{(1.068)^2} = \$343$$

Notice now that the adjusted cash flows result in a real rate of return of 3%:

$$\text{Year 1: } \$697 \times \frac{1.00}{1.03} = \$\ 677$$

$$\text{Year 2: } \$343 \times \frac{1.00}{(1.03)^2} = \frac{323}{\$1,000}$$

Economic depreciation, in real terms, becomes $667 for Year 1 because the present value of the remaining cash flows at the end of Year 1 is $333. This is determined by taking the inflation-adjusted cash flows of $343 at the end of Year 2 and multiplying by .97087, the present value of $1 at 3% to be received in one year, which gives the $333.

The asset thus has a real economic value of $333 at the end of Year 1 before adjusting for the inflation factor. After adjusting for inflation, the real economic value of the asset at the end of Year 1 is $356 ($333 × 1.068).

The $356 real value of the asset, after adjustment for inflation, however, will be far below the inflation-adjusted value (current cost in this case) of the asset if straight-line depreciation is used. After one year, the asset value would be $500 with straight-line depreciation. After adjustment for inflation, the asset would be carried at $534 ($500 × 1.068). Hence, asset values are liable to be overstated well above their real values after adjustment for inflation.

CRITIQUE OF THE ARGUMENT

That constant dollar accounting with straight-line depreciation gives uninterpretable results, as Beaver and Landsman contend, is hardly open to question. They concentrate on the overstatement of the asset value. What should really be at issue is the understatement of the depreciation amount for Year 1: $667 in real economic terms versus $534 in constant-dollar-adjusted terms.

As Beaver and Landsman note, the problem becomes less serious the longer the life of the asset. Their analysis certainly points out the need for more economically realistic depreciation methods, such as sum-of-the-years-digits (which would also greatly alleviate the income tax allocation problem). What is even more strongly implied is calculating depreciation as the change in the current cost of the asset during the period by taking the beginning-of-period current cost (adjusted for the price-level change) from the current cost at the end of the period. This avoids using arbitrary depreciation methods that are not grounded in real economic terms and should also increase verifiability as well as representational faithfulness.

QUESTIONS

1. Is there any reason why current costs should be used in financial statements even if the general level of prices remains relatively flat?
2. Did the AICPA and the AAA favor current costs or constant dollars for supplementary statements in early documents they sponsored?

3. Why did the FASB withdraw its exposure draft on "Financial Reporting in Units of General Purchasing Power"?

4. What was the significance of ASR 190 of the SEC?

5. Why might it be said that both constant dollar and current cost income numbers under SFAS 33 are "disaggregated"?

6. Using the CPI as opposed to a company-specific index for restatements has some disadvantages. What are the disadvantages? In your opinion, why did the board select the CPI?

7. What problems do you see with the choice of the Consumer Price Index (CPI) as a measure of general inflation?

8. The FASB required use of average-for-the-year dollars for SFAS 33 disclosures. Why did it make this choice? Was it a good choice? Why? What other alternatives are available and what are their advantages and disadvantages?

9. How did SFAS 82 and SFAS 89 modify SFAS 33? What do you think the practical effect of SFAS 89 will be?

10. What is the gearing adjustment?

11. What is the danger of having *both* constant dollar and current cost disclosures?

12. What arguments were raised *against* the repeal of the current cost disclosures of SFAS 33?

13. What is direct pricing?

14. What are unit pricing and functional pricing?

15. What are the advantages and disadvantages of using externally developed indexes for current cost estimation?

16. Summarize why SFAS 33 disclosures were not perceived as useful.

17. What reasons underlie the apparent closer correlation of historical cost income — as opposed to current cost income — with changes in security prices?

CASES AND PROBLEMS

1. DeSoto, Inc., manufactures chemical coatings (consumer paints, industrial coatings, and specialty products, which include detergents and other household cleaning products). The company is an important supplier to Sears, Roebuck and Co. Shown on page 407 is information from DeSoto's 1984 annual report on earnings from continuing operations in both historical cost and current cost terms. From this information estimate the following current cost income numbers:
   (a) Distributable income
   (b) Realized income (assume that 20 percent of the total real holding gains have been realized)
   (c) Earning power

2. Shown on pages 408–409 are a note discussing current cost information from the 1985 annual report of the Quaker Oats Company and the consol-

Statement of Earnings Adjusted for Changing Prices
For the Year Ended December 31, 1984
(in thousands of dollars)

	As Reported in the Primary Financial Statements (Historical Cost)	Adjusted for Changes in Specific Prices (Current Cost)
Continuing Operations		
Net sales	$407,439	$407,439
Cost of sales	330,386	330,734
Selling, administrative and general expenses	39,251	39,258
Interest expense	2,998	2,998
Retirement security program	2,321	2,321
Interest income	(2,070)	(2,070)
Provision for Income Taxes	15,800	15,800
Earnings from Continuing Operations	$ 18,753	18,398
Gain From Decline in Purchasing Power of Net Amounts Owed		$ 500
Increase in Specific Prices (Current Cost) of Inventories and Property, Plant and Equipment Held During the Year		$ 3,300
Effect of Increase in General Price Level		6,400
Increase in Specific Prices Over (Under) Increase in the General Price Level		$ (3,100)

Courtesy of DeSoto, Inc.

idated income statement from continuing operations under historical costs and current costs.

Required: Discuss the adequacy of note 17 in terms of explaining Quaker Oats' current cost disclosures.

Note 17
Financial Reporting and Changing Prices (Unaudited)

Financial statements prepared using historical cost accounting principles do not reflect the impact of inflation on a company's financial position and results of operations. Page 41 presents selected financial information using current cost calculations, which attempt to measure this impact.

The current cost method adjusts financial data for the effects of specific price changes for goods and services, in order to reflect the current cost of these items. In developing the current cost data for properties, specific industry indices from sources such as the Construction Cost Index, Producer Price Index, Factory Mutual Building Cost Index, or other appropriate indices, were used. Current cost amounts for inventories are based on year-end market values of raw materials and current production costs. These adjusted values were then used to compute the related depreciation expense and cost of goods sold. The Company uses the translate-restate method to compute inflation-adjusted data for foreign subsidiaries. Current cost is measured first in each subsidiary's functional currency, translated into U.S. dollars at current exchange rates, and then restated into average U.S. dollars using the Consumer Price Index for all Urban Consumers (CPI-U).

Because the development of inflation-adjusted data requires the use of estimation techniques and assumptions, caution should be exercised in comparing the financial data presented herein with that of other companies. Also, since the inflation-adjusted data has been developed using the hypothetical assumption that all fixed assets would be replaced in exactly the same state as they currently exist, it does not reflect how the Company would actually replace existing assets. Technological changes, which significantly influence a company's decision regarding fixed assets replacement, are not considered.

As a result of adjusting pretax earnings for the effects of inflation without adjusting the provision for income taxes, the effective tax rate for fiscal 1985 is 61.9 percent. This compares with a 46.5 percent rate in the historical financial statements. We believe that the data will provide a better understanding of how, in an inflationary environment, the current tax laws reduce the amount of cash available for expansion or replacement of existing assets.

Monetary assets, such as cash and receivables, lose purchasing power during inflationary periods, because the same dollars will purchase fewer goods or services, while monetary liabilities such as accounts payable are satisfied with "cheaper" dollars. Since the Company's monetary liabilities exceeded the monetary assets during the period covered in this report, the Company realized a purchasing power gain. This gain in purchasing power is not included in income from continuing operations, but is shown separately. It is, however, a significant factor and should be considered when evaluating the inflation-adjusted data presented herein.

Courtesy The Quaker Oats Company.

Consolidated Statement of Income from Continuing Operations Adjusted for Changing Prices

		Millions of Dollars
Year Ended June 30, 1985	As Reported in the Primary Statements	Adjusted For Changes in Specific Prices (Current Costs)
Net Sales	$3,520.1	$3,520.1
Cost of goods sold (excluding depreciation expense)	$2,078.3	$2,098.7
Depreciation expense	71.7	112.3
Selling, general and administrative expenses (excluding depreciation expense)	1,021.3	1,021.3
Interest expense—net	52.5	52.5
Other expense	3.6	15.5
Provision for income taxes	136.1	136.1
Net Income	156.6	83.7
Gain from decline in purchasing power of net amounts owed		15.2
Total	$ 156.6	$ 98.9
Increase in current cost of inventories and property, plant and equipment held during the year*		$ 95.3
Effect of increase in general price level**		48.0
Excess of increase in specific prices over the general price level		$ 47.3

*At June 30, 1985, current cost of inventory was $398.3 million and current cost of property, plant and equipment, net of accumulated depreciation, was $1,023.6 million.
**Based on the U.S. Consumer Price Index for All Urban Consumers.

BIBLIOGRAPHY OF REFERENCED WORKS

Accounting Standards Executive Committee (1982). "Accounting and Financial Reporting for Personal Financial Statements," *Statement of Position 82-1* (AICPA).

American Accounting Association (1936). "A Tentative Statement of Accounting Principles Underlying Corporate Financial Statements," reprinted in *Accounting and Reporting Standards for Corporate Financial Statements and Preceding Statements and Supplements* (American Accounting Association, 1957), pp. 59–64.

American Institute of Certified Public Accountants (1953). "Restatement and Revision of Accounting Research Bulletins," *ARB No. 43* (AICPA, 1973).

Beaver, William H., and W. R. Landsman (1983). *Incremental Information Content of Statement 33 Disclosures* (Financial Accounting Standards Board).

Bildersee, John S., and Joshua Ronen (1987). "Stock Returns and Real Activity in an Inflationary Environment: The Information Impact of FAS No. 33," *Contemporary Accounting Research* (Fall 1987), pp. 89–110.

Bublitz, Bruce, T. Frecka, and J. McKeown (1985). "Market Association Tests and FASB Statement No. 33 Disclosures: A Reexamination," *Studies on Accounting Earnings and Security Valuation: Current Research Issues* (supplement to *Journal of Accounting Research*), pp. 1–23.

Burton, John C. (1975). "Financial Reporting in an Age of Inflation," *Journal of Accountancy* (February 1975), pp. 68–71.

Committee on Concepts and Standards Underlying Corporate Financial Statements (1951). "Price Level Changes and Financial Statements," *Supplementary Statement No. 2* (AAA).

Cormier, Denis (1989). "Prescriptive Models of Inflation Accounting Adopted by Standard Setting Bodies: Empirical Results," *Journal of Accounting Literature* (Vol. 8), pp. 293–309.

DeBerg, Curtis L., and Keith A. Shriver (1987). "The Relevance of Current Cost Data: A Review and Analysis of Recent Studies," *Journal of Accounting Literature* (Vol. 6), pp. 55–87.

Fabricant, Solomon (1978). "Accounting for Business Income Under Inflation: Current Issues and Views in the United States," *The Review of Income and Wealth* (March 1978), pp. 1–24.

Financial Accounting Standards Board (1979). "Financial Reporting and Changing Prices," *Statement of Financial Accounting Standards No. 33* (FASB).

———— (1982a). "Financial Reporting and Changing Prices: Foreign Currency Translation," *Exposure Draft* (FASB).

———— (1982b). "Disclosures about Oil and Gas Producing Activities," *Statement of Financial Accounting Standards No. 69* (FASB).

———— (1982c). "Financial Reporting and Changing Prices: Foreign Currency Translation," *Statement of Financial Accounting Standards No. 70* (FASB).

———— (1986). "Financial Reporting and Changing Prices," *Statement of Financial Accounting Standards No. 89* (FASB).

Frishkoff, Paul (1982). *Financial Reporting and Changing Prices: A Review of Empirical Research* (Financial Accounting Standards Board).

Griffin, Paul A., ed. (1979). *Financial Reporting and Changing Prices: The Conference* (FASB).

International Accounting and Financial Reporting (1980). (Institute for International Research Ltd., April 28, 1980.)

International Accounting Standards Committee (1981). "Information Reflecting the Effects of Changing Prices," *International Accounting Standard No. 15* (IASC).

Nobes, Christopher, and R. H. Parker, eds. (1985). *Comparative International Accounting* (Philip Allan/St. Martin's Press).

Paton, W. A., ed. (1932). *Accountants' Handbook*, 2d ed. (Ronald Press).

Securities and Exchange Commission (1976). "Disclosure of Certain Replacement Cost Data," *Accounting Series Release No. 190* (The Commission).

Shriver, Keith (1987). "An Empirical Examination of the Potential Measurement Error in Current Cost Data," *The Accounting Review* (January 1987), pp. 79–96.

Study Group on Business Income (1952). *Changing Concepts of Business Income* (American Institute of Accountants).

Swanson, Edward P., Winston T. Shearon, and Lynn R. Thomas (1985). "Predicting Current Cost Operating Profit Using Component Models Incorporating Analysts' Forecasts, *The Accounting Review* (October 1985), pp. 681–691.

Swanson, Edward P., and Keith A. Shriver (1987). "The Accounting-for-Changing-Prices Experiment: A Valid Test of Usefulness?," *Accounting Horizons* (September 1987), pp. 69–77.

Swieringa, Robert J. (1981). "The Silver-Lined Bonds of Sunshine Mining," *The Accounting Review* (January 1981), pp. 166–177.

Tweedie, David, and G. Whittington (1984). *The Debate on Inflation Accounting* (Cambridge University Press).

Whittington, Geoffrey (1983). *Inflation Accounting: An Introduction to the Debate* (Cambridge University Press).

World Accounting Report (1982). (*The Financial Times*, November 1982), pp. 3–5.

———— (1983). (*The Financial Times*, March 1983), pp. 14–15.

ADDITIONAL READINGS

General Price-Level Restatements

Baran, Arie, Josef Lakanishok, and Aharon Ofer (1980). "The Information Content of General Price Level Adjusted Earnings: Some Empirical Evidence," *The Accounting Review* (January 1980), pp. 22–35.

Davidson, Sidney, Clyde P. Stickney, and Roman L. Weil (1976). *Inflation Accounting* (McGraw-Hill).

Gynther, R. S. (1966). *Accounting for Price-Level Changes: Theory and Procedures* (Pergamon Press).

Hillison, William A. (1979). "Empirical Investigation of General Purchasing Power Adjustments on Earnings Per Share and the Movement of Security Prices," *Journal of Accounting Research* (Spring 1979), pp. 60–73.

Ijiri, Yuji (1976). "The Price-Level Restatement and its Dual Interpretation," *The Accounting Review* (April 1976), pp. 227–243.

Ketz, J. Edward (1978). "The Effect of General Price-Level Adjustments on the Predictive Ability of Financial Ratios," *Studies on Accounting for Changes in General and Specific Prices: Empirical Research and Public Policy* (supplement to *Journal of Accounting Research*, 1978), pp. 273–284.

Vickrey, Don W. (1976). "General Price-Level Adjusted Historical Cost Statements and the Ratio-Scale View," *The Accounting Review* (January 1976), pp. 31–40.

Current Value Accounting

Abdel-khalik, A. Rashad, and James C. McKeown (1978). "Disclosure of Estimates of Holding Gains and the Assessment of Systematic Risk," *Studies on Accounting for Changes in General and Specific Prices: Empirical Research and Public Policy* (supplement to *Journal of Accounting Research*, 1978), pp. 46–77.

Arnold, Donald F., and Ronald J. Huefner (1977). "Measuring and Evaluating Replacement Costs: An Application," *Journal of Accounting Research* (Autumn 1977), pp. 245–252.

Backer, Morton (1973). *Current Value Accounting* (Financial Executives Research Foundation, 1973).

Bromwich, Michael (1977). "The General Validity of Certain 'Current' Value Asset Valuation Bases," *Accounting and Business Research* (Autumn 1977), pp. 242–249.

Friedman, Lawrence A. (1978). "An Exit-Price Income Statement," *The Accounting Review* (January 1978), pp. 18–30.

Ovadia, Arie, and Joshua Ronen (1983). "On the Value of Current-Cost Information," *Journal of Accounting, Auditing and Finance* (Winter 1983), pp. 115–129.

Rosenfield, Paul (1975). "Current Replacement Value Accounting – A Dead End," *Journal of Accountancy* (September 1975), pp. 63–73.

INCOME TAXES AND FINANCIAL ACCOUNTING

ACCOUNTING HAS BECOME far more complex as a result of the federal government's attempt to influence such macroeconomic factors as corporate investment by means of the income taxation process. In this chapter we examine income tax allocation, a topic that has become perhaps even more controversial in accounting theory since SFAS 96 was issued in 1987. The appendix to this chapter deals with the investment tax credit. The investment tax credit was repealed in the Tax Reform Act of 1986 but many assets are still subject to its provisions.

The income tax law of 1913 resulted in many items being recognized in different time periods for tax and book purposes. The efforts to "synchronize" tax and book accounting go back to the 1930s, but it was ARBs 43 and 44 (revised) (1953 and 1958, respectively) that firmly established income tax allocation as a canon of financial accounting. After examining the basic elements of tax allocation, we analyze extensively the principal timing difference: accelerated depreciation for tax purposes and straight-line depreciation for published financial reporting. Various positions on income tax allocation within the context of book–tax timing differences arising from depreciation are examined. The tax allocation portion of the chapter concludes with an analysis of the major aspects of SFAS 96.

INCOME TAX ALLOCATION

The allocation of corporate income taxes is one of the most controversial issues that has ever arisen in financial accounting theory. ARB 43 put it into practice in words that today have an almost archaic-sounding innocence when viewed with the hindsight of thirty years of heated debate:

> Income taxes are an expense that should be allocated, when necessary and practicable, to income and other accounts, as other expenses are allocated. What the income statement should reflect under this head . . . is the expense properly allocable to the income included in the income statement for the year.[1]

Tax allocation is made necessary by the timing differences between when a revenue or expense item reaches the published financial statements as opposed to when it appears on the tax return. In these situations, tax expense is based on the published before-tax income figure. The problem can also be viewed from the perspective of the balance sheet, where the tax basis and book basis of assets and liabilities differ. Hence, the income-tax allocation process acts like a balance wheel between income tax expense and income tax liability numbers with the difference appearing on the balance sheet. We will closely scrutinize the meaning of the income-tax expense number and the balance sheet account arising from the income-tax allocation process.

APB 11 continued the thrust of ARBs 43 and 44 (revised). As long as timing differences arise, tax allocation must take place, despite the possibility of relevant circumstantial differences. This requirement is known as *comprehensive allocation.*

Permanent differences between published statements and tax returns are not subject to the allocation process. In the case of a nontaxable item, such as municipal bond interest, there is no effect on either tax expense or tax liability.

Another aspect of the tax picture is called *intrastatement* or *intraperiod tax allocation.* Where prior period adjustments, extraordinary items, or operations of discontinued segments of a firm have tax effects, these items are shown net of the tax effect. The balance of the total tax expense figure then appears below net income before income taxes and extraordinary items. Intrastatement allocation is relatively easy to employ and probably has relevance for users, so the benefits appear to outweigh the costs. Nothing else of a theoretical nature is involved in intrastatement tax allocation.

There are numerous examples of timing differences (called *temporary differences* in SFAS 96). The tax liability would be greater than tax expense where either revenues are recognized for tax purposes earlier than for published reporting purposes or expenses are recognized more rapidly on the financial statements than on the tax return. Examples include the following:

1. Receipt of cash for rent or subscriptions prior to the period in which services are performed.
2. Warranties recognized for financial accounting purposes when goods are sold and for tax purposes when work is performed.
3. Postretirement benefits other than pensions recognized prior to cash payment.

Conversely, tax expense is greater than tax liability when either revenues are recognized more slowly or expenses more rapidly for tax purposes than for book purposes. These situations would include

---

[1] AICPA (1953, p. 88).

1. Income from long-term construction contracts using the percentage-of-completion approach for financial accounting and the completed-contract approach for income taxes.
2. Installment sale income recognized for financial purposes at the time of sale and when cash is collected for taxes.
3. Accelerated depreciation for taxes and straight-line depreciation for financial accounting.
4. Intangible drilling and development costs deducted when incurred for taxes and capitalized for financial accounting.

THE RATIONALE OF INCOME TAX ALLOCATION

As the name explicitly states, income tax allocation is indeed an allocation. Thomas, in fact, has characterized it in very pithy terms:

> . . . tax allocation embodies the allocation problem in one of its most pathological forms. . . . tax allocation may be perceived as an attempt to make allocation consistent, and its allocation problems are the consequences of other allocations.[2]

Although the language of ARB 43 is not explicit, it appears that income tax allocation is grounded in the matching concept. However, matching, as it is employed in tax allocation, differs from all other applications of matching. In the usual situation, expenses are matched against revenues. The result is expected to at least roughly portray efforts (expenses) that have given rise to accomplishments (revenues). However, the matching that occurs under income tax allocation attempts to normalize income tax expense with pretax accounting income. Hence, after-tax income is also correlated with pretax income. The matching brought about by tax allocation literally occurs at a lower point on the income statement than that of any other expense.

Income tax allocation may smooth income but, because its use is mandatory where timing differences exist, it cannot be construed as a smoothing instrument — since management has no choice but to use it under both APB 11 and SFAS 96.[3] Comprehensive allocation is thus an example of rigid uniformity. It *might* be useful for predicting cash flows, but no empirical studies have been made of the relationship between income using tax allocation and other income measurement methods and future cash flows.

Two articles by Beaver and Dukes, however, examined another aspect of prediction.[4] Their studies concern the effect on security prices of allocation versus nonallocation. They assumed that because of market efficiency, security

---

[2] Thomas (1974, pp. 146–147).
[3] However, under SFAS 96 tax-planning strategies can be employed to determine the specific years when temporary differences are expected to give rise to net taxable or deductible amounts. This can affect the calculation of the total net taxable or deductible amounts. Management must have the ability and intention of implementing these strategies and their costs must be feasible. For further details, see FASB (1987, pp. 10–11 and 44–46).
[4] Beaver and Dukes (1972 and 1973).

price behavior would indicate which method the market perceives to be most appropriate in terms of setting equilibrium prices. In their first study, they found that tax allocation had the highest degree of association with security price behavior, while income without tax allocation was second, and cash flows were last. They thus concluded that the income tax allocation procedure is correct. Their second study also found that income tax deferred earnings had a higher association with security prices than income without allocation. However, they amended their earlier conclusion and suggested that the net-of-tax method (to be discussed shortly) using a tax rate significantly higher than current rates had a higher association with security prices than tax allocation using existing rates.

The general weakness of studies of the type done by Beaver and Dukes — where an attempt is made to measure the association of an accounting method with security prices — lies in the imperfection of the market for accounting information: the "free-rider" problem discussed in Chapter 4. Hence, these studies provide descriptive information but they cannot be relied on for the normative purpose of choosing among competing accounting alternatives.[5]

Viewed from the perspective of the 1990s, matching provides a weak rationale for income tax allocation. However, within the framework of the historical cost approach, and in an era when the arbitrariness of the allocation process was not questioned, a strong case could have been made for income tax allocation. Nevertheless, income tax allocation has been controversial since the late 1950s in its most important application: the use of accelerated depreciation for tax purposes and straight-line depreciation for the financial statements.

TAX ALLOCATION AND ACCELERATED DEPRECIATION

In the early years of the income tax allocation debate, the case favoring allocation was often made by using what was, in effect, a single-asset type of example.[6] For example, assume that an asset with a five-year life and a cost of $15,000 and no salvage is depreciated with a 40 percent tax rate by the sum-of-the-years' digits for tax purposes and by straight-line depreciation for financial accounting. The results are shown in Exhibit 14–1. The fifth column shows an increase in deferred taxes in the first and second years and reversal and elimination in the fourth and fifth years. If this model were representative of real circumstances, the tax allocation situation would present few problems. The extra tax benefits above those stemming from straight-line depreciation received in the early years of the asset's life are paid back in the later years.

Another situation is depicted in Exhibit 14–2 where a new asset acquisition is made each year until the firm reaches a stable point. It is assumed that beyond Year 6 the pattern of acquiring a new asset each year and the disposal

---

[5] Gonedes and Dopuch (1974, pp. 115–116) suggest that where several alternative methods are possible, the one that can be converted to other methods at the least cost may be optimal. In the case of income tax expense, it would be easier for users to transform allocation figures to cash flow than vice versa.
[6] For example, Moonitz (1957, p. 177).

EXHIBIT 14–1
Tax Deferral with a Single Asset

(1)	(2)	(3)	(4)	(5)
Year	Sum-of-the-Years'-Digits Depreciation	Straight-line Depreciation	Excess Tax Depreciation	Deferral of Taxes (40% Tax Rate × Column 4)
1	$ 5,000	$ 3,000	$2,000	$800
2	4,000	3,000	1,000	400
3	3,000	3,000	0	0
4	2,000	3,000	(1,000)	(400)
5	1,000	3,000	(2,000)	(800)
	$15,000	$15,000	$ 0	$ 0

of an old one continues as before. Cost and depreciation methods are the same as in the first example. Beyond Year 5 total accelerated and straight-line depreciation are equal, so the tax benefits occurring in Years 1–3 become permanent when viewed in the aggregate sense. Of course, if the firm continues to expand or if costs of new assets increase, the amount of deferred taxes will continue to increase.[7] In fact, the great bulk of empirical evidence appears to indicate that the deferred tax account does indeed increase over time.[8]

The situation of virtually permanent deferral has presented an enigma to accounting standard setters and theoreticians in terms of interpreting the credit and even calling into question the whole process of tax allocation where the potential for permanent deferral exists.

Interpreting Deferred Tax Credits

Unquestionably, no legal liability arises as a result of using accelerated depreciation for income tax purposes. The federal government's desire in allowing accelerated depreciation as well as shorter guideline lives (the so-called Asset Depreciation Range system prescribing the number of years of tax life for the

---

[7] The classic article discussing the multiasset case and its ramifications is by Davidson (1958).

[8] See Livingstone (1967a, 1967b, and 1969) and Price Waterhouse & Co. (1967). For an opposing view, see Herring and Jacobs (1976). For a refutation of Herring and Jacobs, see Davidson, Skelton, and Weil (1977). The Davidson, Skelton, and Weil (1977) study was updated by Davidson, Rasch, and Weil (1984). Using the Compustat files for 3,108 firms, all of them listed on the major exchanges, plus additional files for approximately 2,000 smaller firms for the years 1974–82, they found that on the average only 7.5 percent of the firms that experienced a change in the deferred taxes account paid additional taxes as a result of a decline in the account resulting from depreciation timing differences. Skekel and Fazzi (1984) replicated the Davidson, Rasch, and Weil (1984) paper but restricted their sample to capital-intensive firms for the years 1974–82. They found that only 4.5 percent of this group, on the average, paid additional taxes as a result of a decline in the deferred taxes account resulting from depreciation timing differences.

EXHIBIT 14–2
Tax Deferral in a Multiasset Situation

	Sum-of-the-Years'-Digits Depreciation					
	Year 1	Year 2	Year 3	Year 4	Year 5	Year 6
Asset A	$5,000	$4,000	$3,000	$2,000	$1,000	
Asset B		5,000	4,000	3,000	2,000	$1,000
Asset C			5,000	4,000	3,000	2,000
Asset D				5,000	4,000	3,000
Asset E					5,000	4,000
Asset F						5,000
Total	5,000	9,000	12,000	14,000	15,000	15,000

	Straight-line Depreciation					
Asset A	3,000	3,000	3,000	3,000	3,000	
Asset B		3,000	3,000	3,000	3,000	3,000
Asset C			3,000	3,000	3,000	3,000
Asset D				3,000	3,000	3,000
Asset E					3,000	3,000
Asset F						3,000
Total	3,000	6,000	9,000	12,000	15,000	15,000
Excess of sum-of-the-years'-digits over straight-line depreciation	2,000	3,000	3,000	2,000	0	0
Deferral (excess × 40% tax rate)	$ 800	$1,200	$1,200	$ 800	$ 0	$ 0

various classes of assets) has been to stimulate economic growth and modernize the nation's productive capacity by raising the internal rate of return on capital investment projects. Nothing is owed the government as a result of "excess" depreciation allowances taken for tax purposes. Moreover, the problem simply disappears if the enterprise uses accelerated depreciation for both tax and book purposes. The definition of legal liability, however, is too narrow for accounting purposes, which are, of course, concerned with portraying economic reality in accordance with user objectives and needs.

Another way of looking at the problem is to view each asset individually rather than looking at the aggregate balance of the deferred tax credit account. This is often referred to as the *rollover* method.[9] From the individual asset

---

[9] For a discussion, see Black (1966, pp. 69–72).

standpoint, the "liability" is paid off even though a new "loan" is received when a new asset is acquired, thereby offsetting the payback on the older asset as its tax depreciation diminishes. Thus, rollover proponents might say that accounts payable are recognized even though accounts that are paid off may be replaced with new payables. However, the rollover view has been strongly criticized because the payoff of each loan on older assets cannot be compared to the accounts payable situation because the debts are paid off individually, which, of course, is not the case with income taxes.[10]

The argument that deferred taxes are not the same as accounts payable weakened the case for comprehensive tax allocation with deferred taxes interpreted as liabilities. Because of this indeterminate status, deferred taxes were viewed as deferred credits in APB 11. As a result, the income statement, under the mantle of the matching concept, took precedence over the balance sheet (which now contained deferred charges that might not be assets and deferred credits that might not be liabilities). The deferred credit approach differs from the liability interpretation under comprehensive allocation in the sense that the deferred credit account is not adjusted if tax rates change, whereas it is adjusted under the liability method if tax rates change. This distinction is in addition to the interpretation of the account itself.

Orientations to Income Tax Allocation

There are several policy positions possible on the income tax allocation issue. One is that allocation is not appropriate. In other words, tax expense equals tax liability. Some theoretical justification for advocating no allocation has been derived from the interpretation that income tax payments are a distribution of income rather than being an expense.[11] However, this has not been a popular position and cannot be strongly defended.

Somewhat related to the idea that income taxes are a distribution of profits rather than an element deducted in arriving at profits is the "new form of equities" position of Graul and Lemke.[12] According to their interpretation, the credit arising under income tax allocation represents a subordinated equity investment in the firm by the federal government. The reason the government makes this investment in the enterprise is to stimulate business investment. Deferred tax credits would be listed as an element of invested capital in the owners' equities section of the balance sheet. There is indeed some logic to this position, but it is simply one possible interpretation and nothing more. The fact that macroeconomic policy has led to certain tax benefits for business does not make government an investor in the firm except in the most limited sense.

Another possibility is the **net-of-tax** method in which income tax expense is equal to the tax liability. However, the book depreciation is increased (or

---

[10] See the comments of Davidson in Black (1966, pp. 117–119).

[11] Suojanen (1954, p. 393). For a broad discussion of this question, see Wheeler and Galliart (1974, pp. 51–56).

[12] Graul and Lemke (1976). For a somewhat similar argument, see Watson (1979).

reduced) according to the following formula in any year by the excess tax benefits received above (or below) those that would have been derived from straight-line depreciation:

$$D_t = S + r(A_t - S) \tag{14.1}$$

where

D_t = net of tax depreciation for period t
S = straight-line depreciation
r = tax rate
A_t = accelerated depreciation for period t

Hence, if accelerated depreciation were $500 for a particular year and straight-line were $400 with a 40 percent tax rate, net-of-tax depreciation would be $440, determined by

$$\$440 = \$400 + .40(\$500 - \$400) \tag{14.1a}$$

Net-of-tax depreciation gives the same bottom-line net income effect as comprehensive allocation but moves the deferred credit over to the asset side as an additional element of accumulated depreciation. This certainly eliminates a large stumbling block of comprehensive allocation — interpreting deferred tax credits. Moreover, there is some theoretical justification for net-of-tax depreciation in a historical cost context.[13] Assume that amortization should concur with benefits received. In the case of fixed assets, two benefits can be postulated: (1) revenue-producing or cost-avoidance potential from productive utilization, and (2) tax reduction. Therefore, if an asset renders relatively even service over its life and accelerated depreciation benefits are taken, there is certainly some justification for net-of-tax depreciation. However, the procedure is still an allocation and not a method of valuation. Along the same line, the numbers cannot be transformed or related to any current value measurements. They might, however, be transformed into general price-level-adjusted depreciation numbers.

Still another possible orientation to the timing difference problem is called *partial allocation*. Under **partial allocation,** only those deferred credits that can reasonably be expected to be paid off in the foreseeable future on an aggregate basis are recorded on the books.[14] Thus, income tax expense for a given year is defined as the total tax costs attributable to the given year's operations, costs that will be levied against the firm, both in the current and future years, on a gross or aggregate basis. Hence, the deferred tax credit is clearly definable as a liability. The balance of the deferred tax liability account represents the amount expected to be paid in the future, which is attributable to the current and past years' operations on a gross basis.

An example should clarify the partial allocation approach. Assume that a

---

[13] See Bierman (1990) for an extended discussion of the rationale underlying the net-of-tax method.
[14] See Jeter and Chaney (1988) and Chaney and Jeter (1989) for further discussion of partial allocation.

EXHIBIT 14–3
Partial and Comprehensive Income Tax Allocation

	Tax	Depreciation		Book	Depreciation		Comprehensive Allocation	Partial Allocation
Year	A_1	A_2	A_3	A_1	A_2	A_3	40%(TD−BD)	
1	$8,000			$5,000			$1,200	$1,120
2	6,000			5,000			400	
3	4,000	$2,400		5,000	$1,500		(40)	
4	2,000	1,800		5,000	1,500		(1,080)	
5		1,200	$8,000		1,500	$5,000	1,080	
6		600	7,000		1,500	5,000	440	

firm's income before depreciation is $20,000 each year and the tax rate is 40 percent. Depreciation is the only timing difference between tax and book figures. The planning horizon is a five-year period. Depreciation figures are shown in Exhibit 14–3 (assets are designated $A_1 \ldots A_n$). All predictions are assumed to be accurate. For comparison and completeness the numbers are also shown for comprehensive allocation. Beyond Year 5 tax depreciation is expected to exceed book depreciation.

Notice that the liability in Year 1 under partial allocation is based on the fact that tax depreciation in Years 3 and 4 is less than book depreciation. This results in an anticipated obligation because tax payments in those years would be greater than the anticipated "normal" amount based on book depreciation. This liability under partial allocation is consistent with the definition of liabilities in SFAC 6, which defines them as ". . . probable future sacrifices of economic benefits arising from present obligations of a particular entity to transfer assets . . . as a result of past transactions or events."[15] Whether deferred tax credits arising under comprehensive allocation are liabilities consistent with the definition above is not entirely clear.[16] Partial allocation is, of course, an example of finite uniformity. The relevant circumstance is whether tax depreciation will be less than book depreciation in any given year. Allocation occurs if, and only if, this condition is expected to exist over the period of the planning horizon. In accordance with the previous example, entries for the first four years that would arise under partial allocation are shown in Exhibit 14–4 along with entries under comprehensive allocation.

---

[15] FASB (1985, p. 13).
[16] Nair and Weygandt (1981, p. 100) do not think that deferred tax liabilities arising under comprehensive allocation are consistent with the liability definition of SFAC 3. However, the statement itself appears to admit the possibility that the comprehensive liability approach is consistent with the liability definition presented there. See FASB (1980, p. 71). It appears that both partial allocation and the comprehensive liability approaches may result in the credits qualifying as liabilities according to SFAC 6. For further coverage, see the discussion of SFAS 96 in this chapter.

EXHIBIT 14–4
Entries Under Partial and Comprehensive Tax Allocation

Partial Allocation			*Comprehensive Allocation*		
Year 1			*Year 1*		
Income Tax Expense	$5,920		Income Tax Expense	$6,000	
			Deferred Tax Credit		
Deferred Tax Liability		$1,120	or Liability		$1,200
Income Tax Liability		4,800	Income Tax Liability		4,800
Tax liability is					
.4($20,000 − $8,000)					
Year 2			*Year 2*		
Income Tax Expense	5,600		Income Tax Expense	6,000	
Income Tax Liability		5,600	Deferred Tax Credit		
			or Liability		400
.4($20,000 − $6,000)			Income Tax Liability		5,600
Year 3			*Year 3*		
Income Tax Expense	5,400		Income Tax Expense	5,400	
			Deferred Tax Credit		
Deferred Tax Liability	40		or Liability	40	
Income Tax Liability		5,440	Income Tax Liability		5,440
.4($20,000 − $6,400)					
Year 4			*Year 4*		
Income Tax Expense	5,400		Income Tax Expense	5,400	
			Deferred Tax Credit		
Deferred Tax Liability	1,080		or Liability	1,080	
Income Tax Liability		6,480	Income Tax Liability		6,480
.4($20,000 − $3,800)					

The obvious question about partial allocation concerns the issue of verifiability since the method predicts a cash flow variable. Buckley has made some progress in this area.[17] He has developed a predictive model embracing the appropriate variables of anticipated capital investment over the planning horizon; tax and book depreciation differentials, including different lives; and expected changes in the tax rate. After setting up matrices for these variables, matrix algebra is used to solve for the predicted annual change in the deferred tax liability account. Tested by five firms in the Los Angeles area, the model had a high degree of predictive accuracy; not surprisingly, the firms found the results useful for cash budgeting and planning. Recent literature has given some

[17] Buckley (1972, pp. 71–101).

support to partial allocation.[18] In addition, the United Kingdom has essentially adopted it for years beginning after January 1, 1979.

Agency theory must also be considered in regard to partial allocation. How likely is it that management will favor an accounting method which lowers the current year's income based upon a future contingency? Furthermore, management could also use the problem of verifiability as an additional prop to support any desire not to lower income in the current year.

One more question remains in terms of partial allocation and comprehensive liability. Since the resulting credits are interpreted as liabilities that mature beyond a year, is discounting of these values appropriate?

Discounting Deferred Tax Liabilities   Long-term liabilities, such as bonds payable and noncancellable leases, are carried at their present values. This is accomplished by discounting future payments by the effective or implicit interest rate. Similarly, APB 21 requires that noninterest-bearing notes receivable must be discounted at their implicit interest rate. Consistency would, therefore, appear to dictate that tax liabilities (not deferred credits, however) under either the comprehensive or partial approaches should likewise be discounted.

In reality, the tax liabilities under either of the two interpretations are interest-free loans. However, the opportunity cost doctrine from economics has been advocated as a justification for discounting by the implicit interest rate: if the funds were not received from the government in the form of lower income taxes through higher depreciation allowances, borrowing from another source would have been necessary.[19] The interest rate on the funds from the next best source would be their **opportunity cost.** The opportunity cost doctrine is used in financial accounting. If an asset is donated to a firm, for example, it is booked at its fair market value with a credit to donated capital. Therefore, from the economic standpoint, it appears to be quite reasonable that deferred tax liabilities should be shown at their present value using the interest rate for a loan of similar duration, repayment schedule, and risk borne by the lender. The implicit interest rate should be on an after-tax basis.[20] We will assume that it is 10 percent. Entries for discounting deferred tax liabilities under partial and comprehensive allocation are shown in Exhibit 14–5.

Under comprehensive allocation, the tax expense consists of current tax liabilities and the present value of future obligations using an individual-asset rollover interpretation. Where partial allocation is employed, the tax expense includes the present value of future obligations where an actual payment above the future years' liabilities is involved because book depreciation of presently owned assets is expected to exceed tax depreciation without a shielding effect

---

[18] See Nair and Weygandt (1981, p. 100).

[19] See Nurnberg (1972, pp. 657–658).

[20] For more background on the appropriate rate, see Nurnberg (1972, pp. 659–665). Williams and Findlay (1974), Wolk and Tearney (1980, pp. 126–127), Findlay and Williams (1981), and Collins, Rickard, and Selby (1990).

EXHIBIT 14–5
Entries for Discounting Deferred Tax Liabilities

Partial Allocation			*Comprehensive Allocation*		
Year 1			*Year 1*		

Partial Allocation			Comprehensive Allocation		
Income Tax Expense	$5,644		Income Tax Expense	$5,731	
Deferred Tax Liability		$ 844	Deferred Tax Liability		$ 931
Income Tax Liability		4,800	Income Tax Liability		4,800

As shown in Exhibit 14–3, reversal occurs in Years 3 and 4 which are 2 and 3 years after Year 1:

$.826 \times \$40 \quad = \$ 33$
$.751 \times 1,080 = \underline{\quad 811}$
$\qquad\qquad\qquad \underline{\$844}$

As shown in Exhibit 14–3, reversal occurs for asset A_1 in Years 3 and 4 after Year 1:

$.826 \times .40 \times \$1,000 = \$330$
$.751 \times .40 \times \$2,000 = \underline{\quad 601}$
$\qquad\qquad\qquad\qquad\quad \underline{\$931}$

Year 2			*Year 2*		

Income Tax Expense	5,600		Income Tax Expense	5,930	
Interest on Deferred Tax			Interest on Deferred Tax		
Liability	84		Liability	93	
Deferred Tax Liability		84	Deferred Tax Liability		423
Income Tax Liability		5,600	Income Tax Liability		5,600

Interest at 10% on the balance of the deferred tax liability is (.10 × $844)

Interest at 10% on the balance of the deferred tax liability is (.10 × $934). The current liability on A_1 reverses in 2 years in Year 4:

$.826 \times .40 \times \$1,000 = \$330$

Year 3			*Year 3*		

Income Tax Expense	5,400		Income Tax Expense	5,319	
Interest on Deferred Tax			Interest on Deferred Tax		
Liability	93		Liability	135	
Deferred Tax Liability		53	Deferred Tax Liability		14
Income Tax Liability		5,440	Income Tax Liability		5,440

Deferred tax liability is credited for interest (.10 × $928) and debited for the $40 reversal.

Interest at 10% on the balance of the deferred tax liability is (.10 × $1,354). The reversal on A_1 is $400. Present value of additional liabilities on A_2 which reverses in Years 5 and 6 is

$.826 \times .40 \times \$300 = \$ 99$
$.751 \times .40 \times \ 600 = \underline{\quad 180}$
$\qquad\qquad\qquad\qquad\quad \underline{\$279}$

(continued)

EXHIBIT 14–5   (continued)

Year 4			Year 4		
Income Tax Expense	$5,400		Income Tax Expense	$5,379	
Interest on Deferred Tax			Interest on Deferred Tax		
Liability	98		Liability	137	
Deferred Tax Liability	982		Deferred Tax Liability	964	
Income Tax Liability		$6,480	Income Tax Liability		$6,480

	Interest at 10% on the balance of the deferred tax liability is (.10 × $1,368). The reversal on A_1 is $1,200. Present value of additional liabilities on A_2 which reverse in Year 6 is (.826 × .40 × $300).
Deferred tax liability is debited for the $1,080 reversal and credited for interest (.10 × $981). The account has a zero balance except for the $1 rounding error.	

---

from assets to be acquired in the future. This would, of course, be in addition to the current year's tax liability.

Summary of Orientations to Income Tax Allocation   In this section, we have reviewed and analyzed a bewildering number of possible approaches to the income tax allocation question. The various positions are shown in Exhibit 14–6. The tax allocation debate can be approached only in terms of such criteria as consistency with other areas of valuation, relevance to users, and verifiability of measurements. Pure deductive logic alone cannot resolve this very perplexing issue.

Present Value Depreciation and Income Tax Allocation

Another theoretical facet of tax allocation concerns present value depreciation, which was discussed in Chapter 12. Use of this depreciation is intended to bring about a constant return on investment throughout the life of an asset. However, income tax allocation is essentially inconsistent with the constant rate-of-return approach.[21] The key point is that present value depreciation evens return on an *after*-tax basis. Thus, any attempt at income tax allocation would destroy the equalized rate of return that is built into the depreciation schedule.

There have been several attempts to make present value depreciation and income tax allocation consistent in terms of maintaining a constant rate of return when both are used.[22] Although these attempts have been tactically suc-

---

[21] Drake (1961).
[22] For example, Bierman and Dyckman (1974), Meyers (1973), and Bullock (1974). Meyers' approach, in particular, is successful. He would discount the pretax cash flows back to the cost of the asset to

---

EXHIBIT 14–6
Summary of Tax Allocation Positions

Major Position	No Allocation	Comprehensive Allocation					Partial Allocation	
Principal Variations	Not Applicable	New Form of Equities	Net of Tax	Deferred	Liability		Liability	
Discounting of Liability	Not Applicable	Not Applicable	Not Applicable	Not Applicable	Yes ↓	No ↘	Yes ↓	No ↘

---

cessful, too many other problems remain. First, combining depreciation theory with capital budgeting analysis is something of a quixotic venture. The latter is a planning method that looks forward for at least several years, while the former is a profit-reporting technique that looks backward for one-year periods. Thus, one is ex-post and the other is ex-ante. Their contexts are completely different. Second, the present value method is somewhat artificial because it is designed to bring about a predetermined rate of return. To put it slightly differently, depreciation becomes a causal agent in the determination of income rather than a residual effect.[23] Closely related to the artificial nature of the write-off is the fact that the increasing charge structure that ordinarily results with present value depreciation is inconsistent with the pattern of benefits ordinarily received from many assets: greatest benefits in the earliest years. Third, the jointness problem among productive assets makes it virtually impossible to pinpoint cash flow generation, a drawback that would make the present value method extremely difficult to implement on a practical basis. This is, of course, the allocation problem once again.

ACCELERATED COST RECOVERY SYSTEM

Prior to the 1981 tax act, corporate balance sheets in the United States were encumbered by hundreds of billions of dollars of deferred tax credits under the comprehensive deferral approach required by APB 11. Whatever its economic merits might have been, the deferred tax credit situation became further aggravated under the 1981 tax act because the period of tax recovery was further shortened.

The new system, called ACRS (Accelerated Cost Recovery System), eliminates the concept of useful depreciable life. Instead, it substitutes six classes of

---

determine its internal rate of return. Annual depreciation would then be equal to the change in the present value of the asset's remaining pretax cash flows, using the internal rate of return as the discount rate. Income tax allocation would then be employed by taking the tax rate times the difference between accelerated and present value depreciation, which would then be added to the tax expense.
[23] This point is discussed in Vatter (1966).

capital assets with prescribed lives. Furthermore, salvage values are not considered. As a result, controversies over useful life between the IRS and corporations have been eliminated. The classes of capital assets as set out in the Tax Reform Act of 1986 are

Class (Years)	Types of Assets
3 years	Short-lived special manufacturing tools and handling devices in some industries. Examples include rubber manufacturing, glass products, fabricated metals, and manufacture of motor vehicles.
5 years	Cars, light trucks, and certain manufacturing equipment: oil drilling, construction, chemical manufacturing, and some clothing manufacturing. Also special tools for selected industries such as boat building.
7 years	Most heavy manufacturing equipment.
10 years	Includes railroad track, electrical generating and transmission equipment, cement manufacturing equipment as well as the food processing equipment for grain, sugar, and vegetable oil.
15 years	Includes gas pipelines and nuclear plants.
20 years	Includes sewer pipes and phone cables.

Depreciation schedules for the various classes are shown in Exhibit 14–7.

THE ASSET–LIABILITY ORIENTATION OF SFAS 96

Dissatisfaction with APB 11 led to the reconsideration of income tax allocation by the FASB.[24] SFAS 96 appeared in December, 1987, after almost five years of assessment and analysis. The standard keeps the comprehensive income tax orientation of APB 11 but substitutes a liability (asset–liability) approach in place of the deferred approach of APB 11. However, SFAS 96 employs some unusual assumptions in moving to the balance sheet focus and away from the matching concept underlying the comprehensive-deferred approach of APB 11. In order to comprehend the current FASB position, we will first examine a simple liability and then a simple asset situation before looking at a more complex situation in order to make a theoretical critique of the standard.

LIABILITIES

Assume that in 1987 installment sales of $600 occur with collection of $300 expected to occur in both 1988 and 1989. If the $600 of income is recognized for financial accounting purposes in 1987, but the tax effects do not occur until

---

[24] See Nair and Weygandt (1981) and Rosenfield and Dent (1983), for example.

EXHIBIT 14–7
ACRS Allowances Under the 1986 Tax Act

Year	3-Year	5-Year	7-Year	10-Year	15-Year	20-Year
1	33.00	20.00	14.28	10.00	5.00	3.75
2	45.00	32.00	24.49	18.00	9.50	7.22
3	15.00[a]	19.20	17.49	14.40	8.55	6.68
4	7.00	11.52[a]	12.49	11.52	7.69	6.18
5		11.52	8.93[a]	9.22	6.93	5.71
6		5.76	8.93	7.37	6.23	5.28
7			8.93	6.55[a]	5.90[a]	4.89
8			4.46	6.55	5.90	4.52
9				6.55	5.90	4.46[a]
10				6.55	5.90	4.46
11				3.29	5.90	4.46
12					5.90	4.46
13					5.90	4.46
14					5.90	4.46
15					5.90	4.46
16					3.00	4.46
17						4.46
18						4.46
19						4.46
20						4.46
21						2.25
	100	100	100	100	100	100

[a]Indicates the year of switchback to straight-line depreciation.

1988 and 1989, a liability is created equal to the $600 times the tax rate — assume 34 percent — or $204. The $102 due in 1988 would be classified as a current deferred tax liability with the 1989 portion being long term.

The FASB is unequivocal about the fact that the transaction above creates a liability. It is the result of a past event that will require resources in the future in order to satisfy the obligation. Furthermore, this temporary difference is not dependent on other possible future events, such as earning financial income in 1988 and 1989.[25] The firm could have a zero level of income but receipt of the cash (an event that is assumed to occur) would require payment of the tax.

ASSETS

The asset and liability situations are not symmetrical. Assume an expense of $500 has been recognized for financial accounting purposes in arriving at financial income of $2,500 during 1987. The amount will be paid in 1990, at which

---

[25] SFAS 96, pp. 79–81.

point it becomes deductible for tax purposes. It is the only temporary difference. Recognition of the deferred tax asset is more complicated than the liability situation. Since no intervening event can be recognized, the $500 must be able to be "carried back" against income of a prior year exactly analogous to a tax loss carryback. Since there is a three-year carryback period, the $500 could be carried back against the taxable income of $2,500 occurring during 1987. It would, therefore, be recognized as a noncurrent deferred tax asset of $170 ($500 × .34). There would also be a deferred tax benefit (reduction) in computing the income tax expense for 1987.

If the $500 were not scheduled for payment until 1991, it could not be recognized as a deferred tax asset during 1987 because only a three-year carryback is allowed. It could become a deferred tax asset during 1988 assuming at least $500 of taxable income arises.

Another route can be taken in recognizing the deferred tax asset during 1987. It could be offset against the payment of a deferred tax liability during the carryback period or carried forward up to a period of fifteen years against payment of future deferred tax liabilities. Assume, for example, that during 1990 book depreciation is $600 and tax depreciation is $100. The $500 deductible amount would offset the liability repayment of $500.

The lack of symmetry between deferred tax liabilities and deferred tax assets was vociferously defended in SFAS 96. The crux of the conservative outlook on deferred tax assets is that financial income must be earned in order to derive the benefits from deferred tax assets (holding aside carrybacks, carryforwards, and offsets against deferred tax liability repayments). However, the earnings of financial income in intervening years has not yet occurred and cannot be inherently assumed.[26] We shall return to this point in the theoretical analysis of SFAS 96. In the interim, more complex situations must be analyzed.

COMPLEX SITUATIONS

In complex situations, in order to determine deferred tax assets or liabilities as well as current tax expense, the complete pattern of temporary differences and their reversals must be set out at the end of the period. The complete pattern of temporary differences, both originating and reversing, for the ABCD Company at the end of 1987 is shown in Exhibit 14–8. Parentheses indicate a deduction from accounting income, and no parentheses an addition to accounting income in order to arrive at taxable income. The sum of the future temporary differences from 1988 to 1995 exactly offsets the decrease of $120 from accounting income to taxable income applicable to 1987. Notice also, in accordance with the 1986 Tax Act, that corporate income tax rates decline from 46 percent to 34 percent.

For 1988 and beyond, temporary differences are subtotaled for each year. The excess of tax deductibility benefits for depreciation and warranties is carried back against the taxable income of 1986, creating a deferred tax asset of

---

[26] SFAS 96, pp. 79–81.

EXHIBIT 14–8
Complex Income Tax Allocation Under SFAS 96

	Prior Years		Current Year	Future Years					
	1985	1986	1987	1988	1989	1990	1991	...	1995
Accounting Income	$1,000	$1,000	$1,120						
Scheduling—Temporary Differences									
Depreciation			(50)°	(120)°	(60)°	$100ᴿ	$130ᴿ		
Bad Debts			100°	(100)ᴿ					
Warranty Accrual			200°	(125)ᴿ	(75)ᴿ				
Installment Sale			(400)°	400ᴿ					
Deferred Compensation			30°						$(30)ᴿ
Subtotals (taxable income for 1987)	1,000	1,000	1,000	55	(135)	100	130		$(30)*
Loss Carryback		(135)			135				
Net Taxable Amount	1,000	865	1,000	55	0	100	130		
Tax Rate	46%	46%	40%	34%	34%	34%	34%		
Tax (A)	460	398	400	19	0	34	44		
Actual Tax in Carryback Period (B)	460	460	400						
Deferred Tax (Asset) or Liability [(A) − (B)]	$ 0	$ (62)	0	$ 19	$ 0	$ 34	$ 44		
Net Deferred Tax Liability			$ 35						
Current Deferred			$ 19						
Long-Term Deferred			16						
Total			$ 35						

Source: Adapted with changes courtesy KPMG Peat Marwick.
*Tax benefit not recognized since deductible amount (a) does not offset taxable amounts from other temporary differences and (b) would result in a refund of taxes paid.
O = Originating; R = Reversing.

$62. This amount is offset against the gross noncurrent deferred tax liabilities of $34 and $44 calculated for 1990 and 1991, creating a long-term deferred tax liability of $16 ($34 plus $44 minus $62). Even though the $62 is a carryback, it is noncurrent because it will originate two years after the current year, in 1989. The $30 of deferred compensation does not enter the picture because it cannot be carried back before 1992 nor do any carryforwards exist at this time. The income tax entries for 1987 would be the following:

Income Tax Expense	$400	
Income Taxes Payable		$400
Deferred Income Tax Expense	35	
Current Deferred Tax Liability		19
Noncurrent Deferred Tax Liability		16

The same computation is done again at the end of the next year (1988) with appropriate adjustment of the deferred tax accounts. Assume that the taxable income for 1988 is once again $1,000. No further temporary differences arise. The only current deferred item is the $62 deferred tax asset carried back to 1986. Long-term deferred tax liabilities of $78 ($34 plus $44) exist. The following would be the tax expense and liabilities for 1988:

Income Tax Expense	$340	
Income Taxes Payable		$340
Current Deferred Tax Liability	19	
Income Tax Expense		19
Current Deferred Tax Asset	62	
Noncurrent Deferred Tax Liability		62

The second entry is for the repayment of the deferred tax liability. Had additional asset acquisitions occurred during 1988, repayment would have been blocked by the creation of additional deferred tax liabilities. The last entry reclassifies the tax asset from the carryback. It has now become current since it is applicable to 1989, one year hence. It was previously an offset totaling $78 against the noncurrent deferred tax liabilities of 1990 and 1991. Notice that the Noncurrent Deferred Tax Liability account now has a balance of $78. Entries for the remaining years would proceed in a similar fashion.

THEORETICAL CRITIQUE

The principal criticism leveled against SFAS 96 is the previously mentioned conservatism toward asset recognition. The standard defends this asymmetric approach by saying that it is completely consistent with the tax laws, but that is not quite correct.[27] SFAS 96, using the example of an installment sale where a future liability *is* recognized and a warranty expense differential where an asset is *not* recognized, makes the following statement:

---

[27] SFAS 96, pp. 79–80.

> Taxes payable . . . at the end of the current year could be eliminated by incurring
> a loss in Year 2 or 3 — but that necessary future event has not yet occurred. A tax
> benefit for the $900 warranty expense difference at the end of the current year
> could be realized by earning a profit in Year 2 or 3 — but that necessary future
> event has not yet occurred. This Statement prohibits anticipation of the future
> tax effects of either incurring losses or earning profits in future years.[28]

However, when the carryback approach is used in recognizing deferred tax assets and when tax rates are declining (exactly as they have been as Exhibit 14–8
illustrates), results are both unrealistic (as previously noted) and nonconserva-
tive. The reason for the lack of conservatism is that deferred tax assets, through
the carryback process, are booked at 46 percent, with a resulting credit to income tax expense, even though they will realistically reverse at the rate of 34
percent. SFAS 96 would have been far more effective if it evenhandedly recognized both deferred tax assets and liabilities and booked them at the rates at
which they are expected to reverse. Thus, the net operating loss approach for
assets is confusing, unrealistic, and can be unconservative if tax rates are declining, as they were quite recently.

Paragraph 109 illustrates the "no future event" approach in SFAS 96 in
situations where both revenue and expense are recognized more rapidly for
accounting than for tax purposes. However, a prepaid revenue item that is taxed
when the cash is received even though revenue recognition does not occur until
the following period does not require an intervening event in order for the
deferred tax asset (really a prepaid tax expense) to be realized. Similarly, if an
expense is recognized more rapidly for tax purposes than for accounting purposes, such as ACRS depreciation for tax purposes and straight-line depreciation for financial reporting, a future event in the form of income being earned
would have to occur in order for the liability to be satisfied. Hence, the analysis
in the standard appears to be intended to justify conservatism but instead is
simply logically incorrect.[29] These relationships — and their incongruous nature — are summarized in Exhibit 14–9.

The larger question of permanent deferral, discussed earlier in the chapter, is an issue that simply cannot be separated from the income tax allocation
issue. Furthermore, there are questions about whether the comprehensive-
liability approach to income tax allocation is consistent with the definition of
liabilities put forth in SFAC 6 of the conceptual framework. Nair and Weygandt
have stated that the comprehensive-liability interpretation is inconsistent with
the definition stated in SFAC 3.[30] Dopuch and Sunder used income tax allocation to make a more fundamental criticism of the conceptual framework definition of liabilities: The definition is simply not complete enough to determine
whether the deferred tax liability should be measured on an individual transac-

---

[28] Ibid., p. 79.
[29] See Wolk, Martin, and Nichols (1989) for further coverage.
[30] Nair and Weygandt (1981, pp. 98–100).

EXHIBIT 14–9
Intervening Event (the Need to Have Taxable Income or Loss in Affected Future Years)
in Order to Extinguish Deferred Tax Assets and Liabilities

Event	Type of Deferral	Intervening Event Needed for Payment of Dfd Tax Liab. or Receipt of Dfd Tax Asset Benefits
*Revenue recognized more rapidly for accounting purposes	Deferred Liability	No
Expense recognized more rapidly for tax purposes	Deferred Liability	Yes
*Expense recognized more rapidly for accounting purposes	Deferred Asset	Yes
Revenue recognized more rapidly for tax purposes	Deferred Asset	No

Source: Adapted from Wolk, Martin, and Nichols (1989, p. 3).
*Illustrated in Paragraph 109 of Statement 96.

tion basis (essentially the rollover view previously mentioned) or in the aggregate in terms of whether an actual repayment is expected (the partial allocation outlook).[31] Even dissenters to SFAS 96 rejected partial allocation on the grounds that it is dependent on future transactions (further acquisition of assets) that have not yet occurred. Thus, the question of liability definition may be a problem of the conceptual framework rather than SFAS 96, but permanent deferral, a problem of comprehensive allocation in both its deferred and liability forms, is closely intertwined with the liability definition problem.

These fundamental problems with SFAS 96 lead to several possible conflicts with the conceptual framework. The inconsistencies and anomalies previously noted raise several questions about the accounting qualities of SFAC 2. Given the conservative recognition of deferred tax assets, which turn out to be unconservative if tax rates are declining, as well as the spectre of permanent deferral, which the empirical — as well as the theoretical — literature has largely confirmed, the question must be raised relative to the user-specific quality of understandability. In other words, will users understand that deferred tax liabilities may still be subject to permanent deferral? If there is user confusion on this point, it also affects the pervasive constraint of the costs of standards exceeding the benefits thereof because the type of analysis of deferred taxes required by SFAS 96 and illustrated in a very simple situation in Exhibit 14–8 may be quite costly. Although the conceptual framework is beyond the pale of GAAP, one would hope that newly forthcoming standards would take it into account. This does not appear to be the case with SFAS 96.

There are other theoretical shortcomings to SFAS 96. APB 11, for all its faults, was at least based on the concept of matching. Matching has essentially been given up for accurate and realistic measurement of deferred tax assets and liabilities. But because of an unwarranted conservatism applied to measuring deferred tax assets combined with an unconservative (and unrealistic) twist if tax rates are declining, this is not really the case. The standard would have served its purpose far better if it had employed a consistent asset and liability viewpoint, booking each at their expected reversal rate if future tax rates are expected to change. The net operating loss approach applied to deferred tax assets is an unrealistic facade.

A last point about SFAS 96 is that noncurrent deferred tax assets and liabilities are not to be discounted. This position is inconsistent with numerous other areas in accounting, for example, pensions, leases, bonds payable, and notes receivable and payable without stipulated interest rates. The decision not to discount was probably dictated by political factors. Thus, this issue might well be addressed by the FASB in the future.[32] If so, one would also hope that

---

[31] Dopuch and Sunder (1980, pp. 6–7).

[32] For difficulties in implementing discounting, see James O. Stepp, "Deferred Taxes: The Discounting Controversy," *Journal of Accountancy* (November 1985), pp. 98–106. For difficulties of predicting reversals that affect both the liability method as well as discounting, see Barry P. Robbins and Steven O. Swyers, "Accounting for Income Taxes: Predicting Timing Reversals," *Journal of Accountancy* (September 1984), pp. 108–110 and 114–118.

measurement of deferred tax assets and liabilities would be made consistent. It would appear at present that conservatism's costs very definitely outweigh its benefits.

It is quite likely that SFAS 96 will be amended in a fashion that will loosen the conservatism in recognizing deferred tax assets. One possibility is that a valuation allowance would be established for potential deferred tax assets if, based upon available evidence at the financial statement date, it is "more likely than not" that at least some of the deferred tax assets will not be realized.

NET OPERATING LOSSES AND INCOME TAX ALLOCATION

A net operating loss arises if deductions exceed gross income for a taxable year. Congress recognized in the 1954 Internal Revenue Code that it was unfair to tax firms in profitable years without allowing any benefits in loss years. Consequently, the 1954 code included provisions for carryback and carryforward of net operating losses. The carryback has been maintained for a three-year period. The carryforward, however, was extended to fifteen years by The Economic Recovery Tax Act of 1981.

Net operating losses raise the problem of income tax allocation relative to affected years. There is no controversy relative to carrybacks. Amounts due on refunds for the three prior years would be booked as a tax benefit receivable with a corresponding income tax credit applicable to the loss year. The receivable arises in the loss year as a result of the loss; hence, there are no theoretical issues with regard to carrybacks. However, the carryforward situation is not quite as simple. APB 11 opposed booking the carryforward in the loss year except where virtual certainty of realization beyond any reasonable doubt exists when the carryforward arises. Thus, in the usual situation (nonbooking until realization occurs), carryforward benefits would be booked when received rather than in the loss year when they arose. Tax allocation and its basis in matching took a back seat to conservatism and realization. Furthermore, APB 11 saw "virtual certainty of realization" as a relevant circumstance that would enable booking of the carryforward in the loss year but gave no further criteria for determining when this situation arises.

SFAS 96 treats tax loss carrybacks similarly to APB 11. The tax benefit of the carryback is recognized in the period of the loss as an asset with an attendant reduction of the operating loss on the income statement. SFAS 96 takes a different view of tax-loss carryforwards than its predecessor. Tax-loss carryforwards are under no circumstances to be treated as assets. They can be used to reduce existing deferred tax liabilities with a reduction of the operating loss on the income statement. However, if the tax-loss carryforward exceeds deferred tax liabilities, the excess cannot be booked.

Since 1986 the Internal Revenue Service has become more restrictive in terms of recognizing NOL carryforwards coming from acquired corporations. Continuity-of-business enterprise requirements are the key. In order to use NOL carryforwards, the loss corporation or the acquiring corporation must either continue the traditional business of the loss corporation or use a significant portion of the loss corporation's assets in a business. Treatment of the NOL in a conservative manner in SFAS 96 now appears to be justified because realization of carryforward benefits is a true future contingency unless virtual certainty of realization of the benefits can be assured. In this latter situation the policy of APB 11 is preferable to SFAS 96.

SUMMARY

Income tax allocation appears to be based on the matching concept. Relevance to users of the allocation process is, however, open to serious question. APB 11 required comprehensive allocation using the deferred method of presentation. Comprehensive allocation is a form of rigid uniformity because the question of loan repayment, a potentially important relevant circumstance, is ignored. The deferral approach simply begs the question of balance sheet interpretation and has been rejected as an appropriate classification in SFAC 3. SFAS 96 adopted a modified asset–liability view, which is unfortunately hindered by very conservative asset-recognition criteria.

Perhaps the principal problem of comprehensive allocation is the growth of the balance sheet credit when accelerated depreciation is used for tax purposes and straight-line for financial reporting purposes. A possible defense of the liability approach is the rollover view, which employs an individual-asset interpretation for tax liabilities. This outlook has been criticized on the grounds that tax liabilities are not like accounts payable. The latter are paid off on an individual basis, whereas the former are not.

Consequently, another view, partial allocation, has arisen. In this situation, allocation is employed only if it is foreseen that there will be a real payback of loans received as a result of total book depreciation exceeding total tax depreciation in specific future years. Hence, partial allocation is really a form of finite uniformity. The main problem with partial allocation is the question of verifiability since future tax and book depreciation as well as the tax rate must be estimated.

Another allocation problem has to do with the tax carryback and carryforward provisions of the law. Carrybacks present no problems; they are booked as income tax credits in the loss year. Carryforwards are more controversial. SFAS 96, like its predecessor, takes a conservative view. Tax-loss carryforwards are used to eliminate deferred tax liabilities.

Conservatism in the recognition of NOL carryforwards may now be warranted — except in the case of virtual certainty of realization — due to more stringent Internal Revenue Service rules for using carryforwards as a tax reduction element by acquiring corporations.

Macroeconomic policy has created another major problem area — the investment tax credit (Appendix 14-A). There are four possible interpretations that are described in Appendix 14-A. If deferral is desired, asset reduction appears to be preferable to the deferred investment credit approach, even though the 1982 tax law caused complications by requiring reduction of the tax base of assets by one-half of the investment tax credit taken in the acquisition year.

APPENDIX 14-A: INVESTMENT TAX CREDIT

The investment tax credit (ITC) was first enacted in 1962. Since that time the provisions of the law have changed several times. As a tool of macroeconomic policy the ITC is seen as a means of stimulating investment and, thus, fighting recession in the short run and combating inflation over the long run. In the latter capacity the investment is seen as the avenue to eventually increasing supplies of scarce resources such as energy — and thus contributing to holding prices in check.

The ITC was eliminated by the Tax Reform Act of 1986. However, it is still applicable to many assets acquired prior to its repeal. Furthermore, it has previously been suspended (1966) and repealed (1969) only to be reenacted (1971). Therefore, it would not be surprising to see it resuscitated again if economic conditions make it an attractive tool of fiscal policy. Hence, it is worthwhile to examine some of the unusual theoretical problems presented by the ITC.

PROVISIONS OF THE ITC FROM THE 1981 AND 1982 TAX ACTS

The ITC permitted a reduction of income tax liability of up to 10 percent of the cost of eligible capital acquisitions (6 percent for property with a three-year amortization period under ACRS). Liability reduction is restricted to the first $25,000 of tax liability plus, for 1982 and thereafter, 85 percent of the excess above the first $25,000 of tax liability. Unused current benefits of the ITC can be carried back for three years and forward for fifteen. It was applicable to depreciable tangible property excluding buildings (except as they are construed to be an integral part of the manufacturing process). Up to $125,000 of used capital acquisitions were eligible for the ITC, up from $100,000 prior to 1981.

The recapture provisions regarding the ITC were changed by the Economic Recovery Tax Act of 1981 in order to align them with ACRS. As a result, three-year property under ACRS received a 6 percent ITC, and five-year and other property a 10 percent ITC. If the property is held for less than the three- and five-year periods, respectively, the firm kept 2 percent for each full year held and had to refund the differential.

The Tax Equity and Fiscal Responsibility Act of 1982 (TEFRA) made one important additional change to the ITC. For assets acquired after December 31, 1982, cost recovery for ACRS purposes must be reduced by 50 percent of the allowable ITC taken on the asset. Instead of reducing the tax basis of the asset by 50 percent, the firm could elect to reduce the allowable investment credit by 2 percent. Hence, assets with three-year ACRS lives would have the ITC reduced to 4 percent and all other assets would be lowered to 8 percent.

Cash flow could generally be maximized by adopted the first alternative: taking the maximum allowable ITC.[33] As will be seen shortly, this presents some thorny conceptual problems.

INTERPRETING THE ITC

The fiasco APBs 2 and 4 caused in choosing an appropriate accounting for the ITC has already been discussed in Chapter 3. There have been at least four interpretations of the transaction:

1. Reduction of the cost of the asset.
2. Allocation by means of a deferred investment credit account.
3. Capital donated by the government.
4. Flow through (immediate recognition of all benefits taken in the year of acquisition).

The first two methods are allocations, while the last two are not.

Reduction of Asset Cost

The apparent intention of the government concerning the ITC was to reduce the cost of capital acquisitions, which, in turn, because it increases the internal rate of return or net present value of potential capital acquisitions, stimulates investment in new plant and equipment. Therefore, a possible treatment is to leave tax expense unaffected by the ITC and reduce the cost of the affected assets by these amounts. The method is somewhat analogous to the net-of-tax approach to income tax allocation.

The method would result in the benefits being taken over the lives of eligible assets in the form of lower depreciation. Of course, depreciation expense under historical cost is an allocation, and the effect of the ITC reduction in terms of user relevance is not clear. Under current value approaches in situations in which depreciation is theoretically equal to the change in the market value of the asset between the beginning and end of the period, the ITC reduction to cost is simply not applicable.

Acceptance or rejection of the asset reduction approach largely hinges on the definition of *cost*. Indeed, SFAC 3 has interpreted the ITC as an asset reduction.[34] Let us examine what this interpretation implies in terms of the meaning of cost. It has linked together two totally separate transactions: (1) the net cash cost of the asset, and (2) the amount of the ITC that is attributable to the particular asset. Although there are numerous other examples linking somewhat separate transactions — interest during construction of buildings in SFAS 34 for one — no other linkage is as "wide" as this one. The cost of the asset is literally dependent upon the firm's making a profit in order for income taxes to be reduced by the ITC. A similar problem occurs in the event of an ITC carryforward because the assignment of the ITC taken during the current year to par-

---

[33] Levy (1982, p. 74).
[34] FASB (1980, pp. 72–73).

ticular assets is arbitrary (another allocation problem). However, if an allocation solution is desired, the balance sheet treatment of the credits as asset reductions does appear to be superior to the deferred investment credit method.

Deferred Investment Credit

This allocation method sets up a deferred investment credit account and writes it off over the life of affected assets by means of reducing (crediting) income tax expense. This account is neither a liability nor an owners' equity account. It is another example of a deferred-credit class of account. However, it differs from deferred tax credits arising under income tax allocation. Deferred credits per se are ruled out by SFAC 3. In the case of tax allocation, the deferred credit can be interpreted as a liability (the rollover view). The deferred credit under the ITC, however, has no liability elements that pertain to it. Although the income result is the same as under the asset reduction method — assuming the amortization methods are the same — the deferred credit nature of the balance sheet account makes it much less desirable than that method.

Donated Capital View

The donated capital view would be implemented by setting income tax expense at the amount it would have been without the investment credit and with an offset to donated capital. As with the "new form of equities" interpretation of income tax allocation, the argument has some plausibility but it is not really convincing. Macroeconomic policy that results in tax reduction does not persuasively lead to the conclusion that this is in effect an investment in the firm by the government.

Flow Through

A reasonable case can at least be made for flow through of ITC benefits. The strongest argument against it is that the benefits should be associated with usage rather than purchase. This is, of course, the matching argument, which underlies the reduction-of-asset-cost and deferred-investment-credit methods — which unfortunately leads to allocation problems and some questionable definitions. Although the government's intention may have been to reduce capital investment costs, it accomplished this by means of tax reduction, and the flow-through interpretation reflects exactly that.

Non-flow-through treatment leads to allocation problems. Assuming efficient markets, it is simply not clear whether these methods provide additional information in the form, for example, of better cash flow predictions. In the absence of this evidence, flow through has the advantage of being less costly than the allocation methods, and its benefits in terms of user relevance appear to be at least on a par with those methods.

ACCOUNTING FOR THE ITC

The provision in TEFRA for reducing an asset's tax base by one-half of the ITC taken leads to some serious results. Assume that the ITC on an asset costing $100,000 is taken in full in the year of acquisition. For financial statement purposes, the asset has a ten-year life and no salvage value. Straight-line depreciation is to be employed. The asset will be written off over five years by means of ACRS for tax purposes. Financial depreciation and the application of ACRS are shown in Exhibit 14–10.

Notice that there is both a timing difference and a permanent difference in the expense amounts shown in Exhibit 14–10. Technically speaking, we are faced with an allocation problem. However, this problem can be most simply handled, given comprehensive income tax allocation, by recognizing for income tax allocation purposes the timing differences first and not recognizing the permanent difference until the tenth year. Recognition of the permanent difference first, however, may obviate any need to allocate income taxes. This may be a pleasing prospect because of the swollen size of the deferred tax credit account on the books of many American corporations.

Because it decreases the tax base of the asset by one-half of the ITC taken in the year of acquisition, TEFRA has led to even more basic problems for accounting for the ITC. If flow through is used, should the reduction of the tax expense be for the gross amount of the tax reduction? Or should this tax expense be reduced by the amount of the depreciation shield lost as a result of the lowering of the tax base? The latter may be more useful in terms of indicating future cash flows but cannot be accomplished without using accruals; hence, it is a modified cash flow approach to the problem.

If accrual (deferral) of ITC benefits is desired, three possibilities present themselves: (1) credit of the entire liability deduction to a deferred investment

EXHIBIT 14–10
ACRS and Financial Depreciation with Different Lives

Year	ACRS	Straight-line Depreciation
1	$14,250[a]	$ 10,000
2	20,900[b]	10,000
3	19,950[c]	10,000
4	19,950	10,000
5	19,950	10,000
6		10,000
7		10,000
8		10,000
9		10,000
10		10,000
	$95,000	$100,000

[a]15% × $95,000
[b]22% × $95,000
[c]21% × $95,000

credit account, (2) reduction of the fixed asset by the entire liability deduction, and (3) splitting of the liability deduction between the fixed asset and a deferred credit account. None of these solutions is entirely acceptable. The deferred investment credit account does not qualify as a liability, a revenue, or a gain under SFAC 6. If the entire credit is to the fixed-asset account, then book and tax bases of assets will differ, as will depreciable lives and depreciation methods. Nevertheless, it still appears to be the most palatable of the deferral approaches. The various solutions to the ITC problem are examined in Problem 1 of this chapter.

Theory has thus far provided us with no definitive criteria for unraveling the ITC problem. The definitional screen for both deferred investment credits and deferred tax credits in SFAC 3 is a useful first step for coping with the dilemma. The broader context of relevance to users is thus far largely unexamined. Whether research can provide insights to the question of user relevance appears to be very doubtful at this time.

THE PRESENT STATE OF ITC ACCOUNTING

As a result of the politics of the ITC, either allocation or flow through is allowable, or even a combination of the two (as a result of the complexities brought about by TEFRA). There does not appear to be a relevant circumstance that differentiates among investment credit transactions.[35] Hence, the ITC would appear to be a viable candidate for rigid uniformity treatment. A reasonable choice, as discussed above, would be flow through. Of course, that would present an interesting situation of two problems having some similar facets — income tax allocation and the ITC — handled on two entirely different bases. Perhaps fresh thinking will lead to the elimination of the ITC if it is ever reconsidered.

QUESTIONS

1. As a type of allocation, why is income tax allocation unique?
2. Relative to depreciation, why is comprehensive allocation an example of rigid uniformity and partial allocation an example of finite uniformity?

---

[35] The only time that relevant circumstances arise would be in the case of carryforwards. APB 2's position on ITC carryforwards is somewhat similar to the treatment of loss carryforwards in APB 11 — that it "... should ordinarily be reflected only in the year in which the amount becomes 'allowable,' in which case the unused amount would not appear as an asset." See AICPA (1962, para. 16). As a result of running ITC carryforwards through income when realized, the carryforwards might reach income faster than through capitalization in the year of acquisition. However, this is still less of a problem than the possibility of constantly revising asset costs whenever ITC carryforwards are realized.

3. Although net-of-tax depreciation gives the same bottom-line result as comprehensive allocation, are there any financial ratios that would be affected by the choice between these methods?

4. How do the deferral and liability methods of implementing comprehensive allocation differ?

5. What is the rollover defense of the liability interpretation of deferred taxes, and how has it been attacked?

6. What is the justification for discounting deferred tax liabilities under either comprehensive or partial allocation?

7. What is the interpretation of income tax expenses under partial allocation?

8. What is permanent deferral?

9. Are the different recognition rules for deferred tax assets and deferred tax liabilities under SFAS 96 justified?

10. Why does a very peculiar situation arise in terms of the recognition of deferred tax assets under SFAS 96 when the tax laws show a decline in corporate tax rates over several succeeding years?

11. Critique SFAS 96 in terms of the qualitative characteristics of SFAC 2 of the conceptual framework.

12. Are loss carryforwards recognized under SFAS 96?

13. Using the asset illustrated in Exhibit 14–10, assume that the appropriate interest rate is 10 percent and the tax rate is 46 percent. Is the enterprise better off by taking the full investment tax credit and reducing the asset's tax base by one-half of the ITC taken or should it take 8 percent on the ITC without the tax basis reduction? Assume that ITC benefits are received immediately and depreciation tax shield benefits occur at year end.

14. Relative to the investment tax credit, why does TEFRA create both a permanent difference and a timing difference relative to depreciation?

15. TEFRA's requirement is that the depreciable tax basis of an asset must be reduced by half the investment tax credit taken. Why does this create problems if a deferral method of accounting for the investment tax credit is desired?

16. List two situations where an intervening event (1) is *not* needed in order to receive the benefits of a deferred tax asset and (2) is needed for payment of a deferred tax liability.

CASES AND PROBLEMS

1. Shown below is an article dated September 22, 1986, from *Business Week*. It concerns reduction in deferred tax accounts in light of the decline in corporate tax rates from 46 percent to 34 percent enacted in the 1986 tax act. Critique and comment on as many points and issues in the article as extensively as you can.

Surprise! A Bonanza for Business
in Tax Reform:
An Accounting Shift Creates a Windfall
of Hundreds of Millions[36]

Phillips Petroleum Co. is stretched pretty thin. Debt is eight times shareholder equity of $1.6 billion. But a little-known wrinkle in the tax bill will sharply reduce one major liability for the company. Deferred taxes — amounts set aside to pay future tax bills — will suddenly be cut by more than $400 million. Phillips isn't alone. Du Pont gets a $600 million windfall, IBM gets $1 billion in relief, and Exxon reaps nearly $3 billion. Indeed, virtually every major company will have its balance sheet and bottom line brightened by Uncle Sam.

"Even for Exxon, another $3 billion in its coffers is a big plus," says William L. Randol, an analyst at First Boston Corp. But for troubled one-line manufacturing companies, he notes, it is a true bonanza. While cash flow will not increase, debt will be sharply reduced and earnings will surge.

The tax bill has generally been thought to be harmful to business. It eliminates the investment tax credit (ITC), and it imposes a new 20% minimum tax to prevent corporations from paying little or nothing. On the positive side, tax rates on profits drop from 46% to 34% beginning on July 1, 1987. The net effect, though, is that business is expected to pay an estimated $120 billion in additional taxes over the next five years.

Capital-intensive companies that have used the ITC will bear much of the burden. But it is just these manufacturers that will benefit the most from this unexpected and largely uncounted windfall. The drop in tax rates means that companies with big deferred tax liabilities — especially oils and utilities — will get a huge one-shot gain. Suddenly, companies that had been accumulating the deferrals assuming a tax rate of 46% find they have to pay only 34%.

Accounting Fiction   For decades companies have legally kept one set of books for shareholders and one set for the tax man. For example, they would write off depreciation faster for the government in order to show lower profits and thus pay lower current taxes. But accelerated depreciation exhausts itself faster than the so-called straight-line method. Because there is less to deduct from profits in later years, earnings actually become higher. In theory, then, companies that take accelerated depreciation aren't really cutting taxes, just deferring them.

In practice, however, deferred taxes have grown and grown. True, the writeoffs diminish for a given piece of equipment. But the company then usually buys a more expensive one. So the accelerated depreciation on the new purchase more than offsets the diminished charges on the old equipment. During the inflationary 1970s, deferred taxes grew fast. A study by accountants Ernst & Whinney showed that deferred taxes as a percentage of shareholder equity grew from 9% in 1970 to 26% by 1979. And the accelerated cost recovery system (ACRS) in the 1981 tax law speeded up write-offs even more.

As a result, some analysts began to dismiss deferred taxes as an accounting fiction, assuming they would never be paid. But the deferrals of past years may finally be coming home to roost. Inflation has eased, and so has capital spending.

---

[36]Reprinted from the September 22, 1986 issue of *Business Week* by special permission, copyright © 1986 by McGraw-Hill, Inc.

The elimination of the ITC will further dampen spending on plant and equipment. Tax-law changes since 1981 have slowed depreciation allowances. Meanwhile, the write-offs on old machinery have long been used up. "Deferred taxes are going to start going the other way, because companies have cut spending and the ability to take accelerated depreciation has lessened," says Warren M. Shimmerlik, an analyst at Merrill Lynch, Pierce, Fenner & Smith Inc.

Exxon's deferred tax liability in 1985 stood at a staggering $11 billion. The tax proposal chops it to $8 billion. But even those who doubt that the $8 billion will ever come due agree that the drop in rates means that at least $3 billion was unnecessarily written off against previous earnings. And some analysts argue that stock prices for Exxon and other companies may have been undervalued because profits were understated.

Two Choices In addition, a perceived claim against the company has been cut, helping the balance sheet and thus potentially increasing the company's access to the capital markets. "Financial ratios would tend to improve," says Solomon B. Samson, a senior vice-president at Standard & Poor's Corp. Southwestern Bell Corp.'s debt as a percentage of equity falls from 161% to 138%. CSX Corp.'s percentage drops from 150% to 130%. And General Dynamics Corp.'s debt-to-equity percentage falls from 233% to 182%. Of course, credit analysts won't blindly boost their ratings of these companies. But commercial bankers, many of whom use rigid financial statistics to grant or withhold loans, may look more kindly on prospective borrowers.

To reflect the windfall, Financial Accounting Standards Board is likely to give companies two options. They can either restate prior years' earnings. Or they can show a one-time gain in 1987. Most would probably elect to do the latter. For example, had the new tax bill been law in 1985, GTE Corp., which lost 95¢ a share in 1985, would have had a $3.20 one-time gain (table). Norfolk Southern Corp., which earned $7.95 a share last year, would have added an additional $10.02 to profits. And Eastman Kodak, which earned $1.46 last year, would have gotten an extra $1.20 a share.

Investors, then, should be aware that 1987 earnings may be much higher than expected, though some companies may use the opportunity to take a big one-time write-off of another kind to offset their windfall. Regardless of how the accountants tally it, the tax proposal, while harsh on some corporations over the next several years, has helped lift a huge weight off the shoulders of business and investors.

2. Martin and Easley Company had a litigation accrual expense of $10,000 that was booked in 1987 but was not expected to be paid until 1990 (when it would be deductible for tax purposes). The company had taxable income of $7,000 in 1985; $10,000 in 1986; and $8,000 in 1987. The tax rate was 46 percent in 1985 and 1986, 40 percent in 1987, and 34 percent in 1988 and thereafter. One other temporary difference arose during 1987. An asset was acquired during 1987 at a cost of $30,000 and with no salvage value. For financial reporting purposes the asset was going to be depreciated over a five-year period on a straight-line basis. For tax purposes the asset was being depreciated on a three-year ACRS basis.

Required:
Make all entries for income taxes for the year 1987 (prepare any other supporting schedules that you deem necessary to support your entries).

3. This problem is a continuation of Problem 2. Assume that in 1988 taxable income was $12,000. One additional temporary difference arose. Another asset was acquired during 1988 that was exactly like the one acquired during 1987. Its cost remained at $30,000 and tax and book depreciation are to be handled in exactly the same fashion for the new asset as for the old one.

Required:
Make all entries for income taxes for the year 1988.

4. Paragraph 20 of SFAS 96 states the following:

> A deferred tax liability or asset shall be adjusted for the effect of a change in tax law or rates. The effect shall be included in income from continuing operations for the period that includes the enactment date.

SFAS 96 is effective for fiscal years beginning after December 15, 1988, although earlier application is encouraged.

Assume that you are the chief financial officer (CFO) for a firm whose fiscal year ends on June 30, 1988. At that time there are $1,000,000 of deferred tax liabilities on your books. The deferred taxes all entered your books when the tax rate was 46 percent; it is presently 34 percent. You expect the tax rate to go back up to 45 percent for 1989 and thereafter.

Required:
Under the circumstances, would you write the deferred tax liabilities down for the year ending June 30, 1988, by applying SFAS 96 or would you wait until 1989? Discuss.

5. You are preparing the tax entries for the ABC Company. The company elected to go with SFAS 96. The firm was formed on January 1, 1986. Taxable income and tax rates for 1986 and 1987 are shown below.

Year	Taxable Income	Tax Rate
1986	$1,000	46%
1987	1,500	40%

The worksheet analyzing temporary differences shows subtotals for 1988 and 1989 as follows (these arose in 1987):

Year	Amount	Designation	Tax Rate
1988	$3,000	Deferred Tax Asset	34%
1989	200	Deferred Tax Liability	34%

Required:
Make all tax entries for 1987 in accordance with SFAS 96.

BIBLIOGRAPHY OF REFERENCED WORKS

Accounting Principles Board (1962). "Accounting for the 'Investment Credit,'" *Accounting Principles Board Opinion No. 2* (APB).

—— (1967). "Accounting for Income Taxes," *Accounting Principles Board Opinion No. 11* (AICPA).

Beaver, William, and Roland Dukes (1972). "Interperiod Tax Allocation, Earnings Expectations, and the Behavior of Security Prices," *The Accounting Review* (April 1972), pp. 320–332.

—— (1973). "Interperiod Tax Allocation and δ-Depreciation Methods: Some Empirical Results," *The Accounting Review* (July 1973), pp. 549–559.

Bierman, Jr., Harold (1990). "One More Reason to Revise Statement 96," *Accounting Horizons* (June 1990), pp. 42–46.

Bierman, Harold, and Thomas Dyckman (1974). "New Look at Deferred Taxes," *Financial Executive* (January 1974), pp. 40–49.

Black, Homer (1966). "Interperiod Allocation of Corporate Income Taxes," *Accounting Research Study No. 9* (AICPA).

Buckley, John (1972). *Income Tax Allocation: An Inquiry into Problems of Methodology and Estimation* (Financial Executives Research Foundation).

Bullock, Clayton (1974). "Reconciling Economic Depreciation with Tax Allocation," *The Accounting Review* (January 1974), pp. 98–103.

Chaney, Paul K., and Debra C. Jeter (1989). "Accounting for Deferred Income Taxes: Simplicity? Usefulness?," *Accounting Horizons* (June 1989), pp. 6–13.

Collins, Brett, John Rickard, and Michael Selby (1990). "Discounting of Deferred Tax Liabilities," *Journal of Business Finance and Accounting* (Winter 1990), pp. 757–758.

Committee on Accounting Procedure (1953). "Restatement and Revision of Accounting Research Bulletins," *Accounting Research Bulletin No. 43* (CAP).

Davidson, Sidney (1958). "Accelerated Depreciation and the Allocation of Income Taxes," *The Accounting Review* (April 1958), pp. 173–180.

—— (1966). "Comments," in H. Black, "Interperiod Allocation of Corporate Income Taxes," *Accounting Research Study No. 9* (AICPA), pp. 117–119.

Davidson, Sidney, Lisa Skelton, and Roman Weil (1977). "A Controversy over the Expected Behavior of Deferred Tax Credits," *Journal of Accountancy* (April 1977), pp. 53–56.

Davidson, Sidney, S. F. Rasch, and R. L. Weil (1984). "Behavior of the Deferred Tax Credit Account, 1973–82," *Journal of Accountancy* (October 1984), pp. 138–142.

Dopuch, Nicholas, and Shyam Sunder (1980). "FASB's Statements on Objectives and Elements of Financial Accounting: A Review," *The Accounting Review* (January 1980), pp. 1–21.

Drake, David (1962). "The Service Potential Concept and Interperiod Tax Allocation," *The Accounting Review* (October 1962), pp. 677–684.

Financial Accounting Standards Board (1980). "Elements of Financial Statements of Business Enterprises," *Statement of Financial Accounting Concepts No. 3* (FASB).

—— (1985). "Elements of Financial Statements," *Statement of Financial Accounting Concepts No. 6* (FASB).

—— (1987). "Accounting for Income Taxes," *Statement of Financial Accounting Standards No. 96* (FASB).

Findlay, M. Chapman, III, and E. E. Williams (1981). "Discounting Deferred Tax Liabilities: A Reply," *Journal of Business Finance and Accounting* (Winter 1981), pp. 593–597.

Gonedes, Nicholas, and Nicholas Dopuch (1974). "Capital Market Equilibrium, Information Production, and Selected Accounting Techniques: Theoretical Framework and Review of Empirical Work," *Studies on Financial Accounting Objectives: 1974* (Supplement to the *Journal of Accounting Research*), pp. 48–129.

Graul, Paul, and Kenneth Lemke (1976). "On the Economic Substance of Deferred Taxes," *Abacus* (June 1976), pp. 14–33.

Herring, Hartwell, and Fred Jacobs (1976). "The Expected Behavior of Deferred Tax Credits," *Journal of Accountancy* (August 1976), pp. 52–56.

Jeter, Debra C., and Paul K. Chaney (1988). "A Financial Statement Analysis Approach to Deferred Taxes," *Accounting Horizons* (December 1988), pp. 41–49.

Levy, Gregory M. (1982). "'TEFRA': Its Accounting Implications," *Journal of Accountancy* (November 1982), pp. 74–82.

Livingstone, John L. (1967a). "Accelerated Depreciation and Deferred Taxes: An Empirical Study of Fluctuating Asset Expenditures," *Empirical Research in Accounting: Selected Studies, 1967* (Supplement to the *Journal of Accounting Research*), pp. 93–105.

―――― (1967b). "A Behavioral Study of Tax Allocation in Electric Utility Regulation," *The Accounting Review* (July 1967), pp. 544–552.

―――― (1969). "Accelerated Depreciation, Tax Allocation, and Cyclical Asset Expenditures of Large Manufacturing Firms," *Journal of Accounting Research* (Autumn 1969), pp. 245–256.

Meyers, Stephen L. (1973). "An Examination of the Relationship Between Interperiod Tax Allocation and Present Value Depreciation," *The Accounting Review* (January 1973), pp. 44–49.

Moonitz, Maurice (1957). "Income Taxes in Financial Statements," *The Accounting Review* (April 1957), pp. 175–183.

Nair, R. D., and Jerry J. Weygandt (1981). "Let's Fix Deferred Taxes," *Journal of Accountancy* (November 1981), pp. 87–102.

Nurnberg, Hugo (1972). "Discounting Deferred Tax Liabilities," *The Accounting Review* (October 1972), pp. 655–665.

Price Waterhouse & Co. (1967). *Is Generally Accepted Accounting for Income Taxes Possibly Misleading Investors?* (Price Waterhouse & Co.).

Robbins, Barry P., and S. O. Swyers (1984). "Accounting for Income Taxes: Predicting Timing Difference Reversals," *Journal of Accountancy* (September 1984), pp. 108–118.

Rosenfield, Paul, and William C. Dent (1983). "No More Deferred Taxes," *Journal of Accountancy* (February 1983), pp. 44–55.

Skekel, Ted, and C. Fazzi (1984). "The Deferred Tax Liability: Do Capital-Intensive Companies Pay It?" *Journal of Accountancy* (October 1984), pp. 142–150.

Stepp, James O. (1985). "Deferred Taxes: The Discounting Controversy," *Journal of Accountancy* (November 1985), pp. 98–108.

Suojanen, Waino (1954). "Accounting Theory and the Large Corporation," *The Accounting Review* (July 1954), pp. 391–398.

Thomas, Arthur (1974). "The Allocation Problem: Part Two," *Studies in Accounting Research #9* (AAA).

Watson, Peter L. (1979). "Accounting for Deferred Tax on Depreciable Assets," *Accounting and Business Research* (Autumn 1979), pp. 338–347.

Wheeler, James, and Wilfred Galliart (1974). *An Appraisal of Interperiod Income Tax Allocation* (Financial Executives Research Foundation).

Williams, E. E., and M. Chapman Findlay III (1975). "Discounting Deferred Tax Liabilities," *Journal of Business Finance and Accounting* (Spring 1975), pp. 121–133.

Wolk, Harry I., Dale R. Martin, and Virginia A. Nichols (1989). "Statement of Financial Accounting Standards No. 96: Some Theoretical Problems," *Accounting Horizons* (June 1989), pp. 1–5.

Wolk, Harry I., and M. G. Tearney (1980). "Discounting Deferred Tax Liabilities: Review and Analysis," *Journal of Business Finance and Accounting* (Spring 1980), pp. 119–133.

ADDITIONAL READINGS

Tax Allocation

Barton, Alan (1970). "Comparing Income Tax and Interperiod Allocation," *Abacus* (September 1970), pp. 3–24.

Beresford, Dennis (1982). "Deferred Tax Accounting Should Be Changed," *The CPA Journal* (June 1982), pp. 16–23.

Bevis, Donald, and Raymond E. Perry (1969). *Accounting for Income Taxes* (AICPA).

Dewhirst, John (1975). "The Tax Allocation Question Answered," *CA Magazine* (November 1975), pp. 43–50.

Drummond, C., and S. Wigle (1981). "Let's Stop Taking Comprehensive Allocation for Granted," *CA Magazine* (October 1981), pp. 56–61.

Greenball, Melvin (1969). "Appraising Alternative Methods of Accounting for Accelerated Tax Depreciation: A Relative Accuracy Approach," *Empirical Research in Accounting: Selected Studies, 1969*, pp. 262–289.

Hope, Tony, and John Briggs (1982). "Accounting Policy Making — Some Lessons from the Deferred Taxation Debate," *Accounting and Business Research* (Spring 1982), pp. 83–96.

Laibstain, Samuel (1971). "A New Look at Accounting for Operating Loss Carryforwards," *The Accounting Review* (April 1971), pp. 342–351.

Lemke, Kenneth, and Paul Graul (1981). "Deferred Taxes — An 'Explicit Cost' Solution to the Discounting Problem," *Accounting and Business Research* (Autumn 1981), pp. 309–315.

Nurnberg, Hugo (1968). "Present Value Depreciation and Income Tax Allocation," *The Accounting Review* (October 1968), pp. 719–730.

—— (1971). *Cash Movements Analysis of the Accounting for Corporate Income Taxes* (Michigan State University).

—— (1989). "Deferred Tax Assets Under FASB Statement No. 96," *Accounting Horizons* (December 1989), pp. 49–56.

Parks, James T. (1988). "A Guide to FASB's Overhaul of Income Tax Accounting," *Journal of Accountancy* (April 1988), pp. 24–34.

Sharp, William M. (1977). "An Analysis of Corporate Transactions Involving Net Operating Loss Benefits," *Indiana Law Review* (no. 5):981–1007.

Subcommittee of the American Accounting Association's Committee on Financial Accounting Standards (1978). *Response to Exposure Draft Number 13 of the International Accounting Standards Committee Entitled "Accounting for Taxes on Income"* (AAA).

Voss, William (1968). "Accelerated Depreciation and Deferred Tax Allocation," *Journal of Accounting Research* (Autumn 1968), pp. 262–269.

Wolk, Harry I., and M. G. Tearney (1973). "Income Tax Allocation and Loss Carryforwards: Exploring Uncharted Ground," *The Accounting Review* (April 1973), pp. 292–299.

Investment Credit

Moonitz, Maurice (1966). "Some Reflections on the Investment Credit Experience," *Journal of Accounting Research* (Spring 1966), pp. 47–61.

Stamp, Edward (1967). "Some Further Reflections on the Investment Credit," *Journal of Accounting Research* (Spring 1967), pp. 124–128.

Throckmorton, J. (1970). "Theoretical Concepts for Interpreting the Investment Credit," *Journal of Accountancy* (April 1970), pp. 45–52.

OIL AND GAS ACCOUNTING

OIL AND GAS ACCOUNTING is an interesting though specialized area, one which demonstrates many theoretical problems of the type discussed in this book. Standard setting in this area has been the subject of controversy for nearly two decades. Moreover, several of the decisions rendered by standard-setting agencies have been extremely dubious. From a theoretical point of view, financial accounting and reporting in the oil and gas industry illustrates very well a situation in which information produced by the historical cost model generally is considered to be much less relevant for decision makers than information produced by some form of current valuation. Because of this factor and the politics of the oil and gas accounting controversy, we have seen more empirical research using security price movements to ascertain the economic impact of an accounting standard in this area than in any other single area of accounting.

In this chapter we first look at an example of the impact on financial statements of full cost (FC) versus successful efforts (SE) accounting (the two broad methods of applying historical cost). Then we take up a discussion of the conceptual differences between the two methods in the application of historical costing. We also review standard setting for oil and gas accounting and the various empirical studies, compare oil and gas accounting to the conceptual framework, and examine the current value approach proposed by the Securities and Exchange Commission that was called *reserve recognition accounting* (RRA). Last, we take up the current status of financial accounting and reporting in the oil and gas industry.

In practice, there are variations in the application of both FC and SE because of such factors as the definition of a cost center (to be discussed later). However, in this chapter the two methods will be examined in their broadest sense. The basic difference between the two is their treatment of incurred exploration costs that do not result in the discovery of oil or gas reserves. Under FC, all the costs of exploration are capitalized, regardless of whether those costs lead to a specific discovery of reserves. The rationale supporting FC is the probabilistic nature of exploration: it may require, on average, that numerous exploratory wells be drilled in order to find a reservoir that can be developed. Therefore, costs of all exploration are included in the cost of successful wells. Under SE, only the exploration costs that result in a producing well are capitalized and those that result in dry holes are expensed immediately. If four exploratory wells are drilled and three are dry holes, the costs of those three will not provide future benefits and therefore should be expensed.

The following example will illustrate the possible impact on financial statements of applying FC versus SE for a relatively young enterprise. XYZ Corporation was formed three years ago and has drilled four exploratory wells per year with a success rate of 25 percent. Depletion expense is 20 percent of beginning-of-year oil properties (that is, XYZ produces 20 percent of its proven reserves each year), and depreciation expense is 10 percent of beginning-of-year other assets. Production cost is 8 percent of revenues. In the current year, 100,000 barrels of oil were sold at $32 per barrel. Four exploratory wells were drilled at an average cost of $525,000. One well was successful. Exhibit 15–1 presents the beginning-of-year balance sheets, 15–2 the current-year income statements, and 15–3 the end-of-year balance sheets under both the FC and SE methods.

Although the illustration is hypothetical, it does point out that the two methods may have a significant impact on financial statements, particularly for a relatively new or developing enterprise. In this illustration assets differ by $4.5 million, or approximately 54 percent (FC as base) at year end. The difference is even more pronounced in stockholders' equity, where SE's stockholders' equity is only 24 percent of FC's. Net income varied by $843,000, or 45 percent.

These results appear unusually large; however, the potential effects are

---

EXHIBIT 15–1
XYZ CORPORATION
Balance Sheets, Beginning of Year

	FC	SE
Assets		
Current Assets	$ 800,000	$ 800,000
Oil Properties	4,880,000	1,220,000
Other Assets	1,000,000	1,000,000
Total	$6,680,000	$3,020,000
Liabilities and Stockholders' Equity		
Current Liabilities	$ 600,000	$ 600,000
Long-term Liabilities	2,000,000	2,000,000
Common Stock	2,000,000	2,000,000
Retained Earnings (Deficit)	2,080,000	(1,580,000)
Total	$6,680,000	$3,020,000

EXHIBIT 15–2
XYZ CORPORATION
Income Statements, Current Year

	FC	SE
Revenues (100,000 barrels at $32)	$3,200,000	$3,200,000
Expenses:		
Production Costs	$ 256,000	$ 256,000
Depletion	976,000	244,000
Depreciation	100,000	100,000
Exploration Costs	—	1,575,000
	$1,332,000	$2,175,000
Net Income	$1,868,000	$1,025,000

substantiated by several studies of the financial statements of operating enterprises. For example, in a study of twenty-eight enterprises, Klingstedt's data revealed that earnings may increase from 10 percent to several hundred percent by merely switching from the SE method to the FC method.[1] Touche Ross & Company found in a study of thirty-six enterprises that net income would be reduced by 20 percent, assets by 30 percent, and stockholders' equity by 16 percent if the enterprises were required to switch from FC to SE.[2] Similarly, the First Boston Corporation's analysis showed net income reductions as high as 55 percent as a result of switching from FC to SE.[3] The Financial Accounting Standards Board staff found similar but smaller variations in a study of its own.[4]

CONCEPTUAL DIFFERENCES BETWEEN FC AND SE

Both FC and SE methods of accounting in the oil and gas industry are allowed under generally accepted accounting principles. The fundamental difference between FC and SE is the size of the cost center used in the capitalize/expense decision for exploration costs. Under FC, the largest possible cost center is the country or even a continent, and all costs of finding oil and gas reserves would be capitalized regardless of whether a specific local effort is successful. Under SE, the smallest possible cost center is the property (lease), reservoir, or field (most SE companies use the field), and all costs of that well would be expensed

[1] Klingstedt (1970, pp. 79–86).
[2] Touche Ross & Co. (1977).
[3] First Boston Corporation (1978).
[4] FASB (1978).

EXHIBIT 15–3
XYZ CORPORATION
Balance Sheets, End of Year

	FC	SE
Assets		
Current Assets	$1,445,000	$1,445,000
Oil Properties	6,004,000	1,501,000
Other Assets	900,000	900,000
Total	$8,349,000	$3,846,000
Liabilities and Stockholders' Equity		
Current Liabilities	$ 401,000	$ 401,000
Long-term Liabilities	2,000,000	2,000,000
Common Stock	2,000,000	2,000,000
Retained Earnings (Deficit)	3,948,000	(555,000)
Total	$8,349,000	$3,846,000

unless oil and gas reserves are found. Establishing a direct cause-and-effect relationship between costs incurred and reserves discovered is not relevant to recording the costs as assets under FC, while such a relationship must exist to record the costs as assets under SE. Both methods eventually will produce the same accounting results because the same costs are incurred and the same discoveries made. The timing of those results, however, may vary significantly.

SE accounting was the only method used prior to the late 1950s and early 1960s. About that time, FC came into use, and by the late 1960s it was widely used. A reason suggested for the increase in the use of the FC method was problems with the application of the historical-cost model.[5] In the oil and gas industry, amounts spent on exploration have no predictable relationship to the value of oil and gas discovered. For example, a large amount may be spent to find nothing, but in another geographical area a small amount spent could result in a large discovery. The motivation for FC was frustration with a historical cost concept that penalizes enterprises for exploration efforts that result in no discoveries and does not reward those efforts that result in discoveries with recognition of the value discovered. Although FC does not accomplish the latter goal, it does accomplish the former by capitalizing all exploration costs as long as discovery values exceed costs on a company-wide basis.

Regardless of the theoretical reason(s) for the increasing use of the FC method, it does have a desirable impact on reported income, not to mention net assets of growing firms as illustrated in Exhibits 15–1, 2, and 3. FC also results in a smoothing of reported income because costs that are written off in the

---

[5] Arthur Young (1977, p. 5).

current period under the SE method are capitalized and amortized against revenues of a number of future periods. Generally, the larger, more mature and fully integrated enterprises in the oil and gas industry use SE, while the smaller, less integrated enterprises use FC. In using FC, the larger enterprises, simply because of their size and the extent of their operations, would receive a relatively smaller smoothing impact than the smaller enterprises. A 1973 survey of approximately 300 enterprises found that nearly one-half used FC.[6] However, a 1972 survey found that SE enterprises were responsible for 87 percent of the oil and gas produced in the United States.[7] A later survey, in 1977, found that only 6 percent of the oil and gas produced in the United States and Canada came from enterprises using the FC method.[8]

This flexibility, with either FC or SE being permissible, caused the FASB to reconsider whether either method of accounting was appropriate:

> Neither full costing nor successful efforts costing reflects success at the time of discovery. Under both methods, success is reported at the time of sale. It might be said, therefore, that both methods tend to obscure, or at least delay, the reporting of success, but that is the consequence of the historical cost basis of accounting, and its adherence to the realization concept.[9]

Not only is the "sale basis" of revenue recognition questionable in the oil and gas industry but the use of acquisition cost as a measure of economic value is gravely deficient. Under the historical cost model, at the time an asset is purchased the value to the purchaser is normally assumed to be measured by the cost. Both SE and FC, although they differ significantly in their treatment of costs, present as assets only the costs incurred in exploration and development. Those costs typically do not have any relationship whatsoever to the economic resources acquired. Because of these problems and the political concern in the United States regarding the compilation of meaningful information on domestic oil and gas reserves, standard-setting bodies have struggled with oil and gas accounting for over two decades.

STANDARD SETTING FOR OIL AND GAS ACCOUNTING

Financial accounting and reporting for the oil and gas industry has been studied by standard setters for a long time. Ijiri put the issue into perspective when he stated that ". . . never in the history of accounting has the choice of an accounting method attracted so much attention as the controversy over full versus successful efforts costing."[10] The issues raised in the standard-setting process for

---

[6] Ginsburg, Feldman, and Bress (1973, p. 31).

[7] Porter (1972, p. 6).

[8] Arthur Young (1977, p. 4).

[9] FASB (1977, para. 152).

[10] Ijiri (1979, p. 20).

oil and gas accounting are all-encompassing. They provide one of the best examples of interaction between accounting researchers and accounting standard setters. Many of the issues involved relate closely to the FASB's Conceptual Framework Project. Another interesting aspect is that political pressure resulted in a breakdown of the standard-setting process in the private sector. After a brief historical review of oil and gas accounting standard setting, we will examine these three broad subjects.

HISTORY OF STANDARD SETTING FOR OIL AND GAS ACCOUNTING

In 1964 the AICPA commissioned an accounting research study of various accounting practices used in the extractive industries in order to make recommendations to the APB. This project represented the first ARS-commissioned study of an industry-related accounting practice as opposed to general accounting practices applicable to all industries. The general recommendation of ARS 11 was that the SE method rather than the FC method should be used.[11]

Following the publication of ARS 11 in 1969, the APB asked its Committee on Extractive Industries to review the ARS 11 recommendations and draft a proposed APB Opinion that would narrow the acceptable accounting practices in the extractive industries. The committee's paper, "Accounting and Reporting Practices in the Petroleum Industry," was published in 1971. Again, the principal recommendation favored the SE method. The APB scheduled a public hearing on the paper for late November, 1971. Just prior to the public hearing, however, the Federal Power Commission issued Order No. 440, which required the FC method for mineral leases acquired after October 6, 1969.[12]

Because of Order No. 440 and mixed reactions to the SE method at the public hearings, the Committee on Extractive Industries was unable to finalize its paper for the APB. Subsequently, the AICPA supported the formation of the FASB, and as a result the APB dropped long-term projects from its agenda, including accounting in the extractive industries. In the meantime, the SEC entered the scene. In December, 1972, it proposed that those enterprises that do not follow SE should disclose what net income would have been under that method.[13] Later, however, the SEC retreated from its proposal, but it was obvious that the SEC favored the use of SE over FC. Although financial accounting and reporting in the extractive industries, in particular the oil and gas industry, was proposed as a subject the newly formed FASB should add to its original agenda, the FASB decided not to do so.

The foreign oil embargo of 1973 had a significant impact on accounting in the oil and gas industry in the United States. During that period, public policy was concerned with attaining self-sufficiency in energy supplies. While pursuing that goal, U.S. oil and gas producers reported substantial increases in

---

[11] Field (1969, pp. 150–151).
[12] Federal Power Commission (1971, 36 F.R. 21963).
[13] SEC (1972, 38 F.R. 1747).

income, an outcome that aroused opposition to the industry and generally caused its reporting practices to be viewed with skepticism. In December, 1975, President Ford signed Public Law 94-163, "The Energy Policy and Conservation Act." The accounting thrust of the act was that the SEC do one of two things, either

> prescribe rules applicable to persons engaged in the production of crude oil or natural gas, or make effective by recognition, or by other appropriate means indicating a determination to rely on, accounting practices developed by the Financial Accounting Standards Board, if the Securities and Exchange Commission is assured that such practice will be observed by persons engaged in the production of crude oil or natural gas to the same extent as would result if the Securities and Exchange Commission had prescribed such practices by rule.[14]

By this time, two months prior to the act, the FASB had added to its agenda a project to promulgate accounting standards for oil and gas enterprises. It worked closely with the SEC and issued a discussion memorandum in December, 1976, and held a public hearing in the spring of 1977. In July, 1977, the FASB issued an exposure draft. The draft required the SE method of accounting. Prior to that issuance, the FASB had begun several empirical research studies. Although the results of the studies were not conclusive, they did indicate that "the method of accounting would not affect their loan officers' investment and credit decisions regarding oil and gas producing companies."[15] The SEC apparently agreed with this conclusion. On August 31, 1977, it issued "Securities Act Release No. 5861," which proposed to amend regulations to incorporate the accounting standards set forth in the exposure draft in the event a statement of financial accounting standards was not issued by December 22, 1977 (the mandatory date established by the act). Subsequently, the FASB issued SFAS 19 in December, 1977. SFAS 19 required SE and eliminated FC. However, bending to political pressure, the SEC effectively circumvented SFAS 19 in ASR 253, which permitted either FC or SE. As a result, SFAS 25, which suspended the mandatory SE provisions of SFAS 19, was issued in February, 1979.

EMPIRICAL STUDIES OF OIL AND GAS ACCOUNTING

There have been numerous empirical research studies of oil and gas accounting. Several of these studies were sponsored by the FASB and represented a major attempt to work with accounting researchers in the standard-setting process and to evaluate the economic consequences of proposed accounting standards.

FASB-Sponsored Studies

Prior to the issuance of the exposure draft but after issuance of the discussion memorandum, the FASB sponsored one research study and conducted another itself. In the former, the purpose was to determine how investment and credit

---

[14] Energy Policy and Conservation Act (1975, SEC 503(b)(2)).
[15] FASB (1977, para. 90).

decisions regarding oil and gas enterprises are made and, in particular, whether the method of accounting, FC or SE, had an impact on those decisions. Academic consultants interviewed various individuals who made investment and credit decisions in the oil and gas industry. Interviewees included loan officers of large and small banks making loans to all sizes of oil and gas enterprises, bank trust department officers, institutional securities underwriters, and security analysts. In general, a wide spectrum of individuals involved in the everyday investment and credit decisions for oil and gas enterprises, but not employees of those enterprises, were interviewed. However, the total number of interviewees was only twenty-four, thus somewhat limiting the conclusiveness of the results. The interviewees indicated that the method of accounting, FC or SE, did not affect the investment and credit decision. To the contrary, most interviewees relied on such factors as their own valuations of oil and gas reserves and cash flow data rather than on reported earnings.[16]

The second study, conducted by the FASB's staff, concerned the application of SFAS 9, "Accounting for Income Taxes — Oil and Gas Producing Companies." SFAS 9 allowed two alternative approaches to tax allocation for certain timing differences. The purpose of the study was to determine whether the approach adopted by an enterprise was correlated to either the method of accounting it used, FC or SE, or its size. The results showed that a correlation did not exist with regard to either variable.[17]

After the exposure draft was issued, the FASB commissioned two additional studies. Both studies were directed toward determining the economic consequences of proscribing the FC method of accounting. An argument frequently given in opposition to the draft was that if FC enterprises were forced to follow SE accounting, their ability to raise capital would be materially hampered and, as a result, their exploration activities would have to be curtailed drastically or eliminated. If true, then the market value of these firms should have declined.

Dyckman conducted research designed to determine whether the release of the draft had a negative impact on the security prices of FC enterprises. Two research designs were employed. In one, the sample enterprises derived more than 50 percent of their revenue from exploration and production activities. In that study, the market prices for twenty-two FC and twenty-two SE enterprises were studied for the eleven-week period prior to issuance of the draft and the eleven-week period after issuance. Testing the differences in security returns, Dyckman found that FC enterprises were somewhat negatively affected around the time the draft was issued, but that negative impact was short term; and for the twenty-two-week period there was no statistically significant difference between FC and SE enterprises.[18] This would be in line with the allocation nature of the differences not affecting prices.

The other approach used different statistical tests and was not limited to enterprises engaged primarily in exploration and production. The sample in-

[16] Ibid.
[17] Ibid.
[18] Dyckman (1979, p. 24).

cluded sixty-five FC and forty SE enterprises. The time period studied was twenty-one weeks, ten prior to and eleven after the issuance of the ED. Although the differences in the security returns of FC and SE enterprises generally were statistically significant at the 10 percent level of probability, they were not at the 5 percent level.[19] Incidentally, Dyckman conducted a similar study after the issuance of SFAS 19. The methodology was identical to his second study and covered seventeen weeks, eight prior to and nine after issuance of SFAS 19. The results indicated that differences between security returns of FC and SE enterprises were not statistically significant at the 10 percent level of probability.[20]

The second study commissioned by the FASB was a telephone interview survey. The survey was of twenty-seven senior executive officers of relatively small and medium-sized SE enterprises. The purpose was to determine whether those executive officers believed that the use of SE had any negative impact on their enterprises' ability to raise capital. None of the executive officers surveyed indicated that the company's use of successful-efforts accounting had hindered its ability to raise capital.[21] Generally, the results of the FASB-sponsored research indicated that few, if any, economic consequences would result from proscribing FC accounting. These findings were used, in part, to justify the elimination of FC in SFAS 19.

Other Research Studies

The majority of non-FASB-sponsored research regarding oil and gas accounting focused on two hypotheses: (1) characteristics of the enterprise determine whether FC or SE is used; and (2) whether proscribing FC would have a negative indirect economic impact on enterprises that use that method. The first hypothesis is concerned with the possibility of relevant circumstances that might justify finite uniformity, and the second with economic consequences of accounting standards.

Many FC enterprises argued that there were significant differences between them and SE enterprises and that those differences would justify continued use of the FC method. The U.S. Department of Justice agreed with them:

> [Uniformity] as a goal can only claim superiority where like entities are being compared. If two entities or groups of entities were significantly dissimilar, attempts to draw simple accounting comparisons would only confuse the analysis.[22]

Deakin studied fifty-three nonmajor oil and gas enterprises. Nonmajor enterprises were chosen because most major oil and gas enterprises use SE and, moreover, the method of accounting has relatively little impact on major enterprises. The study found that it was difficult to distinguish among enterprises. Although some distinguishing characteristics may exist, such as the age of the

---

[19] Ibid., pp. 31–37.
[20] Ibid., pp. 43–44.
[21] FASB (1977, para. 93).
[22] U.S. Department of Justice (1978, p. 18).

enterprise (FC enterprises tend to be younger), Deakin concluded that it would be difficult to promulgate accounting methods based on characteristic differences among the enterprises.[23]

Several other studies, in addition to the FASB's, were made of the economic consequences of proscribing FC accounting. The results are mixed. The Directorate of Economic and Policy Research of the SEC conducted a study of security returns of FC versus SE enterprises. The sample consisted of thirty-five FC and thirty-seven SE enterprises, including both large and small enterprises. Security prices were studied over a period of thirty days following issuance of the exposure draft. The finding was that initially upon issuance the security returns of FC enterprises were negatively affected; however, the impact was short lived and generally disappeared within thirty days.[24] Dyckman and Smith, in another study, also found that FC firms had no significant stock price reaction to the draft.[25]

Smith used a "reversal method" to study the economic impact of SFAS 19 on FC enterprises. The study examined security prices of FC versus SE enterprises *after* the SEC reinstated FC accounting. The hypothesis was that the securities of FC enterprises would be favorably affected by the reinstatement if proscribing FC had a negative impact. The results indicated

> no evidence . . . of "extreme" price effects of the proposed elimination or retention of full cost accounting. The magnitude of the "unexpected" return observations of the reversal test casts serious doubt that there were extreme "information effects" of the accounting change(s) on individual sample full cost firms.[26]

However, Collins, Rozeff, and Salatka used a somewhat different testing approach and found evidence indicating that FC firms had a positive stock price reaction when FC was reinstated.[27]

Collins and Dent conducted a study similar to Dyckman's with two major exceptions: (1) Canadian enterprises were excluded, and (2) the period studied was extended to one year. Their finding was directly opposite to the earlier study. The results showed that

> . . . over the three, six and eight month periods following the issuance of the ED, the average risk-adjusted return of the full cost firms was significantly less than that of the successful efforts firms.[28]

However, Kross, having used the same sample of firms, argued that, when contemporaneous industry effects were controlled for, the exposure draft had no effect on firms using FC.[29]

---

[23] Deakin (1979, pp. 730–733).
[24] Haworth, Matthews, and Tuck (1978).
[25] Dyckman and Smith (1979).
[26] Smith (1981, p. 207).
[27] Collins, Rozeff, and Salatka (1982).
[28] Collins and Dent (1979, p. 24).
[29] Kross (1982).

Lev's study differed from the others in that he used daily rather than weekly stock prices. Lev believed that a week between price observations is too long to identify the impact of a single event, such as the issuance of the draft. He used only seven days, two prior and five after issuance of the draft. The sample comprised forty-nine FC and thirty-four SE enterprises. He found that the issuance of the draft had a negative impact on the stock prices of FC as compared to SE enterprises.[30]

Several additional studies were made in connection with the FC versus SE controversy. Dhaliwal examined seventy-two FC enterprises and forty-one SE enterprises. The objective of his study was to determine the impact of an enterprise's capital structure on management's attitude toward accounting standards. He found that FC enterprises generally were more highly leveraged than SE enterprises and that their managements opposed SFAS 19 more than did the managements of the lower-leveraged SE enterprises, a result consistent with debt-contracting-related incentives hypothesized by agency theory.[31] Lilien and Pastena similarly found that FC is used by more highly leveraged firms and that larger-sized firms use SE.[32] In addition, they suggested that variations in the application of both FC and SE create more of a "continuous choice" of accounting method, and that this *continuum* is associated with income-increasing incentives for highly leveraged firms (due to debt contracts) and income-decreasing incentives for larger-sized firms (due to hypothesized size-related political costs).

Collins, Rozeff, and Dhaliwal also used agency theory to explain the observed decline in stock prices associated with the draft's elimination of FC accounting. The results seem to indicate that stock price declines were associated with an anticipated increase in the cost of supplying information using SE as opposed to FC and with an anticipated negative impact on important financial contracts, such as debt covenants.[33] Two other studies found a negative stock price reaction. Larcker and Revsine argued that the negative returns were associated with negative income effects that could motivate management to reduce exploration costs in order to maintain incentive compensation levels, and Lys suggested that the reaction was due, in part, to the firm's leverage level, which proxies for debt covenant effects.[34]

Three other empirical studies are of interest. Deakin was interested in which FC firms would lobby against the elimination of FC when the discussion memorandum was issued, when the exposure draft came out, and when the FASB's decision to eliminate FC was appealed to the SEC in March, 1978. He found strong evidence indicating that the FC firms that lobbied (as opposed to FC firms that did not lobby) were characterized by larger debt-equity ratios, the presence of management incentive plans that were based on accounting

---

[30] Lev (1979, p. 500).

[31] Dhaliwal (1980, pp. 78–84).

[32] Lilien and Pastena (1982).

[33] Collins, Rozeff, and Dhaliwal (1981, pp. 37–73).

[34] Larcker and Revsine (1983) and Lys (1984).

income, and relatively high activity in oil and gas exploration.[35] These results are in accord with the tenets of agency theory. Johnson and Ramanan were concerned with characteristics of firms that changed from SE to FC between 1970 and 1976, prior to the appearance of SFAS 19.[36] The study centered on nineteen firms that made the switch during the 1970–76 period. Firms that switched (as opposed to those that did not) were characterized by higher leverage (relative usage of debt) and relatively high capital expenditures for oil and gas exploration. Once again, the results are in accordance with agency theory.

Frost and Bernard's study, however, raises some significant questions about debt covenants and economic consequences.[37] They investigated how public and private loan agreements were affected by an SEC ruling in May, 1986, that tightened capitalization of exploration costs by FC firms in light of a steep decline in oil prices during the first full quarter of 1986. The ruling itself was unexpected and occurred after the close of the fiscal period to which it was applicable but prior to the release of financial statements.[38] Thus firms could not take any immediate actions to offset the effects of the decision. As a result of the ruling, debt covenants of the FC firms were adversely affected. In the period immediately before and immediately after the SEC ruling, no difference in cumulative abnormal returns between FC and SE firms was noted. Furthermore, both types of firms (FC and SE) had an upward drift in abnormal returns above that of the market right after the decision was announced. Frost and Bernard did see the possibility of a confounding effect in these surprising results owing to discussions at the time of possible favorable tax law changes for oil and gas firms.[39] Also, it should be noted that their study involved only eighteen firms. Nevertheless, their results are quite interesting.

Overall, it is clear that the numerous stock market studies are inconclusive as to whether there was a negative impact on FC firms when FC was proscribed or, conversely, a positive impact when FC was reinstated. And even assuming there was an impact, the studies are inconclusive as to what caused it. However, the non-stock market research does provide convincing evidence that FC firms strongly favored the FC method for reasons of income-increasing motivation discussed at the outset of this chapter.

RELATIONSHIP TO THE CONCEPTUAL FRAMEWORK

SFAS 19 was issued prior to the issuance of any statements of Financial Accounting Concepts; however, concepts discussed in SFACs 1 and 2 were well formulated in the minds of FASB members and served as background for the decisions reached in SFAS 19. The overall criterion of decision usefulness as discussed in SFAC 1 was clearly the objective of the FASB in promulgating SFAS 19.

---

[35] Deakin (1989).
[36] Johnson and Ramanan (1988).
[37] Frost and Bernard (1989).
[38] Ibid., p. 789.
[39] Ibid., p. 804.

Information about enterprises is much more useful if it is comparable between enterprises than if not. For example, if similar enterprises use dissimilar accounting procedures, although the inputs (transactions and events) into the respective systems may be the same, the outputs (financial statements) will be different and not comparable. Thus, to enhance the usefulness of information reported by oil and gas enterprises, the FASB decided that all enterprises should use the same accounting procedures.

SFAC 2 contains two broad concepts that make accounting information useful — reliability and relevance. To be reliable, information must be faithful to what it purports to represent and it must be verifiable. These two concepts of reliability — representational faithfulness and verifiability — were discussed at length in SFAC 2. Information must affect a decision made by decision makers in order for it to have the quality of relevance. Thus, it must have feedback value and predictive value as well as be timely. Both of the broad concepts — reliability and relevance — weighed heavily on the FASB during its deliberations leading up to SFAS 19.

In the oil and gas industry, most generally agree that the critical event for success is the discovery of reserves. As a result, the FASB considered, but rejected, a method of accounting that would have focused on the discovery of reserves. The method, discovery value accounting, is very similar to an SEC proposal called reserve recognition accounting (RRA), which will be discussed shortly. Although many variations of discovery value accounting exist, the primary thrust of it is that oil and gas reserves would be recorded at their estimated value when discovered. The discovery value would be recorded as revenue from exploration activities and as inventory for future production activities. The inventory would then be charged to the income statement as the reserves are sold.

The FASB rejected discovery value accounting primarily because of the lack of reliability in the measurement process. The measurement process involves estimates of the quantity of reserves, the amount and timing of costs to develop reserves, the timing of production of reserves, the production costs and income taxes, the selling prices, and the discount factor. The board concluded:

> The uncertainties inherent in those estimates and predictions tend to make estimates of reserve values highly subjective and relatively unreliable for the purpose of providing the basis on which to prepare financial statements of an oil and gas producing company.[40]

The board, therefore, was left with the choice between FC and SE. It opted for SE and rejected FC primarily because it believed that SE resulted in more relevant information being reported than did FC. In making decisions about enterprises, investors and creditors are concerned with the relative risk of each enterprise for which a decision must be made. Therefore, financial reports should report information about the relative risk of enterprises. The FASB concluded:

---

[40] FASB (1977, para. 133).

Because it capitalizes the costs of unsuccessful property acquisitions and unsuccessful activities as part of the costs of successful acquisitions and activities, full costing tends to obscure failure and risk. Successful efforts accounting, on the other hand, highlights failures and the risks involved in the search for oil and gas reserves by charging to expense costs that are known not to have resulted in identifiable future benefits.[41]

Another aspect of relevance of information that is discussed in SFAC 2 and was considered by the board in its deliberations on SFAS 19 is neutrality. Neutrality in the context of accounting information means that economic activity should be reported as faithfully as possible without attempting to alter what is being communicated in order to influence behavior in a particular direction. In other words, it is not the purpose of accounting information to influence behavior in any direction other than the direction indicated by the economic activity being reported. Neutrality has a more obvious impact on standard setters than on those preparing accounting information. The standard setters must establish accounting standards that result in the reporting of reliable and relevant information in accordance with the underlying economic activities being reported and must not be influenced by various special-interest groups, including the federal government, whose policies have their own purposes.

There were many, both inside and outside government, who felt that requiring SE and proscribing FC was contrary to national economic policy in the oil and gas industry. The argument was that prohibiting FC would be anticompetitive and thus would result in less exploration and development of reserves. The board rejected this argument because, notwithstanding the fact that it did not accept the economic consequences argument, national policy is best served by limiting acceptable alternatives and promulgating standards that do not obscure economic facts.

POLITICAL PRESSURE

The FC/SE controversy acquired political overtones to a far greater extent than any accounting issue either before or after. Indeed, the ultimate outcome could have seriously harmed the credibility of the FASB; however, such a drastic impact does not appear to have occurred. As noted earlier, an act of Congress empowered the SEC to

> ... take such steps as may be necessary to assure the development and observance of accounting practices to be followed in the preparation of accounts by persons engaged ... in the production of crude oil or natural gas in the United States.[42]

The SEC elected to rely on the FASB, and both groups interpreted the act's charge to mean that a single uniform system of accounting should evolve.

---

[41] Ibid., para. 15b.
[42] Energy Policy and Conservation Act (1975, Sec. 503(a)).

Knowing the recommendation several years earlier by the AICPA Task Force (favoring SE), oil and gas industry representatives pushed their viewpoints in various high-profile ways. They lobbied Congress, sponsored and published studies conducted by the American Petroleum Institute, made their views known in the press, and lobbied government agencies in Washington.

This pressure initially appeared to be of no use because the FASB issued its draft favoring SE, and the SEC announced its intention to incorporate the draft in the regulations in the event the FASB was unable to act fast enough. The FASB, however, did act and issued SFAS 19 promptly. The political pressure did begin to mount shortly after SFAS 19 was issued. The oil and gas industry was under attack for high profiteering and little competition. Many blamed the FASB. Shortly after the issuing of SFAS 19, the Department of Energy held hearings to consider the impact of SFAS 19 on competition; the antitrust division of the Department of Justice also registered its concern about SFAS 19; and the Federal Trade Commission urged the SEC to reject SFAS 19. Even the SEC decided to hold hearings on FC versus SE. The SEC reversed its position and in ASR 253 indicated that it would accept the FC method and planned to develop some form of a discovery value method. Subsequently, in ASRs 257 and 258, the SEC permitted a method of FC as an acceptable alternative to SE and indicated its intention to require reserve recognition accounting (RRA) in the future. At the same time, to avoid harm to the FASB's credibility, the SEC reaffirmed its basic policy of looking to the FASB for leadership in developing and promulgating accounting standards. The FASB subsequently issued SFAS 25, which suspended the mandatory use of SE. In issuing SFAS 25, the FASB bent to the political pressure that was brought to bear. From a practical point of view, it had no other choice.

RESERVE RECOGNITION ACCOUNTING (RRA)

A survey of all financial analysts involved with the oil and gas industry was conducted primarily to determine whether analysts favored FC or SE. Over 40 percent responded, and they overwhelmingly favored the SE method. A secondary finding, however, is perhaps more enlightening. The vast majority of the analysts (83 percent) thought that the value of recoverable reserves should be disclosed in financial reports.[43] This indicates that, for the oil and gas industry at least, the historical cost model simply does not provide adequate information to decision makers. The perceived failure of the historical cost method led the SEC to advocate RRA.

The SEC cited three primary reasons for favoring the development of RRA:

1. historical cost accounting fails to provide sufficient information on financial position and operating results for oil and gas producers;

---

[43] Naggar (1978, pp. 72–77).

2. additional information, outside the basic financial statements, is required to permit assessments of the financial position and operating results of an enterprise in the oil and gas industry and allow comparisons between it and other enterprises;

3. an accounting method based on valuation of oil and gas reserves is needed to provide sufficiently useful information.[44]

Hence the SEC was concerned with providing informative disclosure in terms of oil and gas accounting.

In August, 1978, the SEC issued Release 33-5969, which ushered in RRA on an experimental basis for three years. If successful, the SEC's plan was to require RRA in the primary financial statements. The valuation method required for RRA was as follows:

1. Estimate the timing of future production of proven reserves, based on current (that is, balance sheet date) economic conditions.

2. Estimate future revenue by using the estimate from (1) and applying current prices for oil and gas, adjusted only for fixed contractual escalations.

3. Estimate future net revenue by deducting from the estimate in (2) the costs to develop and produce the proven reserves — on the basis of current cost levels.

4. Determine the present value of future net revenue by discounting the estimate in (3) at 10 percent.

Exhibit 15–4 (page 464) illustrates the format for displaying earnings under RRA suggested by the SEC.

As might be expected, RRA received significant criticism from the oil and gas industry. Most of the criticism was based on concepts discussed in SFACs 1 and 2, which, although not in place at that time, had been disseminated for public comment. Some questioned the relevance of the information because it represented a relatively objective and uniform approach but did not produce fair market value of an enterprise's oil and gas properties. RRA considered only proven reserves rather than total reserves; therefore, significant quantities could be ignored. Moreover, it did not anticipate future price and cost changes and by doing so assumed that changes in costs would result in similar changes in prices. This assumption is not necessarily true for oil and gas operations where the price of oil and gas is significantly influenced by the actions of the Organization of Petroleum Exporting Countries and supply and demand, while costs are influenced more by local inflationary conditions. The selection of a discount rate of 10 percent was nothing more than an arbitrary decision to force rigid uniformity and did not consider any of the enterprise-specific factors, such as risk, that enter into the determination of an appropriate discount rate.

The reliability of the information was the subject of numerous research studies. A study undertaken by Stanley P. Porter was designed to determine the accuracy of annual estimates of proven reserves. It included twenty-seven dif-

[44]SEC Docket (1978).

EXHIBIT 15–4
Earnings Summary of Oil- and Gas-Producing Activities

Year Ended December 31, 19XX		
Revenues from Oil and Gas:		
Sales to outsiders	$XXXX	
Transfers	XXXX	$XXXX
Costs of Production:		
Lifting costs	XXXX	
Amortization of proved properties	XXXX	(XXXX)
Income from Producing Activities		XXXX
Current Additions to Proved Properties		XXXX
Costs of Additions to Proved Properties:		
Exploration costs	XXXX	
Development costs	XXXX	(XXXX)
Income from Current Exploration and		
Development Activities		XXXX
Revisions to Previous Additions to Proved Properties:		
Changes in estimated quantities of proved reserves		XXXX
Changes in rate of production		XXXX
Changes to reflect current prices and costs		XXXX
Holding gains from passage of time		XXXX
Total Revisions		XXXX
Profit Before Income Taxes		XXXX
Provision for Income Taxes		(XXXX)
Profit After Income Taxes		$XXXX

ferent enterprises that together accounted for 54 percent of crude oil and natural gas liquid production and 50 percent of the oil production in the United States in 1978. Participating enterprises were asked to supply information involving the impact of changes in existing reserves on an annual basis. The results reflect the impreciseness of reserve quantity estimates:

1. In 64% of the years studied, reserve revisions were more than 20% of additions and, hence, income was affected by more than 20%; in 46% of the years, the impact was greater than 40%; and in 23% of the years, it was over 100% ...;
2. All companies that reported for the entire ten-year period had at least one year in which the impact of judgement would be in excess of 60% of income on an RRA basis.[45]

---

[45] Porter (1980, pp. 36–37).

Price Waterhouse conducted a study of nine oil and gas enterprises to determine the impact on reported earnings of the various estimates to be made. Some of the findings included:

1. Reserve estimates made in the year of discovery were inaccurate by at least ±50 percent.
2. Generally, RRA income is changed percentage-wise by at least as much as the percentage change in reserve estimate.
3. Income from reserve revisions, ignoring price changes, greatly exceeded income from discoveries.
4. Income from price changes greatly exceeded income from discoveries.[46]

In general, the perception was that RRA's relevance was more than offset by its lack of reliability. As a result, the SEC decided not to require it in primary financial statements. The FASB subsequently added a project to its agenda to develop a comprehensive set of disclosures for oil and gas enterprises.

Two studies investigated the effect of RRA disclosures on security prices. Bell reported that the initial RRA disclosures in 1979 had information content; however, Dharan found that RRA data itself had very little information content above and beyond similar information contained in non-RRA data in the accounting reports.[47] Once again, as has been the case in oil and gas accounting, stock market research provides ambiguous evidence on economic consequences.

CURRENT STATUS OF ACCOUNTING IN THE OIL AND GAS INDUSTRY

The FASB, working with oil and gas representatives and the SEC, moved fairly rapidly in developing a set of required disclosures. The SEC issued ASR 289 on February 26, 1981. It stated that the SEC did not consider RRA as a potential method of accounting in primary financial statements. The FASB added its project on oil and gas disclosure to the agenda on March 4, 1981. By May 15, 1981 it had issued an Invitation to Comment. Public hearings were held in August, 1981; a draft was issued in April, 1982; and SFAS 69, "Disclosures about Oil and Gas Producing Activities," was issued in November, 1982, to take effect for fiscal years beginning on or after December 15, 1982.

SFAS 69 is significant for at least two reasons. First, it represents an attempt by the FASB to combat the *standards-overload* problem. SFAS 69 is not applicable to enterprises that are not publicly traded nor to publicly traded enterprises that do not have significant oil- and gas-producing activities. The reason for exempting those enterprises is "that the costs of providing that infor-

---

[46] Price Waterhouse & Co. (1979, pp. 15–21).
[47] Bell (1983) and Dharan (1984).

mation exceed the benefits."[48] Second, SFAS 69 represents another expansion of the concept of financial reporting. It requires the disclosure of financial information outside the basic financial statements or notes thereto. The reason given by the FASB for this requirement is that the information is not historical cost (the basis of the primary financial statements), and its reliability is not such as to make it comparable with the primary financial statements.[49]

The basic information required from oil and gas enterprises covered by SFAS 69 includes disclosures about these items:

1. Proven oil and gas reserve quantities.
2. Capitalized costs relating to oil- and gas-producing activities.
3. Costs incurred in oil and gas property acquisition, exploration, and development activities.
4. Results of operations for oil- and gas-producing activities.
5. A standardized measure of discounted future net cash flows relating to proven oil and gas reserves. The discount rate to be used is 10 percent.[50]

The standardized measure of discounted future net cash flows is calculated by estimating future cash inflow from proven reserves at current prices less estimated future development and production costs and income taxes relating to the cash inflows, both to be computed using current costs and rates. The amount derived is then discounted at 10 percent. The aggregate change in the discounted future net cash flow during the year must also be disclosed and the sources of that change, if significant, also disclosed. Some likely reasons for a change in the discounted future net cash flow from one year to the next include changes in estimated future sales prices, development and production costs, and income taxes relating to future production as well as revisions of reserve quantity estimates and discoveries.[51] As can be seen, this calculation is very similar to the calculation of income from exploration and development under the SEC's RRA. The FASB did not go so far as the SEC, however, because an earnings statement based on the various estimates is not required. Presumably the reason is the lack of reliability of the information.

Given the turmoil from 1976 to 1982, and the adoption of SFAS's 25 and 69, it came as something of a surprise when the SEC's accounting staff recommended the abolishment of FC in October of 1986. The reasons were pretty much related to uniformity and echoed the sentiment behind SFAS 19. Once again, though, political factors dominated the process. The *Wall Street Journal* reported that two cabinet members pressed the SEC not to drop FC, and, one week later when the SEC commissioners met, they voted 4–1 to retain FC.[52] The "reasons" given also echoed those of the 1970s — the potentially adverse economic consequences on small firms and on the incentive to explore for new oil and gas reserves.

---

[48] FASB (1982, para. 113).
[49] Ibid., para. 116.
[50] Ibid., paras. 10–38.
[51] Ibid., paras. 30–33.
[52] The *Wall Street Journal*, October 24, 1986, p. 8.

SUMMARY

Financial reporting in the oil and gas industry has been the subject of considerable controversy. At the center of that controversy is the adequacy of the historical cost model to provide information for users of financial reports. The most significant event for an oil and gas enterprise is the discovery of oil and gas reserves, not the revenues recognized from oil and gas sales. The historical cost model, however, does not measure or report oil and gas reserves until those reserves have been developed, produced, and sold. A related problem is that the costs incurred to discover oil and gas reserves bear little, if any, relationship to the value of the reserves.

Two accounting methods (FC and SE) evolved in the industry. In many cases, the financial statement impact of FC versus SE is dramatic and results in financial statements that are not comparable among enterprises. The FASB attempted to solve the uniformity and comparability problem by requiring that all enterprises use SE. Its efforts, however, were undermined by political pressure in general and SEC actions specifically. As a result, both FC and SE accounting continue to be acceptable today.

The SEC attempted to overcome the shortcomings of the historical cost model by eliminating its use in the oil and gas industry. In its place, a form of discovery value accounting (RRA) was to be used. However, measurements made under RRA were perceived to be too unreliable for the basic financial statements. The FASB subsequently issued SFAS 69, which requires the disclosure of information similar to the SEC's RRA information outside of the basic financial statements and notes thereto.

The oil and gas controversy has two important ramifications for the standard-setting mechanism today. First, it demonstrates that standard setting is a political process. Second, academic researchers, working together with standard setters, can have a significant impact on the standard-setting process. The decision to press on with SFAS 19 was, in part, due to a finding that there were no adverse economic consequences on FC firms vis-à-vis stock prices or their ability to raise capital.

QUESTIONS

1. What factors make the oil and gas industry in general, and oil and gas accounting in particular, so politically sensitive?
2. Both FC and SE represent applications of historical cost. How do the two methods differ conceptually?
3. Why is FC predominantly used by smaller firms and SE by larger firms, and how does this relate to the alleged economic consequences of mandating SE?
4. The FASB was determined to narrow acceptable practices. Why do you think it opted for SE rather than FC in SFAS 19?

5. Many believe that the historical cost model is inappropriate for the oil and gas industry. What is the difference between the oil and gas industry and other industries that leads to the perception of inadequacy of the historical cost model?

6. The FASB readily admitted that historical-cost-based accounting systems in the oil and gas industry do not meet the overall objective of financial accounting and reporting as stated in SFAC 1. Why, then, did the FASB reject the use of a discovery value method?

7. Define *neutrality* as the term is used by the FASB. Can neutrality exist, and should neutrality be a goal of standard setters?

8. Defend the following statement: the FASB is a public policy-making agency, so the reaction against SFAS 19 was legitimate and the subsequent issuance of SFAS 25 represented good public policy making.

9. To those concerned with the FASB's autonomy, SFAS 25 was a disappointment. Why?

10. What motivated the SEC's push for RRA in 1978, and why was it discontinued in 1981?

11. Oil and gas disclosures in SFAS 69 are not considered part of the basic financial statements or notes thereto and do not require auditor attestation. Why did the FASB adopt this approach?

12. What have been the objectives of stock market research with respect to oil and gas accounting?

13. Despite many studies, it remains an open question as to whether oil and gas accounting standard setting has affected stock prices. What are some reasons for the contradictory findings?

14. Discuss the limitations of using stock market research to evaluate economic consequences of accounting policies.

15. Bismarck said that democracy is not a very pretty thing to watch. How is this apropos to standard setting for the oil and gas industry?

16. FC firms that lobbied against elimination of FC (as opposed to FC firms that did not lobby) were characterized as reported in a study by Deakin by larger debt-equity ratios, the presence of management incentive plans based on accounting income, and relatively high activity in oil and gas exploration. Explain why this is in accordance with the tenets of agency theory.

CASES AND PROBLEMS

1. Consider the following case: The XYZ Corporation was formed and commenced operations last year. It began with $5,000,000 capitalization (cash/capital stock). Oil properties costing $2,000,000 were acquired by issuing long-term debt. Other assets costing $600,000 cash were acquired. Three exploratory wells costing $500,000 cash each were drilled and one was successful. No production occurred and, therefore, no depreciation or depletion was recorded. In the current year, 19XX, three more exploratory wells

costing $525,000 cash each were drilled and one was successful. 100,000 barrels, representing 20 percent of beginning-of-the-year reserves, were produced and sold at $30 per barrel (cash). Production costs average 10 percent of revenues (cash) and depreciation is 12 percent of property and other assets. Ignore income taxes.

Required:
(a) Prepare a balance sheet at end of year 19XX and an income statement for year 19XX under:
   (1) FC method of accounting.
   (2) SE method of accounting.
(b) Discuss the advantages and disadvantages of both methods.

2. Determine the standardized net cash flow required to be disclosed by SFAS 69 using the following information:
(a) Proven reserves are 1,000,000 barrels.
(b) Estimated production is 20 percent per year of proven reserves.
(c) Current selling price is $35 per barrel.
(d) Costs to develop and produce proven reserves are approximately 40 percent of the selling price.
(e) Depreciation and depletion average 75 percent of development and production costs.
(f) Income taxes generally are 38 percent of income before taxes.

3. The Gas Drilling Company (GDC) has asked your opinion as to the appropriate accounting for the following transaction. GDC uses the SE method of accounting.

   GDC is participating in the drilling of an exploratory gas well.

   The drilling arrangement provides that GDC must drill to 20,000 feet in order to earn an interest in any gas found at the drill site.

   During drilling, a producing zone was found at 15,000 feet. However, GDC continued drilling to 25,000 feet. There was no definitive determination of gas reserves below 15,000 feet, and GDC has no specific plans to continue exploration.

   The decision has been made to plug the well back up to 15,000 feet and operate it as a producing well.

   Total costs of drilling the well were $12,000,000, of which $4,000,000 were incurred between 15,000 feet and 20,000 feet, and $5,000,000 were incurred between 20,000 feet and 25,000 feet.

(a) What do you believe should be the appropriate accounting (capitalization versus expense) for the costs incurred below 15,000 feet?
(b) What is the appropriate accounting for the costs incurred beyond 15,000 feet under SFAS 19?

4. Presented below is Exxon Corporation's comments on RRA in its 1979 10-K:[53]

---

[53] Reprinted by permission.

The following information departs significantly from prior reporting of historical information and attempts to portray 1978, 1979 and future activities of Exxon in oil and gas producing in a highly arbitrary fashion. Therefore, Exxon believes it should warn that the remaining data set forth in this section, for reasons further explained below, are not to be interpreted as necessarily representing current profitability or amounts which Exxon will receive, or costs which will be incurred, or the manner in which oil and gas will be produced from the respective reserves. The arbitrary ten percent discount rate used in the determination of the present value of estimated future net revenues represents neither a cost of capital nor a borrowing rate, and, additionally, does not necessarily reflect political risks. Actual future selling prices and related costs, development costs, production schedules, reserves and their classifications, and other matters may differ significantly from the data portrayed or assumed.

The requirement to publish such information regarding future activities is part of the SEC's attempted development of a new method of accounting for oil and gas producing activities called "Reserve Recognition Accounting" (RRA). RRA would depart significantly from historical accounting practices. Exxon has taken exception to the SEC's proposal and has indicated the following major concerns with the concept of RRA:

> Financial reporting for the oil and gas producing segment of the oil industry would include forecasts of future production rates and future investments in an estimation of potential cash flows. Such reporting would be completely different from the historical cost reporting of the remainder of the oil industry and of all other industries.
>
> The difficulties and uncertainties of estimating the volumes of oil and gas reserves and their production rates appear not to have been appropriately considered, making comparability between companies, and segments thereof, very difficult at best. Quantification of reserves is far from a precise science. A variety of methods and techniques are used to estimate reserves and the answers obtained are subject to wide fluctuations because they are dependent on judgmental interpretations of geologic and reservoir data. The same is true of estimates of future production schedules. While, in management's judgment, the quantities reported herein are reasonable, there is no methodology or certification process in place now, or likely to be in place in the near future, which would permit independent verification of such volumes and rates.
>
> The Regulations prescribe that future net revenues be determined by applying December 31, 1979 prices and costs to the projected production schedules for Exxon's net proved oil and gas reserves as of December 31, 1979. The reserves exclude probable reserves as well as reserves in the Canadian Athabasca Oil Sands. In Exxon's opinion, applying these arbitrary assumptions to the estimated future production schedule for the various categories of reserves can only lead to financial reporting which is more likely to mislead than inform.

In addition to these general areas of concern, the following cautions should be noted when reviewing the information:

Care should be exercised when comparing the "Net Revenues From Producing Oil and Gas in 1978 and 1979" with "Future Net Revenues." The 1978 and 1979 information, in accordance with the Regulations, was determined by subtracting only Production (Lifting) Costs from the gross revenues. Future Net

Revenues, in accordance with the Regulations, were determined by subtracting both Development Costs and Production (Lifting) Costs from the gross revenues. Care should also be exercised when using the net revenue data for 1978, 1979 and the future since all applicable costs have not been deducted from gross revenue. The Regulations make no provision for deducting exploration expenses, amortization of acquisition costs (bonus payments), depreciation of capitalized production investments, purchase costs of royalty oil and gas, income taxes, or other payments to governments.

The "Future Net Revenues" and the present value of such revenues, as computed under the Regulations, present neither a true "future value" nor "present value" for the reasons mentioned above in addition to the effect of excluding income taxes from the calculation. In view of Exxon's concern that the absence of this considerable, and in some cases major, cost from the calculation would cause the information to be seriously misunderstood and misleading, particularly in the case of some foreign operations, the undiscounted and present value information presented here is shown on both a before-tax and after-tax basis.

Required:
(a) Evaluate the merits of Exxon's criticism of RRA.
(b) How might political visibility (see Chapter 4) have affected Exxon's attitude toward RRA?

5. In October, 1986, the SEC's accounting staff proposed a reconsideration of banning the FC method. The commission voted not to re-open the matter, as reported in The *Wall Street Journal*, October 31, 1986, p. 4:[54]

> The 4-1 vote against the SEC chief accountant's proposal was a triumph for a coalition of independent producers, which was able to get Energy Secretary John Herrington, Interior Secretary Donald Hodel and numerous oil-state lawmakers to lobby for the preservation of both accounting methods.
>
> They contended that mandating successful-efforts accounting would retard domestic oil and gas exploration and further depress an industry reeling from the oil-price collapse.
>
> Companies using the full-cost method argue that it enables them to undertake risky exploration projects without having sharp swings in their reported earnings. Critics argue that the method inflates earnings and hides the cost of inefficient exploration efforts.
>
> The full-cost companies feared that a mandatory switch would force producers to restate their financial results at considerable cost and to write down billions of dollars in stockholder equity. Even the threat of an accounting change, some said, was depressing stock prices.
>
> "Everybody has been looking for a way to help the industry," said Robert Odle, lobbyist for several independent producers. "Today a federal agency found a way: The SEC removed the uncertainty about what the rules are going to be."

What are the economic consequences that were once again raised in defense of FC?

---

[54]Reprinted by permission of The *Wall Street Journal*. © 1986. Dow Jones & Company, Inc. All Rights Reserved Worldwide.

BIBLIOGRAPHY OF REFERENCED WORKS

Arthur Young (1977). *Successful Efforts' Accounting: Why It Is Needed in the Extractive Industries* (Arthur Young).

Bell, Timothy Barnes (1983). "Market Reaction to Reserve Recognition Accounting," *Journal of Accounting Research* (Spring 1983), pp. 1–17.

Collins, Daniel W., and Warren T. Dent (1979). "The Proposed Elimination of Full Cost Accounting in the Extractive Petroleum Industry: An Empirical Assessment of the Market Consequences," *Journal of Accounting and Economics* (March 1979), pp. 3–44.

Collins, Daniel W., Michael S. Rozeff, and Dan S. Dhaliwal (1981). "The Economic Determinants of the Market Reaction to Proposed Mandatory Accounting Changes in the Oil and Gas Industry: A Cross-Sectional Analysis," *Journal of Accounting and Economics* (March 1981), pp. 37–71.

Collins, Daniel W., Michael S. Rozeff, and William K. Salatka (1982). "The SEC's Rejection of SFAS No. 19: Tests of Market Price Reversal," *The Accounting Review* (January 1982), pp. 1–17.

Deakin, Edward B., III (1979). "An Analysis of Differences Between Non-Major Oil Firms Using Successful Efforts and Full Cost Methods," *The Accounting Review* (October 1979), pp. 722–734.

———— (1989). "Rational Economic Behavior and Lobbying on Accounting Issues: Evidence from the Oil and Gas Industry," *The Accounting Review* (January 1989), pp. 137–151.

Dhaliwal, Dan S. (1980). "The Effect of the Firm's Capital Structure on the Choice of Accounting Methods," *The Accounting Review* (January 1980), pp. 78–84.

Dharan, Bala G. (1984). "Expectation Models and Potential Information Content of Oil and Gas Reserve Value Disclosure," *The Accounting Review* (April 1984), pp. 199–217.

Dyckman, Thomas R. (1979). *The Effects of the Issuance of the Exposure Draft and FASB Statement No. 19 on the Security Returns of Oil and Gas Producing Companies* (FASB).

Dyckman, Thomas, and Abbie Smith (1979). "Financial Accounting and Reporting by Oil and Gas Producing Companies — A Study of Information Effects," *Journal of Accounting and Economics* (March 1979), pp. 45–75.

Energy Policy and Conservation Act (1975). Public Law 94-163, 94th Congress, S. 622 (December 22, 1975).

Federal Power Commission (1971). Order No. 440, 36 F.R. 21963 (November 5, 1971).

Field, Robert E. (1969). "Financial Reporting in the Extractive Industries," *Accounting Research Study No. 11* (AICPA).

Financial Accounting Standards Board (1977). "Financial Accounting and Reporting by Oil and Gas Producing Companies," *Statement of Financial Accounting Standards No. 19* (FASB).

———— (1978). *Appendices to the Additional Comments of the Financial Accounting Standards Board to the Securities and Exchange Commission, Accounting Practices — Oil and Gas Producers* (SEC File 57-715, May 31, 1978).

———— (1979). "Suspension of Certain Accounting Requirements for Oil and Gas Producing Companies," *Statement of Financial Accounting Standards No. 25* (FASB).

———— (1982). "Disclosures about Oil and Gas Producing Activities," *Statement of Financial Accounting Standards No. 69* (FASB).

First Boston Corporation (1978). Statement at the Department of Energy Inquiry (February 21, 1978).

Frost, Carol A., and Victor L. Bernard (1989). "The Role of Debt Covenants in Assessing the Economic Consequences of Limiting Capitalization of Exploration Costs," *The Accounting Review* (October 1989), pp. 788–808.

Ginsburg, Feldman, and Bress (1973). Attorneys for the Ad Hoc Committee (Petroleum Companies), *Comments of the Ad Hoc Committee (Petroleum Companies)* (SEC File No. 57-464, March 14, 1973).

Haworth, H., J. Matthews, and C. Tuck (1978). *Full Cost vs. Successful Efforts: A Study of a Proposed Accounting Changes' Competitive Impact* (SEC Directorate of Economic and Policy Research, February 1978).

Ijiri, Yuji (1979). "Oil and Gas Accounting – Turbulence in Financial Reporting," *Financial Executive* (August 1979), pp. 18–26.

Johnson, W. Bruce, and Ramachandran Ramanan (1988). "Discretionary Accounting Changes from 'Successful Efforts' to 'Full Cost' Methods: 1970–76," *The Accounting Review* (January 1988), pp. 96–110.

Klingstedt, John (1970). "Effects of Full Costing in the Petroleum Industry," *Financial Analysts Journal* (September–October 1979), pp. 79–86.

Kross, William (1982). "Stock Returns and Oil and Gas Pronouncements: Replication and Extension," *Journal of Accounting Research* (Autumn, Pt. II 1982), pp. 459–471.

Larcker, David F., and Lawrence Revsine (1983). "The Oil and Gas Controversy: An Analysis of Economic Consequences," *The Accounting Review* (October 1983), pp. 706–732.

Lev, Baruch (1979). "The Impact of Accounting Regulation on the Stock Market: The Case of Oil and Gas Companies," *The Accounting Review* (July 1979), pp. 485–503.

Lilien, Steven, and Victor Pastena (1982). "Determinants of Intramethod Choice in the Oil and Gas Industry," *Journal of Accounting and Economics* (December 1982), pp. 145–170.

Lys, Thomas (1984). "Mandated Accounting Changes and Debt Covenants: The Case of Oil and Gas Accounting," *Journal of Accounting and Economics* (April 1984), pp. 39–65.

Naggar, Ali (1978). "Oil and Gas Accounting: Where Wall Street Stands," *Journal of Accountancy* (September 1978), pp. 72–77.

Porter, Stanley P. (1972). *"Full Cost" Accounting: The Problem It Poses for the Extractive Industries* (Arthur Young & Co.).

———— (1980). *A Study of the Subjectivity of Reserve Estimates and Its Relation to Financial Reporting* (Stanley P. Porter).

Price Waterhouse & Co. (1979). *Reserve Recognition Accounting* (Price Waterhouse & Co.).

SEC Docket (1978). (Volume 15, No. 12 – Part III, September 10, 1978).

Securities and Exchange Commission (1972). "Proposed Amendment to Regulation S–X to provide for Disclosure of Significant Accounting Policies," *Securities Act Release 5343, Exchange Act Release 9914* (38 F.R. 1747, December 18, 1972).

Smith, Abbie (1981). "The SEC 'Reversal' of FASB Statement No. 19: An Investigation of Information Effects," *Studies on Standardization of Accounting Practices: An Assessment of Alternative Institutional Arrangements* (1981 Supplement to *Journal of Accounting Research*), pp. 174–211.

Touche Ross & Co. (1977). Letter to the Ad Hoc Committee on Full Cost Accounting (March 29, 1977).

United States Department of Justice (1978). "Comments on Accounting Practices – Oil and Gas Producers – Financial Accounting Standards," Before the Securities and Exchange Commission (February 28, 1978).

ADDITIONAL READINGS

Full Cost and Successful Efforts

Bierman, Harold, Roland Dukes, and Thomas Dyckman (1974). "Financial Accounting in the Petroleum Industry," *Journal of Accountancy* (October 1974), pp. 58–64.

Collins, Daniel W., Warren T. Dent, and Melvin C. O'Connor (1978). "Market Effects of the Elimination of Full Cost Accounting in the Oil and Gas Industry," *Financial Analysts Journal* (November–December 1978), pp. 48–56.

Committee on Extractive Industries of the Accounting Principles Board (1973). *Accounting and Reporting Practices in the Oil and Gas Industry* (AICPA).

Dyckman, Thomas (1979). "Market Effects of the Elimination of Full Cost Accounting in the Oil and Gas Industry: Another View," *Financial Analysts Journal* (May–June 1979), pp. 75–80.

Financial Accounting Standards Board (1976). *Discussion Memorandum: Financial Accounting and Reporting in the Extractive Industries* (FASB).

Jain, Prem (1983). "The Impact of Accounting Regulation on the Stock Market: The Case of Oil and Gas Companies: A Further Analysis," *The Accounting Review* (1983), pp. 633–638.

King, Raymond D., and Terrence B. O'Keefe (1986). "Lobbying Activities and Insider Trading," *The Accounting Review* (January 1986), pp. 76–90.

Larcker, David F., Renee E. Reder, and Daniel T. Simon (1983). "Trades by Insiders as Evidence of Economic Consequences of Accounting Standards," *The Accounting Review* (July 1983), pp. 606–620.

Myers, John H. (1974). *Full Cost vs. Successful Efforts in Petroleum Accounting: An Empirical Approach* (John H. Myers).

Patz, Dennis H., and James R. Boatsman (1972). "Accounting Principle Formulation in an Efficient Markets Environment," *Journal of Accounting Research* (Autumn 1972), pp. 392–403.

Sunder, Shyam (1976). "Properties of Accounting Numbers Under Full Costing and Successful Efforts Costing in the Petroleum Industry," *The Accounting Review* (January 1976), pp. 1–18.

Reserve Recognition Accounting

Adkerson, Richard C. (1979). "Can Reserve Recognition Accounting Work?" *Journal of Accountancy* (September 1979), pp. 72–81.

Connor, Joseph E. (1975). "Discovery Value — The Oil Industry's Untried Method," *Journal of Accountancy* (May 1975), pp. 54–63.

——— (1979). "Reserve Recognition Accounting: Fact or Fiction?" *Journal of Accountancy* (September 1979), pp. 92–99.

Cooper, Kerry, Steven Flory, Steven Grossman, and John Groth (1979). "Reserve Recognition Accounting: A Proposed Disclosure Framework," *Journal of Accountancy* (September 1979), pp. 82–91.

Doran, B. Michael, Daniel W. Collins, and Dan S. Dhaliwal (1988). "The Information of Historical Cost Earnings Relative to Supplemental Reserve-Base Accounting Data in the Extractive Industry," *The Accounting Review* (July 1988), pp. 389–413.

Maglio, Joseph (1986). "Capital Market Analysis of Reserve Recognition Accounting," *Studies on Alternative Measures of Accounting Income* (Supplement to *Journal of Accounting Research*), pp. 69–108.

Most, Kenneth S. (1979). "A New Method of Accounting for Oil and Gas Producers," *Management Accounting* (May 1979), pp. 53–58.

Peat Marwick Mitchell & Co. (1979a). *Financial Accounting for Oil and Gas Reserves* (Peat Marwick Mitchell & Co.).

—— (1979b). *1979 Survey by Peat Marwick Mitchell & Co. of Petroleum Investment Analysts* (Peat Marwick Mitchell & Co.).

Porter, Stanley P. (1980). *Highlights of a Study of the Subjectivity of Reserve Estimates and Its Relation to Financial Reporting* (Stanley P. Porter).

Reed, Joel L. (1978). "Exploring for Information on Oil and Gas Companies," *Financial Analysts Journal* (November–December 1978), pp. 42–46.

Touche Ross & Co. (1980). *Oil and Gas Accounting* (Touche Ross & Co.).

Walendowski, George (1980). "RRA – Will It Work?" *Management Accounting* (March 1980), pp. 21–25.

Welsch, Glenn A., and Edward B. Deakin (1977). *A Research Study: Measuring and Reporting the "Replacement" Cost of Oil and Gas Reserves* (Glenn A. Welsch and Edward B. Deakin).

PENSIONS AND OTHER
POSTRETIREMENT BENEFITS

THE CENTRAL QUESTIONS in accounting for the effects of pension plan and other postretirement benefits involve the recognition and measurement of pension expenses and liabilities for the sponsoring company. Pension accounting provides an excellent illustration of the revenue–expense and asset–liability orientations to the financial statements. Previous accounting standards were based on a revenue–expense approach, which emphasized the recognition and measurement of annual pension expense. In SFAS 87, more rigid uniformity has been achieved in expense measurement, and the asset–liability orientation is evident in both expense measurement and the balance sheet recognition of unfunded pension benefits. Postretirement benefits are now subject to accrual accounting as a result of SFAS 106. In most areas, accounting for postretirement benefits is similar to pension accounting.

This chapter reviews the nature of pension plans in the first section. Pension plans are complex, so the review is meant to provide the necessary background for analysis of pension accounting. The second section examines in detail the forty-year development of pension accounting standards. The economic consequences of pension accounting standards are then discussed. After a simple illustration and a discussion of the main facets of SFAS 106, the economic consequences and theoretical aspects of other postretirement benefits are discussed in the final section of the chapter.

OVERVIEW OF PENSION PLANS

A pension plan is an arrangement between an employer and employee for the payment of postemployment income, hereafter called *pension benefits*.[1] There are many characteristics of pension plan design and funding, some of which are very complex. It is not feasible to review all of them, but we will briefly discuss significant areas that bear on pension accounting.

DEFINED CONTRIBUTION AND DEFINED BENEFIT PLANS

An important feature of pension plans concerns the benefit formula and specification of contributions. There are two broad types of plans, and they differ as to how benefits are specified and funded. **Defined contribution** plans are those in which the benefit is defined as the future value of pension fund contributions made on an employee's behalf. The exact value is unknown prior to retirement because it depends on future earnings of pension fund investments. Benefits are solely a function of accumulated contributions, and for this reason the plans are called *defined contribution*. The value of benefits is variable; it is dependent on contribution levels and earnings made on invested contributions.

Contribution rates for defined contribution plans are normally stated as a percentage of wages or salaries. Plans may be either **noncontributory,** in which all contributions are made by the employer, or **contributory,** where funding is shared by the employer and employee. Mandatory contributions must be made to a pension fund for most plans.[2] This means that assets are set aside for the sole purpose of paying pension benefits. The technical arrangements for accomplishing this are through either the establishment of a formal pension plan trust fund or the purchase of insured annuity contracts from insurance companies on behalf of employees. The term *pension fund* will be used to refer to both situations.

The other type of pension plan is called *defined benefit*. In **defined benefit** plans, the pension benefit is defined either as a specific dollar amount or by a general formula based on salary. Benefits may be expressed as a specific dollar amount, normally multiplied by years of membership in the plan (hereafter called *years of service*) to determine the value of the benefit. When benefits are defined by a general formula, two alternatives exist. Benefits can be based on career average salary: in this type of plan, pension benefits are based on career average salary multiplied by years of service. Another type of plan is referred to as *final pay:* pension benefits are based on final salary (usually the average of regular compensation a few years prior to retirement) multiplied by years of

---

[1] There are other benefits in a pension plan; for example, death and disability. These are normally paid for through group insurance contracts. Therefore, pension funding is assumed to refer just to the funding of retirement benefits.

[2] Funding requirements established by the Internal Revenue Service and the Employee Retirement Income Security Act would be applicable to most pension plans.

service. In all types of defined benefit plans, the value of pension benefits is directly related to the employee's years of service.[3]

Benefits in a defined benefit plan may be paid in one of two ways. The benefit may be paid as a single lump sum amount at retirement date. Alternatively, the benefit may be paid as a life annuity.[4] Some plans permit the employee to elect either form of payment. When the benefit is lump sum, the payment represents a multiple of the defined base; for example, final regular salary averaged over five years, multiplied by 15 percent for each year of service. An employee with forty years of service would receive forty times .15 (which is six times final average salary). When benefits are defined as life annuity, the same principle is used. However, the benefit is paid each regular pay period and represents a fraction of the final average salary. For example, a rate of 1.5 percent per year of service and forty years of service would create a lifetime monthly pension equal to 60 percent of final average monthly salary.

VESTING

Vesting refers to a qualifying period of pension plan membership that must be met before pension benefits legally exist. Pension benefits do not come into legal existence before vesting requirements are satisfied. Once benefits vest, there is a formal obligation between the plan and employees as set out in the terms of the plan.

Vested benefits are calculated as follows. The salary base, as defined in the benefit formula, is multiplied by the credited years of plan membership. For example, in a final pay plan, the salary base would be the most recent average salary, rather than final average salary. Because the benefits are not payable until retirement, actuaries compute the present value of vested benefits by discounting them at the assumed rate of interest earned on pension fund investments. Since pension benefits increase with each year of service, the value of vested benefits also increases with each additional year of service after becoming vested. At retirement date, the value of vested benefits will of course be equal to retirement benefits. If an employee withdraws from a plan prior to retirement, statutory requirements dictate that benefits must be frozen in the fund and paid when the employee retires. A permissible alternative is to transfer assets equal to the actuarial present value of vested benefits into the employee's new pension plan.

SINGLE AND MULTIEMPLOYER PLANS

Another characteristic of pension plans is that they can be either single-employer or multiemployer plans. A multiemployer pension plan is one that is subject to collective bargaining agreements in which two or more employers

---

[3] Service credit is normally weighted evenly per year of service, though some plans do weight later years more heavily in order to reward long service. The Employee Retirement Income Security Act sets a limit on the weighting of later years. *Backloading* is the technical term for uneven weighting.

[4] A life annuity may be one of three forms: single, single with a refund provision, or joint with survivorship. See McGill (1984, p. 124).

are plan sponsors. Under statutory requirements, one employer can contribute no more than 50 percent of initial contributions and no more than 75 percent thereafter. There are regulatory differences between the two types of sponsorship, and this does have some accounting implications, which are raised later.

ACTUARIAL FUNDING OF DEFINED BENEFIT PLANS

When benefits in a defined benefit plan are based on either career average or final average salary, it becomes something of a guess as to the value of future benefits. Actuaries are consulted to determine annual contribution levels. The principle of actuarial funding is to derive a time series of annual pension fund contributions that will accumulate to produce a projected pension fund balance sufficient to meet the cost of projected pension benefits. There is no single correct way of doing this. Many different actuarial funding models exist, and each one derives a different funding pattern over time. However, given the same set of plan conditions and actuarial assumptions, each method builds up a pension fund to the same future balance needed to meet expected retirement benefits. The extreme opposite of actuarial funding is called *terminal funding*. With terminal funding, the sponsor funds benefits only at the time of retirement. It is easy to see how yearly cash flows could be very erratic under terminal funding. Actuarial funding achieves a more even cash flow. The methods developed by actuaries to determine contribution levels are referred to as either *actuarial funding methods* or *actuarial cost methods*. The term *actuarial funding method* will be used for the remainder of the chapter.

Actuarial funding methods are analogous to depreciation methods. A depreciation method allocates a given amount over a specified period of years. Each depreciation method produces a different time series of depreciation expense, but they all sum to the same amount (asset cost less estimated salvage). In a slightly more complicated way, the same thing happens with actuarial funding. Each actuarial funding method produces a time series of future contributions that compound to the same future amount. The mathematical differences between actuarial funding methods are in how benefits are assumed to accumulate (increase) with each year of employee service. It is important to emphasize that this is an arbitrary assumption made solely for the purpose of orderly pension funding. Pension benefits do not legally accumulate or increase in value with each year until vesting requirements are met. For funding purposes, however, benefits are assumed to accumulate each year, even prior to vesting. Actuarial terminology refers to the increase in accumulated benefits each period as *service cost* or *normal cost* and the accumulated benefits to date as *actuarial liability*. A very important point to reiterate, though, is that the actuarial calculation of both yearly normal cost and actuarial liability is arbitrary and that each actuarial method produces different amounts.

Funding becomes more complex in three situations: (1) when a plan is started and past service credit is given to employees; (2) when plan amendments are made that alter benefit levels, and the amendments are made retroactive for past years of service credits; or (3) when actuarial assumptions differ from the subsequent experience of the plan (a situation giving rise to actuarial gains and losses). In all three cases, accumulated benefits will exist (as calculated by the actuarial funding method in use) but are not fully funded. Each of the three situations is explained below.

When a pension plan commences, credit is often granted to employees for past years of service. From an actuarial funding viewpoint, accumulated benefits exist for past service, but no funding has occurred. This gives rise to what is called *unfunded past service cost*. It is also called *unfunded benefits* and *unfunded actuarial liability*. The identical situation is encountered when benefit improvements are made; this gives rise to what are called *prior service costs*. For example, the rate of benefit accumulation per year of service might be increased. If the increased rate is applied to prior service as well as future service, accumulated benefits will exist that have not been funded. In both cases, accumulated benefits exceed the existing pension fund balance.

Actuaries deal with the problem of unfunded accumulated benefits in one of two ways. One way is to assume that pension funding dates from the earliest past service credit granted and to continue calculating future contributions (future normal costs) as though this were true. When this is done, however, a supplemental contribution is necessary because future normal costs will be insufficient to fund expected retirement benefits. The total contribution, therefore, will be normal cost plus a yearly supplement (until the deficiency is fully funded). The other solution is to compute a new time series of yearly contributions (normal costs) over the remaining service life — in order to accumulate a pension fund sufficient to meet expected retirement benefits. Supplemental contributions are not necessary because future normal costs are recalculated to make up the deficiency.

Actuarial gains and losses present a similar problem. In applying actuarial funding methods, actuaries must make assumptions about (1) future withdrawals from the plan, (2) the effects of future salary levels on the value of expected retirement benefits (though this is not always done), and (3) the rate of interest to be earned on pension fund investments. If the pension plan experience differs from these assumptions, the pension fund will be either too high or too low. This difference is an actuarial loss if the fund is less than needed and an actuarial gain if the fund is greater. Actuarial gains and losses are treated in the same general way as other unfunded accumulated benefits. For example, if an actuarial loss exists owing to lower-than-expected earnings on fund investments, a supplemental annual contribution could be made over an arbitrary period of years to make up the deficiency. Alternatively, the loss could be funded implicitly by the calculation of a new time series of future contributions that will fully fund the expected retirement benefits.

Actuarial funding methods are summarized in Exhibit 16–1. This is not an exhaustive list, but it includes the major methods.[5] There are two broad types of actuarial funding methods: **accrued benefit** and **projected benefit.**

---

[5] Other funding methods also exist. For example, the **frozen initial liability** method is acceptable for ERISA. Frozen initial liability is a projected benefit method, with supplemental funding of unfunded past service cost. Theoretically, an infinite number of actuarial funding methods exist; that is, there are a limitless number of ways that estimated pension costs could be funded over time.

EXHIBIT 16–1
Actuarial Funding Methods

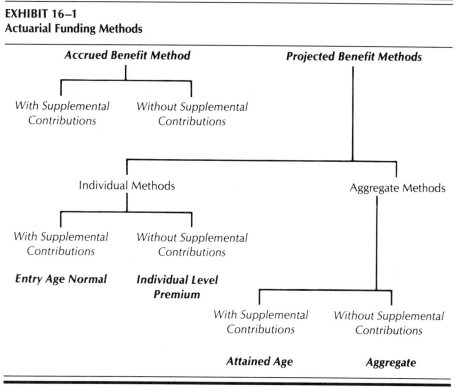

The FASB refers to these two types as the **benefits approach** and the **cost approach,** respectively.[6]

    The accrued benefit method can be used in either of the two ways discussed to deal with unfunded accumulated benefits: a separate contribution may be calculated to supplement normal cost, or normal cost can be recalculated in such a way that the deficiency is implicitly funded as part of future normal costs. The accrued benefit method is so named because the accumulation of benefits is measured using current salary levels and years of service to value current benefits. This approach is a literal measurement of the value of current accumulated benefits based on the benefit formula in a plan. The method has been criticized for not incorporating future salary increases into the calculations. Eventual benefits will be based on future rather than current salaries. However, one variation of the method does use projected future salaries to calculate accumulated benefits and normal costs.

    Projected benefit funding methods are more complex. Each one represents an alternative way of spreading the cost of projected benefits over time. It is for this reason that the projected benefits method is called the *cost approach* by

---

[6] FASB (1985, para. 129).

the FASB. Within this group of methods, the first distinction is between individual and aggregate methods. Individual methods develop contribution rates for individuals, which are then summed to derive the total contribution for the plan. Aggregate methods make funding calculations for the plan as a whole. The other distinction concerns the manner in which unfunded accumulated benefits are funded. Different names have been given to projected benefit methods, depending on whether a supplemental contribution is required to deal with unfunded accumulated benefits. **Entry age normal** and **attained age** both require a supplement to normal cost. **Individual level premium** and **aggregate** do not require a supplement because normal cost is always recalculated to fund implicitly any unfunded accumulated benefits over future periods.

The mathematics of accrued benefit and projected benefit funding methods are defined and illustrated in Appendix 16-A at the end of the chapter. We have emphasized that actuarial funding is arbitrary and is nothing more than a technique for smoothing a sponsor's pension fund contribution. Differences between the accrued benefit and projected benefit methods are illustrated in Appendix 16-A. The exhibits should be reviewed, though the formulae are not essential. In general, the accrued benefit method assigns more cost to later years of employment and a smaller amount to earlier years compared to projected benefit methods. There is a more even distribution of contribution levels with projected benefit methods. Differences between the two are less pronounced for stable, mature pension plans because the mixture of young and old employees tends to even out the results. But the differences become pronounced for very young pension plans or very old pension plans. For very young plans, the accrued benefit method would fund substantially less each year than projected benefit methods, and the reverse would be true for very old plans. Because of the faster pace of funding, it might be inferred that projected benefit methods are better. This is not true, however. All that can really be said is that the accrued benefit method produces a different time series of future normal costs. The alleged superiority of projected benefit methods stems from a misunderstanding about the arbitrary nature of actuarially based pension funding.

EMPLOYEE RETIREMENT INCOME SECURITY ACT OF 1974 (ERISA)

ERISA was a landmark piece of social legislation that was intended to improve access to and the security of pension benefits for employees.[7] The legislation affected four areas: (1) membership eligibility and vesting requirements, (2) mandatory funding requirements, (3) investment diversification requirements, and (4) the guarantee of certain vested benefits in the event of plan terminations. The first area was intended to increase participation levels and to improve the probability of receiving benefits. This was achieved by setting maximum time periods on qualifying years of employment — first to join the plan and then

---

[7] United States Public Law 93-406.

to qualify for pension benefits. Membership eligibility cannot require a higher minimum age than 25 and a longer term of service than three years.

Vesting must follow one of three alternative formulae: (1) 100 percent vested after ten years of membership; (2) graded vesting, in which benefits are 25 percent vested after five years, increasing 5 percent for the next five years, and increasing 10 percent per year thereafter — so that 100 percent vesting occurs in fifteen years; (3) the "rule of 45," in which benefits of an employee with five or more years of membership must be 50 percent vested when the sum of age and years of membership are forty-five, with 10 percent additional vesting for each year of service (subject to a requirement that vesting be 50 percent after ten years and 100 percent after fifteen years).

The objective in the second area was to override discretionary funding clauses in pension plans. ERISA requires that annual funding must occur and be based on an acceptable actuarial funding method. In addition, unfunded accumulated benefits must be funded over a maximum of forty years for single-employer plans in existence on January 1, 1974; thirty years for plans established after that date; and forty years for multiemployer plans. Unfunded accumulated benefits due to actuarial losses must be funded over a maximum of fifteen years.

The third area concerns portfolio diversification. ERISA states that pension fund managers should be concerned with diversification of investments. However, the only specific requirement is to limit investments in the sponsoring company to 10 percent of the total pension fund. This rule is designed to make a plan financially independent of the sponsor. If a sponsoring company fails, accumulated benefits of the company's pension plan should not be in jeopardy. In a general way, diversification also reduces investment risk and increases the security of assets held in the pension fund.

Finally, ERISA created the Pension Benefit Guaranty Corporation (PBGC) as a national insurer of pension plans and empowered it to collect premiums from plans to pay for guaranteed termination benefits. Vested benefits of participants are partially guaranteed by the PBGC if a plan is terminated. There are different guarantees for single-employer and multiemployer plans.[8] If a pension fund cannot meet guaranteed vested benefits, any shortfall is paid by the PBGC. The PBGC, then, has a statutory lien against the sponsor for this shortfall up to a maximum of 30 percent of the sponsor's net worth. Premiums collected by the PBGC are intended to cover termination benefits that are not recouped from the sponsors of terminated plans.

Much of the pension controversy centers on whether ERISA has had any

---

[8] Guaranteed benefits are different for single- and multiemployer plans. The guarantee for single-employer plans was set at $750 a month in 1974, to be adjusted upward annually by a ratio based on the social security income base. In 1988, the guarantee level was a monthly pension of $1,909.09. For multiemployer plans, the guarantee is $5 of monthly pension benefit per year of service, with the next $15 of monthly pension benefit only 75 percent guaranteed. In 1988 the PBGC charged an insurance premium of $16 and $2.60 per employee for single- and multiemployer plans, respectively. The charge is intended to cover operating costs and guaranteed benefits from plan terminations.

effect on the nature of pension plans and the appropriate accounting for pension plans by sponsoring companies. The impetus for review of pension accounting by the FASB came in response to the passage of ERISA.

LEGAL RELATIONSHIPS IN DEFINED BENEFIT PLANS

The parties to a defined benefit pension plan are the sponsoring employer, a pension fund, plan participants (the sponsor's present and past employees or their beneficiaries), and the PBGC for plans subject to ERISA. Pension plans are governed by a formal document that sets out the rights and obligations of the employer and employee. Plans have clauses obligating the sponsor to make annual pension fund contributions. The typical requirement is that funding must be based on the advice of actuaries. However, exculpatory clauses usually exist that give the sponsor the right to determine its own contribution levels, to suspend contributions altogether, and to even terminate the plan with no obligation for further contributions. The effect of these clauses is to shelter the sponsor from a legal pension liability.

Pension plans also state that the payment of benefits is to be made solely from pension fund assets, not from the sponsor's assets. This is one reason for establishing a pension fund. Exculpatory clauses limit the payment of pension benefits to the existing assets of the pension fund, regardless of how much may be earned according to a plan's benefit formula. These clauses also shelter the sponsor from a legal pension liability. ERISA has not changed this basic relationship between sponsors and employees. Sponsors still have a right to terminate plans. Exculpatory clauses still shelter the sponsor from a direct legal liability to employees for pension benefits. However, there is now a minimum level of annual funding and a legal obligation for vested benefits that are guaranteed by the PBGC.

The PBGC is a fourth party to the plan, guaranteeing certain pension benefits upon plan termination and having a claim against the plan's sponsor for reimbursement if there is a shortfall in the pension fund at termination. For continuing plans, a funding obligation also exists because of the PBGC guarantee. If the plan continues, unfunded pension benefits will eventually become funded through statutory annual contributions. Either way, then, guaranteed pension benefits must be funded. The significance of this is that the sponsor has a legally unavoidable funding obligation for pension benefits guaranteed by the PBGC.

In a voluntary termination the sponsor has a legal liability under ERISA for *all* accrued benefits, both vested and unvested.[9] It is only with involuntary plan terminations that the liability is restricted to PBGC-guaranteed *vested* benefits. Involuntary terminations generally occur only when the sponsor is insolvent or in bankruptcy, and they can be initiated either by the company or the PBGC.

---

[9] Although there is no direct obligation to employees, the PBGC does superimpose an obligation to make up the difference if fund assets are deficient at termination.

ACCOUNTING ISSUES RELATING TO DEFINED BENEFIT PENSION PLANS

Defined contribution plans do not present difficult accounting problems. An expense is recognized for the sponsor's contribution made in accordance with the terms of the plan. No further obligation exists because pension benefits attributable to employee service to date are restricted to the accumulation of past contributions. In other words, accumulated benefits are fully funded by the sponsor as long as each year's required contribution is made. An expense and liability should be accrued for the current year's required contribution, and the liability is discharged when the contribution is made.

The major accounting question that emerges in a defined benefit pension plan is this: when the benefits are defined independently of contribution levels, does the sponsor have an obligation (either contractual or implied) to meet the projected cost of pension benefits arising from employee service to date? The implication is that existing contributions (pension fund assets) may be less than accumulated benefits relating to years of service worked to date. Any under-funding of accumulated benefits will have to be made up for in future periods in order for the fund to have sufficient assets to meet expected retirement ben-efits. It can be argued, then, that unfunded accumulated benefits give rise to an accounting liability that should be recognized. This proposition holds aside the difficult question of actually measuring the value of accumulated benefits.

Another accounting question concerns the recognition and measurement of yearly pension expense: is it simply the cash contributed to the pension fund, or is it a more complex accrual based on the yearly increase in accumulated benefits? If a complex accrual is to be made, the problem is one of defining how pension benefits are assumed to accumulate in each period.

The recognition and measurement of pension expenses and liabilities as specified in accounting standards are examined in detail in the next sec-tion, which provides a historical perspective on the development of pension accounting.

DEVELOPMENT OF PENSION ACCOUNTING STANDARDS

ARB 36 (Codified as ARB 43, Chapter 13, Section A)

A cash basis for pension accounting existed prior to any accounting standards. Pension expense was equated with cash contributions to pension funds. The first pension accounting standard was ARB 36 issued in 1948. It was later codi-fied as ARB 43, Chapter 13, Section A.[10] ARB 36 was concerned with the rec-ognition of unfunded accumulated benefits (arising from plan startups) in the

---

[10] Committee on Accounting Procedure (1948).

financial statements. There were three possible methods that could be used to account for unfunded accumulated benefits. One was to make a prior period adjustment – the reason being that the accumulated benefits were related to service given in the past. An alternative followed the same basic argument, but the adjustment was charged to current income and classified as an extraordinary item. These two methods represented the current operating and all-inclusive income concepts, respectively. ARB 36 adopted a third approach, which allocated unfunded accumulated benefits over current and future periods.

The argument in ARB 36 was that the cost of providing pension benefits should be spread over the remaining service life of employees. If unfunded accumulated benefits exist because of a plan startup, the employer's cost of meeting these benefits should be matched against future revenues to be generated from employees' labor. The matching concept is the underlying principle of ARB 36. Since the employer's future costs will increase because of future funding of unfunded accumulated benefits, future sales revenue will have a markup based on these higher pension contributions. The fact that service giving rise to the benefits occurred in the past is unimportant. It is future contributions and revenues that will be affected by the decision of the firm to incur unfunded accumulated benefits.

ARB 36 would not necessarily have changed the cash basis of pension accounting. If firms were expensing the amount of pension fund contributions and if the cash contribution included an element for unfunded accumulated benefits, a cash basis of accounting would still have existed. All ARB 36 did was to reduce flexibility in how the cost relating to unfunded accumulated benefits was dealt with in the income statement.

ARB 47

A pension liability concept was introduced for the first time in ARB 47.[11] The standard recommended that the balance sheet report unfunded vested benefits. It also implied that the income statement should report the increase in unfunded vested benefits as the minimum pension expense for the period. In spite of the change, a de facto cash basis of accounting continued for most companies under ARB 47 because pension funds would normally have been in excess of vested benefits at the time of the standard. Prior to the pension reform movement, which began in the 1960s, it was not uncommon for pension plans to have lengthy vesting periods.[12] As a result, plans would normally have been adequately funded for vested benefits. This was due to the fact that accumulated benefits would be predominantly unvested if lengthy vesting periods existed. A plan would have to have been grossly underfunded in order to be affected by ARB 47.

---

[11] Committee on Accounting Procedure (1956).

[12] Davis and Strasser (1970) report a large Department of Labor survey that indicated that most plans (and particularly larger plans) would not have been radically affected by the vesting requirements of ERISA. However, some plans were significantly affected.

APB 8

A major change in pension accounting occurred with APB 8.[13] In this, standard pension expense was computed using any one of several acceptable actuarial funding methods, regardless of cash contributions.[14] APB 8, then, represented a move from simple cash accounting to a more complex accrual basis. For companies following actuarial funding recommendations, the cash basis of accounting posed no problem. The real concern in APB 8 was for companies not consistently following actuarial funding advice. APB 8 was an attempt to make pension expense recognition consistent between those companies following actuarial funding advice and those that were not.

As has been pointed out, annual pension funding was potentially discretionary prior to ERISA. Using a cash basis of accounting, pension expense could vary from year to year, depending on management funding decisions. Companies might fund more in good years and less in bad years. That this happened has been supported by one research study based on data preceding adoption of APB 8.[15] The reason for mandating an accrual rested on the premise that a quantifiable portion of future pension benefits accumulates with each period of employment, regardless of how much is actually funded. The accountant's task is to make a reasonable estimate of the yearly cost of these accumulating pension benefits. Since this is exactly what actuarial funding methods do, it is understandable why APB 8 endorsed their use for pension expense estimation.

APB 8 was regarded as a successful accounting standard. It utilized a research study as the basis of the accounting standard and brought some uniformity to pension accounting.[16] At the time of its adoption, APB 8 affected companies that were extremely discretionary in funding. However, a major uniformity problem still existed in the measurement of accrued pension expense – because APB 8 permitted flexibility in the choice of actuarial funding methods used to accrue pension expense. Funding methods vary significantly in the calculation of yearly normal cost. These differences are material under certain conditions and can materially affect reported income.[17] Appendix 16-A illustrates the yearly variation between actuarial funding methods.

APB 8 was consistent with the revenue–expense approach and with general principles of expense measurement. The accrual method achieved a "rational and systematic" recognition of pension costs over the working lives of employees, the exact words used in APB 8. It will be recalled that expenses are

---

[13] APB (1966).

[14] The methods are the five listed in Exhibit 16–1.

[15] Beidleman (1973).

[16] APB 8 successfully utilized the two-pronged approach advocated by the Accounting Principles Board. The standard was based on a study of pension accounting by Hicks (1965).

[17] Numerical examples of differences may be found in Hicks (1965), FASB (1981), and Schipper and Weil (1982). Francis (1982) evaluated the yearly differences under a range of simulated conditions and concluded that there can be material effects on the income statement resulting from the choice of actuarial funding method.

recognized in a rational and systematic manner if direct matching to revenue cannot be achieved. (See Chapter 10 in this text and the discussion of expense recognition, in particular APB Statement No. 4.) Under APB 8, pension costs were allocated to the periods of employee service, and in this way an indirect matching of costs to revenues was considered accomplished.

FASB INTERPRETATION 3

FASB Interpretation 3 was issued in response to the passage of ERISA.[18] It reaffirmed APB 8 and concluded that ERISA did not create a pension liability except in the likelihood of plan termination. A liability accrual was required only if termination was probable and if guaranteed termination benefits exceeded pension fund assets. This requirement was a reiteration and interpretation of APB 8, paragraph 18, which required balance sheet recognition of legally unavoidable pension liabilities.

This interpretation was *incorrect*, however, because ERISA created an unavoidable obligation to fund unfunded accumulated benefits. The obligation exists whether the plan is terminated or not. If a plan is not terminated, an obligation still exists in the form of future annual statutory funding requirements (which include an element representing the funding of unfunded accumulated benefits).

SFAS 35

SFAS 35 defines the pension plan as a reporting entity and establishes accounting standards for the measurement and reporting of plan assets and plan obligations.[19] This is considered a landmark standard because it set accounting and reporting standards for a new entity, the pension plan, as separate and distinct from the sponsoring company. Assets are measured at current market values. Plan obligations are defined as accumulated benefits (both vested and unvested) and are measured using the accrued benefit funding method, without taking future salary increases into consideration.

Great care is taken in SFAS 35 to separate clearly the plan (and pension fund) from the sponsor. The nature of the relationship between the sponsor and employee for the payment of pension benefits is carefully avoided. SFAS 35 represents a subtle way of reporting the sponsoring company's pension obligations. It is far less controversial to report a pension obligation of a plan than to report the obligation of a sponsor. This indirect approach to the liability question carried through in SFAS 36, which required information about the "plan's" obligations to be reported as a note in the sponsor's financial statements.

SFAS 36

SFAS 36 amended the supplemental disclosure requirements of APB 8, paragraph 46. The specific disclosure requirements of SFAS 36 were as follows:

---

[18] FASB (1974).
[19] FASB (1980a).

1. Basic plan description.
2. General statement of funding policy (actuarial method not required).
3. Any significant matters affecting comparability between periods; for example, change in accounting methods, changes in actuarial assumptions or funding methods, plan amendments, and actuarial gains or losses.
4. Plan assets, as measured under SFAS 35 requirements (market values).
5. Actuarially calculated accumulated benefits as measured under SFAS 35, separated into vested and unvested amounts.
6. Interest rates used in making the actuarial calculations.
7. Date at which the actuarial calculations were made.

The most significant change was the disclosure of accumulated benefits as measured under SFAS 35 and the segregation of this amount into vested and unvested benefits. However, it was left to the reader to interpret the significance of the data and how, if at all, they related to the sponsor. Disclosure was thus used as an effective way of dealing with a controversial topic.

SFAS 87 AND SFAS 88: SHIFTING TO A LIABILITY ORIENTATION

A revenue–expense orientation dominated pension accounting standards up to and including APB 8. Largely because of ERISA, most firms were funding and accruing similar amounts.[20] In a cash flow sense, then, the accounting can be said to have been uniform among companies. However, in an accrual sense there was no uniformity because the accruals could be based on any of five different actuarial methods – in addition to the effects of differing actuarial assumptions used in applying the methods. Each actuarial funding method accrues accumulated benefits in a different (and arbitrary) manner. The situation is analogous to the arbitrary allocation of costs under alternative depreciation methods. Just as there is no single defensible depreciation method, there is no single defensible actuarial funding method.

The present standard, SFAS 87, has achieved greater uniformity in measuring accrued pension expense by mandating use of one actuarial method, the accrued benefit method (with projected future salaries), or what the FASB calls the *benefits/years-of-service approach*. SFAS 87 uses *service cost* rather than the term *normal cost*. Accrued periodic pension expense is defined as the sum of

1. Service (normal) cost for the year using the accrued benefit actuarial method (with projected future salaries).
2. Interest cost for the year relating to the actuarial present-value increase in accumulated benefits measured using the accrued benefit actuarial method (with projected future salaries) and the assumed discount rate.
3. A reduction for the increase in the fair value of plan assets over the period net of contributions and payments (or an increase in expense if fair value decreased), or, more simply, the effect of the actual return on plan assets.

---

[20] Evidence of this is found in Francis and Reiter (1987), who report that only 29 of 297 firms in their study indicated a divergence between the two policies.

4. Systematic amortization of unrecognized prior service cost (arising from plan adoptions and amendments), with such costs allocated over the remaining period of employee service.
5. Systematic amortization of actuarial gains/losses, with the minimum rate being one divided by the average service of active employees, or the average remaining life expectancy if most of the plan's participants are not active.
6. Straight-line amortization of a transitional "net obligation" or "net asset" at the time of adopting SFAS 87, amortized as in (5) above subject to election of an alternative fifteen-year period if average service is less than fifteen years.

A pension liability is recognized if yearly funding is less than periodic expense, as computed above, and a pension asset is recognized if yearly funding exceeds the periodic expense.

In calculating the first component of pension expense, *service cost*, several important assumptions are necessary. First, future salary levels must be estimated. Second, actuarial assumptions are required with respect to turnover, mortality, early retirement, etc. — all of which relate to the probability of there being a pension obligation. Third, a discount rate (the time value of money) must be assumed for the calculation. The FASB requires that the assumed discount rate be based on the current interest rate required to settle pension benefits. The PBGC publishes such rates on a monthly basis, and these may be used as a guide in selecting the assumed discount rate. The second component of pension expense, *interest cost*, also requires use of the assumed discount rate in accruing interest on accumulated pension benefits. The third component of pension expense, *actual return on plan assets*, requires an estimate of the fair value of pension assets. Fair values are defined as market prices in a nonliquidation setting and estimates of market value for assets with no active market. The fourth component of pension expense, *amortization of unrecognized prior service cost*, is not narrowly specified. Instead, systematic allocation is required and simple straight-line amortization is one acceptable algorithm. The fifth component of pension expense, *amortization of actuarial gains/losses*, is similarly specified in general terms of systematic amortization. In addition, amortization is only required if unrecognized gains/losses exceed the greater of 10 percent of the fair value of plan assets or 10 percent of accumulated pension benefits (measured using the accrued benefit actuarial method with future salary projections). The final component of pension expense, *amortization of the net obligation/asset*, relates to either the effect of transition or the effect of subsequently recognizing a balance liability (discussed below). The consequence of the last three components of pension expense is to smooth the annual accrual of pension expense and reduce the variability caused by unfunded past/prior service costs, actuarial gains/losses, transitional adoption of SFAS 87, and amortization of the intangible asset related to minimum pension liabilities recognized in the balance sheet.

The FASB refers to three distinct types of accrued pension obligations in SFAS 87: projected benefit obligations (measured using the accrued benefit actuarial method with projected future salaries), accumulated benefit obligations (measured using the accrued benefit actuarial method with current salaries), and vested benefit obligations (which are a subset of accumulated benefit obligations). A shift to an asset–liability orientation is evident from the requirement to recognize a minimum pension liability when accumulated benefit obligations exceed the fair value of plan assets (including those at the time of adopting SFAS 87). Note the conservatism, though, in that an asset is not recognized if accumulated benefits are less than the fair value of plan assets. In addition, the minimum balance sheet liability is measured using only *current* rather than projected future salary levels, which understates the liability relative to the actuarial calculation of service cost.

A liability for unfunded benefits is recorded on adoption of SFAS 87 or subsequently, and a corresponding intangible asset is recognized and amortized (as described above). The rationale for recognizing an intangible asset relates to matching arguments but also has the effect of smoothing reported pension expense. In addition, the disclosures of SFAS 87 are oriented toward pension plan assets and obligations. The funded status of plans must be reported showing separately the fair value of plan assets and all three measures of pension benefit obligations (and a reconciling schedule). Also required are disclosures of unrecognized prior service cost, unrecognized actuarial gains/losses, and unamortized net obligations/assets. These disclosures are informative in that they convey information about the likely future levels of funding required to meet pension obligations.

Finally, if a pension plan is to be terminated, or substantially curtailed, SFAS 88 sets out separate rules for recognizing and measuring a gain or loss to the sponsor, after incurring the costs of settlement. The accounting gain or loss is the net effect of closing out balance sheet balances arising from SFAS 87 plus any assets recaptured from the pension plan less any corporate assets required to settle or curtail the pension obligations.

ASSESSING SFAS 87

Before evaluating the SFAS 87 requirement to record a pension liability, we will briefly review the definition of accounting liabilities. SFAC 6 defines accounting liabilities as ". . . probable future sacrifices of economic benefits arising from present obligations . . ." (paragraph 35). The word *obligation* is deliberately used to define an accounting liability and is intended to convey a broader liability concept than that of legally enforceable claims arising from contracts. Obligations ". . . refer to duties imposed legally or socially; to do that which one is bound to do by contract, promise, moral responsibility, etc. . . ." (SFAC 6, footnote 22 to paragraph 35).

Three types of liabilities are identified in the SFAC 6 definition: (1) legally enforceable claims arising from contracts, (2) constructive obligations, and (3) equitable obligations. These were discussed at length in Chapter 10. Three tests, set out in paragraph 36, must also be satisfied before an accounting liability is recognized under the SFAC 6 definition: (1) a duty exists to transfer assets in the future (either on demand, on a fixed date, or on the occurrence of a specified event); (2) the duty is virtually unavoidable; and (3) the obligating event or transaction has already occurred. Recognition occurs in the period when the obligating event or transaction occurs.

The definition of an accounting liability can be related to recent studies in labor economics that have evaluated the nature of pension obligations.[21] In this literature, a distinction is drawn between explicit and implicit liability concepts. Each of these are discussed and related to the SFAC 6 liability definition and the accounting requirements of SFAS 87.

LEGAL LIABILITIES AND EXPLICIT PENSION CONTRACTS

If pension plans are voluntarily terminated, the sponsor has a legal liability under ERISA for *all* accrued benefits, both vested and unvested. For most plans, the termination value is well approximated by the accrued benefit funding method (without future salary projections). Termination or legal liability is also called the *explicit* contract view because accumulated benefits are measured as literally accrued under the explicit terms of the plan. This is, of course, the minimum liability recognized under SFAS 87 and thus corresponds to a legal liability definition. Even if termination is not likely, the sponsor still has a liability to fund the accrued benefits under ERISA funding rules. Either way, then, a legally binding and obligating event occurs as the benefits accumulate each year under the plan's terms, and a virtually unavoidable duty exists to transfer assets. In fact, sponsor insolvency and an involuntary termination of the plan by the PBGC is about the only way out of the obligation, and this of course means that the going-concern assumption would be invalid. So, in spite of the criticism, SFAS 87 really does nothing more than recognize a legally enforceable obligation to transfer assets under the usual assumption that the firm remains solvent.

ECONOMIC LIABILITIES AND IMPLICIT PENSION CONTRACTS

The alternative view characterizes the pension contract as a long-term implicit contract in which the intent is to pay retirement benefits in "real" dollars adjusted for inflation. Measurement of this implicit economic liability is not straightforward. In general, though, the projected benefit family of funding methods and the accrued benefit method (*with* future salary projections) all provide reasonable approximations. Thus, SFAS 87 presumes an implicit contract in calculating accrued pension expense.

The FASB's original 1982 pension proposal represented the implicit contract view since the pension liability would have been measured using the accrued benefit funding method *with* future salary projections.[22] This implicit or

---

[21] See Bulow (1982), Francis and Reiter (1987), Ippolito (1986), and Pesando and Clarke (1984).
[22] FASB (1982).

economic liability could be interpreted as either a constructive or equitable obligation under SFAC 6.[23] The argument basically is that the pension contract is a long-term relationship between employer and employee, and the expectation is that the employer will sufficiently fund the plan in order to meet the promised benefits. Evidence that this represents the pension contract can be found in the fact that benefits are usually linked to future salary levels. In essence, the sponsor is promising a benefit in "real" inflation-adjusted dollars by linking the benefit to future salary levels, and this linkage to the future reflects the long-term implicit nature of the pension contract.

Since accounting liabilities are defined to include this type of constructive or equitable obligation, a case can be made that SFAS 87 underestimates pension liabilities. The FASB's decision not to press on with the economic liability concept is largely due to economic consequences on the balance sheet, which are discussed in the next section, although, as noted above, accrued pension expense is based on the economic liability concept.

ECONOMIC CONSEQUENCES

A number of studies have investigated whether a firm's unfunded pension benefits are interpreted "as if" they are liabilities. If they are, then stock prices should, therefore, be lower in the presence of unfunded benefits since they would lessen the value of residual stockholder claims. Several studies have reported this to be the case.[24] If unfunded pension benefits are interpreted "as if" they are liabilities, then their presence should also affect corporate bond ratings and bond interest rates. There is evidence that bond ratings are lower and interest rates are higher in the presence of unfunded benefits, which is consistent with the market acting as if they are liabilities.[25]

Given the results of these studies, it might appear that there would be little economic consequence from SFAS 87 vis-à-vis balance sheet recognition of pension liabilities. However, Francis documents the balance sheet impact of the original 1982 FASB pension proposal for 218 companies that lobbied against liability recognition: on average, the new debt would have been about 8.9 percent of balance sheet assets, a finding similar to that reported in other studies.[26] Such a large increase could very easily have affected debt covenants in existing lending agreements.

The income statement is also affected by SFAS 87, mainly through a loss of flexibility. Beidleman reported evidence that pre-APB 8 pension expense was used to smooth yearly income, and Hagerman and Zmijewski found that the

---

[23] See Hall and Landsittel (1977) and Lucas and Hollowell (1981) for such interpretations in addition to FASB (1982).

[24] See Daley (1984), Dhaliwal (1986), Feldstein and Seligman (1981), Kemp (1988), Landsman (1986), and Stone (1982) for a review of earlier studies.

[25] Reiter (1985).

[26] Francis (1987). See also Morris and Nichols (1984) and Rue and Volkan (1984).

choice of amortization periods for unfunded prior service cost under APB 8 was associated with an income-increasing strategy for firms with high leverage levels and an income-decreasing strategy for large-sized firms.[27] These findings are supportive of economic consequences vis-à-vis debt contracting and political costs (see Chapter 7). Finally, Francis and Reiter found that long-term pension expense policy, not just the portion of expense pertaining to prior service cost, was associated with the hypothesized income-increasing and income-decreasing incentives of debt and political costs, respectively.[28] Given these research findings, it is not surprising that a loss of flexibility was of concern to many companies lobbying against the FASB's pension proposals that led up to SFAS 87. It was for these reasons that the FASB modified its original proposals and smoothed the effect of actuarial gains/losses in pension expense calculation.

Thus, the FASB's pension project that culminated in SFAS 87 can be seen as an object lesson in the politics of standard setting. The FASB's initial 1982 proposal was so controversial that it was issued under the unique title of "Preliminary Views." It generated over 500 comment letters and two rounds of public hearings even before an exposure draft was issued. The exposure draft was also controversial and resulted in a similar level of negative reaction. Compromises were made, and these, along with a fortuitously rebounding stock market that increased the value of pension fund assets, made the standard more acceptable to affected companies. And, as with leases in SFAS 13, a long four-year transition period was allowed regarding minimum liability recognition. This would permit companies to mitigate potential adverse financial statement consequences prior to mandatory liability recognition under SFAS 87. After the stockmarket crash in late 1987, many pension plans found themselves underfunded once again, and many companies delayed the minimum liability provisions of SFAS 87 as long as possible.

POSTRETIREMENT BENEFITS OTHER THAN PENSIONS

Like pensions, postretirement benefits other than pensions (OPEB) had been handled on a cash basis of accounting prior to SFAS 106, which was passed in 1990. OPEB benefits include health care, life insurance outside of pension plans, and additional welfare benefits such as legal services, housing subsidies, tuition assistance, and day care, though the first two are undoubtedly the most important. Several estimates have been made of the total OPEB liability of American enterprises; the amount is not small, ranging between $140 billion and two trillion dollars.[29] The FASB concluded that OPEB costs are a form of deferred compensation in which the employer receives current services in ex-

---

[27] Beidleman (1973) and Hagerman and Zmijewski (1979).

[28] Francis and Reiter (1987).

[29] Wright (1990, p. x). The OPEB acronym refers to *other postemployment benefits*, which is synonymous with *postretirement benefits other than pensions*.

change for future benefits. As a result, the FASB took an enormous step in SFAS 106 by requiring the recognition and measurement of OPEB costs and obligations.[30] Previously SFAS 81 had required only minimum disclosures relative to OPEB: a description of benefits provided and groups covered, the accounting and funding policies used for those benefits, and the cost of those benefits recognized for the current period.[31] We begin by giving a very simple example of the workings of SFAS 106 and then review the major features of the standard. We follow this with a theoretical critique of the standard.

THE MECHANICS OF OPEB

Assume that a firm has one employee who will be covered by OPEB. The plan is dated January 1, 1993 and goes into effect immediately. There is one active plan participant (covered employee); she is 58 years old and becomes fully eligible for benefits on January 1, 1996 when she will have performed all necessary service to qualify for postretirement benefits.

The employee is expected to retire on December 31, 1996. Postretirement benefits are expected to be $5,000 on December 31, 1997 and $7,716.83 on December 31, 1998 (end-of-year dates are assumed for convenience). The applicable discount rate is 10%. Discounting the two payments back to December 31, 1995 results in a value on that date of $9,930 [($5,000 × .8264) + ($7,716.83 × .7513)]. The $9,930 is then discounted back to its present value on both December 31, 1994 and 1995. One-third of the present value on December 31, 1996 and the following two years on the same date becomes the **service cost.** Interest on the same dates is then added in to arrive at the total OPEB expense as illustrated in Exhibit 16–2.

Notice that service costs are not equal each year but are one-third of the present value at year end (see Case 1A of Appendix C of SFAS 106) even though paragraphs 43 and 246 talk about equal amounts per year during the **attribution period.** The year 1996 has only interest costs. The full eligibility date is analogous to the vesting date under pensions. However, pension service costs would run through 1996, the year when the employee retires. Hence, relative to OPEB the FASB has attempted an asset–liability approach. However, there is a legitimate question concerning whether the entire working period up to the point of retirement should bear its share of OPEB costs.[32] In most pension plans full benefits are not earned until retirement, whereas full benefits in some OPEB plans are earned at a date prior to retirement (the full eligibility date); hence the FASB saw the attribution periods in SFASs 87 and 106 as being consistent. But in many cases the date of retirement and the full eligibility date may coincide.[33] Let us next examine the major aspects of SFAS 106.[34]

---

[30] All paragraphs cited in parentheses refer to FASB (1990).
[31] FASB (1984, p. 2).
[32] This point has also been made by the AAA Financial Accounting Standards Committee. See AAA (1990, p. 113).
[33] Thomas and Farmer (1990, p. 103).
[34] All paragraphs mentioned refer to FASB (1990).

EXHIBIT 16–2
Postretirement Benefit Illustration

	Jan. 1, 1993	Dec. 31, 1993	Dec. 31, 1994	Dec. 31, 1995	Dec. 31, 1996	Dec. 31, 1997	Dec. 31, 1998
				Full Eligibility Date	Retirement Date		
Expected benefit payments						$5,000	$7,716.83
Present value factor of obligation						× .8264	× .7513
						$4,132	$ 5,798
Present value on Dec. 31, 1993, 1994, 1995		$8,206 c	$9,027 b	$9,930 a			
Service cost for year		2,735 d	3,009 e	3,310 f			
Interest for year		—	274 g	602 h	993 i		
Total OPEB expenses		$2,735	$3,283	$3,912	$993		

(Attribution Period spans 1993 through 1995)

a $4,132 + $5,798 = $9,930
b $9,930 × .9091
c $9,930 × .8264
d 1/3 × $8,206
e 1/3 × $9,027
f 1/3 × $9,930
g .10 × $2,735
h .10 × $6,018
i .10 × $9,930

MAJOR FEATURES OF SFAS 106

We first examine whether there is a liability for postretirement benefits and then discuss actuarial assumptions, including interest and discount rates, prior service costs, and disposition of gains or losses.

Postretirement Benefit Obligations Are Liabilities

The first issue is the question of whether postretirement benefits are liabilities. Paragraphs 152–158 make it clear that this is indeed the case. Even though the obligation is equitable in nature rather than a legal liability, there is a duty or requirement to sacrifice assets in the future. Furthermore, even though employers may terminate OPEB plans, they cannot do so very easily without incurring real costs such as negative employee goodwill. The assumption that OPEBs are part of the total compensation package for covered employees clearly stamps them as being attributable to past transactions or events.

Actuarial Assumptions

Our example is obviously as simple as possible. Not only will typical OPEB plans be much more complex, they must be based on numerous actuarial assumptions. Postretirement benefits should take into account trends in health care costs, for example, as well as projected changes in Medicare benefits that may reduce costs. Medical costs are generally going up but changes in medical technology may reduce some costs. For example, triglycerides and other fatty substances in the blood may be eliminated in the future by means of pills rather than by costly angioplasty ("balloon") techniques. Clearly, OPEB costs will not be easy to determine in terms of both the cost of measurement and the reliability of the estimates.

If OPEB levels are based on wages, they should reflect expected wage levels rather than those in effect at the current time. SFAS 106 thus agrees with pension accounting since SFAS 87 employs the projected benefit obligation approach rather than the accumulated benefit obligation method.

Total OPEB expenses may be reduced by earnings from plan assets. *Plan assets* consist of stocks, bonds, and other investments that are segregated — presumably in a trust — for the exclusive purpose of providing for OPEB benefits. The expected long-term rate of return on plan assets should be based on their market value. If fund earnings are taxable, this should also be taken into account. Few OPEB plans are funded at this time because tax laws do not generally provide for a deduction for plan contributions, unlike the pension situation.

The discount rate used in order to show the OPEB obligation at present value should be based on rates of return for high-quality fixed-income investments that are currently available on the market and whose cash flows are generally similar in amount and timing of OPEB payments (para. 31). The AAA Financial Accounting Standards Committee points out that OPEB obligations are largely unsecured and that the discount rate should thus concur with the employer's borrowing rate for unsecured debt with a similar payment structure.[35] This latter rate would most likely be higher than what SFAS 106 calls

---

[35] AAA (1990, p. 114).

for, resulting in a lower present value for the firm's OPEB obligation. Paragraph 42 also notes that discount rates should include an inflationary component geared to the expected general rate of inflation.

Finally, there are many other actuarial assumptions that must be considered, including employee turnover, mortality, and dependency status. Once again, it must be stated that measurement costs will not be inexpensive and verifiability and other aspects of reliability should not be taken for granted.

Plan Amendments and Prior Service Costs

When plan amendments increase (or possibly reduce) employee benefits and these costs are clearly attributable to future periods for active plan participants, they are to be charged to future periods. If plan amendments improve benefits based on service prior to the plan amendment itself or even the plan initiation, as with pensions these are called *prior service costs*. Paragraph 51 provides for these costs to be recognized over the remaining years of service to full eligibility dates of active plan participants. These costs can be amortized over future periods on either a straight-line basis or on the basis of the remaining years of service of active plan participants to their full eligibility, an accelerated method of amortization (illustrated in paragraphs 451–454). Where employees are already retired or are beyond their full eligibility dates, prior service costs are amortized on the basis of the remaining life expectancy of these participants (paragraph 52). The retroactive basis is used, however, where prior service costs are involved relative to measuring the OPEB obligation. That is, prior service is taken into account in measuring the OPEB obligation when the plan is amended.

Gains and Losses

Gains and losses from OPEB plans arise from either differences from assumed experience or changes in plan assumptions. Net gains or losses are not recognized immediately but are amortized to the extent that the net amount exceeds 10 percent of the greater of the accumulated postretirement benefit obligation or the market-related value of plan assets as of the beginning of the year (para. 59). This amortization process for OPEB gains and losses, called the *corridor* approach, is quite similar to accounting for net gains or losses for pensions under SFAS 87.

THEORETICAL ASPECTS OF OPEB ACCOUNTING

Several theoretical considerations of OPEB have already been discussed. Pervading the whole postretirement benefit situation are issues of cost and reliability. There is, however, little question that OPEBs are indeed a liability. The FASB was rather adamant about the importance of recognition of OPEB costs and obligations in the financial statements as opposed to footnote disclosure (para. 164). Hence, the efficient-markets hypothesis was not used as a dodge to avoid responsibilities. It is certainly desirable that the benefits of SFAS 106 will be greater than the costs of preparation and will outweigh problems of reliability.

Economic Consequences of OPEB Recognition

Financial statement preparers strongly opposed OPEB recognition. In addition to costs of preparation, OPEB obligations on the balance sheet mean higher debt-to-equity ratios, which threaten debt covenants on bond issues. In addition, management compensation is affected by SFAS 106. While we are very sympathetic to the need to recognize OPEB costs and obligations, the blow might have been much more palatable to business if discounting were also permitted with deferred tax liabilities. The need to be as consistent as possible in recognizing and measuring different liabilities is extremely important. It is not too late, we hope, to use the conceptual framework more effectively despite the imperfections of that document.

Another point is that the booking of OPEB obligations may well lead to an extensive scaling back of this benefit when the size of the liability is understood. This would be a classic example of shooting the messenger who brings bad news. Wyatt has quite correctly focused on the issue of liability recognition and accrual accounting for OPEB as one of accountability.[36] The FASB's job in examining OPEB costs and obligations is to be neutral while taking into account the benefits/costs matrix. We believe that they have done this. Whether OPEB benefits will be reduced is a separate issue that should not be linked to the FASB's responsibilities.

A last economic consequence to be considered is whether SFAS 106 will put American firms at a competitive disadvantage relative to foreign firms in such areas as cost of capital and pricing of products.[37] We tend to view this issue from a perspective similar to the question of the potential for the reduction of OPEB benefits as a result of SFAS 106. The real issue should not be one of bad economic consequences; it should be one of harmonization of accounting standards. That is, other nations should be using recognition and measurement techniques similar to those of SFAS 106 where applicable (see Chapter 19 for a discussion of harmonization of accounting standards).

SUMMARY

Pension accounting for the sponsors of defined benefit pension plans has been one of the long-standing issues faced by accounting policy makers. The traditional approach has been based on a revenue–expense orientation in which the objective is to accrue yearly pension expense. This leads to the problem of determining how benefits accumulate with the passage of time and how these benefits should be measured. APB 8 sanctioned flexibility by permitting one of five actuarial methods to be used to measure yearly pension expense. This resulted in the same kind of arbitrariness as occurs with multiple depreciation and inventory methods.

---

[36] Wyatt (1990).
[37] See Wright (1990) for further examples of economic consequences as applied to OPEB.

In SFAS 87, the FASB has achieved more rigid uniformity regarding pension expense measurement. Only one actuarial method can be used though some flexibility remains with respect to actuarial assumptions. A shift toward the asset–liability orientation is evident with both expense measurement and the new requirement to recognize a minimum balance sheet liability for unfunded pension benefits. Although the case for recognizing unfunded benefits as a liability is a strong one, disclosures about the effects of pension plan sponsorship on future cash flows would seem to be as useful for determining whether a liability exists and how it should be measured. Such disclosures are now required by SFAS 87. Yet, the existence of disclosure, per se, should not be used as an excuse to avoid addressing the hard question of whether an accounting liability exists for unfunded accumulated benefits. To its credit, the FASB did not skirt the hard question in arriving at SFAS 87, though it may have seriously underestimated the liability by not requiring the use of projected future salary levels in calculating the liability.

SFAS 106 brought accrual accounting to OPEB. Like pension costs, these costs are clearly a liability. In many respects accounting for OPEB is very similar to pension accounting. The costs and reliability of OPEB measurements are important issues as are several other questions involving the economic consequences.

APPENDIX 16-A: MATHEMATICAL DEFINITIONS AND ILLUSTRATIONS OF ACTUARIAL FUNDING METHODS

The following example is a simplified presentation of actuarial pension mathematics.[38] Assume a pension plan is started with ten employees on their 62nd birthday. No new employees will be admitted to the plan. Employees withdraw from the plan at the beginning of each year, and pension fund contributions are made at the end of each year. Retirement is assumed to occur at the end of age 64 (the equivalent of age 65). Benefits are a lump sum amount equal to final year's salary times 10 percent per year of service. Pension fund investments earn 5 percent, which is also the settlement rate. Salary projections are $10,000 at age 62; $20,000 at age 63; and $40,000 at age 64. There are no vested benefits prior to retirement.

Of the ten original members of the plan, ten will survive in employment through age 62, eight will survive in employment through age 63, and four will survive in employment through age 64. At age 62, an employee's probability of surviving to retirement is .4. During age 63, the probability of surviving to retirement is .5, and during age 64, the probability is 1.0. The survival probabilities can also be expressed from entry age to current age. At age 62, the probability of surviving through age 62 is 1.0. The probability of surviving from

---

[38] For an elaboration of pension mathematics, see Winklevoss (1977).

age 62 through age 63 is .8, and the probability of surviving from age 62 through age 64 is .4.

ACCRUED BENEFIT FUNDING METHODS

The principle of actuarial pension funding is to derive a time series of age-based contribution rates. Actuaries refer to these amounts as *normal* or *service costs*. The simplest actuarial method to use is the accrued funding method, without taking future salary increases into consideration. Age-based service costs and accumulated benefits are defined in Equations (16.1) and (16.2).

$$SC_x = B_x - B_{x-1}\phi_x(1 + i)^{-(r-x)} \qquad (16.1)$$

where

$$
\begin{aligned}
SC_x &= \text{service cost at age } x \\
B_x &= \text{estimated retirement benefits based on current salary and} \\
&\quad\text{current years of service} \\
B_{x-1} &= \text{estimated retirement benefits at age } x - 1 \\
\phi_x &= \text{probability at age } x \text{ of surviving in employment to retire-} \\
&\quad\text{ment at age } r \\
(1 + i)^{-(r-x)} &= \text{discount rate based on remaining years to retirement}
\end{aligned}
$$

$$AL_x = B_x\phi_x(1 + i)^{-(r-x)} \qquad (16.2)$$

where

AL_x = actuarially computed accumulated benefits

In applying these two formulae, the current age probabilities of surviving to retirement age are .4 at the end of 62, .5 at the end of age 63, and 1.0 at the end of age 64. The age-based amounts are computed from Equations (16.1) and (16.2), then multiplied by the surviving members each year to derive total pension plan contribution. Plan totals are summarized as shown in Exhibit 16–3. Accumulated benefits in Exhibit 16–3 are the basis for minimum liability recognition under SFAS 87 (if the accumulated benefits at each age are not fully funded).

EXHIBIT 16–3
Accrued Benefit Method (Using Current Period Salaries)

	Service Costs	Accumulated Benefits
Age 62	$ 3,628	$ 3,628
Age 63	$11,429	$15,238
Age 64	$32,000	$48,000

EXHIBIT 16–4
Accrued Benefit Method (Using Projected Salaries)

	Service Costs	*Accumulated Benefits*
Age 62	$14,512	$14,512
Age 63	$15,238	$30,476
Age 64	$16,000	$48,000

Exhibit 16–4 shows the effect of using salary projections in conjunction with the accrued benefit funding method. In other words, a projected retirement salary of $40,000 is used in Equations (16.1) and (16.2) instead of current salary. This is the method required by SFAS 87 in calculating service costs.

PROJECTED BENEFIT FUNDING METHODS

Pension mathematics are more complicated with projected benefit funding methods. There are two main versions, one in which a survivor-adjusted level annuity per year is calculated, and the other in which contribution levels are calculated as a constant percentage of survivor-adjusted salaries. The level annuity method is illustrated. First it is necessary to define the present value of projected retirement benefits. This is calculated at each age and is defined as

$$(PVRB)_x = B_r \phi_x (1 + i)^{-(r-x)} \tag{16.3}$$

where

$(PVRB)_x$ = present value of projected retirement benefits, age x, based on projected retirement salary and years of service, adjusted by survival probability

B_r = estimated retirement benefit based on projected retirement salary and years of service at age r

The function defined in Equation (16.3) is then used to calculate the time series of service costs and accumulated benefits. These are defined in Equations (16.4) and (16.5), respectively.

$$SC_x = \frac{(PVRB)_y}{a_{\overline{y:r-y|}}} \tag{16.4}$$

where

SC_x = service cost at age x
$(PVRB)_y$ = PVRB function at entry age y
$a_{\overline{y:r-y|}}$ = annuity factor representing summation of yearly survival probabilities from entry age y to retirement age r

$$AL_x = \frac{a_{\overline{y:x-y|}}}{a_{\overline{y:r-y|}}} \times (PVRB)_x \tag{16.5}$$

where

AL_x = actuarially computed accumulated benefits

$a_{\overline{y:x-y|}}$ = annuity factor representing summation of yearly survival probabilities from entry age y to current age x

The annuity factors in Equations (16.4) and (16.5), $a_{\overline{y:r-y|}}$ and $a_{\overline{y:x-y|}}$ are necessary in order to determine an age-based level annuity. At age 62, the annuity factor $a_{\overline{y:r-y|}}$ represents the present value of the survival probabilities from entry age through age 62, age 63, and age 64. These survival probabilities are 1.0, .8, and .4, respectively, for ages 62, 63, and 64. To derive present values, the age 64 probability is discounted for two periods, the age 63 probability is discounted for one period, and the age 62 probability is considered to be at present value. This results in a value of 2.125 for the annuity factor $a_{\overline{y:r-y|}}$.

The value of the annuity factor $a_{\overline{y:x-y|}}$ is different at ages 62, 63, and 64. At age 62, it represents the present value of the survival probability through age 62, or 1.0. At age 63, it represents the probability of surviving through age 62, plus the probability of surviving through age 63 discounted to present value at age 62. This results in 1.0 plus .8 times $(1.05)^{-1}$, or 1.762. At age 64, the value is the same as the annuity $a_{\overline{y:r-y|}}$, or 2.125. As with accrued benefit methods, the age-based calculations must be multiplied by the number of employees at that age, in order to determine the total pension plan contribution. Service costs and accumulated benefits are summarized in Exhibit 16–5 (page 504). To verify that a survivor-adjusted level annuity has been calculated, divide each of the yearly normal costs by the number of yearly survivors. This results in a level funding of $2,049 per surviving employee per year.

Service costs and accumulated benefits are significantly different under the three actuarial funding methods illustrated above. One way of summarizing these differences is to calculate the cumulative percentage of retirement benefits that have been funded at each age. This is defined as the ratio of $AL_x/PVRB_x$. These results are summarized in Exhibit 16–6 (page 504).

The allocation of pension costs is quite different under each approach and it is easy to see that material differences in yearly pension expense could occur. Although this example is a simplification of pension plan funding calculations, it shows the basic procedure and illustrates the wide variation possible under alternative actuarial funding methods. There was a lack of uniformity under APB 8 because choice was permitted in the use of actuarial methods. SFAS 87 reduced the uniformity problem by mandating use of the accrued benefit method (future salary increases). Funding decisions continue to be based on any acceptable actuarial method.

QUESTIONS

1. What do the following actuarial terms mean: *accumulated benefits, actuarial liability, vested benefits, service cost,* and *unfunded accumulated benefits*? How are they measured? How are projected benefit obligations, accumulated

EXHIBIT 16–5
Projected Benefit Method (Level Annuity)

	Service Costs	Accumulated Benefits
Age 62	$20,491	$20,491
Age 63	$16,393	$37,908
Age 64	$ 8,196	$48,000

EXHIBIT 16–6
Cumulative Percentage of Accumulated Benefits
Recognized Through Each Period (Present Value at 5 Percent)

	Accrued Benefits (Current Salary)	Accrued Benefits (Future Salary)	Projected Benefits
Age 62	8.3%	33.3%[a]	47.1%
Age 63	33.3%	66.7%[b]	82.9%
Age 64	100.0%	100.0%	100.0%

[a]$14,512/$48,000 × .90703
[b]$30,476/$48,000 × .95238

benefit obligations, and vested benefit obligations defined in SFAS 87, and how are they actuarially calculated?

2. Why is there a pension accounting problem with defined benefit pension plans, but not with defined contribution plans?

3. Explain how previous pension accounting standards were based on a revenue–expense approach to the financial statements.

4. Why did APB 8 only minimally improve uniformity between companies?

5. Why does the revenue–expense approach to accrual pension accounting lead to a theoretical impasse?

6. Why is there not a uniformity problem under an asset–liability approach or a cash basis of pension accounting?

7. How has ERISA affected pension accounting?

8. Given the evidence from the research in the stock market, does it matter whether pension information is disclosed in the formal financial statements or as supplemental disclosure?

9. What economic consequences of SFAS 87 were suggested in the chapter?

10. Why could information about future pension funding in SFAS 87 disclosures be more useful than SFAS 87 liability recognition?

11. Is SFAS 87's argument favoring recognition of a pension liability for accumulated benefits consistent with the Conceptual Framework Project?

12. Evaluate if the implicit contract (economic liability) view of pensions meets the SFAC 6 definition of an accounting liability. What contradiction exists in SFAS 87 regarding the legal versus economic liability viewpoints?

13. Why do the FASB's pension deliberations provide an object lesson in the politics of standard setting?

14. Voluntary pension plan terminations have been increasing [see Hamdallah and Ruland (1986) and Stone (1987)] in which surplus plan assets are recaptured by sponsoring companies after deferred annuities (of equivalent value to accrued benefits) are purchased for plan participants. Why do you think this practice has been criticized by some employee groups, and how might SFAS 87 affect voluntary terminations?

15. What issues of qualitative characteristics of accounting information (SFAC 2) are important relative to accrual accounting for OPEB?

16. What types of economic consequences may arise from accrual accounting for OPEB in SFAS 106?

CASES AND PROBLEMS

1. Verify the calculations of normal costs and accumulated benefits in Appendix 16-A. What is the relationship between accumulated benefits and the pension fund?

   Suppose that a plan was introduced in the second year when eight of the original ten employees remained, and that one year of past service credit was granted. Calculate the required supplemental contribution needed at the beginning of the second year to make up the deficiency if the original service costs (as calculated in Appendix 16-A) are used to fund in years 2 and 3. Why is your answer dependent on the actuarial method used for funding? Using the projected benefit method, calculate a new time series of service costs that will fully fund retirement benefits over the remaining two periods.

2. Assume the following facts concerning a new pension plan: (1) the plan starts with ten employees on their 60th birthday; (2) benefits do not vest until retirement at the end of age 64; (3) no past service credit is granted; (4) funding occurs at the end of each year and investments earn 5 percent; (5) turnover occurs at the beginning of each year; (6) ten employees survive in service through age 60, eight through age 61, six through age 62, five through age 63, and four through age 64; (7) no new employees enter the plan; (8) at age 60, salaries are $26,000 and increase by $1,000 per year. Benefits accumulate at 10 percent of final salary per year of service.

   Required:
   (a) Use the accrued benefit funding method, both with and without salary projections, and prepare the five-year time series of service costs and accumulated benefits.

(b) Prove that service costs compound to the required pension fund balance.

3. Presented below are the balance sheet and 1985 pension-related disclosures of International Harvester Company (now called Navistar) in millions of dollars.

Current Assets	$1,101
Total Assets	$2,406
Current Liabilities	$ 988
Noncurrent Liabilities	1,377
Stockholders' Equity	41
Total Liabilities and Stockholders' Equity	$2,406

The actuarial present value of accumulated plan benefits and plan net assets for the company's defined benefit plans, measured under SFAS 36, were (in millions of dollars)

Actuarial Present Value of Accumulated Plan Benefits:

Vested	$2,072
Nonvested	121
Total	$2,193
Net Assets Available for Benefits	$1,141

Calculate the SFAS 87 impact of recognizing unfunded pension benefits in the balance sheet and the effect on balance sheet ratios. Why might you be motivated to reduce such an accounting liability if you were the manager of a company? What means would be available to accomplish this?

4. Immediately prior to the issuance of SFAS 87, an article appeared in The *Wall Street Journal*, December 6, 1985, p. 6.[39]

> Corporate financial executives are fuming about the controversial pension accounting rule that the Financial Accounting Standards Board is expected to issue soon.
>
> They say the proposed rule is vexing on two counts: It would burden corporate balance sheets by placing a hefty new liability on the books, and it would make bottom-line financial results more volatile. Thus, some companies would have a harder time raising capital, these executives argue. . . .
>
> Norman Weinger, a senior vice president of Oppenheimer & Co., a securities firm that has analyzed prospective effects of the proposed rule, agrees. "The added liability isn't happy news for heavy industrial companies with underfunded pension accounts," Mr. Weinger says. It will "impair several key financial ratios that analysts and bankers use to judge a company's potential for growth and leverage," he adds.
>
> Wall Street analysts also say that market prices for these companies' shares often don't reflect the huge unfunded pension liabilities that could undermine

---

[39] Reprinted by permission of The *Wall Street Journal.* © 1985. Dow Jones & Company, Inc. All Rights Reserved Worldwide.

their financial structures. The stock market is often unaware of these liabilities, says Thornton O'glove, publisher of the Quality of Earnings Report. . . .

"The FASB is trying to force us to put funny numbers on our profit-and-loss statements and our balance sheets," asserts Paul E. Boehk, controller of Champion Spark Plug Co., Toledo, Ohio. "We'd be a lot happier if the rule makers went back to square one and reconsidered this rule."

What sorts of economic consequences are alluded to in the article? Are these issues of concern given the research findings reported in the chapter? What is implied by the statement of Thornton O'glove, and how, if at all, can it be reconciled with research cited in the chapter?

5. Using SFAS 87 and SFAS 106 for additional background, list and briefly discuss as many similarities and differences as you can between pension accounting and OPEB accounting.

BIBLIOGRAPHY OF REFERENCED WORKS

AAA Financial Accounting Standards Committee (1990). "Other Post-Employment Benefits," *Accounting Horizons* (March 1990), pp. 111–116.

Accounting Principles Board (1966). "Accounting for the Cost of Pension Plans," *APB Opinion No. 8* (AICPA).

American Institute of Certified Public Accountants (1981). "Illustrations and Analysis of Disclosure of Pension Information," *Financial Report Survey No. 22* (AICPA).

Beidleman, Carl R. (1973). "Income Smoothing: The Role of Management," *The Accounting Review* (October 1973), pp. 653–667.

Bulow, Jeremy (1982). "What Are Corporate Pension Liabilities?" *Quarterly Journal of Economics* (August 1982), pp. 435–452.

Committee on Accounting Procedure (1948). "Pension Plans – Accounting for Annuity Costs Based on Past Services," *ARB No. 36* (AICPA).

——— (1956). "Accounting for the Cost of Pension Plans," *ARB No. 47* (AICPA).

Daley, Lane Alan (1984). "The Valuation of Reported Pension Measures for Firms Sponsoring Defined Benefit Pension Plans," *The Accounting Review* (April 1984), pp. 177–198.

Davis, Harry, and Arnold Strasser (1970). "Private Pension Plans 1960 to 1969 – An Overview," *Monthly Labor Review* (July 1970), pp. 45–56.

Dhaliwal, Dan S. (1986). "Measurement of Financial Leverage in the Presence of Unfunded Pension Obligations," *The Accounting Review* (October 1986), pp. 651–661.

Feldstein, Martin, and Stephanie Seligman (1981). "Pension Funding, Share Prices, and National Savings," *Journal of Finance* (September 1981), pp. 801–824.

Financial Accounting Standards Board (1974). "Accounting for the Cost of Pension Plans Subject to the Employee Retirement Income Security Act of 1974," *FASB Interpretation No. 3* (FASB).

——— (1980a). "Accounting and Reporting by Defined Benefit Pension Plans," *Statement of Financial Accounting Standards No. 35* (FASB).

——— (1980b). "Disclosure of Pension Information," *Statement of Financial Accounting Standards No. 36* (FASB).

——— (1980c). "Elements of Financial Statements of Business Enterprises," *Statement of Financial Accounting Concepts No. 3* (FASB).

——— (1981). *FASB Discussion Memorandum: An Analysis of Issues Related to Employers' Accounting for Pensions and Other Postemployment Benefits* (FASB).

———— (1982). *Preliminary Views of the Financial Accounting Standards Board on Major Issues Related to Employers' Accounting for Pensions and Other Postemployment Benefits* (FASB).

———— (1983). *FASB Discussion Memorandum: An Analysis of Additional Issues Related to Employers' Accounting for Pensions and Other Postemployment Benefits* (FASB).

———— (1984). "Disclosure of Postretirement Health Care and Life Insurance Benefits," *Statement of Financial Accounting Standards No. 81* (FASB).

———— (1985a). "Employers' Accounting for Pensions," *Statement of Financial Accounting Standards No. 87* (FASB).

———— (1985b). "Employers' Accounting for Settlements and Curtailments of Defined Benefit Pension Plans and for Termination Benefits," *Statement of Financial Accounting Standards No. 88* (FASB).

———— (1990). "Employers' Accounting for Postretirement Benefits Other Than Pensions," *Statement of Financial Accounting Standards No. 106* (FASB).

Francis, Jere R. (1982). "An Analysis of Pension Cost Accruals by Actuarial Methodology" (Ph.D. diss., University of New England).

———— (1987). "Lobbying Against Proposed Accounting Standards: The Case of Employers' Pension Accounting," *Journal of Accounting and Public Policy* (Spring 1987), pp. 35–57.

Francis, Jere R., and Sara Ann Reiter (1987). "Determinants of Corporate Pension Funding Strategy," *Journal of Accounting and Economics* (March 1987), pp. 35–59.

Hagerman, Robert L., and Mark Zmijewski (1979). "Some Economic Determinants of Accounting Policy Choice," *Journal of Accounting and Economics* (August 1979), pp. 141–161.

Hall, William D., and David L. Landsittel (1977). *A New Look at Accounting for Pension Costs* (Richard D. Irwin).

Hicks, Ernest L. (1965). "Accounting for the Cost of Pension Plans," *Accounting Research Study No. 8* (AICPA).

Ippolito, Richard A. (1986). *Pensions, Economics and Public Policy* (Dow-Jones/Irwin).

Kemp, Robert S., Jr. (1988). "An Examination of the Relationship of Unfunded Vested Pension Liabilities and Selected Elements of Firm Value," *Advances in Accounting*, Vol. 5 (JAI Press).

Landsman, Wayne (1986). "An Empirical Investigation of Pension Fund Property Rights," *The Accounting Review* (October 1986), pp. 662–691.

Lucas, Timothy S., and Betsy Ann Hollowell (1981). "Pension Accounting: The Liability Question," *Journal of Accountancy* (October 1981), pp. 57–66.

McGill, Dan M. (1984). *Fundamentals of Private Pensions*, 5th ed. (Richard D. Irwin).

Morris, Michael H., and William D. Nichols (1984). "Pension Accounting and the Balance Sheet: The Potential Effect of the FASB's Preliminary Views," *Journal of Accounting, Auditing and Finance* (Summer 1984), pp. 293–305.

Pesando, James E., and Carol K. Clarke (1983). "Economic Models of the Labor Market and Pension Accounting: An Exploratory Analysis," *The Accounting Review* (October 1983), pp. 733–748.

Reiter, Sara Ann (1985). "The Effect of Defined Benefit Pension Plan Disclosures on Bond Risk Premiums and Bond Ratings" (Ph.D. diss., University of Missouri-Columbia).

Rue, Joseph E., and Ara G. Volkan (1984). "Financial and Economic Consequences of the New Pension Accounting Proposals: Is the Gloom Justified?" *Journal of Accounting, Auditing and Finance* (Summer 1984), pp. 306–322.

Schipper, Katherine, and Roman L. Weil (1982). "Alternative Accounting Treatments for Pensions," *The Accounting Review* (October 1982), pp. 806–824.

Stone, Mary S. (1982). "A Survey of Research on the Effects of Corporate Pension Plan Sponsorship: Implications for Accounting," *Journal of Accounting Literature* (Spring 1982), pp. 1–32.

—— (1987). "A Financing Explanation for Overfunded Pension Plan Terminations," *Journal of Accounting Research* (Autumn 1987), pp. 317–326.

Thomas, Paula B., and Larry Farmer (1990). "OPEB: Improved Reporting or the Last Straw?" *Journal of Accountancy* (November 1990), pp. 102–112.

Winklevoss, Howard E. (1977). *Pension Mathematics with Numerical Illustrations* (Richard D. Irwin).

Wright, David W. (1990). "Accounting Pedagogy Based on Extant Authoritative Rules Versus Decision-Oriented Analysis: The Case of Other Postemployment Benefits," *Journal of Accounting Education* (Fall 1990), pp. 183–205.

Wyatt, Arthur (1990). "OPEB Costs: The FASB Establishes Accountability," *Accounting Horizons* (March 1990), pp. 108–110.

ADDITIONAL READINGS

Bodie, Z., and J. Shoven, eds. (1983). *Financial Aspects of the U.S. Pension System* (National Bureau of Economic Research).

Clark, Hal G., and Leonard Lorensen (1987). *Illustrations of Accounting for Pensions and for Settlements and Curtailments of Defined Benefit Pension Plans* (AICPA).

Danker, Harold, Michael P. Glinsky, John H. Grady, Murray B. Hirsch, and Richard M. Steinberg (1981). *Employer Accounting for Pension Costs and Other Post-Retirement Benefits* (Financial Executives Research Foundation).

Dewhirst, John F. (1971). "A Conceptual Approach to Pension Accounting," *The Accounting Review* (April 1971), pp. 365–373.

Financial Accounting Standards Board (1975). *FASB Discussion Memorandum: An Analysis of Issues Related to Accounting and Reporting for Employee Benefit Plans* (FASB).

—— (1983). *Preliminary Views — A Field Test: Employers' Accounting for Pensions* (FASB).

Hamdallah, Ahmed El-Sayed, and William Ruland (1986). "The Decision to Terminate Overfunded Pension Plans," *Journal of Accounting and Public Policy* (Summer 1986), pp. 77–92.

Ijiri, Yuji (1980). *Recognition of Contractual Rights and Obligations: An Exploratory Study of Conceptual Issues* (FASB).

Leo, Mario, Preston C. Basset, and Ernest S. Kachline (1975). *Financial Aspects of Private Pension Plans* (Financial Executives Research Foundation).

Moonitz, Maurice, and Alexander Russ (1966). "Accrual Accounting for Employers' Pension Costs," *Journal of Accounting Research* (Autumn 1966), pp. 155–168.

Norton, Curtis (1989). "Transition to New Accounting Rules: The Case of FAS 87," *Accounting Horizons* (December 1989), pp. 40–48.

Philips, G. Edward (1968). "Pension Liabilities and Assets," *The Accounting Review* (January 1968), pp. 10–17.

Rue, Joseph C., and David Tosh (1987). "Continuing Unresolved Issues of Pension Accounting," *Accounting Horizons* (December 1987), pp. 21–27.

Skinner, Ross M. (1980). *Pension Accounting* (Clarkson Gordon Chartered Accountants).

Smith, Jack L. (1977). "Actuarial Cost Methods — Basics for CPA's," *Journal of Accountancy* (February 1977), pp. 62–66.

Stone, Mary, and Robert W. Ingram (1988). "The Effect of 'Statement No. 87' on Financial Reports of Early Adopters," *Accounting Horizons* (September 1988), pp. 48–61.

Willinger, G. Lee (1985). "A Contingent Claims Model for Pension Costs," *Journal of Accounting Research* (Spring 1985), pp. 351–359.

LEASES

LEASES HAVE BEEN THE SUBJECT of more accounting standards than any other single topic. The CAP issued one standard, the APB issued five standards, and the FASB issued ten. The attention given to leases in accounting standards reflects the increased use of leasing in the business community and the need to clarify and standardize the accounting for this complex transaction. The first accounting lease standard, ARB 38, was issued in 1949; however, it was only in the 1960s and 1970s that accounting policy makers responded to the lease accounting problem.[1] The basic accounting requirements are unchanged since the comprehensive SFAS 13 was issued in 1976, although lease accounting continues to be controversial in the standards-overload debate.

Leasing has become popular for a number of operating and financial reasons. From an operating viewpoint, some assets are available only under lease; others are too expensive for outright purchase. Two significant financing aspects are the tax advantages (lease payments are fully deductible) and the possibility of off-balance-sheet financing, which occurs when leased assets and lease obligations are not reported in the financial statements. Off-balance-sheet financing results in better debt ratios and higher accounting rates of return than a purchase alternative could produce.

The accounting controversy about leases has focused on distinguishing between the economic substance of leases and their legal form. Prior to ARB 38, the accounting procedure for lease payments was to record them as periodic revenues for lessors and as expenses for lessees. Increasingly, however, some leases came to be viewed as the equivalent of purchases with debt financing. This view now dominates, and the focus of accounting standards has been on defining those situations in which a lease is considered to be a purchase equivalent and in making such leases look like a purchase with debt financing. These types of leases are called *capital leases* and the accounting procedure for them is called *capitalization*. Noncapitalized leases are called *operating leases*, and the lease payments are treated as periodic expenses.

---

[1] Committee on Accounting Procedure (1949).

From a lessor's viewpoint, capital leases may be one of two types, *sales* or *financing*. A sales-type lease arises when a manufacturer or seller of merchandise uses leasing as a financing instrument to effect what is considered to be the equivalent of a sale. In these situations, the accounting standards have first been concerned with defining the criteria for sales recognition and then making the transaction look like the equivalent of a sale with vendor financing. A financing-type lease occurs when a third party finances a lease rather than a manufacturer or seller. In such situations, the financing party is the lessor and the accounting attempts to make the lease look like a loan with income realized through implicit interest in each lease payment. If a lease is not capitalized by a lessor, the payments are recognized as revenues when received.

The chapter begins with an examination of lease contracts and the capitalization argument and then reviews the evolution of lease accounting in the accounting standards, revealing an ever-finer attempt to achieve finite uniformity vis-à-vis operating and capital leases. Separate accounting rules have been developed for the two types. This approach is defended on the grounds of representational faithfulness, in which a lease is interpreted to be either a simple rental agreement or a more complex capital lease. Finally, the chapter concludes with consideration of the economic consequences of lease accounting standards.

THE LEASE CONTRACT

A **lease** is a legal document conveying use of property for a fixed period of time in exchange for rent or other compensation. From a legal viewpoint, a lease is both a conveyance and a contract, with the contractual element dominating.[2] It is a conveyance because the lessee acquires an interest in property for a fixed period of time. It is a contract because the lessor promises the lessee *quiet enjoyment* of the property during the lease term in exchange for the promise of periodic payments. Although it is not possible to define unambiguously a *true lease* in law, Exhibit 17–1 (page 512) lists characteristics regarded as indicators of a true lease. Material variations from the characteristics listed in Exhibit 17–1 may result in a lease being regarded as a conditional sale agreement or a debt instrument rather than a true lease. Capitalization criteria in accounting standards have been concerned with many of these characteristics.

THE EXECUTORY NATURE OF LEASE CONTRACTS

The legal form of a lease contract is an executory (unperformed) contract. A lessor (legal owner) transfers possession of a leased asset to a lessee for a fixed period of time in exchange for a series of rents. A lessee's performance is executory because future rents are due one period at a time. However, the performance question can be argued both ways with respect to the lessor. The distinc-

---

[2] Hawkins and Wehle (1973, p. 51).

EXHIBIT 17–1
Characteristics of a True Lease

The following factors are considered to be indications that a lease agreement is without doubt a true lease:

1. The absence of a provision for the transfer of the title to the lessee.
2. The absence of any mention of interest as a factor in rental charges.
3. Rental charges that are competitive with those charged by other lessors of similar equipment.
4. Rental charges that are reasonably related to the loss of value due to the lessee's use of the equipment or that are based on production or use and not necessarily related to purchase price.
5. The assumption of the risk of loss by the lessor.
6. The lessor is required to bear the cost of insurance, maintenance and taxes.
7. The lessor retains the right to inspect the equipment during the term of the lease.
8. If the lessee has an option to purchase:
   (a) The option price approximates the predicted fair market value of the equipment at the time the option may be exercised.
   (b) Rentals are not applied to the option price.
9. The rentals charged under leasing plans without an option to purchase approximate the rental charged under plans with such an option.
10. Government agencies recognize the lessor as the owner of the leased asset.
11. The lessee considers by his action that he is a lessee and not a purchaser.

Source: Reprinted with permission of Financial Executives Research Foundation (FERF) from its research study entitled *Accounting for Leases* by David M. Hawkins and Mary M. Wehle (1973, FERF, Morristown, N.J.), pp. 52–53.

---

tion is important because it determines whether the contract is mutually unperformed or unilaterally unperformed. As indicated in Chapter 10, mutually unperformed executory contracts have traditionally been excluded from the balance sheet.

It can be argued that a lease contract is fully executed by a lessor when possession of the leased asset is transferred to a lessee. This would make a lease contract unilaterally unperformed by the lessee in the case of default. Such contracts are recognized in the balance sheet because possession of a leased asset is both an obligation and asset of the lessee. SFAC 6 defines assets as probable future economic benefits and liabilities as probable future sacrifices of economic benefits, both arising from past transactions.[3] A fixed-term lease contract grants property use rights, which may create future economic benefits even

---

[3] FASB (1985a).

though property ownership does not exist. In the same manner, a lease contract also obligates the lessee to make future payments.

If a lease is interpreted as a mutually unperformed executory contract, it can be argued that an asset and liability do not exist for the lessee. In such a situation, the lessor would be permitting use for each period at a time only if the rentals are paid by the lessee. This would simply result in expensing current period lease payments. Mutually unperformed future promises would be excluded from the balance sheet on the grounds that these are future transactions that have not yet occurred.

Legal remedies available to lessors in the event of lessee default treat leases like mutually unperformed executory contracts. A lessee is not liable for future lease payments in the event of default. A lessor must first mitigate the loss of rents by selling the asset or leasing it again. The lessee has a legal obligation to the lessor only for any residual losses after the lessor mitigates the loss. This makes leases significantly different from other debt agreements — for example, corporate bonds in which the borrower is obliged for the full amount of unpaid principal plus any accrued interest in the event of default.

The importance of the executory aspect of lease contracts is attested to in the second lease accounting standard, APB 5. The fundamental assumption underlying lease capitalization was noncancellability of the lease contract or other material equity factors such as the presence of a bargain purchase option or a bargain lease renewal option.[4] The existence of noncancellability clauses, it could be argued, supersedes the executory nature of lease contracts. If the promises under a lease contract are noncancellable, the executory nature still exists, but it has been mitigated to some extent; and additional legal rights have been created for both lessee and lessor in the event of nonperformance by the other party.

Although the executory nature of lease contracts is an important legal characteristic, its importance has been supplanted by an overriding concern with the economic substance of lease contracts. This basic approach is the one taken by policy makers since the first lease accounting standard in 1949. ARB 38 recommended that where it was obvious a lease contract was in substance a purchase, both an asset and an obligation should be recognized in the lessee's balance sheet. This general theme has continued in subsequent lease accounting standards.

LEASES COMPARED WITH PURCHASE ARRANGEMENTS

There are legal differences between true leases and purchase arrangements.[5] Purchase arrangements are outright cash sale, credit sale, installment sale, secured credit sale, or a conditional sale agreement. Title passes to the user of the property in all instances except leases and conditional sales. So a lease and con-

---

[4] APB (1964, para. 10).
[5] Cook (1963) and Zises (1973).

ditional sale are very similar in this respect. Title passes in a conditional sale when final payment is made, but this does not necessarily occur with a lease. Leases in which the title passes at the end of the lease term or in which a bargain purchase option exists are virtually the same as conditional sales with respect to legal ownership. Also, leases that are for substantially all of a leased asset's economic life are virtually identical with conditional sales agreements calling for installment payments over the economic life of the asset.

A strong argument for capitalization can be made for leases that resemble conditional sales agreements. Of course, many of these leases would not be considered true leases in the eyes of the law. Even in law, however, the distinction is not always clear between a true lease and a sale. Both the Internal Revenue Service and the courts often deal with disputes about this issue. They interpret some lease contracts as conditional sales agreements, and vice versa. Capitalization of leases that are virtually conditional sales agreements would be consistent with the true legal nature of the transaction rather than with their superficial resemblance to a lease. Capitalization would treat disguised conditional sales like other conditional sales.

In the event of bankruptcy or default, credit sales and installment sales are identical. With both credit and installment sales, the seller is simply a general creditor of the buyer. A secured credit sale gives the seller a preferred claim or lien on the asset and a general creditor status for any amount of the obligation not covered by the value of the asset. In bankruptcy or default, the seller under a conditional sales agreement has a legal right to recover the property because title has not passed. In addition, the seller has a general creditor status for any difference between the unpaid obligation and the asset value. A lessor's claim is limited to provable damages (loss of lease payments), but the lessor must first mitigate these losses either through sale or a new lease of the repossessed property. In this latter way a lease differs from a conditional sales agreement.

LEASE CAPITALIZATION

From a lessee's viewpoint, a lease must be accounted for as either (1) a rental agreement or (2) a purchase equivalent with debt financing. For a lessor, the transaction must be treated as either (1) a rental agreement or (2a) a sale equivalent with debt financing (if it is a sales-type lease) or (2b) a loan equivalent (if it is a financing-type lease). Choice (1) for both lessee and lessor interprets the lease contract as an operating lease and recognizes the mutually unperformed executory nature of lease contracts. Choice (2) treats the lease as a capital lease and recognizes the conveyance and financing aspects of leases. The simplicity of the basic accounting classification system forces a lease to be accounted for in one of these two ways.

The choice of accounting policy has been described in the following manner:

> At one extreme, there is the case of two physically identical items of equipment used by a business, one financed or partly financed by borrowing, and the other financed by a lease that is noncancellable for a period equal to the equipment's useful life. Most every informed person would agree that it doesn't make much sense to report one of these items on the balance sheet and omit the other. At the other end there are ephemeral leases . . . which most everyone agrees should not give rise to a balance sheet item. The problem is to state a principle that will provide a conceptually sound and practical way of drawing a line somewhere between the two extremes.[6]

The heart of the policy is classification of leases as either operating or capital leases — a classic example of attempting to establish finite uniformity and to account representationally for the real substance of the lease transaction rather than its superficial legal form.

One of the major arguments against lease capitalization was verifiability. Specifically, some believed that the use of present value discounting techniques introduced less reliable accounting numbers into the financial statements. This concern was exaggerated, however, because present value calculations are only used to make lease financing look like the equivalent of a loan with an equal repayment schedule. The present value technique as applied to lease accounting is illustrated later in the chapter, and, as we will see, only one verifiability problem exists: the choice of interest rate used to discount the lease payments. There is some inevitable subjectivity in determining a lessee's rate, but it is certainly susceptible to close approximation. For a lessor, there is no subjectivity because the interest rate implicit in the lease is used. Verifiability is not considered to be a major issue with lease accounting today.

CAPITALIZATION FOR LESSEES

Numerous criteria have been proposed to support lease capitalization. A very good survey is found in the FASB's discussion memorandum on leases and is summarized in Exhibit 17–2 (page 516).[7] In general terms, the arguments for lease capitalization invoke the reasoning that certain leases are, in substance, purchases with debt financing. A lease is simply another type of legal instrument to accomplish this end. Different arguments and criteria have been used to define purchase equivalents, but the differences really are little more than alternative points where the line is drawn between operating and capital leases. The many viewpoints can be simplified into three broad approaches: legal, material equity, and substantial transfer of ownership benefits and risks. These represent increasingly broader interpretations of capital leases.

---

[6] Anthony (1962).
[7] FASB (1974, pp. 40–41).

EXHIBIT 17–2
Lease Capitalization Criteria

1. Lessee builds up a material equity in the leased property.
2. Leased property is special purpose to the lessee.
3. Lease term is substantially equal to the estimated useful life of the property.
4. Lessee pays costs normally incident to ownership.
5. Lessee guarantees the lessor's debt with respect to the leased property.
6. Lessee treats the lease as a purchase for tax purposes.
7. Lease is between related parties.
8. Lease passes usual risks and rewards to lessee.
9. Lessee assumes an unconditional liability for lease rentals.
10. Lessor lacks independent economic substance.
11. Residual value at end of lease is expected to be nominal.
12. Lease agreement provides for lessor's recovery of investment plus a fair return.
13. Lessee has the option at any time to purchase the asset for the lessor's unrecovered investment.
14. Lease agreement is noncancellable for a long term.

Legal Approach

One way to resolve the lease classification problem is to treat true leases as described in Exhibit 17–1 as operating leases and to capitalize leases that are not true leases. This approach to lease capitalization resolves the problem by resorting to legal definitions and concepts. However, such an approach does not address the more fundamental question of whether true leases should be capitalized. It has been argued that all noncancellable leases create legal property rights and obligations that should be in a lessee's balance sheet even if they do arise from a lease contract.[8] We also pointed out in Chapter 10 that accounting theory and policy are not confined to legal definitions of accounting elements.

Material Equity

Historically, the argument for lease capitalization has relied on the concept of **material equity.** This means that the terms of the lease are such that the lessee is clearly paying for more than the current period rental value of the asset. In other words, the lessee is acquiring an implicit equity in the leased asset through the periodic lease payments. Evidence for such a situation would be rental payments in excess of yearly economic value or a bargain purchase option. The excess represents payment for the implicit property rights created by the lease. Also, noncancellability and a lease term for a significant portion of the asset's economic life would support the material equity argument. Material equity, as applied in accounting standards in the past, limited capitalization to a small

---

[8] This view is attributed to Myers (1962).

number of leases that were virtually conditional sales agreements with install-ment payments. As a result, there was very little difference between the legal and material equity approaches.

Transfer of the Benefits and Risks of Ownership

SFAS 13 took a broader approach to the capitalization argument. Leases that substantially transfer ". . . all of the benefits and risks incident to the ownership of property should be accounted for as the acquisition of an asset and the incur-rence of an obligation by the lessee and as a sale or financing by the lessor."[9] The current definition has dropped noncancellability as a prerequisite for capi-talization and de-emphasized the concept of material equity. In spite of the at-tempt in SFAS 13 to disassociate the standard from earlier standards, the es-sence of the capitalization argument remains the same as it has been since ARB 38 — that a purchase equivalent has occurred. The difficulty, of course, has been in agreeing on when this occurs. The material equity concept has simply been superseded by a somewhat broader concept and set of tests.

CAPITALIZATION FOR LESSORS

A basic issue with lessor capitalization is symmetry with lessee accounting. Symmetry means consistent accounting by lessees and lessors for capital and operating leases. Some feel that symmetry, per se, is not necessary.[10] Others believe that the basic characteristic of a capital lease should be consistently re-corded by both lessor and lessee.[11] The absence of symmetry suggests that the basic classification of leases as operating and capital is inconsistent. Accounting standards have moved toward symmetry.

For sales-type leases, the same set of criteria applicable to lessees has been proposed for capitalization by lessors because if a sales-type lease is a purchase equivalent to the lessee, it must be a sale equivalent to the lessor. However, additional criteria must also exist before a sale is recognized. These criteria involve the usual assumptions underlying revenue recognition, mainly the cer-tainty of cash collection and the absence of uncertainties regarding unincurred costs relating to the sale.

Financing-type leases present a different situation. The capitalization analogy treats such leases as the equivalent of debt financing. There is no sale revenue with financing-type leases, only interest revenue earned from the debt equivalent. Arguments for capitalization of finance-type leases have related more to the debt characteristic of the lease than to the sale characteristic. The main criterion proposed is the concept of *full payout*, which refers to a set of lease payments that returns a lessor's investment in the leased asset plus a rea-sonable interest on the investment.[12]

---

[9] FASB (1976, para. 60).
[10] Hawkins (1970).
[11] Alvin (1970).
[12] FASB (1974, pp. 95–97).

THE EVOLUTION OF
LEASE ACCOUNTING STANDARDS

A number of standards have been issued since 1949. We review them chronologically, first as they relate to lessees and then as they affect lessors.

LESSEE ACCOUNTING
ARB 38
The first lease accounting standard, issued in 1949, was ARB 38. It was subsequently codified as Chapter 14 of ARB 43.[13] The standard recommended capitalization for certain leases that were, in substance, installment purchases. Although it referred specifically to the installment purchase analogy, it was more
applicable to leases that were de facto conditional sales agreements. The capitalization criteria were any of the following: (1) the existence of a bargain purchase option at the termination of the lease; (2) covenants that permitted the
application of lease rentals to the purchase price; or (3) rental payments so high
that a purchase plan was evident. The first criterion deals with lease terms that
make a lease almost indistinguishable from a conditional sale. The second and
third criteria refer to the material equity argument and could be analogous to
either an installment sale or conditional sale, though in legal terms the resemblance is closer to a conditional sale. No details were given in the standard
concerning the measurement of either the leased asset or lease obligation.

APB 5
As part of the research approach initially adopted by the APB, a study was commissioned on leases. This resulted in ARS 4, issued in 1962.[14] ARS 4 took a
legalistic approach to determining whether a lease was in substance a purchase.
ARS 4 argued that noncancellability of the lease contract creates legal property
rights warranting capitalization. The next accounting standard, issued in 1964,
was APB 5. APB 5 did not accept the basic argument in ARS 4 and reaffirmed
the material equity argument of ARB 38. However, it did introduce noncancellability, except upon the occurrence of some remote contingency, as a precondi-
tion for capitalization. As suggested earlier in the chapter, this condition could
be interpreted as mitigating the executory nature of lease contracts.

APB 5 also modified criteria for capitalization, though the stated objective
was to clarify ARB 43, Chapter 14, not change it. The intent was to capitalize
any lease creating a material equity interest. Either of two primary criteria were
listed: (1) a renewal option covering the useful economic life, or (2) existence of
a bargain purchase option. Some secondary indicators were also identified:
(1) the property was specially acquired by the lessor to meet the needs of the

---

[13] Committee on Accounting Procedure (1953, Chapter 14).
[14] Myers (1962).

lessee, (2) the lease term corresponded to the useful life, (3) the lessee incurred executory costs (insurance, taxes, and maintenance), (4) the lessee guaranteed any lessor obligation with respect to the leased asset, or (5) the lessee treated the lease as a purchase under tax law. Apparently these secondary criteria were ignored in practice because of the way the standard was worded. As a result, APB 5 caused little change in the number of leases that were capitalized, even though it intended the opposite effect.[15]

APB 10

APB 10, issued in 1966, was an omnibus opinion.[16] One paragraph dealt with leases and required the consolidation of certain subsidiaries that were principally engaged in leasing assets to parent companies. This standard was partially an amendment of APB 5, paragraph 12, and was concerned with lease contracts between related entities, such as parent and subsidiary companies. APB 10 required that subsidiaries engaged in sales-type leases to the parent company must be consolidated. In this way it was not possible to avoid the reporting of leased assets by having unconsolidated subsidiaries write lease contracts. However, the consolidation of subsidiaries engaged in financing-type leases was left unresolved. As a result of APBs 5 and 10, financing-type leases could be treated differently by the lessee, depending on whether the lessor was a subsidiary or an independent entity. Some leases were capitalized and some were not. The SEC attempted to resolve this inconsistency with ASR 132, issued in 1972.[17]

APB 31

The next accounting standard for lessees was APB 31, issued in 1973.[18] This standard expanded disclosure of noncapitalized leases. APB 5 had been criticized on the grounds that it excluded many leases that should be capitalized. The disclosures required by APB 31 included the amounts of future rentals at both future values and present values. The effect of this disclosure requirement was to create adequate supplemental disclosure to permit users to informally capitalize noncapitalized lease obligations if they so desired. Although this disclosure expanded the reporting of information concerning noncapitalized lease obligations, it did not go so far as to formally place them in the balance sheet.

The SEC pressured the newly formed FASB to review lease accounting. Shortly after APB 31 was released (it was the last APB Opinion), the SEC issued ASR 147.[19] The SEC was critical of existing lease accounting standards, and ASR 147 amended lease disclosure for statutory SEC filings. ASR 147 was mainly concerned with financing-type leases. As mentioned above, APBs 5 and

---

[15] FASB (1974, pp. 159–160) indicates that there was only a modest increase in the number of leases capitalized after APB 5 was issued and that most of the increase was due to a new type of lease related to Industrial Development Bonds, which met the capitalization criteria.

[16] APB (1966b).

[17] SEC (1972). This requirement extended the reporting of capitalized leases between related parties — and represented an interpretation of APB 5, paras. 10–12.

[18] APB (1973).

[19] SEC (1973).

10 were thought to have resulted in inconsistent capitalization of financing-type leases. ASR 147 required supplemental disclosure of noncapitalized financing-type leases on a basis that was equivalent to capitalization.

SFAS 13 (as Amended Through SFAS 98)

The FASB issued a discussion memorandum on leases in 1974, and after deliberations, SFAS 13 was issued in 1976. Criteria for lessee capitalization were revised again. This time there was a change in both concept and capitalization criteria. Noncancellability and material equity were abandoned in favor of broader tests representing substantive transfers of ownership benefits and risks – although, as indicated earlier, the underlying objective still seems to be the recognition of purchase equivalents. Perhaps the difference between APB 5 and SFAS 13 is better described as a change in where the line is drawn between operating and capital leases. SFAS 13 is quite clearly intended to capitalize more leases. There are four capitalization tests now applicable to both lessees and lessors:

1. Title passes to the lessee at the end of the lease term.
2. The lease contract contains a bargain purchase option.
3. The lease term is at least 75 percent of estimated useful life (with the lease term covering more than 25 percent of the original economic life when new).
4. The present value of minimum lease payments (the sum of minimum rentals excluding executory costs, a bargain purchase payment if one exists, penalty payment for nonrenewal if renewal is unlikely, and any guaranteed residual value at the end of lease term – plus unguaranteed residual value for lessors) is 90 percent of the fair market value of the lease property at the inception of the lease, less any applicable investment tax credit.

For the last test, the discount rate to be used by the lessee is the incremental borrowing rate. However, the lessor's implicit rate in the lease shall be used if it is obtainable and if the implicit rate is lower than the lessee's incremental borrowing rate. This represents conservatism because a lower interest rate will cause a higher present value and could result in lease capitalization under the 90 percent rule. The lessor's implicit rate is defined in SFAS 13, paragraph 5k, and is illustrated later in the chapter. If *any* one of these four tests or conditions is met, the lease must be treated as a capital lease by the lessee.

SFAS 13 also details how leases should be capitalized. The present value of minimum lease payments (defined in point 4 above) is computed using the interest rate determined for test (4) of the list. This amount is debited to leased assets and credited to lease obligations, subject to an upper limit of the asset's fair market value at lease inception. The asset is depreciated over its useful life if tests (1) or (2) are met. Otherwise, the depreciation period is the lease term with total amortization equal to the capitalized amount less any guaranteed residual value at the end of the lease term. During the lease term, each payment is allocated between interest expense and reduction of the lease obligation. The effective interest method described in APB 21 is used.[20] Finally, any executory costs (taxes, maintenance, and insurance) are expensed as incurred. If lease payments include an amount for these costs, it is separated and expensed directly each period.

In this manner, the prescribed accounting seeks to make the lease resemble a purchase of the asset with debt financing. The leased asset is depreciated over its useful life if it is being leased for substantially all its useful life, with 75 percent being the materiality threshold. If the asset is leased for a shorter period, the shorter period is used as the amortization period. Executory costs are separated and expensed in the same manner as would occur with a purchase. Finally, lease payments are separated into the equivalent of principal and interest each period. The purchase analogy is illustrated with a numerical example in Exhibit 17–3 (page 522).

Real estate leases are accounted for somewhat differently. Leases involving only land are capitalized if either test (1) or test (2) in SFAS 13 is satisfied. Otherwise, land leases are classified as operating. Land under lease is not treated as a purchase equivalent unless title is expected to transfer. The reason for this more restrictive test is due to the nondepreciable nature of land. When a lease includes both land and buildings, the capitalization test is more complicated. If test (1) or (2) is not met, an allocation is made between land and building based on relative fair market values. They are capitalized separately. If a real estate lease involving land does not meet test (1) or (2), but the fair market value of the land component is less than 25 percent of the total, the lease is treated as entirely attributable to the building for the purpose of applying tests (3) and (4) of SFAS 13. If either test (3) or (4) is met, the lease is capitalized. In other words, the land component is considered to be immaterial relative to the building component and the entire lease is capitalized. If the land component is 25 percent or more, the land and building are treated separately, with the land being an operating lease and the building being a capital lease if test (3) or (4) is met. These rules represent somewhat arbitrary ways of dealing with nondepreciable land in real estate leases.

In addition to the prescribed accounting for capital leases, a number of supplemental disclosures are required by SFAS 13: (1) gross amounts of assets under capital lease, (2) future minimum lease payments (excluding executory costs) in aggregate and for each of the five succeeding years, (3) total minimum sublease rentals to be received under noncancellable subleases, and (4) total contingent rentals as they are incurred each period. Lease assets and lease obligations are to be reported separately from other assets and liabilities in the balance sheet. Lease obligations are subject to current and noncurrent classification requirements.

A very important question whenever there is a major change in accounting policy is how it will be implemented. With lease capitalization a generous phase-in period was permitted. For new leases written after 1976, capitalization was required if the new tests were met. However, for existing leases, companies

---

[20] APB (1971).

EXHIBIT 17–3
Lease Purchase Analogy

A company may purchase an asset outright for $100,000 with vendor financing. The note payable would be paid off with three year-end payments of $41,634.90. This represents an effective interest of 12 percent. An alternative is to lease the asset for three years with lease payments of $41,634.90 at the end of each year. The asset's economic life is three years, and no salvage is expected.

Loan/Lease Repayment Schedule

(Col. 1) Beginning Principal	(Col. 2) Payment	(Col. 3) Interest (Col. 1 × .12)	(Col. 4) Principal (Col. 2 − Col. 3)	(Col. 5) Ending Principal (Col. 1 − Col. 4)
Year 1 $100,000.00	$41,634.90	$12,000.00	$29,634.90	$70,365.10
Year 2 $ 70,365.10	$41,634.90	$ 8,443.81	$33,191.09	$37,174.01
Year 3 $ 37,174.01	$41,634.90	$ 4,460.89	$37,174.01	- 0 -

Purchase Alternative Year 1			Lease Alternative Year 1		
Asset	100,000		Leased Asset	100,000	
Note Payable		100,000	Lease Obligation		100,000
Note Payable	29,634.90		Lease Obligation	29,634.90	
Interest Expense	12,000.00		Interest Expense	12,000.00	
Cash		41,634.90	Cash		41,634.90
Depreciation Expense	33,333.33		Depreciation—Lease	33,333.33	
Accumulated Depreciation		33,333.33	Accumulated Lease Depreciation	33,333.33	

Year 2			Year 2		
Note Payable	33,191.09		Lease Obligation	33,191.09	
Interest Expense	8,443.81		Interest Expense	8,443.81	
Cash		41,634.90	Cash		41,634.90
Depreciation Expense	33,333.33		Depreciation—Lease	33,333.33	
Accumulated Depreciation		33,333.33	Accumulated Lease Depreciation	33,333.33	

Year 3			Year 3		
Note Payable	37,174.01		Lease Obligation	37,174.01	
Interest Expense	4,460.89		Interest Expense	4,460.89	
Cash		41,634.90	Cash		41,634.90
Depreciation Expense	33,333.34		Depreciation—Lease	33,333.34	
Accumulated Depreciation		33,333.34	Accumulated Lease Depreciation	33,333.34	

were given until December 31, 1980, to retroactively capitalize the leases and restate prior years' financial statements. Supplemental disclosures were required of what the pre-1977 lease assets and obligations would have been during the phase-in period if they had been capitalized. The reason for a long transition period was due to the potential material effects of lease capitalization on some companies. SFAS 13 was less dramatic than expected because the new standard permitted companies some flexibility in complying with the new requirements. There was time to mitigate the impact on the balance sheet of lease capitalization. The final section of the chapter presents some evidence that this type of behavior (avoiding lease capitalization) did in fact occur.

A criticism of lessee accounting under SFAS 13 is that some leases that should be capitalized still are not. It can be argued that all leases in excess of one year should be capitalized because assets and liabilities are created that are consistent with definitions of assets and obligations in SFAC 6.[21] One reason for avoiding this policy may be the costs that would be imposed on companies if all leases were capitalized. An apparent compromise exists on this point in the form of supplemental disclosure. For noncancellable operating leases in excess of one year, SFAS 13 requires the following supplemental disclosures:

1. Future minimum rental payments in aggregate and for each of the succeeding five periods.
2. Total minimum rentals to be received under noncancellable subleases.
3. Rental expense with separate totals for minimum rentals, contingent rentals, and sublease rentals.
4. A general description of the lessee's lease contracts.

Supplemental disclosure of noncapitalized leases is not as great under SFAS 13 as it was under APB 31. The noncancellability requirement will exclude some operating leases, and present value information is not required under SFAS 13. It is unclear why noncancellability was introduced as the overriding criterion for supplemental disclosure of operating leases since it was dropped as a capitalization criterion. Because many more leases will be capitalized under SFAS 13, it may be that the need for supplemental information is not as great as it was prior to the issuance of SFAS 13. Still, it is puzzling why the supplemental disclosures of noncapitalized leases were reduced so much. The weak disclosures of noncapitalized leases create incentives to structure leases in such a way as to avoid both capitalization and supplemental disclosure. If this can be done, off-balance-sheet financing through leases would still be possible. This issue is discussed later in the chapter.

LESSOR ACCOUNTING

The initial impetus for lease capitalization was caused by a concern over lessee balance sheets. In particular, there was a desire to disclose lease obligations as debt equivalents. It was only belatedly that the lessor side of lease transactions was considered in accounting standards.

---

[21] FASB (1985, paras. 25–40).

APB 7

APB 7, issued in 1966, was the first standard to address lessor accounting.[22] The equivalent of lease capitalization was required, but the criteria differed from APB 5. In addition, separate criteria existed for sales-type and financing-type leases. Sales-type leases were capitalized if three conditions were satisfied: (1) credit risks were reasonably predictable, (2) the lessor (seller) did not retain sizable risks of ownership, and (3) there were no important uncertainties regarding either costs or revenues under the lease contract. These three conditions differed from the lessee tests established under APB 5. As a result, it was possible for a lease contract to be capitalized by either the lessee or lessor, but not by both. This asymmetry between lessee and lessor accounting was criticized.

Financing-type leases are those that involve a third party who writes the lease contract. The lessor is the third party, with the other two parties being the lessee and the manufacturer (or seller) of the leased asset. *All* financing-type leases were capitalized by lessors under APB 7; however, some financing-type leases were not capitalized by lessees under APBs 5 and 10. As indicated earlier in the chapter, lessee accounting for financing-type leases was inconsistent under APBs 5 and 10.

Leases capitalized under APB 7 were recognized as aggregate future rentals less the interest implicit in each rental. This represented the net present value of lease payments receivable. The effective interest method, as described in APB 21, was prescribed as the basis of interest revenue recognition. Each payment was separated into principal and interest, just as was required for lessees under APB 5.

Initial direct costs incurred by the lessor in originating a lease contract were deferred and recognized on a proportional basis consistent with the recognition of lease revenue. This applied to all leases and was an attempt to match lease-related costs to the revenue generated over the lease term.

APB 27

Criticisms of APB 7 regarding the noncapitalization of many sales-type leases led to the issuance of APB 27 in 1972.[23] The intent in APB 27 was to broaden the criteria for capitalization. The new criteria were

1. The collectibility of payments was reasonably assured.
2. No important uncertainties surrounded costs yet to be incurred on the lease.
3. Any one of the following:
    (i)   title passed at end of lease term,
    (ii)   a bargain purchase option existed,
    (iii) the leased property or similar property was for sale and the present value of required rentals (excluding executory costs) plus any investment tax credits was equal to or greater than normal selling price, or
    (iv)   the lease term was substantially equal to the remaining economic life of the property.

---

[22] APB (1966a).
[23] APB (1972).

Two of the requirements under both APBs 7 and 27 were similar and dealt with general revenue recognition criteria. Collectibility and the absence of uncertainties are generally assumed when accruing revenue in advance of cash collection. The third requirement of APB 27 replaced the second criterion of APB 7, the transfer of ownership risk, and was satisfied by any one of four conditions. The first two conditions reiterated the capitalization criteria of APB 5 for lessees. The last two were new and provided additional conditions that suggested the lease was a sale equivalent from the lessor's viewpoint. The addition of these two conditions was important because it represented a departure from the material equity argument and looked more broadly at the economic substance of the transaction. However, the newly broadened criteria for lessors was at variance with the narrower criteria for lessees established in APB 5.

SFAS 13

Finally, lessee and lessor accounting achieved near symmetry in SFAS 13. The four capitalization tests discussed earlier, which were only a slight modification of APB 27, were applied to both lessees and lessors. For lessor accounting, the two additional revenue recognition tests of APBs 7 and 27 were also retained in SFAS 13. The existence of these two additional criteria means that it is possible for some leases that are capitalized by lessees to be treated as operating leases by lessors. However, it is unlikely that this would occur very frequently. Inconsistent capitalization of financing-type leases was also eliminated by SFAS 13. It will be recalled that APBs 5, 7, and 10 created the potential for inconsistency.

Some asymmetry still exists between lessor and lessee accounting with respect to the choice of interest rate for calculating the capitalized value of leases. The lessor uses the implicit rate, which equates minimum lease payments plus unguaranteed residual value in excess of any guaranteed amounts with the sales price of the asset less any applicable investment tax credit. The lessee uses the lower of its incremental borrowing rate or the lessor's implicit rate (if it is obtainable), and only the guaranteed residual value is used. As a result, it is possible for the same lease to be measured differently in the financial statements of lessees and lessors. This disparity is justified on the grounds of conservatism since a lower interest rate will increase the amount of the capitalized lease obligation. It can also be defended on the grounds that each party may not have the same interest rates, owing to the different risks involved. Different residual values can also be justified because they represent different values to the lessor and lessee.

An area of apparent inconsistency in lessor accounting concerns initial *direct lease costs*, costs incurred in arranging the lease. SFAS 13 requires expensing of initial direct lease costs if the lease is a sales type. However, for financing-type leases, these costs are amortized over the lease term indirectly through the effective interest method.[24] The justification is that these costs are best matched against interest revenue in the case of financing-type leases because the lessor earns revenue from lease financing. On the other hand, with a sales-type lease,

---

[24] SFAS 13, para 18b, as amended by SFAS 98.

the costs are considered to be selling costs attributable to the arranging of debt finance. The costs are considered necessary to make the sale. This is another example of finite uniformity, in which the same costs are treated differently due to different circumstances. In this case the circumstances have to do with the nature of the lessor's operations and the classification of initial direct lease costs as either selling costs or as reductions of future interest revenue.

Measurement of capitalized leases for lessors is specified in SFAS 13. The first step is to calculate the implicit interest rate in the lease: the rate of interest that equates minimum lease payments with the asset's fair market value at lease inception, reduced for any lessor investment tax credit. The minimum lease payments are defined as the sum of future rentals (less any amounts for executory costs paid by the lessor), plus amounts to be paid under bargain option purchases, plus penalty payment for nonrenewal if renewal is unlikely, plus guaranteed residual value if the asset reverts to the lessor, plus any unguaranteed residual value. The fair market value of the leased asset would normally be the cash selling price for both sales-type and financing-type leases. Minimum lease payments receivable plus unguaranteed residual value are recognized at the gross amount, and a contra-account is created to recognize unearned interest. The net balance represents the present value of minimum lease payments receivable. Unearned interest is recognized each period, as the interest component is separated from the lease payment through the effective interest method. Lessor accounting for a financing-type lease is illustrated in Exhibit 17–4.

The same procedures are used with a sales-type lease to account for the financing aspect of the lease. The present value of minimum lease payments receivable is computed and recognized in the balance sheet. Payments are separated into principal and interest components. However, in addition, revenue is recognized in an amount equal to the fair market value of the asset at lease inception. Normally this would be the cash selling price. The cost of the leased asset is recognized as cost of goods sold. So gross profit on the sales-type lease is recognized in addition to the present value of minimum lease payments receivable and interest revenue on lease payments.

Initial direct lease contract costs are treated differently depending on the type of lease. They are expensed immediately if a lease is a sales type. The rationale is that the costs represent selling costs, rather than financing costs. If a lease is a financing type, the costs are added to the lease payments receivable, and a new implicit interest rate must be calculated that will recognize the remaining unearned interest using the effective interest method. This latter procedure is illustrated in Exhibit 17–5.

For all noncapitalized leases, the lessor must disclose the cost and book value of leased property (the assets are still recorded in the lessor's balance sheet if they are operating leases). Other supplemental disclosures required of lessors are the same required of lessees and reflect the reciprocal nature of capitalized lease contracts. These are minimum future rentals from noncancellable leases, in aggregate and for each of the five succeeding years, and contingent rental income as it is recognized.

EXHIBIT 17–4
Financing-Type Lease

Assume the following:
1. Fair market value at lease inception is $131,540.53.
2. Lease payments are $50,000, at the end of each of the next three years, and include $2,000 for executory costs.
3. Estimated residual value is $13,000, of which $5,000 is guaranteed by the lessee.
4. There are no significant initial direct lease costs.

Step 1—Calculate implicit interest rate.

Fair Market Value = Present Value of (minimum lease payments exclusive of executory costs, guaranteed residual value, and unguaranteed residual value)

$$\$131,540.53 = \frac{\$48,000}{(1 + i)^1} + \frac{\$48,000}{(1 + i)^2} + \frac{(\$48,000 + \$5,000 + \$8,000)}{(1 + i)^3}$$

$$i = .09$$

Step 2—Record gross amounts of minimum lease payments exclusive of executory costs, guaranteed and unguaranteed residual value, and the unearned interest calculated by the implicit rate.

Lease Payments Receivable	157,000.00	
Unearned Interest		25,459.47
Cash		131,540.53

To record asset payment and capital lease

Step 3—Record yearly interest revenue and lease payments.

Year 1

Cash	48,000	
Lease Payments Receivable		48,000
ªUnearned Interest	11,838.65	
Interest Revenue		11,838.65

Year 2

Cash	48,000	
Lease Payments Receivable		48,000
ªUnearned Interest	8,584.13	
Interest Revenue		8,584.13

Year 3

Cash	48,000	
Lease Payments Receivable		48,000
ªUnearned Interest	5,036.69	
Interest Revenue		5,036.69

ªSee Schedule below.

(continued)

EXHIBIT 17–4
(continued)

Year 3

Asset	13,000	
Lease Payment Receivable		13,000

Implicit Principal Repayments Schedule

	Beginning Net Lease Investment (Lease payments receivable less unearned interest)	Payment	Interest	Principal	Net Lease Investment Ending Unearned Interest	Net Lease Investment Ending Lease Payment Receivable
Year 1	$131,540.53	$48,000	$11,838.65	$36,161.35	$13,620.82	$109,000
Year 2	$ 95,379.18	$48,000	$ 8,584.13	$39,415.87	$ 5,036.69	$ 61,000
Year 3	$ 55,963.31	$48,000	$ 5,036.69	$42,963.31	-0-	$ 13,000

The FASB has issued a number of amendments and interpretations to SFAS 13, all of which are concerned with technical and specific issues.[25] In general, these additional rules have clarified the implementation of lease capitalization arising from complex terms in lease contracts. These additional rules are not reviewed since they pertain to narrower technical issues rather than general standards.[26]

SALE AND LEASEBACK

A sale and leaseback occurs when the owner of an asset legally sells it and enters into a lease agreement to lease the asset back. The lessor (new legal owner) and lessee (original legal owner) both use the standard criteria for classifying such a lease as operating or capital. A principle was established in APB 5 that no immediate recognition should be given to any book gains or losses that the lessee might record in such a transaction. The general rule was that any gain or loss should be amortized by the lessee as an adjustment of the lease rental if the lease is an operating lease and as an adjustment of lease depreciation if the lease is capitalized. The deferred gain or loss was reported in the balance sheet as a deferred credit or charge, respectively. One exception to this rule was that a loss was recognized if the asset's book value exceeded the fair market value at the time of the sale-leaseback. This, however, is nothing more than the application

---

[25] Other standards include SFASs 17, 22, 23, 26, 27, 28, and 29. These have been compiled in a single publication (FASB, 1980). A number of technical bulletins related to leases have been issued since 1980, but only two SFASs, 91 and 98.

[26] For example, see Means and Kazinski (1987) for an inconsistency in SFAS 91 in the handling of initial direct costs in financing-type leases. This was subsequently corrected in para. 22, item i of SFAS 98.

EXHIBIT 17–5
Financing-Type Lease with Initial Direct Costs

Assume the same facts as in Exhibit 17–4, except that initial direct lease costs of $1,500 are incurred. The following entry would be made in Year 1:

Lease Payments Receivable	1,500	
Cash		1,500

It is then necessary to calculate a new interest rate using the effective interest method:

$$133,040.53 = \frac{48,000}{(1 + i)^1} + \frac{48,000}{(1 + i)^2} + \frac{(48,000 + 5,000 + 8,000)}{(1 + i)^3}$$

By interpolation, $i = .08395$.

Revised Principal Repayment Schedule

				Net Lease Investment	
Beginning Net Lease Investment	Payment	Interest	Principal	Ending Unearned Interest	Ending Lease Payments Receivable
Year 1 $133,040.53	$48,000	$11,168.75	$36,831.25	$12,790.72	$109,000.00
Year 2 $ 96,209.28	$48,000	$ 8,076.77	$39,923.23	$ 4,713.95	$ 61,000.00
Year 3 $ 56,286.05	$48,000	$ 4,713.95[a]	$43,286.05	-0-	$ 13,000.00

---

[a] Includes adjustment for rounding error due to approximation of the effective interest rate.

---

of conventional accounting conservatism through the lower-of-cost-or-market rule.

The reason for not recognizing a gain or loss is that the sale and leaseback are considered to be one transaction rather than two. Any book gains or losses therefore arise artificially from the accounting necessity of treating the transaction as having two separate parts. Since the lessee has the same asset as before (but leasing rather than owning), it is argued that no gain or loss should be recognized. To recognize such a gain or loss would be the virtual equivalent of selling something to yourself and recognizing a gain or loss on the transaction. This approach was retained in SFAS 13. If a lease is an operating lease, the deferred gain or loss is recognized proportionally to lease payments. If the lease is capitalized, the deferred gain or loss is recognized proportionally to lease depreciation. An example of a sale and leaseback involving book gains and losses is illustrated in Exhibit 17–6 (page 530).

SFAS 13 did establish conditions under which a gain or loss might be immediately recognized in a sale and leaseback. These tests are concerned with leases in which the original owner retains usage of a substantially smaller part of the total asset. It is argued that there really are two separate and distinct transactions when this occurs because the lessee would no longer have the same asset as before.

EXHIBIT 17–6
Sale-Leaseback

Assume the same facts as in Exhibit 17–3. In addition assume that the lessee was the original asset owner and sold the asset for $100,000 to the new owner, who is now the lessor.[a] Assuming the asset had a book value of $79,000 to the original owner (now lessee), the following entries would be required by the lessee in addition to those illustrated in Exhibit 17–3.

1. At sale date:

Cash	100,000	
Asset (book value)		79,000
Deferred Gain on Sale–Leaseback		21,000

2. For each of the three years during the lease term:

Deferred Gain on Sale–Leaseback	7,000	
Depreciation–Lease		7,000

---

[a] Normally, any gain or loss would be the difference between the original owner's book value and selling price. In such cases, losses would always be recognized immediately and the gains deferred. However, it is possible for the sales price to be set at some amount other than market value. For example, suppose in this example the selling price was $85,000 and estimated market value was $75,000. The following entry would be made by the original owner at the time of sale.

Loss on Asset	4,000	
Cash	85,000	
Asset (book value)		79,000
Deferred Gain on Sale–Leaseback		10,000

The effect of this entry is to recognize a loss of $4,000 ($79,000–$75,000) for the adjustment to market value, and to defer the gain of $10,000 representing the payment in excess of market value by the buyer.

LEVERAGED LEASES

Leveraged leases are a special type of financing lease involving three parties instead of the usual two. The procedure is for a lessor to acquire an asset, which is then leased to the lessee. However, the lessor borrows some money for the transaction (usually in excess of 50 percent) from a third party (usually a group of lenders). This debt to the third party is nonrecourse but the lessor assigns a portion of the lease payments to cover the debt and interest payments. The debt to the third party may also be secured by the leased asset and sometimes by a guarantee from the lessee. At issue is whether this transaction should be accounted for as a conventional financing-type lease with an additional debt transaction, or as a unique transaction warranting separate treatment.

From a lessee's viewpoint, a leveraged lease is not any different from other leases. The more difficult question concerns the effect of a leveraged lease on the lessor. One possible effect is that a leveraged lease is the same as a conventional financing-type lease with an additional debt transaction between the lessor and the third party. The other possibility is to regard a leveraged lease as a unique type of lease warranting special rules applicable to its special circumstances. The FASB concluded in SFAS 13 that the financing-type lease plus debt transaction analogy was inadequate to report leveraged leases. It argued that reporting leveraged leases as two separate transactions, a financing lease and a loan, failed to portray the lessor's net investment in the lease. What is required by SFAS 13 is a complex procedure of reporting all aspects of a leveraged lease in a net amount as if it were one transaction. This represents another example of finite uniformity in which relevant circumstances determine the appropriate accounting procedures. The requirements are illustrated in SFAS 13, Appendix E.

ASSESSING SFAS 13

The long-standing criticism of lease accounting is that many leases are not being capitalized but should be. This is no less true under SFAS 13 than it was under ARB 38 or APB 5. An inherent weakness of the finite uniformity approach is that some accounting methods may be preferred by management over others. In these instances, companies will be motivated to manipulate the relevant circumstances in order to get the desired accounting result. With leases, lessees continue to believe that there are advantages to off-balance-sheet financing through leases. This will always motivate companies to try to defeat the capitalization tests of lease accounting standards.

It is not very difficult to structure a lease contract to defeat the four tests of SFAS 13 because the four tests are not stringent. A more challenging task, though, is to defeat lease capitalization tests for the lessee while satisfying them for the lessor. Lessors normally desire to capitalize leases and recognize sales revenue, but lessees prefer the effects of off-balance-sheet financing. One innovative method to accomplish both objectives is the use of third parties to guarantee residual values to the lessor: such a procedure reduces the lessee's obligation under test (4) of SFAS 13 and, if significant enough, could lead to noncapitalization. However, there is no effect on the lessor because the lessor's accounting deals with the estimated residual value in total. No distinction is made between guaranteed and unguaranteed residual value.

Whenever accounting policies force unwanted results on companies, there will be creative activity to circumvent the unpopular policy. This is certainly the case with lease accounting. Because of the existing "let's beat SFAS 13" attitude, a strong case can be made for rigid uniformity. One solution would be to capitalize all leases that exceed one year. This unambiguous policy would eliminate the game playing and would also eliminate the somewhat artificial distinction still being made between capital and operating leases. As has been indicated throughout the chapter, it is somewhat arbitrary where the line is drawn between capital and operating leases. Therefore, a rigid policy of capitalizing all leases is an arguable improvement because it eliminates both the arbitrariness of where the line is drawn and the motivation to circumvent the finite uniformity established in SFAS 13.

ECONOMIC CONSEQUENCES OF
LEASE CAPITALIZATION

From the viewpoint of a company preparing financial statements, there are at least two types of economic consequences of lease accounting. One is the costs of complying with lease capitalization. More detailed analyses will be required by a company and its auditor in classifying leases as operating and capital. Recall that in Chapter 8 we saw that finite uniformity always imposes a higher compliance cost than rigid uniformity. In addition, the accounting entries for each period will be more complicated if leases are capitalized. There has been no direct study of these types of costs; however, in 1973, one large company estimated it would cost $40,000 to install a lease capitalization system and $25,000 to $35,000 a year to operate it.[27]

The more critical concern has been whether lease capitalization might provide disincentives for leasing itself. From a lessee's perspective, leasing offered the possibility of off-balance-sheet financing for most leases prior to SFAS 13. A survey of lessees indicated that the effect on financial statements was a major reason for leasing.[28] Noncapitalization of leases improves debt ratios and accounting rate of return compared with a purchase/debt alternative. Some lessees also believed that noncapitalization of leases increased available capital because these leases do not affect borrowing restrictions in debt covenants and that the lower debt ratios which would be achieved by noncapitalization would result in better debt ratings and lower interest rates in the capital market. A study of pre-SFAS 13 lease accounting found that companies with high leverage levels were more likely to have reported their leases as operating rather than capital leases, which is consistent with the arguments above favoring off-balance-sheet financing.[29]

The argument against lease capitalization was presented to accounting policy makers in the following manner:

> The effects of treating leases as debt would extend beyond lessees to consumers and other parts of the economy. Increases in reported debt would tend to lead to an increase in interest rates and require an increased investment of equity capital requiring an even greater rate of return. This could contribute to inflationary pressures and act as a deterrent to investment in modernized or expanded plant and equipment.[30]

Neutrality tends to mitigate the preceding argument. Commenting on lease accounting, a former SEC chairman made these remarks:

> We recognize the usefulness of leases as a financing device. Economic objectives — including tax considerations — of two parties are frequently better satisfied by a lease arrangement than a purchase or sale.

---

[27] This evidence is anecdotal but was reported in Hawkins and Wehle (1973, p. 100).
[28] Hawkins and Wehle (1973).
[29] El-Gazzar, Lilien, and Pastena (1986).
[30] Committee on Corporate Reporting of the Financial Executives Institute (1971, p. 237).

> But leasing should not be made more attractive than it really is simply
> because of the way it is accounted for.[31]

It should not be the accounting per se that makes leasing attractive. If it is, the
arguments favoring leasing are specious.

The alleged advantages of off-balance-sheet financing have not been
entirely supported by research evidence. For example, a survey of analysts indicated that the debt implication of noncapitalized leases is factored into the
evaluation of companies.[32] In particular, the debt equivalent of leasing for lease-
intensive industries was very well understood by analysts, even prior to SFAS
13. The general feeling was that lessees were usually within reasonable debt
limits, even when lease effects were considered. So the survey evidence suggests
that analysts were not fooled by off-balance-sheet lease financing even though
company management seemed to believe otherwise. Consistent with these
views, there is empirical evidence to support the view of leases "as if" they are
debt equivalents in the pricing of stocks and bonds.[33]

The FASB commissioned a comprehensive research study of the economic and behavioral effects of SFAS 13.[34] One finding was that financial ratios
and accounting rate of return of companies showed the expected changes due
to increased lease capitalization, although the change was smaller than anticipated. It was suggested that SFAS 13 had less impact than anticipated because
pre-1977 leases did not have to be capitalized until 1980. This gave companies
time to restructure leases as operating and to alter their capital structures in
order to lessen the effects of capitalization on ratios. There was strong evidence
that this type of behavior occurred; it reflects a belief in the naïveté of the market. Yet analysts surveyed in the same study professed not to be fooled by lease
accounting differences (operating and capital) having no cash flow differences.
The sophisticated-user viewpoint is also supported by a capital market study
included in the assessment of SFAS 13 that showed no evidence of new information content in lease capitalization; that is, there was no abnormal security
price response to the lease capitalization requirement. This is consistent with
the efficient-markets hypothesis, particularly since similar information was required as footnote disclosure under APB 31 prior to SFAS 13. In other words,
the form of disclosure (footnote as in APB 31 or balance sheet as in SFAS 13) is
not as important as the existence of disclosure per se.

Two other capital market studies offer additional evidence on lease accounting. One found that APB 31 disclosure requirements caused prices of affected companies to drop.[35] This can be interpreted to mean that the new lease
disclosures of APB 31 had information content and that investors responded
negatively to the revelation of hidden debt through lease financing. Such a finding is not surprising since the debt equivalent of most leases was not reported
very well prior to APB 31. The second study found a negative price response

---

[31] Cook (1973).
[32] Hawkins and Wehle (1973).
[33] Abdel-khalik, Thompson, and Taylor (1978) and Bowman (1980).
[34] Abdel-khalik (1981).
[35] Ro (1978).

during the time of the FASB's public hearings on leases in late 1974.[36] It was argued that the negative price response may have been due to restrictive debt covenants that would have been violated if leases were capitalized. Such a situation was hypothesized to have possible adverse indirect cash flow consequences on the firm and its stockholders. This is an agency theory type of argument, and it does contradict survey evidence that analysts are not fooled by alternative accounting policies. The explanation may be that, prior to APB 31, analysts were really unaware of leases because there was very little reporting of them. But after APB 31 it mattered very little if the disclosures were made in footnotes or in the body of the balance sheet.

Another study evaluated the usefulness of lease capitalization in bankruptcy prediction.[37] Financial ratios, with and without lease capitalization, were compared to determine if the lease-adjusted ratios were better predictors. The study was made prior to both APB 31 and SFAS 13, so the effects of lease capitalization had to be approximated from rather limited footnote information. The results are interesting because they suggest that for bankruptcy prediction at least, lease capitalization had no significant effect on the usefulness of accounting information. This finding partly contradicts survey research indicating that users believe lease capitalization is useful in predicting future cash flows and assessing debt paying ability.[38]

Concerns about the adverse effects of lease capitalization seem to have been exaggerated, although the four-year phase-in period may have permitted companies to mitigate the anticipated adverse balance sheet effects. Management continues to believe that noncapitalization offers some advantage, though user surveys and one capital market study suggest that lease capitalization has had no adverse impact. Holding aside the possible impact of lease capitalization on debt covenants, it could be argued that it is irrelevant whether lease information is disclosed as a footnote or in the body of the balance sheet. However, one prominent academic observed that footnote disclosure can give the impression that accountants do not know how to account for leases so they absolve themselves of the problem through extensive disclosures.[39] Difficult accounting problems should not be dealt with through disclosure simply because it is expedient and less controversial. The mandate of standard-setting bodies exists because of their technical competency and expertise in deciding controversial accounting issues. That mandate could easily be revoked if they fail to demonstrate competence and resolve.

The ferment over leases remains quite strong with respect to the so-called standards-overload problem. In a survey of private companies, the FASB reports that SFAS 13 is by far the most objectionable accounting standard to owners and auditors of the private companies surveyed.[40] The FASB has also

---

[36] Pfeiffer (1980).
[37] Elam (1975).
[38] Abdel-khalik (1981).
[39] Anthony (1962).
[40] FASB (1983).

hinted at a comprehensive review of lease accounting from time to time, but so far this has not occurred.

SUMMARY

Lease accounting represents a classic example of the search for meaningful finite uniformity. Using a broad classification of leases as operating or capital, the search has taken the direction of defining the criteria for classification. This has led to an emphasis on economic substance rather than legal form. The substance of capital leases is argued to be a purchase equivalent with debt financing for the lessee. For the lessor, a capital lease is analogous to a sale with vendor financing if it is a sale-type lease, and to a loan equivalent if it is a financing-type lease. It is somewhat arbitrary where the line is drawn between operating and capital leases. Over time, the criteria have changed, which clearly reflects the subjective nature of the criteria and the difficulty in achieving finite uniformity.

Because the distinction between operating and capital leases is somewhat arbitrary, the economic consequences of lease capitalization are very important in evaluating lease accounting standards. Management attitudes show a belief in the market's naïveté — specifically, the advantages of off-balance-sheet financing. The evidence, however, supports the supposition that users are sophisticated with respect to lease reporting and that they are not fooled by lease accounting differences, at least after APB 31. Finally, there is survey and capital market research to support the position that the reporting of capital leases is useful and relevant. However, a strong case can be made for capitalizing all leases extending beyond one year. This type of rigid uniformity would eliminate the attempts to circumvent SFAS 13.

QUESTIONS

1. What is the argument for finite uniformity in accounting for leases? Why is finite uniformity difficult to achieve? Explain what the relevant circumstances are in accounting for different types of leases.
2. Why is the conveyancing aspect of leases emphasized in capital leases and the contractual element in operating leases?
3. What are the similarities and differences between leases and other means of property acquisition? How can these similarities and differences be reported in the financial statements?
4. Is the executory nature of lease contracts important in assessing lease accounting? How have leases been interpreted? Why might noncancellability override the executory nature?
5. Review the evolution of capitalization criteria in lease accounting standards. Why did APB 5 have little impact? What impact has SFAS 13 had?

Has there been an underlying theme in the development of lease accounting?

6. It has been suggested that footnote disclosure in lieu of capitalization may give the impression that accountants and policy-making bodies do not know how to account for leases. Evaluate this comment.

7. Does it matter if capital leases are reported in a footnote or in the body of the balance sheet? What research evidence exists to help evaluate this question?

8. Does symmetry exist between lessors and lessees under SFAS 13? Should symmetry be a goal of lease accounting?

9. How is representational faithfulness achieved in the capitalization requirements of SFAS 13?

10. Is there a measurement reliability (verifiability) problem with lease capitalization?

11. Evaluate the manner in which initial direct lease costs are accounted for under SFAS 13.

12. Why is sale–leaseback considered different from other leases? Explain the rationale for the deferral of gains or losses arising from a sale–leaseback.

13. Why was there some reason to expect negative economic consequences arising from lease capitalization? What is the role of neutrality in such a situation? What has been the response based on research findings to date?

14. Does the reporting of capital leases appear to have value to users of financial statements? Why are there costs of reporting capital leases?

15. What considerations may have motivated the FASB to grant a four-year transitional period in capitalizing pre-1977 leases meeting the capitalization tests of SFAS 13? What other political behavior is evident in the evolution of lease accounting?

CASES AND PROBLEMS

1. The following information was taken from The Kroger Co. 1977 annual report. As indicated in the notes, leases entered into prior to 1977 were not immediately capitalized. SFAS 13 permitted this deferral until 1980. Evaluate the impact of SFAS 13 on the balance sheet of The Kroger Co. if the pre-1977 leases had been capitalized.

	1977	1976
Property, Plant and Equipment		
Land	$ 14,189,891	$ 14,894,621
Buildings	80,476,555	80,464,968
Equipment	509,969,465	463,184,072
Leaseholds and leasehold improvements	116,939,019	159,936,945
Leased property under capital leases	3,403,527	
Total	$774,978,457	$718,480,606

	1977	1976
Allowance for depreciation and amortization	321,710,959	296,363,852
Property, plant and equipment, net	$453,267,498	$422,116,754
Current Liabilities		
Current portion of long-term debt	$ 5,805,154	$ 5,381,265
Notes payable		8,900,000
Accounts payable	343,789,464	289,654,324
Accrued expenses	149,615,964	140,839,659
Accrued federal income and other taxes	37,569,120	32,336,344
Current portion of unredeemed trading stamps	26,926,973	26,985,895
Current portion of obligations under capital leases	62,853	
Total current liabilities	$563,769,528	$504,097,487
Other Liabilities		
Long-term debt	$215,578,291	$232,982,894
Unredeemed trading stamps	26,926,973	216,985,895
Deferred federal income taxes	79,290,159	69,401,864
Employees' benefit fund	31,934,419	34,106,565
Obligations under capital leases	3,313,919	
Total other liabilities	$357,043,761	$363,477,218

Lease arrangements entered into prior to 1977 have been accounted for as operating leases. Had such leases been accounted for in accordance with Statement of Financial Accounting Standards No. 13, the following amounts of assets and liabilities would have been recorded as of the dates indicated:

	Dec. 31, 1977	Jan. 1, 1977
Total capital leases, net of accumulated, amortization	$101,057,000	$105,894,000
Total obligations under capital leases	$103,508,000	$108,010,000

Capitalization of lease arrangements entered into prior to 1977, in accordance with Statement of Financial Accounting Standards No. 13, would have reduced net earnings by an estimated $335,000 for the year ended December 31, 1977, and by an estimated $235,000 for the year ended January 1, 1977.

Source: Accounting Trends and Techniques (American Institutes of Certified Public Accountants, 1978), p. 203.

2. Presented below is a summary of lease accounting for selected years as reported in *Accounting Trends and Techniques:*

Year	Both Capital and Operating Leases Reported	All Operating Leases	All Capital Leases	No Lease Reported	Total Companies
1965	26	266	0	308	600
1968	87	238	0	275	600
1971	89	247	52	212	600
1974	130	314	45	111	600
1977	274	194	59	73	600
1980	357	107	83	53	600
1984	369	110	63	58	600

On the basis of the numbers of companies in each category, what can you determine about the effect of APB 5, APB 7, APB 31, and SFAS 13 on financial statements? Support your analysis by careful reference to specific years.

3. Assume the following facts concerning a sales-type lease:

The lease term is three years and qualifies as a capital lease for both lessor and lessee. The asset reverts to the lessor at the end of the lease term. Assume straight-line depreciation by the lessee.

Payments are $50,000 at the beginning of each year, plus a guaranteed residual value of $10,000 at the end of the lease term. The lessor estimates a total residual value of $15,000. Lease payments include $4,000 for executory costs under a maintenance agreement.

Initial direct costs associated with the lease are $2,700.

Cash sales price of the asset is $137,102.50. Lessor's manufacturing cost is $100,000.

The lessee does not know the lessor's implicit rate, but its own incremental borrowing rate is 11 percent.

Required:

(a) Prepare the accounting entries for both lessor and lessee for the three years. What happens in Year 3 if residual value is only $8,000?

(b) Assume the same facts as above except that the asset is first sold to a finance company, which then leases the asset to the lessee. Prepare the required entries in all three years for lessor and lessee.

(c) Evaluate the differences between requirements (a) and (b) as well as the differences between lessor and lessee.

4. One of the four capitalization tests of SFAS 13 is that the lease term is 75 percent or more of the asset's remaining economic life. *Lease term* is defined as follows in SFAS 13 (as amended by SFAS 98, para. 22a):

The fixed noncancelable term of the lease plus (i) all periods, if any, covered by *bargain renewal options*, (ii) all periods, if any, for which failure to renew the lease imposes a penalty on the lessee in an amount such that renewal appears, at the *inception of the lease*, to be reasonably assured, (iii) all periods, if any, covered by ordinary renewal options during which a guarantee by the lessee of the lessor's debt related to the leased property is expected to be in effect, (iv) all periods, if any, covered by ordinary renewal options preceding the date as of which a *bargain purchase option* is exercisable, and (v) all periods, if any, representing *renewals or extensions* of the lease at the lessor's option; however, in no case shall the lease term extend beyond the date a *bargain purchase option* becomes exercisable. A lease which is cancelable (i) only upon the occurrence of some remote contingency, (ii) only with the permission of the lessor, (iii) only if the lessee enters into a new lease with the same lessor, or (iv) only upon payment by the lessee of a penalty in an amount such that continuation of the lease appears, at *inception*, reasonably assured shall be considered "noncancelable" for purposes of this definition.

Required:
How can this test be circumvented through either the structuring of the lease contract or interpretation of the test? What are other ways in which lease capitalization could be avoided through the structuring of lease terms or interpretation of the tests? What problem does this exercise illustrate?

5. Presented below are examples of reporting operating leases under APB 31 for Crane Co. and SFAS 13 for The American Ship Building Company, respectively.

Crane Co.

The Company and subsidiaries lease buildings and equipment under noncancelable leases providing for annual rentals as follows:

	Total	Operating Leases Machinery and Buildings	Operating Leases Machinery and Equipment	Financing Leases Machinery and Buildings	Financing Leases Machinery and Equipment
			(in thousands)		
1975	$ 7,887	$1,742	$1,441	$ 813	$ 3,891
1976	6,990	1,497	715	1,099	3,679
1977	6,187	1,260	232	1,274	3,421
1978	5,497	1,037	42	1,338	3,080
1979	5,342	860	9	1,513	2,960
1980–84	22,767	3,042	6	6,964	12,755
1985–89	20,052	1,593	—	5,872	12,587
1990–94	14,229	21	—	3,109	11,099
1995–beyond	4,306	—	—	2,559	1,747

The above amounts have been reduced for rental income from noncancelable subleases by approximately $1,209,000 in 1975 and lesser amounts thereafter (total reduction $4,166,000).

Certain of the leases may be renewed for periods of from 3 to 20 years and provide for an option to purchase or for annual rental payments of minimal amounts.

The estimated present values of the net fixed minimum rental commitments for all noncancelable financing leases, net of noncancelable subleases, are as follows:

	December 31	
	1974	*1973*
	(in thousands)	
Buildings	$15,617	$16,268
Machinery and equipment	31,626	31,797
Subleases	(2,108)	(2,807)
Net present value	$45,135	$45,258

The weighted average interest rate used in the computation was 6¼ percent and ranged from 4½ percent to 14½ percent.

If all financing leases had been capitalized, net income for the years ended December 31, 1974 and 1973 would not have been significantly affected.

The American Ship Building Company

Operating Leases

The Company is committed under noncancelable operating leases involving certain facilities and equipment. A major operating lease requires contingent rentals, based upon certain revenues of Tampa Shipyards, Incorporated. The maximum annual contingent rentals is limited by the lease to $675,000. Total rent expense incurred under noncancelable operating leases is as follows:

	1985	*1984*	*1983*
	(amounts in thousands)		
Minimum rentals	$2,079	$1,847	$ 896
Contingent rentals	198	151	294
	$2,277	$1,998	$1,190

Future minimum rental commitments under these operating leases are as follows:

Fiscal Year	*Amounts (in thousands)*
1986	$ 1,802
1987	703
1988	611
1989	492
1990	492
Later Years	15,777
	$19,877

Required:
Compare the informativeness of the two sets of disclosures and evaluate
SFAS 13 with respect to the reporting of noncapitalized operating leases.

6. SFAS 98 containing some amendments to SFAS 13 passed by a 4–3 vote.
The following dissent to the opinion was made:

> Messrs. Beresford, Lauver, and Swieringa dissent because this Statement pre-
> scribes different accounting for certain sale–leaseback transactions based on a
> distinction between active (as defined) and other use of leased property by a
> seller–lessee. That distinction is without economic substance and is used to ar-
> bitrarily preclude sale–leaseback accounting when a seller–lessee subleases the
> leased property.
>
> Paragraph 48 acknowledges that a leaseback is a form of continuing involve-
> ment with leased property but argues that the form of that involvement is dif-
> ferent if the seller–lessee intends to sublease that property. In a sale–leaseback
> transaction, the seller–lessee has exchanged ownership rights for lease rights,
> and the rights to use the leased property and to benefit from that use are the
> same regardless of how that property is used. Moreover, any guarantee of the
> cash flows related to the leased property is lodged in the lease contract and is
> not altered by what the seller–lessee does with that property.
>
> An objective of financial reporting is to achieve greater comparability of ac-
> counting information. Paragraph 119 of FASB Concepts Statement No. 2,
> *Qualitative Characteristics of Accounting Information,* states that this objective "is
> not to be attained by making unlike things look alike any more than by making
> like things look different. The moral is that in seeking comparability accoun-
> tants must not disguise real differences nor create false differences."
>
> Messrs. Beresford, Lauver, and Swieringa believe that this Statement makes
> like things look different by prescribing different accounting for certain sale–
> leaseback transactions based on the distinction between active and other use of
> leased property, a distinction not relevant to the accounting. Because that dis-
> tinction arbitrarily limits the extent to which sale–leaseback accounting is per-
> mitted, the effects of accounting for identical sale–leaseback transactions will be
> different.

The majority's position was expanded upon in paragraph 48 of SFAS 98
in the section on "Basis for Conclusions":

> **48.** Some respondents to the Exposure Draft noted that the nature of the con-
> tinuing involvement associated with a normal leaseback does not change be-
> cause of the seller–lessee's intent to occupy the property. The Board acknowl-
> edges that the leaseback is a form of continuing involvement with the property
> that serves as support for the buyer–lessor's investment.
>
> Accordingly, the Board believes that transactions accounted for as sales
> should be limited when a sale–leaseback of property exists; otherwise, the effec-
> tiveness of paragraph 28 of Statement 66 would be compromised. Occupancy
> of the property by the seller–lessee provides a basis for distinguishing among
> sale–leaseback transactions involving real estate, including real estate with
> equipment.
>
> The Board believes that the intent to sublease the property represents a dif-
> ferent form of continuing involvement than does the intent to occupy and use

the property in the seller–lessee's trade or business. When the property is sub-leased, the form and consequences of the seller – lessee's continuing involve-ment are equivalent to those of a real estate investor or developer whose ulti-mate source, timing, and amount of cash flows from the use of the property are different from those realized by a tenant. Based on those differences, the Board decided to reaffirm the Exposure Draft's provision to allow sale–leaseback ac-counting when the seller–lessee occupies the leased property.

The position of both the majority and the dissenters center on issues of uniformity and comparability.

Required:
Using the perspective on uniformity developed in Chapter 8, analyze the rigid versus finite uniformity approach to the distinction between the two positions.

BIBLIOGRAPHY OF REFERENCED WORKS

Abdel-khalik, A. Rashad (1981). *The Economic Effects on Lessees of FASB Statement No. 13, Accounting for Leases* (FASB).

Abdel-khalik, A. Rashad, Robert B. Thompson, and Robert E. Taylor (1978). "The Impact of Reporting Leases off the Balance Sheet on Bond Risk Premiums: Two Exploratory Studies," *Economic Consequences of Financial Accounting Standards* (FASB), pp. 103–155.

Accounting Principles Board (1954). "Reporting of Leases in the Financial Statements of Lessee," *APB Opinion No. 5* (AICPA).

——— (1966a). "Accounting for Leases in Financial Statements of Lessors," *APB Opinion No. 7* (AICPA).

——— (1966b). "Omnibus Opinion," *APB Opinion No. 10* (AICPA).

——— (1971). "Interest on Receivables and Payables," *APB Opinion No. 21* (AICPA).

——— (1972). "Accounting for Lease Transactions by Manufacturer or Dealer Lessors," *APB Opinion No. 27* (AICPA).

——— (1973). "Disclosure of Lease Commitments by Lessees," *APB Opinion No. 31* (AICPA).

Alvin, Gerald (1970). "Resolving the Inconsistency in Accounting for Leases," *The New York Certified Public Accountant* (March 1970), pp. 223–230.

Anthony, Robert N. (1962). Letter to Weldon Powell, Chairman of the Accounting Prin-ciples Board, 25 October 1962. Cited in *Financial Accounting Standards Board* (1974, p. 39).

Bowman, Robert G. (1980). "The Debt Equivalence of Leases: An Empirical Investigation," *The Accounting Review* (April 1980), pp. 237–253.

Committee on Accounting Procedure (1949). "Disclosure of Long-Term Leases in Financial Statements of Lessees," *ARB No. 38* (AICPA).

——— (1953). "Restatement and Revision of Accounting Research Bulletins," *ARB No. 43* (AICPA).

Committee on Corporate Reporting of the Financial Executives Institute (1971). Cited in *Proceedings of the Accounting Principles Board of the American Institute of Certified Public Accountants: Public Hearing on Leases* (AICPA).

Cook, Donald C. (1963). "The Case Against Capitalizing Leases," *Harvard Business Review* (January–February 1963), pp. 145–162.

Cook, G. Bradford (1973). "The Commission and the Regulation of Public Utilities" (Paper presented to the Financial Forum of the American Gas Association, Monterey, CA, 1974), cited in *Financial Accounting Standards Board* (1974, p. 38).

Elam, Rick (1975). "The Effect of Lease Data on the Predictive Ability of Financial Ratios," *The Accounting Review* (January 1975), pp. 25–43.

El-Gazzar, Samir, Steve Lilien, and Victor Pastena (1986). "Accounting for Leases by Lessees," *Journal of Accounting and Economics* (October 1986), pp. 217–237.

Financial Accounting Standards Board (1974). *FASB Discussion Memorandum: An Analysis of Issues Related to Accounting for Leases* (FASB).

—— (1976). "Accounting for Leases," *Statement of Financial Accounting Standards No. 13* (FASB).

—— (1980). *Accounting for Leases* (FASB).

—— (1983). *Financial Reporting by Privately Owned Companies: Summary of Responses to FASB Invitation to Comment* (FASB).

—— (1985). "Elements of Financial Statements," *Statement of Financial Accounting Concepts No. 6* (FASB).

Hawkins, David (1970). "Objectives, Not Rules, for Lease Accounting," *Financial Executive* (November 1970), pp. 30–38.

Hawkins, David M., and Mary M. Wehle (1973). *Accounting for Leases* (Research Foundation of Financial Executives Institute, 1973).

Means, Kathryn M. and Paul M. Kazinski (1987). "SFAS 91: New Dilemmas," *Accounting Horizons* (December 1987), pp. 63–67.

Myers, John H. (1962). "Reporting of Leases in Financial Statements," *Accounting Research Study No. 4* (AICPA).

Pfeiffer, G. (1980). "The Economic Effects of Accounting Policy Regulation; Evidence on the Lease Accounting Issue." (Ph.D. diss., Cornell University).

Ro, Byung T. (1978). "The Disclosure of Capitalized Lease Information and Stock Prices," *Journal of Accounting Research* (Autumn 1978), pp. 315–340.

Securities and Exchange Commission (1972). "Reporting Leases in Financial Statements of Lessees," *Accounting Series Release No. 132* (SEC).

—— (1973). "Notice of Adoption of Amendments to Regulation S-X Requiring Improved Disclosure of Leases," *Accounting Series Release No. 147* (SEC).

Zises, Alvin (1973). "The Pseudo-Lease — Trap and Time Bomb," *Financial Executive* (August 1973), pp. 20–25.

ADDITIONAL READINGS

Bevis, Herman W. (1965). "Reporting of Leases: Agreement and Disagreement," *Journal of Accountancy* (April 1965), pp. 27–28.

Clay, Raymond J., and William W. Holder (1977). "A Practitioner's Guide to Accounting for Leases," *Journal of Accountancy* (August 1977), pp. 61–68.

Coughlan, John W. (1980). "Regulation, Rents and Residuals," *Journal of Accountancy* (February 1980), pp. 58–66.

Dieter, Richard (1979). "Is Lessee Accounting Working?" *The CPA Journal* (August 1979), pp. 13–19.

Finnerty, Joseph F., Rick N. Fitzsimmons, and Thomas W. Oliver (1980). "Lease Capitalization and Systematic Risk," *The Accounting Review* (October 1980), pp. 631–639.

Goodman, Hortense, and Leonard Lorensen (1978). *Illustrations of Accounting for Leases: A Survey of the Application of FASB Statement No. 13* (AICPA).

Ingberman, Monroe, Joshua Ronen, and George H. Sorter (1979). "How Lease Capitalization Under FASB Statement No. 13 Will Affect Financial Ratios," *Financial Analysts Journal* (January–February 1979), pp. 28–31.

Ma, Ronald (1972). "Accounting for Long-Term Leases," *Abacus* (June 1972), pp. 21–34.

Nelson, A. Tom (1963). "Capitalizing Leases – The Effect on Financial Ratios," *Journal of Accountancy* (July 1963), pp. 49–58.

Rappaport, Alfred (1965). "Lease Capitalization and the Transaction Concept," *The Accounting Review* (April 1965), pp. 373–376.

Richardson, A. W. (1985). "The Measurement of the Current Portion of Long-Term Lease Obligations – Some Evidence from Practice," *The Accounting Review* (October 1985), pp. 744–752.

Shanno, David F., and Roman L. Weil (1976). "The Separate Phases Method of Accounting for Leveraged Leases: Some Properties of the Allocating Rate and an Algorithm for Finding It," *Journal of Accounting Research* (Autumn 1976), pp. 348–356.

Shillinglaw, Gordon (1958). "Leasing and Financial Statements," *The Accounting Review* (October 1958), pp. 581–592.

Vatter, William J. (1966). "Accounting for Leases," *Journal of Accounting Research* (Autumn 1966), pp. 133–148.

Wilkins, Trevor, and Ian Zimmer (1983). "The Effect of Leasing and Different Methods of Accounting for Leases on Credit Evaluations," *The Accounting Review* (October 1983), pp. 749–764.

INTERCORPORATE EQUITY INVESTMENTS

ACCOUNTING STANDARDS FOR intercorporate equity investments represent the most extensive application of finite uniformity in accounting practice. The basic framework is set out in Exhibit 18–1 (page 546). There are three ways to report on intercorporate equity investments: (1) consolidated reporting as if the two separate legal entities are one accounting entity using either the purchase or pooling method (as appropriate), (2) nonconsolidation using the equity method of accounting, and (3) nonconsolidation using the cost method of accounting. We discuss the relevant circumstances that determine the method of reporting in the first section of the chapter, and then go into detail on each of the methods. Finally, we examine the question of what the reporting entity is. This question is central to an unresolved FASB project concerning the definition of the reporting entity and to assessing the role of consolidated financial statements in financial reporting.

RELEVANT CIRCUMSTANCES

The relevant circumstances that justify differential accounting for intercorporate equity investments depend on the level of influence held by the investor. In a seminal study, Moonitz evaluated several criteria, such as percentage of voting stock owned, controlling influence on the board of directors, and operating or managerial control.[1] He concluded that no one dimension can be used to determine the level of investor influence that exists. Not surprisingly, however, standard-setting bodies have focused on a single quantitative criterion, percent-

---

[1] Moonitz (1944, pp. 22–44).

EXHIBIT 18–1
Finite Uniformity for Intercorporate Equity Investments

Ownership of Voting Stock	Accounting Method
>50%	Consolidate per ARB 51 (as amended by SFAS 94), APB 16, and APB 17. For 90 percent- to 100 percent-owned subsidiaries, relevant circumstances require either purchase or pooling accounting as appropriate per APB 16.
*20% to 50%	Equity accounting per APB 18.
<*20%	Cost method per SFAS 12. Different rules apply for "current" and "noncurrent" investments.

*20% is only a guideline, not a rigid rule.

---

age of voting stock owned, as the basis for evaluating the level of influence. For convenience, we shall refer to this as *level of control.*

Three levels of control have been defined along with three distinctly different reporting methods for each level. Traditionally, outright control of the majority of voting stock has been the criterion for consolidated reporting. In fact, the SEC prohibits consolidation of a subsidiary company unless majority ownership exists. ARB 51 took a more cautious view that majority ownership per se did not indicate control if ownership were temporary or if for some reason control did not reside with the majority owner. In addition, ARB 51 specifically permitted separate reporting for *heterogeneous* subsidiaries instead of consolidation; and ARB 43, Chapter 12, permitted a similar exception for foreign subsidiaries. The rationale for these two exclusions was based on the argument that (1) a heterogeneous subsidiary — such as a finance company subsidiary of a manufacturing firm (General Motors Acceptance Corporation and General Motors, for example) — would only distort the reporting of the main operations of the consolidated entity; and (2) in the case of foreign operations, that most foreign assets are in some degree of jeopardy as far as their ultimate realization by U.S. owners is concerned. These exceptions represented a further finite uniformity based on the relevant circumstances of homogeneity versus heterogeneity of operations and whether a domestic or foreign subsidiary is involved. *Accounting Trends and Techniques* has reported that in recent years only about 70 percent of firms consolidated all subsidiaries.[2]

The FASB, in SFAS 94 rejected these exclusionary arguments and now requires *all* majority-owned companies to be consolidated except when control is only temporary or if the majority owner does not have effective control. The effect of SFAS 94 is to bring large amounts of debt onto the consolidated balance sheet that had previously been transferred to the subsidiary, an important

---

[2] American Institute of Certified Public Accountants (1988).

economic consequence.[3] SFAS 94 does not elaborate on the issue of temporary control, but it says that noncontrol by a majority owner may occur if the subsidiary is in legal reorganization or bankruptcy, or operates under foreign exchange restrictions or other governmentally imposed uncertainties that are so substantial as to cast doubt on the owner's ability to exercise control. In defense of SFAS 94, the FASB asserts that investors of a parent company are really investing in a group of affiliated companies as a whole, that consolidated statements are thus more relevant in reporting on the group, and that the omission of certain subsidiaries therefore fails to faithfully represent (representational faithfulness) the group of affiliated companies as a whole.[4] We return to these issues at the end of the chapter when examining the problem of defining the reporting entity.

For less-than-majority-owned companies, the appropriate reporting is either the equity method or the cost method. The relevant circumstance is whether the investor can exercise *significant influence* over operating and financial policies. In other words, effective control leads to consolidated reporting as if the two companies were one separate entity. But a lesser level of control can also exist in which there is significant influence but not effective control. In APB 18 it was presumed that ownership of 20 percent to 50 percent of voting stock was prima facie evidence of the ability to exercise significant influence. However, FASB Interpretation No. 35 clarified that the relevant circumstance is the ability to exercise significant influence and that the 20 percent ownership level is only a guideline, not a hard and fast rule. If there is no significant influence, then the cost method of accounting is required (using the lower-of-cost-or-market rule of SFAS 12 for marketable securities).

CONSOLIDATION

Consolidated reporting is a technique in which two or more entities are reported as if they are one common accounting entity. This is also called a *business combination*. In order to prepare consolidated financial statements, separate sets of individual entity accounting records must be combined and certain other adjustments made to arrive at the consolidated totals. Adjustment procedures are covered at length in advanced financial accounting textbooks. The focus here is on the conceptual foundation of accounting for business combinations, not on the consolidation adjustment procedures themselves.

The central accounting issue in a business combination is the valuation of the assets and liabilities of the separate entities being combined for reporting

---

[3] See Heian and Thies (1989) for an empirical analysis.

[4] It should be noted that SFAS 94 was silent on how to account for unconsolidated majority-owned companies where control is temporary or control is effectively lacking. SFAS 94, para. 11, does continue the general disclosure requirement of APB 18 in which summarized balance sheet and income statement data are to be disclosed for material, unconsolidated subsidiaries.

purposes. In a 1976 discussion memorandum, the FASB outlined three possible methods of accounting. One is to use the book values of the combining entities. This method is called *pooling of interests accounting.* A second method assumes that one entity, the parent company, "purchases" another entity, the subsidiary company. The assets and liabilities of the subsidiary are valued at market value at the time of purchase, and the parent's assets and liabilities are valued at book value. This is called *purchase accounting.* The third method, sometimes referred to as the *new entity approach,* results in all entities' assets and liabilities being revalued to market values at the time the combination originates. The central problem faced by standard-setting bodies is whether there are relevant circumstances to justify use of more than one method to account for different types of business combinations.

Terminology regarding business combinations is not uniform throughout the accounting literature. In this chapter, the following terms suggested by the FASB are used:

Combined enterprise: The accounting entity that results from a business combination.

Constituent companies: The separate business enterprises that enter into a business combination.

Combinor: A constituent company entering into a combination whose stockholders (owners) as a group end up with control of the voting stock (ownership interests) of the combined enterprise.

Combinee: A constituent company other than the combinor in a combination in which a combinor is identifiable.[5]

POOLING OF INTERESTS

The pooling of interests concept of a business combination is based on the premise that no substantive transaction occurs between the constituent companies. Rather, they merely unite their respective ownership interests and continue as if they are a single enterprise. The first applications of the pooling of interests concept resembled an internal reorganization more than a business combination; for example, the combination of two subsidiaries of the same parent enterprise. In such a situation, no new entity was established by the combination; the two already related entities merely added together their previously separate financial statements to effect the combination. Pooling of interests started just that way, but eventually the method began to be applied to the combination of unrelated constituent companies. It was at this juncture that questions about pooling accounting began to arise.

What is the conceptual justification for pooling accounting? A pooling of interests is argued to be simply the formal unification of two previously separate ownership groups. The two agree to combine, or pool, their equity interests

---

[5] FASB (1976a, para.4).

and continue as if they are a single enterprise. That is, there is a swap of equity shares in which the combiner company exchanges its shares for the outstanding shares of the combinee company. There is no purchase by one constituent of the other; thus, the assumption is that no exchange transaction occurs but that assets and liabilities are combined at their book values. Pooling is analogous to the concept of a nonmonetary exchange of similar fixed assets, and, as a result, the pooled assets and liabilities have the same basis of accounting in the combination as they did separately before the combination. The book values of the combined enterprise's assets and liabilities after the combination will be equal to the summation of the combinor's and combinee's respective book values just prior to the combination. Total stockholders' equity of the combined enterprise will also be equal to the sum of the constituent companies' equities immediately prior to the combination. There may be some changes in individual components, depending on the exchange ratio, but in aggregate the combined stockholders' equity is the sum of the precombination totals. Of course, one might equally well argue that as a result of the pooling a new entity exists and a totally new basis of accounting should be used in the consolidated accounting for this new entity (see discussion below).

THE PURCHASE METHOD

In purchase accounting, the assumption is that the combinor is a parent company that purchases the combinee (subsidiary) and must account for the purchase as it would for the acquisition of any asset. The asset, investment in the combinee company, is recorded by the combinor at the latter's cost determined as of the date the combination is consummated.[6] This results in the consolidated reporting of the combinee's net assets at their fair market value at the date of combination. Accounting for the combination, however, may be complicated for several reasons:

1. If part of the price paid is of a noncash nature, the total cost of the combinee may not be readily obvious.
2. The fair value of the combinee's assets and liabilities probably is not readily available because its statement of financial position reports only book values and, in fact, may not report all assets, such as internally developed assets.
3. Frequently, the total cost of the combinee is not equal to the summation of the fair values of its individual assets less liabilities, and the purchase differential must be dealt with in some manner. Traditionally, this difference has been called *goodwill*.

The detailed procedures of APB 16 and APB 17 for applying purchase accounting to consolidated reporting are covered in advanced accounting textbooks

---

[6] If the combinee continues to operate as a separate entity its records are maintained on the basis of the combinee's own historical cost. The proposal (called *push down accounting*) has been to carry the combinee's accounts at the purchase price paid by the combinor. See Thomas and Hagler (1988) for an assessment.

and are not examined here. Generally, these procedures relate to determining the purchase price, revaluing the assets of the combinee (subsidiary) for consolidated reporting purposes, and amortizing the purchase differential in the consolidated statement.

THE NEW ENTITY APPROACH

Another possible method of accounting for a business combination is to regard the combined enterprise as an entirely new entity. This approach results in the use of current values for the assets and liabilities of all the separate entities as of the date the combination is consummated. The reason for such an approach would be that the business combination results in a substantially new accounting entity. In other words, more is involved than merely one entity purchasing and integrating another into its own operation. The very nature of the combination may be such that an entirely new operation has come into existence. This approach to accounting for business combinations is not used in practice (except for statutory mergers), but it was identified as a possibility in the 1976 FASB discussion memorandum on business combinations. In fact, a strong case can be made that a new entity results from a pooling type of combination and also from purchase-type combinations when the subsidiary company is material relative to the parent.

SEARCHING FOR RELEVANT CIRCUMSTANCES: POOLING VERSUS PURCHASE

Three different accounting standards have attempted to delineate the relevant circumstances that would justify the use of pooling rather than purchase accounting, but the task has proven difficult. The current rules (APB 16) have restricted the use of pooling, largely as a reaction to the widespread application in the 1960s of pooling accounting to what were often regarded as purchases of subsidiaries.

ARB 40 (codified as ARB 43, Chapter 7C) was the first standard to indicate that business combinations could be differentiated on the basis of their underlying nature. Its primary distinction between a pooling of interests and a purchase was based on the effect on the ownership interests of the constituent enterprises in the combined enterprise. If substantially all equity interests of the constituent enterprises survived in a combined enterprise, as in a swap of equity stock, then a pooling of interests was presumed to have occurred. On the other hand, if the equity interests of one of the constituent enterprises was substantially eliminated in the combined enterprise, as in an outright stock purchase by the combinor, then a purchase was presumed to have occurred. ARB 40 provided additional guidance for differentiating between a pooling of interests and a purchase. A pooling was more clearly indicated if the relative sizes of the constituent enterprises were similar, if the activities of the constituent enterprises were either similar or complementary, and if the managements of the constituent enterprises both survived in the combined enterprise.

Many felt that the criteria established by ARB 40 to distinguish between a pooling of interests and a purchase were not operational because they were too vague. That led the CAP to reconsider the subject in ARB 48, issued in 1957, which superseded Chapter 7C of ARB 43. ARB 48 stated that a pooling of interests combination

> ... may be described for accounting purposes as a business combination of two or more corporations in which the holders of substantially all of the ownership interests in the constituent corporations become the owners of a single corporation which owns the assets and businesses of the constituent corporations. . . . [7]

The criteria in ARB 48 were intended to be reliable guides for determining when a business combination was a pooling of interests. Shares of stock received by the individual owners of the constituent enterprises should be substantially in proportion to their respective equity interests prior to the combination, and the relative voting rights should not be altered by issuing senior equity or debt securities. As with ARB 40, there should be no intention to retire a substantial portion of the stock issued to effect the combination, and the combined enterprise should not plan to sell a significant portion of one of the constituent's assets, because to do so would not be consistent with the pooling concept. Likewise, managements of all constituents should carry forward in the combined enterprise. The criterion from ARB 40 that the constituents be relatively the same size was not retained in ARB 48. Ironically, many felt that ARB 48 made the criteria established by ARB 40 even less operational than before. Wyatt stated that ARB 48 "presented the criteria in such a manner that any given combination could be supported as either a purchase or a pooling, depending largely upon the intentions or desires of the parties to the transaction." [8] This would, of course, be a classic example of flexibility.

The controversy over accounting for business combinations contributed to the APB's demise (see Chapter 3). Some APB members felt strongly that pooling should be disallowed; other members felt that it should be acceptable accounting for practically any business combination and to disallow it would discourage business combinations. It was thus seen as an issue of economic consequences by the latter group. These opposite positions were eventually resolved and resulted in the issuance of APB 16. That document recognized that both the pooling of interests and purchase methods are legitimate methods but are not interchangeable treatments for the same business combination. Any business combination must be accounted for as a purchase unless it meets all of the conditions established by APB 16 for a pooling of interests. If those conditions are met, the business combination must be accounted for as a pooling of interests. The goal of APB 16 was to prevent abuses and curtail the flagrant use of pooling that had occurred in the 1960s. To achieve that goal, paragraphs 46–48 of APB 16 established strict conditions that a business combination must meet in order to be accounted for as a pooling of interests.

---

[7] Committee on Accounting Procedure (1957, para. 4).
[8] Wyatt (1963, p. 38).

The condition *attributes of the combining enterprises* is presented in paragraph 46. It is subdivided into two criteria:

a. Each of the combining companies is autonomous and has not been a subsidiary or division of another corporation within two years before the plan of combination is initiated.
b. Each of the combining companies is independent of the other combining companies.

The criteria established by paragraph 46 assure that the constituents in a pooling of interests are unrelated enterprises. The underlying motive for that requirement is to prevent an enterprise from fragmenting its organization and pooling only part of it, thereby circumventing the nature of a pooling of interests, which is a uniting of all equity interests.

Paragraph 47, *manner of combining interests*, consists of seven interrelated criteria all established to assure the continuity of ownership interests of the constituent enterprises in the combined enterprise. The criteria are

a. The combination is effected in a single transaction or is completed in accordance with a specific plan within one year after the plan is initiated.
b. A corporation offers and issues only common stock with rights identical to those of the majority of its outstanding voting common stock in exchange for substantially all of the voting common stock interest of another company at the date the plan of combination is consummated.
c. None of the combining companies changes the equity interest of the voting common stock in contemplation of effecting the combination either within two years before the plan of combination is initiated or between the dates the combination is initiated and consummated; changes in contemplation of effecting the combination may include distributions to stockholders and additional issuances, exchanges, and retirements of securities.
d. Each of the combining companies reacquires shares of voting common stock only for purposes other than business combinations, and no company reacquires more than a normal number of shares between the dates the plan of combination is initiated and consummated.
e. The ratio of interest of an individual common stockholder to those of other common stockholders in a combining company remains the same as a result of the exchange of stock to effect the combination.
f. The voting rights to which the common stock ownership interests in the resulting combined corporation are entitled are exercisable by the stockholders; the stockholders are neither deprived of nor restricted in exercising those rights for a period.
g. The combination is resolved at the date the plan is consummated and no provisions of the plan relating to the issue of securities or other consideration are pending.

Criteria in paragraphs 47a, c, e, f, and g are aimed directly at insuring that the stockholder groups of all constituents of the combination receive their proportionate rights in the combined enterprise. Criterion 47a is designed to prevent a situation in which some stockholders of the constituent enterprises receive more (or less) than their proportionate ownership interest in the combined enterprise in a multiple-step pooling. For example, assume 40 percent of the stockholders of one company agree to an exchange rate of 2 for 1, while the remaining 60 percent hold out for a better exchange offer. If the latter group subsequently gets an exchange rate of other than 2 for 1, the combination could not be treated as a pooling of interest. Criterion 47c is designed to prevent at least two situations contrary to the nature of a pooling. One situation that would proscribe pooling of interests accounting would occur when one of the constituent enterprises distributes a dividend greater than normal prior to the business combination, thus distributing part of its assets and pooling the remainder. Another situation proscribing pooling of interests is the reacquiring by one of the constituents of its own stock and then reissuing it in order to obtain a new stockholder group that will agree to the business combination.

Criteria 47e and 47f insure that the constituent stockholder groups maintain their proportionate right to control management of the combined enterprise. They require, for example, that if an individual owns 25 percent of one of the combined enterprises, he or she must receive 25 percent of the shares that are exchanged in the combination. Moreover, those shares must have the same rights as all other combinor shares, and the rights must not be restricted for any period of time. Criterion 47g prohibits contingent consideration agreements based on events subsequent to the date the combination is consummated. This criterion is designed to prevent the dilution of any of the ownership interests in the combined enterprise.

Criteria 47b, 47c, and 47d are aimed directly at insuring that all equity interests are combined in order for a business combination to be accounted for as a pooling of interests. Criterion 47b is designed to make certain that substantially all (90 percent) of the constituents' ownership interests are pooled. Criterion 47d prevents use of treasury stock in pooling-of-interests business combinations to insure that all equity interests are combined and, as with criterion 47c (see earlier discussion), to prevent realigning equity interests to obtain a new stockholder group that will agree to the combination.

Paragraph 48, *absence of planned transactions*, is designed to prevent structuring a business combination as a pooling of interests and then, once that accounting is accomplished, violating the nature of a pooling of interests (that is, not uniting all equity interests). Three criteria are listed in paragraph 48:

a. The combined corporation does not agree directly or indirectly to retire or reacquire all or part of the common stock issued to effect the combination.

b. The combined corporation does not enter into other financial arrangements for the benefit of the former stockholders of a combining company, such as a guaranty of loans secured by stocks issued in the combination, which in effect negates the exchange of equity securities.

c. The combined corporation does not intend or plan to dispose of a significant part of the assets of the combining companies within two years after the combination other than disposals in the ordinary course of business of the formerly separate companies and to eliminate duplicate facilities or excess capacity.

Without criterion 48a, one company could exchange its stock for the stock of another company and, subsequent to the combination, reacquire the stock issued to effect the business combination and thus disguise a purchase as a pooling of interests. Criterion 48b is designed to prevent one of the constituent stockholder groups from being disproportionately rewarded because of the business combination. Although a violation of criterion 48c may not result in a situation that is unfavorable or disproportionate to a particular constituent group, it would be inconsistent with a pooling of all assets and the noncash nature of a pooling.

In summary, APB 16 accepted the legitimacy of the pooling concept. But, in practice, it established the most extensive set of qualifying criteria that exists in accounting standards. Indeed, the criteria read like a checklist of the ways in which pre-APB 16 poolings were structured so as to violate the spirit of a pooling. The tenor of APB 16 is clearly oriented toward restricting the application of pooling to more or less straightforward swaps of equity stock in which holders in the combinee company exchange their voting common stock for voting common stock in the combinor company.

RESEARCH ON POOLING AND PURCHASE ACCOUNTING

Earlier in the chapter we stated that pooling of interests accounting was viewed as an important motivation for business combinations. A FASB survey found that 66 percent of enterprises having made combinations believed that the combinations would not have occurred if purchase accounting had been required.[9] Pooling of interests generally produces more favorable financial statements than purchase accounting because combined assets are not revalued. Pooled financial statements would thus report higher income since depreciation, cost of goods sold, etc., would *not* be calculated on the basis of higher valued assets, nor would there be any amortization of the purchase differential (goodwill). In addition, return on investment would be greater owing to both a higher income level and a lower asset base.

Research has also been conducted to determine the attitude of financial statement users toward the two accounting methods. Interestingly, the two methods are favored about equally. A FASB survey found 40 percent preferred pooling of interests; 45 percent, purchase accounting; and 15 percent, a new accounting basis for both combinor and combinee.[10] Another survey of financial analysts found 46.7 percent preferred purchase accounting and 43.3 percent favored pooling of interests.[11] Although some academic researchers have taken a very critical stance on pooling of interests, it is interesting to see that the method has a following with financial analysts.[12] *Accounting Trends and Techniques* has reported that approximately 90 percent of combinations in recent years are accounted for as purchases.[13]

Finally, there has been some limited research to determine how the two

---

[9] FASB (1976a, para. 138).

[10] Ibid., para. 110.

[11] Burton (1970, p. 75).

[12] For example, Briloff (1967).

[13] AICPA (1988).

accounting methods affect the security price of the combinor company. One study found no evidence that pooling accounting caused higher stock prices. In other words, the stock market did not appear to be fooled by the higher income reported under the pooling method.[14] This finding is consistent with capital market research regarding the sophistication of users of accounting information. However, there is also some evidence to support the contention that APB 16's restricting the use of pooling may adversely affect the combinor with respect to covenants in its debt contracts, and that this potential economic consequence could further explain companies' preferences for pooling accounting.[15]

What insight does empirical research give into the purchase/pooling question? Management seems to prefer pooling because of its favorable financial statement effect. However, security price research has shown that the market is not fooled or deceived by book profits arising solely from the way in which business combinations are accounted for. If the market is not fooled, one could argue that it makes no difference which method is used, so long as the method is disclosed. This is the efficient-market school of thought. Yet, if it really makes no difference, why bother having two methods of accounting for similar but subtly different phenomena since it has proved difficult to specify the relevant circumstances that would justify the two very different accounting methods?

FASB DISCUSSION MEMORANDUM

Although the FASB has not established any standards other than technical bulletins on purchase versus pooling accounting, it has addressed the subject. Shortly after formation, the FASB issued an open letter to all interested parties requesting views on existing APB Opinions and ARBs. The letter stated in part, "The Board is interested in learning of the experiences of users, preparers, and auditors of financial statements which would indicate that these existing pronouncements need (1) interpretation, (2) amendment or (3) replacement." The replies to that letter indicated that APB opinions 16 and 17 most needed the FASB's attention. Accordingly, the FASB decided to reconsider accounting for business combinations and purchased intangibles and in 1976 issued a discussion memorandum entitled "Accounting for Business Combinations and Purchased Intangibles." It was a comprehensive document, covering all relevant areas in accounting for business combinations. After public hearings in 1977, the FASB deferred action on the project pending development of the Conceptual Framework Project. Subsequent to that decision, the FASB dropped the project from its agenda, citing its low priority in relation to other existing and potential projects. This action is disappointing given the problem of defining relevant circumstances that would justify finite uniformity in accounting for business combinations.

---

[14] Hong, Kaplan, and Mandelker (1978).
[15] Leftwich (1981).

THE EQUITY METHOD

The equity method of accounting for investments in equity securities is used whenever the investor has the ability to exercise significant influence over the investee. If the investor's investment does not establish control (that is, ownership is not greater than 50 percent), consolidated financial statements are not required. Rather, what is frequently referred to as a *one-line consolidation* takes place: the investment account is used to reflect the investor's underlying book value of equity in the investee. Many of the mechanical adjustments that are required for consolidated financial statements (for example, recognition and amortization of goodwill) are also required for a one-line consolidation — except that only the net effect of those adjustments is reported in the investment account rather than a consolidated reporting of all of the individual accounts actually involved. Thus, the income statement under equity accounting is the same as if consolidated reporting had been used (after deducting minority interest in consolidated income). However, because of the absence of effective control, the investee's assets and liabilities are not reported as if they are owned outright as occurs with consolidated reporting. Rather, the investment account simply mirrors the net change in investee book value.

The investment is recorded at cost plus transaction costs. At the time of the investment, the investor must determine if more (or less) was paid than the underlying book value acquired. For example, assume P Company purchased 25 percent of S Company's voting stock for $100,000 when S Company's book value was $300,000. P Company paid $25,000 over the underlying book value of S Company [$100,000 − ($300,000)(.25) = $25,000]. An attempt should be made to determine what specific assets of S Company are undervalued; however, as is more often the case, the $25,000 is arbitrarily assumed to be attributable to goodwill and amortized over a maximum of forty years as allowed by APB 17.

Three events must be recorded in the investment account for each reporting period: (1) proportionate share of investee's income or loss for the period, (2) proportionate share of investee's cash dividend for the period, and (3) amortization of the amount of the cost of the investment that is different from the underlying book value acquired (for example, the $25,000 above). The investor's proportionate share of the investee's net income is recorded as a debit to the investment account and a credit to income from equity investments. The investor's proportionate share of the investee's cash dividends is recorded as a debit to cash and a credit to the investment account. The excess cost over book value of the investment is amortized over its estimated useful life by debiting income from equity investments and crediting the investment account. Intercompany profits and losses are eliminated and other adjustments typically made in consolidation also are recorded. The result is that one line on the balance sheet, the investment account, and one line on the income statement, the income from equity investments account, are reported as if consolidation had occurred.

In terms of both relevance and representational faithfulness, one may question the usefulness of the equity method. The investment account represents neither the cost nor the market value of that investment. Moreover, one cannot determine from the income statement the amount of actual dividends received from investments. Information under the equity method, however, might be as important to financial statement users as is the amount reported as income using purchase accounting. A market price valuation approach would be superior to the equity method because it would display the current value of the investment as well as its current cash-generating ability. Empirical studies have reached a similar conclusion.[16]

THE COST METHOD

If APB 18 is not applicable and there is no significant influence, then the cost method is required for intercorporate equity investments. The cost method presumes only nominal influence or control exercisable by the investor, and, as a result, income is recognized only from investee dividends. Although the investment is carried at original cost, SFAS 12 does require that the lower-of-cost-or-market (LCM) rule be applied to investments in *marketable* equity securities accounted for by the cost method. The LCM rule is applied on a portfolio basis, and all marketable equity investments are divided into two portfolios:

1. current, which includes those investments that are readily marketable and that management expects to convert into cash within the next year (or within the operating cycle, whichever is longer) and
2. noncurrent, which includes all other equity investments.

For the current portfolio, declines in market prices below cost are reported in the income statement as losses, which increases in market price (above previous declines) are reported in the income statement as reverses of previous losses. In other words, an increase in market price is handled as a change in the estimate of a previously reported loss. The LCM rule is applied similarly to the noncurrent portfolio except that losses (and their reversal) are reported in a separate component of the equity section of the balance sheet, thus bypassing the income statement. The FASB's logic is that changes in the market price of equity investments in the noncurrent portfolio will not affect cash flow in the near future and therefore should not be included in income determination, while similar changes in the current portfolio will be realized imminently and therefore should be accrued.

Under the cost method, the investment is recorded at cost, including transaction costs. No subsequent adjustments (other than LCM adjustments) are made for such events as the investee's income or loss and dividends. When

---

[16] See, for example, Lloyd and Weygandt (1971); and Copeland, Strawser, and Binns (1972).

an investee declares a cash dividend, the investor records its proportionate amount of that dividend as income on the date of record.

SFAS 12 is a step in the right direction — that is, away from a purely cost-basis valuation — but it does not go far enough toward a market basis of accounting. The LCM rule, as applied in SFAS 12, is obviously a conservative approach because losses are anticipated and accrued while unrealized gains are ignored. Even the terminology denies the anticipation of gains. The recovery of previously recognized losses is assumed to be a correction of a previous loss estimate rather than the recognition of a gain. Moreover, the practice of treating market declines differently (depending on the classification of the investment) does not appear justified by the underlying relevant circumstances. Certainly a case may be made that market declines in the noncurrent portfolio do not readily affect cash and therefore should not affect earnings. If that argument is accepted, however, then why recognize the market declines at all? The presumption is, after all, that the investment will be held indefinitely, and any immediate market declines will not necessarily affect ultimate cash flows. Another weakness in this dual approach to the recognition of market declines is that it is based on an arbitrary classification of each particular investment, and that classification certainly is susceptible to management manipulation. If available, market valuations for all equity investments would provide more relevant information to financial statement users, would be less arbitrary, would remove from the balance sheet an ambiguous element (that is, the separate component of stockholders' equity representing market declines on noncurrent investments), and would be less susceptible to management manipulation.

DEFINING THE REPORTING ENTITY

SFAS 94, in justifying mandatory consolidation for *all* majority-owned investments, reiterated the rationale of ARB 51:

> The purpose of consolidated statements is to present, primarily for the benefit of the shareholders and creditors of the parent company, the results of operations and the financial position of a parent company and its subsidiaries essentially as if the group were a single company with one or more branches or divisions. There is a presumption that consolidated statements are more meaningful than separate statements and that they are usually necessary for a fair presentation when one of the companies in the group directly or indirectly has a controlling financial interest in the other companies.[17]

Thus, the FASB maintains that consolidated reporting is the most appropriate way to report, but this is little more than an assertion or presumption.

At the heart of the consolidation issue is a deeper question concerning the definition of the reporting entity. To its credit, the FASB recognized this and in

---

[17] FASB (1987, para. 1).

1986 added the question of the reporting entity to its agenda (though the board also made clear in doing so that it was not reopening the purchase–pooling debate). However, SFAS 94 was issued *before* any conclusion was reached concerning the reporting entity, which undermines the logic of that standard. Consolidation reporting presumes, then, that the accounting fiction of a group entity is more meaningful than defining the reporting entity in legal terms: that is, as the parent company alone, perhaps supplemented with the separate financial statements of other companies that are majority owned.

So SFAS 94 simply asserts, rather than demonstrates, that consolidated reporting (and the fictional accounting entity thus created) is more relevant to investors than are separate entity statements in which the reporting entity is the legal entity. Walker has evaluated the following seven propositions concerning the alleged usefulness of consolidated reports compared to separate entity statements of the parent and/or subsidiary companies:

1. Consolidated income statements provide a better basis for reporting parent company income than parent company statements.
2. Consolidated income statements (alone or in conjunction with parent company income statements) provide a better basis for predicting a parent company's earnings than parent company statements (alone).
3. Consolidated balance sheets assist shareholders of a parent company to assess the likely profitability of that firm by providing information as to the pattern of the parent company's investments.
4. Consolidated balance sheets assist shareholders to assess the volatility of parent company earnings' relative to fluctuations in operating income.
5. Consolidated income statements (in conjunction with the income statements of subsidiary companies) provide a better basis for predicting the earnings of those subsidiaries than the subsidiaries' income statements (alone).
6. Consolidated balance sheets provide creditors and potential creditors with a better basis for assessing the risks attaching to claims than would parent company statements (alone).
7. Consolidated balance sheets (in conjunction with subsidiary company balance sheets) provide creditors and potential creditors of subsidiaries with a better basis for assessing the risks attaching to claims than would the subsidiary company statements (alone).[18]

Walker's analysis rejects outright the claims in propositions 1 and 5 and offers only partial or conditional support for the other propositions. The support is conditional mainly because it is not self-evident that consolidated statements are always, under all conditions, superior to separate entity statements, especially when subsidiaries are less than 100 percent-owned or when there are no cross-guarantees of debt between the parent and subsidiary companies.

The preceding discussion suggests that the consolidation question should

---

[18] Walker (1976) and (1978).

not be reduced to a question of whether it is the right or only way of reporting. Rather, consolidation is a useful way of summarizing overall results *as if* an affiliated group were one legal entity. But such a method necessarily fails to report on the *real* separate legal entities, and for this reason there is bound to be a loss of information with respect to the separate legal entities.[19] SFAS 94 recognizes that consolidated statements do cause a loss of detail through the aggregation process and that the reporting entity project is considering the possibility of disaggregated disclosures.[20] In fact, a number of studies have found that disaggregated data (by product line) are more useful in forecasting earnings and in valuing the firm.[21] There are reasons to believe the same to be true with respect to separate legal entity reporting.

Consider the situation where there are *no* cross-guarantees of debt between a parent company and its majority-owned (subsidiary) companies. In this situation, consolidated statements are misleading with respect to the debt situation of the parent company because the parent's assets are completely sheltered from any liability claims of the subsidiaries' debt holders. Indeed, this is one motivation for establishing a subsidiary structure as opposed to a divisional structure for the firm. A simple example will illustrate the problem. Assume a 60 percent-owned subsidiary with assets of $2,000,000 and liabilities of $1,000,000 and a parent company with assets of $2,000,000 (excluding its investment in the subsidiary) and liabilities of $1,000,000. On a parent-only basis, which is the *legal* situation with respect to parent company debt, the ratio of debt to assets is 38.5 percent (parent debt of $1,000,000 divided by parent assets of $2,000,000 plus the parent's 60 percent equity in the *net* assets of $1,000,000). But on a consolidated basis, the ratio increases to 50 percent (parent debt of $1,000,000 plus subsidiary debt of the same amount divided by parent assets of $2,000,000 plus subsidiary assets of $2,000,000). Of course, when there are cross-guarantees of debt, it follows that consolidated statements are *more* informative than separate entity statements. Indeed, there is some evidence that cross-guarantees of debt may have, at least in part, led to the voluntary adoption of consolidated reporting before it was required by regulation.[22]

The point that emerges here is simply that it is naive to presume consolidated reporting is always, under all conditions, preferable to reporting of the separate legal entities. Yet, this is exactly how consolidated statements have come to be viewed in the United States. Consolidated reporting emerged in the early 1900s in response to the growth of holding (parent) companies, and consolidated statements had already been substituted for parent-only statements by

---

[19] See Pendlebury (1980) and Francis (1986).

[20] SFAS 14 disaggregates consolidated data by product line and geographical area, but not by separate legal entity.

[21] See Mohr (1983) for a summary of relevant empirical research, and Kim (1987) for a theoretical development of the argument.

[22] See Whittred (1986) and (1987), though Francis (1986) reports that less than 10 percent of New York Stock Exchange companies cross-guarantee debt.

the time the Securities Acts of 1933 and 1934 were passed.[23] By contrast, holding companies and consolidation accounting came onto the British scene at the time of an already-existing regulatory framework, the British Companies Acts. As a result, consolidated reporting did not substitute for parent-only statements but was required as a *supplement* to them. In fact, parent-only statements are still required, and separate subsidiary company statements can still be reported in lieu of consolidation, though consolidation is virtually the universal way of reporting subsidiary companies.

SUMMARY

Accounting rules for intercorporate equity investments have evolved into an elaborate system of finite uniformity. The relevant circumstance centers on the notion of investor control, but, in practice, the magnitude of ownership has been the guiding criterion. All three of the accounting methods — cost, equity, and consolidation — have serious deficiencies. The cost method establishes a doubtful distinction between current and noncurrent investments and is biased in recognizing unrealized losses but not recognizing unrealized gains. The equity method lacks representational faithfulness inasmuch as the book value of intercorporate investments accounted for under the equity method is an artificially constructed accounting attribute that has no market referent. Attempts to create finite uniformity within consolidation accounting through the purchase or pooling methods have been an unmitigated disaster. Yet the FASB, in declining to readdress this issue as part of its reporting entity project, has endorsed thirty years of standard-setting folly. Finally, while consolidated statements have emerged as the primary basis of financial reporting, they have not proven to be universally relevant to the point of doing away with the reporting of separate parent and/or subsidiary statements. Thus, dual reporting — both parent-only and consolidated statements — as occurs in Britain (and Australia) seems to be a more complete approach to financial reporting for business combinations.

QUESTIONS

1. What general circumstances are used to justify accounting for a business combination as a pooling of interests as contrasted with a purchase?
2. Review the development of criteria for pooling accounting and how these criteria changed from ARB 40 to ARB 48.
3. Evaluate the criteria for purchase versus pooling accounting in APB 16.

---

[23] Prior to 1982, the SEC did, in very limited instances, require supplemental parent-only statements. But this last gesture to dual reporting was dropped in ASR 302.

4. Pooling accounting originated between affiliated companies. APB 16 prohibits pooling for affiliated companies that combine. What caused this change?

5. The logic of pooling rests heavily on the assumption that no substantive economic transaction occurs between the combinor and stockholders of the combinee. Evaluate this assumption.

6. Why may companies *not* be indifferent to purchase and pooling accounting, and what do we know about this issue from research studies?

7. A third accounting method is rarely discussed: a new accounting basis for both combinor and combinee. Why might this be the best way to account for a business combination?

8. There are two methods of accounting for unconsolidated investments in equity stock — the cost and the equity methods. Discuss the rationale behind the two methods and how to determine which method to apply.

9. The equity method reports neither the investor's cost nor the market value of the investment. Do you believe the equity method provides useful information? Why, or why not?

10. The LCM rule is applied differently depending on the classification of the investment. Evaluate the rationale for this finite uniformity.

11. What is meant by the term *one-line consolidation*? What differences occur in financial statements when a one-line consolidation is used rather than full consolidation?

12. What are some reasons why consolidated reports are thought to be relevant?

13. Discuss the limitations of consolidated financial statements and why dual reporting (consolidated and separate entity statements) as well as other forms of disaggregated reporting, such as SFAS 14, make sense.

14. Why does the FASB's reporting entity project logically precede any conclusion regarding consolidated financial reporting?

15. Describe the implicit assumption made in SFAS 94 about the reporting entity.

16. What is push down accounting?

CASES AND PROBLEMS

1. In 1987, the FASB issued SFAS 94, which requires the consolidation of all majority-owned subsidiaries. An article in The *Wall Street Journal*, November 2, 1987, page 10, reported on why it is a controversial standard:[24]

   The Financial Accounting Standards Board issued a controversial rule that forces all companies to consolidate in their financial statements the results of all majority-owned subsidiaries.

---

[24] Reprinted by permission of The *Wall Street Journal*. © 1987. Dow Jones & Company, Inc. All Rights Reserved Worldwide.

Many companies in the auto, retail and consumer-products businesses continue to oppose the rule because it will load a lot more debt on their balance sheets from finance, insurance and other subsidiaries.

Some of the companies affected by the ruling are General Motors Corp., Ford Motor Co., Chrysler Corp., General Electric Co., J. C. Penney Co., ITT Corp., Xerox Corp. and International Business Machines Corp.

"A lot of companies with nonconsolidated subsidiaries that are in far different business from the parent are going to be upset with this rule," said Pat McConnell, an accountant and an associate director of Bear, Stearns & Co., a securities firm. . . .

Bernard R. Doyle, manager of corporate accounting services for GE, Fairfield, Conn., said the new FASB rule will "produce information overload." He added: "GE's consolidated statements aren't really going to be intelligible because the FASB now requires that we add together nonhomogeneous operations."

Mr. Doyle noted that GE owns not only a finance subsidiary — General Electric Credit Corp. — but 80% of Kidder, Peabody & Co., the securities firm, and a reinsurance company, all of which aren't currently consolidated in the financial statements. "Consolidating them on our balance sheet as required by the FASB will be quite confusing," he said.

Larry Brooke, an FASB project manager, said the FASB doesn't believe that the GE financial statement after all subsidiaries are consolidated will be any more confusing than it is now. "We don't think that a balance sheet which combines a broadcasting company with a maker of light bulbs and jet engines is that monolithic or homogeneous," Mr. Brooke said. . . .

Some companies already have begun to change their corporate structure to avoid having the new FASB rule force them to change their debt covenants. Early last month, Houston-based Tenneco Inc. created a holding company that will permit it under the new FASB rule to keep separate the debt of its pipeline business with heavy debt from its other businesses.

The FASB's Mr. Brooke said the FASB is aware of Tenneco's action to sidestep the new rule but doesn't know of any other company taking similar action.

Required:

(a) Evaluate the "homogeneity" argument as a basis for excluding certain subsidiaries from consolidation.

(b) What economic consequences are alluded to in the article, and what are some ways that companies might respond to such consequences?

(c) Why might companies now have incentives in certain instances, to report supplemental separate entity statements as a result of SFAS 94?

2. Examine the 1987 and 1988 annual reports of one of the companies mentioned in Case 1: General Motors Corp., Ford Motor Corp., Chrysler Corp., General Electric Co., J. C. Penney Co., ITT Corp., Xerox Corp., and IBM. Determine the effect of SFAS 94 on operating ratios, profitability ratios, liquidity ratios, and leverage ratios. Evaluate whether the impact is as substantial as suggested in Case 1.

3. The following items pertain to a parent company and its 60 percent-owned subsidiary at year end. There are no cross-guarantees of debt between the parent and subsidiary.

	Parent	*Subsidiary*
Current Assets	$ 500,000	$1,000,000
Noncurrent Assets		
(Excluding Subsidiary Investment)	5,000,000	2,000,000
Current Liabilities	750,000	250,000
Noncurrent Liabilities	2,000,000	750,000
Revenues	1,700,000	1,500,000
Expenses	1,600,000	900,000
Dividends	100,000	600,000

Required:

Explain and illustrate how consolidated reporting using the data above can be misleading.

4. In 1983, the FASB became concerned with procedures used to account for business combinations in the thrift (savings and loan) industry. Purchase-type combinations restate acquired assets and liabilities at current market values at the time of combination. Assets of thrifts are predominantly low-yielding mortgages and must be discounted to present values using current interest rates. The discount is then recognized as income as the mortgages are written up to face value over the remaining period to maturity. This is analogous to a discount on investments in bonds. Liabilities (customer deposits) are likely to be at market values.

Frequently, combinors simply acquired the assets and liabilities (sometimes not even paying any cash). Because of the discounted assets, it was common for liabilities to exceed assets, in which case purchased goodwill was recognized to balance the entry. Under APB 17 goodwill can be amortized over forty years. The accounting problem was described in an article that appeared in *Business Week*, April 18, 1983, page 97:

> "Under the old rules," says Bertill A. Gustafson, senior vice-president and controller of Great Western Savings, based in Beverly Hills, California, "the discounted mortgage portfolio would slowly increase in value as maturity approached, usually over about 10 years, creating income each year. Yet the related goodwill would be 'expensed' over a much longer time period, as much as 40 years." The result: bookkeeping profits for the first decade after the acquisition.

In response to this anomaly, the FASB issued SFAS 72, which limits the amortization period of goodwill in the thrift industry to the maturity period of the mortgages. It also requires use of what it called the "interest" method to amortize goodwill. This is not clearly explained, but it appears to mean that goodwill is amortized in the same proportion as income is recognized over the period to mortgage maturity. It has been suggested that the new rule may inhibit future combinations in the thrift industry because of the loss of accounting income. The *Business Week* article continued:

> "There were a few abuses," acknowledges a senior executive at a New York bank. "Two sick banks got together and all of a sudden both were profitable on

paper," he says. "That's why the FASB acted." But the executive says the new rule will effectively discourage numerous transactions that otherwise make economic sense. "I know of many banks that were planning acquisitions, but now they're just baffled."

Required:
(a) Create an example to show how accounting income was computed before the change, and how the change will affect income.
(b) What does goodwill represent here in the accounting sense? How does it conform to asset definitions?
(c) Evaluate SFAS 72 accounting requirements in terms of accounting theory, particularly the effect on the balance sheet and income statement.
(d) What might be some economic consequences as a result of SFAS 72?

5. *Accounting Trends and Techniques* (AICPA) summarizes accounting practices for 600 large publicly traded corporations. For selected years the number of new business combinations accounted for using pooling versus purchase accounting was as follows:

	1962	1967	1971	1975	1985
Pooling	31	144	100	31	24
Purchase	36	116	131	75	200

Required:
(a) What does the data indicate concerning the general frequency of business combinations during the 1960s, 1970s, and early 1980s?
(b) APB 16 was adopted effective late in 1970. Given the discussion in the chapter, are the data consistent with the motivation underlying APB 16?
(c) During the debate leading to APB 16, it was claimed that the elimination (or reduction) of pooling would result in fewer combinations and that this was an undesirable economic consequence. Does the above data support or refute this claim?
(d) In the 1980s, business combinations often took the form of hostile corporate takeovers, which were unheard of before then. Why may this explain the virtual disappearance of pooling accounting by the mid-1980s?

BIBLIOGRAPHY OF REFERENCED WORKS

Accounting Principles Board (1970a). "Business Combinations," *APB Opinion No. 16* (AICPA).

———— (1970b). "Intangible Assets," *APB Opinion No. 17* (AICPA).

———— (1971). "The Equity Method of Accounting for Investments in Common Stock," *APB Opinion No. 18* (AICPA).

American Institute of Certified Public Accounts (1988). *Accounting Trends and Techniques* (AICPA).

Briloff, Abraham J. (1967). "Dirty Pooling," *The Accounting Review* (July 1967), pp. 489–496.

Burton, John C. (1970). *Accounting for Business Combinations* (Financial Executives Research Foundation).

Committee on Accounting Procedure (1950). "Business Combinations," *ARB No. 40* (AICPA).

———— (1957). "Business Combinations," *ARB No. 48* (AICPA).

———— (1959). "Consolidated Financial Statements," *Accounting Research Bulletin No. 51* (AICPA).

Copeland, Ronald M., Robert Strawser, and John G. Binns (1972). "Accounting for Investments in Common Stock," *Financial Executive* (February 1972), pp. 36–46.

Financial Accounting Standards Board (1975). "Accounting for Certain Marketable Securities," *Statement of Financial Accounting Standards No. 12* (FASB).

———— (1976a). *FASB Discussion Memorandum: An Analysis of Issues Related to Accounting for Business Combinations and Purchased Intangibles* (FASB).

———— (1976b). "Financial Reporting for Segments of a Business Enterprise," *Statement of Financial Accounting Standards No. 14* (FASB).

———— (1981). "Criteria for Applying the Equity Method of Accounting for Investment in Common Stock," *Interpretation No. 35* (FASB).

———— (1983). "Accounting for Certain Acquisitions of Banking and Thrift Institutions," *Statement of Financial Accounting Standards No. 72* (FASB).

———— (1987). "Consolidation of All Majority-owned Subsidiaries," *Statement of Financial Accounting Standards No. 94* (FASB).

Francis, Jere R. (1986)."Debt Reporting by Parent Companies: Parent-Only Versus Consolidated Statements," *Journal of Business Finance and Accounting* (Autumn 1986), pp. 393–403.

Heian, James B., and James B. Thies (1989). "Consolidation of Finance Subsidiaries: $230 Billion in Off-Balance-Sheet Financing Comes Home to Roost," *Accounting Horizons* (March 1989), pp. 1–9.

Hong, H., R. Kaplan, and G. Mandelker (1978). "Pooling vs. Purchase: The Effects of Accounting for Mergers on Stock Prices," *The Accounting Review* (January 1978), pp. 31–47.

Kim, Jae-Oh (1987). "Segmental Disclosures and Information Content of Earnings Announcements: Theoretical and Empirical Analysis" (Ph.D. diss., University of Iowa).

Leftwich, Richard W. (1981). "Evidence on the Impact of Mandatory Changes in Accounting Principles on Corporate Loan Agreements," *Journal of Accounting and Economics* (March 1981), pp. 3–36.

Lloyd, Michael, and Jerry Weygandt (1971). "Market Value Information for Nonsubsidiary Investments," *The Accounting Review* (October 1971), pp. 756–764.

Mohr, R. (1983). "The Segmental Reporting Issue: A Review of Empirical Research," *Journal of Accounting Literature* (Spring 1983), pp. 39–71.

Moonitz, Maurice (1944). *The Entity Theory of Consolidated Statements* (American Accounting Association).

Pendlebury, M. (1980). "The Application of Information Theory to Accounting for Groups of Companies," *Journal of Business Finance and Accounting* (Spring 1980), pp. 105–117.

Securities and Exchange Commission (1981). "Separate Financial Statements Required by Regulation S-X," *Accounting Series Release No. 302* (November 6, 1981).

Thomas, Paula B., and J. Larry Hagler (1988). "Push Down Accounting: A Descriptive Assessment," *Accounting Horizons* (September 1988), pp. 26–31.

Walker, Robert G. (1976). "An Evaluation of Information Conveyed by Consolidated Statements," *Abacus* (December 1976), pp. 77–115.

———— (1978). *Consolidated Statements: A History and Analysis* (Arno Press, 1978).

Whittred, Greg (1986). "The Evolution of Consolidated Financial Reporting in Australia," *Abacus* (September 1986), pp. 103–120.

———— (1987). "The Derived Demand for Consolidated Financial Reporting," *Journal of Accounting and Economics* (December 1987), pp. 259–285.

Wyatt, Arthur R. (1963). "A Critical Study of Accounting for Business Combinations," *Accounting Research Study No. 5* (AICPA).

ADDITIONAL READINGS

Bachman, Jules (1970). "An Economist Looks at Accounting for Business Combinations," *Financial Analysts Journal* (July–August 1970), pp. 39–48.

Baxter, George C., and James C. Spinney (1975). "A Closer Look at Consolidated Financial Statement Theory," *Canadian Chartered Accountant* (January 1975), pp. 31–36.

Catlett, George R., and Norman O. Olson (1968). "Accounting for Goodwill," *Accounting Research Study No. 10* (AICPA).

Chambers, R. (1968). "Consolidated Statements Are Not Really Necessary," *Australian Accountant* (February 1968), pp. 89–92.

Cunningham, Michael E. (1984). "Push Down Accounting: Pros and Cons," *Journal of Accountancy* (June 1984), pp. 72–77.

Dipchand, C., G. Roberts, and J. Viscione (1982). "Agency Costs and Captive Finance Subsidiaries in Canada," *The Journal of Financial Research* (Summer 1982), pp. 189–198.

Gagnon, Jean-Marie (1971). "Purchase-Pooling Choice: Some Empirical Evidence," *Journal of Accounting Research* (Spring 1971), pp. 52–72.

Livnat, Joshua, and Ashwinpaul C. Sandhi (1986). "Finance Subsidiaries: Their Formation and Consolidation," *Journal of Business Finance and Accounting* (Spring 1986), pp. 137–147.

Mohr, Roseanne M. (1988). "Unconsolidated Finance Subsidiaries: Characteristics and Debt/Equity Effects," *Accounting Horizons* (March 1988), pp. 27–34.

O'Connor, Melvin C., and James C. Hamre (1972). "Alternative Methods of Accounting for Long-Term Nonsubsidiary Intercorporate Investments in Common Stock," *The Accounting Review* (April 1972), pp. 308–319.

Rosenfield, Paul, and Steven Rubin (1985). *Consolidation, Translation, and the Equity Method: Concepts and Procedures* (John Wiley and Sons).

Storey, Reed K., and Maurice Moonitz (1976). "Market Value Methods for Intercorporate Investments in Stock," *Accounting Research Monograph No. 1* (AICPA).

Walker, R. G. (1978). "International Accounting Compromises: The Case of Consolidation Accounting," *Abacus* (December 1978), pp. 97–111.

ISSUES IN INTERNATIONAL ACCOUNTING

INTERNATIONAL TRADE AND INVESTMENT during the last quarter century have increased at a staggering rate. For example, exports of merchandise by the United States have gone from 19.6 billion dollars in 1960 to 322.2 billion dollars in 1988. Similarly, imports have gone from 15 billion dollars in 1960 to 441 billion dollars in 1988 (measures of both imports and exports are in unadjusted dollars).[1] In a like fashion, during the same period there has been an extensive increase in direct investment by U.S. firms in overseas operations and by foreign enterprises in the United States. In fact, the increase of foreign investment in the United States by some twenty-fold during this period, symbolized by the sale of Rockefeller Center to the Japanese, has caused considerable consternation in this country. Our concern is with the importance of this huge increase in international trade and investment upon financial accounting and reporting.

We begin by examining the problem of foreign currency translation as it pertains to U.S. multinational firms. SFASs 8 and 52 and their ramifications are scrutinized in this context and a discussion of consolidation accounting is continued from Chapter 18. Since this text has examined the standard-setting mechanism and process in the United States, the second section of the chapter is a brief introduction to accounting regulation in other English-speaking nations. Finally, we conclude by examining the efforts arising from the increased interdependence among national economies to harmonize accounting standards from a transnational perspective.

---

[1] Statistical Abstract of the United States (1990, p. 804).

TRANSLATION OF FOREIGN OPERATIONS

Translation of foreign-based operations and holdings into U.S. dollars has been addressed by all three standard-setting bodies. The CAP issued two ARBs on the subject (4 and 43); the APB issued APB 6 and discussed the subject at length in 1971 but did not issue a pronouncement; and the FASB has issued three SFASs (1, 8, and 52). The accounting issue is how to report foreign-currency-denominated operations in consolidated financial statements that are expressed in U.S. dollars. Hence, exchange rate differentials are critical.

Exchange rates between currencies of different countries were essentially fixed by the Bretton Woods Agreement from just prior to the end of World War II until 1971. While Bretton Woods brought stability, extreme pressure on the dollar and unrealistically low valuation of the Yen and Deutschemark has led us into a system of managed floating exchange rates.

What determines the exchange rate between currencies of different countries? Exchange rates are assumed to be the result of two factors: (1) different nominal interest rates arising from differences in expected inflation rates occurring in different countries, and (2) the ratio of the relative prices of a common "market basket" of goods and services of two particular countries as expressed by the price level of one country divided by the price level of the second country.[2] Purchasing power parity — constancy of the price level ratio between different currencies — was expected to be stable, but it now appears that purchasing power parity does not hold in either the short run or the long run.[3] Both as a result of different expected rates of inflation in different countries and the lack of purchasing power parity, there is an instability in foreign exchange rates that has the potential to create large translation gains and losses. Hence, what exchange rate to use and how to dispose of the differential resulting from the translation process become key questions.[4]

There are numerous approaches to the translation of foreign operations, but all stem from the basic orientation one adopts. A **U.S. dollar orientation** requires an enterprise to account for foreign operations as if those operations actually occurred in U.S. dollars. That is, foreign-currency-denominated assets, liabilities, revenues, and expenses are reported as if originally recorded in

---

[2] See Houston (1989, pp. 26–27) for further details.

[3] Ibid., p. 31.

[4] Beaver and Wolfson, in a deductive analysis under the assumption of perfect and complete markets, show that only in a system where current values are employed and translation occurs at current exchange rates will the results be both symmetrical and economically interpretable. The former is defined as a situation where two "economically equivalent investments" — one in the foreign market and the other in the investment market — will lead to the same financial statement numbers when translation into a common currency is made. Economic interpretability occurs only if the balance sheet values are equal to the present value of future cash flows for all balance sheet elements. If historical cost elements are translated at the historical rate, the results will be symmetrical. If accounts kept on a historical cost basis are translated at the current rate, the results are neither economically interpretable nor symmetrical. The problems of extending their analysis to incomplete and imperfect markets, including imperfections in exchange rates themselves, are duly noted by the authors. Beaver and Wolfson (1982).

U.S. dollars. On the other hand, a **foreign currency orientation** recognizes that the foreign operations occurred in a foreign currency and that those operations may not affect U.S. dollars; therefore, accounting should be consistent with the foreign-currency economic impact of the operations. Foreign-currency-denominated assets, liabilities, revenues, and expenses are assumed to be measured in the foreign currency but are translated to U.S. dollars for reporting purposes. Consistent with the foreign orientation is the notion that exchange rate changes do not affect operations or cash flows until the net assets are exchanged. Therefore, the effects of changing exchange rates should not be reported in income until the net assets are exchanged.

SFAS 8

SFAS 8 and previous standards were consistent with the U.S. dollar orientation. The **temporal** method of translation was required by SFAS 8: all balance sheet items that were carried at current or future exchange prices (for example, monetary items, inventories at market price, and investments at market price) were translated at the current exchange rate, while items carried at past prices (for example, fixed assets) were translated at exchange rates existing at the time the item was acquired (that is, the historical exchange rate). Income statement items were translated at the average exchange rate for the reporting period — except that items related to balance sheet accounts which were translated at historical exchange rates (for example, cost of goods sold and depreciation) were also translated at the historical rates. The exchange adjustment, the amount required to balance the statements due to different translation rates, was reported each period on the income statement as an exchange gain or loss. This complex translation was necessary to convert foreign currency account balances to their U.S. dollar equivalent; that is, to arrive at the same dollar amount as if dollars had been used as the accounting basis all along.

SFAS 8 was faithful to the historical cost accounting model but from an economic viewpoint it produced illogical results. For example, assume a Swiss subsidiary of a U.S. enterprise borrows $100 million in Swiss francs to finance the construction of a plant that costs $120 million in Swiss francs. Swiss franc revenues generated from use of the new plant will be used to retire the Swiss franc debt; therefore, no U.S. dollars will be used. If the franc appreciates 10 percent against the U.S. dollar, the liability would be written up to $110 million and an "accounting loss" of $10 million would be reported in the consolidated financial statements in accordance with SFAS 8. Because the cost of the plant is translated at the historical rate, however, no recognition would be given to the fact that the plant may be "worth" more in terms of its future net revenue stream in francs that will be used to retire the debt.

The preceding transaction may be viewed in two ways economically: (1) a gain of $2 million occurred because the building is "worth" $12 million more, while the debt owed is only $10 million more; or (2) no gain or loss occurred because the Swiss subsidiary is self-contained and its operations do not affect the U.S. parent's cash flows, nor do exchange rate changes affect the subsidiary's cash flows. As can be seen, accounting numbers produced by SFAS 8, although faithful to the historical cost model, did not necessarily reflect the perceived economic impact of the foreign operations.

A number of empirical studies were made of the economic impact of SFAS 8 on American multinational enterprises. Although the studies were directed to many facets of the subject, the only aspect that was found to have any possible impact dealt with foreign exchange risk and management policies regarding hedging of foreign currency exposures. Foreign currency exposure may be defined as either accounting or economic exposure. **Accounting exposure** is the exposure to exchange gains and losses resulting from translating foreign-currency-denominated financial statements into U.S. dollars (for example, the $10 million we have just been considering). **Economic exposure** is the exposure to cash flow changes resulting from dealings in foreign-denominated transactions and commitments (for example, the need to use more U.S. dollars to settle a foreign-currency-denominated debt).

In general, accounting exposure does not affect foreign currency cash flows nor does it affect reporting currency cash flows (that is, U.S. dollars). Rather, it results in "paper" debits and credits. An example is the translation of the $110 million liability of the preceding example; it would result in reporting a $10 million loss but would not affect either Swiss franc or U.S. dollar cash flows. On the other hand, economic exposure does directly affect consolidated cash flows. An example would be if the $110 million Swiss franc debt were settled using U.S. dollars rather than Swiss francs.

Many studies found that multinational enterprises adopted policies of minimizing accounting exposure through hedging activities.[5] Unfortunately, accounting exposure and economic exposure frequently were opposite; for example, there might be a short accounting exposure and a long economic exposure. The result, then, was that many enterprises were risking cash resources through forward exchange contracts to hedge a noncash exposure at the sacrifice of economic exposure. Those enterprises, in essence, were transferring a foreign exchange loss under SFAS 8 into an interest cost and simultaneously risking greater economic exposure.

SFAS 52

In May, 1978, the FASB requested comments from constituents regarding the first twelve SFASs. Eighty-eight percent of the comments received requested that the board reconsider SFAS 8. The primary complaints about SFAS 8 were similar to those illustrated in the preceding example: exchange gains and losses are reported when from an economic viewpoint the reverse had occurred.

SFAS 52 changes drastically the means of accounting for foreign currency operations. It adopts a functional currency orientation rather than a U.S. dollar orientation. The **functional currency** is the currency of the subsidiary's "primary economic environment" where cash is primarily received and spent.[6]

---

[5] See, for example, Evans, Folks, and Jilling (1978); and Shank, Dillard, and Murdock (1979).
[6] FASB (1981, para. 162).

If the foreign entity's currency is the functional currency, this means that net income is measured in the foreign currency and then restated into dollars at the average exchange rate for the period. All balance sheet items are translated at the current exchange rate at the end of the period. Any exchange adjustment resulting from translating balance sheet and income statement items at different exchange rates is displayed as a separate component of stockholders' equity, not as a gain or loss on the income statement. The separate component of stockholders' equity is taken into income only upon complete or substantially complete liquidation of the foreign investment by the U.S. parent. At that time, it is included in the gain or loss on disposition of the investment (for example, net proceeds from sale minus carrying amount of the investment minus debit component of equity equals gain or loss on disposition).

The objective of translation under SFAS 52, then, is to avoid reporting (1) accounting exchange gains and losses when an economic gain or loss has not occurred, and (2) not to report foreign-currency-denominated operations as if they had occurred in U.S. dollars. Thus, if the results of foreign-currency-denominated operations will not affect U.S. dollar cash flows, no exchange gain or loss is recorded. Moreover, assets, liabilities, revenues, and expenses that are denominated in a foreign currency are measured in that currency and then translated to U.S. dollars.

The key question brought up in SFAS 52 involves determination of the functional currency. The FASB has stated that where an enterprise's operations are ". . . relatively self-contained and integrated within a particular country, the functional currency generally would be the currency of that country."[7] This wouldn't always be the case, however, particularly if the foreign operations are a mere extension of the operations of the parent. SFAS 52 does not provide "unequivocal" criteria for determining the functional currency, but it does provide extensive guidelines. The six guidelines or economic factors do have, as the discussion in the standard indicates, a differential cash flow orientation:

1. Cash flow indicators
   a. Foreign Currency — Cash flows related to the foreign entity's individual assets and liabilities are primarily in the foreign currency and do not directly impact the parent company's cash flows.
   b. Parent's Currency — Cash flows related to the foreign entity's individual assets and liabilities directly impact the parent's cash flows on a current basis and are readily available for remittance to the parent company.
2. Sales price indicators
   a. Foreign Currency — Sales prices for the foreign entity's products are not primarily responsive on a short-term basis to changes in exchange rates but are determined more by local competition or local government regulation.
   b. Parent's Currency — Sales prices for the foreign entity's products are primarily responsive on a short-term basis to changes in exchange rates; for example, sales prices are determined more by worldwide competition or by international prices.

---

[7] Ibid., para. 6.

3. Sales market indicators

a. Foreign Currency — There is an active local sales market for the foreign entity's products, although there also might be significant amounts of exports.

b. Parent's Currency — The sales market is mostly in the parent's country or sales contracts are denominated in the parent's currency.

4. Expense indicators

a. Foreign Currency — Labor, materials, and other costs for the foreign entity's products or services are primarily local costs, even though there also might be imports from other countries.

b. Parent's Currency — Labor, materials, and other costs for the foreign entity's products or services, on a continuing basis, are primarily costs for components obtained from the country in which the parent company is located.

5. Financing indicators

a. Foreign Currency — Financing is primarily denominated in foreign currency, and funds generated by the foreign entity's operations are sufficient to service existing and normally expected debt obligations.

b. Parent's Currency — Financing is primarily from the parent or other dollar-denominated obligations, or funds generated by the foreign entity's operations are not sufficient to service existing and normally expected debt obligations without the infusion of additional funds from the parent company. Infusion of additional funds from the parent company for expansion is not a factor, provided funds generated by the foreign entity's expanded operations are expected to be sufficient to service that additional financing.

6. Intercompany transactions and arrangements indicators

a. Foreign Currency — There is a low volume of intercompany transactions and there is not an extensive interrelationship between the operations of the foreign entity and the parent company. However, the foreign entity's operations may rely on the parent's or affiliates' competitive advantages, such as patents and trademarks.

b. Parent's Currency — There is a high volume of intercompany transactions and there is an extensive interrelationship between the operations of the foreign entity and the parent company. Additionally, the parent's currency generally would be the functional currency if the foreign entity is a device or shell corporation for holding investments, obligations, intangible assets, etc., that could readily be carried on the parent's or an affiliate's books.[8]

The FASB research report by Evans and Doupnik found that the six criteria provided adequate guidance for determining the functional currency. Furthermore, the respondents to the study agreed very strongly.[9] Of the six indicators, the four that were most heavily weighted were the first four discussed above.[10] Only a small percentage of the participants had difficulty in determining the functional currency in many cases. In terms of the extent of numbers of functional currencies that had to be determined, the maximum number was in the lower fifties and the mean number was fourteen.[11] Hence,

---

[8] Ibid., para. 42.
[9] Evans and Doupnik (1986, pp. 7–8).
[10] Ibid., p. 6.
[11] Ibid., p. 5.

determining the functional currency as well as actually doing the translating can be an extremely significant problem.

If the functional currency of a foreign operation is judged to be U.S. dollars, a different approach is taken. For example, if a foreign subsidiary of a U.S. parent is, in reality, an extension of the parent (that is, it is nothing more than a sales branch selling the U.S. parent's products and remitting the sales proceeds to the U.S. parent), then although the subsidiary's records are kept in a foreign currency, the functional currency is the U.S. dollar, and the accounting records must be converted into U.S. dollars. This is called **remeasurement** and is done by following the approach in SFAS 8 discussed previously. As a result, exchange gains and losses arising from translation from the currency of record into the functional currency would be recognized on the income statement. Thus, in certain situations, SFAS 52 will result in the same reporting as SFAS 8.

Although remeasurement may appear inconsistent with the approach adopted in SFAS 52, it is entirely consistent on theoretical grounds. The theory behind the functional currency concept is that some foreign subsidiaries are self-contained and that exchange rate fluctuations affect neither them nor their U.S. parent companies until cash is exchanged. On the other hand, however, if the functional currency is really the U.S. dollar, the presumption is that the foreign operation is not self-contained but rather an extension of the parent. Consequently, exchange rate fluctuations will affect cash flows and should be reported on the income statement as was done under SFAS 8. Remeasurement in SFAS 52 is an example of finite uniformity.

A problem does occur with the functional currency concept and the use of current exchange rates whenever the functional currency is too unstable to be used as a measurement base. This problem is referred to as "the disappearing asset problem" and is present when the functional currency is experiencing rapid inflation much in excess of that experienced in the reporting currency. For example, assume an Argentine subsidiary purchased a fixed asset in December, 1974 when the Argentina peso–U.S. dollar exchange rate was $.20. The asset cost 20,000,000 pesos and would be translated as $4,000,000. By September, 1982, the exchange rate was .000040; thus, the asset would be translated at $800.

At least three approaches are available for accounting for the disappearing asset problem. It could be ignored — so the asset would be translated at $800. The original exposure draft leading up to SFAS 52 adopted this position, but most of the comment letters received by the FASB objected. In the second exposure draft, the FASB proposed to adjust cost of the asset in pesos for the effects of changing prices and translate the adjusted amount at the current exchange rate. Although this approach probably is sound theoretically, it too met with considerable objection because it would result in introducing onto U.S. consolidated financial statements something that is not permitted for changes in prices denominated in U.S. dollars. Finally, the FASB, in SFAS 52, specified that in highly inflationary economies (defined as those with a cumulative inflation rate of approximately 100 percent over three years), the U.S. dollar should be used as if it were the functional currency. Translations, therefore, are similar to the SFAS 8 approach and fixed assets are translated at the historical rate (for example, .20 in the preceding example).

THE INTERNATIONAL SCENE

In order to gain a fuller understanding of the standard-setting process in other English-speaking countries, we briefly review the regulatory scene in the United Kingdom and several other members of the Commonwealth.[12] There are, of course, numerous other issues concerning accounting institutions and governance throughout the world.[13]

THE UNITED KINGDOM

The United Kingdom consists of England, Wales, Scotland, and Northern Ireland. The accounting profession in the United Kingdom consists of six major organizations. They are

The Institute of Chartered Accountants in England and Wales

The Institute of Chartered Accountants of Scotland

The Institute of Chartered Accountants in Ireland

The Association of Certified Accountants

The Institute of Cost and Management Accountants

The Chartered Institute of Public Finance and Accountancy

It is particularly interesting to note that the Institute of Chartered Accountants in Ireland, which was established prior to partition, still embraces both Northern Ireland and the Republic of Ireland. No standard-setting body existed in England prior to 1970, but several scandals occurring in the 1960s led to the possibility of government regulation of accounting standards. As a result, the three chartered institutes set up a standard-setting body, which is now called the Accounting Standards Committee (ASC). By 1976, the other three organizations also had representatives on the ASC.

The ASC resembles the APB much more than it does the FASB. ASC members serve on a part-time basis and are unpaid, similar to the APB. The ASC's standards, called *Statements of Standard Accounting Practice* (SSAPs), must

---

[12] Much of the information for the last two sections was derived from Holzer (1984); Evans, Taylor, and Holzmann (1985); Nobes and Parker (1985); and AlHashim and Arpan (1988).

[13] One important area in the international accounting realm concerns experience and educational requirements for licensure throughout the world. For an extended discussion, see Heaston (1984).

be approved by the governing boards of the six establishing organizations. Nevertheless, through 1988 a total of twenty-four SSAPs had been passed, two of which were later withdrawn.

Another difference between the regulatory scene in the United Kingdom and our own is that there is no British counterpart to the SEC. As a result, Solomons has noted that the ASC must look to the stock exchange and the six organizational bodies for its enforcement powers.[14] In the case of the stock exchange, it is a condition of listing that in the case of a qualified report due to a departure from an ASC standard, the firm must explain the reason for the departure to its shareholders. As for the auditors, any conflict with SSAPs must be disclosed and justified if the auditor concurs with the departure.

To a greater or lesser extent, standard setting in other countries in the British Commonwealth has been influenced by the United Kingdom model.

AUSTRALIA

There are two major accounting organizations in Australia: the Institute of Chartered Accountants in Australia and the Australian Society of Accountants. Both organizations issued their own statements independently until 1966. At that time, they jointly founded the Australian Accountancy Research Foundation, which is responsible for drafting and issuing accounting standards, called *Australian Accounting Standards.* The standards are issued in the name of both sponsoring organizations. Through 1988, twenty-three Australian Accounting Standards had been issued as well as two Provisional Accounting Standards. The latter deal with certain current value data that are recommended as supplementary disclosures in published financial statements.

CANADA

Since the 1940s, the Canadian Institute of Chartered Accountants (CICA) has used committees to establish accounting standards. In 1973, two important groups were established: the Auditing Standards Committee and the Accounting Research Committee. The accounting and auditing "recommendations" of these two groups are published in the CICA Handbook.

The Accounting Research Committee does have members from the Financial Executives Institute of Canada as well as the Society of Industrial Accountants of Canada. To this extent, it bears a resemblance to the FASB. Both Canadian committees also use a system of exposure drafts for the purpose of receiving input from affected parties. The two committees also require a two-thirds vote before a recommendation can be issued.

CICA recommendations often parallel American standards. Research and development costs are expensed, as in the United States, except for situations where technical feasibility of production is established. Only in this situation

---

[14] Solomons (1986, p. 56).

are development costs capitalized. The categorization and classification of leases as capital leases or operating leases is essentially similar to our own.

NEW ZEALAND

New Zealand's professional body of accountants is the New Zealand Society of Accountants. Although a committee of this body had been issuing statements on accounting practice since 1951, a new group, the Board of Research, was formed in 1961, which issued Statements on Accounting Practice. Finally, in 1973 the council of the New Zealand Society began issuing its current series, called *Statements of Standard Accounting Practice*, the same title used in the United Kingdom. Twenty-one standards had been issued through 1988.

INTERNATIONAL HARMONIZATION OF ACCOUNTING STANDARDS

Revolutionary developments in transportation and communications have been bringing the world closer together, closer to what has been called a "global village." In addition, a forty-five-year era marked by a large growth in international trade and other forms of interdependency among nations have had enormous significance for many facets of our lives. In a general way, these developments have a homogenizing effect upon many customs, practices, and institutions. In business several specific conditions have led to a desire to harmonize accounting standards among nations. *Harmonization* refers to the degree of coordination or similarity among the various sets of national accounting standards and methods and formats of financial reporting.[15]

Among the factors underlying the desire for harmonization is the rise in importance of the multinational firm. General similarity of accounting standards and procedures would facilitate coordination among the parts of the multinational enterprise. In particular, consolidated financial reporting would certainly be made easier if the accounting rules applicable to the various parts of the multinational firm were more consistent. Complementary to the rise of the multinational corporation is the internationalization occurring within the public accounting profession. Many firms have offices and practices throughout the world. The greater the degree of harmonization, the more the auditing function is facilitated. Finally, cross-border financings have increased as has the listing of securities of foreign enterprises for trading on the major stock exchanges in many countries. The International Organization of Securities Commissions

---

[15]Meek and Saudagaran (1990, pp. 168–169) make a distinction between standardization and harmonization. The former refers to uniform standards in all countries, which makes the concept similar to absolute uniformity as developed by AlHashim and Arpan. Harmonization, according to Meek and Saudagaran, refers to reconciling different national viewpoints as long as there are no logical conflicts. Wallace (1990, pp. 10–11) presents five degrees of harmonization within the context of the International Accounting Standards Committee's limitations and goals.

(IOSCO), an organization of stock exchanges throughout the world, is actively concerned with promoting harmonization of accounting standards.

While harmonization is primarily concerned with promoting similarity among sets of national accounting standards, the issue of uniformity has also arisen. Three proposed models of uniformity at the international level are

1. Absolute uniformity.
2. Circumstantial uniformity.
3. Purposive uniformity.[16]

Absolute uniformity means one set of standards as well as one financial statement format should prevail throughout the international economic community without regard to different economic circumstances or user needs. Capitalist societies, as one might expect, have responded coolly to the absolute uniformity approach. The circumstantial uniformity model would, on a transnational basis, allow different accounting methods where different circumstances are present. This is similar to finite uniformity (Chapter 8) but employed on an international basis. The third approach, purposive uniformity, would take into account both different underlying circumstances as well as different user needs and purposes.

Although these three models are somewhat useful as a philosophy for coordinating accounting standards from the international perspective, they do present problems. Absolute uniformity, for example, must squarely face the problem of national sovereignty relative to standard setting. At the other end of the spectrum, the purposive model may be too diffuse to employ successfully if both different circumstances and different user needs are to underlie accounting standards. Circumstantial uniformity, while certainly not easy to employ, at least avoids the extreme dangers of the other two models. At this time, international accounting standard setting has not reached the point where any of these models have been specifically selected. Let us, then, examine the two bodies that have been concerned with international harmonization of accounting standards.

THE INTERNATIONAL ACCOUNTING STANDARDS COMMITTEE

The IASC was formed in 1973 by professional accounting organizations from nine nations: Australia, Canada, France, Germany, Japan, Mexico, the Netherlands, the United Kingdom and Ireland, and the United States. The AICPA (rather than the FASB or the SEC) is the American organization holding membership in the IASC. At the present time, sixty accounting organizations from forty-seven nations are members of the IASC. The members have pledged to use their "best endeavors" to bring the adoption of IASC standards to their countries. It should be noted, however, that no nation or any professional body

---

[16]For further coverage, see AlHashim and Arpan (1988, pp. 42–47).

from any nation has surrendered its accounting standard-setting sovereignty to the IASC.[17] As of fall 1990, thirty international accounting standards had been issued by the IASC. These are listed in Exhibit 19–1 (page 580).

The IASC is playing an important role in the drive toward harmonization. This has been accentuated by the release in 1989 of Exposure Draft 32, which attempts to decrease the number of acceptable alternatives in its previous twenty-five standards in order to increase comparability among the financial statements of corporations complying with IASC standards. Many previously acceptable alternative treatments would be eliminated, although in several cases an allowed alternative treatment is acceptable. For example, in the case of positive goodwill, immediate adjustment against shareholders' interests has been eliminated and capitalization of goodwill has been required. Amortization of goodwill may in no case exceed twenty years. In the case of pensions, the accrued benefit valuation method is preferred but the projected benefit valuation approach is the allowed alternative.[18]

It should also be noted that the IASC has recently promulgated a conceptual framework. The similarity of the IASC conceptual framework to that of the United States has been noted by Agrawal, Jensen, Meador, and Sellers.[19] They note that several user groups are identified but only those objectives that are common to all users are emphasized. The principal qualitative characteristics are similar to those in SFAC 2. Likewise, the IASC lists several possible measurement bases, such as historical cost, replacement cost, exit value, and present value, and notes that historical cost is the most prevalent basis although it may be combined with other approaches.

Several studies have attempted to measure the progress of harmonization.[20] The general conclusion appears to be that harmonization is increasing, but vastly different ways of measuring harmonization have been employed and there have been questions raised relative to the validity of the data in some of the studies.[21]

One of the impediments to the harmonization process is nationalism. Standard-setting organizations in the various countries attempt to maintain independence and sovereignty in the promulgation of accounting regulations. A further compounding factor is the growth of regional groups, such as the Eu-

---

[17] For an excellent analysis of IASC's survival strategies and mode of operations, see Wallace (1990).

[18] Rivera is somewhat pessimistic about the ability of the IASC to bring about harmonization. The issuance of standards at the national level has not been synchronized with the IASC. In addition, the IASC may be overly reliant on American and British models. Finally, enforcement of IASC standards was going to receive the "best endeavors" on the part of the founding member nations but there has been little real attempt to bring about compliance. Departures from IASC standards were to be noted in audit reports but there has been very little, if any, observance of this practice. Rivera (1989, pp. 325–328).

[19] Agrawal, Jensen, Meador, and Sellers (1989, pp. 243–246).

[20] Studies attempting to measure changes in harmonization include Nair and Frank (1980); Nair and Frank (1981); Choi and Banishi (1982); Taylor, Evans, and Joy (1986); Moung-Yin Chan (1986); Al-Najjar (1986); and Doupnik (1987). See van der Tas (1988) for a discussion of how to measure harmonization.

[21] Nobes (1983).

EXHIBIT 19–1
International Accounting Standards

Standard Number	Subject	Date of Issue
IAS 1	Disclosure of Accounting Policies	Jan. 1975
IAS 2	Valuation and Presentation of Inventories in the Context of the Historical Cost System	Oct. 1975
IAS 3	Consolidated Financial Statements	June 1976
IAS 4	Depreciation Accounting	Oct. 1976
IAS 5	Information to Be Disclosed in Financial Statements	Oct. 1976
IAS 6	(Superseded by IAS 15)	
IAS 7	Statement of Changes in Financial Position	Oct. 1977
IAS 8	Unusual and Prior Period Items and Changes in Accounting Policies	Feb. 1978
IAS 9	Accounting for Research and Development Activities	July 1978
IAS 10	Contingencies and Events Occurring After the Balance Sheet Date	Oct. 1978
IAS 11	Accounting for Construction Contracts	March 1979
IAS 12	Accounting for Taxes on Income	July 1979
IAS 13	Presentation of Current Assets and Current Liabilities	Nov. 1979
IAS 14	Reporting Financial Information by Segment	Aug. 1981
IAS 15	Information Reflecting the Effects of Changing Prices	Nov. 1981
IAS 16	Accounting for Property, Plant and Equipment	March 1982
IAS 17	Accounting for Leases	Sept. 1982
IAS 18	Revenue Recognition	Dec. 1982
IAS 19	Accounting for Retirement Benefits in the Financial Statements of Employers	Jan. 1983
IAS 20	Accounting for Government Grants and Disclosure of Government Assistance	April 1983
IAS 21	Accounting for the Effects of Changes in Foreign Exchange Rates	July 1983
IAS 22	Accounting for Business Combinations	Nov. 1983
IAS 23	Capitalization of Borrowing Costs	March 1984
IAS 24	Related Party Disclosures	July 1984
IAS 25	Accounting for Investments	March 1986
IAS 26	Accounting and Reporting by Retirement Benefit Plans	Jan. 1987

(continued)

EXHIBIT 19–1
(continued)

IAS 27	Consolidated Financial Statements and Accounting for Investments in Subsidiaries	April 1989
IAS 28	Accounting for Investments in Associates	April 1989
IAS 29	Financial Reporting in Hyperinflationary Economies	April 1989
IAS 30	Disclosures in the Financial Statements of Banks and Similar Institutions	August 1990

ropean Community (EC), which try to promote harmonization within their member-nation groups. In order to understand the need for harmonization, we next examine some of the possible factors underlying differences in accounting standards among various nations and national groupings.

CULTURAL AND OTHER IMPEDIMENTS TO HARMONIZATION

The desire for harmonization of financial accounting standards leads to a very obvious question: Why do accounting standards differ among nations? A growing body of research has attempted to shed light on this question. Most of the approaches have been of a "top down" nature. By this labeling, we mean that researchers have attempted to identify economic and environmental or cultural characteristics of a nation and then to determine deductively the effect upon the accounting system. For example, Mueller identified four economic/professional dimensions to accounting development in advanced Western nations with market-oriented economies:

1. The macroeconomic pattern.
2. The microeconomic pattern.
3. The independent discipline approach.
4. The uniform accounting approach.[22]

In the macroeconomic pattern, private-sector accounting is closely linked to national economic policies. In the microeconomic pattern, accounting is seen as an aspect of managerial economics with decision-making overtones. Accounting is a service-type function deriving from business practice in the independent discipline orientation. Finally, it is a control and administrative tool in

---

[22] As discussed by Gray (1988, p. 2).

the uniform accounting category.[23] Nobes added further depth and discriminating characteristics to Mueller's basic model.[24]

Perhaps the most common approach to national accounting differentiation has emphasized the cultural dimension developed by Hofstede.[25] The cultural orientation emphasizes similar social understanding, values, beliefs, and symbols shared by the members of a particular culture.[26] Hofstede's cultural dimensions consist of

1. individualism versus collectivism,
2. large versus small power distance,
3. strong versus weak uncertainty avoidance,
4. masculinity versus femininity.[27]

Collectivism indicates a tightly knit social grouping, whereas individualism implies a looser and freer social framework and resulting modes of action by members of the society. In large power-distance societies, the place of individuals within the society is accepted by the participants; whereas much more unrest and turmoil relative to the power vested in institutions and organizations is present in small power-distance cultures. In weak uncertainty-avoidance cultures, people feel relatively secure; whereas in strong uncertainty-avoidance societies, people have a stronger desire to manage the future and hedge or avoid risks than in the weak uncertainty-avoidance culture. In masculine societies, qualities such as heroism, assertiveness, and financial and other forms of success are strongly desired; whereas in feminine-oriented cultures, altruism and similar forms of behavior prevail.[28]

Gray attempted to extend Hofstede's cultural dimension to the values of the accounting subculture. His accounting values include professionalism, uniformity, conservatism, and secrecy.[29] In terms of professionalism, a greater degree leads to professional self-regulation and a lesser degree points toward government regulation. The higher the degree of uniformity, the more accounting rules are applied in a "cook book" fashion and the less professional judgment is employed. Conservatism influences measurement practices. More conservative leans toward well-specified measurement practices (historical costs, for example), whereas less conservative would veer toward current values. The degree of secrecy in a culture affects the extent of disclosure.[30]

Perera has restated Hofstede's cultural dimension and Gray's accounting

---

[23] Ibid.
[24] Nobes (1983).
[25] Hofstede (1987).
[26] Perera (1989, p. 43).
[27] Hofstede (1987, pp. 4–5).
[28] Perera (1989, pp. 44–46).
[29] Gray (1988, pp. 8–11).
[30] As discussed in Perera (1989, p. 47).

subculture into a number of hypotheses that should shed light on these relationships. For example, he hypothesizes that the greater the uncertainty avoidance and the less the individualism, then the greater should be the conservatism exhibited by the accounting subculture.[31]

Although these approaches to deducing national characteristics are quite interesting and may later bear considerable fruit, they have not as yet been able to zero in on particular accounting practices within a nation, much less provide specifics about whether harmonization can occur and how best to accomplish it. At this point, this research appears to be leading to the coalescing of countries into various groupings based on the cultural dimension combined with the values of the accounting subculture.[32] An appreciation and understanding of cultural groupings can be useful in terms of guiding the harmonization process as well as determining its limits.

However, the cultural dimension — as discussed above — is not the only area being investigated in terms of determining differences in national accounting systems and standards. Rebmann-Huber sees the nature of financial markets within nations as being a key determinant of financial reporting.[33] The crucial distinction that she sees is between capital-based financial markets where long-term investment is dominated by individual investors in the capital market, and credit-based financial markets where the bulk of long-term funds are provided by government or financial institutions. In the former situation, financial reporting would be geared more toward providing information useful to actual and prospective investors. Secondary factors underlying financial reporting include the division between private and state regulation of the standard-setting process and the participation of the accounting profession in the setting of standards.

Finally, Most and Salter argue that financial reporting is grounded in the legal system of the nation.[34] For example, the Companies Acts dominate in the United Kingdom with the result that audited financial statements must be approved by the shareholders and that auditors be appointed by the shareholders.[35] In continental Europe, however, conformity with tax laws has been a dominating factor.[36] This may account for why leases are not capitalized in France and are seldom even disclosed.

Many of the analyses of why national accounting systems differ may overlap. For example, legal institutions surely have a cultural basis. Clearly, we are at a very early stage in the evolution of this important aspect of international accounting research. We now briefly examine other organizations involved with various aspects of international accounting.

---

[31] Ibid., p. 49.
[32] Gray (1988, pp. 11–13). See also Donleavy (1990).
[33] Rebmann-Huber (1990).
[34] Most and Salter (1990).
[35] Ibid., p. 4.
[36] Ibid.

THE INTERNATIONAL FEDERATION OF ACCOUNTANTS

IFAC was formed in 1977. In terms of its objectives, it is quite complementary to the IASC. Like the IASC, the members are accounting organizations from the nations of the world. At the end of 1986, ninety-seven accounting organizations from seventy-one nations belonged to IFAC. Forty-two international guidelines on such subjects as auditing practices, education, and ethics have been issued. Like the IASC, IFAC guidelines cannot be imposed on any member organization or nation.

Since the IASC and IFAC are so closely concerned with complementary international accounting issues, the possibility of their merger has arisen. Though this has not occurred, both organizations continue to cooperate and work together on their mutual interests.

OTHER ORGANIZATIONS INVOLVED WITH INTERNATIONAL ACCOUNTING ISSUES

Several other organizations, in addition to IASC and IFAC, are concerned with international accounting issues. The European Economic Community (EEC or Common Market) has issued certain directives that, when passed by its Council of Ministers, become binding on its member nations. The Fourth Directive concerns basic issues of financial reporting that are applicable to companies within the EEC community. In addition to providing standard formats for financial statements, the directive states that financial statements be based on four concepts: consistency, going concern, prudence, and accrual accounting. It also permits current value statements in addition to historical costs. The United Nations has also taken an interest in international accounting. Its efforts have been restricted to the presentation of both accounting and nonaccounting information by multinational corporations.

Another organization concerned with promoting harmonization is the Organization for Economic Cooperation and Development (OECD). This organization is made up of twenty-four members coming mainly from the large, industrialized Western nations. Although it has been mainly focused on fiscal and economic matters, it has begun taking an interest in accounting practices. In 1978 it formed an Ad Hoc Working Group on Accounting Standards, which was concerned with formulating standards for multinational enterprises. It has begun working with standard-setting agencies within its member nations and also the IASC, whose efforts it supports.

Despite the limited power held by such organizations as the IASC and IFAC, we would expect increased activity in the regulatory process by international organizations. However, it is quite clear that national accounting organizations will maintain and not surrender their standard-setting powers. Furthermore, cultural and socioeconomic factors will probably militate against a very close harmonization of accounting standards. Lease accounting provides an example of a cultural difference affecting accounting standards. In the United States, for example, the attempt is made to analyze leases from the economic standpoint, resulting in the dichotomy of capital leases and operating leases.

However, in many overseas countries legal form takes precedence over economic substance resulting in noncapitalization of *all* leases.[37] Cultural differences are not easy to overcome. Even more troublesome than cultural differences are socioeconomic differences. In socialist countries, enterprises often must utilize a uniform chart of accounts to facilitate measurement of gross national product and related statistical and national income accounting data. However, even in a capitalist nation like France, a uniform system of accounts along with model financial statements are used by virtually all businesses. Cultural and socioeconomic considerations, not to mention nationalism itself, will tend to slow harmonization.

SUMMARY

SFAS 8 developed a system of foreign currency translation that employed current exchange rates for current assets and liabilities and monetary items and historical exchange rates for fixed assets. The result of this method was that gains or losses were created as a result of the translation process. For firms having a functional currency that is *not* the U.S. dollar, this created accounting exposure but generally not economic exposure.

SFAS 52 corrected some of the problems of SFAS 8. If the functional currency is not the U.S. dollar, translation is done at the current exchange rate for all balance sheet items. Income is measured in the foreign currency and translation occurs at the average exchange rate for the period. Any exchange differential resulting from this process would be a separate item of stockholders' equity rather than a gain or loss for the period. If the U.S. dollar were the functional currency resulting from a factor like frequent remission of funds to the American parent, then the method of SFAS 8 would be used.

Harmonization means increasing the coordination or similarity of accounting standards and reports throughout the world. To accomplish this, three types of uniformity models have been suggested. Absolute uniformity throughout the world would be virtually unattainable. Purposive uniformity, which would take into account differences both in circumstances and in user groups, would also be extremely difficult to attain. The IASC is an organization that drafts international accounting standards that are intended to bring about harmonization. Member nations are pledged to attempt to bring their own national standards in line with IASC standards although the task will certainly not be an easy one.[38] The IFAC is an organization whose functions in areas such as auditing practices, ethics, and education are complementary to the IASC. Other organizations of a transnational variety are also concerned with bringing about harmonization. Although the evidence indicates that more harmonization is

---

[37] AlHashim and Arpan (1988, p. 101).

[38] Problems of bringing about harmonization as seen from the national standard-setting perspective are discussed by Beresford (1990).

occurring, economic, cultural, and environmental differences have led to a lack of similarity in accounting regulations and financial reporting at the national level.

QUESTIONS

1. What are the differences between a foreign currency orientation and a U.S. dollar orientation regarding the translation of foreign currency operations?
2. How do accounting exposure and economic exposure differ?
3. Why would balance sheets prepared under SFAS 8 lack additivity?
4. Why does SFAS 52 provide an example of finite uniformity in terms of the use of remeasurement?
5. What is the disappearing asset problem?
6. What does the term *functional currency* mean?
7. Why did SFAS 8 present an enormous problem in the area of economic consequences?
8. What does harmonization of accounting standards mean?
9. Why would it be extremely difficult to implement purposive uniformity in terms of the harmonization of accounting standards?
10. Are rigid uniformity (Chapter 8) and absolute uniformity identical concepts?
11. What factors make it difficult to bring about a high degree of harmonization among accounting standards?
12. In what ways is the U.K. method of setting accounting standards rather unwieldy?
13. How do the cultural impediments to harmonization described by Hofstede relate to the economic/professional dimension developed by Mueller?
14. What other factors, aside from the cultural and economic/professional, affect accounting standards at the national level?
15. What is the relationship between the IFAC and IASC?

CASES AND PROBLEMS

1. Three models of uniformity have been proposed for the harmonization of standards: absolute uniformity, circumstantial uniformity, and purposive uniformity. In Chapter 8 two approaches to uniformity were discussed: finite uniformity and rigid uniformity. Write an essay on the purposes of uniformity at both the national and international levels covering (but not necessarily restricted to) the following issues:
    (a) The role of uniformity and comparability at the national level relative to setting standards.
    (b) The relationship between the terms *harmonization* and *uniformity*.

(c) The interrelation between the three types of harmonization and the two types of uniformity.
2. Why do the six criteria or guidelines for determining the functional currency in SFAS 52 provide a good example of finite uniformity? Discuss in depth.

BIBLIOGRAPHY OF REFERENCED WORKS

Agrawal, Surendra P., Paul H. Jensen, Anna Lee Meador, and Keith Sellers (1989). "An International Comparison of Conceptual Frameworks of Accounting," *The International Journal of Accounting* (Vol. 24, No. 3), pp. 237–250.

AlHashim, Dhia, D., and Jeffrey S. Arpan (1988). *International Dimensions of Accounting* (PWS-KENT Publishing Company).

AlNajjar, Fouad (1986). "Standardization in Accounting Practices: A Comparative International Study," *The International Journal of Accounting* (Spring 1986), pp. 161–176.

Beaver, William H., and Mark A. Wolfson (1982). "Foreign Currency Translation and Changing Prices and Perfect and Complete Markets," *Journal of Accounting Research* (Autumn 1982, Pt. II), pp. 528–550.

Beresford, Dennis (1990). "Internationalization of Accounting Standards," *Accounting Horizons* (March 1990), pp. 99–107.

Choi, Frederick D. S., and Vinod B. Bavishi (1982). "Financial Accounting Standards: A Multinational Synthesis and Policy Framework," *The International Journal of Accounting* (Fall 1982), pp. 159–183.

Donleavy, G. D. (1990). "Prospects for Accounting Harmonization in the Asia Pacific Region in the 1990's," presented at Global Economic Alliances: The Implications for Accounting Education, Standard Setting and Practice (Montreal 1990), pp. 1–13.

Doupnik, Timothy S. (1987). "Evidence of International Harmonization of Financial Reporting," *The International Journal of Accounting* (Fall 1987), pp. 47–67.

Evans, Thomas G., and Timothy S. Doupnik (1986). *Determining the Functional Currency Under Statement 52* (FASB).

Evans, Thomas G., William R. Folks, Jr., and Michael Jilling (1978). *The Impact of Financial Accounting Standards No. 8 on the Foreign Exchange Risk Management Practices of American Multinational Firms: An Economic Impact Study* (FASB).

Evans, Thomas G., Martin E. Taylor, and Oscar Holzmann (1985). *International Accounting and Reporting* (Macmillan Publishing Company).

Financial Accounting Standards Board (1975). "Accounting for the Translation of Foreign Currency Transactions and Foreign Currency Financial Statements," *Statement of Financial Accounting Standards No. 8* (FASB).

———— (1981). "Foreign Currency Translation," *Statement of Financial Accounting Standards No. 52* (FASB).

Gray, S. J. (1988). "Towards a Theory of Cultural Influence on the Development of Accounting Systems Internationally, *Abacus* (April 1988), pp. 1–15.

Heaston, Patrick H. (1984). "Qualification Requirements for Public Accounting in Selected Foreign Countries: A Comparison with the United States," *The International Journal of Accounting* (Fall 1984), pp. 71–94.

Hofstede, Gert (1987). "The Cultural Context of Accounting," in *Accounting and Culture* (American Accounting Association, 1987), pp. 1–11.

Holzer, H. Peter, ed. (1984). *International Accounting* (Harper and Row).

Houston, Carol Olson (1989). "Foreign Currency Translation Research: Review and Synthesis," *Journal of Accounting Literature* (1989), pp. 19–29.

Meek, Gary, and S. Saudagaran (1990). "A Survey of Research on Financial Reporting in a Transnational Context," *Journal of Accounting Literature* (Vol. 9, 1990), pp. 145–182.

Most, Kenneth S., and Stephen B. Salter (1990). "Classification Research in International Accounting and Its Relevance to European Accounting Harmonization," presented at Global Economic Alliances: The Implications for Accounting Education, Standard Setting and Practice (Montreal 1990), pp. 1–9.

Moung-Yin Chan, Anthony (1986). "The Patterns of the Theoretical Basis of IAS: Accounting Theory Models at the International Level," *The International Journal of Accounting* (Fall 1986), pp. 101–117.

Nair, R. D., and Werner G. Frank (1980). "The Impact of Disclosure and Measurement Practices on International Accounting Classifications," *The Accounting Review* (July 1980), pp. 426–450.

———— (1981). "The Harmonization of International Accounting Standards, 1973–1979," *The International Journal of Accounting* (Fall 1981), pp. 61–77.

Nobes, C. W. (1983). "A Judgmental International Classification of Financial Reporting Practices," *Journal of Business Finance & Accounting* (Spring 1983), pp. 1–19.

Nobes, C. W., and R. H. Parker (1985). *Comparative International Accounting* (Philip Allan/St. Martin's Press).

Perera, M. H. (1989). "Towards a Framework to Analyze the Impact of Culture on Accounting," *The International Journal of Accounting* (Vol. 24, No. 1), pp. 42–56.

Rebmann-Huber, Zelma (1990). "The Relationship Between Financial Markets and Financial Reporting Systems: Model and Empirical Test for 16 Countries of the OECD," presented at Global Economic Alliances: The Implications for Accounting Education, Standard Setting and Practice (Montreal 1990), pp. 1–18.

Rivera, Juan M. (1989). "The Internationalization of Accounting Standards: Past Problems and Current Prospects," *The International Journal of Accounting* (Vol. 24, No. 4), pp. 320–342.

Shank, John K., Jesse F. Dillard, and Richard J. Murdock (1979). *Assessing the Economic Impact of FASB No. 8* (Financial Executives Research Foundation).

Solomons, David (1986). *Making Accounting Policy* (Oxford University Press).

Statistical Abstract of the United States (1990). (United States Government Printing Office).

Taylor, Martin, Thomas G. Evans, and Arthur C. Joy (1986). "The Impact of IASC Accounting Standards on Comparability and Consistency of International Accounting Reporting Practices," *The International Journal of Accounting* (Fall 1986), pp. 1–9.

van der Tas, Leon G. (1988). "Measuring Harmonization of Financial Reporting Practice," *Accounting and Business Research* (Spring 1988), pp. 157–169.

Wallace, R. S. (1990). "Survival Strategies of a Global Organization: The Case of the International Accounting Standards Committee," *Accounting Horizons* (June 1990), pp. 1–22.

ADDITIONAL READINGS

Foreign Currency Translation

Brown, Betty (1985). "The Relationship Between Firm Attributes and Early Adoption of the Foreign Currency Translation Standard, SFS No. 52: An Empirical Investigation," *International Journal of Accounting* (Fall 1985), pp. 1–19.

Dukes, Roland E. (1978). *An Empirical Investigation of the Effects of the Statement of Financial Accounting Standards No. 8 on Security Return Behavior* (FASB).

Houston, Carol Olson, and Gerhard G. Mueller (1988). "Foreign Exchange Rate Hedging and SFAS No. 52 — Relatives or Strangers?" *Accounting Horizons* (December 1988), pp. 50–57.

Lorensen, Leonard (1972). *Reporting Foreign Operations of U.S. Companies in U.S. Dollars* (AICPA).

Peat, Marwick, Mitchell & Co. (1977). *A Survey of the Economic Impacts of FASB Statement No. 8*, "Accounting for the Translation of Foreign Currency Transactions and Foreign Currency Financial Statements" (Peat, Marwick, Mitchell & Co.).

Wyman, Harold E. (1976). "Analysis of Gains or Losses from Foreign Monetary Items: An Application of Purchasing Power Parity Concepts," *The Accounting Review* (July 1976), pp. 545–558.

Ziebart, David A. (1985). "Exchange Rates and Purchasing Power Parity: Evidence Regarding the Failure of SFAS No. 52 to Consider Exchange Risk in Upper-Inflationary Countries," *International Journal of Accounting* (Fall 1985), pp. 39–51.

Harmonization of Accounting Standards

Aitken, Michael J., and Trevor D. Wise (1984). "The Real Objectives of the International Accounting Standards Committee," *The International Journal of Accounting* (Fall 1984), pp. 171–177.

Evans, Thomas G., and Martin E. Taylor (1982). "'Bottom Line Compliance' with the IASC: A Comparative Analysis," *International Journal of Accounting* (Fall 1982), pp. 115–128.

Fitzgerald, Richard D. (1981). "International Harmonization of Accounting and Reporting," *The International Journal of Accounting* (Fall 1981), pp. 21–32.

Golub, Steven (1982). "A Global Perspective to Financial Reporting," *International Journal of Accounting* (Fall 1982), pp. 37–44.

Nobes, C. W. (1981). "An Empirical Analysis of International Accounting Principles: A Comment," *Journal of Accounting Research* (Spring 1981), pp. 268–270.

Purcell, Thomas J., III, and James P. Scott (1986). "An Analysis of the Feasibility of Harmonizing Reporting Practices Between Members of the EEC and OECD," *International Journal of Accounting* (Spring 1986), pp. 109–131.

Soeters, Joseph, and Hein Schreuder (1988). "The Interaction Between National and Organizational Cultures in Accounting Firms," *Accounting, Organizations and Society* (Vol. 13, No. 1), pp. 75–85.

Vangermeersch, Richard (1985). "The Route of the Seventh Directive of the EEC on Consolidated Accounts — Slow, Steady, Studied, and Successful," *International Journal of Accounting* (Spring 1985), pp. 103–118.

AUTHOR INDEX

Abdel-khalik, A. R., 47, 48, 94, 107, 109, 163, 191, 203, 220, 411
Adkerson, R., 474, 533, 534, 542
Agrawal, S., 193
Aitken, M., 589
Ajinkya, B., 47
Albrecht, W. S., 287, 294
AlHashim, D., 575, 577, 578, 585, 587
AlNajjar, F., 579, 587
Altman, E., 209, 220
Alvin, G., 517, 542
Anderson, A., 241, 253
Anderson, G., 69, 74
Anderson, R., 208, 220
Andrews, F., 82, 109
Anthony, R., 119, 132, 141, 329, 515, 534, 542
Anton, H., 157, 191, 346
Archibald, T. R., 203, 220
Armstrong, M., 89, 107
Arnold, D., 411
Arpan, J., 575, 577, 578, 585, 587
Arrow, K., 87, 90, 107
Ashton, R., 143, 223
Atiase, R., 245, 253

Bachman, J., 567
Backer, M., 342, 345, 370, 382, 411
Ball, R., 197, 201, 203, 220, 223
Bamber, L., 245, 253
Baran, A., 209, 220, 411
Barden, H., 329

Barlev, B., 143
Barnea, A., 185, 191
Barton, A., 160, 191, 447
Baskin, E., 379, 382
Basset, P., 509
Bavishi, V., 579, 587
Baxter, G., 567
Beaver, W., 40, 42, 46, 127, 142, 165, 186, 191, 196, 197, 201, 202, 206, 207, 209, 220, 235, 243, 244, 253, 383, 398, 410, 414, 445, 569, 587
Becker, S., 127, 142
Bedford, N., 50, 74, 143, 194, 255
Beidleman, C., 330, 379, 382, 487, 494, 507
Bejan, M., 255
Bell, P., 35, 46, 352, 358, 360, 370, 382
Bell, T., 32, 47, 465, 472
Benston, G., 80, 97, 107, 109, 243, 247, 253
Bentz, W., 48
Beresford, D., 447, 585, 587
Bernard, V., 459, 472
Bernstein, L., 144
Bernstein, M., 91, 107
Bevis, D., 447
Biddle, G., 203, 220
Bierman, H., 26, 383, 419, 424, 445, 474
Biggs, S., 302, 328
Bildersee, J., 40, 46, 206, 207, 398, 410
Binns, J., 557, 566
Bird, F., 144
Black, H., 417, 418, 445
Blackburn, J., 384

Blough, C., 76
Boatsman, J., 32, 47, 144, 379, 382, 474
Bodie, Z., 509
Borst, D., 150, 191
Boudreaux, K., 330
Bourn, M., 372, 382
Bowen, R., 197, 221
Bowers, P., 83, 107
Bowman, R., 533, 542
Bradford, W., 384
Braeutigam, R., 110
Breyer, S., 109
Briggs, J., 447
Briggs, R., 48
Briloff, A., 82, 107, 554, 565
Brinkman, D., 383
Bromwich, M., 109, 247, 253, 411
Brown, B., 588
Brown, P., 68, 74, 92, 107, 186, 191, 197, 201, 220, 221
Brown, R., 203, 221
Brownlee, E. R., 243, 253
Bruns, W., 383
Bublitz, B., 398, 410
Buckley, J,. 48, 421, 445
Buckman, A., 216, 223
Bullock, C., 424, 445
Bulow, J., 492, 507
Burgstahler, D., 197, 221
Burton, J., 75, 193, 388, 410, 554, 566
Buzby, S., 255
Byington, J. R., 320, 328

Cadenhead, G., 230, 253
Campbell, W., 342, 346
Canning, J., 119, 141, 301, 328
Castanias, R., 94, 108
Caplan, E., 35, 46
Carey, J., 75
Carlson, M., 48, 114, 141
Carnap, R., 35, 46
Carroll, T., 296
Cassidy, D., 203, 221
Catlett, G., 567
Caws, P., 114, 119, 141
Chambers, R., 10, 27, 41, 46, 116, 117, 141, 143, 187, 191, 255, 300, 328, 337, 345, 352, 355, 382, 383, 567
Chandra, G., 256
Chaney, P., 419, 445, 446

Chang, L., 208, 221
Chasten, L., 330
Chatfield, M., 118, 130, 141
Chatov, R., 76, 109
Chewning, E., 110
Choi, F., 579, 587
Chow, C., 109
Christenson, C., 33, 46
Clancy, D., 330
Clark, H., 509
Clarke, C., 492, 508
Clarke, R., 201, 220
Clarkson, G., 342, 345
Clay, R., 543
Coates, R., 186, 191
Coe, T., 193, 255
Coffee, J., 244, 253
Collins, B., 422, 445
Collins, D., 128, 142, 204, 221, 457, 458, 472, 474
Comiskey, E., 203, 221
Conner, J., 69, 74, 474
Cook, D., 513, 533, 542
Cook, T., 209, 221
Cooper, D., 94, 107, 110
Cooper, K., 474
Copeland, R., 557, 566
Coughlan, J., 330, 543
Courmier, D., 398, 410
Cullather, J., 36, 46
Cunningham, M., 567
Cushing, B., 110, 247, 254, 255
Cyert, R., 194, 235, 254

Daley, L., 181, 182, 191, 197, 221, 493, 507
Danker, H., 509
Davidson, L., 144
Davidson, S., 384, 411, 416, 418, 445
Davis, H., 486, 507
Davis, S., 218, 221
Deakin, E., 457, 459, 472, 475
DeAngelo, L., 286, 295, 297
DeBerg, C., 397, 398, 410
DeCoster, D., 347
Deinzer, H., 115, 116, 141
Demsetz, H., 88, 107
Demski, J., 42, 46, 88, 107, 110, 165, 191, 216, 221, 223, 247, 254, 255
Dent, W. C., 426, 446, 457, 472, 474

Desai, H., 256
Deskins, J., 384
Devine, C., 27, 34, 46, 48, 124, 141, 186, 191, 256
Dewhirst, J., 447, 509
Dhaliwal, D., 204, 221, 458, 472, 473, 474, 493, 507
Dharan, B., 465, 472
Dickens, R., 384
Dieter, R., 543
Dillard, J., 571, 588
Dipchand, C., 567
Donleavy, G. D., 583, 587
Dopuch, N., 67, 74, 83, 88, 108, 165, 181, 191, 208, 222, 248, 254, 384, 415, 433, 445
Doran, B. M., 474
Doupnik, T., 573, 579, 587
Drake, D., 384, 424, 445
Drtina, R., 346
Drummond, G., 447
Dukes, R., 202, 203, 207, 220, 221, 414, 445, 474, 588
Dyckman, T., 40, 46, 66, 74, 224, 424, 445, 452, 457, 472, 474
Dye, R., 285, 295

Edwards, E., 352, 358, 360, 370, 382, 384
Eisley, L., 30, 46
Elam, R., 186, 191, 209, 221, 534, 543
El-Gazzar, S., 532, 543
Elgers, P., 206, 221
Elliott, J., 297
Ellyson, R., 69, 74
Epstein, M., 82, 109, 208, 221
Eskew, R., 206, 221
Evans, T., 571, 573, 575, 579, 587, 589

Fabricant, S., 388, 410
Fama, E., 196, 197, 221
Farmer, L., 495, 509
Fazzi, C., 416, 446
Feldstein, M., 493, 507
Feltham, G., 48, 223, 224
Field, R., 452, 472
Findlay, M. C., 422, 445, 446
Finnerty, J., 543
Fisher, L., 209, 221

Fitzgerald, R., 589
Fitzsimmons, R., 543
Flesher, D., 68, 75
Flory, S., 474
Folks, W., 571, 587
Foster, G., 110, 186, 192, 200, 201, 203, 221, 222, 223, 318, 328
Francis, J., 196, 197, 222, 487, 489, 492, 493, 494, 508, 560, 566
Frank, W., 185, 192, 579, 588
Fraser, I., 194
Frecka, T., 398, 410
Freeman, R., 245, 253
Fremgen, J., 120, 141
Friedman, L., 411
Frishkoff, P., 144, 282, 295, 399, 410
Fromm, G., 110
Frost, C., 459, 472

Gaa, J., 85, 108, 179, 180, 192, 194
Gagnon, J., 567
Galliart, W., 418, 446
Gans, M., 157, 158, 193
Gellein, O., 330
Gerboth, D., 193
Gilman, S., 119, 141
Glinsky, M., 509
Goldberg, L., 143, 144
Golub, S., 242, 253, 589
Gombola, M., 346
Gonedes, N., 83, 88, 108, 207, 208, 216, 222, 274, 346, 415, 445
Goodman, H., 543
Gordon, M., 48, 196, 222
Gosman, M., 342, 345
Grady, J., 509
Grady, P., 58, 74, 122, 141, 237, 254
Graham, W., 255
Graul, P., 418, 446
Grawoig, D., 120, 142
Gray, J., 48, 185, 193
Gray, S., 581, 582, 583, 587
Greenball, M., 186, 192, 447
Greenberg, R., 197, 222
Griffin, C., 48
Griffin, P., 94, 108, 224
Gringyer, J., 384
Grossman, S., 474
Groth, J., 474

Gujarathi, M., 302, 328
Gynther, R., 144, 357, 382, 411

Hagerman, R., 494, 508
Hagler, L., 549, 566
Hakansson, N., 35, 46, 82, 108, 216, 222
Hall, W., 493, 508
Hamdallah, A., 509
Hamre, J., 330, 567
Hand, J., 202, 222, 288, 295
Harcourt, G., 353, 382
Haring, J., 76
Hatfield, H., 119, 142
Hawkins, D., 342, 346, 511, 517, 532, 533, 543
Haworth, H., 457, 473
Healy, P., 287, 295
Healy, R., 51, 74
Heaston, P., 575, 587
Heath, L., 193, 346, 356, 383
Heian, J., 547, 566
Hendershott, P., 209, 221
Henderson, M. S., 329
Hendriksen, E., 123, 141, 255, 359, 383
Herring, H., 416, 446
Hicks, J., 30, 46, 487, 508
Hillison, W., 411
Hines, R., 208, 222
Hirsch, M., 509
Hofstede, G., 581, 587
Hofstedt, T., 128, 141
Holder, W., 543
Hollowell, B., 493, 508
Holthausen, R., 79, 108
Holzer, H. P., 575, 587
Holzman, O., 575, 587
Hong, H., 203, 222, 555, 566
Hope, T., 447
Horngren, C., 89, 108, 110, 144, 296, 305, 329
Horrigan, J., 209, 222
Hoskin, R., 274, 296
Houston, C., 569, 587, 589
Huefner, R., 346, 411
Hughes, J., 274, 296, 302, 329
Hughes, G. D., 128, 141
Hussein, M., 92, 97, 108

Iino, T., 143
Ijiri, Y., 11, 12, 26, 27, 48, 114, 141, 155, 159, 186, 192, 194, 225, 235, 254, 302, 329, 347, 411, 452, 473, 509
Imdieke, L., 330
Ingberman, M., 229, 254, 544
Ingram, R., 110, 181, 192, 509
Ippolito, R., 492, 508

Jacobs, F., 416, 445
Jaedicke, R., 11, 12, 26, 27, 347
Jaenicke, H., 269, 272, 295
Jain, P., 474
Jennings, A., 113, 141
Jensen, M., 79, 108
Jensen, P., 579, 587
Jeter, D., 419, 445, 446
Jilling, M., 571, 587
Johnson, G., 197, 222
Johnson, O., 347
Johnson, W. B., 459, 473
Joy, A., 579, 588
Joyce, E., 183, 192

Kachline, E., 509
Kafer, K., 347
Kaplan, R., 203, 209, 222, 224, 372, 382, 555, 566
Kazenski, P., 306, 329, 528, 543
Keller, T., 255
Kelley, A., 36, 46
Kelly, L., 110
Kelly-Newton, L., 110
Kemp, P., 129, 141
Kemp, R., 493, 508
Kennelly, J., 186, 191
Kettler, P., 40, 46, 206, 207, 220
Ketz, J. E., 92, 97, 108, 333, 346, 411
Kim, J., 560, 566
King, E., 54, 74
King, R., 474
Kircher, P., 48
Kirk, D., 67, 75, 89, 108
Klingstedt, J., 450, 473
Kochanek, R., 347
Koeppen, D., 193
Kohler, E., 53, 75
Konner, M., 38, 46

Kripke, H., 194
Krislov, S., 89, 108
Kross, W., 457, 473
Kuhn, T., 43, 46
Kulkarni, D., 296

Laibstain, S., 447
Lakonishok, J., 209, 220, 411
Lamb, J., 48, 114, 141
Lambert, R., 297
Lambert, S., 143
Landsittel, D., 493, 508
Landsman, W., 398, 410, 493, 508
Langenderfer, H., 255
Larcker, D., 458, 473, 474
Largay, J., 333, 346, 383
Larson, K., 9, 26
Lawson, G. H., 340, 346
Lee, C., 246, 254
Lee, T., 38, 39, 46, 208, 222, 340, 342, 346, 347, 383
Leftwich, R., 79, 108, 110, 205, 222, 287, 296, 555, 566
Lemke, K., 369, 382, 418, 446
Leo, M., 509
Leone, R., 110
Lev, B., 48, 206, 222, 224, 244, 253, 458, 473
Levy, G., 437, 446
Lewis, B., 224
Lewis, W. A., 384
Li, D., 131, 141
Libby, R., 183, 192, 209, 222, 224
Lilien, S., 458, 473, 532, 543
Lindahl, F., 110, 203, 220
Linn, S., 196, 197, 222
Littleton, A., 118, 119, 123, 125, 128, 134, 142, 145, 192
Livingstone, J. L., 383, 416, 446
Livnat, J., 567
Lloyd, M., 557, 566
Loeb, S., 39, 47
Lookabill, L., 287, 294
Lorensen, L., 509, 543, 589
Lowe, H., 384
Lowe, T., 110
Lucas, T., 493, 508
Lys, T., 458, 473

Ma, R., 329, 544
MacNeal, K., 119, 142
Maglio, J., 474
Mandelker, G., 203, 222, 555, 566
Marshall, R., 247, 254
Martin, D., 430, 446
Mason, P., 347
Mathews, J., 457, 473
Mathews, R., 48
Mattessich, R. 10, 26, 27, 29, 46, 48, 114, 142
Mautz, R., 48, 113, 114, 115, 142, 255, 256
May, G., 278, 296
May, R., 42, 46, 83, 108
May, W., 256
Mayer-Sommer, A., 39, 47
McDonald, D., 12, 26
McEnroe, J., 68, 75
McGill, D., 478, 508
McIntyre, E., 40, 47
McKee, A. J., 32, 47
McKeown, J., 203, 220, 287, 294, 398, 410, 411
McNichols, M., 297
Meador, A., 579, 587
Means, K., 306, 329, 528, 543
Meckling, W., 79, 108
Meek, G., 577, 588
Melcher, B., 330
Menon, K., 218, 221
Merino, B., 33, 47, 84, 108, 255
Metcalf, R., 143
Meyer, P., 68, 75
Meyers, S., 424, 445
Milburn, J. A., 369, 382
Miller, H., 152, 192
Miller, H. E., 161, 165, 192
Miller, M., 196, 221, 222
Miller, M. C., 329
Miller, P., 110, 177, 178, 192, 226, 254, 255
Mills, P., 48
Mobley, S., 296
Mock, T., 27
Modigliani, F., 196, 222
Mohr, R., 207, 222, 342, 346, 560, 566, 567
Moody, S., 68, 75

Moonitz, M., 27, 60, 75, 110, 154, 192, 268, 296, 329, 330, 354, 383, 415, 446, 447, 509, 545, 566, 567
Moore, U., 119, 142
Morgan, G., 218, 221
Morgenstern, O., 114, 142
Morris, M., 493, 508
Morse, D., 224, 246, 254
Most, K., 126, 142, 194, 208, 221, 296, 475, 583, 588
Moung-Yin Chan, A., 579, 588
Mueller, G., 589
Munter, P., 320, 328
Murdock, R., 571, 588
Murphy, G., 144
Murray, D., 206, 221
Musolf, L., 89, 108
Myers, J., 124, 142, 296, 474, 516, 518, 543

Nabes, W., 194
Naggar, A., 462, 473
Nair, R., 246, 254, 420, 422, 426, 430, 446, 579, 588
Neimark, M., 33, 47, 84, 108
Nelson, A. T., 544
Nelson, C., 34, 47
Neuhausen, B., 319, 329
Newman, D. P., 76
Newman, M., 330
Ng, D., 78, 108
Nichols, A., 120, 142
Nichols, D., 372, 382
Nichols, V., 430, 446
Nichols, W. D., 493, 508
Nielsen, O., 27
Nikolai, L., 68, 75
Nobes, C., 402, 410, 575, 579, 582, 587, 589
Norgaard, C., 347
Norton, C., 509
Nurnberg, H., 279, 296, 347, 422, 446, 447

O'Connor, M., 128, 142, 330, 474, 567
Ofer, A., 209, 220, 411
Ohlson, J., 209, 216, 223, 224
O'Keefe, T., 474
O'Leary, T., 110
Oliver, T., 543

Olson, N., 567
Olson, W., 255
Ou, J., 205, 206, 223, 224
Ovadia, A., 411
Owen, B., 110

Pacioli, L., 5
Pany, K., 128, 142
Parker, R., 352, 382, 402, 410, 575, 588
Parks, J., 447
Pastena, V., 458, 473, 532, 543
Paton, W., 6, 26, 118, 123, 128, 131, 132, 134, 142, 145, 192, 386, 410
Pattillo, J., 127, 142
Patz, D., 474
Peasnall, K., 34, 47, 162, 192, 248, 254
Peloubet, M., 129, 142
Peltzman, S., 110
Pendlebury, M., 560, 566
Penman, S., 205, 206, 223, 224
Perera, M., 582, 588
Perry, R., 447
Pesando, J., 492, 508
Pfeiffer, G., 205, 223, 534, 543
Philips, G. E., 270, 296, 384, 509
Phillips, S., 110
Pines, J. A., 76
Popoff, B., 143
Porter, S., 452, 464, 473, 475
Posner, R., 110
Powell, W., 230, 239, 254
Prakash, P., 384
Pratt, D., 384
Previts, G., 76
Purcell, T., 589
Puro, M., 110
Puxty, A., 110

Radosevich, R., 12, 26
Ramanan, R., 459, 473
Ramanathan, K., 94, 97, 108
Ramesh, K., 197, 222
Rappaport, A., 544
Rasch, S., 416, 445
Rayburn, F., 181, 192
Rayburn, J., 197, 223
Rebmann-Huber, Z., 583, 588
Redding, R., 110
Reder, R., 474

Reed, J., 475
Reiter, S., 209, 223, 489, 492, 493, 494, 508
Revsine, L., 129, 142, 152, 160, 185, 192, 255, 359, 360, 370, 372, 382, 383, 384, 458, 473
Rickard, J., 422, 445
Ricks, W., 203, 223, 224, 274, 296
Richardson, A. W., 544
Richardson, F., 237, 254
Rittenberg, L., 246, 254
Rivera, J., 579, 588
Ro, B., 533, 542
Robbins, B., 433, 446
Roberts, G., 567
Robertson, J., 144
Rockness, H., 68, 75
Roll, R., 200, 223
Ronen, J., 185, 191, 194, 230, 233, 235, 247, 254, 286, 296, 398, 410, 411, 544
Rose, J., 127, 142
Rosen, L., 347
Rosenfield, P., 411, 426, 447, 567
Ross, S., 79, 108
Rozeff, M., 204, 221, 457, 458, 472
Rubin, S., 567
Rudner, R., 35, 47
Rue, J., 493, 508, 509
Ruland, R., 180, 182, 193
Ruland, W., 509
Russ, A., 509

Sack, R., 69, 75
Sadan, S., 185, 191, 230, 254, 286, 296
Salamon, G., 347
Salatka, W., 457, 472
Salter, S., 583, 588
Samuels, W., 165, 193
Samuelson, R., 364, 382
Sanders, T., 119, 142
Sandhi, A., 567
Saudagaran, S., 577, 588
Savage, H., 297
Schattke, R. W., 155, 193
Schipper, K., 285, 296, 487, 508
Schneider, G., 278, 296
Scholes, M., 40, 46, 206, 207, 220
Schreuder, H., 34, 47, 94, 97, 108, 589
Schuetze, W., 76
Scott, J., 589

Scott, R., 330
Seidler, L., 82, 109
Selby, M., 422, 445
Seligman, S., 493, 507
Sellers, K., 579, 587
Shank, J., 571, 588
Shanno, D., 543
Sharaf, H., 113, 142
Sharp, W., 447
Shaw, W., 297
Shearon, W., 399, 410
Sherer, M., 94, 107
Shillinglaw, G., 544
Shoven, J., 509
Shriver, K., 395, 396, 397, 398, 410
Simmons, J., 185, 193
Simon, D., 474
Singhvi, S., 256
Skekel, T., 416, 446
Skelton, L., 416, 445
Skinner, R., 125, 142, 509
Skousen, K. F., 76
Smith, A., 457, 473
Smith, C., 144
Smith, J., 509
Smith, R., 330
Snavely, A., 297
Soeters, J., 589
Solomons, D., 32, 47, 89, 93, 109, 110, 173, 177, 179, 193, 301, 329, 352, 370, 383, 576, 588
Sorter, G., 127, 142, 157, 158, 193, 229, 235, 254, 305, 329, 347, 544
Spacek, L., 55, 75, 76
Spinney, J., 567
Sprouse, R., 69, 75, 76, 129, 142, 193, 227, 255, 268, 329, 347, 354, 383
Stamp, E., 38, 47, 187, 193, 302, 329, 447
Stark, A., 347
Staubus, G., 22, 26, 132, 142, 155, 193, 329
Steinberg, R., 509
Stepp, J., 433, 446
Sterling, R., 12, 13, 26, 33, 36, 38, 39, 42, 47, 48, 110, 120, 125, 142, 163, 171, 177, 187, 193, 194, 234, 255, 329, 352, 355, 369, 382, 384
Stewart, J., 319, 329
Stickney, C., 384, 411
Stigler, G., 79, 91, 109

Stone, M., 207, 223, 493, 508, 509
Storey, R., 50, 51, 53, 75, 194, 296, 330, 567
Strand, W., 330
Strasser, A., 486, 507
Strawser, R., 557, 566
Summers, E., 384
Sundem, G., 42, 46, 83, 108
Sunder, S., 67, 74, 165, 181, 183, 191, 192, 203, 223, 248, 254, 384, 433, 445, 474
Suojanen, W., 418, 445
Swanson, E., 395, 396, 399, 410
Sweeney, H., 119, 143
Swieringa, R., 394, 410
Swyers, S., 433, 446

Taylor, M., 575, 579, 587, 589
Taylor, R., 533, 542
Tearney, M., 422, 447
Thies, J., 547, 566
Thomas, A., 210, 223, 272, 296, 337, 346, 414, 446
Thomas, B., 347
Thomas, L., 399, 410
Thomas, P., 495, 509, 549, 566
Thompson, D., 206, 207, 223
Thompson, R., 533, 542
Throckmorton, J., 447
Tietjen, A., 143
Tinic, S., 202, 223
Tinker, A., 33, 47, 94, 109
Titman, S., 297
Tosh, D., 509
Tranter, T., 181, 182, 191
Tritschler, C., 365, 383
Trueblood, R., 76
Trueman, B., 297
Tuck, C., 457, 473
Tweedie, D., 208, 222, 399, 410

Urwitz, G., 209, 222

Vagts, D., 76
Vancil, R., 372, 383, 384
van der Tas, L., 579, 588
Vangermeersch, R., 589
Vatter, W., 115, 128, 133, 143, 425, 544
Verrechia, R., 216, 217, 223

Vickrey, D., 27, 411
Viscione, J., 567
Volkan, A., 493, 508
Voss, W., 186, 191, 447

Walendowski, G., 475
Walker, M., 48
Walker, R., 329, 559, 566, 567
Wallace, R., 577, 579, 588
Wallace, W., 78, 109
Warrell, C., 329
Watson, P., 418, 446
Watts, R., 31, 33, 34, 41, 47, 79, 90, 92, 95, 109, 110, 111, 287, 296
Wehle, M., 511, 532, 533, 543
Weil, R., 351, 370, 372, 383, 384, 411, 416, 445, 544
Wells, M., 43, 47
Welsch, G., 475
Weygandt, J., 383, 420, 422, 426, 430, 446, 557, 566
Wheeler, J., 418, 446
Wheeler, S., 128, 142
White, L., 111
Whittington, G., 401, 411
Whittred, G., 560, 561
Wigle, S., 447
Wilkens, T., 544
Wilkes, T., 209, 223
Willett, R., 30, 47
Williams, D., 34, 47
Williams, E., 422, 445, 446
Williams, P., 48
Williams, T., 48
Willinger, G. L., 509
Wilmott, H., 110
Wilson, G. P., 297
Windal, F., 296
Winklevoss, H., 500, 509
Winters, A., 194
Wise, T., 589
Wishon, K., 66, 75
Wolfson, M., 569, 587
Wolk, H., 48, 422, 431, 446, 447
Wright, D., 475, 494, 509
Wright, F. K., 117, 143, 370, 383, 384
Wright, H., 237, 254
Wright, W., 201, 209, 220, 223
Wyatt, A., 231, 255, 499, 509, 551, 567
Wyman, H., 589

Young, S. D., 243, 253
Yu, S., 144, 347

Zecher, R., 110
Zeff, S., 50, 52, 61, 70, 75, 94, 109, 111, 143, 330, 359, 383, 384

Ziebart, D., 589
Zimmer, I., 209, 223, 544
Zimmerman, J., 31, 33, 34, 47, 48, 79, 90, 92, 95, 109
Zimmerman, V., 347, 384
Zises, A., 513, 543
Zmijewski, M., 494, 508

SUBJECT INDEX

A Statement of Basic Accounting Theory (ASOBAC), 147–153
Accelerated Cost Recovery System (ACRS), 425–426
Accountability, 78, 186. *See also* Agency theory
Accounting changes, 203–205, 278–279
Accounting entity, 121–122, 558–561
Accounting policy making. *See* Standard setting
Accounting Principles Board, 56–62, 112–113
Accounting research (role of), 28–29, 39–43, 397–398
Accounting Standards Executive Committee (AcSEC), 65–67
Accounting theory
  as art or science, 36–38
  contrast with practice, 38–39
  definition of, 6–7, 148
  normative vs. descriptive, 32–34
  relation to policy making, 7–8
  role of research, 8. *See also* Accounting research
  scientific revolution, 42–43
  scope of, 34–35
Additivity, 308, 314, 355. *See also* Measurement
Agency theory, 41–42, 78–79
Allocations, 210–211, 272–273, 489
American Accounting Association, 70, 147
American Institute of Certified Public Accountants, 50–51, 69

Articulation (of financial statements), 261–265
Asset-liability approach to financial statements, 265, 426–428, 489
Assets, 298–309
  criteria for recognition, 302
  definition of, 299
  measurement, 302, 308–309

Balance sheet, 298–330
Behavioral accounting research, 40
Bias, 151. *See also* Neutrality
Bonds. *See* Debt; Liabilities
Business combinations. *See* Consolidated reporting

Capital asset pricing model, 198
Capital leases. *See* Leases
Capital maintenance, 30, 367–369
Capital market research, 39–40, 79–80, 197–208, 397–398, 454–459
Capture theory, 91. *See also* Regulation
Cash flow statement, 331–347
Cash flow valuation model. *See* Firm value; Discounted cash flows
Cash flows, 335–342
  definition of, 338
  research, 340–342
Classification
  in balance sheet, 321–322
  in cash flow statement, 338–339
  in income statement, 275

Classification (*continued*)
  in statement of changes in financial
    position, 333
Classification system (of financial state-
    ment), 263
Committee on Accounting Procedure, 6,
    52–56
Comparability, 129, 171
Concepts, 59–60, 118–119. *See also* Pos-
    tulates; Principles
Conceptual Framework Project, 166–183
Congressional inquiries, 67–69
Conservatism, 125, 171
Consistency, 125–126, 129–130, 171
Consolidated reporting
  business combinations, 60–61, 547–
    548
  defining reporting entity, 558–561
  new entity approach, 550
  parent-only statements, 560–561
  pooling of interests, 548–549
  purchase method, 549–550
  relevant circumstances (pooling vs.
    pooling), 550–554
  research, 554
Constant dollar disclosures, 390–391
Contingencies. *See* Liabilities
Contributed capital, 316. *See also* Owners'
  equity
Cost method. *See* Investments
Current cost disclosures, 391–392
Current value accounting, 19–22, 359,
    391–392
Current value (cost) approaches
  distributable income, 359, 364–365
  earning power income, 360, 365–366
  realized income, 360, 365–366

Debt
  early extinguishment, 284–285
  measurement of, 312–314
  restructuring, 284
  usefulness of accounting for creditors,
    209
  See also Liabilities
Debt-equity swaps, 287–289
Decision-maker approach, 163
Decision model approach, 162–163. *See
  also* Information economics
Decision usefulness, 162–163
Deductive reasoning, 29–30, 35–36
Default risk, 209

Deferred charges, 308
Deferred credits, 311, 416
Deferred tax credits. *See* Income tax allo-
  cation
Depletion. *See* Oil and gas accounting
Depreciation, 306, 370–371, 377–380,
    404–405
Development stage enterprises, 283
Disclosure, 126, 152, 240–246
Discontinued operations, 279–280
Discounted cash flows, 22–23, 196–197
Discounting deferred taxes, 422–424
Distributable income. *See* Current value
  approaches
Dividend valuation model, 196. *See also*
  Firm Value

Earning power income. *See* Current
  value approaches
Earnings. *See* Income
Earnings management, 285–286. *See also*
  Income smoothing
Earnings per share, 282
Economic consequences, 94–95, 181–
    183, 461–462, 493–494, 532–535
Efficient-markets hypothesis, 197, 234.
  See also Capital market research
Emerging Issues Task Force, 66–67
Entity theory. *See* Equity theories
Entry valuation, 352–354
Equity method. *See* Investments
Equity theories, 130–133
  entity theory, 131–132
  fund theory, 133
  proprietary theory, 131
  residual equity theory, 132–133
Ethics, 38–39
Events, 227–228
  complex, 228
  simple, 228
Executory contracts, 301, 511–513
Exit valuation, 19, 354–355
Expenses, 270–273
Externalities, 83
Extinguishment of debt, 284–285
Extraordinary items, 276–277

Feedback value, 170
Financial Accounting Foundation, 62–
  65

Financial Accounting Standards Advisory Council, 64
Financial Accounting Standards Board, 6–7, 62–67
Financial Analysts' Federation, 68
Financial Executives Institute, 70
Financial instruments, 318–321
Finite uniformity. *See* Uniformity
Firm value (models of), 196–197
Flexibility. *See* Uniformity
Foreign operations, 569–575
Free-rider problem, 83
Full cost. *See* Oil and gas accounting
Fund theory. *See* Equity theories
Funds, 331–335. *See also* Cash flows

Gains. *See* Revenues
General price-level accounting (GLPA), 16–19, 359, 362–364, 390–391
Generally accepted accounting principles, 122
Going concern, 156
Goodwill, 60–61

Harmonization, of international accounting standards, 577–583
Historical costing, 15–16, 122
Holding gains and losses, 357–358

Income
    all-inclusive, 273
    comprehensive, 273–274
    current operating, 275–276
    definition of, 266–267
    earnings, 175
    nonoperating, 276–281
Income smoothing, 286–287
Income statement, 261–289
Income tax allocation, 412–425
Inductive reasoning, 30–32, 35–36
Inflation, 55, 348
Inflation accounting, 348–411
    in Australia, 402
    in Canada, 401
    in New Zealand, 402
    in the U.K., 400–401
    in the U.S., 386–399
Information content, 198. *See also* Capital market research

Information economics, 42, 163, 212–217
Information overload, 152
Intangible assets, 307–308
International Accounting Standards Committee, 399, 578–581, 584
International Federation of Accountants, 584
Inventories, 304–305. *See also* LIFO choice
Investment tax credit, 58, 436–440
Investments
    cost method, 303, 557–558
    equity method, 303, 556–557
Investor surveys, 208, 399

Lease accounting
    economic consequences, 532–535
    history of standard setting, 518–525
    lessees, 518–523
    lessors, 523–528
    leveraged leases, 530–531
    sale and leaseback, 528–530
Leases
    capitalized, 514–517
    compared with purchases, 513–514
    criteria for capitalization, 516
    executory contract, 511–513
    operating, 510–511
    true, 511
Liabilities
    definitions of, 309–310
    measurement of, 311–314
    recognition criteria, 311
    See also Pensions; Postemployment obligations; Debt
LIFO choice, 203–204
Losses. *See* Expenses

Market failure, as need for regulation, 81–83
Marketable securities, 303
Matching concept, 124
Materiality, 126–127, 172
Measurement
    conceptual framework, 177–178
    definition, 6–7
    problems of SFAS 33, 395–397, 403–406
    role in theory, 8–13

Meta theory, 148, 235. *See also* Statement of Basic Accounting Theory
Monetary assets and liabilities. *See* Purchasing power gains and losses

Naive investor hypothesis, 202
National Association of Accountants, 70
Net operating losses and income tax allocation, 434–435
Net realizable value, 303
Neutrality, 171
Nonmonetary exchanges, 306–307
Nonoperating income, 276
Notes payable. *See* Debt; Liabilities

Objectives of accounting
  APB Statement No. 4, 154
  SFAC 1, 167–168
  Statement of Basic Accounting Theory, 148–150
  Trueblood Report, 156–161
Objectivity, 11, 128
Off-balance-sheet financing. *See* Leases; Financial instruments
Oil and gas accounting, 448–475
  full cost, 450–452
  history of standard setting, 452–454
  research into, 454–459
  reserve recognition, 462–465
  successful efforts, 450–452
Operating leases. *See* Leases
Optimal accounting standards, 247–248
Owner's equity, 315–318
  definition of, 315
  recognition criteria, 315–316

Pension accounting
  accounting issues, 485
  asset-liability orientation, 489
  benefits approach, 481
  cost approach, 481
  economic consequences, 493–494
  history of standard setting, 485–489
  implicit liabilities, 492
  legal liabilities, 492
  revenue-expense orientation, 489
  terminations, 491–492

Pension benefits
  actuarial funding of, 479–482, 500–503
  defined benefit plans, 477
  defined contribution plans, 477
  Employee Retirement Income Security Act (ERISA), 482–484
  Pension Benefit Guaranty Corporation, 483
  vested, 478
Political economy of accounting, 93–95, 195
Politics of standard setting, 8, 89–93, 461–462
Pooling of interests, 548–549, 554–555
Portfolio theory, 198
Positive accounting, 31, 33. *See also* Inductive Reasoning; Agency theory
Postemployment benefits, 494–499. *See also* Pension accounting
Postulates of accounting, 57, 113–116, 134–135
Predictive value, 170, 185–186
Price indexes, 349–351
Price-Level Accounting. *See* Inflation Accounting
Principles of accounting, 57, 116–118, 122–123, 136–139. *See also* Postulates of accounting
Prior period adjustments, 281
Proprietary theory. *See* Equity theories
Public goods, 83
Purchasing power gains and losses
  long-term debt, 372–376
  monetary items, 355–357
  SFAS 33, 390

Receivables, 303
Recognition, 123–124, 173, 176–177
Regulation, 81–95. *See also* Political economy of accounting
  of financial reporting, 77
  market failures, 81–83
  paradox of, 87–89
  regulatory process, 89–93
  social goals, 84
Relevance, 150, 168, 170, 233–234. *See also* Feedback value; Predictive value
Relevant circumstances. *See* Uniformity

Reliability, 170, 233–234. *See also* Measurement

Replacement cost. *See* Current value approaches

Representational faithfulness, 170–171, 180

Reserve recognition accounting. *See* Oil and gas accounting

Retained earnings, 315

Revenue – expense approach to financial statements, 264, 489

Revenues
definition of, 267
recognition criteria, 268–270

Rigid uniformity. *See* Uniformity

Risk
accounting-based, 206–207
beta, 198
default, 209
systematic, 198
unsystematic, 198

Scientific method, 28–36

Securities and Exchange Commission, 6–7, 51–52, 54, 58, 69, 241–245

Self-constructed assets, 305

Signalling theory, 79

Social responsibility accounting, 97–98

Standard setting, 85, 145, 179–183, 452–454, 577–583

Standard setting in other countries
Australia, 576
Canada, 576
New Zealand, 577
United Kingdom, 575–576

Standards overload, 88, 245, 465

Statement of Accounting Theory and Theory Acceptance (SATTA), 161–166

Stewardship. *See* Agency theory

Stock dividends, 318

Stock options, 316

Stock warrants, 314

Successful efforts. *See* Oil and gas accounting

Tax allocation. *See* Income tax allocation

Theory. *See* Accounting Theory

Timeliness, 12, 170

Treadway Commission, 68

Treasury stock, 317

Troubled debt restructuring, 284

Trueblood report, 62

Uniformity, 226–240
definition of, 130
finite, 130, 231, 515, 531
finite and rigid compared, 232–233
flexibility, 237–240
relevant circumstances, 229–231, 545–547, 550
rigid, 130, 231

User diversity, 164–165, 187–189, 195

User Orientation, 147–148, 233

Valuation systems, 14–24. *See also* Inflation accounting

Verifiability, 151, 170. *See also* Measurement; Reliability

Wheat Committee, 61–62